Reader's Digest
The Origins of Words & Phrases

Reader's Digest
The Origins of Words & Phrases

Nudge nudge wink wink!

Contents

Everybody will be world famous for 15 minutes.

Features

Behind every English word and phrase there is a story, perhaps going back thousands of years or simply to last year. THE ORIGINS OF WORDS & PHRASES has more than 3,000 of the most intriguing, amusing and surprising of those stories, compiled by the people who know best – the researchers of Oxford Dictionaries. This book delights in both the historical depth and the sheer quirkiness of English, so whether you simply want to go straight to a word for its origin or dip in and out for entertaining enlightenment, you will find it all in these pages.

The story of English

No other language is as rich and vibrant as English. It is a bubbling stew of influences, reflecting the many influxes of peoples into the island of Britain, from the Celts, Romans, Anglo-Saxons, Vikings and Normans of distant history to the Jews, West Indians and Asian peoples of more recent times. The language has also been spiced up by Britain's long story of overseas expansion, trade and adventure, so that English is steeped in tastes from places as far flung as India, China, Iran, South Africa and Japan. Then there are the English-speaking countries historically close to Britain, such as the USA, Canada, Australia, New Zealand and South Africa, which have beefed up the recipe with their own distinct linguistic ingredients.

How it all started

More than 6,000 years ago around the Black Sea, among the inhabitants on the edge of what is now eastern Europe and Asia, a new language stirred. It was the genesis of what you are reading now – English. Few traces of that prehistoric people, and

WORD SHAPERS

Geoffrey Chaucer (c.1342-1400) was the first great English poet. He is known particularly for the *Canterbury Tales*, a cycle of linked stories told by a group of pilgrims who meet in a London tavern before their pilgrimage to the shrine of St Thomas à Becket in Canterbury. He also wrote *Troilus and Criseyde* (1385) and served at court and in a number of official posts, including Member of Parliament. Among the words that he is credited with introducing are ***flute***, ***harmony***, ***jingle***, ***laxative***, ***magic***, ***misery***, ***munch*** and ***nicety***.

English is spoken by up to 400 million people around the world

none of their writing, remain, but the language, now known as **Indo-European**, has developed into what is today spoken by between 350 and 400 million people. English is the world's most common second language, and only outstripped as a first tongue by Chinese. This global popularity brings many new influences to bear on English, and constantly expands its vocabulary.

The journey to Europe begins

Evidence that Indo-European existed lies in the similarities between most European languages and some Asian ones, such as Persian and Hindi. A number of everyday words in English echo with these primeval origins. *Feather*, for instance, can be traced back thousands of years to a root shared by Latin *penna* 'feather', Greek *pteron* 'wing' and even *patra*, which meant 'wing' in ancient Indian **Sanskrit**. Going back even further, *deer* has a root that meant simply 'breathing creature'.

Around 2000 BC Indo-European split into branches, one of which was **Germanic**. The Germanic-speaking peoples moved from their homeland to northern Europe. Those who settled to the north laid the foundations for the Scandinavian languages and the western branch spoke what became German and Dutch. Later the overseas adventures of these people would have a huge impact on Britain, its inhabitants and how they spoke.

Invaders from over the sea

At the time of these Germanic movements the people of Britain spoke **Celtic** languages, the ancestors of Welsh and Gaelic. A little survives in place names derived from Celtic words such as *penno*, 'hill' or 'headland' (Penzance, 'holy headland', in Cornwall), and *egles*, 'church' (Eccles in Lancashire). This ancient Celtic world was turned upside down in AD 43 when the Emperor Claudius sent an expedition that established a Roman presence in Britain lasting until the early 5th century, when the troops were recalled to a Rome under attack from the Goths.

Although Roman roads, villas and fortifications were left behind, not much **Latin** remained, except in place names such as Portsmouth (from *portus*, 'a port') and Lincoln (from Lindum, its Roman name). With the Romans gone, the Britons, speaking the Celtic tongues that had survived occupation, were attacked from the north by Picts and Scots and decided to look abroad for help. Their king, Vortigern, invited the Germanic-speaking

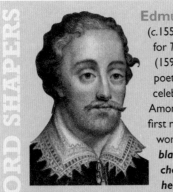

WORD SHAPERS

Edmund Spenser (c.1552-99) is known for *The Faerie Queene* (1590-6), a six-book poetic romance that celebrates Elizabeth I. Among the 500 words first recorded in his work are **amenable**, **blandishment**, **cheerless**, **dismay**, **heedless**, **indignant**, **jovial**, **tambourine** and **thrilling**, as well as an early example of 'crocodile tears':

A cruel crafty crocodile,
Which in false grief hiding his harmful guile,
Doth weep full sore, and sheddeth tender tears.

Saxons from across the North Sea to come and settle strategic parts of England, and they landed near Ramsgate in Kent in AD 449. Soon Angles, Saxons and Jutes from parts of modern Germany, Denmark and the Netherlands were taking over the land, and spreading their language.

English starts to take shape

By the end of the 7th century this language, which we now know as **Old English**, had carved out its own identity. There were many dialects, but the kind spoken in southern England, or Wessex – the kingdom of the West Saxons – became the main form when Alfred the Great began to unite England in the 9th century. The majority of the words we use most frequently, and the basic elements of nearly any sentence, date from this time. Old English words tend to be short and express simple concepts, such as *the*, *to*, *be*, *a*, *from* and *with*. The commonest nouns, such as *thing*, *time*, *man*, *year* and *day*, and verbs, for example *be*, *do*, *say*, *get* and *have*, are all Old English.

Fragments of Old English can still be read and understood, but it has many distinctions from modern English. Grammar and word order are different, and Old English had three letters we no longer use – *ash* (æ), representing a sound similar to the vowel sound of *cat*; *thorn* (þ), pronounced like the *th* in *thin*; and *eth* (ð), like the *th* in *leather*. Old English also used distinctive compounds, known as *kennings*, usually made up of two word elements. Some were quite evocative: a ship might be called a *wægflota*, 'wave floater', or *sæhengest*, 'sea steed', while the sea was the *hronrade* or 'whale road'.

Words from the fringes

Such was the Anglo-Saxon domination that few Celtic words entered Old English. No one is sure whether the Britons were driven out or simply had their language replaced, but Celtic languages were certainly pushed to the margins of the British Isles, to Scotland, Wales, Cornwall and the Isle of Man. In contrast Latin staged a small revival when monks arrived from Rome to convert the Anglo-Saxons to Christianity, headed by the mission of St Augustine, which landed in Kent in 597, and St Aidan's arrival in the north at Lindisfarne around 635. In particular they brought with them words of a religious nature such as *amen*, *candle* and *hymn*.

WORD SHAPERS

William Shakespeare (1564-1616), the greatest dramatist in English, has given more to the language than any other person. As well as his comedies, historical plays, Greek and Roman plays and great tragedies, including probably the most quoted play, *Hamlet*, he wrote more than 150 sonnets. Around 2,000 words are first recorded in his works, including *amazement*, *assassination*, *go-between*, *inaudible*, *laughable* and *stealthy*. See feature on page 299.

> The majority of the words we speak most frequently are Anglo-Saxon

PERYGL! DIM NOFIO YN YR AFON

DANGER! DO NOT SWIM IN THE RIVER

Welsh, a Celtic language, has survived the dominance of English across Britain.

The longboat on a village sign for Ormesby St Margaret in Norfolk gives away its Viking origins – Ormesby means 'Ormr's farmstead'.

A stronger influence on Old English was the **Old Norse** spoken by the Vikings, who set sail from Norway, Sweden and Denmark to attack the south and east of England at the end of the 8th century. Fighting continued until Alfred the Great agreed a treaty with their leader Guthrum in 886, which established the Danelaw, an area of England subject to Danish laws that covered what is now East Anglia, the east Midlands and the north up to the River Tees. Hundreds of Scandinavian place names survive there, many of them, such as Rugby and Grimsby, ending in *-by*, the Old Norse word for 'farmstead' or 'town'. Numerous other Viking words barged their way into Old English, including *arrow*, *bull*, *cross*, *fellow*, *outlaw* and *wrong*.

A flavour of France

The Norman invasion of England in 1066 heralded the rise of a new French-influenced language, **medieval** or **Middle English** – one that is much easier for us to understand today than Old English. Look in Geoffrey Chaucer's *Canterbury Tales*, written at the end of the 14th century, and many phrases and sentences will read just like oddly spelled modern English.

For nearly 300 years French was the language of the Crown and the nobility, and thousands of French words flooded into English, most in turn derived from Latin. The characteristic starts and ends of our words date from this time – prefixes such as *con-*, *de-*, *dis-*, *ex-*, *pre-*, *pro-* and *trans-*, and suffixes like *-able*, *-ance*, *-ence*, *-ant*, *-ent*, *-ity*, *-ment* and *-tion* came via French from Latin. The Norman influx is a major reason why English has such an incomparably large vocabulary, as it added new ways of saying the same thing – as well as *asking* (Old English), you could now *enquire* (from French) or *query* (from Latin), for example.

There was no conformity to this hybrid language – many regional dialects were spoken, and words could be spelled in any of a number of ways, with no comprehensive dictionary to dictate standards. As the influence of London, the capital, began to grow, though, and its civil servants produced more and more official documents, the dialect of the southeast became increasingly prestigious and spelling more fixed.

In the 15th century there was also a change in the way that many English words were pronounced, known as the Great Vowel Shift. Before this time the *a* in *fame* sounded like the *a* in

WORD SHAPERS

John Milton (1608-74) completed his three major poems after he had gone blind in 1652. *Paradise Lost* (1667) is an epic on the fall of man, *Paradise Regained* (1671) covers Christ's temptations, and *Samson Agonistes* (1671) deals with the final years of the biblical figure Samson. In *Paradise Lost* Milton coined words such as **impassive**, **jubilant**, **pandemonium**, **satanic** and **unaided**, and was the first to use **dreary** in its modern sense – before then it had meant 'bloody or cruel' and 'sad, melancholy'.

For nearly 300 years French was the language of the English ruling classes

present-day *father*, the *i* in *fine* like the *ee* in *fee*, and the *o* in *so* like the *aw* in *saw*. This change is a cause of the seeming peculiarity of many English spellings we use today, which are still based on the rules of early medieval English pronunciation, before the shifting of the vowels.

Print and the word of God

In 1476 William Caxton, an English merchant who had studied the art of printing in Cologne, set up a press in Westminster, London, and began to print books in English. For the first time English was available for wide consumption, helping to establish a more stable version and imposing order on how it was transcribed. This was the beginning of **early modern English** – the language of Henry VIII, the Elizabethans and Shakespeare.

It is also the language of the Authorised Version of the Bible, or King James Bible, an English translation made in 1611 at the order of James I, and for more than 300 years the version used in church and at home. The beauty of its prose, the most widely read in the land, gave English dozens of memorable phrases, such as 'a fly in the ointment', 'feet of clay' and 'salt of the earth'. Another influential work, absorbed by a God-fearing population, was the official service book of the Church of England, the Book of Common Prayer, first issued in 1549 and revised in 1662. It has remained largely unchanged, with many phrases such as 'speak now or forever hold your peace' and 'till death us do part' deeply etched in English.

William Caxton reads a proof hot off his printing press. He printed nearly 100 publications, including Geoffrey Chaucer's *Canterbury Tales* and Thomas Malory's *Le Morte D'Arthur*, bringing a more standard form of English to a wide audience.

New worlds of words

While Caxton was turning out the first printed English pages, the Renaissance, a 'rebirth of learning', was flourishing in Continental Europe and spreading slowly to Britain. Latin and Greek, revered as the languages of intellectual pursuit, were plundered for words to express new concepts, such as *chaos*, *democracy*, *encyclopedia*, *pneumonia*, *skeleton* and *vacuum*. Artistic and scientific advances made on the Continent also caused contemporary European languages such as French, Italian and Spanish to become a rich source of new words and a channel for others from further afield, including *elegy*, *guitar*, *madrigal*, *minaret*, *ode*, *opera*, *optician* and *zero*.

The spread of words into English continued with the great age of exploration, spurred on by the first

WORD SHAPERS

Sir Walter Scott (1771-1832) established the historical novel in Britain. His works, such as *The Heart of Midlothian* (1818) and *Ivanhoe* (1819), were hugely popular, not only in Britain but also across Europe and as far as the USA and Australia. Scott was influential in his use of regional speech, introducing hundreds of Scots terms such as *clansman*, *Glaswegian* and *sporran* to a wider readership and being credited with the first use of **comradeship**, **far-away**, **gadabout**, **harrowing** and **Norseman**, and phrases such as 'back of beyond' and 'cold shoulder'.

English adventurers trade with the people of a Caribbean island in the 16th century. The novel crops they saw, such as potatoes and tobacco, soon entered English.

voyage of Christopher Columbus in 1492. Europeans visited Africa, the Americas and the Far East for the first time, bringing back to the Old World new produce that required new names – *cocoa*, *chocolate*, *tobacco*, the *potato* and the *tomato* from South America and the Caribbean, and the *banana* from Africa. Contacts with North Africa and the Middle East led to the appearance of Arabic words like *alcove*, *harem* and *hashish*, and *horde*, *kaftan* and *yogurt* from Turkish, while Persian contributed *bazaar*, *caravan* and *turban*, and Hebrew *hallelujah* and *shekel*.

Fruits of empire

Trade and colonial expansion from the 16th century onwards took English far beyond the shores of Britain. American English was the first major new variety to emerge, followed soon by others as the British Empire expanded to the Caribbean, Canada, Australia, Africa and southern Asia. The willing sponge of English soaked up many words from these new places, such as *bungalow* and *pyjamas* (Hindi), *ketchup* and *kowtowing* (Chinese), and *boor* and *trek* (Afrikaans).

When America won its independence from Britain in 1776 the US dictionary writer Noah Webster saw it as a chance for the new nation to establish its own linguistic identity, and his *American Dictionary of the English Language* (1828) featured many spellings that differed from British ones. He favoured simplified spellings like *center*, *color* and *maneuver*, which are now the standard forms in American English rather than *centre*, *colour* and *manoeuvre*.

The language goes contemporary

By 1800 English had become recognisably modern. Read a novel or a letter by Jane Austen and there are few obvious differences from today's language. The most noticeable distinctions between **modern English** and earlier varieties are in vocabulary, with thousands of new words appearing with each passing year. From the time of the Industrial Revolution, which began in England in the late 18th century, science and technology in particular have been a fruitful source of new terms, with computers (*geek*, *icon*), the internet (*blog*, *podcast*) and mobile phones (*texting*, *smileys*) merely the latest in a succession of inventions to contribute words and phrases.

WORD SHAPERS

Jane Austen
(1775-1817) wrote witty novels, such as *Sense and Sensibility* (1811), *Pride and Prejudice* (1813) and *Persuasion* (1818), which were a success at the time and, apart from a few periods out of fashion, have remained popular ever since. Among the words first found in her work are **coddle**, **doorbell**, **irrepressible**, **outsider**, **raffish**, **smarten** and **stylish**. In *Northanger Abbey* (1818) she even makes an unexpected reference to baseball: 'It was not very wonderful that Catherine … should prefer cricket, base ball, riding on horseback, and running about the country at the age of fourteen, to books.' This is one of the earliest mentions of baseball, then a children's game, in print.

Slang is another constant source of fresh language, particularly among the young, and especially since the birth of the teenager in the 1950s. The increasing informality of modern life is reflected in our use of English – we are today more likely to say *bike*, *pub* and *bra* than *bicycle*, *public house* and *brassiere*. If enough people use a word, English will absorb it. No official body monitors our language, unlike French, which has been supervised and protected by the Académie française since 1635.

English takes on the world

The democratic nature of English now is shown by the freedom with which journalists and advertising copywriters invent words, particularly by combining two others. These 'blends' include *adultescent* (a middle-aged person with interests and clothing more often associated with adolescents), *docudrama* and *infotainment* – more established ones are *breathalyser* (breath + analyse) and *smog* (smoke + fog).

The manipulation of existing language provides more than half of our new words. Old words also often gain new senses – for example, *issues* developed the meaning 'personal problems' in the 1980s, and in the 1990s a *text message* became a *text* and then quickly transformed into a verb (I *texted* her). From *bad* meaning 'good' in the 1920s to the popularity of terms from hip-hop music in the 1990s, urban black street culture, particularly in the US, has taken even more liberties with the language. In turn this is aped by other English speakers, famously parodied by the comic character Ali G, a member of the Staines *massive*, or gang, who likes to think he is a *gangsta*.

In the 21st century English is the global language of the internet, business, science, technology, air traffic control and pop music. American English, through the worldwide reach of its music, films and television, is the most influential form, but emerging varieties such as Hinglish (English used by speakers of Hindi), Japlish (Japanese English), Singlish (spoken in Singapore) and Polglish (Polish English) are further transforming the language. We still need a standard English so that we can speak to one another – but this most diverse of languages is set to become ever more colourful.

Rudyard Kipling (1865-1936), the novelist, short-story writer and poet, was born in India. He wrote tales about the Raj, poems from the point of view of the British soldier, and children's stories such as *The Jungle Book*. He gained a reputation as the voice of Empire, which made him revered and much quoted at home, while his popularity abroad brought him the Nobel prize for literature in 1907. Many of the expressions he coined, such as 'never the twain shall meet' and 'the white man's burden', are still popular. In 1995 his poem 'If' was voted Britain's favourite in a BBC poll.

WORD SHAPERS

More than half of new words are made from existing words

P. G. Wodehouse (1881-1975) wrote for more than 70 years. His best-known works are humorous stories set in the 1920s, in the leisured upper-class world of Bertie Wooster and his valet, Jeeves. During the Second World War Wodehouse was interned by the Germans, and was later accused of being a traitor after making radio broadcasts from Berlin. His books contain the first recorded uses of **fifty-fifty**, **lame-brained** and **ritzy**, and he is remembered also for quotes like 'It is never difficult to distinguish between a Scotsman with a grievance and a ray of sunshine.'

WORD SHAPERS

About this book

Like any dictionary, *The Origins of Words & Phrases* is arranged A-Z to make it easy to find what you want. Each entry, based on a **headword** (in red print), will give you the ultimate origin, where known, of the word or phrase and how and why it has developed into what we use today. Any other words that have spun off from the headword, or are related to it in some way, are picked out in **larger, bold type**. Those words referred to that have their own entry elsewhere in the book are printed in SMALL CAPITALS.

---

parrot

The origin of **parrot** may lie in the tendency to give pet birds human names. The word, recorded in the early 16th century, could represent French *Pierrot*, a form of *Pierre* 'Peter'. People often address a pet bird as 'Pretty Polly', and the name **Polly** has been used to mean 'a parrot' since the early 19th century; it is a longer form of **Poll**, first recorded as a parrot's name in 1600. See also SICK.

parson see PERSON.

Unlike other dictionaries, this book includes 38 features on key influences in the English language, from advertising slogans to Yiddish words. They pull together many of the words and phrases that those influences have injected into the way we speak, and also steer you to entries in the book (indicated by SMALL CAPITALS) that cover even more examples. See the 'Contents' page for a list of all the features.

Glossary of linguistic terms

Indo-European Lost language from which most European languages and some others derive, spoken around the Black Sea before 4000 BC.

Germanic Ancestor of English, German, Dutch and the Scandinavian languages.

Sanskrit Ancient Indian language in which the Hindu scriptures are written, the source of Hindi and Urdu.

Celtic Group of languages spoken in much of Europe before the Romans, and the source of Irish, Scottish Gaelic, Manx, Welsh, Cornish and Breton.

Greek Language of classical Greece and the source of modern Greek, written in an alphabet borrowed from the Phoenicians of Lebanon and Syria.

Persian Spoken in the ancient Persian empire and the source of modern Persian or Farsi, used in modern Iran and written in a version of Arabic script.

Latin Language of ancient Rome and its empire, the medium of communication for educated Europeans in the Middle Ages and still used in biology, medicine and law. Ancestor of Italian, French, Spanish, Portuguese and Romanian.

Old Norse Language of medieval Norway, Iceland, Denmark and Sweden, from which the modern Scandinavian languages are derived.

Old English Development of the language brought over to England by the Angles, Saxons and Jutes in the 5th century. Spoken until around 1150. Known also as Anglo-Saxon.

Old French Spoken in France until around 1325. A form of Old French was used by the Normans and became the language of the English nobility after the conquest of 1066.

Medieval or **Middle English** Much more similar to modern English than Old English; the language of Chaucer's *Canterbury Tales*.

Early modern English Language of Shakespeare and the Authorised Version of the Bible.

Modern English Form of English we speak today.

abacus

The **abacus** that we know today, a calculating device with rows of wires along which you slide beads, is an ancient object that was used by the Babylonians, Greeks and Romans and is still found in many parts of the world. The earliest abacus was probably a board covered with sand, on which a clerk could draw figures and then rub them out again, and this was what the word first referred to in English. The word **abacus** was borrowed from Latin, but came before that from Greek *abax* 'board, slab, plate', and probably ultimately from Hebrew *ābāq* 'dust'.

abet

If you **abet** someone these days you are very likely to be up to no good, but this was not always the case. Since the late 18th century the word has mainly occurred in the phrase **aid and abet**, 'to help and encourage someone in some wrongdoing', but in its early use to abet someone was simply to urge them to do something, not necessarily something bad. It comes from the Old French word *abeter*, which could also mean 'to encourage a hound to bite'. **Bait** has a similar root.

abhor

Imagine that you dislike or are revolted by something so much it actually makes you shudder. This is what **abhor** literally means. It derives from Latin *ab*- 'away from' and *horrere* 'to shudder with fright', which is also the basis of HORROR. In Shakespeare's day **abhor** could also mean 'to cause horror': 'It does abhor me now I speak the word' (*Othello*).

abominable

People used to think that **abominable** came from Latin *ab*- 'away from' and *homo* 'human being', and so literally meant 'inhuman or beastly'. Until the 17th century it was frequently spelt *abhominable*, and appears in this form in the works of Shakespeare. In fact, the word comes via Old French from Latin *abominari*, meaning 'to regard something as a bad omen', and is related to **omen** and **ominous**.

Abominable Snowman is another name for the Yeti, a large ape-like creature alleged to inhabit the high reaches of the Himalayan mountains. The name was brought back from the expedition that the Royal Geographical Society mounted in 1921 to Mount Everest, which found mysterious footprints in the snow. Abominable Snowman is a translation of Tibetan *Meetoh Gangmi*, the name the Sherpa porters gave to the animal responsible for the tracks. **Yeti** is from Tibetan *yeh-the* 'little man-like animal'.

abracadabra

These days **abracadabra** is just a fun word said by magicians as they do a trick, but as far back as the 17th century it was much more serious – a magic word that was supposed to be a charm against fever and was often engraved on an amulet worn around the neck. **Abracadabra** was written so that it formed a triangle, beginning with 'A' on the first line, 'AB' on the second, and so on. It ultimately goes back to ancient times, first recorded in a Latin poem of the 2nd century AD. See also PRESTO.

```
A B R A C A D A B R A
  A B R A C A D A B R
    A B R A C A D A B
      A B R A C A D A
        A B R A C A D
          A B R A C A
            A B R A C
              A B R A
                A B R
                  A B
                    A
```

absurd

One sense of the Latin word *absurdus* was 'out of tune', and in the 17th century **absurd** was occasionally used with just this meaning. From this Latin sense it developed the meaning 'out of harmony with reason, irrational'.

The term **Theatre of the Absurd**, describing drama by writers such as Samuel Beckett, Eugène Ionesco and Harold Pinter that aims to convey the futility of human existence in a meaningless universe, was coined by the critic Martin Esslin in 1961. Probably the best-known example of the genre is

Beckett's play *Waiting for Godot* (1952), which portrays two tramps, Estragon and Vladimir, who wait endlessly for the arrival of a mysterious person named Godot.

abysmal

The original literal sense of **abysmal**, in the 17th century, was 'very deep', and people did not start using it to describe something utterly appalling, 'the pits', until the beginning of the 20th century. The word is related to **abyss**, which is from Greek *abussos* 'bottomless'.

academy

An **academy** today is a place of learning or culture. It is fitting, then, that the word originated with one of the most influential scholars who ever lived, the Greek philosopher Plato. During the 4th century BC he taught in a garden in Athens called the *Akadēmeia*, which was named after an ancient hero called Akadēmos and gave its name to the school Plato founded, known in English as the Academy. See also PLATONIC.

An **Academy award** is an OSCAR. It is a statuette awarded annually by the Academy of Motion Picture Arts and Sciences of Hollywood since 1928 for achievement in various areas of the film industry.

accent

English and many other languages distinguish the different parts or syllables of a word by stressing one of them, but the ancient Greeks pronounced them with a distinct difference in musical pitch. Syllables marked with a grave accent (for example *à*, from Latin *gravis* 'heavy, serious') were spoken at a comparatively low pitch, those with an acute (*á*, from Latin *acutus* 'sharp, high') at a higher pitch, and those with a circumflex (*â*, from Latin *circumflexus*, 'bent around') began at the higher pitch and descended during the pronunciation of the syllable. This gives some explanation of why the root of **accent** is Latin *cantus* 'song', which was a direct translation of the Greek word *prosÿidia*. Quite a few languages (technically known as 'tonal' languages) still have this musical way of speaking, among them Chinese and Swedish: anyone familiar with the 'sing-song' speech of the Swedish chef in *The Muppet Show* will know what this sounds like.

accident

An **accident** was originally simply 'an event, something that happens', not necessarily a misfortune or mishap. It came into English in the Middle Ages via Old French from Latin, ultimately deriving from Latin *cadere*, meaning 'to fall', which also gave us words such as **cadaver**, CHANCE, **decay**, **incident** and **occasion**. The idea of an event 'falling' remains in the English word **befall**. Later the meaning of **accident** evolved into 'something that happens by chance', as in the phrase **a happy accident**, and by the 17th century the modern meaning had become established in the language.

The full form of the proverb **accidents will happen**, which dates from the early 19th century, is **accidents will happen in the best-regulated families**. According to Mr Micawber in Charles Dickens's *David Copperfield* (1850), 'Accidents will occur in the best-regulated families; and in families not regulated by . . . the influence of Woman, in the lofty character of Wife, they must be expected with confidence, and must be borne with philosophy.' See also ADVENTURE.

accolade

The Provençal word *acolada* is the source of **accolade**. This literally meant an embrace or a clasping around the neck, and described the gesture of a friendly hug that was sometimes made when knighting someone, as an early alternative to the more familiar stroke on the shoulder with the flat of a sword. The ultimate root of the Provençal word is Latin *collum* 'neck', from which we also get **collar**.

ace

An **ace** was originally the side of a dice marked with one spot. The word comes from Latin *as*, meaning 'unit'. Since an ace is the card with the highest value in many card games, the word often suggests a sense of excellence. An ace was also a wartime fighter pilot who brought down many enemy aircraft, and is now anyone who excels at something. In tennis an ace is a service that your opponent is unable to reach, and in golf it is a hole in one.

If you have an **ace up your sleeve** (or in American English **an ace in the hole**) you have a secret resource ready to use when you need it. A cheating card player might well hide an ace up their sleeve to use at an opportune moment. To **hold all the aces** is to have all the advantages, again from the idea of a card game: a player holding all four aces in their hand is likely to be in a winning position. To be **within an ace** of doing something is to be on the verge of doing it. This comes from the idea of an ace being a single spot on a playing card and hence a tiny amount.

ache

The word **ache** is a good example of the way that English spelling and pronunciation have developed and in many cases have diverged from each other. The noun comes from Old English and used to be pronounced 'aitch' (like the letter H), whereas the verb was originally spelled *ake* and pronounced the way **ache** is today. Around 1700, though, people started pronouncing the noun like the verb. It is the spelling of the noun that has survived, but the word is said in the way the verb (*ake*) used to be. The modern spelling is largely due to Dr Johnson, who mistakenly assumed that the word came from Greek *akhos* 'pain'. Other pairs of words that have survived into modern English with *k*-for-the-verb and *ch*-for-the-noun spellings include **speak** and **speech** and **break** and **breach**.

acid

The word **acid** originally meant 'sour-tasting', and came from Latin *acidus*. The term seems to have been introduced by the 17th-century scientist Francis Bacon, who in 1626, for example, described sorrel as 'a cold and acid herb'. The chemical sense came along at the end of that century because most common acids taste sour.

The **acid test** was originally a method of testing for gold using nitric acid. An object made of gold will show no sign of corrosion if immersed in nitric acid, unlike one made of some other metal. By the end of the 19th century the expression had come to denote any situation that proves beyond doubt a person's or thing's suitability or quality. The Australian expression **put the acid on**, meaning 'to extract a loan or favour from', is a reference to such a test – the would-be borrower is seen as 'testing' their victim for resistance or weakness.

acme

In Greek *akmē* meant 'point' or 'pinnacle, highest point'. Its use in English dates from the late 15th century, although for the next hundred years or so it was consciously used as a Greek word, and written in Greek letters. For many people their first exposure to the word came from the 'Looney Tunes' cartoons featuring characters like Bugs Bunny and Wile E. Coyote. In emergency the characters resort to objects labelled as 'Acme' that very often turn out to be disastrously faulty. 'Acme' was a real brand name for various US firms in the last two decades of the 19th century.

Wile E. Coyote, the creation of the animator Chuck Jones, uses an Acme product in yet another futile attempt to catch Road Runner.

Acne, the skin condition, has a similar root. The idea is that all those red pimples are little points sticking up from someone's face.

acorn

An Old English word, related to **acre** and meaning 'fruit of the open land or forest'. It was later applied to any fruit, then subsequently restricted to the most important fruit produced by the forest, the acorn. The spelling of the word, originally *aecern*, evolved into its modern form because people thought the word must have something to do with OAK and CORN.

acrobat

The earliest **acrobats** were tightrope walkers, which explains why the word derives from Greek *akrobatos*, meaning 'walking on tiptoe'. The *akro-* part of *akrobatos* meant 'tip, end or summit' and is found in several other English words. The **acropolis** of a Greek city, most famously Athens, was the fortified part, which was usually built on a hill. **Acrophobia** is fear of heights. An **acronym** is a word such as *laser* or *Aids* formed from the initial letters of other words, and an **acrostic** is a poem or puzzle in which certain letters in each line form a word or words.

adamant

The Greek word *adamas*, originally meaning 'invincible or untameable', came to be applied to the hardest metal or stone and to diamond, the hardest naturally occurring substance. Latin *adamas* (the source not only of the English word **adamant** but also of DIAMOND)

15

carried this meaning over. In Old English **adamant** was the name given to a legendary rock or mineral so hard that it was believed to be impenetrable. The modern use, with its notion of unyielding conviction, is much more recent, probably dating from the 1930s.

Adam Adamant was the hero of the 1960s TV series *Adam Adamant Lives!* Adam, played by Gerald Harper, was an Edwardian adventurer deep-frozen for 60 years by his evil enemy the Face and thawed out in the Swinging Sixties. In the late 1970s a young punk called Stuart Goddard divided the hero's surname to become **Adam Ant**.

IT'S AN ADOLESCENT — APPARENTLY ALL THEY DO IS EAT AND GRUNT

adder

One of the words Anglo-Saxons used for a snake was *naedre*, which became *nadder* in medieval times. At some point during the 14th or 15th century the word managed to lose its initial *n*, as people heard 'a nadder' and misinterpreted this as 'an adder'. A northern dialect form *nedder* still exists. A similar process of 'wrong division' took place with words such as APRON and UMPIRE, and the opposite can happen too, as with, for example, NEWT and NICKNAME. In time **adder** became the term for a specific poisonous snake, also known as the VIPER. See also DEAF.

addled

An **addled** egg is rotten and produces no chick, whereas if your brain is addled you are confused. Originally, though, a rotten egg was described as an **addle egg**. In Old English *addle* was liquid mud or dung, the sort of stuff you might come across in a farmyard, and which came to describe rotten eggs because of its nasty smell.

admiral

The first recorded meaning of **admiral**, dating from the early 13th century, refers to an emir or Muslim commander, and the word ultimately comes from Arabic *amir* 'commander'. The Arabic word was used in various titles of rank, such as *amir-al-bahr* ('commander of the sea') and *amir-al-ma* ('commander of the water'). Christian scholars, not realising that the *-al-* part simply meant 'of the', thought that *amir-al* was a single word meaning 'commander', and accordingly anglicised it as **admiral**. The modern maritime use comes from the office of 'Ameer of the Sea', created by the Arabs in Spain and Sicily and later adopted by the Genoese, the French and, in the form 'Amyrel of the Se' or 'admyrall of the navy', by the English under Edward III. From around 1500 the word **admiral** on its own has been used as the naval term.

adolescent

Both **adolescent** and **adult** come from Latin *adolescere*, 'to grow to maturity'. The root of the Latin word is *alescere* 'to grow up', which in turn derives from *alere* 'to nourish or give food to'. So the idea of coming to maturity is closely related to the idea of feeding yourself up.

adventure

The meaning of **adventure** has changed over the centuries. In the Middle Ages it meant 'anything that happens to someone by chance' or 'chance, fortune or luck', deriving from Old French *aventure*, from Latin *advenire* 'to arrive'. Gradually the idea of 'risk or danger' became a stronger element in the word's meaning, which later evolved into 'a dangerous or hazardous undertaking' and still later into 'an exciting incident that happens to someone'. See also ACCIDENT.

aeroplane

An **aeroplane** is literally an 'air wanderer'. Coined in the late 19th century, the word is from French *aéro-* 'air' and Greek *-planos* 'wandering', and so the short form PLANE has the less than reassuring meaning of 'wanderer'. See also PLANET.

aficionado see AMATEUR.

affiliate

We talk about parent companies, so why not child companies? This is literally what an **affiliated** company is. The first meaning of **affiliate**, back in the early 17th century, was 'to adopt as a son', and the word ultimately came from Latin *filius* 'son', from which we also get **filial**. By the mid 18th century **affiliate** was being used to mean 'to adopt as a subordinate member of a society or company'.

affluent

Arriving in the English language via Old French from Latin *affluere* 'flow towards', **affluent** was originally used to describe water either flowing towards a place or flowing freely without any restriction. It later came to mean 'abundant' and then 'wealthy', a meaning which dates from the mid 18th century.

affray

Although an **affray** is now a disturbance of the peace caused by fighting in a public place, its first meaning was 'alarm, fright or terror', and it used to be a verb as well, meaning 'to disturb, startle' and 'to alarm, frighten'. Its root is the old Norman French word *afrayer*, and **afraid** was originally its past participle form, then spelled *affrayed*.

aftermath

The **aftermath** was originally the crop of new grass which springs up after the harvest or after a field has been mowed in early summer. John Buchan, the Scottish writer of adventure stories like *The Thirty-Nine Steps*, wrote about 'Meadowland from which an aftermath of hay had lately been taken'. *Math* was an old word meaning 'a mowing'. The modern meaning of **aftermath**, 'the unpleasant consequences of an event', developed in the middle of the 19th century.

aghast

Gast (originally *gaestan*) was an Old English word meaning 'to frighten or terrify'. It was still being used in this sense in Shakespeare's day: 'Or whether gasted by the noise I made, Full suddenly he fled' (*King Lear*). This gave rise to **agast**, which had the same meaning. The spelling **aghast** (probably influenced by the spelling of GHOST) was originally Scottish but became generally used after 1700.

agnostic

This is one of those words that was actually invented by a specific person and then successfully entered the language. It was coined by the Victorian biologist Thomas Huxley (1825-95) to describe his own beliefs: he did not believe in God but did not think you could say for sure that God did not exist. Before Huxley came up with **agnostic** there was no word for such a religious position. He is said to have first used it in 1869 at a party held in Clapham, London, prior to the formation of the Metaphysical Society. Huxley formed the word from the Greek *a-* 'not' and *gnostos* 'known'.

Sch . . . you know who

The history of advertising is full of creative wordplay. The best slogans stick in the mind, entertaining – or irritating – us, and take on a life beyond the product.

Some slogans have such resonance that they have become a shorthand for their time. We are the Ovaltineys, happy girls and boys was the theme song to a 1930s show on Radio Luxembourg, promoting the Ovaltine drink. Its success was largely due to the feeling it evoked of childhood innocence and joy that chimed with the pre-war era.

After the war, television took over as the main source of slogans that burrow into the public mind. Drinka pinta milk a day (National Dairy Council), Cool as a mountain stream (Consulate cigarettes), I'm only here for the beer (Double Diamond), Your flexible friend (Access credit card), It's good to talk (British Telecom) and I'm loving it (McDonalds) each carry associations of the decades they belong to, from the 1950s right up to the 21st century.

The slogans that people vote for as the most memorable are those that pack a punch in few words. Nike's Just do it, the National Lottery's It could be you and L'Oreal's Because I'm worth it have all lodged in the public mind.

Sometimes innuendo proves stronger than the direct appeal. In 1994 billboards for the Playtex Wonderbra, featuring the model Eva Herzigova's cleavage and the line Hello boys, caused a stir and allegedly even traffic accidents. Such wordplay was nothing new – Castlemaine lager has been using Australians wouldn't give a XXXX for anything else since the 1980s, a successor to Clairol's Does she ... or doesn't she? and Heineken refreshes the parts other beers cannot reach.

If an ad is truly successful its slogan may become part of the language. Since the late 1980s the wood preservative manufacturer Ronseal has seen It does exactly what it says on the tin become a catch-all phrase for anything which unpretentiously does what it claims to. Va va voom, the Renault slogan that imitates the revving of a car's engine, has also become entrenched as an expression for pep or sex appeal. Renault did not invent the phrase – it dates back to the 1950s as an expression of admiration for a woman's curvaceous figure – but it changed perceptions of the brand.

See also BEAN, EGG, NAUGHTY, NICE.

agog

If you are **agog** you are now very eager or curious to hear or see something, but originally you were having a lot of fun. The word comes from Old French *en gogues*, 'in mirth, in a merry mood'. The 1960s phrase **a gogo**, meaning 'galore', has a similar origin.

agoraphobia

What could be more distressing to someone with a fear of crowded places than the bustle of market day? **Agoraphobia**, a psychiatric term coined in the 19th century, is literally 'fear of the market place', from Greek *agora* 'a market place' and the English suffix *-phobia* (from Greek *phobos* 'fear'). In ancient Greece an *agora* was a public open space used for markets and assemblies.

air

A good example of a word in which different meanings come from different sources. The main modern sense of **air**, 'the invisible gaseous substance surrounding the Earth' entered English via Old French and Latin from Greek *aēr*. **Aerial**, meaning 'a rod or wire by which signals are transmitted or received' and 'existing or happening in the air', comes from the same source. The senses 'an impression or manner' and 'a condescending manner' (as in 'she gave herself airs') are probably from a completely different word, Old French *aire* 'site, disposition', which derives from Latin *ager* 'field', the root of English words such as **agriculture**. The Italian word *aria* (used in English for a long operatic solo song) gave us the English sense 'tune or melody'. See also GAS.

akimbo

You might think that the odd-looking word **akimbo**, 'with hands on the hips and elbows turned outwards', derives from an African language. In fact it appeared in medieval English in the form *in kenebowe* or *a kembow* and was probably an alteration of an Old Norse phrase meaning 'bent in a curve, like a horseshoe'.

albatross

The spelling of **albatross** was influenced by Latin *albus*, 'white'. The large white seabird was originally called the **alcatras**, a name which was also applied to other water birds such as the pelican and which came from Spanish and Portuguese *alcatraz*, from Arabic *al-gattās* 'the diver'. In golf an albatross is a score of three under PAR at a hole. Other *alb-* words with an element of whiteness in their meaning include **albino**, ALBION and ALBUM. See also AUBURN, CANDID.

Albion

A poetic or literary name for Britain or England which today is particularly associated with the names of soccer teams such as West Bromwich Albion and Brighton and Hove Albion. **Albion** probably derives from Latin *albus* meaning 'white', and alludes to the white cliffs of Dover. The phrase **perfidious Albion**, translating the French *la perfide Albion*, refers to England's alleged treachery in international affairs and is attributed to the Marquis de Ximénès (1726-1817). See also ALBUM.

album

In 1968 the Beatles released their classic album *The Beatles*, better known, because of its completely white cover, as *The White Album*. As it happens, the very first albums were all white. The Latin word *albus* 'white' was used as a noun meaning 'a white (or, rather, blank) marble tablet' on which public notices were written. Brought into English as **album**, the word has subsequently been used to describe various blank books used for compiling a collection of items, such as stamps or photographs, and in the 1950s became applied to a collection of recorded pieces of music. See also ALBION, BEAT.

alcohol

Arabic *al-kuhl* gave us the modern English word **alcohol**, but there were several changes in meaning along the way. *Al* in Arabic means 'the', and *al-kuhl* means 'the kohl', referring to a powder used as eye make-up. By extension, the term was applied to a fine powder and then to a liquid essence or spirit obtained by distillation.

alert

This comes from the Italian military phrase *all' erta*, 'on the lookout' or, more literally, 'to the watchtower'. It was originally a military term in English too, before it acquired its more general meaning. **Alert** was first used as an adverb, so you could say that the later expression **on the alert** strictly means 'on the on the lookout'.

---

airy-fairy

Once upon a time, **airy-fairy** meant 'delicate or light as a fairy' – 'Airy, fairy Lilian, Flitting, fairy Lilian', wrote Lord Tennyson in 'Lilian' (1830). Then along came a more scornful meaning, 'impractical and foolishly idealistic' – 'He had already an airy-fairy knowledge of the whole affair', wrote D.H. Lawrence in *The Lost Girl* (1920).

algebra

Bone-setting does not seem to have much to do with mathematics, but there is a connection in the word **algebra**. It comes from the Arabic *al-jabr* 'the reunion of broken parts', used specifically to refer to the surgical treatment of fractures and to bone-setting. **Algebra** was used in this meaning in English in the 16th century. The mathematical sense comes from the title of a 9th-century Arabic book *ilm al-jabr wa'l-mukabala,* 'the science of restoring what is missing and equating like with like', written by the mathematician al-Kwarizmi. See also ZERO.

alibi

This is recorded from the late 17th century, as an adverb in the sense 'elsewhere', and was originally a Latin word with the same meaning and spelling. A typical example of its use comes from John Arbuthnot's *History of John Bull* (1727): 'The prisoner had little to say in his defence; he endeavoured to prove himself Alibi.' The noun use, 'a piece of evidence that a person was somewhere else when a crime was committed', dates from the 18th century.

alimony

Today **alimony** means 'provision for a husband or wife after divorce' (what is usually called **maintenance** in Britain), and is chiefly used in the USA. Originally, though, in the early 17th century, it simply meant 'nourishment or means of subsistence'. It comes from Latin *alere* 'nourish', which is the root of words such as ADOLESCENT, **adult** and **coalesce**.

all

A little Old English word found in a host of popular phrases. The Latin equivalent was *omnis* (see OMNIBUS), which gives us words such as **omnivorous**, literally 'all-eating'.

Although with the Second World War, **the all-clear** dates from the very beginning of the 20th century. It refers to a signal such as a siren that indicates enemy aircraft have left the area, making it safe to come out into the open again from bomb shelters or other places of refuge.

All animals are equal, but some animals are more equal than others comes from George Orwell's *Animal Farm* (1945), a satire on Communism as it developed under Stalin. In Orwell's fable the animals, led by the pigs, revolt against and expel the cruel farmer Mr Jones. They establish a free society for which one of the principles is 'All animals are equal'. Gradually, though, the pigs take control, acquiring the rights of rulers, and one day the original statement of absolute equality is modified to read: 'All animals are equal, but some animals are more equal than others.'

All done with mirrors means 'performed or achieved by trickery or illusion'. One of the earliest examples of the phrase comes from a 1908 play by G.K. Chesterton called *Magic*, about a conjuror working out how an effect might be created, but it probably goes back to 19th-century magicians.

All human life is there was an advertising slogan used by the British tabloid newspaper the *News of the World* in the 1950s. The phrase had been used earlier by the novelist Henry James in *The Madonna of the Future* (1879). A maker of statuettes says of his wares, 'Cats and monkeys – monkeys and cats – all human life is there!'

The first things to be described as **all-singing, all-dancing** were film musicals. Posters for *Broadway Melody* (1929) carried the slogan 'All Talking All Singing All Dancing'. These days something 'all-singing, all-dancing' is generally an advanced computer or other gadget.

The proverb **all good things must come to an end** dates back to the 15th century, usually in the form 'All things must come to (or have) an end'. Jonathan Swift wrote in 1738, 'All Things have an End, and a Pudden has two', a 'pudden' or 'pudding' being a kind of sausage. The inclusion of the word 'good' in the proverb appears to be a 20th-century development.

All's well that ends well is first recorded in the 14th century as 'If the end is well, then is all well'.

alligator

Our English word **alligator** comes from two Spanish words *el lagarto*, 'the lizard'. The first record of its use is from an account of his travels written by a 16th-century English adventurer called Job Hortop. Hortop was press-ganged to sail to the Americas on a slaving voyage when he was only a teenager, and wrote vividly of the strange animals he encountered, among them the alligator.

aloof

It now has a sense of steering clear of something or keeping your distance, but **aloof** was originally a nautical term for an order to steer a ship as close as possible towards the wind. It literally means 'to windward', *loof* (or *luff*) being an old term meaning 'windward direction'. The idea was that keeping the bow of the ship close to the wind kept it clear of the shore or some other obstacle that it might be blown towards.

alphabet

The first two letters of the Greek **alphabet** are *alpha* and *beta*. In Greek these two letters were combined to make the word *alphabētos*, which was taken as a name for all 24 letters of the Greek alphabet as a whole, just as English-speaking children are taught their **ABC**. From this we got the English word **alphabet**.

amateur

An **amateur** does something for love rather than for money. The idea of love was certainly there from the moment the word entered the language. Borrowed from French in the 18th century, and ultimately deriving from Latin *amator* 'lover', it was originally used to describe a person who loves or is fond of something. Later on it came to be used of a person who practises an art or sport as a hobby, rather than professionally, and also of someone who is inept at a particular activity. The original meaning of **amateur** was similar to the modern one of **aficionado**. This is a Spanish word, from *aficionar*, 'to become fond of', which came from Latin *affectio* 'affection'. In English an aficionado was originally a person devoted to bullfighting.

Amazon

In Greek legend the Amazons were a race of female warriors who were supposed to exist in the unexplored regions of the north. In Homer's *Iliad* their queen, Penthesilea, came to the aid of Troy and was killed by Achilles. The word **Amazon** is Greek for 'without a breast' – the connection is the story that the women cut off their right breasts so that they could draw their bows more easily. Nowadays an Amazon is any tall, strong or athletic woman. The River Amazon was given its name by European explorers because of stories that a race of female warriors lived on its banks.

amber

A yellowish fossilised resin deriving from prehistoric coniferous trees, which has been used in jewellery since ancient times. The word **amber** comes from Arabic *'anbar*, which also meant 'ambergris'. This is a wax-like substance that originates as a secretion in the intestines of the sperm whale, found floating in tropical seas and, despite its unpromising description, used in the manufacture of perfume.

Much more appealing is **amber nectar**, which was popularised as an advertising slogan for Fosters lager from 1986. It goes back much further than that, though, and has been a slang term for beer since the 1890s, especially in Australia.

ambidextrous

As anyone left-handed knows, we live in a right-handed world. The bias towards right-handedness is present in the language too. While the positive word DEXTEROUS or 'skilful, good with the hands' comes from the Latin for 'right-handed', the rather more negative SINISTER comes from the Latin for 'left-handed'. And if you are **ambidextrous**, it is as though you have got two right hands: the word is from Latin *ambi* 'both, on both sides' and *dexter* 'right, right-handed'. At one time **ambidextrous** could also be used to mean 'double-dealing, trying to please both sides', as in 'a little, dirty, pimping, pettifogging, ambidextrous fellow' (Laurence Sterne, 1768).

ambiguous

The Latin word *ambiguus*, from which we get the English **ambiguous**, had the meaning 'doubtful, shifting, going from one place to another', and ultimately came from *ambigere* 'to waver or go round'. The English word, which appears to have been coined by the English scholar and statesman Sir Thomas More in the early 16th century, originally meant 'indistinct, obscure'.

ambition

Ambitious politicians are known for tirelessly canvassing for votes, and the origin of the word **ambition** certainly ties in with this. It comes from Latin *ambire*, literally meaning 'to go round or go about' (also the source of **ambient**), but with the more specific sense of 'to go round canvassing for votes', from which developed the idea of eagerly seeking honour or advancement.

An Amazon warrior prepares to draw her bow.

ambulance

First used in the Crimean War, an **ambulance** was originally a mobile temporary hospital – a field hospital – that followed an army from place to place. The term was later applied to a wagon or cart used for carrying wounded soldiers off the battlefield, which in turn led to its modern meaning. **Ambulance** comes from the French *hôpital ambulant*, literally 'walking hospital': the root is Latin *ambulare*, 'to walk', which gave us words such as **alley**, **amble** and **ambulate** (a formal way of saying 'walk').

Ambulance chaser is a wry nickname for a lawyer who specialises in bringing cases seeking damages for personal injury. The first example of the term, from 1897, tells us that 'In New York City there is a style of lawyers known to the profession as "ambulance chasers", because they are on hand wherever there is a railway wreck, or a street-car collision . . . with . . . their offers of professional services.'

amethyst

It was traditionally believed that putting an **amethyst** in your drink could prevent you getting drunk. Presumably you were not supposed to swallow it. The word, first found in medieval English, ultimately derives from the Greek word *amethustos*, meaning 'not drunken'.

amok

If someone **runs amok** they rush about behaving uncontrollably and disruptively. The word **amok** comes via Portuguese from a Malay word *amuk* meaning 'fighting furiously' or 'rushing in a frenzy'. It was first used in English as a noun in the 17th century, referring to a Malay person in a murderous frenzy after taking opium.

ampersand

A corruption of 'and *per se* and', an old phrase that used to be chanted by schoolchildren as a way of learning the character &, which we now call the **ampersand**. *Per se* is Latin for 'by itself', so the phrase can be translated '& by itself is *and*'. The word is recorded from the mid 19th century, while the symbol itself is based on a Roman shorthand symbol for Latin *et* 'and'.

amphibian

Amphibians live both in water and on land, and it is the idea of 'living in both' that gives us the word, which comes from Greek *amphi* 'both' and *bios* 'life'. Before it was applied specifically to frogs, toads and newts, **amphibian** simply meant 'having two modes of existence, of doubtful nature'.

amuse

In its early senses **amuse** had more to do with deception than entertainment or humour. Dating from the late 15th century and deriving from an Old French word meaning 'to stare stupidly', it originally meant 'to delude or deceive'. In the 17th and 18th centuries to amuse someone usually meant to divert their attention in order to mislead them. In military use it meant to divert the attention of the enemy away from what you really intend to do, as illustrated by this quotation from Lord Nelson, writing in 1796: 'It is natural to suppose their Fleet was to amuse ours whilst they cross from Leghorn.'

'We are not amused' is associated with Queen Victoria, who reigned from 1837 to 1901. It is first recorded in *Notebooks of a Spinster Lady* (1919) by Caroline Holland – Victoria is supposed to have made the stern put-down in 1900 to a man who had made an inappropriate joke. There is no firm evidence that she said it, though, and her biographer Stanley Weintraub claimed that 'she was often amused'. Her reputation for being humourless may come from the many stern paintings and sculptures of her in public buildings and spaces.

anachronism

Spotting an **anachronism**, something which is wrongly placed in a particular period, in films is good fun – maybe cavemen fighting dinosaurs, or a Roman soldier wearing a watch. The word comes from Greek *anakhronismos*, from *ana-* 'backwards or against' and *khronos* 'time'. The latter is the source of other time-related words such as **chronicle**, **chronological** and **synchronise**.

anatomy

At first **anatomy** was not just the study of the structure of the human body, it was specifically the practice of cutting up human bodies to learn about them. The word came into English in the 14th century via Old French and Latin from Greek *anatomia*, from *ana-* 'up' and *tomia* 'cutting'. **Anatomy** used also to be applied to a skeleton, and in this meaning it was commonly found in the contracted form **atomy**, as in 'His sides . . . looked just like an atomy, ribs and all' (J. Fenimore Cooper, 1863).

anecdote

Part of the pleasure of an **anecdote** can be the feeling that you are hearing something indiscreet or secret. This characteristic is borne out by the word's origin, Greek *anekdota* 'unpublished things'. This was applied by the 6th-century historian Procopius to his *Unpublished Memoirs* of the Byzantine emperor Justinian, which consisted chiefly of tales of the private life of the court. When the word came into English during the late 17th century it was only used in the plural, and meant 'secret or hitherto unpublished details of history'. About a hundred years later people starting using it in the singular, to mean 'an item of gossip'.

angel

The traditions of Christianity, Judaism, Islam and other religions all include angels. They are messengers from God, and the word **angel** comes ultimately from Greek *angelos* 'messenger'. An **angel** was also the name given to an old English gold coin (known in full as the **angel-noble**) minted between the reigns of Edward IV and Charles I and stamped with the image of the Archangel Michael standing over and slaying a dragon.

To be **on the side of the angels** is to be on the side of what is right. In a speech in Oxford in 1864 the British statesman Benjamin Disraeli referred to the controversy that was then raging about Charles Darwin's book *On the Origin of Species*, saying: 'Is man an ape or an angel? . . . I am on the side of the angels.' See also ANGLE.

angina

The Latin word *angere*, 'to choke, squeeze or strangle', is the source of a number of English words. The most obvious is perhaps **angina**, which originally denoted quinsy (an inflammation of the throat) and later referred to **angina pectoris**, a condition characterised by a feeling of suffocation and severe pain in the lower left side of the chest. Nervous tension can produce feelings of tightness in the throat and chest, which explains why *angere* is indirectly the root of **anguish** and **anxiety**.

angle

The **angle** meaning 'the space between two intersecting lines' and the one meaning 'to fish with a rod and line' or 'to prompt someone to offer something' are different words. The first comes from Latin *angulus* 'corner' and the second is an Old English word from ancient Germanic roots.

The **angles** were a people who journeyed to England from Germany during the 5th century and founded kingdoms in the Midlands and East Anglia, eventually giving their name to England and the English. They came from the district of Angul, on the long, curved peninsula that is now called Schleswig-Holstein, and are thought to have acquired their name from the fact that either Angul or Schleswig-Holstein were shaped like a fish hook – **angle** is also an old name for such a hook.

Pope Gregory the Great (*c*.540-604) is said to have been quite taken by the appearance of some English slaves in Rome. When told they were Angles, he reportedly declared that the fair-haired captives were 'Not Angles, but Angels'.

animal

Animals are so called simply because they breathe. The word, used as an adjective in English before the noun became established, originally described any living being, as opposed to something inanimate. Its source is the Latin word *animalis*, 'having the breath of life', from *anima* 'air, breath or life'. As a noun, the word was hardly used in England before the end of the 16th century – the older **beast** was the usual term – and does not appear in the King James Bible of 1611. See also MESMERISE.

annihilate

Hidden in the middle of **annihilate** is the Latin word *nihil*, meaning 'nothing', which is at the heart of the English word's meaning: to **annihilate** something is to destroy it completely so that there is nothing left. Deriving in the 14th century from the Latin *annihilatus* 'reduced to nothing', it was first used as an adjective with the meaning 'destroyed or annulled'. A couple of centuries later **annihilate** started to be used as a verb, replacing an earlier form **annihil**. *Nihil* is also the source of NIL.

annoy

Something that annoys you is rather unpleasant, but originally it was worse – it was hateful. **Annoy** came into English in medieval times from Old French *anoier*, but was based on Latin *in odio*, from the phrase *mihi in odio est*, 'it is hateful to me'.

ante

The expression **up the ante**, meaning 'to increase what is at stake', comes from the world of card games and gambling. *Ante* is a Latin word meaning 'before' and is a component of English words such as **ante-room** and **antenatal**. **Ante** was originally used in English by American players of poker and similar card games in the early 19th century as a term for a stake put up by a player to start the betting before drawing the cards. 'Upping' (or 'raising') the ante is putting up a higher stake than your opponent in order to put more pressure on them.

antelope

Before 17th-century zoologists gave the name to a fast-running horned animal, an **antelope** was a fierce mythical creature with long serrated horns that was believed to live on the banks of the River Euphrates and was often depicted in heraldic designs. It was said to be able to use its saw-like horns to cut down trees. Although the word came into English via Old French and medieval Latin from Greek *antholops*, the origin and meaning of the Greek word is a mystery.

antenna

On old Mediterranean sailing ships certain types of triangular sail (called lateen sails) were supported by long yards or poles at an angle of 45 degrees to the mast. These sailyards reminded the ancients of an insect's antennae. The Latin word *antenna* was an alteration of *antemna* 'sailyard' and was used by writers to translate the Greek *keraioi* 'horns of insects'. **Antenna** was adopted into English in the 17th century, and when Marconi and others developed radio in the 1890s the word was quickly taken up, along with **aerial**, to refer to a rod or wire by which signals were transmitted or received. See also AIR.

anorak

The **anorak** has come a long way – from Greenland, where the Inupiaq language of the Eskimos gave us the word for a hooded waterproof jacket. The shabby anoraks worn by trainspotters and others with unfashionable and largely solitary hobbies led to such people being called anoraks from the early 1980s.

anthology

An **anthology** is literally a collection of flowers. The Greek word *anthologia* (from *anthos* 'flower' and *logia* 'collection') was applied to a collection of the 'flowers' of verse, in other words poems or epigrams by various authors that had been chosen as being especially fine or appropriate examples. Writing in 1580, the French essayist Montaigne uses the same metaphor: 'It could be said of me that in this book I have only made up a bunch of other men's flowers, providing of my own only the string that ties them together.' See also POSY.

Antipodes

Think of a person standing on the other side of the world, exactly opposite the point on the Earth's surface where you are standing. The soles of their feet are facing the soles of your feet. This is the idea behind the word **Antipodes**, which came into English via French or Latin from the Greek word *antipous*, meaning 'having the feet opposite'. Writing in 1398, John de Trevisa described the Antipodes who lived in Ethiopia

as 'men that have their feet against our feet'. Nowadays it is used more specifically to refer to Australia and New Zealand, by inhabitants of the Northern Hemisphere. See also OCTOPUS.

ape

Until MONKEY came into the language in the 16th century, the Old English word **ape** applied also to monkeys. The verb use 'to imitate unthinkingly' was formed when 'ape' still meant 'monkey', and was suggested by the way that monkeys sometimes mimic human actions.

The expression **go ape**, meaning 'to become wildly angry, run amok', is often thought to be a reference to the 1933 film *King Kong*, in which a giant ape-like monster goes on a destructive rampage through New York, but the phrase is not recorded until quite a bit later: US newspaper reports from 1954 and 1955 both say that 'go ape' is current teen slang. The cruder version **go apes**— is recorded from 1951.

aplomb

If you do something with **aplomb**, you do it with self-assurance. This use of the word has developed from its early literal sense of being perpendicular or steady, ultimately from the French phrase *à plomb*, 'straight as a plumb line'. Going back even further into the history of the word, Latin *plumbum* 'lead' is also the source of words such as PLUMB, **plumber** and **plummet**, presumably because plumb lines were weighted with lead.

appal

Like ABHOR, **appal** has its origin in the physical effect of being horrified or revolted by something. Old French *apalir* meant both 'to grow pale' and 'to make pale', and these senses were carried over into the English word in the 14th century. As shock or disgust can make the colour drain from your face, **appal** soon acquired its current meaning.

appendix

In humans the **appendix**, a tube-shaped sac attached to the lower end of the large intestine, has no known function, although in rabbits and some other herbivores it is involved in the digestion of cellulose. The word comes directly from Latin and is based on *appendere* 'to hang on', the source of other English words such as

append and **appendage** – the idea is of something being attached or added at the end, as if it were being hung on. In the sense 'section of extra matter at the end of a book or document' **appendix** is recorded in the mid 16th century, with the anatomy term appearing early in the next century.

apple

Originally the Old English word **apple** could be used to describe any fruit. The **forbidden fruit** eaten by Adam and Eve in the Garden of Eden is generally thought of as an apple, and pictured as such, but the 1611 King James Version of the Bible simply calls it a fruit.

The apple is the predominant fruit of northern Europe, and many common phrases involve it. A **rotten apple** (or a **bad apple**) is someone who is a bad influence on the rest of a group, from the idea of a rotten apple spoiling other fruit. The idea can be traced back at least as far as the days of the early printer William Caxton in the 15th century. The **apple of your eye** was once a term for the pupil, which people used to think of as a solid ball. They later applied the expression to anything considered to be similarly delicate and precious, or to someone you are very proud or fond of. The proverb **an apple a day keeps the doctor away** dates from the 19th century, as does the alternative form 'eat an apple on going to bed, and you'll keep the doctor from earning his bread'.

The Australian expression **it's** (or **she's**) **apples** means everything is fine, there is nothing to worry about. This derives from *apples and rice* (or *apples and spice*), rhyming slang for 'nice'. Another example of rhyming slang is **apples and pears** for 'stairs'.

The city of New York has been known as **the Big Apple** since the 1920s, possibly from the idea that there are many apples on the tree but New York is the biggest. Other famous 'Apples' include the computer company Apple, maker of the iPod, which was founded in 1976 in California. The Beatles called their record label Apple, and in 2004 the actress Gwyneth Paltrow and singer Chris Martin named their baby daughter Apple Blythe Alison Martin.

appliance

Until the manufacturer Zanussi introduced its slogan 'The appliance of science' in the 1970s the use of **appliance** to mean 'the application of something' had become rare if not obsolete. This sense was the original one, dating from the mid 16th century, but had fallen out of use, and **appliance** generally meant 'a device designed to perform a specific task'. No doubt

unintentionally, the marketing folk at Zanussi reintroduced this original sense to English, and now it is commonly used without conscious reference to the advert, as in 'the heroic belief that heaven on Earth is attainable through the appliance of science' (*New Scientist*, 1990).

apricot

The Romans called the **apricot** the *malum praecocum* or 'the apple that ripens early'. The second part of the Latin name, meaning 'early ripening', is also the root of the word PRECOCIOUS. Over the centuries *praecocum* gradually mutated in a multilingual version of Chinese whispers. In Byzantine Greek the name of the fruit became *perikokkon*, in Arabic *al-birquq*, in Spanish *albaricoque* and in Portuguese *albricoque*. In the 16th century the word was adopted into English from Portuguese in the form **albrecock**. The modern spelling was probably influenced by French *abricot*, and perhaps by Latin *apricus* 'ripe'.

apron

What we now call an **apron** was known in the Middle Ages as a *naperon,* from Old French *nape* or *nappe* 'tablecloth' (also the source of **napkin**). Somewhere along the line the initial *n* got lost, as people heard 'a naperon' and misinterpreted this as 'an apron'. A similar process of 'wrong division' took place with words such as ADDER and UMPIRE.

aquamarine

In Latin *aqua* means 'water' and *marina* means 'of the sea, marine'. Put them together and you get **aquamarine**, a precious stone the blue-green colour of sea water.

arc

A number of English words comes from Latin *arcus* 'a bow, arch or curve', among them **arc** and **arch**. **Arc** was originally a term for the path of the sun or some other celestial object from horizon to horizon. Given the shape of a bow for shooting arrows, it should not be surprising that **archer** has the same Latin source. Another meaning of **arch**, 'chief or principal' (as in **archbishop** or **arch-enemy**), has a different derivation, coming from Greek **arkhos** 'a chief or ruler'. The Greek word can also be seen in **anarchy**, which literally means 'the state of having no ruler'.

Arctic

If you were told that **arctic** ultimately comes from Greek *arktos* 'bear', you might think that this was because of all the polar bears that live up in the

Sugar with your coffee

From medieval times merchants brought Arabic words to the West along with new goods and materials, including some of our household staples. Today, the Arab world continues to exert its influence on English.

Coffee derives from Arabic *qahwa*, although it entered English in the late 16th century via Turkish *kahveh*. Muslims had taken wild plants from Ethiopia and cultivated them in Arabia, from where the drink spread throughout the Arab world and Turkey, becoming particularly popular in the international metropolis of Constantinople.

Sugar has been in English much longer than coffee, coming in the 13th century by way of Old French and Italian from Arabic *sukkar*. Candy, the North American term for 'sweets', is another Arabic word, from *qandī* 'candied', or clarified and crystallised by repeated boiling.

Another vital commodity was cotton, or in Arabic *qutn*, known in Britain by the 14th century. More exotic were mohair, which in Arabic was *mukayyar*, literally 'choice, select', and saffron, or *za'faran*. A sequin was originally a Venetian gold coin whose name came from Arabic *sikka*, 'a die for making coins'. Trade often involves customs and tariffs, so it is no surprise that the word tariff itself is from Arabic.

In Arabic *al-* means 'the', reflected in the spellings of ALBATROSS, ALCOHOL, alcove and ALGEBRA, and also in many proper names. Al-Qaeda means literally 'the base' – a reference to the training camp or base in Afghanistan used by the mujahideen, or guerrillas, fighting the Russian occupiers, from which the terrorist group developed.

Islam and Muslim are both from the same word, *aslama*, meaning 'to submit, surrender', or 'to submit to Allah or God', and both were first recorded in English in the early 17th century. An ayatollah is a Shiite religious leader in Iran. The word has been used since around 1950 in English, and many people only became aware of it when Ayatollah Khomeini led the Iranian revolution in 1979.

A much more established word in English is imam, the leader of prayers in a mosque, known since the 17th century. The word's root is *amma* 'to lead the way'.

Fatwa was in use in English as early as the 17th century, but it was an obscure and unfamiliar word until 1989, when it suddenly gained new and widespread currency. In this year Ayatollah Khomeini issued a fatwa sentencing the British writer Salman Rushdie to death for publishing *The Satanic Verses*, a novel regarded by many Muslims as blasphemous. Fatwa is a generic term for any legal decision made by an Islamic religious authority, but, because of the particular way in which the English-speaking world became familiar with it, is sometimes wrongly thought to refer to a death sentence.

See also ELIXIR, GIRAFFE, LEMON, MAGAZINE, ORANGE, SOFA, ZERO.

---

northern polar regions. In fact it has nothing to do with polar bears. The bear in question is the Great Bear, the constellation Ursa Major, which can always be seen in the north.

arena
The word **arena** has a gory origin. Roman amphitheatres, used for staging gladiatorial combats and other violent spectacles, were strewn with sand to soak up the blood spilled by the wounded and dead combatants. The word for 'sand' in Latin was *harena* or *arena*, and after a time this came to be applied to the whole amphitheatre.

argent
This heraldic word for silver comes from Latin *argentum* 'silver'. The country **Argentina** is so called because of the silver found there, especially in the region of the River Plate, which in Spanish is *Río de la Plata*, literally the 'silver river'.

argy-bargy
It is the Scots who first engaged in **argy-bargy**, or noisy quarrelling, but before that they had **argle-bargle**. Both words date from the late 19th century, but go back to **argle**, a Scots dialect form of **argue** that was used as long ago as the 16th century.

ark
Aerc was the Old English word for a chest, from Latin *arca* 'a chest or box'. This developed into **ark**, as in the **Ark of the Covenant**, the wooden chest in which the tablets of the laws of the ancient Israelites were kept, and the **Holy Ark** in a synagogue, a chest or cupboard

which contained the scrolls of the Torah or Hebrew scriptures. A ship may be thought of as a floating container, hence **Noah's Ark**, the vessel built by Noah to escape the Flood. The Latin word is also the source of **arcane**, which describes something hidden, concealed or secret, as if it were shut up in a box which only a few people can open.

arm

Although they may seem connected, **arm** meaning 'part of the body' and **arm** meaning 'a weapon' are different words. The former is Old English, and the latter came into medieval English from French and ultimately Latin.

The long arm of the law is the police force. The phrase was first recorded in *Rob Roy* by Sir Walter Scott (1817) as 'the arm of the law', but the more usual form was 'the strong arm of the law', as in this example from *The Pioneers* by James Fenimore Cooper (1823): 'If the idlers in the village take it into their heads to annoy him, as they sometimes do reputed rogues, they shall find him protected by the strong arm of the law'. The first example of the 'long' form is in Charles Dickens's *The Old Curiosity Shop* of 1841.

If something **costs an arm and a leg** it is extremely expensive. The traditional story connects the expression with portrait painting. A pose in which the sitter's arms and legs were all visible might be more difficult to paint, making the portrait more expensive than one where some of the limbs were hidden out of sight. A more likely explanation is that the phrase originates in the idea that a person's arms and legs are very precious to them. It may be an insensitive punning reference to 'lost an arm and a leg', a phrase which was all too common in reports of wartime casualties. There is a similar thought behind the much older expression **give your right arm for** something, meaning 'to want something very much and be willing to pay a high price for it'.

aroma

A walk past any Indian restaurant will confirm that spices have a definite aroma, and it is 'spice' that was the original meaning of **aroma**. From the 13th century, when the word entered English via Latin from Greek *arōma*, 'spice' was the only meaning, and the modern

sense 'a distinctive pleasant smell' did not appear until the beginning of the 19th.

arrive

Until about 1550 the main meaning of **arrive** was 'to come ashore or come into port after a voyage'. You could also talk about 'arriving' a ship or a crew or a group of passengers, meaning to bring them to shore or into port. Only later did the more general sense of 'to reach a destination, come to the end of a journey' develop. **Arrive** comes from the Old French word *ariver*, ultimately from Latin *ad-* 'to' and *ripa* 'shore'. RIVER is also descended from *ripa*.

armadillo

'The little armed man' is the meaning of **armadillo** – a good description for an animal with a body encased in armour-like bony plates. The word was originally the diminutive form of Spanish *armado* 'armed man'. In 1577 John Frampton, an English trader, explained the unfamiliar zoological term: 'He is called the Armadillo, that is to say a beast armed.'

arse

Like BUM, **arse** was not originally a rude slang word. It dates back to before 1000 in English, and is connected to various old German and Scandinavian forms that were probably linked to Greek *orros* 'the rump or bottom'. So **arse** is an ancient word that was perfectly respectable until the 17th century, even though these days it is considered rather crude.

To **go arse over tip** (the original form, rather than **tit**) and **not know your arse from your elbow** are first found in the early 20th century. **My arse!**, that eternal refrain of Jim Royle in the TV comedy *The Royle Family*, is first recorded in the 1920s, though all these expressions are probably older.

The American spelling is **ass**, which is nothing to do with **ass** meaning 'donkey'. The latter is from an Old English word that is related to EASEL and goes back to Latin *asinus*, as in **asinine** or stupid.

arsenic

As it is understood today, the chemical element **arsenic** is a brittle steel-grey substance with many highly poisonous compounds, but its root word means 'gold'. In English the word first referred to a compound of arsenic called arsenic sulphide or yellow orpiment, which was formerly used as a dye and artist's pigment. The word comes from Greek *arsenikon*, from Arabic *az-zarnīk*, the root of which was Persian *zar* 'gold'.

art

Originally **art** was simply 'skill at doing something'. Its use in the modern sense dates from the early 17th century. The word comes from Latin *ars*, from a base which meant 'to put together, join, or fit'.

The phrase **art for art's sake** conveys the idea that the chief or only aim of a work of art is the self-expression of the artist who creates it. It was the slogan of the Aesthetic Movement, which flourished in England during the 1880s and rejected the notion that art should have a social or moral purpose. Among its chief exponents were Oscar Wilde and Aubrey Beardsley. The Latin version of the phrase, *ars gratia artis*, is the motto of the film company MGM, and appears around the roaring lion in its famous logo.

asbestos

In Greek **asbestos** meant 'unquenchable'. In English it originally referred to a mythical stone that once set alight was impossible to extinguish. This was probably a distorted reference to what happens when cold water is poured on quicklime – it reacts to form calcium hydroxide with a lot of heat and fizzing. The word was revived in the 17th century to refer to the fibrous mineral used for making fireproof material.

The victorious Australian cricket team celebrate regaining the Ashes after defeating England in December 2006.

ash

The two meanings of **ash**, the powder and the tree, started out as two completely different words. In Old English *aesce* or *aexe* referred to the powder and *aesc* referred to the tree.

When something **turns to ashes in your mouth** it becomes bitterly disappointing or worthless. The origins of this phrase can be traced back to medieval times. In John de Mandeville's *Travels*, a 14th-century work claiming to be an account of the author's travels in the East, there is a description of a legendary fruit known as the Dead Sea fruit, sometimes also referred to as the apple of Sodom. Although the fruit was apparently attractive and appetising to look at, it was said to dissolve into smoke and ashes as soon as anyone tried to eat it.

Bitter disappointment has often been the feeling of English cricket fans after a series of **the Ashes**, the competition played roughly every other year between England and Australia. The name of the contest comes from a mock obituary notice published in the *Sporting Times* newspaper on September 2, 1882, after the Australians had sensationally beaten the English team at the Oval:

In Affectionate Remembrance of English Cricket Which Died at the Oval on 29th August, 1882. Deeply lamented by a large circle of sorrowing friends and acquaintances. R.I.P. N.B. – The body will be cremated and the ashes taken to Australia.

During the subsequent 1882-3 Test series in Australia the captain of the English team declared that his mission was to recover the Ashes for England. During the tour a group of women presented him with a wooden urn containing the ashes of a bail or stump, which has since been kept at Lord's Cricket Ground in London. Despite what many people think, this urn does not contain a relic of the famous Australian victory of 1882.

ask

Like many short but vital words, **ask** is Old English. Variations of the saying **ask a silly question and you get a silly answer** date back to at least the 13th century. It has a biblical source, 'Answer a fool according to his folly, lest he be wise in his own conceit', from the Book of Proverbs.

A **big ask** is a difficult demand to make of someone, a lot to ask. The phrase originates in Australia, where it was first recorded in 1987, but has spread quickly into British English, and is a favourite of sports players, commentators and writers, as in the example 'If we get four wins we will make the play-offs, but it's a big ask' (*Bolton Evening News*).

asparagus

The vegetable we now know as **asparagus** was originally called *sparagus* (from medieval Latin), which was soon turned into the more English-sounding **sparrow-grass**. This process is called folk etymology, where people modify the form of an unusual word to make it seem to be derived from familiar ones. **Sparrow-grass** remained the polite name for the vegetable during the 18th century, with only botanists sticking to the spelling **asparagus**. As the compiler of a pronunciation dictionary wrote in 1791, '*Sparrow-grass* is so general that *asparagus* has an air of stiffness and pedantry.' It wasn't until the 19th century that **asparagus** returned into literary and polite use, leaving **sparrow-grass** to survive as an English dialect form.

aspersion

To engage in **casting aspersions** is almost literally mud-slinging. **Aspersion** originally meant 'sprinkling water or other liquid on someone', especially in baptism, and came from Latin *spargere* 'to sprinkle'

(the root of **disperse** and **intersperse**). Sprinkling a person with water developed into the idea of spattering them with something less pleasant, such as mud or dung. This in turn led to the notion of soiling a person's reputation by making false and damaging insinuations against them. See also SLUR.

ass see ARSE.

assassin

During the Crusades political and religious leaders were targeted for murder by a fanatical sect of Ismaili Muslims led by Hassan-i-Sabbah (known as the 'Old Man of the Mountains'). Members of the sect were said to prepare themselves for these deeds by smoking or chewing hashish or cannabis, although this would surely be more likely to subdue their militant zeal, and were accordingly known in Arabic as *hashīshī*, 'hashish-eaters', which was filtered through French and eventually became our word **assassin**. The first recorded example of the word in its more familiar meaning comes from the 1530s.

asterisk

The Greeks had two words for 'star', *astēr* and *astron*. They go right back to an ancient root that is also the source of the Latin word *stella*, which gave us STAR itself and also **stellar**.

An **asterisk** is a symbol that looks like a little star, so it is not surprising that it comes from a Greek word (*asteriskos*) which means exactly that. *Asteriskos* itself is derived from *astēr*, which is also the root of *asteroeidēs*, 'star-like'. This came into English in the early 19th century as **asteroid**, a term that the astronomer William Herschel coined for the small rocky bodies orbiting the sun. *Astēr* also gave us our name for the plant aster, which has purple or pink flowers whose petals radiate out from the centre rather like an asterisk.

Words beginning with *astro-* come from *astron*. In the Middle Ages **astronomy** covered not only astronomy but astrology too. The Greek word it descends from meant 'star-arranging'. By the 17th century the modern distinction between astronomy (the scientific study of the stars and planets) and astrology (the art of interpreting how the movements the stars and planets may influence people's lives) was established.

Rather poetically, an **astronaut** is literally a 'star sailor'. The word dates from the 1920s and comes from Greek *astron* 'star' and *nautēs* 'sailor'. It was modelled on **aeronaut**, an old word for a traveller in a hot-air balloon or an airship. **Cosmonaut**, a later term for a

Russian astronaut, literally means 'sailor in the cosmos', a traveller in outer space.

athlete

In Greek *athlon* meant 'prize', and the word *athlētēs*, from which we get **athlete**, literally meant 'someone who competes for a prize'. It originally referred to one of the competitors in the physical exercises – such as running, leaping, boxing and wrestling – that formed part of the public games in ancient Greece and Rome.

atlas

Atlas was a Titan, or giant, in Greek mythology who was punished for taking part in a rebellion against the gods by being made to bear the entire weight of the Universe on his shoulders. He also gave his name to the Atlas Mountains in Morocco, which are so high that they were imagined to be holding up the sky. A collection of maps is called an **atlas** because early works of this kind were published with an illustration of Atlas bearing the world on his back on the title page. The first person to use the word in this way was probably the map-maker Gerardus Mercator in the late 16th century.

The **Atlantic Ocean** also gets its name from Atlas. The word **Atlantic** originally referred to Mount Atlas in Libya, then to the sea near the west African coast, and later to the whole ocean.

Charles Atlas was the assumed name of Angelo Siciliano (1893-1972), an Italian who emigrated to the USA with his parents when he was ten. Small and puny as a young man, he decided to take up bodybuilding and in 1922 won a national contest as 'America's most perfectly developed man'. He developed a correspondence course for bodybuilding which he publicised widely, especially in comics, describing how he had had sand kicked in his face on a beach by a lifeguard who then stole his girlfriend.

Charles Atlas

atom

Long before scientists were able to prove the existence of atoms, ancient Greek philosophers believed that matter was made up of tiny particles that could not be broken down into anything smaller. The word the Greeks used for this hypothetical particle was *atomos* 'indivisible, that cannot be cut up', from *a-* 'not' and *temnein* 'to cut'. By way of Latin *atomus*, this came into English in the 15th century as **atom**. The word was used in the early 19th century by the British chemist John Dalton when he gathered evidence for the existence of these building blocks of matter. A century later the physicist Ernest Rutherford disproved the theory that the atom could not be divided when he split the atom for the first time, in 1919.

The power unleashed by this splitting, or fission, paved the way for the atom bomb and its use against the cities of Hiroshima and Nagasaki in August 1945. The term **atom bomb** was first recorded in *The Times* on August 7, 1945, the day after the Hiroshima blast. Japan surrendered on August 15, the date when **the Bomb** first appeared in a headline in *The Times* – 'Victory and the Bomb'.

H. G. Wells was writing about an 'atomic bomb' as early as 1914.

atrocious

Whereas nowadays **atrocious** tends to describe something like bad weather or poor English, it used to be a stronger word which referred to great savagery, cruelty or wickedness, as in Charles Darwin's reference to 'Atrocious acts which can only take place in a slave country' (1845). The source of the word was Latin *atrox* 'fierce or cruel', based on *ater* 'black' and literally meaning 'black-looking'.

auburn

The root of our word **auburn** is Latin *albus*, which actually meant 'white'. Based on this, medieval Latin formed the word *alburnus* 'whitish', which in Old French became *alborne* (or *auborne*) 'yellowish-white' and was subsequently adopted into English. In the 16th and 17th centuries it was written down in a number of different ways, including **abron**, **abrune** and **abroun**, and these spellings must have put into people's minds the idea that auburn was in fact a kind of brown.

Digger dialect

Australian and New Zealand English is fun and informal. TV shows such as *Neighbours* have helped spread it across the globe – so now a Putney pom is as likely as a Sydney sheila to toss a shrimp on the barbie.

Hundreds of indigenous languages have enriched Australasian English. The 18th-century journals of the explorer Captain Cook record kangaroo as a name used for the animal by Aboriginals in what is now North Queensland. A later suggestion that the word actually meant 'I don't understand', given as a reply to an enquiry in English, took people's fancy but it now seems to be an invented story.

In Australia one way of suggesting that someone is mad or eccentric is to say that they have kangaroos in the top paddock. This is something of a zoological contrast with the British 'bats in the belfry'.

When European settlers first came across the Aboriginal word budgerigar for the colourful little native bird they had absolutely no idea how they should spell it, and early attempts included *betshiregah*, *budgery garr* and *budgregore*. The Maori word kiwi entered English in the 1830s. People started using the bird as the emblem of New Zealand at the end of the 1890s, and New Zealanders have been known as Kiwis since shortly after that.

The larrikin is one of the Australian stereotypes – the maverick with an apparent disregard for convention, or the boisterous young man. The word could have been brought over from England – it is recorded in Cornish dialect in the 1880s – or based on Larry, a form of the man's name Lawrence common in Ireland and the Irish Australian community.

During the First World War Australian and New Zealand soldiers were referred to as diggers, in the sense 'miner', which was used of gold and opal miners in Australasia. In peacetime

digger became a friendly form of address for a man, like cobber, which probably came from English dialect *cob* 'to like'.

One of the things that friends do together is drink, and if they have too much they may chunder, or vomit, in the dunny. The first is probably from rhyming slang *Chunder Loo* = 'spew'. Chunder Loo of Akim Foo was a cartoon character devised by Norman Lindsay (1879-1969) that appeared in advertisements for Cobra boot polish in the early 20th century. Dunny, or 'toilet', was originally a dunnekin, an English dialect word from dung and ken, meaning 'house'.

Australians may refer to a Brit as a Limey or a pom. The former comes from the rations of lime juice given to Royal Navy seamen to ward off scurvy, while the latter term probably derives from POMEGRANATE, as a near rhyme for 'immigrant'. The red, sunburnt cheeks of new arrivals may also have reminded people of the fruit.

If an Australian or New Zealander tells you to rattle your dags, you would be well advised to hurry up. Dags are locks of wool clotted with dung at the rear end of a sheep, which can rattle as they move. The word may be related to tag, and goes back to medieval England, when dags were pointed divisions on the edge of a fashionable garment. Today an entertaining or eccentric person can also be called a dag, as can someone who is untidy or dirty-looking, or an awkward adolescent.

Australian bushmen used various women's names for a bundle or 'swag' of personal belongings, but Matilda is the one whose name stuck, especially after 1893 when A.B. 'Banjo' Paterson wrote the song 'Waltzing Matilda'. To waltz (or walk) Matilda is to travel the roads carrying your swag. The other woman's name forever associated with Australia is Sheila, an Irish name that has meant 'a girl or woman' since the 1820s.

kangaroos in the top paddock

One of Australia's best-loved exports, via the *Neighbours* soap opera, has been the singer Kylie Minogue. Some of her fans may be unaware that in Western Australia a kylie is a boomerang. The word is from the Aboriginal language Nyungar.

See also ANTIPODES, BLUE, BUNG, DINKUM, LAIRY, MOCKER, PIKE, POSSUM, TUCKER.

The word has always been used to describe hair, but its meaning gradually changed from 'yellowish-white' to 'golden-brown or reddish-brown'. See also ALBUM, BAIZE, BROWN.

auction

In an **auction** the bids are steadily increased until an item is sold. This aspect is embodied in the word's origin, as it derives from Latin *auctio* 'an increase', from *augere* 'to increase', also the source of **augment** and AUTHOR – the idea of a sale by ever-increasing bids was already captured in Latin usage.

audacious

Today **audacious** means 'willing to take surprisingly bold risks' and 'showing a lack of respect, impudent', but it originally had a more direct sense of 'bold, confident, daring'. The root is Latin *audax* 'bold', from *audere* 'to dare'.

audience

When people go to the theatre they generally talk about going to 'see' a play, but in former times the usual verb was 'hear'. In keeping with this idea, the oldest meaning of **audience** is 'hearing, attention to what is spoken'. **Audience** is based on the Latin word *audire* 'to hear', as are a number of other English words, the best known of which is **audible**, 'able to be heard'. An **auditorium**, originally a Latin word, was a place for hearing something. Before it meant a trial performance of an actor or singer, **audition** was the act of hearing or listening. And an **audit** was originally a hearing, in particular a judicial hearing of some kind – it was later used as the term for the reading out of a set of accounts, hence the modern meaning.

auspicious

In Roman times people tried to predict future events by watching the behaviour of animals and birds. An *auspex* was a person who observed the flight of birds for omens about what to do in important matters, and gave advice according to them. A related word, *auspicium*, meant 'taking omens from birds'. Like *auspex*, it was derived from *avis* 'bird' and *specere* 'to look'. *Auspicium* came into English in the 16th century as **auspice**. It was originally used to translate the Roman concept, but later came to mean 'a premonition or forecast, especially of a happy future'. The adjective **auspicious** accordingly meant 'fortunate or favourable'. If the ancient Roman auspex's omens were favourable, he was seen as the protector of a particular enterprise, hence the expression **under the auspices of**, 'with the help, support or protection of'. An auspex

was also known as an *augur* (again, *avis* 'bird' is the root of this word, together with *garrire* 'to talk'). If something **augurs** well, it is a sign of a good outcome. See also AVIATION, INAUGURAL.

Australia

Since the days of the ancient Greeks, travellers speculated on the existence of an 'unknown southern land', or in Latin *terra australis incognita*, from *australis* 'of the south'. Portuguese sailors may have reached Australia in the 16th century, but the first Europeans known to have visited it were the Dutch in 1606. At first the continent was called New Holland, and it was not officially named Australia until 1824.

author

In medieval English the **author** of something was the person who originated, invented or caused it. God was sometimes described as 'the Author of all'. The word came into English via Old French from Latin *augere* 'to increase or originate'. **Augment** has the same source, as does AUCTION. In time **author** came to be applied specifically to the writer of a book.

Some purists feel that it is wrong to use **author** as a verb meaning 'be the author of'. It is very well established, though, and has been in use since the end of the 16th century. The first recorded example comes from George Chapman's translation of Homer's *Iliad*, dated 1596.

autopsy

In an **autopsy** someone seeks to find out how a person died by seeing the body with their own eyes. An early sense of the word was 'personal observation', and this is the key to the word's origin. It comes from Greek *autoptēs* 'eyewitness', based on *autos* 'self' and *optos* 'seen', which means that it is related to other English words like **optic** and **optician**.

autumn

We now call the season between summer and winter **autumn**, a word that is recorded in English from the 14th century and comes via Old French from Latin *autumnus*. HARVEST, an older word, was the usual name for the season until **autumn** displaced it in the 16th century. Americans call it FALL, which was originally a British expression, first recorded in 1545, for the season in which leaves fall from the trees, and travelled over to the New World with the first colonists.

average

Originally a shipping term, meaning either the duty payable by the owner of goods about to be shipped or the financial liability for any goods lost or damaged at sea, **average** came into English in the 15th century from French *avarie* 'damage to a ship or cargo, customs duty'. The ultimate source was Arabic *awar* 'damage to goods'. All this may seem a long way from the modern meaning of **average**, but the word came to be applied to the fair splitting of the financial liability between the owners of the vessel and the owners of the cargo, which in time led to the modern senses.

aviation

The Latin word for 'bird', *avis*, is the root of a number of English words that relate to birds, such as **aviary** and **avian**. It is also the source of words connected with the idea of flying, such as **aviation** and **aviator**, both 19th-century borrowings of French words. See also AUSPICIOUS.

avocado

Look at an **avocado** – does it remind you of anything? The name of the avocado in the Aztec language Nahuatl was *ahuacatl*, also the word for 'testicle' and applied to the fruit because of its shape. In the 16th century the Spanish conquerors of Central America adopted this word but converted it into the form *aguacate* and then to the more familiar-sounding *avocado*, the Spanish word for 'a lawyer' (and related to the English **advocate**). The word came into English in the mid 17th century.

awe

The battle plan for the 2003 invasion of Iraq by US-led forces was dubbed **shock and awe**. The phrase was not invented by President George W. Bush or Secretary of Defense Donald Rumsfeld, but came from *Shock and Awe: Achieving Rapid Dominance* (1996), by the US strategic analysts Harlan K. Ullman and James P. Wade. The Old English word **awe** originally meant 'terror or dread'. Gradually people started to use it to express their feelings for God, a being who inspired some fear but also great respect and wonder, and now we might be in awe of an impressively powerful or talented person, or of some wonder of nature.

Both **awful** and **awesome** have become weaker in meaning over the centuries. **Awful** was originally used to describe things that caused terror or dread – Winston Churchill used it in this sense when he referred to 'the grim and awful cataclysm of war'. Other old meanings included 'awe-inspiring' and 'filled with awe'; the modern sense 'extremely bad' dates from the early 19th century. **Awesome** dates from the late 16th century, when it meant 'filled with awe'. It later came to mean 'inspiring awe', and in the 1960s took on the

rather weaker meaning of 'overwhelming, remarkable, staggering'. Now it can just mean 'great, excellent', especially in the USA.

awkward

There used to be a word **awk**, based on an Old Norse *afugr*, that meant 'turned the wrong way round'. So **awkward** meant 'in an awk direction', 'in the wrong direction, in reverse order, upside down'. It could be applied, for instance, to an animal that was on its back and was unable to get up. The meaning 'clumsy or ungainly' dates from the 16th century, followed by other meanings such as 'embarrassing' or 'difficult to deal with'.

axe

Since Anglo-Saxon times an **axe** has been a tool or weapon, but since the 1950s it has also been a musical instrument. Jazz fans started referring to saxophones as axes, but now an axe is generally an electric guitar. Many people will feel that the threat of **the axe**, meaning a measure intended to reduce costs, especially by making people redundant, is a particularly modern one, but the term goes back at least to 1922. In that year the *Glasgow Herald* reported on 'military officers . . . who are the unhappy victims of the Geddes economy "axe"'.

A person who **has an axe to grind** has a private reason for doing something. The phrase is thought to come from an 18th-century cautionary tale in which a passing stranger takes advantage of a bystander and, by flattering him, tricks him into turning a grindstone to sharpen his axe.

axis

In Latin *axis* means 'axle' or 'pivot'. That is really what an axis is – an imaginary line through a body, around which it rotates, rather like an invisible axle. In the Second World War **the Axis** was the alliance of Germany and Italy, later also including Japan and other countries, which opposed the Allies. The connection with an axis was the idea of the relations between countries forming a 'pivot' around which they revolved. The reference to the concept, in *The Times* for November 3, 1936, mentions 'the Rome-Berlin axis'. See also EVIL.

baby

Both **baby** and **babe** probably come from the way that the sound *ba* is repeated by very young children, and both are medieval words. A person's lover or spouse has been their **baby** since the middle of the 19th century, in the USA. The sense 'someone's creation or special concern' dates from later in that century – in 1890 artificial silk was referred to as its inventor's 'new-born baby'.

The proverb **don't throw the baby out with the bathwater**, 'don't reject the essential with the inessential', is from German. The first known appearance in English is from the Scottish historian and political philosopher Thomas Carlyle, who wrote in 1853 that 'The Germans say, "You must empty out the bathing-tub, but not the baby along with it"'.

Babe originally just meant 'child', and only later became restricted to a child too young to walk. Inexperienced people in a situation calling for experience are **babes in the wood**, from characters in an old ballad *The Children in the Wood*, whose wicked uncle wanted to steal their inheritance and abandoned them in a wood. The proverbial phrase **out of the mouths of babes** is used when a precocious child says something unexpectedly appropriate. It has biblical origins – 'Out of the mouth of babes and sucklings', in Psalms and the Gospel of Matthew.

A **babe** today is generally an attractive young woman, or occasionally a man. Actually, the first babes *were* men. In the 1870s the youngest member of class of US military cadets was called the babe, rather like 'the baby of the family'. The term was then used as a friendly form of address between men before it came to mean a sexy girl. See also BIMBO.

bachelor

The word **bachelor** was adopted from French in the early Middle Ages. The earliest meaning was 'a young knight serving under another's banner', one who was not old or rich enough to have his own band of followers. The sense 'unmarried man' is known from the late Middle Ages – Geoffrey Chaucer wrote in *The Canterbury Tales* that 'bachelors have often pain and woe'.

back

As you would expect with such a common and fundamental word, **back** is as old as English itself – and even older than that. Over its long history it has been prolific in forming compounds, phrases and popular expressions.

If you **get someone's back up** you make them annoyed. The image is that of a cat arching its back when angry or threatened. The idea is recorded as early as 1728: a character in *The Provok'd Husband*, a comic play of that year by John Vanbrugh and Colley Cibber, remarks, 'How her back will be up then, when she meets me!'

People often exaggerate the remoteness of a place by saying it is at the back of somewhere that is already remote. To Australians the back of beyond is **back o' Bourke**, Bourke being a remote town in New South Wales. In America there have been **backwoods** since the early 18th century.

Failure has sent people **back to square one** since the 1950s. This possibly comes from a board game such as Snakes and Ladders, in which the board has some squares that send a player who lands on them back to the beginning or to an earlier position. **Back to the drawing board** does not seem to have been used until the 1940s, though drawing boards themselves have been known by that name from the early 18th century.

Andrew Johnson, the 17th President of the USA, gave us the phrase to **take a back seat**. He said in 1868 that 'in the work of Reconstruction traitors should take back seats' (the Reconstruction was the period 1865-77 following the American Civil War). In the 20th century the car brought with it the **back-seat driver**. By the 1950s the term appears in other contexts: in 1955 *The Times* reported a comment that 'it was contrary to democracy for elected members to consult "pressure groups" and "back-seat drivers"'. See also KITCHEN, NIMBY.

The novelist Sir Walter Scott was the first person to use the back of beyond, in 1816.

bacon

The word **bacon** was adopted from French in the 14th century, but it is not ultimately from Latin, as most French words are. It can be traced back to an ancient German root that links it to BACK. In early use it could mean fresh meat, what we now call pork, as well as cured, and could also refer to a pig's carcass.

To **bring home the bacon**, 'to supply food or support', first appeared in the USA during the early years of the 20th century. It may have developed from to **save one's bacon** ('to escape danger or difficulty'), an older expression which dates from the mid 17th century.

bad

Homophobia may lie at the root of the meaning of **bad**. The word first appeared in the 13th century, and at that time had two syllables, like **baddy**. This suggests that it may be a shortening of Old English *bæddel* 'effeminate man'.

Bad was specifically applied to coins with a reduced content of precious metal. This gives us the **bad penny**, which 'always turns up'. Debased coinage also features in the proverb **bad money drives out good**, also known as Gresham's law, after Queen Elizabeth I's chief financial adviser Sir Thomas Gresham. He observed that people tended to hang on to coins of a high intrinsic value, like gold sovereigns, while being happier to spend those of a lower intrinsic worth but equal face value.

At the end of the 19th century **bad** underwent a complete reversal of meaning in US black slang, and in the 1920s jazz enthusiasts began to use it as a term of approval – something 'bad' was now 'good'. Compare the development of FUNK and WICKED.

bag

The first record of **bag** comes from the early medieval period, and it may date back to an older Scandinavian word. Some phrases in English derive specifically from its use to mean a hunter's game bag, such as having something **in the bag**, 'as good as secured'. Another sense, 'a particular interest or distinctive style', as in 'Dance music isn't really my bag', is probably jazz slang of the late 1950s. In the sense 'an unattractive woman', **bag** or **old bag** was originally American, and was first recorded in the 1890s.

baize

Today we think of **baize**, the material used for covering billiard tables, as green in colour. But originally it must have been brown, as the word comes from the French *bai* 'chestnut-coloured'. Bai is also the root of the English word **bay**, used to describe a brown horse with black mane and tail.

bail

The spelling **bail** represents several different words. The one meaning 'temporary release of an accused person' came via French from Latin *bajulus*, 'a carrier', and is related to **bailiff**. The Latin word is also ultimately the source of **bail** (in Britain also spelled **bale**) meaning 'to scoop water out of a boat'. The **bailey** or outer wall of a castle has a quite different origin, but it is connected with the third **bail**, a crosspiece on a cricket stump: originally this **bail** meant the same as **bailey**. The ultimate origin of both of these appears to be Latin *baculum*, 'a rod or stick'.

Bailing out from an aircraft may be a development of the 'to scoop water' sense. It was at first spelled **bale out**, though, and could come from the idea of letting a bale of straw though a trapdoor in a barn. The first written record dates from 1930.

baker's dozen

This expression, meaning 'thirteen', arose in the 16th century. It was a traditional bakers' practice to add an extra loaf to every dozen sold to a shopkeeper – this bonus, thirteenth loaf was the source of the retailer's profit when the loaves were sold on to customers. The surname Baxter derives from a female form of the word **baker** (with *-ster* as in spinster), though historically people used it of bakers of either sex.

bald

Words related to **bald** in other northern European languages suggest that its core meaning was 'having a white patch or streak'. This may survive in the phrase **as bald as a coot**. The coot is not actually bald (few birds are, not even the bald eagle): it has a broad white area on its forehead extending up from the base of its bill. Descriptions of people as being **as bald as a coot** appear as far back as the 15th century.

ball

The spherical **ball** dates from the early Middle Ages, and comes from an old Scandinavian word that was the ultimate root of Italian *ballotta*, from which English took **ballot** in the mid 16th century, and also of French *ballon* and Italian *ballone* 'large ball', one of which was the source of BALLOON. The **ball** at which people dance is completely unrelated. It came later, in the early 17th century, from French, and goes back to Latin *ballare* 'to dance'. This was also the source of **ballad** and **ballet**.

In America a ball game is a baseball match and a ballpark a baseball stadium. These have entered even British English in phrases such as **a whole new ball game**, 'a completely new set of circumstances', **in the (right) ballpark**, 'a particular area or range', and a **ballpark figure** (an approximate figure).

The dancing sense has notably given us **have a ball**, meaning 'enjoy yourself a lot'. This was originally an American expression of the 1930s, but is now used nearly everywhere that English is spoken.

Testicles have been **balls** since the Middle Ages, but the slang sense 'nonsense' is Victorian. The meaning 'courage, determination' is more recent still, dating only from the 1950s. People often claim that the phrase **cold enough to freeze the balls off a brass monkey** comes from a former naval custom of storing cannonballs on a brass rack or 'monkey'. When the weather was very cold the rack could contract and eject the cannonballs. There are some severe problems with this explanation, though. First, cannonballs were stored on a wooden rack, not a brass one. Second, it would have to be extremely cold to cause sufficient contraction in the metal for this to happen. And third, the earliest recorded versions of the phrase (dating from the 19th century) feature noses and tails rather than balls, suggesting that the reference is to a brass statue of a monkey, and that the 'balls' are testicles rather than cannonballs. See also BOLLOCK, COB, GOLDEN.

ballistic

Two ancient engines of war, a catapult for hurling large stones and a large crossbow firing a spear, were each known as a **ballista**. The Latin source, *ballista*, from Greek *ballein* 'to throw', gave us **ballistic**. As a technical term this dates from the 18th century, but it only became widely known in the mid 20th century with the development of the **ballistic missile**, a missile which is initially powered and guided but falls under gravity on to its target. In the 1980s to **go ballistic** began to be used meaning 'to fly into a rage'.

balloon

The **balloon** that carries passengers in a basket is older than the one used as a children's toy. In 1782 the brothers Joseph and Jacques Montgolfier built a large balloon from

linen and paper and successfully lifted a number of animals, and the following year people, whereas the toy version did not appear until the middle of the next century. The word was adopted from French or Italian in the late 16th century, and originally referred to a large inflatable leather ball used in a game of the same name. It goes back to the same Scandinavian root as BALL.

The phrase **when the balloon goes up**, 'when the action or trouble begins', has been used in Britain since the 1920s. It may refer to the release of a balloon to mark the beginning of a race. By contrast, to **go down like a lead balloon** is American in origin: **lead balloon** appears as a term meaning 'a failure, a flop' in a comic strip of 1924 in which a man who had been sold dud shares discovered they were 'about to go up as fast as a lead balloon'. The British rock group Led Zeppelin took their name from a joking comment made by Keith Moon, drummer with the Who. He quipped that the new group would probably go down 'like a lead zeppelin'.

banana

Africa is the original home of the **banana**. The word travelled to English through Portuguese and Spanish from Mande, a language group of West Africa, arriving in the 16th century.

The fruit was too exotic for its name to enter into slang expressions in the first few centuries of its English life, but in the 20th century it began to inspire the linguistic imagination. American people began to **go bananas** with excitement, anger or frustration in the 1950s. The **top banana**, 'the most important person in an organisation', derives from US theatrical slang.

It referred to the comedian with top billing in a show, a use first recorded in 1953 from a US newspaper, which also mentions **second** and **third bananas**. People have been slipping on a **banana skin** since the beginning of the 20th century: the comic writer P.G. Wodehouse referred in 1934 to 'Treading upon Life's banana skins'. The **banana republic**, a small state, especially in central America, whose economy is almost entirely dependent on its fruit-exporting trade, was referred to as early as 1904.

band

Musicians take note: in early use a **band** usually consisted of armed men, robbers or assassins. The first groups of musicians called a band (in the 17th century) were attached to regiments of the army. The word is related to **banner**, and has always had military connections.

A **bandwagon** was once really for a band – it was a wagon used for carrying the band in a parade or procession. The word now occurs more often in phrases such as to **jump on the bandwagon**, referring to an activity or cause that has suddenly become fashionable or looks likely to become successful. This use developed in America in the late 19th century.

bang

The word **bang** imitates the sound, though it may have been taken from an old Scandinavian form. The American expression **bang for your buck**, 'value for money, return on your investment', was originally used in the early 1950s of military spending, especially on nuclear weapons. A nuclear explosion was referred to as the **big bang** in John Osborne's 1957 play *Look Back in Anger*: 'If the big bang does come, and we all get killed off . . .'. Nowadays the **Big Bang** is more usually the explosion in which the Universe originated. It was originally a term of ridicule, used by the scientist Fred Hoyle in 1950, but is now the standard term for a respectable theory. In 1986 it was also the name given to the major changes in trading on the Stock Exchange introduced that year.

Banger has had several slang senses since the beginning of the 1800s. It was first a gross or blatant lie, what we would now call a 'whopper'. It was also a loud or forceful kiss, or a 'smacker', and in US college slang it was a cane or club. The meaning 'sausage' is originally Australian, and was probably suggested by the tendency of fat sausages to 'pop' if not pricked before cooking. The 'old car' sense is surprisingly recent, not being recorded before the 1960s. See also WHIMPER.

> **Bang on, meaning 'exactly right, excellent', originated in air force slang, and referred to dropping a bomb exactly on target.**

bank

The very different uses of **bank** are all ultimately related. The **bank** beside a river or stream was adopted from a Scandinavian word in the early Middle Ages, and is related to **bench**. The earliest use of the **bank** or financial institution referred to a money-dealer's counter or table. This came from French or Italian in the late 15th century, but goes back to the same root as the first **bank**. A **bank** of oars or of lights represents yet another related form. It came into English in the early Middle Ages from French, and originally meant a bench or a platform to speak from.

bankrupt

The earliest form of **bankrupt**, in the mid 16th century, was **bankrout**. This reflects the word's origin in Italian *banca rotta*, which really means 'a broken bench'. The reference was to the breaking up or abandonment of a trader's business – originally a counter or table, as described at BANK – because he could not pay his liabilities. The word was altered early on in its history in English, through association with Latin *ruptus* 'broken'.

bar

There are few more functional words than **bar**. It gives us bars of soap and chocolate, bars serving drinks, bars that we can put criminals behind, and in Britain members of the Bar who can help to put them there. The word entered English from French in the early Middle Ages, but beyond that its history is unknown. Its earliest use was for fastening a gate or door. People used it for various kinds of **barrier** – a related word. In a court a bar marked off the area around the judge's seat, where prisoners were brought to be charged – hence **prisoner at the bar**. At the Inns of Court, where lawyers were trained in England, a bar separated students from those qualified, and a student was 'called to the bar' to become a fully fledged **barrister**. From this **the Bar** came to mean the whole body of barristers, or the barrister's profession, as early as the 16th century. At this time a bar was also a barrier or counter from which drink was served.

From barring doors and barring a person's way, it took a small step for **bar** to mean 'to prohibit', as in **no holds barred**, and 'except': **bar none** means 'without exception'.

barbarian

It is nothing new for people to despise or scoff at foreigners and their speech and customs. The ancient Greeks were high achievers, with a high opinion of themselves and a correspondingly low one of other peoples. They called everyone who did not speak Greek *barbaros* or 'foreign', which is where we get **barbarian** and related words **barbaric**, **barbarity** and **barbarous**. The word *barbaros* originally imitated the unintelligible language of foreigners, which to the Greeks just sounded like *ba, ba, ba*.

barber

No one now would go to a hairdresser to have a tooth or bullet extracted, but originally barbers were also regular practitioners of surgery and dentistry, as well as cutting and trimming beards – the word **barber** goes back to French *barbe*, 'a beard'. The Company of Barbers was given a charter by Edward IV in 1461. Under Henry VIII the title was altered to 'Company of Barbers and Surgeons', and in 1745 they were divided into two distinct livery companies.

In the 16th and 17th centuries, long before glossy magazines, barbers provided lute or guitar music for customers waiting their turn. Naturally some would sing along. This **barber's music** was not always pleasant to listen to, and the term was quite insulting. In America standards seem to have been higher: the term **barbershop** for close-harmony singing is first recorded in the early 20th century.

barge

A **barge** was originally a small seagoing vessel rather than a humble flat-bottomed boat for carrying freight. The word is French and probably comes ultimately from Greek *baris*, which referred to a kind of Egyptian boat used on the Nile. The verb sense 'move forcefully or roughly', which dates from the end of the 19th century, refers to the way a heavily laden, unwieldy barge might collide with the bank or other traffic at a port or lock.

If you **wouldn't touch something with a bargepole** you refuse to have anything to do with it. An early example in a diary of 1893 expressed the opinion that 'It will be a long while before any political party touches Home Rule again with the end of a barge pole'. The equivalent expression in America says that you **wouldn't touch something with a ten-foot pole**.

Barbershop quartet

bark

Dogs have always barked, so it is not surprising that **bark** is a prehistoric word. It may be an imitation of the sound, though it is also possible that it is related to **break**.

If **someone's bark is worse than their bite** they are not as ferocious as they appear or sound. The contrast between barking and biting also appears in the proverb **a barking dog never bites**. Forms of this are recorded from the 16th century, and there are also similar proverbs in French and Latin.

Short-tempered schoolteachers and sergeant majors are often described as barking orders. But barking is often a waste of time: you can **bark at the moon** or **bark up the wrong tree**. The first of these, meaning 'to make a fuss with no effect', is first recorded in the 17th century. The second, 'to be pursuing a mistaken or misguided course of action', is from the 19th century and is originally American.

People have been **barking** or **barking mad** since the 1930s. The idea is that they have lost control so completely that they are barking like a dog.

The bark of a tree is possibly related to the name of the **birch** tree. **Bark** or **barque** is also an old-fashioned word for a boat, from which we get **disembark** and **embark**.

barnacle

A **barnacle** was originally what we would now call a **barnacle goose**. The name appeared in English in the early Middle Ages, but its ultimate origin is unknown. The barnacle goose breeds in the arctic tundra of

Greenland and similar places, but for a long time its place of origin was something of a mystery. People thought it hatched from the shell of a particular crustacean that attaches itself to objects floating in the water and has long feathery filaments protruding from its shell, which presumably suggested the notion of plumage. The shellfish itself started to be called a **barnacle** in the 16th century.

barrel

Before refrigerators and other mod cons made life easier, the **barrel** used for storage, and dating back to Latin *barriclus* 'small cask', was a more familiar object. Various phrases refer back to those earlier days. To **have someone over a barrel** is to have them in a helpless position, at one's mercy. People rescued from drowning would be laid face down over a barrel to help the water to drain out of their lungs, and it is possible that the idea of helplessness developed into one of coercion, although the phrase could derive from the idea of someone forced to lie over a barrel to be flogged. If you **scrape the barrel** (or **the bottom of the barrel**) you are reduced to using things or people of the poorest quality because nothing else is available. Neither of the expressions is recorded until the early 20th century.

barricade

Barricades now tend to be associated with protests against governments, and to **man the barricades** is to stage a protest of a kind particularly associated with France. The word is indeed French, formed from *barrique* 'cask' – barrels were part of the assemblage of objects, furniture and stones thrown up to block the streets. The French word came ultimately from Spanish *barrica*, and the form *barricado* was formerly used in English as well as **barricade**. Both are recorded from the late 16th century.

base

Along with the words **basic** and **basis**, **base** comes via Latin from the Greek form *basis*, which meant 'step, walk' and 'pedestal'. Its first meaning was 'the pedestal of a statue'.

Although **baseball**, which goes back to the beginning of the 19th century, is primarily an American game, phrases drawn from its terminology are familiar elsewhere. A notable example is to **touch base**, 'to briefly make or renew contact with something or somebody'. Other phrases using **base** include to **get to first base**, 'to achieve the first step towards your objective', and **off base**, 'mistaken', though these are still primarily American. See also BAT.

basic

For such a basic word, **basic** has been around for a relatively short time – it did not emerge until the mid 19th century. The catchphrase **back to basics**, calling for a return to fundamentals, first appeared in the USA in the 1940s. Such calls have a way of going wrong, and an example was the 'back-to-basics' campaign of the British Prime Minister John Major in 1993, which took a high moral tone over personal behaviour. Its launch was fairly promptly followed by a series of scandals involving members of his own government.

bastard

In the past **bastard** was the standard term for an illegitimate child, but now this use is old-fashioned, and the word is mainly a term of abuse. It probably derives from medieval Latin *bastum* 'packsaddle' (a horse's saddle which was adapted for supporting loads) – the French equivalent was *fils de bast* or 'packsaddle son'. The reference was to a loose-living mule driver who used a packsaddle for a pillow and the next morning was off to the next town (and girl). See also BAT.

bat

The nocturnal flying mammal was originally not a **bat** but a **back**. The earliest form, adopted in the early Middle Ages from a Scandinavian word, was altered to **bat** in the 16th century.

The creature has inspired numerous expressions. You could be **as blind as a bat** from the 16th century – before then the standard comparison was with a beetle. From the early 20th century you could **have bats in the belfry**, 'be mad', or, in the same vein, be **bats** or **batty**.

The first recorded example of **like a bat out of hell**, 'very fast and wildly', is from the *Atlanta Constitution* of February 3, 1914: 'One day we saw an automobile go down the street like a bat out of hell and a few moments later we heard that it hit the last car of a freight train at the grade crossing.' In 1977 the singer Meat Loaf gave the title *Bat Out of Hell* to his second album. It has sold more than 34 million copies worldwide, making it one of the most successful records of all time.

An old-fashioned name for a bat is **flittermouse**, meaning literally 'flying mouse'. Dutch *vledermuis* and German *Fledermaus* are matching terms in other languages.

The other **bat**, the implement for hitting a ball, is a word adopted from French in the Old English period, and is related to **batter** and BATTERY. If you do something **off your own bat** you are using a cricketing phrase; it originally referred to the score made by a player's own hits, and so 'at your own instigation'. But if you did something **right off the bat**, 'at the very beginning, straight away', you would be taking a term from baseball.

Batman has been a comic character and superhero since 1939. The less glamorous batman was a British army officer's personal servant. This **bat** is unrelated to the other two. It came through French from medieval Latin *bastum* 'a packsaddle' (which is probably the ultimate source of BASTARD) and originally referred to a man in charge of a *bat-horse*, which carried the luggage of military officers.

bated

A shortened form of **abated**, meaning 'reduced, lessened'. The idea behind the phrase **with bated breath** is that the anxiety or excitement you experience while waiting for something to happen is so great that you almost stop breathing. The word is sometimes spelled **baited**, from a mistaken association with a fisherman's bait.

bath

The city of **Bath** in the west of England derives its name from its hot springs, where people immersed themselves for health reasons. The word and the place name were both known in Old English times. Baths are much more everyday things than they once were. The British order of knighthood the **Order of the Bath** has this name because recipients took a bath before being installed – it was a special event. Nowadays sports players usually take a bath after each game. If they take **an early bath** they have been sent off by the referee. This is particularly associated with the 1970s English Rugby League commentator Eddie Waring, who was also famous for his catchphrase 'It's an up and under!'

baton

The original **baton** was a club or cudgel, used as a weapon. Now it is a less dangerous object. The baton used to direct an orchestra or choir was first mentioned by the historian of music Charles Burney (father of the novelist Fanny Burney) in 1785. The baton passed from hand to hand in a relay race is first mentioned by that name in 1921. This use gives rise to to **pass on the baton**, 'to hand over a particular duty or responsibility', and to **take up** (or **pick up**) **the baton**, 'to accept a duty or responsibility'.

The French name of **Baton Rouge**, the capital of Louisiana, means 'Red Stick' in English. It comes from a red-stained Indian boundary marker seen by early French explorers of the area.

battery

The root of **battery** is Latin *battuere* 'to strike, beat', and in the Middle Ages the word referred to metal articles shaped with a hammer. The military soon adopted the term to mean a succession of heavy blows inflicted upon the walls of a city or fortress with artillery, and so it came to have the sense 'a number of pieces of artillery combining in action'. It is this idea of combining to produce a result that is behind the use in electrical batteries. The original electrical battery was a series of Leyden jars, glass jars with layers of metal foil on the outside and inside, used to store electric charge. Benjamin Franklin mentioned the device in a letter of 1748. Sir Humphry Davy developed the later **galvanic battery**, using chemical action to produce electric current, and described it in 1801. An electrical battery is a container with one or more cells, and this no doubt prompted the use of the word for a series of cages for laying hens, and later for calves.

battle

Along with **battalion**, **batter** and BATTERY, the word **battle** goes back through French to Latin *battuere* 'to strike, beat'. It has been known in English since the early Middle Ages.

Battles have been all too frequent throughout history, and the word appears in many phrases. We say that we are fighting **a losing battle** when a struggle is bound to end in failure, or that something that contributes to success is **half the battle**. A fiercely contested fight or dispute is a **battle royal**, which was originally a fight with several combatants.

'The battle of Waterloo was won on the playing fields of Eton' is a comment popularly attributed to Arthur Wellesley, the 1st Duke of Wellington, implying that the essential foundations of courage and determination are fostered by school sport. But the earliest version of it was not recorded until 1856, and Wellington died in 1852.

bay

Hounds have bayed since the Middle Ages. Like BARK, the word probably imitates the sound it refers to. People can now also **bay for blood**, when they call loudly for someone to be punished. The related phrase **at bay** comes from hunting and means 'cornered, forced to face one's attackers'. It is often used now in to **hold someone at bay**, 'to prevent someone from approaching or having an effect'.

beam

As well as referring to a piece of wood, **beam** originally also meant 'a tree', a use that survives in the name of the **hornbeam**, a member of the birch family. Sailors understood a beam to be one of the timbers stretching from side to side of a ship, supporting the deck and holding the vessel together. From there **beam** came to mean a ship's greatest breadth. This is why you can call someone **broad in the beam**, 'wide in the hips'. A ship that is **on its beam ends** is heeled over on its side, almost capsized, and so if a person is on their beam ends they are desperate or in a very bad situation.

The **beam in your eye**, the fault that is greater in yourself than in the person you are finding fault with, comes from the Bible. Matthew contrasts the large beam unseen in someone's own eye with the mote ('speck') noticed in the eye of another.

When someone is **way off beam** they are mistaken, on the wrong track. Here they are being likened to an aircraft that has gone astray from the radio beam or signal used to guide it.

beam me up, Scotty

The phrase will forever be associated with the American television series *Star Trek*, as Captain Kirk asks Lieutenant Commander Scott to 'beam' or transport him from a planet back to the starship USS *Enterprise*. But these exact words do not occur in any of the scripts. The nearest equivalent is 'Beam us up, Mr Scott.'

bean

In spite of the long history of the **bean** in Europe, many of the phrases in which it is now used are from America. An example is to **spill the beans**, 'to reveal a secret'. Britain did give us some expressions, though, including **full of beans**, 'lively, in high spirits', first recorded in the mid 19th century. This originally referred to horses, because beans were one of their staple foods and a well-fed horse would be full of energy and vitality. As an insulting term for an accountant, **bean-counter** is another US term, originating in the 1970s. The rather dated **bean** meaning 'the head' is also originally from the US. It lives on in the close-fitting hat the **beanie**.

For 30 years the Heinz company used the slogan 'Beanz Meanz Heinz' to advertise its baked beans. First used in 1967, the full jingle was:

A million housewives every day
Pick up a can of beans and say
Beans Meanz Heinz!

bear

The verb **bear**, meaning 'to carry or support', comes from the oldest possible source, the ancient ancestor of languages spoken over most of Europe and Asia and as far as northern India. Related forms are found in Sanskrit, the ancient language of India, as well as in Latin and Greek. The core meaning is 'to carry'. In English it is related to **bier**, the frame carrying a coffin or corpse. From early times **bear** has also been used of mental burdens, of suffering or toleration. Wise people have encouraged us to **bear and forbear**, 'be patient and endure', since the 16th century, and from the mid 19th century others have told us more briskly to **grin and bear it**.

Bear meaning a large animal is a different Old English word that also goes back to ancient times. In stock exchange terminology a bear is a person who sells shares hoping to buy them back later at a lower price (the opposite of a BULL). The use is said to be from a proverb warning against 'selling the bear's skin before one has caught the bear'.

beard

As well as referring to a man's facial hair, **beard**, which is related to Latin *barba* 'beard', is used of the chin tuft of certain animals, such as a lion and a goat. These uses come together in the phrase to **beard the lion in his den** or **lair**, 'to confront or challenge someone on their own ground'. To invade someone's personal space enough to be able to touch or pull their beard was always an aggressive or provocative act – in 1587 the English sailor and explorer Francis Drake described his expedition to Cadiz as 'the singeing of the King of Spain's Beard'. In the Middle Ages to **run in someone's beard** was to defy him, and by the 16th century you could simply 'beard someone'. Clearly this stopped being fearsome enough, and lions were introduced in the 18th century.

beat

An Old English word related to BEETLE in the sense 'heavy mallet'. It is extremely unlikely that the Beatles had this fact in mind when they chose their name – it was a combination of the insect's name and musical 'beat', with possibly a reference to the Crickets, Buddy Holly's backing band. See also ALBUM.

The **beat generation** was a group of unconventional artists and writers of the 1950s and early 1960s, among them Jack Kerouac and Allen Ginsberg, who valued free self-expression and liked modern jazz. Here the **beat** probably originally meant 'worn out, exhausted' rather than referring to a musical rhythm.

The first people to **beat about the bush** were the 'beaters' who tried to disturb game birds so that they would fly up to be shot at. The first use of the phrase outside hunting referred to preliminary operations, and so to approaching something in a roundabout way. Now it means specifically 'to discuss a matter without coming to the point'.

Beaters beat bushes, but soldiers beat drums. This is the origin of the phrase to **beat a hasty retreat**. To 'beat a retreat' was to sound the drums in a way that signalled to soldiers that they should withdraw from the battle. The drumming also helped them to retreat in an orderly manner.

beauty

The Latin word *bellus*, 'beautiful', is the root of **beauty**, and also of **beau** and **belle**. Beauty plays a significant role in human relationships, and has its full share of wise thoughts and reflections. The idea that **beauty is in the eye of the beholder**, that what one person finds attractive might not appeal to someone else, is very old indeed, appearing in the works of the ancient Greek poet Theocritus. In English the proverb as we know it today is recorded from the 18th century. The warning that **beauty is only skin-deep** (and no guarantee of good morals or a good temper) is known from the early 17th century. Anthony Price wrote in *The '44 Vintage* (1978), 'Beauty is only skin-deep, but it's the only skin you see'.

The **beautiful game** is soccer. The phrase is from the title of the 1973 autobiography *My Life and the Beautiful Game* by Pelé, the Brazilian football star.

beck

If you are **at someone's beck and call** you have to be ready to obey their orders immediately. The phrase is known from the 19th century, but **beck** itself is much older. It is first recorded in the Middle Ages, when to **beck** someone was a shortening of **beckon**. The northern English word **beck**, meaning a stream or brook, is unconnected, and comes from Old Norse.

bed

The core idea of this Old English word may be 'digging', as if the very first beds were dug-out lairs or hollows. Medieval uses of to **make a bed** refer to the preparation of a sleeping place on the floor of an open hall, one which would not have existed until 'made'. The term **bed and breakfast** first appeared in the late 19th century – in 1910 a 'residential hotel' is recorded offering 'Bed and breakfast from 4/-' (4 shillings or, in modern British currency, 20 pence). In the 1970s the phrase began to describe the financial practice of **bed-and-breakfasting**, in which dealers sell shares late in the day and buy them back early the next morning to gain a tax advantage.

bedlam

The word is a corruption of *Bethlehem*, but the uproar and confusion signified by **bedlam** were not in the Middle East. They were at the Hospital of St Mary of Bethlehem, also known as Bethlem Royal Hospital, in London – what used to be known as an asylum. People did not regard the mentally ill with much compassion at that time, even visiting such hospitals as an entertainment, to watch the disturbed antics of the unfortunate inmates. In the 17th century **bedlam** became a term for any mental hospital, and from that for any scene of mad confusion. See also CHAOS, PANDEMONIUM.

bee

A form of **bee** is found in almost all the languages that are closely related to English, and the familiar insect has inspired numerous familiar phrases. A worker is **as busy as a bee**, a comparison made from at least the 16th century. People used to describe an obsessive person as having **a head full of bees**, whereas we now say that you **have a bee in your bonnet**.

Before close studies of insect behaviour, people believed that bees instinctively take a straight line when returning to the hive. This is the origin of **beeline**. If you **make a beeline for** a place, you hurry directly to it.

A **spelling bee** is a spelling contest, and a **sewing bee** a gathering for people to do their sewing together. This use to mean 'a meeting for communal work or amusement' was suggested by the insect's social nature, and is first recorded in the USA in the 1760s.

beef

A teacher may have told you that after the Norman Conquest people used French words for an animal's meat and the English word for the animal itself. If they did, they probably gave **beef** as an example. In this case it is true. **Beef** is from French, and COW and **ox** are native English words, whereas BULL was adopted from Scandinavian.

Beef meaning 'a complaint' or 'to complain' was originally American, from the mid 19th century. The first person to write of the kind of **beef** possessed by a muscular man was another American, Herman Melville, author of *Moby-Dick*.

The British are so well known for eating beef that a French insult for an Englishman is *un rosbif* ('a roast beef'). In English too, **beefeater** was originally a term of contempt for a well-fed domestic servant. Now a beefeater is a Yeoman Warder or Yeoman of the Guard at the Tower of London, a nickname first used in 1671.

beer

The ancestor of **beer** came from a Latin term used in monasteries. This is not as surprising as it might seem, if you consider that Belgian Trappist monks still brew some well-known beers, such as Chimay. The source of that monastic word, classical Latin *bibere* 'to drink', is also behind **beverage**. Although **beer** appears in

Old English, it was not common before the 16th century – the usual word in earlier times was **ale**. See also BITTER, LAGER.

beetle

The meaning of the source word for the insect is 'biter', and it is closely related to BITE. The other word **beetle**, 'a heavy mallet', is unrelated. It comes ultimately from the ancestor of BEAT, 'to strike'. See also EARWIG.

The **Beetle** is an affectionate name for a type of small Volkswagen car that was first produced in 1938. The term started as a nickname, and was not officially adopted by the company until the 1960s. A review of the car in *Motor* magazine during 1946 said: 'It has the civilian saloon body on the military chassis with the higher ground clearance, and it looks rather like a beetle on stilts.'

belfry

Although you will find bells (as well as bats) in a belfry, the Old English word **bell** is not related to **belfry**.

Never-ending stories

Thriller, history book, work of faith, all-time best-seller – the Bible is all of these and more. It contains enough stories to keep anyone cast away on a desert island happy for years, and its words of wisdom fill our everyday conversations.

At the beginning of his reign King James I gave orders for a new translation of the Bible to be made. What we now call the Authorised Version or the King James Bible, published in 1611, is the version from which readings in church were taken for more than 400 years, and many phrases from it have become part of the fabric of our language. A fly in the ointment, lean years, a man after your own heart – these and many other expressions show how often we quote the Bible without knowing it.

We call a charitable or helpful person a good Samaritan, after the man from Samaria who stopped to help a Jewish traveller who had been beaten and robbed, despite the traditional hostility between Samaritans and Jews. Jesus tells the parable of the Good Samaritan in the Gospel of Luke, where he also gives the story of the prodigal son, who left home to live an extravagant lifestyle but later returned poor and repentant. The father's forgiving response, when he ordered a grand feast to be prepared in celebration, is remembered when we talk about killing the fatted calf.

The virtuous elder brother, who had stayed at home, resented their father's generosity, and failed to turn the other cheek – to take the course recommended by Jesus in the Gospel of Matthew: 'Whosoever shall smite thee on thy right cheek, turn to him the other side.' He was not yet ready to offer his erring brother an olive branch.

In the Acts of the Apostles we read how Saul, persecutor of the early Christians, became the Apostle Paul. He experienced a sudden and complete conversion while on his way to Damascus, and the story has given us the idea of someone's road to Damascus as the moment at which they decide to embrace what they have previously rejected.

We may well reach for biblical wording when describing someone's essential character. A person seen as kind, honest and reliable is often said to be salt of the earth. On the other hand, someone might reveal by their actions that they have feet of clay – even if they did not go so far as the deliberate hypocrisy of a whited sepulchre, or the concealed danger of a wolf in sheep's clothing.

A belfry was originally a movable wooden tower used in the Middle Ages by armies besieging a fortification. The word originally had an -r- not an -l- in the middle, and came from Old French *berfrei*. The first part probably meant 'to protect' and the second 'peace, protection'. The first belfry connected with a church was a separate bell tower: the word began to be used for a room or storey where the bells were hung in the middle of the 16th century. See also ISLAND.

belt

An Old English word that can be traced back to Latin *balteus*, 'girdle'. It is unlawful for a boxer to land a punch below his opponent's belt, and people often use the phrase **below the belt** about a critical or unkind remark. Margot Asquith, wife of the Liberal Prime Minister Herbert Asquith, once remarked of another Liberal Prime Minister, Lloyd George: 'He can't see a belt without hitting below it'.

If you take a **belt and braces** approach to something you make doubly sure that nothing will go wrong. The reference is to someone so anxious that their trousers will fall down that they wear both a belt and braces.

The old school punishment of **belting** a pupil, or hitting them with a belt, is behind the verb sense 'to strike, hit', and probably also the meaning 'to move very fast'. **Belt up**, or 'be quiet', seems to have started life as RAF slang, in the 1930s.

benefit

The source of **benefit** is Latin *benefactum*, 'a good deed', and that was the original meaning in English, in the late Middle Ages. The ordinary modern sense is recorded from the early 16th century. To **give someone the benefit of the doubt** originally meant to give a verdict of not guilty when the evidence was not conclusive (the presumption of innocence). Now it is used more generally for assuming that someone must be believed if you cannot be certain that they are wrong.

It is tempting to criticise those who fall short of an ideal. We may at times need to separate the sheep from the goats in distinguishing good from bad, but we should not be ready to cast the first stone. We probably also need to be wary of impatience if we are someone who does not suffer fools gladly, or if we find that a person is a constant thorn in the side.

Someone trying to fulfil an objective without proper resources might complain that they have been asked to make bricks without straw, like the Israelites in Egypt. But in this story from the Old Testament book of Exodus, being expected to make bricks 'without straw' meant 'without having straw provided' – the Israelites had to gather the straw themselves – and a misinterpretation has led to the current sense. Nevertheless, a determined person would not give up, but would be ready to go the extra mile, an expression which probably goes back to the encouragement in the Gospel of Matthew: 'And whosoever shall compel thee to go a mile, go with him twain [two].'

In difficult circumstances you may kick against the pricks, resenting hardship. You might even be described as raising Cain over your difficulties, in reference to the eldest son of Adam and Eve in the book of Genesis, the jealous Cain who murdered his brother Abel. But there may be help at the eleventh hour, even if the relief you receive does not qualify as manna from heaven, the food which in Exodus was miraculously supplied to the Israelites in the wilderness.

A number of biblical phrases relate to how clearly we can see the nature of something. We may be tempted by the illicit pleasures of forbidden fruit, but sooner or later the scales fall from our eyes. We might realise that we had been dangerously near to giving up something of great value in exchange for a mess of pottage. Alternatively, our mistake might lie in offering something precious to someone unable to appreciate it – casting pearls before swine, in an allusion to the warning in the Gospel of Matthew: 'Give not that which is holy unto dogs, neither cast ye your pearls before swine, lest they trample them under their feet.'

a wolf in sheep's clothing

See also FOOT, FRUIT, HOUR, KICK, MESS, OLIVE, SALT, SCALE, SHEEP, STONE, SUFFER, THORN, WASH, WHITE, WOLF.

berk

This British slang term for a stupid person is generally regarded as fairly acceptable in polite society, but it has a very rude origin. It is an abbreviation of *Berkeley* or *Berkshire Hunt*, rhyming slang for c—. The first written example dates from the late 1920s.

berserk

A **berserker** was an ancient Norse warrior who fought with wild, uncontrolled ferocity – he went **berserk**. The name came from an old Scandinavian word, *berserkr*, which probably meant 'bear coat' or 'bearskin', a suitably rugged garment for a terrifyingly unhinged Viking. An alternative possibility is that the first element is the equivalent of 'bare', referring to fighting without armour. The phrase to **go berserk** is first recorded in 1896.

berth

When we **give someone a wide berth**, or stay away from them, we are using a nautical expression. **Berth** shares a root with BEAR, 'to carry'. Originally, in the early 17th century, it meant 'sea room', or space to turn or manoeuvre. It developed the sense 'a ship's allotted place at a wharf or dock', and could also mean the place where seamen stowed their chests, then later the space where the sailors themselves slept.

bib

A **bib** for a baby is recorded from the late 16th century. It probably derived from the old word *bib* 'to drink', from Latin *bibere*, also meaning 'to drink'. Towards the end of the 17th century adults too were wearing bibs, often as part of an apron. Women could decorate this with a **tucker**, a piece of lace worn round the top of the bodice – 'The countrywoman . . . minds nothing on Sundays so much as her best bib and tucker' (1747). Soon men too were described as wearing their **best bib and tucker**, their smartest clothes.

bidet

British people are famous on the Continent for not knowing what a bidet is for – washing the genitals and bottom – or for using it to wash their feet. Well, few people know the word's origin, either. In French and originally in English it meant 'pony, small horse' – the link was the way that people sat astride both the animal and the basin.

Ursula Andress in one of the world's most memorable bikinis, from the James Bond film *Dr No*.

big

Like many small words, **big** appeared from nowhere. It is first recorded in the early Middle Ages meaning 'strong, powerful', and clear examples referring just to size do not emerge until the 16th century.

The sense 'elder' as in **big brother** or **big sister** is first found in the 19th century. In George Orwell's novel *Nineteen Eighty-four* the head of state is called Big Brother, and 'Big Brother is watching you' is the caption on posters showing his face. The novel was published in 1949, and very quickly people started using **Big Brother** to refer to any person or organisation exercising total control over people's lives. The reality TV show *Big Brother*, which films a group of people constantly for weeks on end, picked up on this idea of 24-hour surveillance. It was first shown in Holland in 1999.

Various phrases involving **big** refer to an important or influential person, such as **big cheese**, which first came into use in American slang during the early 1900s. It almost certainly has no connection with food – the word **cheese** here probably comes from Urdu and Persian *cīz*, which just means 'thing'.

bigwig

People of importance in the 17th and 18th centuries wore large wigs that covered their heads and came down to their shoulders. These were the original 'big wigs'. In Britain this type of headdress can still be worn by judges, the Lord Chancellor and the Speaker of the House of Commons. In the 18th century **bigwig** began to refer to the person wearing the wig, and the word has outlived the fashion.

bikini

In 1946 the USA exploded an atom bomb at Bikini, an atoll in the Marshall Islands in the western Pacific. Not long after, a scanty two-piece swimming costume caused a sensation on the beaches of France. Its effect was so great that the French dubbed it the *bikini*. The word seems to have appeared first in English in a US newspaper, the *Waterloo Daily Courier*, on June 26, 1947. In an article on swimwear it reports: 'The French, it seems, have a new suit planned that is about twice as wide as a piece of string. It's so explosive that they call it the Bikini.' In 1950 the *News of the World* reported that an unnamed woman 'made an unsuccessful attempt yesterday to swim in a Hampstead Heath pond in her home-made "Bikini" costume'. The **bikini** had arrived on British shores.

In the early days of the garment a memorable bikini scene could earn a film actress eternal star status. Brigitte Bardot wore one for *And God Created Woman* (1956), while Ursula Andress emerged from the sea wearing a bikini in the James Bond film *Dr No* (1962) and Raquel Welch snipped away at her fur bikini between takes of the prehistoric adventure *One Million Years BC* (1966) to make it more revealing.

bill

During the Middle Ages a **bill** was any written statement or list, an early sense that survives in **a clean bill of health**. The master of a ship about to sail from a port where various infectious diseases were known to be common would be given an official certificate before leaving, to confirm that there was no infection either on board the ship or in the port. The nautical term spread from the ports, and can now refer to any statement that someone is healthy or something is sound. See also BULLETIN.

The Old Bill is British slang for the police, with the first written evidence arriving in the 1950s. The original Old Bill was a cartoon character of the First World War, portrayed as a grumbling Cockney soldier with a walrus moustache. The 'police' meaning may have arisen from subsequent use of the cartoon character, this time wearing police uniform, on posters in a Metropolitan Police recruitment campaign, and then during the Second World War giving advice on wartime security. Apparently police officers before the Second World War often wore 'Old Bill' moustaches, and this could provide another connection.

bimbo

Bimbos these days are attractive, if not too bright, young women, but in Italian a *bimbo* is a baby, and in English **bimbo** was originally an American slang term for a fellow or chap, especially a foolish one. In 1947 P.G. Wodehouse wrote of 'Bimbos who went about the place making passes at innocent girls after discarding their wives'. This meaning is first recorded in 1918, and by the 1920s the modern sense was being used. In the 1980s the word **himbo** was coined to mean 'a male bimbo', but it never really caught on. See also BABY.

binge

Binge drinking is generally thought of as a modern problem, but some people have always drunk to excess, and the word **binge** has been around since at least the 1850s. It was originally a dialect term in the English Midlands, first meaning 'to wash or soak', which was taken up by boozy students at Oxford University.

bird

The origin of **bird** is unknown, and there are no parallel forms in any of the languages related to English. Old English *brid* (with the *r* before the *i*) meant only a chick or a nestling: an adult bird was a **fowl**. The form *brid* existed alongside **bird** in the literary language into the 15th century, but after that it survived only in dialect. Meanwhile **fowl** stopped being a general term, and it now refers only to specialised groups such as wildfowl and waterfowl.

The first record of the proverb **a bird in the hand is worth two in the bush** comes in the mid 15th century. In **birds of a feather flock together**, first recorded a century later, the word **a** means 'one' or 'the same'.

The British slang use of **bird** to mean a young woman or a man's girlfriend is associated with the 1960s and 1970s, but goes back as far as the Middle Ages. In those days there was another word **bird**, also spelled *burd*, that meant a young woman, which people confused with the familiar **bird**. The Virgin Mary could be described in those days as 'that blissful bird of grace'. The modern use, recorded from the beginning of the 20th century, appears to be something of a revival.

The earliest version of the expression **give someone the bird**, meaning to boo or jeer at them, is **the big bird**, which was used by people working in the theatre in the early 19th century. The big bird referred to was a goose, a bird well known for its aggressive hissing when threatened or annoyed. The booing and hissing of the audience at an actor's poor performance might well have suggested a flock of angry geese.

Bird meaning 'a prison sentence' is a shortening of **birdlime**, a sticky substance spread on twigs to catch birds, although that is not why it refers to capture and imprisonment. The word was also used in rhyming slang to mean 'time'. So if you were 'doing bird' or 'doing birdlime', you were 'doing time', a sense known from the mid 19th century.

In golf a **birdie** is a score of one stroke under par at a hole. See PAR.

biscuit

The basic meaning of **biscuit** is 'twice cooked', coming into English from French in the Middle Ages. The name refers to the original process of making biscuits – the cakes were first baked and then dried out in a slow oven so that they would keep. This produces the flat crisp cake that is a biscuit to the British. In America a biscuit is a small, soft round cake, like a scone.

bite

There are words related to **bite** in many other European languages. Their ancestor also gave us **bit** and BITTER, and it probably meant 'to split, to cleave'.

To **bite the bullet** now means 'to face up to something unpleasant'. Its origin is in battlefield surgery. Before anaesthetics, wounded soldiers would be given a bullet or some other hard object to bite on to prevent them from crying out or harming themselves when the pain became unbearable. Another phrase involving biting something unusual is to **bite the dust**, 'to be killed or come to an end'. Nowadays people are likely to associate it with westerns and gunfights, but it is used by the novelist Tobias Smollett in 1750, and similar expressions such as to **bite the ground** and **bite the sand** are found even earlier.

Man bites dog is a much-used tongue-in-cheek newspaper headline, which harks back to the quote: 'When a dog bites a man, that is not news, because it happens so often. But if a man bites a dog, that is news.' This was said by the American journalist John B. Bogart (1848-1921).

The **bit** in computing, a unit of information expressed as either a 0 or 1, is a contraction of **binary digit**. **Bit** and **bite** were combined to give **byte**, a group of eight bits.

bitter

Like **bit**, **bitter** is related to BITE, and comes from the Old English period, when it already had its modern meaning of 'not pleasing or sweet in taste'. The sense 'painful', also Old English, is appropriate in the phrase **to the bitter end** 'until something is finished, no matter what', but this is probably not the origin of the expression. It derives instead from a nautical term **bitter**, meaning the last part of a cable, that goes around the 'bitts' or fastening points for ropes on board ship. The biblical quotation 'her end is bitter as wormwood' may have helped popularise the phrase.

Many Englishmen love their pint of bitter, or 'warm beer', as those who prefer **the amber nectar** tend to call it. This use seems to have started life as Oxford University slang in the 1850s, when students would talk of 'doing bitters'.

black

Since the Middle Ages the word **black** has had connotations of gloom, foreboding and anger, and since Shakespeare's time it has been associated with wickedness. It is also a perennially stylish colour, though, and the **little black dress** has been a byword of fashion from the very beginning of the 20th century.

The car manufacturer Henry Ford was not motivated by any of these associations when he said of his Model T Ford, 'Any customer can have a car painted any colour that he wants so long as it is black' – nor was he trying to impose uniformity. Black simply dried quicker than any other paint.

To **be in someone's black books** is to be out of favour. Since the 15th century various types of official book were known as black books, especially those used to note down misdemeanours and punishments. The relevant books here are probably the black-bound books in which Henry VIII's commissioners recorded accounts of scandals and corruption within the English monasteries in the 1530s. These books provided the evidence to support Henry's plan of breaking with the Pope and the Church of Rome, allowing him to dissolve the monasteries and marry Anne Boleyn.

Not all things called black are black in colour. An aircraft's **black box**, its flight recorder, for instance, is not. **Black** here refers to the mystifying nature of the device to anyone but an aeronautical engineer. The first use of **black box** is as RAF slang for a navigational instrument in an aircraft which allowed the pilot and crew to locate bombing targets in poor visibility. See also PLAGUE.

blackmail

Blackmail was originally a form of protection racket. Scottish chiefs in the 16th century exacted a tribute from farmers and small landowners in the border counties of England and Scotland, and along the Highland border. The money was in return for protection or immunity from plunder. The second part of the word has nothing to do with a postal service. It means 'tribute, rent' and comes from an old Scandinavian word *mál*, meaning 'speech, agreement'. **Black** may have been a joke on **white money**, the silver coins in which legitimate rents were paid.

blancmange

In medieval times a **blancmange** was a dish of white meat or fish in a cream sauce – the 'dessert' sense seems to have come into use in the middle of the 16th century. The word comes from Old French and literally means 'white food'.

blanket

As with BLANCMANGE, the root of **blanket** is French *blanc* 'white'. Originally **blanket** referred to undyed (hence 'white') woollen cloth used for clothing, not to bedclothes. A dampened blanket would sometimes be used to extinguish a fire before going to bed. This is the origin of a **wet blanket**, 'someone who spoils other people's fun by refusing to join in or by showing disapproval'.

blatant

A word first used by the Elizabethan poet Edmund Spenser in *The Faerie Queene*, as a description of a thousand-tongued monster, offspring of the three-headed dog Cerberus and the fire-breathing Chimaera. Spenser used this monster as a symbol of slander, and called it 'the blatant beast'. He may just have invented the word, or taken it from Scots *blatand* 'bleating'. **Blatant** was subsequently used to mean 'clamorous, offensive to the ear', and did not take on its modern meaning 'unashamedly conspicuous' until the late 19th century.

blaze

The **blaze** meaning 'a bright flame' and the one referring to a white streak on a horse's face are probably related, through the idea of shining or brightness. In America the latter one came to apply to a white mark chipped in a tree to indicate a path or boundary. This is where we get to **blaze a trail**, 'to set an example by being the first to do something'. The phrase does not refer to creating a path by burning scrubland. The exposed white marks on the trees allowed people coming behind to follow the same route.

Cricketers and other sportsmen wore a type of coloured, often striped jacket called a **blazer** in the late 19th century. The name came from the brightness of the cloth, although nowadays most blazers are a little more subdued.

blind

In the sense 'unable to see' **blind** is an Old English word. Blinds that are hung on windows were first mentioned in the early 18th century, and Venetian blinds (the ones made up of horizontal slats) at the end of that century.

To **turn a blind eye to**, 'to pretend not to notice', goes back to the Battle of Copenhagen in 1801. The British admiral and naval hero Horatio Nelson, who was leading the attack against the Danes, had lost the sight in one eye in action several years before. His superior, Sir Hyde Parker, feared that his men would suffer very heavy losses and so hoisted the signal for Nelson to halt his attack and withdraw. Nelson avoided seeing the signal by putting a telescope to his blind eye, and continued the battle. An hour later he was victorious. See also EXPECT and KISS for more sayings attributed to Nelson.

The *-fold* of **blindfold** is not the *fold* meaning 'to bend over on itself'. It derives from **fell**, 'to knock or strike over'. The Old English word from which **blindfold** developed meant 'to strike blind'. By the 16th century people stopped understanding **blindfell**, and substituted the more familiar **fold**. See also BUFF.

block

In the early Middle Ages a **block** was a log or tree stump. The word came from French *bloc*, which English readopted in a different sense as **bloc**, 'a group of countries that have formed an alliance', in the early 20th century. By the late Middle Ages a block was often a large lump of wood on which chopping, hammering – and beheading – were performed. We refer to an executioner's block when we use the phrase to **put your head** (or **neck**) **on the block**, 'to put yourself at risk by proceeding with a particular course of action'.

A block of buildings, bounded by four streets, dates from the late 18th century in North America. This use has given rise to numerous popular phrases: the **new kid on the block** and the person believed to **have been around the block a few times** (to have a lot of experience). It also gave us the **blockbuster**. Although this now means 'a great commercial success', in the 1940s it was a huge aerial bomb capable of destroying a whole block of streets.

Block has meant head, as in to **knock someone's block off**, since the 17th century. In Australia, to **do** or **lose your block** is to lose your temper.

Blighty

British soldiers serving in India at the beginning of the 20th century first started calling their homeland **Blighty**. The word was an alteration of Urdu *bilāyatī* 'foreign, European', which came from Arabic *wilāyat* 'country, district'. During the First World War soldiers hoped for a **blighty** – a wound not too serious but bad enough to allow safe passage home.

blonde

Long before it referred to fair-haired women who were DIZZY or DUMB, **blonde** simply meant 'yellow'. *Blond* or *blonde* means 'fair-haired' in French, but the word was descended from medieval Latin *blondus* 'yellow'. The adjective was adopted by the English at the end of the 15th century, but the noun use, 'a blonde woman', dates only from the 19th century, since when the desirability of blondes has become almost proverbial. *Gentlemen Prefer Blondes* was the title of a 1925 book by Anita Loos, which in 1953 was made into a film starring Marilyn Monroe and Jane Russell, and the album *Blondes Have More Fun* was released by Rod Stewart in 1978. See also BOMB, DIAMOND.

blood

Something so vital to life is bound to play a large part in the language. Blood represents violence, genetic inheritance and, in **blood, sweat and tears**, hard work and sacrifice – in 1940 Winston Churchill announced to Parliament that he had 'nothing to offer but blood, toil, tears and sweat'.

Nowadays **bloody** is a relatively mild swear word, but it used to be virtually unprintable. In the 19th century, and well into the 20th, it was on a par with obscene language and caused deep offence. Its use by George Bernard Shaw in *Pygmalion* (1913), where Eliza Doolittle says, 'Walk! Not bloody likely', caused a sensation, and indeed the play's stage directions mark the word 'Sensation' after the line in question. This reaction probably arose because people thought the word contained a blasphemous reference to the blood of Christ, or was a corruption of **by Our Lady**. In fact the most likely origin lies in the aristocratic rowdies, or 'bloods', of the late 17th and early 18th centuries. Most of the earliest examples, in the second half of the 17th century, involve someone being 'bloody drunk', which probably simply meant 'as drunk as a blood'.

blouse

Women and girls did not originally wear blouses. When it first appeared in English, in the early 19th century, the word referred to the blue blouse traditionally worn by French workmen, and **blouse** is indeed French. In the course of the 19th century the word began to apply to various smocks and tunics worn by English farm labourers, and in 1870 came the first reference to a blouse 'for a young lady'. Testimony to the fact that it is now fundamentally a female garment comes in **a big girl's blouse**. In Britain this is an insult for a man regarded as weak, cowardly or oversensitive.

blow

One of the more colourful phrases involving **blow** is to **blow hot and cold**, or keep changing your mind, which comes from Aesop's fable of the man and the satyr. A traveller lost in a forest meets a satyr, a type of woodland god that looked like man with a goat's ears, tail, legs and horns. The satyr offers him lodging for the night, promising to lead him safely out of the woods in the morning. On the way to the satyr's home the man blows on his hands. The satyr asks him why he does this, to which he replies, 'My breath warms my cold hands.' At the satyr's home they sit down to eat some steaming hot porridge. The man blows on his first spoonful and again the satyr asks him why. 'The porridge is too hot to eat and my breath will cool it,' he answers. At this the satyr orders him to leave, saying 'I can have nothing to do with a man who can blow hot and cold with the same breath.' See also GAFF.

blue

The English **blue** and French *bleu* are ultimately the same word, which goes back to ancient Germanic and is related to the *blae-* in **blaeberry**, a Scottish and northern English spelling of **bilberry**. The word occurs in a number of phrases, in particular those relating either to depression and melancholy or to the blue of the sky, as in **out of the blue**, 'as a total surprise'. See also BOLT.

Something occurring **once in a blue moon** is something very rare. A blue moon sounds fanciful but it is a phenomenon that does occur occasionally, due to large amounts of dust or smoke in the atmosphere.

A particularly Australian use of **blue** is as a surreally humorous nickname for a red-haired person. This is first recorded in 1932, although **bluey** can be found earlier, in 1906.

Depression or melancholy have always been around, but no one called these feelings **the blues** until the mid 18th century, although people have been feeling blue since as early as the 1580s. **The blues** was a contraction of **blue devils**, which were originally baleful demons punishing sinners. In the 18th century people fancifully imagined them to be behind depression, and later also to be the apparitions seen by alcoholics in delirium tremens. The first printed record of the name of the melancholic music style is in the 'Memphis Blues' of 1912, by the American musician W.C. Handy, who later set up his own music publishing house and transcribed many traditional blues. Its later development, **rhythm and blues**, appeared in the 1930s.

Obscene or smutty material has been known as **blue** since the mid 19th century. The link may be the blue gowns that prostitutes used to wear in prison, or the blue pencil traditionally used by censors.

Blue-chip shares are considered to be a reliable investment, though less secure than **gilt-edged** stock (see GILT). Blue chips are high-value counters used in the game of poker.

In America a **blue-collar** worker is someone who works in a manual trade, especially in industry, as opposed to a **white-collar** worker in an office. Traditionally office workers would always wear white shirts, while manual workers would be free to wear coloured ones, often blue. See also MURDER.

bluestocking

During the 17th and 18th centuries men favoured blue worsted stockings for informal daytime wear, but never on formal occasions, when black silk stockings were in order. In about 1750, though, the botanist and writer Benjamin Stillingfleet was asked to an assembly for literary conversation at Montagu House in London. These gatherings were notable for being attended by women with literary and intellectual tastes. Stillingfleet felt he had to refuse the invitation as he was too poor to afford the formal dress required, but his hostess told him to come as he was, in his informal day clothes. So he turned up in his everyday blue worsted stockings and started a trend. Some people sneered at the assemblies, using such terms as **bluestocking assemblies** and **bluestocking ladies**, and an intellectual woman soon became just a **bluestocking**.

bluff

The earliest meaning of **bluff**, in the late 17th century, was 'to blindfold, hoodwink'. The word was adopted from Dutch *bluffen* 'to brag, boast'. During the mid 19th century poker players in the USA began to use it – when players 'bluffed' in the game they tried to mislead others as to how good their hand of cards really was. The game of poker itself was called **bluff**. To **call someone's bluff** meant making another player show their hand to reveal that its value was weaker than their heavy betting had suggested. From this developed the sense of challenging anything you suspect to be false or mere bravado. See also BUFF.

blunder

The original medieval meaning of **blunder**, 'to move blindly, flounder', gives a clue to its origin. It is likely to be related to BLIND. Clumsiness was a central part of the word's original meaning, and towards the end of the 15th century was added clumsiness in speech, with the

meaning 'to say thoughtlessly, to blurt out'. The modern sense developed in the early 18th century. In his poem 'The Charge of the Light Brigade' (1854), Lord Tennyson wrote of one of history's greatest blunders:

> Forward, the Light Brigade!
> Was there a man dismayed?
> Not though the soldier knew
> Some one had blundered.

blurb

Not many words are simply made up, but **blurb**, 'a short description written to promote a book or other product', is one of them. It was invented by the American humorist Gelett Burgess in 1914, although the jacket of one of Burgess's earlier works carried an image of a young lady with the facetious name of 'Miss Blinda Blurb'.

board

It is more difficult to cheat at cards if your hands are clearly visible above the table. This is where the expression **above board** comes from. **Board** is an old word for table, and if a card player was playing 'above board' they were showing that they were not trying to cheat. The members of the **board** that runs a company typically sit round a large table in the boardroom, and it is again the meaning 'table' that gives them their name. See also CABINET.

The expression **across the board** originally comes from horse racing. A bet made 'across the board' is one in which you stake equal amounts of money on the same horse to win a race, to come second or to finish in the first three. The board here is one on which bookmakers write up the odds.

Go by the board was originally said at sea of masts and pieces of rigging that fell overboard. The board in this case was the side of the ship, and is used also in **on board**, **overboard** and **shipboard**.

bob

Short words are often the hardest to pin down, and this is the case with **bob**, which has many uses. Some imply 'short', for example the hairstyle, which became fashionable in the 1920s. Before that people had used **bob** for a horse's docked tail, a short bunch of hair or curls, and a short wig, and the **bob** in **bobcat**, **bobsleigh** and **bobtail** also means 'short'. Another set of uses involves a quick, short movement. People and things **bob up and down**, and boxers **bob and weave**. The British **bob**, 'a shilling', dating from the late 18th century, does not appear to be related to any of these, and its origin remains a mystery.

bodice

The original form of **bodice** was bodies, the plural of **body**. This referred to an item of clothing for the upper body from the mid 16th century, when the pronunciation of **bodies** would have been like that of **bodice**. A similar thing happened with DICE, which is in origin the plural of **die**.

A **bodice ripper** is a sexy romantic novel with a historical setting, often having a cover featuring a woman with revealingly torn clothes swooning in the arms of a masterful man. The term was not used until the start of the 1980s.

boffin

All that is known for sure about **boffin** is that it originated in the Second World War as naval slang for an older officer. In 1945 there was the first reference to a person engaged in complex scientific or technical research, when *The Times* wrote of 'A band of scientific men who performed their wartime wonders at Malvern and apparently called themselves "the boffins"'. These days a boffin is any person with great skill or knowledge in a difficult or obscure area. But however clever the dictionary boffins are, they still cannot find the origins of the word.

The US slang term **boff**, dating from the 1920s and meaning 'to have sex with', is unrelated. It first meant 'to hit or strike', and arose as an imitation of the sound of a blow.

bog

In Gaelic **bog** means 'soft', and this is the source of our word. In the slang sense 'toilet', **bog** was originally **bog-house**, which is recorded as early as 1665.

The British Labour Party spin doctor Alistair Campbell caused widespread offence in 2001 when he said that 'The day of the bog-standard comprehensive school is over'. **Bog standard** is first recorded in print as recently as 1968, although people working in the British motor industry remember it being used a little before this. It may be a reference to **bog** in the sense 'toilet', but it is more likely to be an alteration of **box standard**, meaning either 'made in a standard form and packaged in a box' or 'shaped like a box, plainly designed and without refinements'.

Bob's your uncle

Do something easily and you might say, 'Bob's your uncle'. The true Bob, short for Robert, has proved elusive. He may have been Lord Salisbury, who in 1887 appointed his nephew, Arthur Balfour, then only 39, Chief Secretary for Ireland. But the first examples appear only in the 1930s.

bogus

Originally an American word, which first appeared in the late 18th century in reference to an apparatus for making counterfeit coins. The source could have been **tantrabogus**, a New England word for any strange-looking apparatus or object that possibly came from **tantarabobs**, which was brought over by colonists from Devon and meant 'the devil'. The source would have been another dialect name for the devil, Bogey, which gave us **bogey** and **bogeyman**. In golf a **bogey** is a score of one stroke over PAR at a hole.

Also American is the modern slang sense 'bad', which came to a wide audience in the name of the 1991 film comedy *Bill & Ted's Bogus Journey*, starring Keanu Reeves. It seems to have originated as a term used by young computer hackers in the 1960s for anything useless or incorrect.

bohemian

The English novelist William Makepeace Thackeray was apparently the first to use **bohemian** to mean 'a socially unconventional person', in the mid 19th century. He took it from French *bohémien*, which meant 'a person from Bohemia' (now part of the Czech Republic) and also GYPSY. Gypsies do not originate in Bohemia, though this may be what people believed, nor do they come from Egypt, as their English name suggests, but from northern India. People probably called them Bohemians because that was one route by which they reached western Europe.

For many, the word will always be associated closely with the 1975 single 'Bohemian Rhapsody' by Queen. It was certainly unconventional – a 5 minute 56 second medley of opera, rock and ballad.

bollock

Bollocks used to be **ballocks**, and in that spelling they go back to the time of the Anglo-Saxons. The word is related to BALL, and like many rude words it was perfectly standard English until around the 18th century. It is now used in a number of colourful expressions. A **bollocking**, or severe telling-off, is more genteely written as a **rollicking**, and it is more refined to **make a Horlicks of** something than to **make a bollocks of** it. **The dog's bollocks** is a coarse version of expressions like **the bee's knees** or

the cat's pyjamas, meaning 'an excellent person or thing', which was popularised in the late 1980s by the grown-up comic *Viz*.

bolt

In Old English **bolt** meant 'an arrow'. This is the bolt in **bolt upright**, 'with the back very straight'. Why this comparison was made is not clear – bolts are held more or less horizontally to fire, or at least not straight up, which would be dangerous to the archer. To **have shot your bolt**, 'be able to do no more', is also taken from archery. The completely unexpected **bolt from the blue**, on the other hand, is a thunderbolt, a flash of lightning with a simultaneous crash of thunder. Such a bolt coming from a totally clear and unclouded sky would indeed be a shock. See also BLUE.

bomb

In terms of origin, a **bomb** goes **boom** – the word probably goes right back to Greek *bombos* 'booming, humming'. The first bombs, in the late 17th century, are what we would call 'shells'. Soldiers ignited their fuses and fired them from mortars. Before they were dramatically unexpected events or sexy blondes, **bombshells** were originally the casings of such devices. Bombs as we know them came to prominence in the First World War. It was not until after the Second World War, though, that to **go like a bomb** began to be used for 'to go very fast', or **cost a bomb** for 'be very expensive'. See also ATOM.

bombastic

Although it now means 'high-sounding language with little meaning', **bombast** originally referred to raw cotton or cotton wool. The connection was probably the puffed-out, inflated look of the cotton. So you could say that someone talking in a **bombastic** way is just being **woolly**. See also WOOL.

bonfire

A **bonfire** was originally a **bone fire**, on which people burned animal bones. People would collect bones through the year to make a big fire for annual celebrations, which is how we get the modern meaning. The modern spelling is due to Dr Johnson, who thought the word was from French *bon* 'good'. See also GUY.

bonk

The fun word **bonk** simply came about as an imitation of the sound of a solid object striking a hard surface. It first appeared as a verb, meaning 'to shell', in the First World War. The sexual sense does not seem to have been used before the mid 1970s, but has become very established, perhaps because people feel it is an acceptable term that is not too rude. The link with **bonkers**, 'mad', probably comes from the idea of a mad person having been 'bonked' on the head one too many times.

book

The forerunners of the modern book would have been scrolls of papyrus or parchment, or engraved tablets – the first example of what we might recognise as a book came in Roman times. The English word **book** goes back to Old English and has related forms in most of the other northern European languages of the time. Their ancestor was probably a word related to **beech**, which would have been a wood that people used for engraving inscriptions.

A **bookmaker** is someone who 'makes a book'. Bookmakers keep a record of bets made with different people, which was originally carried out using a memorandum book.

boor

Before the Norman Conquest a *gebūr* was a peasant or tenant farmer. The second part of the word is also found in NEIGHBOUR, and it is the source of **boor**, 'a rough and bad-mannered person'. The Normans swept away the Anglo-Saxon social structure, and with it the word, until in the mid 16th century English readopted it from related Dutch and German words meaning a peasant or rustic. Much later, in the 19th century, the Dutch word *boer* gave rise to the **Boer** farmer of southern Africa.

booty

The original core of **booty** was 'to distribute'. Victors in war divided the booty stolen from an enemy among themselves. The modern American word meaning 'a person's bottom or buttocks' is unconnected. It is probably an alteration of **botty** in the same sense, itself an alteration of **bottom**. If someone urges you to **shake your booty**, they want you to dance energetically. A sexy woman has been **bootylicious** since 1994, although the word was popularised by the single of the same name by Destiny's Child, featuring Beyoncé Knowles, in 2001.

booze

People have been boozing for a long time. The spelling **booze** dates from the 18th century, but as *bouse* the word entered English in the 13th century, probably from Dutch. We have been going to the **boozer**, or pub, since the 1890s.

botch

A person who botched something did not originally do it badly. The first meaning of **botch** was simply 'to repair', with no implication of clumsiness or lack of skill. By the 17th century it seems to have taken on its modern meaning, and Shakespeare's use of the noun in *Macbeth* makes this clear: 'To leave no rubs nor botches in the Work.' **Bodge** is the same word as **botch**, but always had the negative meaning.

bother

The origins of **bother** are in Ireland. It is probably related to Irish *bodhaire* 'deafness' and *bodhraim* 'to deafen, annoy'. Its first record is in the late 17th century, meaning 'noise, chatter'. In the 18th century emphasis moves to worry, annoyance and trouble. The word quickly spread out of its Anglo-Irish confines, and in the 19th century appears as a common mild oath in the works of Dickens and Thackeray.

The late 1960s gave us the cockney pronunciation of **bovver**, 'deliberate troublemaking'. The **bovver boy** (a hooligan or skinhead) wore **bovver boots**, heavy boots with a toe cap and laces. Since 2004 many television viewers have enjoyed the catchphrase **Am I bovvered?** from *The Catherine Tate Show*.

bottle

The word **bottle** goes back to Latin *buttis* 'cask, wineskin', the origin of **butt** and also of **butler**. To **have a lot of bottle** and the related phrases to **lose your bottle** and to **bottle out**, meaning 'to lose your nerve', date back to the 1950s. 'Bottle' here may be from rhyming slang **bottle and glass**, 'arse'.

boudoir

Originally a **boudoir** was a place where a woman sulks. The word was adopted from French in the late 18th century, and literally means 'sulking place', from *bouder* 'to sulk, pout'.

boulevard

The first boulevards referred to in English were in Paris, in the mid 18th century. They were wide avenues planted with trees, originally on the top of demolished fortifications. The word **boulevard** then meant 'the horizontal portion of a rampart' in French. It derives from the same German and Dutch word as **bulwark**, and its elements are related to **bole**, 'the stem or trunk of a tree', and WORK. In the late 19th century the French boulevard also gave us the **boulevardier**, a person who frequented the boulevards, and so a wealthy, fashionable socialite.

boutique

Small shops started being called boutiques in French during the mid 18th century. The French word goes back through Latin to Greek *apothēkē* 'a storehouse'. This is ultimately the source of **apothecary** and of *bodega*, a shop in Spain selling wine. In the 1950s **boutique** came to be used particularly of a shop selling fashionable clothes. Other small businesses claiming exclusive clienteles began to call themselves boutiques: the **boutique winery** appeared in the United States in the 1970s, and an early mention of a **boutique hotel**, in New York, dates from 1989.

bow

The bow of a ship has nothing to do with a person bowing in respect or a support bowing under pressure. The nautical **bow** is in fact related to **bough**, the limb of a tree. Its immediate source, in the later Middle Ages, was German or Dutch. The phrase **a shot across the bows**, 'a warning statement or gesture', has its origins in the world of naval warfare. A shot fired across the bows of a ship is one which is not intended to hit it but to make it stop or alter its course. See also BUXOM.

Boxing Day

This is not a day on which people fought, or went to see others fight. The first working day after Christmas Day was the one on which well-off households traditionally gave presents of money or other things to tradespeople and employees. Such a present was called a **Christmas box**, from the custom of collecting the money in an earthenware box which was broken after the collection had been made and the contents shared out.

boycott

In Ireland during the late 19th century the Irish Land League was campaigning for lower rents and land reform. One of its tactics was to ostracise people, or refuse to have any dealings with them. In September 1880 a land agent called Captain Charles C. Boycott became one of the first to be shunned in this way. The word **boycott** was born. Newspapers took up the term immediately and enthusiastically, and other European languages quickly borrowed it. French, for example, has *boycotter*, Dutch has *boycotten* and German *boycottiren*.

brand

Something that is **brand new** is really being likened to something hot and glowing from a fire: Shakespeare used the similar phrase *fire-new*. **Brand** existed in Old English in the senses 'burning' and 'a piece of burning wood'. The sense 'mark permanently with a hot iron' gave rise to 'a mark of ownership made by branding', hence the current use 'a type of product manufactured under a particular name'.

brave

In Old English people with all the attributes of bravery were 'bold'. In the Middle Ages they could also be 'courageous', but it was not until the late 15th century that they became **brave**. The word came through French from Italian or Spanish *bravo* and goes back to Greek *barbaros*, the source of BARBARIAN.

The phrase **brave new world** refers to a new or hopeful period of history brought about by major changes in society – usually implying that the changes are in fact undesirable. It is taken from the title of a satirical novel by Aldous Huxley, published in 1932. Huxley himself borrowed the phrase from a line in Shakespeare's *The Tempest*. Miranda has grown up isolated on an island with her magician father Prospero, the monster Caliban and some spirits. On first encountering some other humans she exclaims:

> How beauteous mankind is! O brave new world
> That has such people in it!

bread

In Old English **bread** was not the standard term for the familiar food. That was LOAF, which has since become restricted to a lump of bread. The sense 'money', suggested by the similar use of **dough**, was originally 1930s underworld slang in the USA.

breeches

Breeches are old-fashioned trousers that are now worn for riding or as part of ceremonial dress. Like **trousers** and **pants**, the word is now always plural, but it used to be singular. Until the 16th century a **breech** was a garment covering the groin and thighs, like a loincloth or kilt. A breech was also a person's bottom, a sense which survives in **breech birth**, in which the buttocks or feet of a baby are delivered first. The idea of 'back' or 'end' is also preserved in the breech of a gun, the back part of the barrel.

breeze

A **breeze** was originally a north or northeast wind, especially a trade wind on the Atlantic seaboard of the West Indies and the Caribbean coast of South America. This is the meaning of the Spanish and Portuguese word *briza* from which **breeze** probably derived, in the 16th century. In the following century it began to refer to any gentle wind.

The breeze in **breeze block** is totally unconnected. It referred to small cinders, coke dust and the like, and came in the late 16th century from French *braise* 'burning charcoal, hot embers'. Breeze was often mixed with sand and cement to make lightweight building blocks.

bride

In Old English **bride** was *bryd*. The **bridegroom** did not necessarily take care of horses – the original form was *brydguma*, from *guma* 'man'. This second part was always a slightly poetic word, and by the end of the Middle Ages people would not have recognised it. So they substituted a word they did know, **groom**.

One of the things that many people like best about weddings is the drinking. The origin of **bridal** shows that this has always been the case. The word comes from Old English *bryd-ealu* 'wedding feast', from *bryd* 'bride' and *ealu* 'ale-drinking'.

brief

Briefs or underpants, which were first worn in the 1930s, are literally 'shorts'. **Brief** comes from the Latin word *brevis*, meaning 'short', a root shared by **abbreviate** and the musical note **breve**.

brigadier

The high-ranking and no doubt respectable **brigadier** and the lawless **brigand** are related. Both words go back to Italian *brigare* 'to contend, strive'. This gave *brigata* 'a troop, company', from which French took *brigade* and which English adopted as **brigade** in the mid 17th century. French *brigade* also gave us **brigadier**. **Brigand** has been around since the late Middle Ages. It came through French from Italian *brigante* 'foot soldier', which is formed from *brigare*. Originally a brigand could be a lightly armed irregular foot soldier, but this use was rare after the 16th century and finally died out. The bandits and desperadoes won the day.

Bristol

The city in southwest England has been a leading port since the 12th century. Its history is the background to the phrase **shipshape and Bristol fashion**, or 'in good order, neat and clean'. Something in a pleasing or well-ordered state would be described as Bristol fashion because sailors regarded the city as a model of prosperity and success.

One of the city's two soccer teams, Bristol City, is the reason that a woman's breasts are sometimes called **bristols**. The word is rhyming slang, from *Bristol Cities* = *titties*.

British

The Latin word for Britain was *Britannia*, and its inhabitants were the *Brittones*. These words gave English both **Britain** and **Briton** during the Anglo-Saxon period, and **Brittany** in northern France has the same origin. **British** originally referred to the ancient Britons or their Celtic language; the later inhabitants, descended from Angles, Saxons, Jutes and Normans, as well as from the native Celtic peoples, were not described as **British** until the later Middle Ages. See also ENGLISH.

brochure

Although now associated particularly with holidays, **brochure** is a French word meaning 'stitching' or 'stitched work'. The connection is that the first brochures, in the 18th century, were little booklets that were roughly stitched together rather than properly bound. The root, Latin *brocchus* or *broccus*, meaning 'projecting', connects **brochure** with **broach** and **brooch**.

brown

In Old English **brown** simply meant 'dark' – limitation to the distinct colour we are now familiar with did not occur until the medieval period. The idea of darkness developed into a further sense of 'gloomy or serious', and this is the sense that occurs in the 16th-century phrase **a brown study**, 'absorbed in one's thoughts'. The use of 'study' is puzzling to us today. Here it is not a room for reading or working in, but a state of daydreaming or meditation, a meaning that has long been out of use in English. See also AUBURN, BAIZE.

buck

In poker a **buck** is an article placed as a reminder in front of a player whose turn it is to deal at poker. This is the buck in to **pass the buck**, 'to shift the responsibility to someone else' – to pass the buck is to hand over the responsibility for dealing the cards to the next player. The original buck may have been the handle of a buckhorn knife used as a marker. A related expression is **the buck stops here**, meaning that the responsibility or blame for something cannot or should not be passed to someone else. The US President Harry S Truman had this as the wording of a sign on his desk, indicating that the ultimate responsibility for running the country lay with him.

buccaneer

Forget swashbuckling, at first a **buccaneer** was a hunter of oxen in South America or the Caribbean. He cooked the meat on a wooden frame, or *boucan*, which came via French around 1650 from Tupi, a language of the Amazon basin. Later the same century buccaneers changed career to pirates, working the Spanish American coasts.

budget

When the British Chancellor of the Exchequer holds up the battered case holding details of his Budget speech, he may or may not know that he is making a gesture towards the origin of the word. A **budget** was originally a pouch or wallet. The word came from French in the late Middle Ages, and goes back to Latin *bulga* 'leather sack, bag', from which English also gets **bulge**. Most of the earliest uses referring to the government's budget occur in the phrase to **open the budget**, showing that the idea of a pouch was still to the fore, but the modern sense seems to have been firmly established by the end of the 18th century.

buff

The word **buff** originally meant 'a buffalo or other type of wild ox', and **buff leather**, often shortened to simply **buff**, was leather made from the hide of such an animal. This leather was very strong, with a fuzzy surface and a pale yellowish-beige colour. It was used to make military uniforms, and so soldiers would be described as 'wearing buff' or 'in buff'. The combination of these descriptions and the similarity of the leather's colour to that of a white person's skin led to **in the buff**, 'naked'. **The buff** meaning 'the bare skin' dates from the mid 17th century. The slang sense 'good-looking, fit and attractive', which appeared in California at the beginning of the 1980s, comes from the idea of 'buffing' or polishing something, originally with a cloth of buffalo leather.

Another buff uniform gave rise to the **buff** who is enthusiastic and knowledgeable about a particular subject. The original buffs were, in the words of *The New York Sun* in 1903, 'men and boys whose love of fires, fire-fighting and firemen is a predominant characteristic'. The volunteer firemen in New York City formerly wore buff. Now film buffs and computer buffs are more familiar, and not so well dressed.

The **buff** in the game **blind man's buff** is an old word for 'a blow, a buffet' which survives only in this context. It is not surprising that people want to change the word to something more familiar, and in America the game is called **blind man's bluff**.

In medieval times a **buffer** was a person who stammered. These days it is an old man, especially a rather foolish or old-fashioned one.

bugger

A **bugger** was originally a heretic – this was the meaning of Old French *bougre*. The word ultimately comes from *Bulgarus*, which was the Latin term for a Bulgarian, in particular one who belonged to the Orthodox Church, which was regarded by the Roman Catholic Church as heretical. **Bugger** was first used in English in reference to members of a heretical Christian sect based in Albi in southern France in the 12th and 13th centuries, the Albigensians. The sexual use of the term arose in the 16th century from an association of heresy with forbidden sexual practices.

bull

In stock exchange terminology a **bull** is a person who buys shares hoping to sell them at a higher price later, the opposite of a BEAR. The latter term came first, and it seems likely that *bull* was invented as a related animal analogy.

Nowadays people might associate **bull** in the sense 'nonsense' with the rather cruder term **bulls—**, which means the same thing. **Bull** is much older, though, being first recorded in the early 17th century, in the sense 'an expression containing a contradiction in terms or a ludicrous inconsistency'. An **Irish bull** was a fuller name for this. Where this bull comes from is unknown, though the experts are sure it has nothing to do with a **papal bull** (an order or announcement by the pope), which is from medieval Latin *bulla*, 'a sealed

document'. The modern use appears about the same time as **bulls—**, in the early years of the 20th century. See also BULLETIN.

bulldozer

To **bulldoze** someone first meant to intimidate them, and a **bulldozer** was a bully who intimidated others. Early examples often use the spelling **bulldose**, and the reference may have been to a severe 'dose' of flogging. In the 1890s **bulldozer** seems to have become attached to various devices for pushing things such as piles of earth or snow, and then around 1930 to the heavy tractor we are familiar with. See also DOSE.

bulletin

The word **bulletin** derives from Italian *bulletta* meaning 'official warrant or certificate' – something like a passport today. The root is the Italian and medieval Latin word *bulla* 'seal, sealed document', the source of BILL meaning 'written statement of charges' and of BULL meaning 'papal edict'. The original Latin meaning of *bulla* was 'bubble', and this is the basis of **bowl** in the sense 'ball' and of **budge**, **bullet**, **bullion** and **ebullient**.

bully

People originally liked bullies. When it came into the English language in the 16th century, probably from an old Dutch word *boele* 'lover', **bully** was a term of endearment, much like 'sweetheart' or 'darling'. At the end of the 17th century it was being used to mean 'admirable or jolly', and finally the more general sense of 'first-rate' developed. Today this survives only in the expression **bully for you!**, 'well done! good for you!' The usual modern sense dates from the late 17th century, probably from its use as an informal way of addressing a male friend, or referring to a 'lad' or 'one of the boys'.

bum

There are two different words spelled **bum**. To a Brit, the **bum** is their bottom. Unfortunately, the origin is unknown. From the Middle Ages until around the 18th century bum in this sense was not regarded as a rude word: Shakespeare used it, and a treatise on surgery could refer to '[pulling] the feathers from the bums of hens or cocks'. In the BBC TV comedy series *The Fast Show* Arabella Weir played a variety of women, from High Court judge to nun, united only in asking every week, 'Does my bum look big in this?'

The American **bum** is a tramp or vagrant. The origin of this one is known – it is probably from **bummer**, which now chiefly means 'a disappointing or unpleasant situation' but in the USA first referred to a vagrant. It comes from German *bummeln* 'to stroll about'.

The British slang word **bumf**, meaning 'tedious printed material' was originally bum fodder, 'toilet paper'. The novelist Virginia Woolf wrote in a letter of 1912, 'Is this letter written upon Bumf? It looks like it.' See also ARSE, BUTT.

bundle

In the mid 18th century anatomists and physiologists started using the Old English word **bundle** for a set of muscle or nerve fibres running in parallel. The phrase **a bundle of nerves** is common in US sources from the 1880s, and it also appears in Wilkie Collins's *The Woman In White* (1860): '"I am afraid you are suffering to-day," said the Count. "As usual," I said. "I am nothing but a bundle of nerves dressed up to look like a man."'

The phrase to **go a bundle on** someone or something, or be very fond of them, comes from the world of betting and horse racing. **Bundle** is a slang term for 'a large sum of money', first used in the US around 1880. If a person 'goes a bundle on a horse' they bet a lot of money on it.

bung

The spelling **bung** represents three different words. **Bung** meaning 'a stopper for closing a hole in a container' comes from an old Dutch word. The origin of **bung** as in 'to throw casually' or 'a bribe' is unknown. The 'bribe' sense is first found in the 1950s: it is now generally associated with shady goings-on in the world of sport, but was originally slang used by criminals. The third **bung** is restricted to Australia and New Zealand, and means 'dead', bankrupt' or 'ruined, useless'. It is probably from Yagara, an Aboriginal language of southeast Queensland.

bungee

A **bungee** was originally a rubber or eraser. In the 1930s the word came to mean an elasticated cord for launching a glider, and by the 1960s the bungee or bungee cord, with a hook at each end, was used for securing articles. By the late 1970s a similar band (and some brave or mad people) allowed the development of **bungee jumping**, the sport of jumping from a high place secured by a band round the ankles.

bunk

A shortening of **bunkum**, which also means 'nonsense' but is now dated. **Bunkum**, originally also spelled **buncombe**, refers to Buncombe County in North Carolina, USA. Around 1820 the congressman for the county mentioned it in an inconsequential speech, just to please his constituents. **Buncombe** immediately became a byword for tedious nonsense. **Bunk** meaning 'a kind of bed' and **bunk** as in **bunk off** are different words, both of unknown origin. See also HISTORY.

bunny

The first recorded example of **bunny**, in 1606, reads, 'Sweet Peg . . . my honey, my bunny, my duck, my dear'. The word was originally a term of endearment for a person, and was not found as a pet name for a rabbit until late in the 17th century. It is itself a pet form of **bun**, a dialect word for a squirrel or a rabbit. That word is unlikely to be connected with **bun** 'a small cake', which is also of obscure origin. The 1987 film *Fatal Attraction*, in which Glenn Close's character, rejected by Michael Douglas, boils his pet rabbit, gave us the term **bunny boiler** for a woman who acts vengefully having been spurned by her lover. See also PLAY.

bureau

The French word *bureau* originally meant 'baize', a material that was used for covering writing desks, and probably comes from a form of *buire* 'dark brown'. In the early 18th century **bureau** entered English both as a writing desk and as an office, a place where writing desks are found. In North America the piece of furniture called a **bureau** is a chest of drawers rather than a desk. The word is common there in the official titles of some government offices, for example the Federal Bureau of Investigation or FBI. See also BAIZE.

burn

The **burn** meaning 'to be on fire' and the Scottish word for a small stream are not connected, although both are Old English. To **burn the midnight oil**, 'to read or work late into the night', and to **burn the candle at both ends**, 'to go to bed late and get up early', both recall the days before gas and electricity, when houses were lit by candles and oil lamps. To **burn your boats** (in Britain also to **burn your bridges**) derives from military campaigns. Burning the boats or bridges that a force used to reach a particular position would mean that they had destroyed any means of escape or retreat: they had no choice but to fight on.

Ticking all the boxes

The language of the business world is noted for well-worn cliché and impenetrable jargon. Office English, or Offlish as it has been called, may be full of inflated phrases that mean little to an outsider, but it can also be highly creative in its use of vivid images to drive home a message.

Like teenage slang, business jargon can be useful shorthand for insiders. Abbreviations such as B2B (business to business) and COLA (cost-of-living adjustment) and even the well-worn formulas of picking the low-hanging fruit (meeting easy targets), being ahead of the curve (from the image of a graph charting average growth) or pushing the envelope (see ENVELOPE) deliver the message required to those in the know.

Among the most colourful business phrases in recent years, most coming from the USA, have been prairie-dogging, the act of peeking over a partition wall to check on a colleague's activity, much as prairie dogs post sentinels to guard their colony, and dropping your pants or opening your kimono – respectively, lowering the price of a product in order to close a sale, and putting all your cards on the table. To push the peanut forward is to make a difference, a term that may derive from a game in which players have to push a peanut with their nose. Employers give a duvet day to some workers as an unplanned day off if they are too tired to work. A square-headed girlfriend is a computer, while a chair plug is someone who sits at a meeting but who contributes nothing.

To think outside the box is to view a situation with a fresh perspective, without preconceptions. The image almost certainly comes from a traditional puzzle from as far back as the early 20th century, known as the 'nine-dots puzzle'. The challenge was to connect the dots without lifting your pen from the page. The puzzle was easily solved, but only by thinking laterally and drawing the lines outside the confines of the square suggested by the dots. Blue-sky thinking is a similar idea – blue-sky has been used since the 1920s to mean 'visionary and theoretical, unconstrained by practicalities'.

The business world is constantly generating new idioms. Thanks to the speed with which they proliferate, the latest game at meetings is known as buzzword bingo. In the game bored attendees cross off a business buzzword from their list every time it is used.

to go for a burton

This first appears in RAF slang in the 1940s, when it was used to mean 'be killed in a crash'. The most plausible explanation is that it was a reference to going for a pint of Burton's beer. Burton-upon-Trent in Staffordshire, England, was – and is – a well-known centre of the brewing industry. Another suggestion is that it referred to a suit from the British men's clothing firm Burton's, but there is no known record of to **go for a Burton's suit,** as you might expect if this were the origin of the phrase, and 'gone for a pint' is a much more likely euphemism for a young man's sudden death.

bus see OMNIBUS.

bushel

If a **bushel** is a measure of capacity, how can you **hide your light under a bushel**? The answer is that the word here is used in an old sense, 'a container used to measure out a bushel'. The origin is biblical, from the Gospel of Matthew: 'Neither do men light a candle, and put it under a bushel, but on a candlestick; and it giveth light to all that are in the house.'

business

Old English *bisignis* meant 'anxiety'. Businessmen and women might say that **business** still causes it. But the main early sense, which lasted from the Middle Ages down to the 18th century, was 'the state of being busy'. The modern senses began to develop in the later Middle Ages, and the meanings existed happily in parallel for several hundred years. Then people began to feel that a clear distinction needed to be made between simply being busy and having business to attend to. In the early 19th century this resulted in the form **busyness** – the exact equivalent of *bisignis*.

busk

Busking used to take place not in shopping centres but at sea. The word **busk** comes from Italian *buscare* or Spanish *buscar*, which both mean 'to seek'. Its earliest use in English was in the nautical sense 'cruise about, tack'. This became extended to mean 'go about selling things', and then, in the middle of the 19th century, 'go about performing'.

bust

Real women used not to have busts. Originally **bust** referred only to sculpture, usually a piece of sculpture representing a person's head, shoulders and chest. The term came into English in the 17th century through French from Italian *busto*. The Latin source of the Italian word was even further from warm flesh and blood: *bustum* meant 'a tomb, a sepulchral monument'. When in the early 18th century a living person was described as having a bust, there was usually some comparison with marble or a sculpture. It was not until the later 19th century that the word appeared in the context of dress and fashion, and the measurement of a woman's bosom for clothing sizes.

butcher

The origin of **butcher** may tell us something about the diet of early Europeans. It goes back to a French word meaning 'male goat' that is probably related to **buck** 'male deer'. **Butcher** entered English in the Middle Ages. A butcher was originally more a slaughterman than a salesman, and the word quickly came to refer to a person responsible for the slaughter of many people, a brutal murderer. See also SHAMBLES.

In the phrase to **have a butcher's**, 'to have a look', **butcher's** is short for **butcher's hook**, rhyming slang for 'a look'. The first printed example dates from the 1930s.

butt

The **butt** of something is its end, such as a cigarette stub or the part of a rifle that you hold. In America your butt is your bottom, a meaning that goes back to medieval England. The word is related to **buttock**, which is even older. See also ARSE, BUM.

The brimstone, whose colour may have influenced the word butterfly.

butterfly

The word **butter** has been known in Britain since Saxon times. It goes back to Greek *bouturon*, and before that possibly to the Scythians, an ancient people from the area of the Black Sea. The **butterfly** may get its name, used since the Old English period for a butter-coloured flying creature, from the brimstone butterfly and other yellow or cream-coloured butterflies.

The idea of likening a feeling of nervousness to having a butterfly or butterflies in one's stomach dates from the early 20th century, though the exact formulation **butterflies in one's stomach** is not recorded before the 1950s.

'Who breaks a butterfly on a wheel?' was the headline of the leader article in *The Times* of June 1, 1967, written in defence of the Rolling Stones singer Mick Jagger, who had been arrested for possession of cannabis. The article is now often cited as an indicator of the social change that took place in the 1960s, in that the editor of the traditional 'Establishment' newspaper was defending the long-haired singer of the archetypal rock rebels. The phrase was not original, but was a quotation from 'An Epistle to Lord Arbuthnot' (1735) by Alexander Pope.

Muhammad Ali described his boxing strategy as 'Float like a butterfly, sting like a bee'. The quote first appeared in *The Cassius Clay Story* (1964 – Cassius Clay was Ali's original name), possibly coined by Ali's trainer Drew 'Bundini' Brown. See also CHAOS, MOTH.

buxom

Today **buxom** describes a woman's physical appearance, but originally it would have described her character. From the early Middle Ages and into the 19th century **buxom** meant 'obedient, compliant' and applied to both sexes. The word comes from the root of **bow**, 'to incline the head or body' and originally 'to bend'. From 'compliant' it moved to 'obliging, amiable', and then in the 16th century it became more active and positive, taking in 'bright, cheerful, lively'. Good spirits depend on good health, and soon a buxom woman was one full of health, vigour and good temper. And since plumpness has a traditional association with health, she became plump or large-breasted.

cab

A **cab** was originally a **cabriolet**, which is now a car with a roof that folds down but was at first a kind of light two-wheeled carriage with a hood, drawn by one horse. The motion of the carriage suggested its name, which is from French *cabriole* 'a goat's leap' – the root is Latin *caper* 'goat'. See also CAPER, HANSOM, TAXI.

cabaret

Samuel Pepys wrote in his diary, 'In most cabaretts in France they have writ upon the walls "*Dieu te regarde*", as a good lesson to be in every man's mind'. He was referring to French inns, which is what the word **cabaret** meant in the 17th century. The modern sense of an entertainment in a nightclub dates from before the First World War. **Cabaret** is from the Old French word for a wooden structure such as a shed – a far cry from what we now associate with the term.

cabinet

The modern meaning of 'a piece of furniture' developed from the original sense 'little cabin' or 'small room'. The use of **cabinet** to refer to the small select body of chief ministers who meet to discuss government policy dates from the 17th century. Confidential advisers of the monarch or chief ministers of a country used to hold their meetings in a private room, and in time the term for the room came to be applied to the politicians themselves. See also BOARD.

caboodle

The **caboodle** in the expression **the whole caboodle** or **the whole kit and caboodle**, meaning 'the whole lot', is a mysterious word. The phrase was originally **the whole kit**, and later **the whole kit and boodle**. **Boodle** meant 'a lot, a crowd' or 'money', and may be connected to Dutch *boedel*, meaning 'possessions'. See also KIT.

cacophony

The word **cacophony**, meaning 'a harsh discordant combination of sounds', came into English via French from Greek *kakophonia*. *Kakos* was Greek for 'bad', and *phōnï* meant 'sound' – it is the root of words like **euphonious**, **symphony** and **telephone**.

cadge

The first recorded use of **cadge** was the English dialect sense 'to carry about'. This was formed from the noun **cadger**, which had existed since the late 15th century and meant, in northern English and Scots, 'a pedlar or dealer who travelled between town and country'. From this developed the verb sense 'to hawk or peddle' and eventually the modern sense, 'to ask for something that you are not strictly entitled to'. **Codger**, meaning an elderly man, is probably a variant of **cadger**.

Caesar

Roman emperors from Augustus, the first emperor, to Hadrian were known by the title **Caesar**. The word came simply from the name of Julius Caesar, who was Augustus's predecessor as ruler of Rome. It is the root of both the German **Kaiser** and the Russian **Tsar.**

A person who should be above suspicion can be referred to as **Caesar's wife**. According to the story recounted by the Greek biographer Plutarch, Julius Caesar's wife Pompeia was accused of adultery with Publius Clodius, a notorious womaniser, causing a great scandal. Although he did not believe his wife was guilty, Caesar divorced Pompeia anyway. His justification for this was, 'I thought my wife ought not even to be under suspicion'. A **caesarean section** is so called because Julius Caesar is supposed to have been delivered by this birth method. See also YEAR.

cahoots

To be **in cahoots** with someone is to be working in collusion with them. It is an American expression, recorded in the early 19th century in the neutral sense of 'in league or partnership', as in 'He wished me to go in cahoots in a store'. Nowadays the expression invariably suggests dishonesty and conspiracy. Where **cahoots** comes from is uncertain. It might derive from the French word *cahute*, meaning 'a hut or cabin', with the idea of plotting together in an intimate closed environment. Or it may be an alteration of **cohort**, based on the notion of a group of people working closely together to achieve something.

cake

The first **cakes** were small flat bread rolls baked hard on both sides by being turned during the baking process – you can see the idea of a rounded flattened shape surviving in **fishcake** and **potato cake**. The word occurs in many common expressions as a metaphor for something pleasant or desirable. The phrase **cakes and ale**, for example, means 'merrymaking, a good time'. It comes from Shakespeare's *Twelfth Night*, when the roistering Sir Toby Belch says to the puritanical steward Malvolio: 'Dost though think because thou art virtuous there shall be no more cakes and ale?'

The idea behind the saying **you can't have your cake and eat it** is that you cannot enjoy both of two equally desirable but mutually exclusive things. Once the cake is eaten, it is gone and you no longer have it. Here is an early version from John Heywood, writing in 1546: 'Would you both eat your cake, and have your cake?'

let them eat cake

Did Marie-Antoinette, Louis XVI's wife, say this when told that her people had no bread? The story is suspect. She may really have used the French word *brioche* – a light, sweet roll rather than a cake. Also, Louis XIV's wife may have said 'Why don't they eat pastry?' in a similar situation.

calculate

The Latin word *calculus* meant 'a small pebble', specifically one used on an ABACUS. This is the base of Latin *calculare* 'to count', from which **calculate** comes. Long before a **calculator** was an electronic device for performing calculations, it meant a person who calculates, just as a computer was a person who computes. **Calculus** has become an English word in its own right, as the name of a branch of mathematics.

calendar

The ultimate source of **calendar** is Latin *kalendae*, which referred to the first day of each month of the Roman calendar, when debts were due to be paid and accounts had to be settled. Rather than days of the week, this calendar had three significant monthly dates, the **calends**, the **nones** (the 5th or 7th of the month) and the **ides**, the 15th or 13th day of the month. Julius Caesar was assassinated on the Ides of March, despite having been warned by a fortune teller to 'Beware the Ides of March'. See also YEAR.

calibre

Calibre, now meaning 'the quality of someone's character or the level of their ability' and 'the internal diameter or bore of a gun barrel', went on a long and eventful journey around the Mediterranean and Middle East before arriving in English during the 16th century. It may have started in Greece, from where the word *kalapous*, 'shoemaker's last', migrated east and became Arabic *qālib*, 'mould for casting metal'. The jump to Italy or Spain and then France produced the spelling **calibre**, and from there it was only a short hop to England, where the word first meant 'social standing or importance'.

call

To **call the shots** or **call the tune** is to dictate how something should be done. The original form, **call the tune**, is a shortened form of the saying **he who pays the piper calls the tune**, meaning that if you are paying a musician you are the one to decide what tune they play. **Call the shots** is more recent, and is not recorded before the 1920s. It comes from sports and games, possibly from pool, billiards and snooker or from shooting. In pool to **call your shots** is to say in advance which ball you intend to hit into which pocket. In target shooting it means to announce which part of the target you are going to hit; if someone else **calls the shots** you have to aim at the bit they choose.

callous

Someone who is **callous** is literally 'hard-skinned'. This is what Latin *callosus* (from *callum* 'hard skin') meant and how the English word was originally used. Its modern meaning, 'unfeeling, insensitive to others' feelings', developed from this. The similar-sounding **callus**, also derived from Latin *callum*, is the word we use for a hardened and thickened area of skin.

callow

You would not think of a **callow** youth as someone who was bald, but that is what Old English *calu* meant. A later use referred to young birds and meant 'not yet able to fly, unfledged'. The idea of fluffy young birds must have put people in mind of the down on a youth's cheek and chin, which led to the present sense 'immature or inexperienced'.

calm

The origin of **calm** can be traced back to the idea of the heat of the midday sun in a hot climate. This is the time when people are indoors taking a rest and everything is quiet and still. **Calm** actually emerged from the heat of the Mediterranean. It came into English via Italian, Spanish or Portuguese from Greek *kauma* 'heat of the day', and was perhaps also influenced by Latin *calere* 'to be warm'.

camel

Our term for the **camel** derives from Greek *kamïlos*, which itself probably came from an Arabic or Hebrew word. When it was adopted into Old English it replaced the existing word for the animal, *olfend*. This sounds suspiciously like **elephant**, and it seems that people often got the two animals confused, not being very familiar with either. Talking of mixing animals up, an archaic name for a giraffe was a **camelopard**, from Greek *kamelopardalis*, from *kamïlos* 'camel' and *pardalis* 'female panther or leopard'. People thought that a giraffe's spotted skin looked like that of a leopard. See also CHAMELEON, ELEPHANT, GIRAFFE.

Alec Issigonis, the designer of the Morris Minor and Mini cars, said that 'A camel is a horse designed by a committee'. He was making a point about his dislike of working in teams.

camera

A **camera** was first a council or legislative chamber in Italy or Spain. The word is borrowed from Latin, where it meant 'vault or chamber', and is also the source of **chamber**. In legal contexts the Latin phrase *in camera* is used to mean 'in the judge's private chamber' instead of in open court. The photography sense comes from the **camera obscura** (literally 'dark chamber'), a device popular in the 18th century for recording visual images – the first example of the modern sense comes in the 1840s.

campaign

Latin *campania* meant 'open countryside' and was based on *campus* 'a field'. It is the source of the English word **campaign**, which originally referred to a tract of open land and is a close relative of French *champagne*, both an area of open country and the winemaking region. The connection between countryside and fighting is that armies tended to spend winter in quarters in a fortress or town, leaving it until the start of summer before 'taking the field' to seek battle. Hence the countryside became associated with military manoeuvres, and the main meaning of **campaign** changed.

There is a similar story with the word **camp**, which is also descended from Latin *campus*. The Latin word was used not only to mean 'a field, level ground' but, more specifically, 'an open space for military exercises'

– the most famous one was the Campus Martius, or Field of Mars, in Rome. This developed into the idea of a place where soldiers are housed. **Campus** itself came into English in the 18th century as the term for university or college grounds. See also CHAMPION.

can

Nowadays a **can** is a cylindrical metal container, but its ancestor, Old English *cann*, was a general word for a container for liquids, of any material, shape or size. See also CANNON.

If someone **carries the can** they take responsibility for a mistake or misdeed. The origin of this expression is uncertain, but it probably started life as early 20th-century naval slang. One theory is that it refers to the beer can or keg which one sailor carried for all his companions. An early version was to **carry the can back**, which might have referred to returning the empties.

In film-making and recording you can talk about something being **in the can** when it has been captured on tape or film to a satisfactory standard. Though videotape and digital recordings are not stored in cans, the older expression has been transferred to them. See also CUNNING, WORM.

canary

How do you get from a dog to a canary? The **canary** acquired its name from the Canary Islands, which is where the ancestors of our cage birds originate. The name of the islands comes from Latin *canaria insula*, which meant 'island of dogs' and came from *canis* 'dog', one of the islands having had a large population of dogs. *Canis* is also the source of words including **canine** and **kennel**.

cancer

The pattern of swollen veins around malignant tumours gave them the name **cancer** because they looked like the limbs of a crab – called *cancer* in Latin. In English **canker** was the usual form for the disease until the 17th century, when **cancer** replaced it, with **canker** becoming the term for various plant diseases. See also CRABBED.

candid

'The stones came candid forth, the hue of innocence', wrote the poet John Dryden around 1700. He was using the word **candid** in its original meaning 'white', which is also what its source, Latin *candidus*, meant. Over time the English word developed the senses 'pure and innocent', 'unbiased' and 'free from malice', before finally settling on the meaning 'frank'. **Candour** has a similar history, its meaning developing from 'whiteness' to the current 'openness and honesty in expression'. See also ALBUM.

These days someone running for an important office needs to be 'whiter than white'. Certainly the candidates in Roman times were, since the word **candidate**, like **candid**, is based on *candidus* 'white'. A *candidatus* was a white-robed person, a candidate for office who was traditionally required to wear a pure white toga or robe.

candle

The Old English word *candel*, later to become **candle**, came from Latin *candela*, from *candere* 'to be white, shine, glisten', and so is related to CANDID. A person who **cannot hold a candle to** someone else is nowhere near as good as them. Before the invention of gas or electric lighting an assistant might stand next to his superior with a candle to provide enough light to work by, and so the idea of holding a candle to someone became synonymous with helping them as a subordinate or in a menial way.

We say that something is **not worth the candle** when we think it is not worth doing because of the trouble or cost involved. The expression originated as a translation of the French phrase *le jeu ne vaut pas la chandelle*, 'the game is not worth the candle'. The 'game' was a game of cards involving betting, and would not be worth playing if the expense of candles to provide light for it was likely to exceed the expected winnings.

'Candle in the Wind' is the title of a 1973 song by Elton John, originally written about Marilyn Monroe and in 1997 reworked as a lament for Diana, Princess of Wales, and sung at her funeral. The use of the image of a wavering flame is much older, though. John Bunyan, the 17th-century author of *The Pilgrim's Progress*, wrote in a verse: 'But candles in the wind are apt to flare, and Christians in a tempest to despair.'

cannibal

The explorer Christopher Columbus brought back the word **cannibal** to Europe. On landing in the West Indies he encountered the warlike Caribs, and gained the impression they were cannibals. His interpretation of their name was *Canibales*, which entered English in a translated account of his voyage written in 1553. The Caribs gave their name to the Caribbean sea and region.

cannon

The barrel of a **cannon** consists of a long tube, and this is what its root, Latin *canna*, meant. This is also the

source of **cane**, **channel**, the tube-shaped pasta **cannelloni** and possibly CAN.

Soldiers have been called **cannon fodder**, no more than material to be used up in war, since the late 19th century – the expression is a translation of German *Kanonenfutter*. Shakespeare did encapsulate a similar idea much earlier, with his phrase 'food for powder' in *Henry IV Part 1*.

canopy

Conopeum, the Latin word from which **canopy** derives, referred to a mosquito net over a bed. The ultimate source is the Greek word *kōnōps* 'mosquito'. Since the 14th century the English word has developed various meanings based on the idea of a covering suspended over something, such as an awning or other cloth covering, the uppermost layer of branches in a forest and the expanding umbrella-like part of a parachute.

canter

Our word **canter** began as a shortened form of **canterbury pace** or **canterbury gallop**, the term for the gentle rate at which mounted pilgrims made their way to the shrine of St Thomas à Becket at Canterbury in the Middle Ages. To win something **at a canter** is to do so with the greatest ease. In horse racing a horse easily wins a race if it is able to run the final stretch at the pace of a canter rather than having to gallop.

canvas

You can smoke cannabis, or, more legally, make **canvas** out of its fibre. The versatile cannabis plant, also known as hemp, gives its name to the fabric, as both come from Latin *cannabis*.

To win a race or competition **by a canvas** is to win it narrowly. The canvas here is the tapered front end of a racing boat, covered with canvas to keep water out.

In the early 16th century the verb **canvass** meant 'to toss someone in a canvas sheet', as a punishment or as part of a game. Other early meanings included 'to beat' and 'to criticise severely'. This led on to the idea of discussing an issue, and then to proposing something for discussion. Finally, the word acquired the meaning 'to seek support', as in 'to canvass for votes' at an election.

A leaf of the cannabis plant, source of the fibre used to make canvas.

cap

We get our word **cap** from Latin *cappa*, which may be related to Latin *caput* 'head'. **Cape**, 'a sleeveless cloak', also derives from *cappa*.

Saying **if the cap fits, wear it** is a way of suggesting that you should accept a description or remark if you feel that it applies to you – the cap in question was originally a dunce's cap, of the kind that poor performers at school had to wear as a mark of disgrace. Americans use the version **if the shoe fits, wear it**.

caper

Two frisky animals are behind the word **caper**, meaning 'to dance about in a lively way'. It was adapted in the 16th century from **capriole**, a movement performed in riding in which the horse leaps from the ground and kicks out with its hind legs. The origin of this was Italian *capriola* 'leap', which was based on Latin *caper* 'goat'. Members of the Victorian underworld seem to have been the first to use the word in the sense 'an illicit or ridiculous activity'. In an 1867 edition of the *London Herald* a policeman is quoted as saying: 'He'll get five years penal for this little caper.'

Edible capers are something quite different – the word comes from Greek *kapparis*. See also CAB.

capital

The first meaning of **capital** was 'to do with the head or the top of something'. From this evolved such modern meanings as 'the large form of a letter' and 'the chief city or town in a country'. The word comes from Latin *capitalis*, from *caput* 'head'. Capital in the financial sense was originally the *capital stock* of a company or trader, meaning their main or original funds. The use as an adjective meaning 'very good', now extremely old-fashioned, dates from the mid 18th century.

To **capitulate** is to admit that you are defeated and surrender. When it first entered the language it meant 'to parley or draw up terms', having come via French from medieval Latin *capitulare* 'to draw up under headings'. Like **capital**, its ultimate root is Latin *caput* 'head', source also of CAP, CHAPTER and **chief** (the 'head' of a group of people).

caprice

A **caprice** is a sudden unaccountable change of mind, a whim. But what can this possibly have to do with hedgehogs? Well, if you put the Italian words *capo* 'head' and *riccio* 'hedgehog' together you get the word *capriccio*, or 'hedgehog-head'. In other words, a head with the hair standing on end, like a hedgehog's spines.

This is what can happen if you are terrified by something, so *capriccio*, the source of English **caprice**, came to mean 'horror or shuddering'. Over time this eventually became 'a sudden start, a sudden change', perhaps influenced by Italian word *capra* 'goat'. See also CAPER.

caption

Latin *capere*, 'to take or seize', is the source of many English words such as **capture**, **catch**, **chase**, **perceive** and **receive**, and also gave us **caption**, which originally meant 'seizing or capture'. The word came to be applied to an arrest or the warrant for someone's arrest, then in the 17th century to a certificate attached to a legal document and stating where, when and by whose authority a person had been arrested. This led to the sense 'heading or attached wording' in the late 18th century.

car

The earliest recorded uses of **car**, dating probably from the 14th century, referred to wheeled vehicles such as carts or wagons. The word came into English from Old French *carre*, based on Latin *carrus* 'two-wheeled vehicle', the source of words such as CAREER, **cargo**, **carriage**, **carry**, **charge** and **chariot**.

From the 16th to the 19th centuries **car** was mainly used in poetic or literary contexts to suggest a sense of splendour and solemnity. Lord Tennyson used it to describe the funeral carriage bearing the body of the Duke of Wellington at his state funeral: 'And a reverent people behold / The towering car, the sable steeds' ('Ode on the Death of the Duke of Wellington', 1852). The first self-propelled road vehicle was a steam-driven carriage designed and built in France in 1769, but such vehicles were not called **cars** until the 1890s.

carbuncle

A **carbuncle** is both a severe abscess and a bright red gem, particularly a garnet. The word comes from Old French *charbuncle*, from Latin *carbunculus* 'a small coal' – the core idea is the redness of a lighted coal. In 1984 Prince Charles famously described a proposed extension to the National Gallery in London as 'A monstrous carbuncle on the face of a much-loved and elegant friend'.

card

A medieval word that comes via French *carte* from Latin *charta* 'papyrus leaf or paper', the source of **chart** and **charter**. Its first recorded sense was 'playing card', and many expressions we use today are rooted in the world of the card table.

To have a **card up your sleeve** is to have a plan or asset that you are keeping secret until you need it. If someone **holds all the cards** in a situation, they are in a very strong position, just like a card player who has a hand guaranteed to win. Someone who is secretive and cautious about their plans or activities might be said to be **keeping their cards close to their chest**. The image here is of a card player trying to prevent the other players from looking at their hand. If you **play your cards right** you make the best use of assets and opportunities to ensure that you get what you want, whereas to **lay your cards on the table** is to be completely open and honest in saying what your intentions are.

Rather different from the above expressions is **on the cards** (in the US, **in the cards**), meaning 'possible or likely'. The cards being referred to here are ones used for fortune telling, tarot cards perhaps. In Britain a person unlucky enough to **get** or **be given their cards** is sacked from their job. The cards referred to are the National Insurance details and other documents that were formerly retained by the employer during a person's employment.

A politician who is said to **play the race card** exploits the issue of race or racism for their own ends. The expression originates in a letter written by Lord Randolph Churchill in 1886 on the question of Irish Home Rule. Referring to the Orange Order of Protestant Loyalists, he said that 'the Orange card would be the one to play'. In the years since then, many types of cards have been played for political purposes.

Charles Dickens was fond of using **card** in the sense 'an odd or eccentric person', and his *Sketches by Boz* (1836) provides the first written use. It comes from **sure card**, meaning a person who was sure to succeed.

cardinal

The connection between a **cardinal**, 'a senior Roman Catholic priest', and **cardinal**, 'fundamental or most important', is a door hinge. The word derives from Latin *cardinalis*, from *cardo* 'hinge', and its various senses share the idea of something being of pivotal importance, the crucial thing on which everything else turns or depends. So the ecclesiastical cardinals were thought of as the 'pivots' of the life of the Roman Catholic Church.

career

The core idea behind the various meanings of **career** is that of progressing along a course of some kind. But at one time the notion of doing this at speed was also a key element in the word's meaning. Based on Latin *carrus*, 'wheeled vehicle', **career** was first used in

English to mean both 'a racecourse' and 'a short gallop at full speed, a charge'. There was an old expression to **pass a career**, or make a charge on horseback at a tournament or in a battle. From these senses developed the modern use, referring to the stages in a person's professional employment, the course of their working life. The verb use, 'to rush headlong, to hurtle', preserves the old sense. See also CAR.

carnival

Before the word came to be applied to any festival involving a procession, a **carnival** was, in Roman Catholic countries, specifically the period preceding Lent, a time of public merrymaking and festivities. The word is recorded from the mid 16th century and comes from medieval Latin *carnelevamen* 'Shrovetide'. The base elements of the Latin word are *caro* 'flesh or meat' and *levare* 'to put away', so the idea was that this was a time to feast and party before all the meat was removed and the fasting of Lent began. There is a popular belief that **carnival** is from *carne vale*, 'farewell, meat', but this is mistaken. Other meat or flesh-related words that derive from *caro* include **carnivore**, **carnage**, **carnation** (from the flower's 'fleshy' colour) and **incarnation**.

carpet

It was originally tables or beds, not floors, that were covered by a **carpet**, made of a thick woollen fabric, and it is the early 'tablecloth' meaning that is behind the expression **on the carpet**, 'being severely reprimanded by someone in authority'. This might make you think of standing in the middle of the boss's office getting a ticking off, but the phrase originally had another meaning, 'under consideration or discussion', which referred specifically to the covering of a council table, where official documents for discussion were placed. A matter up for discussion at a meeting was **on the carpet**, just as we might now say **on the table**. The idea of a person in trouble being 'on the carpet' could have come from them being summoned before the members of a council seated at their table to get an official reprimand.

The more familiar **carpet**, though, is definitely the one being referred to in another common expression. When you **sweep something under the carpet** you hide or ignore a problem in the hope that it will be forgotten. The word **carpet** is from old Italian *carpita* 'woollen bedspread', which was based on Latin *carpere* 'to pluck, pull to pieces', the source of **carp**, 'to criticise', and **excerpt**. See also HARVEST.

Curiouser and curiouser

When the writer Lewis Carroll sent Alice down a rabbit hole in *Alice's Adventures in Wonderland* (1865) and through a mirror in *Through the Looking-Glass* (1871) she entered worlds full of fantastic creatures and invented words. Many of them are still part of our language today.

Someone with a broad fixed smile is sometimes said to grin like a Cheshire cat. The expression may go back to the face of a smiling cat traditionally stamped on Cheshire cheeses. It was popularised by Carroll's Cheshire Cat, which disappeared as Alice watched it, 'beginning with the end of the tail, and ending with the grin'.

The title of the nonsense poem 'Jabberwocky' in *Through the Looking-Glass* has given us a word for invented or meaningless language, jabberwocky. The poem itself offers a range of new words. Many of them are 'portmanteau words', created by blending the sounds and combining the meanings of other words. In *Through the Looking-Glass* Humpty-Dumpty explained the process to Alice, who has asked about the word slithy. He told her that it meant 'lithe and slimy', and added: 'You see it's like a portmanteau – there are two meanings packed up into one word.'

Some of Carroll's portmanteau words are now so familiar that it is hard to believe that they were not invented until the late 19th century. They include galumph, chortle and mimsy, a blend of *miserable* and *flimsy* that means 'feeble and prim or affected'.

In 'Jabberwocky' the hero encounters the monstrous Jabberwock, and kills it with his 'vorpal sword'. Afterwards 'He left it dead, and with its head / He went galumphing back.' Galumph here is a blend of *prance* and *triumph* which was intended to suggest his exultant return, but once the word had established itself the meaning shifted, and we would now use galumph to suggest a clumsy noisy progress rather than a triumphant one.

In the poem the hero's father is as delighted as his son by the boy's success. '"O frabjous day! Callooh! Callay!" he chortled in his joy.' Chortle is probably a blend of *chuckle* and *snort*, and its meaning today retains the element of pleasure and self-congratulation as well as of humour.

Perhaps Carroll as a wordsmith did in fact resemble his own character Humpty-Dumpty, who told Alice that 'When I use a word, it means just what I choose it to mean – neither more nor less.'

See also CURIOUS, JAM, TWEEDLEDEE AND TWEEDLEDUM.

cart

Our word **cart**, deriving from Old Norse *kartr* and related to CAR, was originally used to talk about a carriage of any kind, even a chariot, rather than the humble vehicle we are familiar with. If you **put the cart before the horse**, an expression first recorded in the early 16th century, you are doing things in the wrong order. A medieval version was **set the oxen before the yoke**.

cartoon

Lovers of art will know that cartoons were not originally meant to be funny. Long before the days of Mickey Mouse, Bugs Bunny and friends, a **cartoon** was a full-size drawing made on paper as a design for a painting, fresco or tapestry – cartoons by artists such as Raphael and Leonardo da Vinci are now prized and exhibited as artworks in their own right. The word seems to have become attached to cartoons in the more usual modern sense of satirical or humorous drawings in the 19th century, with the first record of its use coming from the magazine *Punch* in 1843. The word was applied to animated films in the early years of the 20th century – Walt Disney's first Mickey Mouse film, *Steamboat Willie*, was released in 1928, and the first full-length animated film, *Snow White and the Seven Dwarfs*, in 1937.

The word is from Italian *cartone*, literally 'big card', from Latin *carta* or *charta*, the source of CARD. **Carton** comes from the same source, although it arrived in English via French: the connection was that cartons are typically made of light cardboard.

casino

Nowadays a **casino** is chiefly associated with gambling, but originally it was a public room used for dancing and music. The word is borrowed from the Italian for 'little house', which is ultimately from Latin *casa* 'cottage', the source of **chalet**.

castle

Our word **castle** goes back to Latin *castellum*, which was from *castrum* 'fort'. To build **castles in the air** is to have daydreams or unrealistic fantasies. The idea derives from a Latin phrase by St Augustine, who became bishop of Hippo in North Africa in AD 396. Another version, originally a translation from medieval French, is to build **castles in Spain**. This country was probably chosen just not as a good place to invest in property abroad but because it was a distant place where it would have been extremely unrealistic to build a palace – most of it was under the rule of the Moors at the time the phrase was first used in French.

cat

The Anglo-Saxons had a word *catt* or *catte*, though the history of **cat** goes back much further than that. There seems to have been a similar word for the animal in most European languages as far back as written records go. The original source, though uncertain, may well have been an Egyptian word – ancient Egypt was the earliest home of the domestic cat.

Like the DOG and the HORSE, the cat features in many colourful English expressions. The saying **a cat may look at a king**, meaning 'even a person of low status or importance has rights', is recorded from the mid 16th century. A 1590 use offers the slightly longer version 'a Cat may look at a King, and a swaine's eye hath as high a reach as a Lord's look', a swain being a country youth or peasant. It crops up also in Lewis Carroll's *Alice in Wonderland*, where the cat in question is the Cheshire Cat and the king is the King of Hearts. See also COXSWAIN.

If you **let the cat out of the bag** you reveal a secret, especially carelessly or by mistake. The French have a similar metaphorical use of 'bag' in the phrase *vider le sac*, literally 'empty the bag', meaning 'tell the whole story'.

When the cat's away the mice will play might be said in a situation where it is likely that people will take advantage of the absence of someone in authority to do as they like. The saying dates from the 15th century. There is an even earlier French proverb with very much the same message: *ou chat na rat regne*, 'where there is no cat the rat is king'.

To **put the cat among the pigeons** is to say or do something that is likely to cause trouble or controversy. The expression was first recorded in 1706, and appears then to have referred to a man causing a stir by surprising a group of women.

You can emphasise how small and cramped a space is by saying that there's **no room to swing a cat**. This probably refers not to the animal but to a cat-o'-nine-tails, a form of whip with nine knotted cords which was formerly used to flog wrongdoers, especially at sea.

Something really good might be called **the cat's whiskers**, **the cat's pyjamas** or, in North America, **the cat's miaou**. Like the **bee's knees**, these expressions were first used in the era of the 'flappers', the 1920s. Black people in America started calling each other **cats** from the middle of the 19th century, a meaning that jazz musicians and fans took up. See also CATERPILLAR, DUDE, RAIN.

catalogue

You can spend ages leafing through the pages of a **catalogue**, trying to choose what goodies you would like to order. It is this idea of choosing that lies behind

TIDDLES AND I GO BACK A LONG WAY

the origin of the word. It is based on Greek *katalogos*, from *katalegein* 'to choose or pick out'.

cataract

Latin *cataracta* (from Greek *kataraktes*, 'rushing down') meant both 'waterfall or floodgate' and 'portcullis'. The first meaning led to the 'large waterfall' sense of the English word **cataract**, and the second is probably behind the medical sense describing the clouding of the lens of the eye. A person's vision is blocked by this condition as if a portcullis had been lowered over the eye.

catch-22

In Joseph Heller's 1961 novel *Catch-22* an American air force pilot tries to avoid dangerous combat missions by feigning insanity. Unfortunately for him, expressing a desire to avoid combat duty was taken as obvious proof that he was sane, and so fit for duty. The phrase **Catch-22 situation** has entered the language to describe a dilemma or difficulty from which there is no escape because it involves two mutually conflicting or dependent conditions. Here is an example from the *New Scientist* in 1997: 'It's a catch-22 situation: you cannot get the job without having the relevant experience and you cannot get the experience without having first done the job.'

caterpillar

The **caterpillar** first appeared in English, in the 15th century, in the form *catyrpel*, which was probably an alteration of the Old French word *chatepelose*, literally 'hairy cat'. English used to have a word *piller*, meaning 'a plunderer or ravager' (related to **pillage**) and, given the amount of damage that caterpillars do to plants, it is likely that this influenced how the word came to be spelled.

cathedral

First used in the term **cathedral church**, a church containing the bishop's throne. **Cathedral** comes from the Latin word for a seat or throne, *cathedra*, and is closely related to **chair**. The term **ex cathedra**, meaning 'with the full authority of office', is a reference to the authority of the pope; its literal meaning in Latin is 'from the chair'.

cauliflower

Looking at the white head of a cauliflower, you can see where the 'flower' part of the vegetable's name comes from. **Cauliflower** is a modified form of the Italian *cavoli fiori*, literally 'cabbage flowers' – *cavoli* comes from Latin *caulis* 'cabbage', the source also of **kale**

and **cole** (as in **coleslaw**). In fact, the original 16th-century English forms *colieflorie* and *cole-flory* had their first element influenced by the word **cole**, and it was only later that the spelling was changed to match the older Latin root.

cave

Latin *cavus*, 'hollow', is the origin of a number of English words, including **cave**, **cavern** and **cavity**. **Cave** is the oldest of these and can be traced back to the 13th century. **Cavern** is also a medieval word, although **cavity** is more recent, dating from the mid 16th century. In the days when more people knew Latin, there was a second English word spelled **cave**. This one, pronounced **kah-vay**, meant 'beware!', and was used by schoolchildren to warn their friends that a teacher was coming.

cemetery

A **cemetery** is literally a place for sleeping. The word came from Greek *koimētirion*, 'dormitory', from *koiman* 'to put to sleep'. It was early Christian writers who first gave it the meaning of 'burial ground', applying it to the underground cemeteries or catacombs in Rome.

centre

When you draw a circle with a pair of compasses, you use the point on one of the arms to prick a dot in the centre of the circle. The Greek word *kentron* meant 'sharp point', specifically the one on a pair of compasses, and for this reason the words descended from it, including the English **centre**, came to refer to the centre of a circle. What is now the American form **center** is in fact the older spelling, found in the works of Shakespeare. It was Dr Johnson's dictionary in 1755 that established **centre** as the preferred British spelling.

century

In English a **century** is a period of a hundred years or a score of one hundred, but its Latin ancestor *centuria* (from *centum* 'hundred') was used to refer to a company in the ancient Roman army, made up of one hundred men. Early usage of the English word carried the meaning 'a hundred', as in Shakespeare's 'a century of prayers' in *Cymbeline*. The 'one hundred years' sense dates from the early 17th century, when it was used as a shortened form of the phrase 'a century of years'. A batsman who scores a century in cricket, a hundred runs, perpetuates the older sense. See also HUNDRED.

chalk

Old English *cealc*, the forerunner of **chalk**, also meant 'lime'. It derived from Latin *calx* 'lime', which is also the source of **calcium**. The meaning of the English word transferred to the soft white chalk (a kind of limestone) found abundantly in southeast England.

When we say **by a long chalk**, meaning 'to a great degree, by far' (and **not by a long chalk**, 'not at all'), the 'long chalk' refers to the length of a line of chalk marks or tallies drawn on a blackboard. This may originally have been in the context of a pub game, where points scored were marked up on the blackboard, or perhaps in the classroom, with a teacher chalking up pupils' marks for schoolwork. In either case, a long line of chalk marks against your name would mean you were a long way ahead of the others.

chameleon

A chameleon, a lion and a giraffe – no, it is not the start of a joke, but there is a connection. They all feature in the history of the lizard's name. **Chameleon** is derived via Latin from Greek *khamaileon*, from *khamai* 'on the ground' and *leōn* 'lion'. So a chameleon was a 'ground lion'. It was often spelled *camelion*, which sometimes got mixed up with **camelopard**, an old word for a giraffe. So for a time, in the 14th and 15th centuries, a *camelion* was also a name for the giraffe. From the 16th century people have been described as **chameleons** if they were fickle or continually changing their opinions. See also CAMEL, GIRAFFE, LION.

champion

Title-deciding boxing matches are often contested between the challenger and the defending champion, the holder of the title. But, historically, both boxers would have been described as **champions**, as the word originally meant 'a fighting man'. It came from medieval Latin *campio* 'fighter or gladiator', from Latin *campus* 'a field, place of combat'. See also CAMPAIGN.

chance

The ultimate source of **chance** is Latin *cadere* 'to fall', which is also the root of many other words including ACCIDENT, **cadaver**, **decay**, **incident** and **occasion**. In medieval times it could mean 'an accident' as well as 'the way things happen, fortune'.

There are a number of stories associated with the origin of the phrase **chance your arm**, meaning 'to take a risk'. One suggestion is that it was a slang expression used by tailors who, in rushing the job of sewing in a sleeve, risked the stitches coming loose. Or it may refer to the stripes on the sleeve of a military uniform that indicate a soldier's rank. Doing something

that broke military regulations might put an officer at risk of being demoted and losing one of his stripes. The most colourful explanation, though, links the phrase with a feud between the Irish Ormond and Kildare families in 1492. According to the story the Earl of Ormond had taken refuge in St Patrick's cathedral in Dublin. The Earl of Kildare, wishing to end the feud and make peace, cut a hole in the cathedral door and put his arm through. The Earl of Ormond accepted his offer of reconciliation and shook his hand rather than cutting it off.

change

The word **change** comes from Old French and before that from Latin *cambire*, 'to exchange or barter'. The ultimate origin could be Celtic, which would mean that the Romans picked up the word when they invaded the lands of the ancient Gauls and Britons.

We say **a change is as good as a rest** to mean that a change of work or occupation can be just as refreshing as a period of relaxation. One of the earliest recorded uses of the saying is by Sir Arthur Conan Doyle in 1890: 'Well, I gave my mind a thorough rest by plunging into chemical analysis. One of our greatest statesmen has said that a change of work is the best rest. So it is.' See also RING.

chaos

A **chaos** was originally 'a gaping void, chasm or abyss'. The word later came to refer to the disordered, formless matter out of which the universe was thought to have been originally formed, from which developed the current meaning, 'utter confusion and disorder' – Shakespeare was the first to use it, in *Troilus and Cressida*. **Chaos** came originally from Greek *khaos* 'vast chasm, void'. See also GAS.

In the 1980s scientists pondered the notion that a butterfly fluttering its wings in Rio de Janeiro could start a chain of events that would eventually change the weather in Chicago. They dubbed this **the butterfly effect**. It is a central idea of **chaos theory**, a branch of mathematics that deals with complex systems whose behaviour is highly sensitive to slight changes in conditions. See also BEDLAM, PANDEMONIUM.

chap

A **chap** is now an ordinary man, but he was originally 'a buyer or customer'. The word was an abbreviation of **chapman** 'a pedlar', which came from Old English *ceap*, 'bargaining, trade', also the origin of CHEAP and of English place names such as Chipping Norton and Chipping Ongar. The current sense dates from early 18th century. In 1905 the English journalist and novelist Edmund Clerihew Bentley neatly summarised the difference between geography and biography: 'Geography is about Maps / But Biography is about Chaps.'

chapel

The first place to be called a **chapel** was named after the holy relic preserved in it, the cape of St Martin, which was highly valued by the Franks, a Germanic people who conquered Gaul in the 6th century. The Latin word *cappella*, meaning 'little cape', was applied to the building itself and eventually to any holy sanctuary. It entered English in the 13th century in the form **chapel**. **Chaplain** is a related word, which referred to an attendant entrusted with guarding the cape. The Latin form remains unchanged in the musical term **a cappella**, which means 'sung without instrumental accompaniment' but is literally 'in chapel style'.

A pedlar or 'chapman', the first kind of 'chap'.

chapter

Latin *capitulum* literally meant 'little head' ('head' was *caput*), but could also be used to mean, among other things, 'a heading, a section of writing or a division of a book'. This is the origin of our word **chapter**, though the immediate source was Old French *chapitre*.

If you want **chapter and verse** for a statement or piece of information, you want to be given an exact reference or authority for it. The phrase originally referred to the numbering of passages in the Bible. See also CAPITAL.

charity

Charity begins at *carus*, the Latin word for 'dear'. This was the base of Latin *caritas*, 'dearness, love', which eventually gave us the English word. The early sense of **charity**, in the 12th century, was 'Christian love of your fellow men'.

The saying **charity begins at home**, 'a person's first responsibility is for the needs of their own family and friends', dates back to the 14th century. A version

in Beaumont and Fletcher's play *Wit without Money* (1625) goes 'Charity and beating begins at home'.

charlatan

If you claim to have specialist knowledge or skill that you do not actually possess, you are a **charlatan**. The word first appeared in English, in the early 17th century, as a term for a fast-talking seller of quack remedies. It comes via French from Italian *ciarlatano*, from the verb *ciarlare*, meaning 'to babble'.

charm

In the Middle Ages a **charm** was an incantation or magic spell, and did not acquire its modern meaning of 'a quality of fascinating or being attractive to people' until the 17th century. The word comes from Latin *carmen* 'song or incantation'.

In the late 1970s people started talking of politicians mounting a **charm offensive** – a campaign of flattery and friendliness designed to gain the support of others. This is a fine example of an **oxymoron**, a figure of speech in which apparently contradictory terms appear together.

chat

In medieval times **chat** was formed as a shorter version of **chatter**, which itself started life as an imitation of the sound made by people chatting away, rather as **jabber** and **twitter** imitated the sound they described. **The chattering classes** are liberal, well-educated people, often working in the media, who are fond of expressing their views on any and every subject. This name for them has been around since the early 1980s.

chauvinism

Nicolas Chauvin was a French war veteran well known for his extreme patriotism and his devotion to Napoleon Bonaparte. He was popularised as a character in *La Cocarde Tricolore* (1831) by the French playwrights the Cogniard brothers, and it did not take long for his name to become synonymous with the idea of fanatical or blind patriotism. In the 1950s **chauvinism** broadened its meaning to 'a prejudiced support or loyalty for your own cause, group or sex'. The phrase **male chauvinism** caught on in the 1970s, to describe prejudice against or inconsiderate treatment of women, since when **chauvinism** can simply be used to mean 'sexism'.

chav

Baseball cap, fake designer sportswear, cheap jewellery – that is the uniform of the **chav**, a loutish, obnoxious youth who barged his way into the British consciousness in 2004. Popularised by websites and the tabloid press, the term caught on quickly, and soon women and older people too were being described as chavs. Big Brother contestant Jade Goody and TV actress Daniella Westbrook became 'chav celebrities', with Westbrook horrifying the upmarket clothing company Burberry by being photographed dressed from head to toe in their distinctive checked garments.

New words appear all the time, but **chav** caused great excitement to word scholars when it came on the scene. It seems to have been popular around Chatham in Kent during the late 1990s, and some people think that it is an abbreviation of the town's name, while others suggest it comes from the initial letters of 'Council House And Violent'. The most plausible suggestion is that it is from the Romany word *chavi* or *chavo*, 'boy, youth'. The related dialect word **chavvy** 'boy, child' was used in the 19th century, and more recently popped up in an episode of the long-running TV comedy *Only Fools and Horses*. The northeast equivalent of **chav**, **charver**, has been around since at least the 1960s, and **chav** can mean 'mate, pal' in Scots dialect. **Chav** was probably knocking around as an 'underground' expression for a long time before it was taken up as a new way of insulting people. See also YOB.

cheap

Nowadays something that is **cheap** is inexpensive or of low value. In Old English, though, *ceap* (derived from Latin *caupo* 'small trader, innkeeper') meant 'bargaining or trade'. CHAP is based on the same word. The obsolete phrase **good cheap** meant 'a good bargain', and it is from this that the modern sense developed. In place names such as Cheapside and Eastcheap, **cheap** means 'market'.

If you say that something is **cheap at the price**, you mean that it is well worth having regardless of the cost. A stronger alternative version of this is **cheap at twice the price**, and you will also hear the inversion **cheap at half the price**.

cheat

This started out as a shortening of **escheat**, a legal term for the reverting of property to the state when the owner dies without heirs. As an extension of this, the word came to mean 'to confiscate', and then 'to deprive someone of something unfairly'. Finally, the senses 'to practise deception' and 'to try to get an advantage by breaking the rules' came to the fore.

check

Chess has given the word **check** its oldest meanings. It came into English via Old French *eschec* from Persian *šāh* 'king' (the origin of **shah**, as in the Shah of Iran), and was first used by chess players to announce that the opponent's king had been placed under attack. From there the meaning gradually broadened to 'to stop, restrain or control' and 'to examine the accuracy of'. A squared pattern is described as **checked** or a **check** because of the appearance of a chessboard.

Checkmate derives from Persian *šāh māt*, 'the king is dead'. **Chess** itself came into English during the 12th century from Old French *eschec*, or rather its plural form, *esches*, but probably goes back ultimately to the ancient Indian language Sanskrit. The game seems to have begun in India or China around the 6th century AD and to have been adopted in Persia, spreading to the West through the Arabs. The game was popular in medieval England, and appears in the works of the poet Geoffrey Chaucer. See also EXCHEQUER.

cheeky monkey!

The affectionate reprimand is particularly common in Lancashire, and often used by Betty Turpin, barmaid since 1969 in the Manchester-based soap opera *Coronation Street*. A variation of the expression was popularised in the 1950s by the comedian Al Read, whose catchphrase was 'Right, monkey!'

cheek

The Old English word **cheek** came to mean 'rude or disrespectful behaviour' in the mid 19th century. The sense probably comes from the idea of a person's cheeks moving as he rudely answers a superior back. **Cheeky** was first used around the same time.

In **cheek by jowl**, meaning 'very close together', **jowl** simply means 'cheek'. In fact the original form of the phrase was **cheek by cheek**. To **turn the other cheek** is to make a deliberate decision to remain calm and not to retaliate when you have been attacked or insulted. The expression comes from the Gospel of Matthew: 'But I say to ye, That ye resist not evil; but whosoever shall smite thee on thy right cheek, turn to him the other.'

cheer

In medieval English the word **cheer** meant 'face'. People came to use it to refer to the expression on someone's face, and hence to their mood or demeanour. This could be in either a positive or negative sense; you could talk, for example, about a person's 'sorrowful cheer' or 'heavy cheer'. '**What cheer**?' was once a common greeting meaning 'how are you?', and in the 19th century this eventually became worn down to **wotcha**. Over time **cheer** developed the specific meaning of 'a good mood' and then 'a shout of encouragement or joy'.

A **Bronx cheer** is a rude noise made by blowing through closed lips with the tongue between them – what is also called a RASPBERRY.

chemical

Alchemy was a medieval science that looked to transform matter, in particular to convert base metals into gold or find a universal 'elixir of life'. It was the medieval equivalent of chemistry, and was also the origin of the word **chemistry**. **Alchemy** came via Old French and medieval Latin from Arabic *al-kīmiyā*, which was from Greek *khēmia* 'the art of transforming metals'. See also ELIXIR.

cherry

The root of **cherry** is Old French *cherise*, and at first *cherise* or *cheris* was the English word for the fruit too. When people heard this word, though, they seem to have thought that it must be a plural and so decided that the word for one of these fruit was **cherry**. PEA is another example of the same process.

The cherry is one of the small number of fruits native to Britain, and although delicious it has a short fruiting season. For these reasons it represents something pleasant or desirable in a number of common expressions. To have **two bites** (or **a second bite**) **at the cherry** is to have more than one attempt or chance to do something. An extremely pleasant or enjoyable experience can be described as **a bowl of cherries**. And the **cherry on the cake** is an attractive feature that provides the finishing touch.

chess see CHECK.

chest

The Greek word *kistï*, 'box or basket', is the source of **chest**. Not until the 16th century was the same word applied to the part of your body enclosed by the ribs and breastbone, acting as a protective 'box' for the heart, lungs and other organs.

chestnut

Chestnuts are nothing to do with chests – the ultimate source is the Greek word *kastanea* 'chestnut'. A frequently repeated joke or story is known as **an old chestnut**. First recorded in the 1880s, the phrase probably comes from a play called *The Broken Sword*, written by William Dimond in 1816. In one scene a character called Zavior is in the throes of telling a story: 'When suddenly from the thick boughs of a cork tree –'. At this point he is interrupted by another character, Pablo, who says: 'A chestnut, Captain, a chestnut . . . Captain, this is the twenty-seventh time I have heard you relate this story, and you invariably said, a chestnut, till now.'

chicken

An Old English word that probably has the same ancient root as COCK. **Don't count your chickens before they're hatched** is an instruction not to expect that success is certain until it actually happens. Although it is recorded from the 16th century, it refers to one of Aesop's fables of 2,000 years earlier, in which a girl carrying a pail of milk to market dreams about buying chickens with the profit from the milk and becoming rich through selling eggs. In her daydream she sees herself as being so wealthy that she would simply toss her head at all her would-be lovers, at which point she tosses her head and spills the milk.

When we talk about **chickens coming home to roost**, we are suggesting that someone's past mistakes or wrongdoings will eventually rebound on them. The full form of the proverb, dating from the 14th century, is **curses, like chickens, come home to roost**.

child

In Anglo-Saxon times **child** frequently meant a newborn baby, a sense we retain in **childbirth**. In the 16th century it was sometimes used to specify a female infant: 'A very pretty bairn. A boy or a child, I wonder?' (Shakespeare, *The Winter's Tale*). On a similar theme, the familiar saying **children should be seen and not heard** was applied originally not to children but to young women. It was described as early as 1400 as 'an old English saw' (or saying) in the form 'A maid should be seen, but not heard'. It was not until the 19th century that children became the subject.

All the tea in China

The creativity of Chinese civilisation, stretching back until at least the 3rd millennium BC, has given us paper, the compass, gunpowder and printing, not to mention china, or porcelain, itself. It has also injected many Far Eastern flavours into English.

For English-speaking peoples, maybe the greatest contribution that China and its language have made to the Western world is tea. The drink is first mentioned in English in 1655. The Chinese source *chá* also gives us the slang term char, as in 'a nice cup of char', used from the early years of the 20th century. The Chinese connection is remembered in the emphatic refusal not for all the tea in China, first found in US English in the early 20th century.

People drinking something stronger than tea might say chin-chin, or 'cheers!' This is a mangled pronunciation of *qing qing*, a Chinese greeting. Another 'doubled' word is chop-chop, or 'quickly'. *Chop* is a pidgin Chinese rendition of Chinese *kuài* 'quick, nimble', also found in chopstick.

Our range of savoury relishes was extended when traders introduced us to ketchup at the end of the 17th century. The name may come from Chinese *k'é chap* 'tomato juice'. Contact with imperial China in the early 19th century introduced Westerners to the Chinese custom of kowtowing – kneeling down and touching the forehead on the ground in worship or submission. The word means literally 'to knock the head'.

Gung-ho, meaning 'unthinkingly enthusiastic and eager, especially about fighting', dates from the Second World War. It is from Chinese *gōnghé* 'to work together', and was adopted as a slogan by the US Marines fighting in the Pacific under General Evans Carlson. He organised 'kung-hoi' meetings to discuss problems and explain orders to promote cooperation.

Increasing interest in our living spaces in the 1990s led to the popularity of feng shui, the ancient Chinese system of designing buildings and arranging objects in rooms to achieve a positive flow of energy and so bring happiness or good luck. It goes back a long way in English, and even had an entry in the *Encyclopaedia Britannica* of 1797.

Not all our Chinese words are ancient, though. China's first manned space flight in 2003 gave us taikonaut, a Chinese astronaut – *taikong* means 'outer space'.

See also MANDARIN, TYPHOON, YEN.

chintz

An advertising campaign in the 1990s by the Swedish furniture business Ikea urged us to **chuck out the chintz**, meaning to discard fussy, dated decor in the home in favour of their sleek modernist furniture and accessories. Chintz may not be terribly fashionable now, but for a long time it was in great demand as an exclusive fabric, originally a painted or stained calico, imported from India. The source was the Hindi word *chīmt*, literally 'spattering, stain', which in English became *chint*. The plural of this unfamilar word, being more frequently used, came over time to be mistaken for a singular and written *chints* and eventually **chintz**. The related word **chintzy** means 'resembling or decorated with chintz' in British English, but in America it means both 'cheap and of poor quality' and 'miserly, mean'.

chip

A person who is thought to resemble one of their parents in their character or behaviour can be described as **a chip off the old block**. The phrase was originally found in the forms **chip of the same block** and **chip of the old block**, as in the politician Edmund Burke's observation following the maiden speech of Pitt the Younger in Parliament in 1781: 'Not merely a chip of the old "block", but the old block itself.'

To **have a chip on your shoulder** is to be aggressively sensitive about something, usually some long-standing grievance or cause of resentment. The expression is first recorded in American English in the mid 19th century. An explanation can be found in the *Long Island Telegraph* of May 20, 1830: 'When two churlish boys were determined to fight, a chip [of wood] would be placed on the shoulder of one, and the other demanded to knock it off at his peril.'

Another meaning of **chip** is 'a counter used in gambling games, representing money', and such gambling chips, especially as used in the game of poker, feature in a number of common phrases. If someone **has had their chips**, they are beaten or out of contention. The idea is of having run out of gambling counters or chips with which to place a stake. Similarly, **when the chips are down** you find yourself in a very serious and difficult situation. To **cash in your chips** is to die – you are no longer 'in the game'.

Deep-fried slices of potato have been known as **chips** since the time of Dickens. You might think of the phrase **cheap as chips** as being a recent invention, but it too goes back until at least the 1850s, when it was used in an advert in *The Times*.

chivalry

The word **chivalry** springs from the world of medieval knights. Although we continue to remember one of a knight's attributes in our use of the word today, namely his code of courteous behaviour, it is a quite different characteristic that lies behind the word's origin – the fact that he rode a horse. **Chivalry** came into English from medieval Latin *caballerius*, which was based on Latin *caballus* 'horse'. **Cavalry** and **cavalier** can also be traced back to the same Latin word. In its early use **chivalry** could describe knights, noblemen and horsemen collectively, as in 'The eleven kings with their chivalry never turned back' (Thomas Malory, *Le Morte D'Arthur*, 1485), and could mean 'the position of being a knight'. Later it came to refer to the qualities associated with an ideal knight, especially courage, honour, loyalty and courtesy.

chock

A **chock**, as in 'chocks away!', is a wedge or block placed against a wheel to prevent it from moving or to support it. It is probably from Old French *çouche* or *çoche*, meaning 'block or log'. **Chock-a-block**, 'crammed full', was originally a nautical expression which referred to a pair of pulley blocks with ropes threaded between to form a hoist or tackle – when they have been pulled so close together that the two blocks touch, further lifting is impossible. The expression was probably influenced by **chock-full**, a much older term meaning 'filled to overflowing'. Where this comes from

chipolata

The little sausage has nothing to do with chips – its name comes from Italian *cipollata*, meaning 'flavoured with onion' (the Italian for 'onion' is *cipolla*, which is related to English **chives**). And there is no 'chip' relation to **chipmunk**, also a completely different word, from the Native American language Ojibwa.

is uncertain, though 'chock' here may have been a form of **choke**, from the idea of being so full that you are almost choking.

chocolate

Before it was a sweet, **chocolate** was a drink. The first recorded use in English, in the early 17th century, is 'a drink made from chocolate', and chocolate was a fashionable drink in the 17th and 18th centuries. Here is Samuel Pepys, writing in his diary in 1664: 'To a Coffee-house, to drink jocolatte, very good.' The word comes from French *chocolat* or Spanish *chocolate*, from Nahuatl (the language spoken by the Aztecs of Mexico) *chocolatl* 'food made from cacao seeds'. **Cacao** and **cocoa** are basically the same word, also from Nahuatl. Not from Mexico, though, is the expression **I should cocoa**. It is cockney rhyming slang for 'I should say so'.

chop

In the sense 'to cut something into small pieces' **chop** is a variant of the closely related word **chap**, 'to become cracked and sore', as in 'chapped lips'. Similarly, while a **choppy** sea nowadays is a fairly rough one, with the surface broken up by many small waves, in the early 17th century the adjective meant 'full of cracks or clefts'.

To **chop and change** is to keep changing your opinions or behaviour without warning and often for no good reason. Both **chop** and **change** once meant 'barter or exchange', and they were used together in this phrase (which originally meant 'to buy and sell') from the 15th century onwards. As time went on, **change** came to be interpreted in its more usual sense, with **chop** reinforcing the idea of abruptness.

Australians and New Zealanders refer to something not very good as being **not much chop**. The **chop** here is a different word, which comes from Hindi *chāp* 'stamp, brand'. Europeans in the Far East used the Hindi word for documents such as passports which were given an official stamp, and it came to mean something that was genuine or had quality or class.

Chopstick is from a quite different word again, being based on the Chinese dialect term *kuaizi*, meaning 'nimble ones'. The *chop-* part (*kuai* in Chinese) means 'quick' – hence **chop-chop**, also originally based on a Chinese dialect expression.

Christ see MESSIAH.

chronic

You can be sure that words beginning **chron-** have something to do with time: the root of them all is Greek *khronos* 'time'. A **chronic** illness is one that persists for a long time. In informal British English the word can also mean 'of very poor quality', as in 'the film was chronic', a sense developing from the idea of unending tedium. On the same dictionary page you can find such other time-related words as **chronicle**, 'a written record of events in the order they happened', **chronology** 'the order in which a series of events happened' and **chronometer** 'a timepiece'. See also CRONY.

chuffed

If you are really pleased or satisfied you are **chuffed**. This word dates from the 1950s and is from the English dialect word **chuff** meaning 'plump or pleased'. To confuse matters, though, there is an entirely different dialect use of **chuff** with the opposite meaning of 'surly or gruff'. So for a while **chuffed** was also being used to mean 'displeased or disgruntled': 'Don't let on they're after you, see, or she'll be dead chuffed, see? She don' like the law' (Celia Dale, *Other People*, 1964).

chum

Before it came to mean 'a friend', **chum** was a slang word, used at Oxford University, for 'a room-mate'. It was probably a shortened form of **chamber-fellow**. See also CRONY.

church

The Old English word **church**, then spelled *circe* or *cirice*, is related to German *Kirche*, Dutch *kerk* and Scots **kirk**. The source of all these words is medieval Greek *kurikon*, from Greek *kuriakon dōma*, 'Lord's house', based on *kurios* 'master or lord'.

cider

Although we are often told that real 'scrumpy' cider is a fine drink, for many of us **cider** is something that we liked as teenagers and have not been able to face since. Not the most likely word to have a distinguished and ancient origin, then, and yet **cider** goes back to Greek *sikera*, a word used by Christian writers to translate Hebrew *sēkār*, which meant 'strong drink'. Few teenagers will be surprised by its literal meaning.

cinch

The first recorded use of **cinch**, 'something that is easy to achieve', was as a term for a girth for a saddle that was made from separate twisted strands of horsehair.

It was used in Mexico and the western USA, and is a Spanish word. The link between the original meaning and the modern one is the idea of having a firm or secure hold on something.

cinema

A **cinema** shows moving pictures, and movement is the root idea of the word. The Greek verb *kinein* 'to move' (the source of **kinetic** and other *kine-* words related to movement) is the base, and was used by the French brothers Auguste and Louis Jean Lumière to form the word *cinématographe* for their invention of an apparatus that showed moving pictures, which they patented in 1895. *Cinématographe* was anglicised to **cinematograph**, which in turn was abbreviated to **cinema** (first recorded in English in 1909).

circle

The root of **circle** is Latin *circulus* 'small ring', from *circus* 'ring', the source of our word **circus**. A Roman circus was nothing like our familiar family entertainment. It was a rounded or oval arena lined with tiers of seats, where chariot races, gladiatorial combats and other, often cruel, contests took place. Names like Piccadilly Circus were given to open, more or less circular areas in towns where streets converged.

Come or **turn full circle**, meaning 'to return to a past position or situation', is a reference to 'The Wheele is come full circle' in Shakespeare's *King Lear*. The wheel is the one thought of as being turned by the goddess Fortune and symbolising change.

circumference

A circle's **circumference** is the boundary or line that encloses it. The term comes from Old French *circonference*, from Latin *circumferentia*. The base elements here are *circum*, meaning 'around', and *ferre*, meaning 'to carry'. English words beginning **circum-** all share some idea of 'going around' in their meaning. A **circumflex** accent (the one like a little hat) bends around the top of a letter. To **circumscribe**, meaning 'to draw a line around something' or 'to restrict', derives from Latin *circum* 'around' and *scribere* 'to write'. **Circumspect**, 'wary or watchful', literally means 'looking around', and **circumcise** 'to cut round'. If you **circumvent** a problem (from Latin *venire* 'to come'), you find a way round it.

clam

It is not easy to prise apart a **clam**, and this tight grip lies behind the origin of the word. **Clam** originally meant 'a clamp', and probably had the same source as **clamp**. There is also an English dialect word **clam**, meaning 'to be sticky or to stick to something', which is related to **clay**. It is also where **clammy** – which was originally spelled *claymy* – comes from. See also HAPPY.

clap

The sound of clapping is the clue to the origin of **clap**, an Old English word whose ancestor first imitated the sound of something striking a surface. The sense 'to strike the palms of your hands together' developed from this around the 14th century.

Claptrap, 'nonsense, rubbish', was first used in the 18th century for something a person says or does just to get applause – a trap to catch a clap.

To **go like the clappers** is to go very fast or very hard. **Clapper** here probably refers either to the striking part of a bell or to a device in a mill for striking or shaking the hopper to make the grain move down to the millstones. Whether a set of pealing bells or a mill in full operation, the clappers would be moving very fast. The expression was first found in RAF slang in the 1940s.

claret

The Old French term *vin claret* 'clear wine' was originally applied to a light red or yellowish wine, as distinct from either a red or white wine. **Claret** was used in English with this meaning until around 1600, when people started using the word to talk about red wines generally. Nowadays the term refers particularly to the red wines imported from Bordeaux.

In books or films about London gangsters you might come across **claret** used as a slang term for 'blood'. It seems like a recently coined cockney expression, but in fact goes back at least as far as 1604, and was originally boxing slang.

clean

To **make a clean breast of it** is to confess all of your mistakes or wrongdoings. People used to think that the breast, or chest, was where a person's conscience was located.

In the proverb **cleanliness is next to godliness**, 'next' means 'immediately following'. The saying is quoted by John Wesley in one of his sermons, on the subject of dress: 'Slovenliness is no part of religion . . . Cleanliness is indeed next to godliness' (1791).

cliffhanger

A **cliffhanger** is a dramatic and exciting ending to the episode of a serial, which leaves the audience in suspense and anxious not to miss the next instalment.

In the US in the 1930s a **cliffhanger** was a serialised adventure film in which each episode ended with the hero or heroine in a desperate situation, such as dangling off the edge of a cliff.

cloak

The source of **cloak** was Old French *cloke*, a variant of *cloche* meaning 'bell' and, because a cloak has a rather bell-like shape, 'cloak'. The ultimate origin is medieval Latin *clocca* 'bell'. See also CLOCK.

The expression **cloak-and-dagger** is used in relation to plotting, intrigue and espionage. As **cloak-and-sword**, a translation of the French phrase *de cape et d'épée*, it dates from the early 19th century. It originally referred to stories and plays featuring intrigue or melodramatic adventure, in which the main characters tended to wear a cloak and be armed with a dagger or a sword.

clobber

The **clobber** meaning 'to hit someone hard or defeat them completely' dates from the Second World War. Although the origin is uncertain, it seems to have been RAF slang, and probably described striking a place hard in a bombing raid. The other sense of **clobber**, 'clothing or belongings', is a different word which dates from the late 19th century and is again of unknown origin.

clock

Like CLOAK, **clock** comes from medieval Latin *clocca* 'bell'. The English word originally meant 'bell', later taking on the sense 'the striking mechanism of a watch'. Gradually **clock** came to be applied not to the sound made by an instrument for telling the time but to the instrument itself.

The verb sense 'to punch or hit in the face', first recorded in the 1920s, is originally Australian from the slang use of **clock** to mean 'a person's face' (see also DIAL). The meaning 'to notice or watch', from the 1930s, refers to a person checking the time on a clock.

clog

The earliest meaning of **clog**, from the beginning of the 15th century, was 'a lump or block of wood', especially one fastened to the leg or neck of an animal to stop it moving too far. The term for a wooden-soled shoe arose around the same time and probably first referred to the thick wooden sole alone. The verb was first used to mean 'to hamper or impede something', and from this developed the idea of hindering free passage through something by blocking it or choking it up.

Clogs were formerly worn by factory and manual workers in the north of England. **From clogs to clogs in three generations** is said to be a Lancashire proverb, meaning that it takes one generation to found a business, the next to build it and the third to spend the profits, leaving the family penniless again.

clone

In 1997 Dolly the sheep hit the headlines. The unassuming ewe was the first mammal to have been successfully cloned – she grew from a cell taken from another sheep rather than as a consequence of two animals mating. The word **clone**, from Greek *klȳn* 'twig, cutting from a plant', is first recorded in 1903, when it referred to a group of plants produced by taking cuttings or grafts from an original. It has been used in the context of the genetic duplication of mammals since the early 1970s. Nowadays it can also be used to describe a person who slavishly copies someone else (as in 'a Kylie clone') and a computer designed to simulate another more expensive model (as in 'an IBM clone'). In gay culture a clone is a gay man who adopts an exaggeratedly macho look and style of dress.

Dolly, the cloned sheep

closet

Although **closet** is now the usual word in American English for a cupboard or wardrobe, it originally referred to a small private room, such as one used for study or prayer. This idea of privacy led to the sense of hiding a fact or keeping something secret, which goes right back to the beginning of the 17th century. A person who is hiding the fact that they are gay has been described as **in the closet**, or as a closet homosexual, since the late 1960s. To **out** someone, meaning to reveal that they are gay, is a shortened way of saying 'to force them out of the closet'.

cloud

The Old English word **cloud** was first used to refer to a mass of rock or earth, a hill. Only around the end of the 13th century did the meaning 'visible mass of condensed watery vapour' develop, presumably because people could see a resemblance in shape between a cloud and a lump of rock. The Anglo-Saxons *did* have a word for a cloud – it was *wolcen* or *weolcen*, which survives in **the welkin**, 'the sky or heavens', used now mainly by poets.

Being **on cloud nine** means you are extremely happy. A possible source of the expression is the classification of clouds given in a meteorological guide published in 1896 called the *International Cloud Atlas*. According to this guide there are ten basic types of cloud, cumulonimbus being the one numbered nine. Cumulonimbus clouds are the ones that form a towering fluffy mass, and they perhaps suggested a comfortable cushion. 'Cloud nine' is said to have been popularised by the Johnny Dollar radio show in the USA during the 1950s. Johnny Dollar was a fictional insurance investigator who got into a lot of scrapes. Every time he was knocked unconscious he was taken to 'cloud nine', where he recovered.

Cloud cuckoo land, used to describe a state of over-optimistic fantasy, is a translation of Greek *Nephelokokkugia* (from *nepheli* 'cloud' and *kokkux* 'cuckoo'). This was the name the ancient Greek dramatist Aristophanes gave to the city built by the birds in his comedy *The Birds*.

According to the proverb **every cloud has a silver lining**, even the gloomiest outlook contains some hopeful or consoling aspect. The saying is recorded from the 19th century, though John Milton expresses a similar sentiment in *Comus* in 1643: 'Was I deceiv'd or did a sable cloud / Turn forth her silver lining on the night?'

clove

You might have two different types of **clove** in your kitchen cupboard, one in a jar on the spice rack and one in a garlic bulb. These are two different words. The spice clove comes from Old French *clou de girofle*, meaning 'nail of the clove tree'. You can see why – cloves look quite like nails. The clove of garlic is an Old English word related to **cleave** and **cloven**.

clown

In the earliest recorded uses of **clown**, in the mid 16th century, it means 'an unsophisticated country person'. Before long it was being applied to any rude or ill-mannered person, and by 1600 the word was also being used to refer to the character of a fool or jester in a stage play, from which the comic entertainer in a circus developed.

For some reason, perhaps a bad childhood experience, quite a few people seem to be afraid of clowns, and a word for the condition has been coined, **coulrophobia**. The first element was borrowed from a Greek word for a stilt-walker, clowns not being known in the classical world.

club

In the sense 'a heavy stick with a thick end' **club** comes from Old Norse *clubba*, and is related to **clump**. The use of the word to refer to a society or association of people who share a particular interest dates from the early 17th century. It appears to have derived gradually from the idea of a group of people forming into a mass like the thick end of a club.

clue

Our word **clue** is a modern spelling of the old word **clew**, 'a ball of thread'. The idea here is of string or thread being used to guide a person out of a maze by tracing a path through it. The most famous example is that of the Greek hero Theseus, who killed the monstrous bull-headed Minotaur in its lair and then escaped from the Labyrinth, an underground maze of tunnels. This he was able to do because the princess Ariadne gave him a ball of twine, which he unravelled as he went in and followed back to find his way out again. If we follow the thread of the word **clue** we find that in time it comes to refer to any piece of information that helps to solve a puzzle, mystery or criminal investigation. The board game **Cluedo** was launched in 1949, based on an idea presented a few years earlier to Waddingtons Games in Leeds by Anthony E. Pratt, a retired solicitor's clerk.

coach

Believe it or not, **coaches** are named after a small town in Hungary. The first vehicles to be called coaches were horse-drawn carriages, which in the 16th and 17th centuries were usually royal state vehicles. The word comes from French *coche*, from Hungarian *kocsi szekér*, which means 'wagon from Kocs', the Hungarian town of Kocs being renowned for making carriages and wagons. When other, similar forms of transport such as railway carriages and single-decker buses were invented, in the 1830s and 1920s respectively, they were called coaches too. The use of the word to refer to a tutor (and later a trainer in sport) is related to the above meanings, based on the idea that a tutor 'carries' or 'drives' a student through an examination.

coal

The Old English word *col* meant 'a glowing ember', and this is where **coal** comes from. The expression **haul over the coals** means 'to reprimand severely'. This is a metaphorical extension of what was once an all-too-real form of torture that involved dragging the victim over the coals of a slow-burning fire.

You might use the expression **taking coals to Newcastle** when talking about some action that is obviously superfluous or redundant. Coal from Newcastle-upon-Tyne in northeast England was abundant even long before the Industrial Revolution, and 'to carry coals to Newcastle' has been an expression since the mid 17th century.

coast

The Latin word *costa* meant 'rib or side', which is why **coast** meant 'rib' and 'the side of the body' from Anglo-Saxon days right up until the start of the 19th century. The phrase **coast of the sea** – meaning 'side of the sea' – gave rise to the modern use, 'the part of the land adjoining the sea'. The verb originally meant 'to move along the edge of something' and 'to sail along the coast'.

People say **the coast is clear** when there is no danger of being observed or caught. The expression originally signalled that there were no enemies or coastguards guarding a sea coast who would prevent an attempt to land or embark by sailors or smugglers.

cob

A small word, but one with many distinct meanings, among them a loaf of bread, the central part of an ear of corn, a male swan and a short-legged horse. What these senses all have in common is probably the underlying idea of being stout, rounded or sturdy. The word, which may be related to Old English *copp* 'top or head', was originally used to refer to a strong man or leader.

Cobble, as in a rounded stone used for paving, derives from **cob**. **Cobbler**, 'a person whose job is mending shoes', is unconnected, and its origin is unknown, although it is related to **cobble** meaning 'to repair shoes' and 'to assemble roughly'. **Cobblers**, 'rubbish', is rhyming slang from **cobbler's awls**, 'balls'.

cobalt

A hard silvery-white magnetic metal, often found in the ground alongside deposits of silver. The name comes from German *Kobalt*, a variation of the word *Kobold* meaning 'goblin or demon', and related to **goblin**. Medieval silver miners gave the metal this name because of the trouble it caused them. They believed that cobalt was harmful both to the silver ores with which it occurred and to their own health, though these effects were mainly due to the arsenic and sulphur with which it was frequently combined.

cobweb

An old word for a spider was a *coppe* or *cop*. This was a shortened form of the Old English *attercop*, also referring to a spider and literally meaning 'poison head', which turns up in a song sung by Bilbo Baggins in J.R.R. Tolkien's *The Hobbit*. A spider's web came to be called a *coppeweb* or *copweb*, and this was later modified to **cobweb**.

coccyx

Your **coccyx** is the small triangular bone at the base of your spine. The name comes via Latin from Greek *kokkux* 'cuckoo', because the shape of this bone looks like a cuckoo's beak.

cock

The ancient root of the word **cock** was probably suggested by the sound the bird makes. The same root is likely to have given us CHICKEN as well.

If you are **cock-a-hoop** you are extremely pleased, especially after some success or triumph. The expression dates from the 17th century and comes from an earlier phrase **set cock a hoop**. **Cock** here may be used in the sense of a tap for stopping the flow of liquid, so that the expression refers to turning on the tap of a beer barrel and allowing beer to flow freely before a drinking session.

A **cock-and-bull story** is a ridiculous and implausible tale. The expression 'talk of a cock and a bull' is recorded from the early 17th century, and apparently refers to some rambling story or fable, a 'shaggy dog story', which is now lost. Laurence Sterne ends his novel *Tristram Shandy* (1759-67) with the words: 'L—d! said my mother, what is all this story about? – A Cock and a Bull, said Yorick – And one of the best of its kind, I ever heard.' This explains the title of the 2005 film version of Sterne's novel, *A Cock and Bull Story*.

To **cock a snook**, first recorded in 1791, is to show open contempt or lack of respect for someone or something, originally by touching your nose with your thumb and spreading out your fingers. **Cock** here means 'to stick out stiffly', but the origin of **snook** is not known. Because it is such an unfamiliar word,

people have often taken to saying **snoot** (slang for 'nose') instead of **snook**.

cockney

A **cockney** was originally a pampered or spoilt child. This use may derive from a similar word, *cokeney* 'a cock's egg', which, since cocks do not lay eggs, actually meant a poor specimen of a hen's egg, a small and misshapen one. The 'pampered child' meaning developed into an insulting term for someone who lives in the town, regarded as effeminate and weak, a bit of a wimp, in contrast to hardier country dwellers. By the beginning of the 17th century the word was being applied to someone from the East End of London, traditionally someone born within the sound of Bow Bells (the bells of St Mary-le-Bow church in the City of London).

coconut

Look at the base of a coconut and you will see three holes. These are the inspiration for its name. It was originally known as a coco, a Spanish and Portuguese word meaning 'a grinning face'.

cockpit

At first a **cockpit** was a place for holding cock fights, so from the beginning the word had connotations of bloodshed and injury. This accounts for it being applied in the early 18th century to the area in the aft lower deck of a man-of-war where wounded sailors were treated during a battle. Then it came to be used for the well from which you steer a sailing yacht. Finally, in the 20th century, **cockpit** acquired its modern meaning, the area or compartment that houses the controls of an aircraft or racing car.

cockroach

The early written form of **cockroach** was *cacaroch*, from the Spanish *cucaracha* 'cockroach'. People adapted the spelling to make it fit in better with the more familiar English words COCK and **roach**, the freshwater fish.

cocktail

The original use of **cocktail** was as a term to describe a creature with a tail like that of a cock, in particular a horse with a docked tail. Hunting horses and stagecoach horses generally had their tails shortened in this way, which led to the term being applied to a racehorse which was not a thoroughbred but 'of mixed blood', with a cock-tailed horse somewhere in its pedigree. It may be that the current sense of an alcoholic drink with a mixture of ingredients, which dates from the early 19th century, comes from this use, though the exact origin of the term is unknown.

codswallop

Meaning 'nonsense or drivel', **codswallop** seems to be a fairly recent addition to English, with the earliest recorded use appearing in a 1959 script for *Hancock's Half Hour*, the radio and TV comedy starring Tony Hancock. It is sometimes said that the word comes from the name of Hiram Codd, who in the 1870s invented a bottle for fizzy drinks, although the evidence for this is sketchy. The *wallop* part may relate to the word's use as a 1930s slang term for beer or other alcoholic drink.

coffin

Coffin comes from the Old French word *cofin* meaning 'a little basket', and in medieval English could refer to a chest or casket. The sense 'a box in which a dead body is buried or cremated' dates from the early 16th century. A closely related word is **coffer** – both words share the same source, Greek *kophinos* 'a basket'.

cold

The Old English word **cold** goes back to an ancient root that was shared by Latin *gelu* 'frost', the root of **congeal** and **jelly**, and also by COOL. It appears in many common expressions, a number of which refer to parts of the body. If someone **gives you the cold shoulder** they are deliberately unfriendly. This may be short for 'a cold shoulder of mutton', the sort of unappetising meal that would be served to an unwelcome guest. Much more likely, though, is that the phrase refers to a dismissive gesture of the body, involving a jerk or shrug of the shoulder. **Cold-hearted** first appeared in Shakespeare's play *Antony and Cleopatra*. The proverb **cold hands, warm heart** is much more recent: the earliest example is from the late 19th century.

The origin of **cold comfort**, meaning 'poor or inadequate consolation', is the idea that charity is often given in a cold or uncaring way. The English writer Stella Gibbons used it in the title of her comic novel *Cold Comfort Farm*, published in 1932, about an isolated farm populated by a cast of odd characters, each with their own particular problem, which a sensible, modern girl called Flora Poste tries to sort out. To **go cold turkey** is suddenly to give up taking a drug that you are addicted to, which can be an unpleasant process involving bouts of shivering and sweating that cause goose pimples reminiscent of the flesh of a dead plucked turkey. The expression dates from the 1920s.

The Cold War was the state of political hostility that existed between the Soviet countries and Western powers from 1945 to 1990. The term was used by George Orwell in a 1945 issue of the left-wing magazine *Tribune*, but earlier examples date it to the beginning of the Second World War.

colossal

Kolossos was the Greek word for 'a gigantic statue', and was originally used to describe the statues of Egyptian temples. The most famous example of such ancient statues was the huge bronze figure of Apollo that stood beside the harbour entrance at Rhodes, one of the Seven Wonders of the World. It was completed in 280 BC, but destroyed by an earthquake soon after, in 224 BC. This statue was known as the Colossus of Rhodes, **colossus** being the Latin, and subsequently English, version of the word. The idea that the statue stood astride the entrance to the harbour is widely held, but wrong. Nevertheless, it has given us the phrase **bestride like a colossus**, which is from Shakespeare's *Julius Caesar*: 'Why man, he doth bestride the narrow world / Like a Colossus.'

Colossal, meaning 'huge or gigantic', is an 18th-century development. The **Colosseum** has been the name since medieval times of the Amphitheatrum Flavium, a vast amphitheatre in Rome begun by the Emperor Vespasian around AD 75 and used for gladiatorial combats, fights between men and beasts and mock battles.

colour

In Old French it was spelled *colour*, in Latin *color*. The main English spelling has been **colour** since the medieval period, though **color**, now the usual spelling in American English, was sometimes used from the 15th century onwards.

Since the late 16th century the distinguishing flag of a ship or regiment has been known as its **colours**, a meaning that lies behind a number of common English expressions. To **show your true colours** is to reveal your real character or intentions, especially when these are disreputable or dishonourable. A ship engaged in illegal trading or in time of war might fly a bogus flag to deceive the authorities or the enemy, a practice known as 'sailing under false colours'. If the ship subsequently revealed itself to the enemy by firing on them or fleeing, it was 'showing its true colours'.

The phrase **nail your colours to the mast**, meaning 'to declare openly and firmly what you believe or support', also relates to naval practice: a ship in battle might nail its flag to the mast so that there was no possibility of it being lowered in defeat. And to **come through with flying colours** is to come successfully through a test, like a victorious warship returning to port with its flag unscathed.

And now for something completely different

Catchphrases – they are repeated endlessly in pubs, playgrounds and workplaces, and forever adapted by journalists and advertising copywriters. Although today most catchphrases come from TV comedy, they have peppered the language since radio comedy was king and as far back as Victorian and Edwardian music halls.

The risqué music hall comic Max Miller (1894-1963) is remembered for It's the way I tell 'em and Now there's a funny thing. The 1940s BBC radio comedy *ITMA* (It's That Man Again), featuring Tommy Handley, gave the world Can I do you now, Sir?, I don't mind if I do and TTFN (ta-ta for now). You rotten swines and You silly twisted boy were two of the catchphrases of *The Goon Show* of the 1950s and 1960s (see GOON), a surreal programme which influenced the British television show *Monty Python's Flying Circus*.

With the exception of And now for something completely different, which became the title of their first film in 1971, *Monty Python* did not specialise in catchphrases, although many of their lines are remembered and re-enacted. One is Nudge nudge, which, sometimes in the longer version Nudge nudge wink wink, is used to draw attention to a sexual innuendo. It was coined by Eric Idle, who plays a leering character who detects sexual suggestions in the most innocent of social exchanges.

Monty Python star John Cleese's next project was *Fawlty Towers* (1975), which gave us Don't mention the war, a warning against raising a topic known to be upsetting or controversial. Cleese, as the manic hotelier Basil Fawlty, briefs his staff about a party of lunch guests: 'They're Germans. Don't mention the war.' Inevitably, he then repeatedly refers to the forbidden topic.

Fawlty Towers was only one of a number of classic TV sitcoms in the 1970s that spawned a string of catchphrases.

Dad's Army provided Don't panic! and Permission to speak, sir!, both spoken by the elderly Corporal Jones. The catchphrase of the much-loved Morecambe and Wise was What do you think of it so far?, to which the usual answer was 'Rubbish!' Others from this period were Tommy Cooper's Just like that!, I'm free! from *Are You Being Served?*, and, from *The Fall and Rise of Reginald Perrin*, I didn't get where I am today without . . . and a bit of a cock-up on the catering front.

In the 1980s the hapless servant Baldrick in *Blackadder* would always attempt to raise spirits by saying I have a cunning plan, while Harry Enfield's Loadsamoney! epitomised the Thatcher years (see LOAD). One of the performers in Harry Enfield's show was Paul Whitehouse, whose quick-fire 1990s series *The Fast Show* consisted of little other than catchphrases, among them Scorchio!, Suits you sir! and I'll get me coat (see also BUM and JUMPER).

Children enjoy repetition, and many children's programmes rely on repeated catchphrases, such as Are you sitting comfortably? Then I'll begin, which started every episode of the BBC radio programme *Listen with Mother* (1950-82). The presenters in *Blue Peter*, from 1963, relied on the phrase Here's one I made earlier when demonstrating how to make something from sticky-backed plastic and detergent bottles. The fox puppet Basil Brush, famous for ending jokes with Boom boom!, appealed to adults as well as children, as do *The Simpsons*, the source of Eat my shorts! and Doh!

Science fiction has also been a rich source, beginning with Take me to your leader, found in innumerable stories. The refrains of the daleks, which appeared in *Doctor Who* from 1963, were Exterminate, exterminate! and Resistance is futile! The US series *Star Trek* (1966-9) gave us To boldly go where no man has gone before and Space, the final frontier. The six *Star Wars* films from 1977 onwards share a catchphrase, May the force be with you, a reference to the life force harnessed by the Jedi knights. And from 1993 the catchphrase of *The X Files* was The truth is out there.

See also ARSE, DIRT, EVEN, FABULOUS, GRAVE, INQUEST, LIFE, NICE.

Nudge nudge wink wink!

comet

We get the word **comet** from Greek *komïtïs* 'long-haired'. The ancient Greeks gazed into the night sky and observed a comet's long tail, made up of particles of ice and dust lit up by the sun's rays. To their eyes it resembled streaming hair, hence their name for what they called 'the long-haired star'.

commando

In early use, from the beginning of the 19th century, **commando** was a word for an armed unit of Boer horsemen in South Africa. During the Second World War the name was adopted to describe troops specially trained to repel the threatened German invasion of England. The word came into English from Portuguese, but is based on Latin *commandare* 'to command'.

To **go commando** is to wear no underpants. This curious phrase dates back to the 1980s and probably originated as American college slang, although it was popularised by its use in an episode of the TV comedy *Friends*. It derives from the practice of not wearing underpants that is supposedly common among military commandos.

commute

In early use **commute** meant 'to interchange two things'. Its source is Latin *commutare*, from *com-* 'altogether' and *mutare* 'to change', the root of English words such as **moult**, **mutant** and **permutation**. The modern meaning, 'to travel between home and your place of work', comes from **commutation ticket**. This was the American term for a season ticket, where a number of daily fares were 'commuted' to, or changed into, a single payment. The Americans have been braving the rush hour and commuting since the 1860s, but the term did not make its way over to Britain until the 1930s.

companion

A **companion** is literally 'a person who you eat bread with'. The word comes from Old French *compaignon*, from Latin *com-* 'together with' and *panis* 'bread'. Other English words that derive from *panis* include **pannier** and PANTRY.

compost

Garden **compost** and fruit **compôte** do not seem to have much in common, but they both derive from French *compôte* 'stewed fruit'. This comes from Old French *composte*, from Latin *compositum* 'something put together' – **composite** has a similar root. **Compost** has been used in the gardening sense since the late 16th century.

computer

The first computers were not machines, but people. In the 17th century a **computer** was a person who makes calculations, in particular someone employed to do this in an observatory or in surveying. The word was used in the late 19th century as a name for a mechanical calculating machine, and the modern sense dates from the 1940s. Its base is Latin *computare*, 'to calculate'. See also COUNT.

comrade

If a COMPANION is, literally, someone you share bread with, then a **comrade** is someone you share a room with. The origin of the word is Spanish *camarada* 'a room-mate', from Latin *camera* 'a room'. Your comrade was originally someone who shared the same room or tent as you, often a fellow soldier. See also CAMERA.

confetti

It was the custom during Italian carnivals and public celebrations for people to throw little sweets, known as **confetti**. The Italian word comes from Latin *confectum* 'something prepared'. As time went on people threw small plaster balls instead of sweets, which were meant to break open in a cloud of white dust when they hit someone. Charles Dickens describes the custom in 1846: 'The spectators . . . would empty down great bags of confetti, that descended like a cloud, and . . . made them as white as millers.' By the end of the 19th century English had borrowed the Italian word to refer to the coloured paper shapes that wedding guests shower on the bride and bridegroom after the marriage ceremony. A related word is **confectionery**.

confiscate

The original meaning of **confiscate** was 'to take someone's property for the public treasury as a punishment'. It comes from Latin *confiscare* 'to store in a chest' or 'to take something for the public treasury', based on *con-* 'together' and *fiscus* 'chest or treasury', also the root of **fiscal**. Later the more general sense developed of a person in authority taking something away from someone, as a schoolteacher might confiscate a pupil's mobile phone.

congregate

The Latin word for a herd or flock was *grex*, hence the verb *congregare*, meaning 'to collect into a herd or flock, to unite'. This is where our word **congregate** comes from. GREGARIOUS, meaning 'fond of company', is also descended from *grex*.

Everybody's gone surfing

Once, browsing was done only by animals, the net was for fish and the web belonged to a spider. The dizzying speed with which computer technology has developed means that language has to run to keep up, giving us a whole new terminology that continues to grow day by day.

From the 1970s the US Defense Department operated a computer network that consisted of a number of smaller networks and was referred to as the internet. Out of this governmental system evolved the global computer network the internet, which provides the information and communication facilities known as the World Wide Web.

Surf originally seems to have come from the obsolete word suff, used in the 16th and 17th centuries. To surf the net or the web is to move from site to site on the internet. It originated from the US expression channel-surfing (the British tend to channel-hop), which describes the practice of constantly switching TV channels using a remote control.

You would hardly expect to see a mild-mannered computer geek biting the head off a live chicken or snake, but in the early 20th century that is exactly what he would do in a US carnival or circus. The word, probably a variant of the English dialect term geck 'a fool', was applied to overly diligent students in the 1950s, and to computer obsessives from around 1984.

As chat rooms, blogs (web logs, or online diaries) and computer gaming communities have grown, so each has developed its own language, often as a code to keep out the uninitiated. Among computer gamers, hierarchies are defined by labels such as leets (short for the 'elite') and newbies or weenies (newcomers), while muggles are those lacking in skill. This comes from the Harry Potter books of J.K. Rowling, where a muggle is a non-wizard. The image is extended with wizard – a person who has particular knowledge of a topic, or a piece of software which guides a naive user through a complex task.

conjure

The earliest meanings of **conjure** were 'to call on in the name of some divine or supernatural being' and 'to appeal solemnly to, entreat' – the -jure bit of the word is from Latin jurare 'to swear', which gave us words such as JURY. A more familiar early meaning was 'to call on a spirit, demon or ghost to appear by means of a magic ritual', from which the sense 'to make something appear as if by magic' developed. **A name to conjure with** is the name of a person who is important or famous in a particular field. The idea is of someone summoning the spirit of an influential or powerful person by saying their name out loud.

conker

Children originally played conkers – or a game very like it – not with horse chestnuts but with snail shells. The word **conker** is first recorded in the 1840s as a dialect word for a snail shell, and may have originally come from **conch**, a kind of mollusc, which is probably also the origin of **conk**, meaning 'the nose'. On the other hand, **conker** could be related to **conquer**, which was how **conker** was often spelled. Indeed, an alternative name for the game at one time was **conquerors**. Horse chestnuts seem to have replaced snail shells late in the 19th century.

connive

When someone **connives** at something wrong, they secretly allow it rather than punishing it or, to put it another way, they turn a blind eye to it. The word comes from French conniver or Latin connivere meaning 'to shut your eyes to something'. An early meaning of **connivance** was 'winking'.

consider

You used to **consider** with your eyes rather than your brain. Latin considerare meant 'to observe or examine something', but had an earlier meaning 'to observe the stars' and was based on sidus 'a star or constellation'. The earliest meaning of its English descendant **consider** was 'to look at something very carefully', but this soon widened to the notion of thinking carefully about something.

Cracker, a person who breaks security on a computer system, was coined in the 1980s by hackers who protested against the use of hacking to mean criminal activity. Its original meaning in the computing world was someone with a high level of skill. A hack, meanwhile, is a rough and hurried fix to a problem that displays enough flair to raise it above the kludge, an unsophisticated solution. The latter probably derives from German *klug*, meaning 'clever', mixed in with the associations of fudge and bodge.

Equally strange at first sight is foo, an all-purpose substitute for other words in technical discussions. The word has quite a history in pre-Second World War comic strips and particularly in the US Smokey Stover cartoons of the 1930s onwards. The cartoons' creator used foo as a nonsense word in phrases such as 'where there's foo there's fire' and 'he who foos last foos best'. Thereafter foo took on a life of its own: in the 1940s foo fighter was used by the US military for a mysterious object which would today be called a UFO, and in 1995 Dave Grohl, former drummer with Nirvana, formed the rock band the Foo Fighters.

Just after the Second World War a moth caused a fault in Navy equipment. As the logbook entry proves, the term bug for a fault in machinery was already around – the technician wrote, alongside the actual moth taped to the page, that this was 'the first actual case of bug being found'. The use can be traced back further, to the inventor Thomas Edison's time. An article in the *Pall Mall Gazette* of 1889 notes that 'Mr. Edison, I was informed, had been up the two previous nights discovering "a bug" in his phonograph – an expression for solving a difficulty, and implying that some imaginary insect has secreted itself inside and is causing all the trouble.'

Computers and the internet have added a new layer of unconventional richness to English. They may not mean much to the uninitiated, but few could argue about the colour of phrases such as a banana problem or an Easter egg. The first is not knowing when to bring a program or computing creation to a close, and comes from the story of the little girl who said: 'I know how to spell banana, but I don't know when to stop.' The year-round Easter egg is a message hidden in a program's code as a joke, and designed to be hunted out with as much enthusiasm as Easter eggs might be.

See also APPLE, COUCH POTATO, ICON, MOUSE, SEE, WEAVE, YAHOO.

conspire

You can imagine a group of people conspiring, or secretly plotting, to do something, huddled in the shadows, whispering to one another, with their heads close together. They are practically breathing the same air. This notion can be traced back to the origin of the word **conspire**. It comes via French from Latin *conspirare* 'to plot', made up of *con-* 'together with' and *spirare* 'to breathe'. *Spirare* is the root of several other English words such as **aspire**, **expire**, **inspire** and **perspire**, and also SPIRIT.

constable

Mounted police officers are in some ways the true descendants of the original **constables**. The Latin phrase *comes stabuli* originally meant 'officer in charge of the stable'. One of the earliest uses of the English word, dating from the 13th century, was as the title of the governor or warden of certain royal castles, a title that is still used today. It was used as a term for a police officer in the modern sense from the mid 19th century.

contemptible

In modern English **contemptible** is still widely used, whereas its root word, **contemn**, 'to treat or regard with contempt', is now rare and restricted to literary contexts. In 1914 the Kaiser of Germany supposedly referred to the British Army as **a contemptible little army**, in an order for his troops to 'walk all over General French's contemptible little army'. In fact the text, which became widely known and resented, appears to have been created by British propaganda. The veterans of the British Expeditionary Force of 1914 later became known as the Old Contemptibles.

contrite

To feel **contrite** is to feel remorse. The Latin word *contritus* meant 'ground down' and was based on *con-* 'together' and *terere* 'to rub or grind', also the source of TRITE. The 'remorseful' meaning of **contrite** developed from the idea of a person's spirit being crushed or broken by a sense of sin.

conundrum

The origin of **conundrum**, 'a confusing and difficult problem', is a conundrum. In 1596 the English political writer Thomas Nashe used it as a term of abuse for a crank or pedant: 'So will I . . . drive him to confess himself a Conundrum, who now thinks he hath learning enough to prove the salvation of Lucifer.' The word later came to refer both to a whim and a pun. The current sense of 'a riddle or puzzle' dates from the late 17th century.

convent

The word **convent** was originally spelled *covent*, a spelling that survives in the London place name **Covent Garden**. A convent is now a religious community of nuns, but until the 18th century it could also be one of monks. The word came into English via Old French from Latin *conventus* 'an assembly or company', based on *convenire* 'to come together'. **Convene**, 'to call people together for a meeting', has the same origin, as does **coven** or 'gathering of witches' – a long way from the residents of a **convent**.

conversation

In Latin *conversare* meant 'to mix with people'. This is the source of our word **conversation**, which once meant 'living among' and 'familiarity or intimacy'. The poet John Milton used the word in this latter sense when he refers in 1645 to 'the good and peace of wedded conversation'. It could also at one time mean 'sexual intercourse', and **criminal conversation** was a legal term for adultery. The 'talking' sense dates from the late 16th century. See also CHAT.

cook

The Old English *coc* – the early form of **cook** – was always male. The word was applied either to the domestic officer in charge of the preparation of food in, for example, a large household, monastery or ship, or to a tradesman who prepared and sold food. Women who prepared dinner started being called cooks in the mid 16th century. The root of the word is Latin *coquus*, also the source of **concoct** and BISCUIT.

Cook has been used to mean 'to tamper with' since the 1630s, hence the expression **cook the books**, meaning 'to alter records or accounts dishonestly'. The proverb **too many cooks spoil the broth**, meaning that if too many people are involved in a task it will not be done well, dates back to the 16th century. It is not certain where the phrase **cook someone's goose**, meaning 'to spoil someone's plans or cause their downfall', comes from. The reference could be to a goose being reared and fattened up for a forthcoming special occasion. Anyone who killed and cooked the goose before the proper time would have ruined the plans for the feast.

cool

As early as the 1880s **cool**, an Old English word related to COLD, was being used by black Americans to mean 'excellent, pleasing' and 'stylish'. It only became more widely known when people started associating it with jazz musicians with a restrained and relaxed style in the 1940s. It then declined in popularity for a decade or two before regaining its position as the top all-purpose affirmative, meaning 'all right, OK', for the young and young-at-heart, who may be unaware of its long history.

In 1996 the magazine *Newsweek* called London the coolest city on Earth, and Britain was briefly dubbed **Cool Britannia** (a pun on *Rule Britannia*), in recognition of its image as a stylish and fashionable place and the international success of bands, artists and designers such as Oasis, Blur, Damien Hirst and Alexander McQueen. The relatively young Tony Blair was elected Prime Minister in 1997, and promptly

The actress Patsy Kensit and Oasis frontman Liam Gallagher on the cover of *Vanity Fair* in March 1997 at the height of Cool Britannia.

invited Oasis guitarist Noel Gallagher to a reception at Downing Street. The concept was soon mocked, and the veteran British Labour MP Tony Benn said in 1998: 'When I think of Cool Britannia, I think of old people dying of hypothermia.' **Cool Britannia** was not invented by Tony Blair – it was the title of a 1967 song by comedy rock act the Bonzo Dog Doo-Dah Band.

coop

The Latin word *cupa* 'barrel' is the forerunner of **coop**, 'a cage or pen in which poultry are kept', and also gave us **cooper**, meaning 'barrel-maker'. In medieval English a coop was a kind of basket that you placed over chickens that were sitting or being fattened.

cope

Nowadays to **cope** with something is to manage or deal with it effectively, but the word used to mean 'to meet in battle' or 'to come to blows'. Its source is the Latin *colpus* 'a blow', which is also the root of **coup**, meaning 'a sudden seizure of power from a government' and often used in its French form *coup d'état*.

copper

The verb **cop**, meaning 'to catch', comes from a northern English dialect word *cap* meaning 'to capture or arrest'. This probably goes back to Latin *capere*, 'to take or seize'. So a **copper** was a catcher, which is why it became an informal word for a police officer in the 1840s. Apprehended villains have been saying 'it's a fair cop!' since the 1880s. See also CAPTION.

Copper, the reddish-brown metal, comes from Latin *cyprium aes* 'Cyprus metal'. The island of Cyprus was the Romans' main source of copper.

cordial

The Latin word *cordis* meant 'to do with the heart', and this is the source and original meaning of **cordial**. It was not long before the adjective was being used to describe drinks as 'comforting' or 'stimulating the heart', and the core 'heart' meaning came to be applied to people too, in connection with actions or behaviour that seemed sincere and heartfelt – 'from the heart'. The root, Latin *cor* 'heart', is the source of many words, including **accord** and COURAGE. HEART itself and **cardiac**, 'of the heart', came from the same ancient root.

corgi

Not many English words derive from Welsh, but **corgi** is one of them. Others include **coracle**, **flummery**, FLANNEL (probably) and PENGUIN (perhaps). A **corgi** is literally 'a dwarf dog', from Welsh *cor* 'dwarf' and *ci* 'dog'.

cormorant

Picture a glossy black **cormorant**, a large diving bird with a long neck, greedily gobbling down great quantities of fish, and you might agree that the description 'sea raven' seems rather fitting. This is indeed the meaning of the Latin *corvus marinus*, the source of the bird's name. Since the 16th century the word has also been used to describe an insatiably greedy person or thing. 'Why, what a cormorant in love am I', says a character in William Congreve's play *The Old Bachelor* (1693).

corn

Meaning 'the seed of wheat and similar plants', **corn** is an Old English word whose root may date back as far as farming itself. And there is a rural link when we call something old-fashioned or overly sentimental **corny**. This is a development of an earlier sense of **corny**, dating from the 1930s, that described something, especially music, of a simple and unsophisticated type that appealed to people living in the country.

The other kind of **corn**, the small area of thickened horn-like skin on your foot, comes from Latin *cornu* 'horn'. *Cornu*, which could also mean 'tip' or 'corner', is the source too of **corner** – you can think of a corner as the part of something that sticks out or forms the tip.

The trumpet-like instrument the **cornet** is now made from brass, but it was originally a wind instrument made out of a horn, and Latin *cornu* is again the source. An ice-cream **cornet**, so called since the early 20th century, owes its name to its shape, which resembles that of the instrument. One brand of ice cream is called a **Cornetto** ('little horn'), and this Italian word was also the name of an old musical instrument, a straight or curved wooden wind instrument with finger holes and a cup-shaped mouthpiece. See also HORN.

coronary

In the 17th century **coronary** had the meanings 'like a crown' or 'suitable for making garlands', from Latin *corona*, 'a crown or wreath'. In medical contexts the term came to refer to blood vessels, nerves or ligaments that encircle a part of the body like a crown, in particular the arteries surrounding the heart. A **coronary thrombosis**, frequently abbreviated just to **coronary**, is a blood clot forming a blockage in one of these arteries. Other crown-related words that descend from *corona* are **coronation**, **coronet** and **coroner** (originally an official responsible for safeguarding the private property of the Crown), not to mention the word CROWN itself.

corpse

At one time **corpses** did not have to be dead. Until the early 18th century a corpse (from Latin *corpus* 'body') could be the living body of a person or animal, as in 'We often see . . . a fair and beautiful corpse but a foul and ugly mind' (Thomas Walkington, 1607). You would need to specify 'a dead corpse', 'a lifeless corpse' or some similar expression if you were talking about a dead body. In time, you could simply say 'a corpse' and people would assume that you meant a dead person.

The *p* used to be silent and the final *e* was rare before the 19th century. In fact, **corpse** and **corps** ('a division of an army') are basically the same word. Latin *corpus* has given us several words, among them **corporation**, **corpulent** or 'fat' and **incorporate**. A **corporal** is in charge of a 'body' of troops, and this is the link with *corpus*.

corridor

Corridors are nothing to do with doors. They are 'running places'. The word comes from Italian *corridore*, from Latin *currere* 'to run'. It started out as a military term for a strip of land along the outer edge of a ditch, protected by a parapet. The modern sense of 'a long passage in a building' dates from the early 19th century. See also CURSOR.

Corridors of power refers to the senior levels of government or the civil service, where all the important decision-making takes place behind the scenes. It was popularised by the title of C.P. Snow's novel *The Corridors of Power* (1964), though Snow did not coin the expression.

corrode

The second part of **corrode** is the same as the first part of RODENT – a clue to the meaning of the Latin word *rodere* from which both the English words are descended. It means 'to gnaw', so when something is corroded it is gradually worn away, as if by gnawing.

cosset

In the 16th century a lamb brought up by hand as a pet was known as a **cosset**. The term was later used to refer to a spoiled child, and this is where the modern verb use, 'to pamper someone', came from. The origin of the word is probably Old French *coscet* 'cottager'. See also PET.

cot

We have the British Empire to thank for **cot**, which started life as an Anglo-Indian word for a light bedstead. The origin is the Hindi word *khāt* 'bedstead or hammock'. A less familiar **cot** is an old word for a small, simple cottage, used nowadays as a term for a small shelter for livestock. Closely related to this word are **cottage** and **cote** (as in **dovecote**, though that too once meant 'cottage').

couch potato

Someone who spends all day at home sitting in front of the television can be described as a **couch potato**. The phrase was coined in the US around 1976. It is actually a more ingenious expression than it might seem: a potato is a type of tuber (a vegetable that grows from a thick underground stem), and the slang term **boob tuber** was used at the time to refer to someone who was addicted to the **boob tube** or television.

Ricky Tomlinson plays Jim Royle, the ultimate 'couch potato', in the TV sitcom *The Royle Family*.

count

The verb to **count** is from Latin *computare* 'to calculate', the root also of COMPUTER. The title of the **count** or foreign nobleman, corresponding to the English EARL, is a completely different word, which was used by the Normans and comes from Latin *comes* 'companion, overseer, attendant'. **County** is from the same root, and seems originally to have referred to the lands or territory of a count, or to a meeting held to discuss the business of the county. See also CHICKEN, DUKE.

country

The source of **country** is medieval Latin *contrata terra*, meaning 'the land lying opposite, the landscape spread out in front of you'. This is based on Latin *contra* 'against or opposite' and *terra* 'land', the source of **mediterranean** and **terrestrial**.

A **country fit for heroes to live in** is a phrase associated with the British politician David Lloyd George. What Lloyd George said, as Prime Minister in a speech of November 23, 1918, was 'What is our task? To make Britain a fit country for heroes to live in.'

A person from a rural background who is unfamiliar with, and alarmed by, urban life can be called a **country mouse**. The allusion is to one of Aesop's fables, which contrasts the country mouse with the streetwise city-dwelling town mouse. In the fable each mouse visits the other, but is in the end convinced of the superiority of its own home.

coupon

Our word **coupon** is borrowed from the French word meaning 'a piece cut off', from *couper* 'to cut'. In early use a coupon was a detachable portion of a stock certificate which you handed over in return for a payment of interest. It came to be applied to any ticket or voucher that entitles you to something or that you can exchange for goods or cash.

courage

Braveheart, the title chosen by Mel Gibson for his 1995 film about the Scottish national hero William Wallace, sums up neatly both the meaning and origin of the word **courage**. It comes from Old French *corage*, from Latin *cor* 'heart'. In the Middle Ages the English word referred to the heart as the centre of a person's character, feelings or thoughts, as in Geoffrey Chaucer's line, 'Such a great courage had this knight to be a wedded man'. See also CORDIAL.

courteous

Medieval courts were associated with good manners, hence the early meaning of **courteous**, 'having manners fit for a royal court'. It derived from Old French *corteis*, based on *cort* 'court'. **Courtesy**, 'the showing of politeness towards others', is from the same root.

cousin

Our word **cousin** is from Old French *cosin*, which in turn comes from Latin *consobrinus* 'mother's sister's child'. By the time the word had entered English it was not simply restricted to the mother's side – a cousin could be on your father's side too. It came to be used of any relative more distant than your brother or sister, and particularly in the past to a nephew or niece: 'How now brother, where is my cosen, your son?' (Shakespeare, *Much Ado About Nothing*).

Coventry

There was obviously something so bad about the city of Coventry that sending someone there was synonymous with refusing to associate with or speak to them. The phrase **send someone to Coventry** may be connected with the English Civil War (1642-49), although it is not recorded until the 1760s. The garrison of Parliamentarian soldiers stationed in Coventry was apparently deeply unpopular with the city's inhabitants, who refused to associate with them socially. Another theory is that this staunchly Parliamentarian city was where many Royalist prisoners were sent to be held in secure captivity.

cow

The female animal is an Old English word. The verb **cow**, meaning 'to subdue someone by bullying them', is a different word, probably from Old Norse *kúga* 'to oppress'. See also BULL.

The expression **till the cows come home**, 'for an indefinitely long time', dates from at least the 16th century. 'I warrant you lay a bed [in bed] till the cows came home', wrote Jonathan Swift in 1738.

coward

The Latin word *cauda* 'tail' is the source of **coward**. This may be from the idea of a frightened animal drawing its tail between its legs or 'turning tail' in flight. In heraldry **lion coward** is the term for a lion depicted with its tail drawn between its hind legs. Despite the similarity in spelling and meaning, the verb **cower** has a completely different origin, coming from German *kūren* 'lie in wait'. See also YELLOW.

coxswain

The **cox** or **coxswain** is the person who steers a racing boat or similar craft. The *cox* part is from the old word **cock** 'small boat', which is not related to the bird but to Latin *caudex* or *codex* 'block of wood'. The second half of the word, **swain**, now means 'a country youth or peasant' but was originally 'a young man attending a knight' and 'a male servant or attendant'. It is also the second half of **boatswain** (often abbreviated to **bo'sun**), a ship's officer in charge of equipment and the crew.

crabbed

The crab is at the root of **crabbed**. Both original senses, the medieval 'perverse or wayward' and the later 'cantankerous and bad-tempered', come from aspects of a crab's behaviour, the way it walks sideways and its habit of snapping. **Crabby** is a later word, also derived from **crab**. See also CANCER, CRAYFISH.

crack

In Old English **crack** meant 'make a sudden sharp or explosive noise'. The drug known as crack, or crack cocaine, is a hard crystalline form of cocaine broken into small pieces and smoked. It gets its name from the 'cracking' noises the crystals make as they are heated. You do not need the help of crack or any other drug to enjoy the crack or lively socialising in a pub – this is an Irish use, first recorded in the 1920s and sometimes written **craic**, that comes from the Scottish sense 'chat, conversation'.

You can talk about a time very early in the morning as the **crack of dawn**. The expression is first recorded in the late 19th century, in the form **crack of day**. The crack here is the crack of a whip, with an additional echo perhaps of break of day and daybreak, and the notion of the sky cracking or breaking open to reveal a sliver of light. The **crack of doom** is a peal of thunder which, according to the biblical Book of Revelation, will announce the Day of Judgement. See also PAPER.

craft

In Old English the word **craft** meant 'strength or skill'. The sense 'a boat or ship', initially in the expression 'small craft', dates from the 17th century, and may originally have referred to vessels that only needed a small amount of skill to handle, in contrast to large ocean-going ships. People came to use **crafty** to mean 'skilful', and over time this developed the more negative sense of 'cunning or sly' that it has today.

crane

The first meaning of **crane**, in the Middle Ages, was as the name for the long-legged long-necked wading bird that was then common in marshy places. What is quite surprising, though, is that the tall machine with a long arm used for lifting heavy objects was also being called a **crane** as early as the 14th century. The appearance and movement of the mechanical device must have reminded people of the bird.

cranky

If you described someone as **cranky** in the late 18th century you meant that they were sickly or in poor health. The word came to be applied to things that were shaky or out of order and subsequently to people who were either bad-tempered or eccentric. The noun **crank**, meaning 'an eccentric person', probably comes from this last sense of **cranky**.

cravat

The short, wide strip of fabric that men wear round the neck tucked inside an open-necked shirt has its origins in the Balkans. It comes from the French word Cravate, meaning 'Croat'. The link between the two is that Croatian mercenaries in the French army during the 17th century wore a linen scarf round their necks, which subsequently became fashionable among the French population at large.

crater

The Greeks and Romans preferred to drink their wine mixed with water, and thought it very uncivilised, and possibly dangerous, to drink it neat. To make this ancient spritzer they used a large wide-mouthed bowl called in Greek a *kratēr* and in Latin a *crater*. English adopted the word in the early 1600s as the term for the bowl-shaped hollow that forms the mouth of a volcano.

crayfish

A **crayfish** is not a fish but a freshwater crustacean that looks like a small lobster. Its name came into medieval English from Old French *crevice*, and was probably related to CRAB (although not to **crevice**, which is from Old French *crever*, 'to burst or split'). The spelling was altered in the 16th century simply because people thought that it made more sense: it lives in water, so it must be a fish.

crazy

The root here is the verb to **craze**, which is now 'to drive mad, send crazy' or 'to develop a network of small cracks' but originally meant 'to break in pieces, shatter'. So a crazy person has had their sanity shattered. **Crazy** formerly meant 'broken, damaged' and 'frail, unwell, infirm' – in *Henry VI Part 1* Shakespeare wrote of 'Some better place / Fitter for sickness and for crazy age'. See also DAFT.

creature

The earliest recorded sense of **creature** in English is 'anything created', whether living or not, and the word is from Latin *creatura* 'a created being'. This is the meaning the poet William Cowper had in mind when he wrote in 1783, 'The first boat or canoe that was ever formed . . . was a more perfect creature in its kind than a balloon at present.' The verb **create** comes from Latin *creare* 'to produce', and originally meant 'to form out of nothing'.

credit

People first used the word **credit** (ultimately from Latin *credere* 'to believe or trust') to mean 'belief' and 'trustworthiness'. The modern sense developed from the idea of, say, a shopkeeper's trust that a customer is able to pay for goods at a later time. *Credere* also gave us **creed**, **credence** and **incredulous**.

You can say **credit where credit is due** to show that you think someone deserves to be given praise. The earlier form of the saying was 'honour where honour is due', a phrase from the Bible, from the Epistle to the Romans: 'Render therefore to all their dues: tribute to whom tribute is due; custom to whom custom; fear to whom fear; honour to whom honour.'

crescent

The Romans referred to the thin curve of the waxing moon early in its cycle as *luna crescens*, 'growing moon'. *Crescens* comes from Latin *crescere* 'to grow', the source of many English words such as **crescendo** and **increase**. Our word **crescent** came to be applied first to the waxing moon and subsequently to anything that had the same shape, including a street or terrace of houses. See also CREW.

crest

Crest comes from Latin *crista*, meaning 'a tuft or plume'. **Crestfallen**, meaning 'dejected', is an extension of its original use to describe an animal or bird with a drooping crest. **Crease** is probably an alternative form of **crest**, the idea being that a fold in a length of cloth forms a ridge or crest.

crew

When **crew** came into English in the 15th century it initially referred to a band of soldiers acting as reinforcements. The origin of the word is Old French *creue* 'an increase', ultimately derived from Latin *crescere* 'to grow or increase'. By the 16th century the word was being applied to any organised armed band or, more generally, a company of people. See also CRESCENT.

A **crew cut** is so called because this closely cropped hairstyle was first adopted by rowing crews at Harvard and Yale universities in the late 1930s. The **crew neck** came from the same source – US university rowers wore sweaters with close-fitting necks.

cricket

Evidence suggests that the game of **cricket** was being played back in the 16th century. The word is first recorded in an official document of 1598 in which a man of 59 swears that when he was a schoolboy he used to play cricket and other games on a particular bit of land in Guildford, Surrey. This would take the game back to the reign of Henry VIII. Cricket would have been very different then: the bats were more like hockey sticks, the wicket consisted of two stumps with one long bail and the ball was trundled along the ground rather than 'bowled' in the way that we understand. The word appears to be closely related to French *criquet* 'a stick', although whether this originally referred to the wicket or the bat is not entirely clear.

The idea of cricket being the epitome of honourable behaviour, as in 'It's just not cricket!', dates from the mid 19th century. In 1867 *The Cricketer's Companion* told its readers: 'Do not ask the umpire unless you think the batsman is out; it is not cricket to keep asking the umpire questions.'

The other **cricket**, the grasshopper-like insect, is a completely different word. It comes from Old French *criquet* 'a cricket', based on *criquer* 'to crackle, click or creak', probably suggesting the chirping sound the insect makes. See also OAF.

crime

The early meanings of **crime** were 'wickedness' and 'sin'. The word comes via Old French from Latin *crimen* 'judgement or offence', which was based on *cernere* 'to judge' (as in **concern** and **discerning**).

The expression **crime doesn't pay** was a slogan associated with the 1930s American radio crime series *The Shadow*, in which it was spoken by the Shadow at the end of each broadcast. It originated earlier, though, and was the title of a silent film in 1912.

crimson

The colour **crimson** was originally a deep red dye used in colouring fine cloth and velvet and obtained from an insect called the kermes, whose body was dried and ground up to produce the dye. The name of the insect came ultimately from Arabic *qirmiz*. See also PURPLE, VERMILION.

crisis

At one time a **crisis** was specifically the turning point of a disease, a change that leads either to recovery or death. The source is Greek *krisis* 'a decision', from *krinein* 'to decide, judge'. Its more general sense 'decisive point' dates from the early 17th century. *Krinein* is also the root of **critic** and **critical**.

Crisis? What crisis? is often attributed to the British Prime Minister James Callaghan, but it was in fact coined by a headline writer in the newspaper *The Sun*. Returning to London from a meeting in the Caribbean in January 1979, during the 'Winter of Discontent' when the country was plagued by strikes and economic problems, Callaghan was interviewed at London Airport. He gave the comment 'I don't think other people in the world would share the view there is mounting chaos.' The next day *The Sun*'s headline read: 'Crisis? What Crisis?'. See also WINTER.

crisp

To the Anglo-Saxons curly or frizzy hair was **crisp**. The word comes from Latin *crispus* 'curled'. It started to be used to mean 'brittle' in the early 16th century, though it is not entirely clear why.

Potato crisps first appeared under that name during the 1920s. The first edible crisps, though, were described in medieval cookery books and were crisp pastries made by dropping batter into boiling fat. **Crisp** was also an old term for the 'crackling' of roast pork, and this may be the sense behind the phrase **burned to a crisp**.

crocodile

The name of the **crocodile** comes from Greek *krokodilos* 'worm of the stones', from *krokï* 'pebble' and *drilos* 'worm'. This is a reference to the crocodile's habit of basking in the sun on the shingly banks of a river. In medieval English the spellings *cocodrille* and *cokadrill* were common.

If you accuse someone of shedding **crocodile tears**, you mean they are putting on a display of insincere sorrow. The expression dates from the mid 16th century and stems from the ancient belief that crocodiles wept while luring or devouring their prey. According to a 16th-century account of the sailor John Hawkins's voyages, the crocodile's nature 'is ever when he would have his prey, to cry and sob like a Christian body, to provoke them to come to him, and then he snatcheth at them'.

crony

This derives from Greek *khronios* 'long-lasting', which was based on *khronos* 'time'. In the 17th century **crony** was Cambridge University slang for 'an old friend' or 'a contemporary'. CHUM is the Oxford University equivalent. The first record of **crony** is found in the diary of Samuel Pepys, a former Cambridge man, for May 30, 1665: 'Jack Cole, my old school-fellow . . . who was a great chrony of mine.' His spelling showed the word's direct relationship with the original Greek. The political sense of **cronyism**, 'the appointment of your friends and associates to positions of authority', originated in the US during the 19th century. See also CHRONIC.

crook

A **crook** was originally a hooked tool or weapon. The source is Old Norse *krokr* 'hook'. The word used to mean 'dishonest trick, guile' in medieval English, and although this sense had fallen from use by the 17th century it gave rise to our **crooks** and **crooked** villains. The 'criminal or swindler' meaning first appeared in the late 19th century in the USA.

In Australia and New Zealand **crook** has meant 'bad, unpleasant', 'dishonest, unscrupulous', and 'ill, unwell' since the late 1890s. These uses might come from the old British thieves' slang sense 'stolen'.

crop

From around AD 700 to the late 18th century **crop** had a sense 'flower head, ear of corn', which gave rise to the main modern meaning 'a cultivated plant grown on a large scale' and also to senses referring to the top of something, such as the verb uses 'to cut very short' or 'to bite off and eat the tops of plants'. The sense 'a very short hairstyle' goes back to the late 18th century but is particularly associated with the 1920s, when the **Eton crop**, reminiscent of the style then worn at the English public school Eton, was fashionable for young women.

A crocodile cries its insincere tears in a Victorian illustration.

croquet

Different as they seem, **croquet** and **crochet** are probably the same word. **Croquet** is thought to be a form of French *crochet* 'hook, shepherd's crook', which can mean 'hockey stick' in parts of France and in English refers to a handicraft in which yarn is made up into fabric with a hooked needle. The lawn game in which you drive balls through hoops with a mallet seems to have been invented in France but introduced to Ireland, from where it spread to England in the 1850s and quickly became a popular sport among the aristocracy.

cross

The word **cross** was initially used in English to refer to a monument in the form of a cross. The source is Old Norse *kross*, which in turn goes back to *crux*, a Latin word that gave us CRUCIAL, **crusade** and EXCRUCIATING.

People **cross their fingers** to ward off bad luck. What they are doing is making a miniature 'sign of the cross', whether they know it or not. To **cross someone's palm with silver** is to pay them for a favour or service. It probably comes from the idea of tracing the shape of a cross on a fortune teller's palm with a silver coin before you are told what the future has in store.

In 49 BC Julius Caesar, having defeated the Gauls in the Gallic wars, brought his army south to fight a civil war against Pompey and the Roman Senate. When he crossed the Rubicon, a small river marking the boundary between Italy and the Roman province of Gaul, he was committed to war, having broken the law forbidding him to take his troops out of his province. To **cross the Rubicon** is to take an irrevocable step, leaving no possibility of turning back.

Cross meaning 'annoyed' dates back to the 17th century. It derives from the nautical idea of a wind blowing across the bow of your ship rather than from behind, which produced the senses 'contrary, opposing' and 'adverse, opposed', and then 'annoyed, bad-tempered'.

crossword

A **crossword** was originally a **wordcross**. The puzzle is said to have been invented by the journalist Arthur Wynne, whose first crossword appeared in a Sunday newspaper, the *New York World*, on December 21, 1913. Some people are addicted to **cryptic** crosswords, whereas others find them totally obscure. Their meaning is literally 'hidden', which is the translation of the Greek root *kruptos*, also the source of **crypt** and **grotto**. See also KRYPTON.

come a cropper

The 19th-century hunting slang term **cropper**, 'a heavy fall', may be behind this calamitous phrase. Cropper probably came from **neck and crop**, meaning 'completely or thoroughly' and originally used for a horse's fall. **Crop** was either the horse's hindquarters or the rider's whip.

crown

A **crown** is now usually a grand jewelled affair, but the original idea was probably closer to a simple garland or headdress. The root was Latin *corona* 'wreath' (see CORONARY), which is from Greek *korōnē* 'something bent' – the Greek crown was a laurel branch or wreath of flowers bent around the head to honour a victor or official. See also TIARA.

crucial

The Latin word *crux*, 'a cross', is the source for **crucial**. It was originally a technical term, especially in anatomy, meaning 'cross-shaped', and a close relative appears in the name of the knee's **cruciate ligament**. The meaning 'decisive' or 'very important', as in 'at a crucial stage', can be traced back to the Latin phrase *instantia crucis* 'crucial instance', coined in the early 17th century by the English statesman and philosopher Francis Bacon. His metaphor was based on the idea of a signpost at a crossroad – a place where you have to choose which way to go next. See also CROSS.

crumb

The word **crumb** did not always have a *b* at the end: this was added in the 16th century, influenced partly by the related word **crumble** and partly by words like **dumb** and **thumb**. The dated exclamation **crumbs** is a euphemism for 'Christ' and dates from the late 19th century. **Crummy**, now meaning 'unpleasant' and 'in poor condition', was originally spelled **crumby** and meant 'crumbly' or 'covered in crumbs'.

crystal

The transparent substance, and the name for the highest-quality glass, started out as a term for ice or a mineral that looks like ice. **Crystal** comes from Old French *cristal*, and ultimately from Greek *krustallos* meaning 'ice, crystal'. Its use as a term in chemistry date from the early 17th century.

cubicle

A **cubicle** is now any small partitioned-off area, but at first it was specifically a little place for lying down or a bedroom. The source is Latin *cubiculum*, from *cubare* 'to lie down'. **Incubate** is based on the same Latin word, as is **concubine**, meaning someone you go to bed with.

cuckoo

The **cuckoo** is one of those birds whose name echoes the sound of its distinctive call – other examples are **curlew**, **hoopoe**, **kittiwake** and **peewit**. You can describe an unwelcome intruder in a place or situation as a **cuckoo in the nest**. This comes from the female cuckoo's habit of laying her eggs in another bird's nest. Once hatched, the cuckoo fledgling pushes the other bird's fledglings out. **Cuckold**, referring to the husband of an unfaithful wife, also derives from *cucu*, and plays on the same cuckoo-in-the-nest idea, although it is not actually the husband who is being the 'cuckoo'.

Kook, 'an eccentric person', is short for cuckoo. It was first recorded in the 1920s but only really became common in the late 1950s.

The reason that a silly or mad person is described as a cuckoo, or is said to have **gone cuckoo**, is probably that the bird's monotonously repeated call suggests simple-mindedness. See also CLOUD, COCCYX.

cuff

Before it came to refer to the end of a sleeve, **cuff** meant 'a glove or mitten'. Its origin is unknown, and it does not appear to be connected to the verb sense of the word 'to hit or punch'.

The expression **off the cuff**, meaning 'without preparation', dates from the 1930s and was first used in the USA. It comes from the idea of a person making a speech and relying on notes jotted down on their shirt cuffs rather than reading out a prepared script.

culprit

Formerly in England, when a prisoner in court pleaded not guilty the Clerk of the Crown said: 'Culprit, how will you be tried?' This expression, first recorded in 1678, may have started out as a mistake in reading the written abbreviation *cul. prist.*, which stood for Old French *Culpable: prest d'averrer notre bille*, '(You are) guilty: (We are) ready to prove our indictment.' *Cul prit* (later **culprit**) came to mean 'a guilty person'.

cunning

If you described someone as **cunning** in the Middle Ages you meant they were skilful or learned – there was no implication of slyness or deceit. The word probably comes from Old Norse *kunnandi* 'knowledge', from *kunna* 'to know', which is related to the verb **can**. Witches and wizards used to be known as 'cunning women' and 'cunning men', from an old sense of the word 'possessing magical knowledge or skill'.

cup

An Old English word, from Latin *cuppa*. As early as 1640 **cup** could mean 'a sports trophy in the form of a cup', originally for horse racing.

To be **in your cups** is to be drunk. In the past you could also use the phrase to mean 'during a drinking bout'. It is unclear which meaning is intended in this passage in the biblical Apocrypha on the strength of wine: 'And when they are in their cups, they forget their love both to friends and brethren, and a little after draw out swords.'

cupboard

In the late Middle Ages a **cupboard**, as its spelling might suggest, was a BOARD, or table, on which you displayed cups, plates and other pieces of crockery. We would now call this a sideboard. The modern meaning of **cupboard** – a piece of furniture with a door, and perhaps shelves, for storing things – emerged in the 16th century.

curate

The word **curate**, 'an assistant to a parish priest', comes from medieval Latin *curatus*, from Latin *cura* 'care', the source of **cure** and **secure**. You can describe something that is partly good and partly bad as a **curate's egg**. This is one of those rare expressions whose origin can be precisely identified. A cartoon in an 1895 edition of the magazine *Punch* features a meek curate at the breakfast table with his bishop. The caption reads:

BISHOP: I'm afraid you've got a bad egg, Mr Jones.

CURATE: Oh no, my Lord, I assure you! Parts of it are excellent!

Only ten years later the phrase had become sufficiently familiar to appear in a publication called *Minister's Gazette of Fashion*: 'The past spring and summer season has seen much fluctuation. Like the curate's egg, it has been excellent in parts.'

curb

A **curb** was a strap passing under the jaw of a horse and fastened to the bit, used for checking an unruly horse. This caused the horse to bend its neck, an action that produced the word. It derives from Old French *courber* 'to bend or bow', from Latin *curvare* (also the source of **curve**). The idea of 'holding back' led to the more general sense of a check or restraint.

Curb is also the American spelling of what in British English is a **kerb**, a stone edging to a pavement or path. The original idea here was of a border or frame, for example around the top of a well or a trapdoor.

cure

Both the verb and noun **cure** come via Old French from Latin *curare* 'to take care of', from *cura* 'care'. The noun originally meant 'care or concern', and was especially used to suggest spiritual care. In late medieval English the senses 'medical care' and 'successful medical treatment' gradually emerged. Other English words that descend from Latin *cura* include CURATE and CURIOUS.

curfew

Today a **curfew** is sometimes imposed during periods of emergency or conflict, as a way of keeping people off the streets, usually at night. Anyone found outdoors after the time of the curfew is liable to be arrested or shot. In the Middle Ages, though, the curfew was the time by which people had to put out or cover the fire in their hearth – the objective was not to keep order but to stop houses burning down. **Curfew** is an Old French word, from *cuvrir* 'to cover' and *feu* 'fire'.

curious

A word that came into the language in the 14th century, in the sense 'eager to know or learn something'. Its source is Latin *curiosus* 'careful', from *cura* 'care'. The word has had a variety of meanings over the centuries, including 'skilfully made', 'very accurate or precise' and 'having an exquisite taste'. The sense 'strange or unusual' appeared early on in the 18th century. Among booksellers **curious** used to be a euphemistic term for erotic or pornographic works.

The Curious Incident of the Dog in the Night-Time is the title of a best-selling 2003 novel by Mark Haddon, about an autistic boy who turns detective when a neighbour's dog is mysteriously killed. The words originate in one of Sir Arthur Conan Doyle's Sherlock Holmes mysteries. In the story *Silver Blaze* (1884), Holmes draws Watson's attention to 'the curious incident of the dog in the night-time'. When Watson protests that 'the dog did nothing in the night-time', Holmes responds: 'That was the curious incident.'

The point, clear to the detective, if not to his slower friend, is that the dog did not raise the alarm because he already knew the person who had disturbed him.

The saying **curiosity killed the cat**, meaning that being inquisitive about other people's affairs might get you into trouble, is first recorded around 1900. The older form is **care killed the cat**, which is first recorded in Ben Jonson's 1598 play *Every Man in His Humour*.

Curiouser and curiouser is a quotation from Lewis Carroll's *Alice in Wonderland* (1865). '"Curiouser and curiouser!" cried Alice (she was so much surprised that for a moment she quite forgot how to speak good English).'

current

When the adjective **current** first appeared on the scene via Old French *corant* it meant 'running or flowing'. The word ultimately derives from Latin *currere* 'to run', the source of many English words, including CORRIDOR, **course**, **courier**, CURSOR and **occur**.

curry

The **curry** that you eat comes from *kari*, a word meaning 'sauce' in the South Indian and Sri Lankan language Tamil. Travellers were bringing back tales of this spicy new food as early as 1598, and in 1747 a book called *The Art of Cookery* told its readers how 'To make a Currey the Indian way'. See also VINDALOO.

If you **curry favour** you try to win favour by flattering someone and behaving obsequiously. The expression dates from the early 16th century and has nothing at all to do with Indian cuisine. It comes from a different word, also spelled **curry**, meaning 'to groom a horse with a coarse brush or comb', which came into English from Old French. **Curry favour** itself is an alteration of the medieval form *curry favel*. Favel or Fauvel was the name of a chestnut horse in a 14th-century French tale who became a symbol of cunning and deceit. So 'to groom Favel' came to mean to handle him in just as cunning a way, by flattering him or behaving in an ingratiating way.

cursor

Nowadays we call the movable indicator on our computer screen the **cursor**. The word has been around for a long time, though. In medieval English a cursor was a running messenger: it is a borrowing of the Latin word for 'a runner', and comes from *currere* 'to run', the source of a great many English words including CORRIDOR, **course**, **courier**, **current** and **occur**. From the late 16th century **cursor** became the term for a sliding part of a slide rule or other instrument, marked with a line for pinpointing the position on a scale that you want, the forerunner of the computing sense.

curt

'In more temperate climes, hair is curt', writes Sir Thomas Herbert in his 1665 account of his travels in Africa and Asia, reflecting **curt**'s original meaning, 'short or shortened'. The word comes from Latin *curtus* 'cut short, abridged'. By the 19th century you could use **curt** to describe people who were not only concise or brief in what they were saying, but rudely so.

cushion

You can tell that the Romans knew a thing or two about reclining in comfort when you discover that they had separate words for a hip cushion (*coxinum*) and an elbow cushion (*cubital*). The former word, from Latin *coxa* 'hip or thigh', gave rise to Old French *cuissin*, from which we get **cushion**.

cusp

When we say someone is **on the cusp of** something we mean that they are at a point of transition between two states, as in 'She was on the cusp of adulthood'. This probably comes from the astrological use of **cusp** as the term for the division between one astrological sign and another. The word comes from Latin *cuspis*, meaning 'a point', and can also be applied to the pointed end where two curves meet, such as the tip of a crescent moon.

custard

A **custard** was originally a pie. Spelled *crustarde* or *custarde*, this was an open pie that contained meat or fruit in a spice or sweetened sauce thickened with eggs. Over time the name gradually came to be applied to the sauce rather than the pie itself. The origin of the word was Old French *crouste* 'a crust', which is also where our word **crust** comes from.

custom

Both **custom** and **costume** come from the same root, Latin *consuetudo* 'custom, habit' – **costume** was originally the decor and clothing appropriate to a painting with a historical theme. A **customer** was a person who habitually bought from a particular tradesman, and **customs** were payments traditionally made to a lord or king.

cut

There is evidence for the verb **cut** from the end of the 13th century. It may well have existed before that in Old English, but there are no written examples to prove it.

You say something is **cut and dried** when it is completely settled or decided. There used to be a distinction between the cut and dried herbs sold in herbalists' shops and those that had been freshly gathered.

The **cut of someone's jib** is their appearance or expression. A jib is a triangular sail set forward of the mast on a sailing ship or boat. It could be short and squat, tall and narrow, or anything in between. The characteristic shape of a particular jib helped to identify the ship it belonged to. Hence the term came to be applied to the impression given by a person's appearance.

We say that something **cuts the mustard** when it comes up to expectations or meets the required standard. In early 20th-century US slang **mustard** had the meaning 'the best of anything'.

Cut to the chase, meaning 'come to the point', comes from film-making. The idea is that, rather than getting bogged down with the build-up, you move straight away to the most exciting or important part – like the chase scene in a film.

cute

This started out in the 18th century as a shortened form of **acute** and originally meant 'clever or shrewd'. The sense 'attractive or pretty' dates from the late 19th century as an American use. **Cutesy**, meaning 'cute in a sickly or sentimental way', is also American, and was first recorded in 1914.

cynic

The original Cynics were members of a school of ancient Greek philosophers who displayed a contempt for wealth, luxury and pleasure, believing that such things distracted a person from the quest for self-knowledge. The word comes from Greek *kunikos*. The Greek word probably derives from the name of the school where one of their founders, Antisthenes, taught. This is more likely than the traditional story that the word comes from the Greek word for dog, *kuōn*, and so means 'dog-like or churlish'. The term **cynic** came to be used for someone who doubts that people are ever sincere and believes that they are only motivated by self-interest. See also EPICURE, STOIC.

daft

In Old English a **daft** person was mild and gentle, qualities which sterner and tougher folk have often interpreted as signs of foolishness or mental incapacity. **Deft** was a related word, which first meant 'mild, meek' as well as 'skilful'. **Daft** came to refer to lack of intelligence during the Middle Ages, and from the 16th century it could also imply madness. It could also mean playfulness – the festivities of Christmas used to be referred to as **the daft days**. See also CRAZY, SILLY.

daisy

Daisies close at night and open again in the morning, revealing the yellow disc at their centre. This gives them their name, as **daisy** is a contraction of *day's eye*.

Being dead and buried loses some of its solemnity and fear when you are **under the daisies** or are **pushing up daisies**. This light-hearted expression dates from the early 20th century, and the First World War poet Wilfred Owen alludes to its use by soldiers in the trenches.

If you are alive and well you can be **fresh as a daisy**. Like the name of the flower itself, this relates to the opening of the daisy in the morning, and to its welcome appearance in spring. The freshness of daisies has been mentioned by writers since at least the 14th century, when it appears in the works of the poet Geoffrey Chaucer.

dame

In its earliest use **dame** meant 'a female ruler'. It comes ultimately from Latin *domina* 'mistress', the root of which also gave us DANGER, **dominate**, **dominion** and DUNGEON. Dame was used as a form of address to a woman of rank from the Middle Ages, and in the 17th century became a legal title – it is now the title given to a woman with the rank of Knight Commander or holder of the Grand Cross in the Orders of Chivalry. Alongside this elevated use ran a more popular strand, where a dame was the mistress of a house or school, or any elderly or mature woman. This gave us the **pantomime dame**, the comic middle-aged character usually played by a man who makes her first appearance in print in the early 20th century. **Dame** is used in the USA for any girl or woman – as Oscar Hammerstein II told us in his 1949 song from the musical *South Pacific*, 'There is nothin' like a dame'. See also BABY, DAMSEL.

damn

The word **damn** goes back to Latin *damnare* 'to inflict loss on'. Originally to damn someone was to condemn them, but associations with being condemned to hell have coloured much of the later history of the word. The desire to avoid profanity led to less offensive alternatives, such as **darn**, used since the 18th century. The older sense of 'to condemn' survives in the phrase to **damn with faint praise**, which was popularised by the 18th-century poet Alexander Pope in his 'An Epistle to Dr Arbuthnot'. It means to give someone or something such unenthusiastic praise that you are really criticising them.

Dan Leno (1860-1904), the most successful of Victorian and Edwardian pantomime dames.

damp

We do not think of something **damp** as being dangerous, but the word originally meant a noxious gas. This use survives in **firedamp**, a name for methane gas, especially when it forms an explosive mixture with air in coal mines. Damp did not come to refer to wetness until the 18th century.

The **damp squib** which failed to go off has probably always marred firework displays – a squib is a small firework that burns with a hissing sound before exploding. From the middle of the 19th century the phrase began to be used of situations and events that were much less impressive than expected. See also FIASCO, LEAD, LEMON.

damper

It can stop the vibration of piano strings, absorb shock in cars and regulate the draught in chimneys, but originally a **damper** was a person or thing that dampened the spirits. This is what to **put a damper on** refers to. Dampers can also take the edge off the appetite. In Australia and New Zealand an unleavened loaf or cake of flour and water was used for this purpose, and in the early 19th century this plain item of food acquired the name **damper**.

damsel

Any knight in shining armour worth his salt in a tale of chivalry scoured the country looking for a **damsel in distress** to rescue. Nowadays she may be less helpless, but a girl can still get into trouble and need a helping hand. **Damsel** is based on Latin *domina* 'mistress', which is also the source of DAME and of modern French *mademoiselle*.

dance

The word **dance** stepped into English from French in the Middle Ages. Many dances have since been danced, but none more sinister than the **dance of death**. This was a medieval image in which Death led all types of people to the grave, emphasising that everyone was equally faced with death. It was also known under its French name **danse macabre** (see MACABRE).

The unlucky person who had to **dance attendance on someone** was kept waiting in an antechamber before being called in to speak to the elevated personage they had come to see. There they would no doubt fidget and kick their heels, as if dancing.

dandy

Dandies emerged in the late 18th century. The word is perhaps a shortened form of **Jack-a-dandy**, a 17th-century term for a conceited fellow, where **dandy** is a pet form of the name Andrew. The original dandies, such as Beau Brummel, were not flamboyant, but understated and elegant. They reacted against the wigs and knee breeches of an older generation, and pioneered the forerunner of the business suit. Dandy quickly became a term of approval for anything of high quality, a use which continues in US expressions such as **fine and dandy**. See also DUDE.

dandelion

The toothed leaves of the dandelion give it away. The name came into English in the late Middle Ages from French **dent-de-lion**, 'lion's tooth'. In France, though, the usual term for the flower is the less poetic **pissenlit**, which has a parallel in English **pissabed**, also a name for the dandelion. The plant has long been known as a diuretic.

danger

From the early Middle Ages into the 19th century **danger** meant 'jurisdiction, power', originally 'the power of a lord and master, power to harm'. This reflects its origin in Latin *dominus* 'lord', the root of which also gave us DAME, **dominate**, **dominion** and DUNGEON. In the later Middle Ages **danger** developed into 'the possibility of suffering harm or injury', which is the main modern sense.

Darby and Joan

An anonymous poem of 1735 in *The Gentleman's Magazine* contained the lines:

Old Darby, with Joan by his side,
You've often regarded with wonder:
He's dropsical, she is sore-eyed,
Yet they're never happy asunder.

People quickly began to use the names, whose exact origin is unknown, for any devoted old married couple.

dare

This is a word with the deepest roots, related to forms in Greek and in Sanskrit, the ancient language of India. It originally meant 'to have the courage to do something'. By the late 16th century there also existed the sense 'to challenge or defy someone', which is the meaning behind **daredevil**, a contraction of 'someone ready to dare the devil'. This sort of formation is also seen in **cut-throat** and **scarecrow**.

dark

The origins of **dark** are mysterious, although it may be related to German *tarnen* 'to conceal'. Ideas of secrecy and mystery are behind such phrases as to **keep someone in the dark** and **a dark secret**. Also mysterious is the **Dark Lady**, the anonymous woman to whom Shakespeare dedicated some of his sonnets. Although there have been various suggestions as to who she was, the lady has never been certainly identified.

A **dark night of the soul** is a period of great depression or soul-searching. The phrase was used by F. Scott Fitzgerald, author of *The Great Gatsby*, in 1936: 'In a real dark night of the soul it is always three o'clock in the morning.' It originated in the title of a poem by the Spanish mystic and poet St John of the Cross, *Noche oscura*, 'Dark Night', which was rendered by a Victorian translator as 'Dark Night of the Soul'.

One of the most famous opening lines in literature is 'It was a dark and stormy night', which begins *Paul Clifford* (1830) by the British novelist and politician Lord Edward Bulwer-Lytton. Today his name is a byword for bad writing, and there is an annual Bulwer-Lytton Fiction Contest for bad writing in the USA, but in his lifetime he was a successful writer who also became an MP and coined the phrases 'the great unwashed' and 'the pen is mightier than the sword'.

Davy Jones's locker

A sailors' term for the bottom of the sea, especially as the last resting place of drowned sailors. The earliest recorded use of the phrase is in Tobias Smollett's novel *The Adventures of Peregrine Pickle*, published in 1751, where Davy Jones is described as 'the fiend that presides over all the evil spirits of the deep'. One suggestion is that Davy is the devil, because both words contain the letters *d* and *v*. Another has Jones as an alteration of the name Jonah, recalling the tale of Jonah and the whale in the Bible. Colourful though these ideas may be, it is just as likely that the original Davy Jones was simply a pirate who drowned at sea: as with many phrases, we will never know the truth.

day

The ancient word **day** is related to Dutch *dag* and German *Tag*, both meaning 'day'. Their root may have meant 'to burn', through association with the heat of summer.

The **working day** came with increasing industrialisation, in the early 19th century. This is the day you refer to if you **call it a day**, 'decide to stop doing something'. In the mid 19th century, when working people had fewer holidays, the expression was to **call it half a day**. If something unusual is **all in a day's work**, it is taken in your stride, as part of your normal routine. Jonathan Swift's *Polite Conversations*, which mocked the clichés of 18th-century society, suggest that the phrase was in circulation even then.

Daylight dawned in the early Middle Ages. It was always associated with seeing, and in the mid 18th century **daylights** appeared as a term for the eyes. This is not the meaning in to **beat the living daylights out of someone**, where 'daylights' are the vital organs, such as the heart, lungs and liver. The phrase implies a beating so violent that it would cause severe internal injuries. The word 'living' is a later addition to the phrase, from the late 19th century.

Days of wine and roses are times of pleasure, which will inevitably pass. The phrase comes from a line in a poem by the 19th-century poet Ernest Dowson: 'They are not long, the days of wine and roses'.

dead

An Old English word related to Dutch *dood* and German *Tod* 'death', and to **death** itself. Their shared ancestor is the origin of DIE.

Often it is not enough to be dead: someone must be **as dead as a doornail** or as a DODO. The comparison with the extinct dodo is understandable enough, but it is not clear why doornails are particularly associated with death. A doornail was one of the large iron studs that were once used on doors to give additional strength or simply for decoration. It may also have been the large stud struck by the knocker, which, subject to constant pounding, could be considered well and truly dead. The phrase goes right back to the Middle Ages and was used by Shakespeare, in whose time a person could also be **as dead as a herring**.

> That **nothing is certain but death and taxes** has been a view since the early 18th century.

Death has prompted many reflections on the human condition. The Roman poet Claudian wrote *omnia mors aequat*, 'death levels all' – in English **death is the great leveller**. Shakespeare's *The Tempest* contains the line 'He that dies pays all debts', a thought that had become **death pays all debts** by the time of the novelist Sir Walter Scott.

deadline

Modern deadlines are frightening enough for most people, but the original **deadline** was grimmer still. It was a line drawn around a military prison, beyond which any prisoner was liable to be shot. It is first mentioned in a document of the 1860s.

deaf

The ancient ancestor of **deaf** also produced Greek *tuphlos* 'blind'. It probably referred to general dullness in perception, rather than dullness in any particular sense.

Emphatic comparisons include **as deaf as an adder** and **as deaf as a post**. The traditional deafness of an adder is based on an image in the Psalms, 'the deaf adder that stoppeth her ear'. Actually, all snakes are deaf, not just the adder – they 'hear' by means of sensors that pick up vibrations in the ground such as footsteps.

decade

One of the works of the Roman historian Livy, who lived at the time of Christ, was in ten parts, and the name for each division was translated into English as **decade**. The earliest uses of the word in English, from the late Middle Ages, refer to the sections of a literary work with ten books or parts. The word did not come to refer to a period of ten years until the early 17th century. The root of **decade**, Greek *deka* 'ten', is also that of **decimal**, DECIMATE and of the first element of units such as the **decilitre** and **decimetre**.

decimate

When Roman legions mutinied, they would be decimated – one in every ten men would be selected by lot and executed. In its first recorded use in English, in the late 16th century, **decimate** refers to this practice, but by the mid 17th century people were using it of other acts of killing, destroying or removing one in ten. They then lost sight of the military context, and soon any severe loss or destruction could be described as decimation. See also DECADE.

deck

Originally **deck** was a material such as canvas that was used as a covering, especially on a ship. The word then came to mean the covering itself, and by the end of the 15th century also the platform of planks extending across a ship.

A pack of cards is usually called a deck in the USA, and the term was formerly also British – it is recorded in Shakespeare. The definition in Dr Johnson's *Dictionary of the English Language,* published in 1755, indicates the idea behind the term: 'A pack of cards piled regularly on each other'. The cards are like the decks of a ship. In the USA a person who is **not playing with a full deck** is very unintelligent. In Britain they would be **not the full shilling** (see SHILLING).

As a verb **deck** meant 'to decorate, adorn', as in 'Deck the halls with boughs of holly', from the early 16th century. In the 1940s a new meaning arose in the USA , 'to knock someone to the ground with a punch', probably from the naval expression **hit the deck**, which originally meant 'jump out of bed for a morning roll call'.

decoy

A **decoy** was originally a pond with net-covered channels into which ducks and other wildfowl were enticed to be captured. The wildfowl were attracted by a **decoy duck**, a tame duck trained for the purpose or an imitation duck placed on the water. **Decoy** dates from the early 17th century and probably comes from Dutch *de kooi* 'the decoy', the second element of which goes back to Latin *cavea* CAVE.

In military use a decoy may be a fake tank designed to be mistaken by bomber aircraft for a real one, or a merchant ship with concealed weapons, of a kind which the British and Americans used against German submarines in the First and Second World Wars. The defenceless appearance of the decoy vessel would encourage a U-boat to surface and attack it, whereupon the decoy would unveil its guns and sink the submarine. The decoy vessels were also called **Q-ships** – the reason for the 'Q' is unknown.

deep

The word **deep** is related to **dip** and in Old English could also mean **depth**. The phrase **in deep water**, 'in trouble or difficulty', has biblical origins. The writer of one of the Psalms begged, 'Let me be delivered from them that hate me, and out of the deep waters'. The deep waters of a swimming pool did not provide linguistic inspiration until the 20th century, when pools became familiar facilities, often with a diving board at the deep end. If you **go off the deep end** you have an emotional outburst, especially of anger, and to **jump** (or **be thrown**) **in at the deep end** is to face a difficult undertaking with little or no preparation or experience.

degree

The source of **degree** is a French word based on Latin *de-* 'down' and *gradus* 'step'. Early senses of the word include 'step, tier', 'rank' and 'relative state'. The use of **degree** for an academic qualification arose from the medieval Mastership or Doctorate, which was attained in stages or degrees.

deign

To **deign** is to do something that you consider beneath your dignity, and the word is bound up with 'dignity'. It goes back to Latin *dignare* 'to judge to be worthy', which was formed from *dignus* 'worthy', the source of **dignity** and **dignify** and similar words.

deliberate

The word **deliberate** 'done intentionally' is older than the closely related, but slightly differently pronounced, **deliberate** 'to engage in long and careful consideration'. The first appeared in the Middle Ages, the second in the mid 16th century. Both go back to a Latin word formed from *libra* 'scales', which captured the idea of weighing something up before coming to a conclusion. See also LIBRA.

In the early 18th century the essayist and dramatist Joseph Addison wrote that 'When love once pleads admission to our hearts . . . The woman that deliberates is lost'. This is the forerunner of the modern proverb **he who hesitates is lost**, which is not recorded until more than 150 years later.

delight

For the first three centuries of its life **delight** was spelled *delit*, as was its French original. The *-gh-* spelling emerged in the 16th century, on the model of **light** and other native English words. **Delight** has no direct connection with LIGHT, though, but goes back ultimately to Latin *delectare* 'to charm'.

The English name of the sweet **Turkish delight** was originally **lumps of delight** (recorded from 1861). It was still a novelty when Charles Dickens wrote in his unfinished novel *The Mystery of Edwin Drood*: '"I want to go to the Lumps-of-Delight shop." "To the —?" "A Turkish sweetmeat, sir."' The first known written record of the name Turkish delight is from 1872.

deliver

In the Middle Ages **deliver** emerged from French, but it goes back to Latin *liber* 'free', which is also the source of LIBERTY. The word has been used for taking and handing over letters and goods since the late Middle Ages. The phrase to **deliver the goods**, 'to provide what is promised and expected', is from the USA, and the first known examples are from political debate in the 1870s. Highwaymen really did tell their victims to **stand and deliver** – the phrase is mentioned in an early 18th-century account of the lives of highwaymen.

deer

To an Anglo-Saxon a **deer** could be any four-footed creature. Then, in the Middle Ages, the meaning narrowed down to the grazing animal we know today. The word itself goes far back to the oldest ancestor of European and Indian languages, to a root that meant simply 'breathing creature'.

delta

The triangular area of sediment at the mouth of some rivers takes the name **delta** from its shape, which is like that of the fourth letter of the Greek alphabet, called delta. The original delta was at the mouth of the River Nile, which was called **the Delta** from the mid 16th century. The shape of the Greek letter also gave its name to the **delta wing**, a triangular swept-back wing fitted on some jet aircraft, immediately after the Second World War.

demagogue

In ancient Greece a **demagogue** was a leader or orator who stood up for the ordinary people against any other party in the state. The Greek word was formed from *dēmos* 'the people' (also the root of DEMOCRACY) and *agōgos* 'leading'. It would have been familiar to the educated people of the 17th century, whose chief subject of study was the classics. At the time of the English Civil War supporters of Charles I began to use **demagogue** with negative overtones, as an insult to his Parliamentary opponents, implying a political agitator who appeals to emotions rather than reason to promote his own interests. This is the primary sense that the word bears to this day.

democracy

The word **democracy** came directly from French in the mid 16th century, but it goes back to Greek *dēmokratia*, from *dēmos* 'the people' (also part of DEMAGOGUE and **epidemic**) and *kratia* 'power, rule'. There have been many critics of this system of government, and democracy has taken different forms in different places and at different times. Winston Churchill summed it up in a speech to the House of Commons in 1947 when he said: 'It has been said that democracy is the worst form of government except all those other forms that have been tried from time to time.'

demon

The Greek word *daimōn* is the root of **demon**. In ancient Greek thought a demon or daemon was a divine or supernatural being of a kind between gods and humans, or an attendant spirit or inspiring force. These demons were not evil at all. The evil kind did not appear until the writing of the Septuagint, a Greek version of the Old Testament, in the 3rd and 2nd centuries BC.

In Australia and New Zealand **demon** is a word for a police officer. This could be from **Van Dieman's Land**, an early name for Tasmania, or from **dee**, an old slang term for a detective, and MAN. Either way, the criminals who first used it probably considered the usual sense of demon to be appropriate. See also DEVIL.

denigrate

To **denigrate** someone is to blacken their reputation. The original meaning of the word, in the late Middle Ages, was 'to make black or dark in colour'; the modern sense developed in the early 16th century. The root of the word is Latin *niger* 'black'.

denim see JEANS.

depot

Latin *depositum*, 'something put down', is the source of both **depot** and **deposit**, although **depot** entered English from French *dépôt*. The earliest meaning of **depot** was 'an act of depositing' rather than 'a place for storage', as it is now. The earliest depots were military establishments, for stores, assembled recruits and even prisoners of war.

Derby

The 12th Earl of Derby founded the Epsom Derby, an annual race for three-year-old horses, in 1780. The simple form **Derby** as the name of the race is not recorded until the mid 19th century; 50 or so years later horse races in other countries, such as the Kentucky Derby in the USA, acquired the title. The significance of the event invited comparisons, and in the early 20th century different sporting events appropriated the name. In 1914 *The Daily Express* referred to 'a local Derby between Liverpool and Everton' – always keen footballing rivals.

Derby is also the US name for a bowler hat, and people attribute this to American demand for a hat of the type worn at the English Derby. The name first appeared in the late 19th century.

desert

There are three words spelled **desert**, two of which are related. The word for 'a waterless, desolate area' and the (differently pronounced) word meaning 'to abandon' both ultimately go back to Latin *deserere* 'to leave, forsake'. The third **desert** usually appears in phrases such as to **get your just deserts**, 'to receive what you deserve, usually appropriate punishment'. It derives from Latin *deservire* 'to serve well', the source

of **deserve**. The **dessert** with two s's, meaning 'a sweet course served at the end of a meal', is from French *desservir* 'to clear the table'.

desperado

It looks like a Spanish word, but **desperado** is almost certainly one hundred per cent English – a pseudo-Spanish alteration of **desperate**, probably created to sound more impressive and emphatic. Between the early 17th and early 18th centuries a *desperate* was a desperate or reckless person, just like a desperado. An earlier meaning was 'a person in despair or in a desperate situation', which developed into 'a person made reckless by despair'. In both senses **desperate** is earlier than **desperado**, but the more exotic form ousted the original. The ultimate origin of **desperate** is Latin *desperare* 'to deprive of hope', the source of **despair**.

detective

The development of an organised police force demanded a word such as **detective**, and it was duly formed in the 1840s from **detect**. The first occurrences are in **detective police** and **detective policeman**; simple **detective** is a shortening of the latter. Charles Dickens was one of the earliest to draw attention to this innovation, reporting in his magazine *Household Words* in 1850 that 'To each division of the Force is attached two officers, who are denominated "detectives".' See also PRIVATE, SLEUTH.

deuce

Where the deuce did **deuce** come from? The answer is: from Latin *duus* 'two', by two routes. The earliest meaning of the word, from the late 15th century, was 'a throw of two at dice'. The immediate source was the French word for 'two' (modern *deux*). In the mid 17th century this was reinforced by German *duus*, meaning 'bad luck or mischief' and by association 'the devil'. The connection arose because two is the worst or unluckiest throw you can have when playing with two dice. Expressions where deuce is interchangeable with devil (as in 'where the deuce . . .' or 'a deuce of a . . .') are now rather old-fashioned.

When the term entered English in the late 16th century, **deuce** was a stage in the original form of tennis, now known as real tennis, which is played with a solid ball on an enclosed court. In real tennis deuce is five or more games all; in modern tennis it is 40 points all, where either side must win two consecutive points to win the game. See also LOVE.

device

The original sense of **device**, recorded from the Middle Ages, was 'desire, intention', which is found now only in to **leave a person to their own devices**. It does occur in the title of the novel *Devices and Desires* by the crime writer P.D. James, taken from the *Book of Common Prayer*: 'We have erred, and strayed from thy ways like lost sheep. We have followed too much the devices and desires of our own hearts.'

The source of **device** is a French form based on Latin *dividere* 'to divide'. Its sense developed from 'desire, intention' to 'a plan, scheme, trick' and then the usual modern meaning of 'a thing made or adapted for a particular purpose'.

devil

The English word **devil**, like the corresponding Dutch form *duivel* and German *Teufel*, goes back to Greek *diabolos* 'accuser, slanderer', the source also of **diabolic** and similar words. In the Septuagint, a Greek version of the Hebrew Bible written in the 3rd and 2nd centuries BC, *diabolos* translated the Hebrew word for 'Satan'.

The devil permeates popular wisdom. **The devil finds work for idle hands to do** appears first in the *Divine Songs* of the 18th-century hymn-writer Isaac Watts, but goes back to the letters of St Jerome, who lived *c*.342-420. **Why should the devil have all the best tunes?** is a question that has been attributed to the Victorian evangelist Rowland Hill, who encouraged the singing of hymns to popular melodies.

The words **speak** or **talk of the devil** are often uttered when a person appears just after being mentioned. The expression dates back to the mid 17th century and comes from the superstition that if you speak the devil's name aloud he will suddenly appear.

The expression **the devil to pay**, 'serious trouble to be expected', is often said to have a nautical origin. The seam near a ship's keel was sometimes known as 'the devil', and because of its position was very difficult to 'pay', or seal with pitch or tar. There is not much evidence for this theory, though, and it is more probable that the phrase was a reference to a pact made with Satan, like that of Faust's, and to the inevitable payment to be made to him in the end.

Shakespeare used the proverb **needs must when the Devil drives**, 'sometimes you have to do something that you would rather not', in *All's Well that Ends Well*, but he did not invent it: it is first found in a medieval work called *The Assembly of the Gods*. **Needs must** here means 'one needs must', or in today's language 'one must' or 'you must'. See also ANGEL, DEMON, DEUCE, EVERY, FALL.

dexterous

The first meaning of **dexterous** was 'clever, mentally agile'. A little later it began to refer to physical coordination, and 'having skill with the hands' remains the primary modern sense. The word goes back to the Latin word *dexter* 'on the right', which is also the root of **dexterity**: people have traditionally associated right-handedness with manual skill. See also AMBIDEXTROUS, SINISTER.

play devil's advocate

Pope Sixtus V appointed the first devil's advocate in 1587 to challenge any proposal to turn a dead person into a saint. The aim was to present everything known about the candidate, including negative aspects, and so make sure the case was examined fairly from all sides.

dial

The earliest senses of **dial** were 'a mariner's compass', 'sundial' and 'the face of a clock or watch' – all round objects marked out with gradations. The old slang meaning 'a person's face' would have been suggested by the fact that faces are roundish. The word's immediate source was medieval Latin *diale* 'clock dial', which came from Latin *dies* 'day', also the source of **diary**. See also CLOCK.

diamond

The name of the gem derives from a medieval Latin alteration of Latin *adamans* ADAMANT. Adamant was a legendary rock or mineral with many supposed properties. One of these was hardness, which was a reason why people in the 15th and 16th centuries sometimes identified it with diamond.

A diamond is forever was used as an advertising slogan for De Beers Consolidated Mines from the late 1940s onwards, and in 1956 Ian Fleming used *Diamonds are Forever* as the title of his latest James Bond thriller, but the idea was first expressed by the American writer Anita Loos, in *Gentlemen Prefer Blondes* (1925):

I really think that American gentlemen are the best after all, because kissing your hand may make you feel very very good but a diamond and safire bracelet lasts forever.

Marilyn Monroe shows off her rocks in the film *Gentlemen Prefer Blondes*.

'Diamonds are a Girl's Best Friend' was a song written by Leo Robin and Jule Styne for the 1949 stage musical *Gentlemen Prefer Blondes*. Marilyn Monroe made the song her own in the 1953 film version. See also EMERALD, ROUGH.

diaper

In the USA babies wear diapers not nappies. This is because the pads were originally made of **diaper**, a linen or cotton fabric woven in a repeating pattern of small diamonds. Napkins, towels and cloths could also be diapers in Britain from the late 16th century, but **napkin** (which later became **nappy**) came to predominate in babywear. Before the 15th century diaper appears to have been a costly fabric of silk woven with gold thread, not something to warm and protect a baby's bottom. The original elements of the word are Greek *dia-* 'through, across' and *aspros* 'white', the overall sense being either 'white at intervals' or 'pure white'.

dice

Originally – and still in the USA – a gambler would throw two **dice** but one **die**. This singular form is now rare in British English, surviving mainly in **the die is cast**, 'something has happened that cannot be undone'. The word came from Latin *datum* 'something given', a form of *dare* 'to give'. This was interpreted as 'something given by chance or fortune' and applied to the dice determining the outcome of chance. See also BODICE.

Playing or gambling with dice is the idea behind **dicing with death**. Journalists began to use the expression in the early 20th century to convey the risks taken by racing drivers in the pursuit of success in their risky sport. It is probably the source of the adjective **dicey** meaning 'dangerous', first used by RAF pilots in the 1950s.

dicky

The informal British word **dicky**, meaning 'not strong, healthy or functioning reliably', dates from the late 18th century, when it had the sense 'almost over'. The origin is not certain, but it may be from the given name Dick, in the old saying **as queer as Dick's hatband**. The pet form of Richard may also be behind **dicky bird**, a child's name for a bird. In **not a dicky bird**, 'nothing at all', it is rhyming slang for 'word'.

dictionary see feature on DR JOHNSON'S DICTIONARY.

diddle

In the farce *Raising the Wind* (1803) by the Irish dramatist James Kenney, the character Jeremy Diddler constantly borrows and fails to repay small sums of money. The informal term **diddle**, 'to swindle or cheat', appeared soon after the play's production, and is probably testimony to the impact the character made. The name Diddler may be based on an earlier word **diddle** (more often **daddle**), which meant 'to walk unsteadily'.

die

In surviving Old English texts the usual way of saying 'to stop living' is to STARVE or to **swelt**, or by a phrase incorporating the word DEAD. The form **swelt** survived in dialect, but has probably now died out. **Die** appeared in the early Middle Ages and came from an old Scandinavian word.

To **die hard**, 'to disappear or change very slowly', is now generally used of habits or customs, but its origins lie in public executions. It was originally used in the 1780s to describe criminals who died struggling to their last breath on the infamous Tyburn gallows in London. A few years later, during the Peninsular War (fought between France and Britain in Spain and Portugal from 1808 to 1814), Lieutenant-Colonel Sir William Inglis, commander of the 57th Regiment of Foot, lay severely wounded on the front line of the Battle of Albuera. He refused to be carried to safety, and urged his men to 'Die hard!' They followed his brave example, sustaining heavy loss of life, and all of the dead were found with their wounds on the front of their bodies. The battle was eventually won, and their heroism earned them the nickname 'the Die-hards'. In the early 20th century political circles took up the name to describe those who were determinedly opposed to reform, and the term **diehard** can still refer to someone who is stubbornly conservative or reactionary. *Die Hard* was also the title of the first of a trilogy of action movies released between 1988 and 1995 and starring the US actor Bruce Willis.

diet

In the context of food **diet** reaches back to Greek *diaita* 'way of life'. In the context of government and administration, for example as the name of the legislative assembly in some European countries, **diet** comes from medieval Latin *dieta*, which meant both 'a day's work or pay' and 'councillors'. Martin Luther committed himself to the cause of Protestant reform at the **Diet of Worms**, a meeting of the imperial diet of the Holy Roman Emperor Charles V in 1521 in the German town of Worms on the Rhine.

different

The word **different** came ultimately from a form of Latin *differre*, which gave us both **defer** and **differ**. The modern proverb **different strokes for different folks** is of US origin. It came to prominence in newspaper reports of comments made by Muhammad Ali about his knockout punches in fights with Sonny Liston, Floyd Patterson and Karl Mildenberger during the 1960s. In the saying **strokes** means 'comforting gestures of approval or congratulation', but Ali was making a pun on the word's other meaning, 'blows'. The phrase was popularised by the band Sly and the Family Stone in their 1968 hit 'Everyday People', and was used as the title of the US sitcom *Diff'rent Strokes*, which ran from 1978 to 1986.

digest

In AD 529 the Byzantine emperor Justinian ordered earlier Roman law to be gathered together and arranged systematically. Part of this codification was the *Digesta*, or opinions of lawyers – in Latin *digesta* meant 'matters methodically arranged'. Justinian's was the first **digest** known to English, and thereafter other collections of statements or information came to be called digests. In 1922 *The Reader's Digest* appeared in the USA. It was the first to use the name for a periodical consisting of condensed versions of pieces of writing or news that had been previously published elsewhere.

digit

We all count on our fingers, and the ten Arabic numerals from 0 to 9 neatly correspond to them. This is how Latin *digitus*, 'finger, toe', came down to us as **digit**, 'numeral', in the late Middle Ages. **Digital** dates from the late 15th century, and the technical use of the word in communications arose in the mid 20th century.

dilemma

Recorded from the early 16th century, **dilemma** was originally a technical term of rhetoric and logic. It referred particularly to a form of argument involving a choice between equally unfavourable alternatives. The expression **on the horns of a dilemma** captures this notion of double difficulty. The word came into English from Greek *dilēmma*, from *di-* 'twice' and *lēmma* 'premise, assertion'. In popular use it came to mean 'a situation in which a difficult choice between alternatives has to be made', and now is even simply 'a difficult situation or problem'. See also HORN.

diminish

This is a medieval English blend of two obsolete words that share its meaning, 'to lessen': **diminue** and **minish**. Both ultimately go back to Latin *minutus* 'small', the source of MINUTE in the same sense.

In economics **the law of diminishing returns** draws attention to the point at which profits are less than the amount of money invested. It originated in the first half of the 19th century with reference to profits from agriculture.

dinkum

In the late 19th century **dinkum**, an English dialect word meaning 'hard work, honest toil', travelled to the other side of the world and took up residence in Australasia. It retired during the 20th century, but lived on in numerous popular expressions. In **fair dinkum** it can describe an honest, straightforward person, a genuine article or acceptable behaviour, and is particularly used to emphasise or seek confirmation of the genuineness or truth of something.

Dinky toys negotiate Piccadilly Circus in an advertisement from the 1950s.

dinky

In Scottish and northern English dialect **dink** meant 'neatly dressed, spruce, trim'. Its origins are unknown, and it remained restricted to northern Britain. But from the late 18th century its derivative **dinky** spread: throughout Britain it means 'attractively small and neat', in the USA 'disappointingly small, insignificant'. In 1934 **Dinky toys** appeared, and these small but perfectly formed model cars are probably the first thing that come to many people's minds when they hear the word.

In the 1980s another word **dinky** appeared, meaning 'a partner in a well-off working couple with no children'. This is formed from elements of 'double income, no kids yet', and was inspired by YUPPIE.

dinner

Our words **dine** and **dinner** are both from the same root, Old French *desjeuner* 'to have breakfast', which survives in modern French as *déjeuner*, 'lunch', and *petit déjeuner*, 'breakfast'. The root was *jēun* 'fasting', which goes back to Latin *jejunus* 'fasting, barren'.

In Australia, New Zealand and Canada to be **done like a dinner** is to be utterly defeated or outwitted – the British equivalent is **done like a kipper**. The messy and unappetising appearance of food set out for a dog is behind the expressions **a dog's dinner** (or **breakfast**), meaning 'a poor piece of work, a mess', and **dressed up like a dog's dinner**, 'wearing ridiculously smart or ostentatious clothes', which date from the 1930s.

dinosaur

The word **dinosaur** was coined in 1841, from Greek words meaning 'terrible lizard'. People or things that have not adapted to changing times have been condemned as dinosaurs since the 1950s.

dint

The phrase **by dint of** 'by means of' has violent origins. A **dint** was originally a stroke or blow with a weapon, and by dint of meant 'by force of', as in **by dint of sword**, an obsolete way of saying 'by force of arms'.

dirt

The origin of **dirt** is old Scandinavian *drit* 'excrement'. In its earliest uses the English word retained both the meaning and the form, but gradually dirt superseded drit. Its history here parallels that of BIRD (earlier *brid*). By the time **dirty** appeared, in the later Middle Ages, *dirt* appears to have been the only form in use. The sense 'obscene, pornographic, smutty' dates from the 16th century, though most familiar phrases such as **dirty joke** and **dirty weekend** are first recorded in the 20th century.

disappear

The usual sense of **disappear**, 'to cease to be visible', appeared in the late Middle Ages. In the late 20th century English acquired a new construction, in which a person could be 'disappeared' – abducted or arrested for political reasons and secretly killed or detained without public knowledge. This came from Latin America, especially Argentina, and involves a translation of American Spanish *desaparecido*, a word which was applied to the many people who 'disappeared' under military rule in the 1970s.

disc

Disc goes back to Latin *discus*, which is the source of **discus** and also of DISH and **desk**. Its earliest sense in English was the seemingly flat, round form that the sun, moon and other celestial objects present to the eye. The anatomical **disc**, the sort that people 'slip', dates from the late 19th century, as does the type that turns on a record player. In the USA the usual spelling is disk, and this is now used everywhere with reference to computers, as in **floppy disk** and **disk drive**. See also JOCKEY.

discretion

In Latin *discretio* developed from 'separation' to 'fine judgement', an ability to separate ideas. This is essentially the sense in which it entered English in the Middle Ages. The proverb **discretion is the better part of valour** was familiar in Shakespeare's time. His fat, jolly, debauched – and cowardly – character Sir John Falstaff declares: 'The better part of valour is discretion; in the which better part, I have saved my life.' The idea is even older, having a parallel in the works of the Greek dramatist Euripides in the 5th century BC.

disease

At first **disease** was 'lack of ease, inconvenience, trouble', the meaning of the word in French, from which English adopted it in the early Middle Ages.

The 'lack of ease' soon became associated with illness, and the original sense became obsolete.

disgruntled

Disgruntled people may go round muttering to themselves and complaining. Originally the word involved comparison with a pig making small or subdued grunts. The main element of **disgruntled** is **gruntle**, a dialect word used of pigs from the Middle Ages and of grumbling people from a little later. In the 17th century someone added *dis-* as an intensifier and created **disgruntled**. In the 20th century the comic novelist P.G. Wodehouse removed the *dis-* again and introduced the humorous **gruntled**, 'pleased'. In *The Code of the Woosters*, published in 1938, he wrote: 'I could see that, if not actually disgruntled, he was far from being gruntled.'

dish

Despite appearances, **dish** is related to **desk**, which explains why corresponding forms in Dutch and German (*disch* and *Tisch*) mean 'table'. All derive from Latin *discus* (see DISC), which English took directly from Latin. Dishes remained containers until the 20th century, when technology gave us the dish-shaped aerial and the modern satellite dish. The sense 'a good-looking person' took off in the USA in the early 20th century, as did **dish the dirt**, 'to reveal scandal or gossip'.

discotheque

France gave us the **discothèque**. At first it was a record library, on the model of **bibliothèque** 'library', then a club where people danced to recorded music. English writers commented on the French discothèque in the 1950s, and by the 1960s the English-speaking world had opened its own discotheques. The USA quickly shortened the word to disco.

dishevelled

In the pre-shampoo days when no respectable man or woman would dream of going out without a hat, headscarf or similar head covering, anyone seen bare-headed would be regarded as very scruffy and **dishevelled**. The word comes from Old French *chevel* 'hair', from Latin *capillus*, the source also of **capillary**. The original sense was 'having the hair uncovered', then, referring to the hair itself, 'hanging loose', hence 'disordered, untidy'.

dismal

This word originally referred to 24 days, two in each month, that medieval people believed to be unlucky. The name derives from Latin *dies mali* 'evil days', and first appeared in English in the early Middle Ages as **the dismal**. This was quickly spelled out more clearly as the **dismal days**. Soon dismal days could be any time of disaster, gloom or depression, or the time of old age. In 1849 the Scottish historian and political philosopher Thomas Carlyle nicknamed the difficult subject of economics (then known as 'political economy') the **dismal science**. In the 20th century the word lightened up to take in 'pitifully bad', as in the performance of many a football team.

distance

The distant origin of **distance** lies in Latin *distare* 'to stand apart'. The apartness may be physical, as in the distance between two places, or intellectual. The earliest senses of **distance** in English are 'discord, debate' and 'a disagreement, a quarrel'.

The expression to **go the distance**, 'to last for a long time', has its roots in the world of boxing, although it is also used in other sports. A boxer who 'goes the distance' manages to complete a fight without being knocked out, while a boxing match similarly described is one that lasts the scheduled length. In baseball, the phrase is used to mean 'to pitch for the entire length of an inning', and in horse racing a horse that can 'go the distance' can run the full length of a race without tiring.

ditto

A Tuscan dialect form of Italian *detto* 'said', from Latin *dictus*, is the root of **ditto**. In the 17th century it meant in Italian '(in) the aforesaid month'. English merchants began to use it in accounts and lists, where the word is usually represented by double apostrophes (**ditto marks**) under the word or figure to be repeated: the symbol would be read out as 'ditto'. In the later 18th century clothiers and tailors used it as shorthand for 'the same material', and a **suit of dittos** was a suit of the same material and colour throughout.

divan

The **divan** travelled across Europe from the court of the Ottoman Empire in the East. The Ottoman divan was its privy council, presided over by the Sultan or his highest official, the grand vizier. Travellers first referred to it in English in the late 16th century. Turkish *dīvān* came from a Persian word with a range of meanings: 'brochure', 'anthology', 'register', 'court' and 'bench'. The last gave rise to the usual sense of **divan** in English, a piece of furniture. Originally, a divan was a low bench

or raised part of a floor forming a seat against the wall of a room, a style which was common in Middle Eastern countries. European imitations of this led to the sense 'a low flat sofa or bed' in the late 19th century.

divide

English adopted **divide** from Latin *dividere* 'to force apart, remove' in the Middle Ages. The maxim **divide and rule**, recommending that a ruler or government set factions against each other so that they will not unite against the powers that be, is also of Latin origin: *divide et impera*. People often attribute it to the Renaissance Italian statesman and political philosopher Machiavelli (see MACHIAVELLIAN), but in fact he denounced the principle. See also WIDOW.

divorce

In early times **divorce** covered many ways of ending a marriage: one spouse could simply leave or send the other away; the marriage could be annulled, declared invalid from the beginning (as in the divorce of Henry VIII from Catherine of Aragon); or the couple could formally enter into a legal separation. The word itself is recorded from the late Middle Ages and came from Latin *divortium*, based on *divertere* 'to turn in separate ways'. A divorced person has been a **divorcee** since the early 19th century. The term came from French, and at first usually appeared in its French forms, *divorcée* for a woman and *divorcé* for a man.

dizzy

A **dizzy** Anglo-Saxon was 'foolish'. In the Middle Ages you could have 'a whirling feeling in the head', which led to 'scatterbrained' and in late 19th-century USA to the **dizzy blonde**, an expert performer and danger to respectable men. The blonde who had been dizzy from the 1870s became the **dumb blonde** in the 1930s.

dock

In a criminal courtroom **dock** is the official term for the enclosure where a defendant stands or sits. It was not always so orderly: originally a dock was crammed full of the thieves and petty criminals whose trial was scheduled for the day. The word may well be identical with Flemish *dok* 'chicken coop, rabbit hutch'. The **dock** meaning 'area of water for the loading, unloading or repair of ships' has a parallel in Dutch *dok* and early German forms, but its earlier history is lost. The plant **dock**, effective against nettle stings, is the oldest of the group, being recorded in Old English.

doctor

The Latin word *doctor* meant 'teacher', and its root, *docere* 'to teach', is the source of **docile**, **doctrine** and **document**. In medieval English **doctor** first meant 'teacher' or 'learned person', although the medical meaning arose in the later medieval period. See also APPLE.

dodo

The **dodo** was a large, heavily built flightless bird found on the island of Mauritius in the Indian Ocean until it was hunted to extinction. The reason for its fate was apparently its lack of fear of human beings. When sailors and colonists came to the island in the 16th and 17th centuries they discovered that the unfortunate bird was very easy to catch and kill, a characteristic which gave it its name: **dodo** comes from Portuguese *duodo*, meaning 'simpleton'. By the end of the 17th century the dodo had died out. Its fate prompted the expression **as dead as a dodo**, 'completely dead or extinct'. See also DEAD.

doff

To **doff**, 'to remove an item of clothing, especially a hat', is a contraction of to **do off**. It has an exact parallel in **don**, 'to put on', which was originally to **do on**. Both forms date from the late Middle Ages.

dog

The word **dog** appears only once in surviving Old English literature, and until the Middle Ages HOUND was the ordinary word for a dog. Many proverbial images and sayings take their inspiration from this sometimes loved, sometimes despised animal. In the past dogs would have been ownerless animals living on their wits on the fringes of human habitation, sometimes tolerated and sometimes driven away. They were generally poor, scorned creatures, as is shown by phrases like **a dog's life**, **not have a dog's chance**, and **to treat someone like a dog**. For something to **go to the dogs** is certainly undesirable, but even such luckless animals might sometimes get hold of a tasty treat or a warm bed, for **every dog has its day**.

Dogs can be savage, and **dog eat dog** signifies a situation of fierce competition in which people are willing to harm each other in order to succeed. This rather chillingly makes reference to, and reverses, the proverb **dog does not eat dog**, which dates back to the mid 16th century in English and has a precursor in Latin *canis caninam non est*, 'a dog does not eat dog's flesh'. **Every dog is allowed one bite** is based on the rule, probably dating from the 17th century, by which an animal's owner was not liable for harm done by it unless he knew of its vicious tendencies.

A **dog in the manger**, 'a person inclined to prevent others having or using things that they do not want or need themselves', derives from a fable in which a dog lies in a manger to prevent the ox and horse from eating hay. People have invoked the idea since the 16th century.

The idea of the dog being **man's best friend** seems to be a Victorian one. A pet dog is a faithful and well-loved animal, and for many owners it is a case of **love me, love my dog**. See also BOLLOCK, CANARY, DINNER, HAIR, HAVOC.

doldrums

To most people **the doldrums** refers to a state or period of stagnation or depression, but to sailors it is an equatorial region of the Atlantic Ocean with calms, sudden storms and light unpredictable winds. In the days of sailing ships, being becalmed in the doldrums was a serious occupational hazard. The earliest form of the word, in the late 18th century, was singular *doldrum*, and it meant 'a dull, sluggish or stupid person'. It may come from **dull**, which originally meant 'stupid'.

doll

The word Doll started life as a pet form of the name Dorothy, and a **doll** was originally a man's 'pet' or lover. The sense 'small model of a human figure' dates from the late 17th century – before this time people used **poppet** or PUPPET to refer to the child's toy. The sense 'attractive girl' is US slang from the 1840s. See also BABY, DAME.

dolphin

The name for this small whale goes back through French and Latin to Greek *delphin*. The form **delphin** existed in English from the early Middle Ages, but **dolphin**, from its French equivalent, appeared in the later Middle Ages and finally ousted the earlier word during the 17th century. In another guise the French word entered English as **dauphin**, the eldest son of the king of France. This is from the family name of the lords of the Dauphiné, an area of southeast France. In 1349 the future Charles V acquired the lands and title of the Dauphiné, and when he became king he ceded both to his eldest son, establishing the pattern of passing them to the Crown prince.

dome

Latin *domus* 'house' entered English directly as **dome** in the 16th century in the sense 'a stately building'; it also passed through Italian *duomo* and French *dôme* to enter English for a second time as **dome** 'a rounded vault' in the mid 17th century. In Italian a duomo is a cathedral.

Towards the end of the 20th century **the Millennium Dome** was the name given to the circular structure built in Greenwich, London as part of the 2000 millennium celebrations and now a distinctive London landmark.

don see DOFF.

donkey

Before the late 18th century a donkey was an ASS. At first the word **donkey** was used only in slang and dialect, and its origin is lost. Early references indicate that it rhymed with MONKEY, and this has prompted some to suggest that it comes from the colour **dun** or from the man's name Duncan. The expression **for donkey's years**, 'for a very long time', is a pun referring to the length of a donkey's ears and playing on an old pronunciation of *ears* which was the same as that of *years*. The British expression **yonks**, with the same meaning, may derive from **for donkey's years**. See also EASEL.

doodle

If you are a doodler, you may not be pleased to know that the original meaning of **doodle** was 'a fool, a simpleton'. The word came from German *dudeltopf* or *dudeldopp* in the early 17th century. The modern senses, 'to scribble absent-mindedly' and 'a rough drawing', date from the 1930s.

The Second World War **doodlebug**, or German V-1 flying bomb, may have got its name from the 1930s slang sense 'a small car or railway locomotive', or from the English dialect use 'cockchafer'. A cockchafer is a large beetle which flies around slowly at dusk, making a deep hum.

doom

The ancient root of **doom** meant 'to put in place' and is also the root of **do**. By the time that written English records began the emphasis had narrowed to putting law and order in place: the Old English senses of **doom** include 'a law, statute', 'a judicial decision' and 'the right to judge'. In the context of the end of the world the word **judgement** was not used until the 16th century – before that the usual term for Judgement Day was **doomsday** (other early formulations include **the Last Day** and **the Day of Wrath**). In the Middle Ages this was also shortened to **doom**, a use that survives only in **the crack of doom**.

In 1086 William I (William the Conqueror) ordered his officials to gather information relating to all the land in his new kingdom of England, including its extent, value and ownership. The result was the **Domesday Book**. Domesday is an old spelling of Doomsday, and people apparently gave it this name about a century later because they regarded it as a final authority, like Judgement Day.

'We're doomed!' was the catchphrase of the gloomy Scottish undertaker Frazer, played by John Laurie, in the BBC TV comedy *Dad's Army* (1968-77). The 1947 musical *Finian's Rainbow* popularised **doom and gloom** (or **gloom and doom**), which became a catchphrase when it was made into a film (starring Fred Astaire, with Tommy Steele as a leprechaun) in 1968. The idea seemed appropriate to a world threatened by nuclear war.

dose

The Greek physician Galen, who lived between 129 and 99 BC, used *dosis*, the Greek word for 'a gift', for 'a portion of medicine'. This is the sense in which **dose** entered English in the late Middle Ages.

In **like a dose of salts**, 'very quickly and efficiently', the salts referred to are Epsom salts, or magnesium sulphate. They have had a variety of medicinal uses since the 18th century, most notably as a very effective and fast-acting cure for constipation. The name Epsom salts comes from the town of Epsom in Surrey, where the crystals were first found.

dot

The word **dot** appears only once in Old English manuscripts, meaning 'the head of a boil'. It then disappears until the late 16th century, when it re-emerges in the sense 'a small lump or clot'. The sense 'small mark or spot' dates from the mid 17th century. In **on the dot**, 'exactly on time', the dot is one appearing on a clock face to mark the hour. Writers and printers sometimes use a dot in place of a number or letter that they do not know or do not want to specify, and this may be the origin of **the year dot**, 'a very long time ago' – the dot could also be a zero.

doubt

In English **doubt** goes back to Latin *dubitare* 'to hesitate, waver', from *dubium* 'doubt' (from which **dubious** also derives). The immediate sources were French forms in which the -*b*- had been lost, and people never pronounced the -*b*- in **doubt** – it was a learned spelling to show that the writer knew the original Latin word.

The first **doubting Thomas** to refuse to believe something without proof was the apostle Thomas. In the biblical account Thomas refused to believe that Christ was risen again until he could see and touch the wounds inflicted during the Crucifixion.

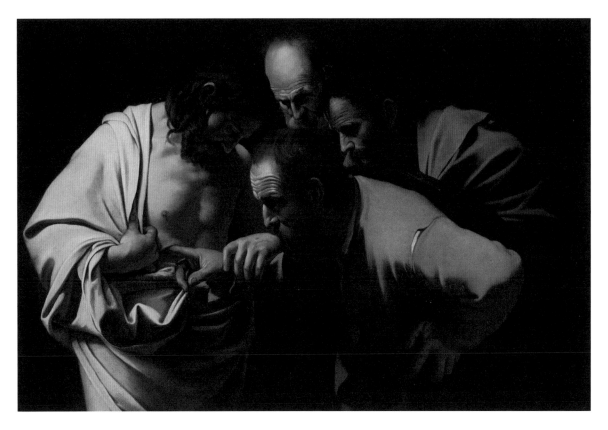

The apostle 'doubting Thomas' touches one of Christ's wounds in a painting by the Italian artist Caravaggio (1573-1610).

dove

In politics a **dove**, a person who advocates peaceful or conciliatory policies, contrasts with a HAWK, a more warlike hardliner. The terms emerged in the early 1960s at the time of the Cuban missile crisis, when the Soviet Union threatened to install missiles in Cuba within striking distance of the USA. More generally, the dove has long been a symbol of peace and calm, in reference to the dove sent out by Noah after the Flood. The first time she went out she was unable to find any dry land, and returned to the Ark, but when Noah sent her out again a week later she came back with an olive branch in her beak, indicating that the treetops were now above the level of the water. See also COT.

down

Downs are gently rolling hills. The word **down** may be of Celtic origin and related to early Irish *dún* and obsolete Welsh *din* 'fort', which go back to an ancient root shared by TOWN. The everyday **down**, 'towards a lower place', is also Old English, but was once not distinct from **down** 'hill'. It is a shortening of **a-down**, itself a reduction of **off down** 'off the hill'.

The phrase **down and out**, 'completely without resources, defeated in life', probably comes from boxing. It referred to a boxer who was knocked out by a decisive blow. Since the late 19th century a **down-and-out** has been a person without money, a job or a place to live.

The fluffy **down** that forms the first covering of a young bird is unrelated. It came in the Middle Ages from an old Scandinavian word.

draconian

Draco was a Greek lawmaker of the 7th century BC. His drafting of Athenian law was notorious for its severity, with the death penalty imposed even for trivial crimes. Since the late 19th century **draconian** has described excessively severe laws and punishments, although that was not when people first made the comparison – **draconic** was used in the same way from the early 18th century.

drag

The word **drag** comes from the same Old Norse root as **draw**. The sense 'a boring or tiresome person or thing' developed in the early 19th century from the idea of an attachment that drags or hangs heavily and hinders progress. The cumbersomeness of contemporary women's dress may also be behind the use of **drag** for 'women's clothing worn by a man', which is recorded from the 1870s.

A street has been a **drag** since the middle of the 19th century. A description of London life in 1851 records a woman 'whose husband has got a month for "griddling in the main drag" (singing in the high street)'. The term later became better known in the USA, especially in **the main drag**.

dragon

Dragon goes back to Greek *drakōn* 'serpent', and this was one of the first senses in English, in the Middle Ages. In early texts it can be difficult to distinguish the genuine large snake or python (at that time known only from report) from the mythical fire-breathing monster.

The dragon is a popular Chinese symbol, and this is behind the expression to **chase the dragon**, 'to smoke heroin'. A 1961 *Narcotic Officer's Handbook* explains: 'In "chasing the dragon" the heroin and any diluting drug are placed on a folded piece of tinfoil. This is heated with a taper and the resulting fumes inhaled through a small tube of bamboo or rolled paper. The fumes move up and down the tinfoil with the movements of the molten powder, resembling the undulating tail of the mythical Chinese dragon.'

dread

The original word for 'to fear greatly, regard with awe' was **adread**, shortened to **dread** in the Middle Ages. Dread meaning 'extreme fear, great awe' appeared at much the same time.

Among Rastafarians, members of a Jamaican cult that believes Emperor Haile Selassie of Ethiopia was the Messiah, dread is dread of the Lord, and more generally a deep-rooted sense of alienation from contemporary society. Rastafarians wear **dreadlocks**, a hairstyle in which the hair is washed but not combed, and twisted while wet into tight braids. Dreadlocks are sometimes simply dreads. These uses were originally Jamaican, but came to wider attention in 1974 in 'Natty Dread', a song performed by Bob Marley and the Wailers. See also NATTY.

In the early 19th century, a dreadnought could be a fearless person or a warm coat worn in cold weather.

The most familiar **dreadnought** is a type of large, fast battleship equipped with large-calibre guns, the first of which, HMS *Dreadnought*, was launched in 1906.

dream

Although it corresponds to Dutch *droom* and German *Traum*, **dream** is not recorded in Old English, as many shared words are. In the main modern sense **dream** did not appear until the Middle Ages, although an earlier word **dream** meaning 'joy' and 'music' did occur in Old English and may be related.

Dreams are often pleasant, sometimes unrealistically so, and numerous popular phrases refer to this. If something goes **like a dream**, it goes very well or successfully; the phrase is recorded from the early 20th century. Expressing a desire or hope for something may elicit the ironic response **in your dreams**; this use is recorded from the 1980s.

The **city of dreaming spires** is Oxford. The name comes from a line in the poem 'Thyrsis' (1866) by Matthew Arnold: 'And that sweet City with her dreaming spires'. See also NIGHTMARE.

dreary

Something **dreary** is not particularly pleasant, but it was worse in Saxon times, when the sense was 'gory, bloody'. It came from a word meaning 'gore' which was related to Old English *drēosan* 'to drop, fall', the source of dreary **drizzle**. The modern sense 'depressingly dull and bleak' did not develop until the mid 17th century.

drop

In the course of its history people have dropped all sorts of things: bombs, names, aitches, goals, LSD, hints, stitches and more. Since the 1940s they have been dropping clangers, although the slightly less obtrusive brick has also been let slip since the 1920s. To **drop a clanger** is 'to make an embarrassing mistake or tactless remark'. Clangers only turn up in this phrase, but presumably they are things that make a very loud noise on hitting the ground and so draw immediate attention to the person responsible for dropping them.

drown

Although it makes its first appearance in the Middle Ages, **drown** probably existed in Old English. It was originally a northern English form, and is related to the old Scandinavian word *drukkna* 'to be drowned', which comes from the same root as **drink**, in which people sometimes **drown their sorrows**.

The idea that **a drowning man will clutch at a straw**, that people grab at the slightest chance even when all hope is slipping away, has been expressed since the 16th century. Before the 20th century the proverb involved 'catching' at straws: clutch adds a vivid sense of desperation.

'Not waving but drowning' is the title of a 1957 poem by the English poet and novelist Stevie Smith (1902-71): 'I was much too far out all my life / And not waving but drowning.' Smith also popularised the phrase 'A good time was had by all', which was the title of a collection of poems in 1937.

drum

Recorded from the late Middle Ages, **drum** is probably from Dutch or German *tromme*, which imitates the sound of a drumbeat. The English word may be an alteration of **drumslade**, from German *trommelslag* 'drumbeat'.

In Australia and New Zealand **drum** is a term for 'a piece of reliable inside information'. The meaning dates from the early 20th century, and perhaps derives from the use of the musical instrument to give signals.

The idea behind **drumming up** support is that of a person going around beating a drum to attract attention. We talk of someone being **drummed out** of a place or institution with reference to the military drum beat that accompanied the ceremony of dismissing a soldier from a regiment. And a lesson is **drummed into** someone in the regular, repetitive way that a drum is beaten.

dub

It has been possible to **dub** someone a knight since the Norman Conquest: the king conferred the rank by ceremonially touching the person being honoured on the shoulder with a sword. The word **dub** came from a shortened form of Old French *adober* (modern *adouber*) meaning 'to equip with armour' or 'to repair'. The sense of giving an unofficial title, name or nickname to someone developed from this ritual conferring of a knighthood. See also NICKNAME.

Since the 1920s to **dub** a film has been to provide it with an alternative soundtrack, now usually in another language. Dub is also a kind of reggae music in which some vocals and instruments are removed and the bass guitar accentuated. In these uses **dub** is a shortening of **double**.

duck

The name of the waterbird and **duck** meaning 'to lower the head and body quickly' go back to the same ancient root. The earliest sense of the latter was 'to suddenly go underwater and emerge, to dive', which connects directly with the behaviour of ducks – a duck is a bird that 'ducks' underwater.

Stock exchange traders in the mid 18th century originally used the expression **lame duck** to describe a person or company unable to pay their debts. The idea behind it may be that a lame duck could easily fall victim to a hunter or predator: in the case of a debtor, he would be at the mercy of his creditors. Since the 19th century **lame duck** has also described a politician or government in their final period of office, after their successor has been elected. In November 2000, following the election of his successor George W. Bush, Bill Clinton remarked: 'People say I will be a lame duck but I've got another ten weeks to quack', reminding the public that his term of office extended until January 2001.

In cricket a **duck** is a batsman's score of nought. This is short for **duck's egg**, used for the figure 0 because of its similar outline. To **break your duck** is to score the first run of your innings. See also GOOSE, LOVE, WATER.

dude

This slang term is probably from German dialect *Dude* 'fool'. It appeared in New York at the beginning of 1883 for a man who was the equivalent of the English DANDY, fastidious in his dress. At the same time the word was applied to a non-westerner or city-dweller spending his holidays on a ranch in the western USA, a 'dude ranch'. In the 20th century it came to mean simply 'a man, a guy'. See also CAT.

duff

People have obviously long found the sound of **duff** expressive, and it has a wide variety of uses. One of them begins with **duffer** 'a useless person or thing'. This is recorded from the mid 19th century and may be an alteration of **dowfart**, an old Scottish term meaning 'a stupid person', from **dowf** 'spiritless'. Golfers shortened **duffer** to **duff** in the early 19th century and used it to mean 'to mishit a shot or ball', which spread into the wider community as 'to make a mess of something, bungle'. This **duff** may be the source of **duff** 'of poor quality, worthless', or may link to another set of words, also going back to a **duffer**. In this sense **duffer** appeared in the mid 18th century as thieves' slang for a person who sells worthless articles and passes them off as valuable. The origin is unknown, but it seems to have travelled to Australia and reappeared in the mid 19th century as 'a cattle rustler'. The phrase **up the duff** 'pregnant' may be related: it shares the Australian connections, as it is first recorded in Australia in the mid 20th century. The violent **duff**, as in to **duff someone up**, is recorded from the 1960s and may also be connected, though this is less likely.

Everything about **duff** is hedged about with uncertainty, and the only **duff** whose history is known for certain is that of **plum duff**, a northern English dialect form of **dough**. It is enough to make the lexicographer feel a duffer.

duke

The word **duke** is recorded in Old English, but it goes back to Latin *dux* 'leader', which is related to *ducere* 'to lead'. The earliest meaning of **duke** was 'the ruler of a duchy' – it referred to sovereign princes in continental Europe, and did not describe a member of the British nobility until the end of the 14th century. See also COUNT, EARL, PRINCE.

dumb

In Old English **dumb** signified 'unable to speak', and could apply to both humans and animals. The sense 'stupid, unintelligent' dates from the Middle Ages. These days the 'stupid' sense has come to dominate the word to such an extent that it has overshadowed the 'unable to speak' meaning, so using it in the latter context is likely to cause offence. **Speech-impaired** or a similar alternative is safer.

A person considered stupid began to be called a **dumbo** in the USA in the 1950s, probably inspired by the 1941 Disney cartoon film *Dumbo*, which featured a flying elephant. The elephant's name was probably based on JUMBO.

Worry about things being **dumbed down**, or having their intellectual content reduced so as to be accessible to a larger number of people, seems very recent, but the phrase goes back to 1933. In *Forum* magazine the US cartoonist H.T. Webster referred to 'Hollywood gag men' discussing a comedy which is too subtle and which 'they determine they must dumb . . . down'. See also BLONDE, DIZZY.

dunce

In the Middle Ages the Scottish theologian and scholar John Duns Scotus was a profoundly influential figure. His works were university textbooks, and his followers so numerous that they had a name, Scotists. But from the 16th century the Scotists' views became old-fashioned and they were attacked and ridiculed, especially for making unnecessarily fine distinctions. The Scotists acquired a new name: Dunsmen or Dunses. A Duns was a 'hair-splitter', 'a dull pedant' and 'a person who is slow at learning'. The last is the sense of **dunce** which survives to this day.

dungeon

The word **dungeon** had two main senses when it was first used in the 14th century, 'the great tower or keep of a castle' and 'an underground prison cell'. The first is now usually spelled **donjon** and regarded as a separate word. The core meaning was 'lord's tower', and the word goes back to Latin *dominus* 'lord, master', through which it is related to DAME, DANGER and **dominion**.

dust

Our word **dust** is related to Dutch *duist* 'chaff, meal dust, bran', and the ancient meaning appears to have been 'material that rises in a cloud of smoke'. Various biblical uses of **dust** have settled in the language. To **shake the dust off your feet** derives from the Gospel of Matthew: 'And whosoever shall not receive you, nor hear your words, when ye depart out of that house or city, shake off the dust of your feet.' The phrase **dust and ashes**, used to convey a great sense of disappointment or disillusion, is found in the books of Genesis and Job. It refers back to the legend of the Sodom apple or Dead Sea fruit, whose attractive appearance tempted people but which tasted only of dust and ashes when eaten.

A **dusty answer** is a curt and unhelpful reply. The expression comes from the 1862 poem 'Modern Love' by George Meredith: 'Ah, what a dusty answer gets the soul When hot for certainties in this our life!'

Dutch

From the Middle Ages up to the 17th century **Dutch** was not restricted to the people and language of the Netherlands, but referred to much of north and central Europe, taking in the peoples of modern Germany and the Low Countries. In 1579 the seven provinces that form the basis of the republic of the Netherlands gained independence and united, adopting the kind of German spoken in Holland as their national language. This change in the political landscape led to the more specific uses of **Dutch** in modern English.

During the 17th century there was great rivalry between the English and the Dutch. The English attributed various undesirable characteristics to their neighbours, including **Dutch courage**, 'strength or confidence gained from drinking alcohol', which managed to imply that the Dutch were both cowards and drunkards. Their language was insulted in **double Dutch**, 'gibberish'. In some phrases the Dutch appear to have been singled out simply because they are foreign, as in **I'm a Dutchman**, used to express disbelief. In the American expression **Dutch uncle**, 'a kindly but authoritative figure', the choice serves to emphasise that the person referred to is not a blood relation. The original wording was 'I will talk to him like a Dutch uncle', meaning 'I will give him a lecture'. Another expression that was originally American is **go Dutch**, 'to share the cost of something equally', first recorded in 1914 – the implication, more obvious in **Dutch treat**, was presumably that the Dutch were mean.

dye

Both main uses of **dye**, 'a substance used to add or change colour' and 'to add a colour to', are recorded in Old English. Soon afterwards they both disappeared, the first until the late 16th century, the second until the late Middle Ages. The world in the meantime was not colourless, so the absence of **dye** from writing is a puzzle.

The basis of **dyed in the wool**, 'unchanging in a belief or opinion', is the fact that yarn dyed in its raw state, before it is woven into a piece of fabric, has a much more even and permanent colour. The practice goes back many centuries, and the sense of 'unchanging' is also very old. Nowadays people often use the expression to refer to someone's political or sporting affiliation, as in the following example from *The Scotsman* newspaper: 'Voters and dyed-in-the-wool Tories are crying out for some "red meat" policies they can believe.'

Going Dutch

Is your boss a bit gruff, or does he snoop? Time to pack him off on a cruise on his yacht, maybe to Holland, where all of these words come from.

The 'boss' of all our Dutch words is boss, which comes from *baas* 'master'. It started life in the USA at the beginning of the 19th century, and when it arrived in Britain was restricted to workmen's slang. If the boss is addicted to snooping he is now spying, but originally he would be stealing tasty items of food and eating them on the sly – the meaning of the Dutch source *snoepen*, and the first English use in the 1840s.

BOOZE is a Dutch word, and so are two of our most popular drinks. The full name for brandy was originally brandy wine, a term that entered English in the early 17th century from Dutch *brandewijn*, literally 'burnt wine'. 'Burning' referred to the heating of low-strength alcohol over a fire so that the alcohol was given off as a vapour that condensed as brandy.

Gin is flavoured with juniper berries, and was traditionally made in the Netherlands. In the early 18th century the word was spelled genever or geneva, which came via Dutch from Old French *genevre* 'juniper'. To avoid confusion with Geneva in Switzerland the drink was sometimes called Hollands geneva or just Hollands.

Many words to do with the sea and sailing came the short distance across the North Sea to Britain, most of them in the 17th century. The source of cruise was probably Dutch *kruisen* 'to cross', which is related to CROSS itself. The names of the corvette, the sloop, the smack and the yacht are all Dutch: the last of these is from *jaghte* 'light sailing vessel', which was derived from *jaghtschip* 'fast pirate ship'.

In English frolic first meant 'playful, happy' when it entered the language in the early 16th century from Dutch *vrolijk*. A less cheerful word is gruff, originally meaning 'coarse'. It started life in Scotland rather than England, in the late 15th century. In Dutch a bumpkin is either 'a little tree' or 'a little barrel' – either way, it probably referred to the ungainly figure of a short, stout countryman.

See also CABOODLE, EASEL, GROOVE, LOTTERY, SNOOP, TREK, WAGON.

eagle

In Latin *aquila* meant **eagle** but also referred to the figure of an eagle that was used as the standard of a legion, a division of the ancient Roman army. *Aquila* also gave us **aquiline** – an aquiline nose is one that is hooked like an eagle's beak.

Renowned for its keen sight and soaring flight, the eagle is considered the king of birds. The **bald eagle** is the emblem of the USA, and *Eagle* was the name of the lunar module during the first moon landing, on July 20, 1969. The phrase **the eagle has landed** was said by astronaut Neil Armstrong on that day: 'Houston, Tranquillity Base here. The Eagle has landed.' It was used by Jack Higgins in 1975 as the title of his thriller about an attempt to assassinate Winston Churchill.

In golf an eagle is a score of two under par, or rather one less than a mere **birdie**, but one more than an **albatross**. See PAR.

ear

Unsurprisingly, since their meanings are so dissimilar, the **ear** that allows you to hear and the one that bears seeds are different words. The first is an Old English word that goes right back to an ancient root that was shared by Latin *auris*, from which we get **aural**. The second seems to come ultimately from the same root as Latin *acer*, meaning pointed or sharp.

To **earmark** something is to set it aside for a particular purpose. Originally, though, it referred to the practice of marking the ear of an animal as a sign of ownership.

You might say that **your ears are burning** if you are subconsciously aware of being talked about or criticised. This phrase has been around in English since at least the early 1600s, but the idea is an ancient one, which the 1st-century Roman scholar Pliny mentioned in his *Natural History*. There have been various folk beliefs about burning ears: that only your left ear was sensitive, or that a burning left ear meant that you were being criticised, while a burning right one meant you were being praised. They do not seem reliable, though, as the sides were sometimes reversed. In 1738 Jonathan Swift wrote, 'Miss, didn't your Left Ear burn last Night? . . . Because . . . you were extolled to the Skies.'

earl

In Saxon days an **earl** was a man of noble rank, as opposed to a **churl** or ordinary peasant, or a **thane**, who was a man granted land by the king. At the time of King Canute the governor of a large division of England such as Wessex was called an earl. As the court started to be influenced by the Normans, the word was applied to any nobleman who held the continental title of COUNT. See also DUKE.

early

Like **late**, **early** is an Old English word, and is found in many idioms and proverbs. **The early bird gets the worm** is first recorded in 1636, and **early to bed, early to rise, makes a man healthy, wealthy, and wise** goes as far back as 1496.

Early doors, meaning early on in a game or contest, has become a cliché of sports reporting, but was not invented by a pundit. It originally referred to admission to a music hall some time before the start of the performance, which was more expensive but gave you a wider choice of seating. The first record of its use is from 1883. The practice died out in the 1950s but the phrase was resurrected in footballing circles in the 1970s in its current sense, with the legendary English soccer manager Brian Clough providing the first recorded example.

earth

It is impossible to tell which meaning of **earth** came first in English: the senses 'the ground', 'our planet' and 'soil' are all found in Old English. Related words in other languages are German *Erde* and Dutch *aarde*, as in **aardvark** or 'earth pig'. Earth meaning 'the underground lair of a badger or fox' dates from the late Middle Ages.

'The earth' has been used in idioms like **pay the earth**, **cost the earth** and **expect the earth** since the 1920s. Many of the earliest examples are by the comic novelist P.G. Wodehouse – he probably did not invent them, but spotted new slang expressions among the 'bright young things' and 'flappers' of the day.

We think of **earthling** as being a term from science fiction, but it actually goes back at least as far as 1593: 'We (of all earthlings) are God's utmost subjects' (Thomas Nashe, *Christ's Tears*).

earwig

Earwigs have nothing to do with wigs. The *-wig* bit is related to WIGGLE, which makes a lot more sense. It was once thought that the insect crawled into people's ears, and the same idea is found in other languages: in French an earwig is a *perce-oreilles*, literally 'ear-piercer', and in German it is *Ohrwurm*, or 'ear worm'. See also BEETLE.

easel

You would never guess by looking at it, but an **easel** is literally a donkey, coming into English in the 1630s from Dutch *ezel*. The use is similar to that of HORSE in **clothes horse**, where the load-bearing object is likened to a beast of burden.

east

All of the words for compass points are Old English. **East** is from an ancient root shared by the Latin word for dawn, *aurora* (as in the **Aurora Borealis**, or Northern Lights). It is also related to **Easter**, another Old English word, which is probably connected with *Ēastre*, the name of a Germanic goddess associated with spring and the dawn.

The title of the James Dean film *East of Eden* (1955) is taken from the Book of Genesis: 'And Cain went out from the presence of the Lord, and dwelt in the land of Nod, on the east of Eden.' See also NOD, TWAIN.

eat

For such a fundamental concept, it is unsurprising that **eat** is an Old English word, with an ancient root shared by Latin *edere* 'to eat'. This is the source not only of **edible** but also **comestible** (something edible), **edacious** (a rare word for 'greedy') and **obese**.

There are many phrases associated with eating. **Eat drink and be merry, for tomorrow we die** is a combination of two Biblical sayings, 'A man hath no better thing under the sun, than to eat and to drink, and to be merry' (Ecclesiastes) and 'Let us eat and drink; for tomorrow we shall die' (Isaiah).

You are what you eat, recently the title of a TV programme on healthy eating, is a proverb that first appeared in English in the 1920s. It is a translation of the German phrase *Der Mensch ist, was er isst*, 'Man is what he eats', which was said by the philosopher Ludwig Feuerbach (1804-72).

If you **eat your heart out** you suffer from excessive longing or grief. As **eat your own heart** the phrase was first used in Edmund Spenser's *The Faerie Queene* (1590-6): 'He could not rest; but did his stout heart eat.' See also FRET, WORD.

eaves

In Old English **eaves**, then spelled *efes*, was a singular word, but the *-s* at the end made people think it was a plural, which is how we treat it today. If you **eavesdrop** you secretly listen to a conversation. The word was formed in the early 17th century from the old word **eavesdropper**, 'a person who listens from under the eaves'. **Eavesdropper** came from the noun **eavesdrip** or **eavesdrop**, 'the ground on to which water drips from the eaves'. This was a concept in an ancient law which banned building closer than two feet from the boundary of your land, in case you damaged your neighbour's land by 'eavesdrop'.

eccentric

Rather eccentrically, **eccentric** started life as a noun, meaning 'a circle or orbit not having the earth precisely in its centre', before taking on its main modern meaning of 'unconventional and slightly strange' in the mid 17th century. It comes from Greek *ekkentros*, from *ek* 'out of' and *kentron* 'centre'.

MMM, THAT TOBLERONE WAS DELICIOUS

YOU ARE WHAT YOU EAT

echo

In Greek mythology **Echo** was the name of an oread or mountain nymph whom the goddess Hera deprived of speech to stop her chattering. The unfortunate creature was left able only to repeat what others had said. She fell in love with the handsome Narcissus (see NARCISSISM), and when he rejected her she wasted away with grief until there was nothing left of her but her voice. In another, nastier version of the story she was loved by the god Pan but turned him down; in revenge he drove a group of shepherds mad and made them tear her to pieces. The fragments were hidden in the earth, including her voice, which could still imitate other sounds. The name of the goddess was probably a personification of the Greek word *ēkhÿ*, which was related to *ēkhē* 'a sound'.

ecology

The word **ecology** is thought to have been invented in 1869 by the German biologist Ernst Haeckel. Originally spelled **oecology**, it is based on the Greek word *oikos* 'house' – in this case the natural environment is seen as the home of all the plants and animals that live within it.

economy

Like ECOLOGY, **economy** and **economical** come from Greek *oikos* 'house', and in the 15th century they were spelled **oikonomy** and **oikonomical**. **Economy** was then 'the art or science of managing a household' and 'the way in which household finances are managed'. The sense expanded in the 17th century to cover the management of a country's finances.

Being **economical with the truth** is a euphemism for lying or deliberately withholding information. Mark Twain commented in *Following the Equator* (1897), 'Truth is the most valuable thing we have. Let us economize it.' The phrase itself did not gain widespread popularity until its use in 1986 during a government attempt to prevent the publication of *Spycatcher*, a book by a former MI5 officer, Peter Wright. Giving evidence at the trial, the head of the British Civil Service reportedly said of a letter: 'It contains a misleading impression, not a lie. It was economical with the truth.'

ecstasy

The base of the word **ecstasy** is Greek *ekstasis*, which meant 'standing outside yourself'. **Ecstasy** first referred to a state of frenzy or distraction, of literally being 'beside yourself' with fear, passion or other strong emotion. This meaning is now encountered only rarely, but was famously used by Wilfred Owen in his war poem 'Dulce et Decorum Est' (written in 1917): 'Gas! Gas! Quick, boys! – An ecstasy of fumbling, Fitting the clumsy helmets just in time.' The word came during the 16th and 17th centuries to mean a condition of emotional or religious frenzy or heightened emotion: if you were **in ecstasy** you were transported by any emotion, not just happiness or pleasure.

The illegal drug **Ecstasy** is first referred to in 1985, in the *Los Angeles Times*. It gained its 'street' name because of its euphoric effects – the chemical name is methylenedioxymethamphetamine, or MDMA.

edify

In the Middle Ages to **edify** was to construct a building. This reflected the word's origin, Latin *aedificare*, from *aedis* 'house, dwelling' and *facere* 'to make'. It quickly took on the extended sense of 'building up' someone in moral or intellectual terms. *Aedis* also gave us **edifice**, a formal word for a large building.

effete

Today an **effete** young man is affected and rather effeminate, but the word originally referred to animals and meant 'no longer fertile, too old to bear young'. It comes from Latin *effetus*, from *ex-*, meaning 'out', and *fetus* 'breeding, childbirth, offspring' – the same word as English **fetus**. The meaning developed into 'having exhausted strength or vigour' and in the late 18th century on to 'feeble, over-refined'.

egg

In the Middle Ages the Old Norse word **egg** started to take over from the earlier **ey** or **eye** (plural **eyren**). The two terms were used side by side for some time, and in 1490 the printer William Caxton wrote about how difficult it was to decide which word to use. See also COCKNEY.

If you **have egg on your face** you look foolish or ridiculous. The phrase does not go back very far – the first recorded example is from 1950s America. It probably comes from the idea of a messy eater having traces of food around their mouth, but it could also refer to a bad actor being pelted with eggs.

Calling someone a **good egg** or **a bad egg** is now associated with the 1920s and writers such as P.G. Wodehouse, but the expressions are older than that. A disliked or unpleasant person was first called a bad egg in the 1850s; the first person to reverse the words and come up with good egg seems to have been Rudyard Kipling, in 1903.

The advertising slogan **Go to work on an egg**, used in Britain by the Egg Marketing Board during the 1960s, is often credited to the novelist Fay Weldon,

The Egg Marketing Board pushes the breakfast benefits of an egg.

who used to work as an advertising copywriter. She now says that it was written by another member of her team.

The proverb **don't teach your grandmother to suck eggs** has been in use since the early 18th century to caution someone against giving unwanted advice, in particular trying to tell a more experienced or knowledgeable person how to do something that they already know. Why your grandmother should be sucking eggs in the first place is not certain, but presumably the suggestion is that she has no teeth.

An intellectual or highbrow person is sometimes called an **egghead** because of the association of an egg-like bald head with age and wisdom. The use dates from the early years of the 20th century.

Egg as in to **egg someone on** is a different word. It comes from Old Norse *eggja* 'to incite'.

elastic

First recorded in the 1650s, **elastic** was originally used to describe the way that gas is able to expand spontaneously to fill whatever space is available. In those days some people thought that gas particles acted like a coiled spring, an idea that led to **elastic** being 'stretched' to take on its modern sense. The word comes from Greek *elastikos*, from *elaunein* 'to drive'.

elbow

An **elbow** is literally 'an arm-bend': well, it was in Old English, when it was spelled *elboga* or *elnboga*. The first part of the word also gave us **ell,** a former measure of length in the textile industry, equivalent to six hand breadths. The second part became **bow**, as in **tying a bow** and **bow and arrow**.

electricity

The word **electric** seems to have come before **electricity**, having been first used by the scientist William Gilbert in a Latin treatise called *De Magnete* (1600). Gilbert, the man who discovered how to make magnets and coined the term **magnetic pole**, spelled it as *electricus*. **Electricity** is first recorded in 1646, in the writings of the physician Sir Thomas Browne. Both were based on the Latin word *electrum* 'amber', the connection being that rubbing amber produces an electric charge which will attract light objects.

elegant

These days someone **elegant** will generally be well dressed, but the basic idea behind the word is of being discerning and making careful choices. It comes from Old French *élégant* or Latin *elegans*, from **eligere** 'to choose or select', which was the origin of **elect**, **eligible** and **elite**.

element

Latin *elementum* 'principle, rudiment' is the source of **element**. Modern science has identified more than one hundred elements that are basic constituents of matter, but in medieval times people thought that everything was made up from four elements: earth, air, fire and water. They also believed that each kind of living creature had a natural affinity with one of these elements: most commonly these were air and water, although the salamander, for example, was supposed to live in fire. From this idea came that of a person's natural or preferred environment, and of **being in your element** if you are doing something that you love. **The element** was sometimes used specifically to mean 'the sky', and **the elements** became a term for strong winds, heavy rain and other kinds of bad weather.

Elementary is particularly associated with Sherlock Holmes saying 'Elementary, my dear Watson', although the phrase is not actually found in any of Sir Arthur Conan Doyle's books. Holmes did certainly say 'My dear Watson', and he said 'Exactly, my dear Watson' in three different stories; but the famous phrase does not appear until 1915, in the comic novel *Psmith, Journalist* by P.G. Wodehouse.

elephant

Perhaps surprisingly, **elephant** did not come to us from an African or Indian language, but via Latin from Greek. The Greek word *elephas* meant both 'ivory' and 'elephant'. It goes back a long way, being found in the work of the poet Homer, who probably lived in the 8th century BC, and may have been taken up by the Greeks from an ancient language of the Middle East. **Elephant** appeared in English in the 14th century, but before that people called tuskers **oliphants** or **elps**. The related word **olfend** was used to mean 'a camel' – in those days northern Europeans had only vague notions of exotic animals. See also CAMEL, CHAMELEON, GIRAFFE, ROOM, WHITE.

elf

An Old English word related to German *Alp* 'nightmare'. Elves were formerly thought of as more frightening than they are now: dwarfish beings that produced diseases, caused nightmares and stole children, substituting changelings in their place. Later they became more like fairies, dainty and unpredictable, and in the works of J.R.R. Tolkien they are tall, noble and beautiful.

Originally an **elf** was specifically a male being, the female being an **elven:** Tolkien revived **elven** and used it to mean 'relating to elves'. **Elfin,** meaning 'relating to elves' and also used to describe a small, delicate person with a mischievous charm, was first used by Edmund Spenser in *The Faerie Queene* (1590-6). See also OAF.

elixir

The root of both **elixir** and **Xerox** is Greek *xēros* 'dry'. **Elixir** came into English via Arabic *al-'iksīr*, from Greek *xīrion* 'powder for drying wounds'. It was first used in alchemy, as the name of a sought-after preparation that was supposed to change ordinary metals into gold, and one that could prolong life indefinitely (the **elixir of life**). **Xerox,** a name for a copying process that uses dry powder, dates from the early 1950s. See also CHEMICAL.

embargo

A Spanish word, from *embargar* 'to arrest'. When it was first used in English, at the start of the 17th century, **embargo** referred to an order prohibiting ships from entering or leaving a country's ports, usually just before a war. These days it is an official ban on trade with a particular country.

embarrass

Although it came into English from French, **embarrass** was probably based on Portuguese *baraço* 'halter'. The first English sense was 'to encumber or impede': the notion of difficulty or problems led to the use of **embarrassed** to mean 'in difficulties through lack of money', as in **financially embarrassed.** The familiar modern meaning was not recorded until the early 19th century.

emerald

Emerald can be traced back to Greek *smaragdos*, and ultimately to an ancient Hebrew verb meaning 'flash or sparkle'. In early English examples the word's meaning is vague, and does not necessarily refer to a green stone. Ireland has been called **the Emerald Isle**, on account of its lush greenery, since as long ago as 1795. See also DIAMOND.

emotion

The modern meaning of **emotion** is surprisingly recent, and the original meaning was very different. In the 16th century the word first meant 'a public disturbance or commotion', as in 'There were . . . great stirs and emotions in Lombardy' (1579). The root is Latin *movere*, 'to move', and the second sense was 'a movement or migration'. The main current meaning of 'a strong feeling such as joy or anger' was not used in writing until the early 1800s. See also TIRE.

emperor

The root of **emperor** is the Latin word *imperare* 'to command', which is also the ultimate source of **empire**, **imperative**, IMPERIAL and **imperious**. **Emperor** comes from Latin *imperator* 'military commander', which in Roman times was given as a title to Julius Caesar and to Augustus, the first Roman emperor, and was adopted by subsequent rulers of the empire. In English **emperor** first referred to these Roman rulers, and then to the head of the Holy Roman Empire. See also EVIL, ROOM.

empty

In Anglo-Saxon times **empty** meant 'at leisure', 'unoccupied' and also 'unmarried' as well as 'not filled'. It came from Old English *æmetta* 'leisure'. The proverb **empty vessels make most noise**, meaning that foolish people are always the most talkative, dates back to the work of the 15th-century poet John Lydgate.

emulsion

Nowadays we tend to think of it mainly as a household paint for walls and ceilings, whose name comes from the scientific sense of 'a fine dispersion of minute droplets of one liquid in another', but **emulsion** was originally a milky liquid made by crushing almonds in water. Its root is the Latin word *mulgere* 'to milk'.

enchant

The immediate source of **enchant** is French *enchanter*, from Latin *incantare*, which was based on *cantare* 'to sing'. These Latin words gave us **chant** and **incantation**. The original meanings of **enchant** were 'to put under a spell' and 'to delude', and it could also be spelled **inchant**.

encyclopedia

An **encyclopedia** is literally a 'circle of learning'. In ancient Greece a child was expected to receive a good all-round education, an *enkuklios paideia* in Greek. The word came to be spelled *enkuklopaideia* and made its way into English in the 1530s. Its first English meaning was 'general course of instruction', the meaning 'large work of reference' not appearing until 1644. The Latin-style spelling **encyclopaedia** is still sometimes used, partly because some encyclopedias, notably the *Encyclopaedia Britannica* (first published in 1768), use it in their title.

end

To **make ends meet** or **make both ends meet**, 'earn enough money to live on', was formerly also **make the two ends of the year meet**. It probably refers to the idea of making your annual income stretch from the beginning to the end of the year. The phrase goes back to at least 1661.

If you are **at the end of your tether** you have no patience or energy left to cope with something. People in North America tend to say that they are **at the end of their rope**. The image behind both expressions is that of a grazing animal tethered on a rope so that it can move where it likes, but only within a certain range. When it reaches the end of its tether – when the rope is taut – it can go no further.

At the end of the day has become one of those clichés that enrage teachers and linguistic purists. It is now continually parroted by sports players and commentators, but does not seem to have been used before the 1970s.

enemy

An **enemy** is not your friend. So far, so obvious, but this is in fact the derivation of the word. It came into the language at the end of the 13th century from Old French *enemi*, from Latin *inimicus*, which was based on *in-* meaning 'not' and *amicus* 'friend'. *Inimicus* is the

source of INIMICAL or 'hostile', and *amicus* of **amicable** or 'friendly'.

engage

Gage is an old word that means 'a valued object deposited as a guarantee of good faith' and, as a verb, 'to give as a pledge'. An Old French word related to WAGE and WED, it is the root of **engage**, formerly also spelled **ingage**, which has been used in English since the late medieval period. **Engage** originally meant 'give as a pledge' and 'pawn or mortgage', later coming to express the ideas 'to pledge or guarantee' and 'to enter into a contract'.

People have been getting engaged to be married only since the start of the 18th century. The novelist Henry Fielding provides the first example in print.

engine

An **engine** is certainly an **ingenious** device, and the two words are linked. **Engine** is from Old French *engin*, from Latin *ingenium* 'talent, device', the source also of INGENIOUS. Like many English words that now start with **en-**, it could also be spelled **in-**. Its original senses were 'ingenuity, cunning' and 'natural talent, wit, genius', which survives in Scots as **ingine**. From there it became 'the product of ingenuity, a plot or snare' and also 'a tool or weapon', specifically a large mechanical weapon, such as a battering ram or heavy catapult, constructed by **engineers**. By the first half of the 17th century something like our idea of an engine had arisen, a fairly complex device with moving parts that worked together.

English

England and the English get their names from the Angles, an ancient Germanic people who came to England in the 5th century AD and founded kingdoms in the Midlands, Northumbria and East Anglia. Their name came to refer to all of the early Germanic settlers of Britain – the Angles, Saxons and Jutes – and their language, which we now call Old English. The first written example of **English** (spelled *Engliscne*) comes from *The Treaty of Alfred and Guthrum*, an agreement between King Alfred the Great and Guthrum, the Viking ruler of East Anglia. Its exact date is uncertain, but it was probably written around 880. For an account of how the Angles got their name see ANGLE, and see also BRITISH.

engross

As you might imagine from its form if not its meaning, the word **engross** is related to **gross**. Both come ultimately from the Latin word *grossus* 'large'. Engross comes from the Latin phrase *in grosso* 'wholesale' and originally meant 'to buy up the whole of a commodity in order to sell it at a monopoly price'. It is also linked to **grocer** – a grocer was originally a person who sold things 'in the gross' or in large quantities.

enigma

An **enigma** is now a person or thing that is mysterious or difficult to understand, but it was originally a riddle, or an obscure speech. The word came from Latin, based on Greek *ainissesthai*, 'to speak allusively'. See also RIDDLE.

The British composer Sir Edward Elgar said that his *Enigma Variations* (1899) were dedicated 'to my friends pictured within'. The work consists of 14 musical portraits, each headed with initials or a pseudonym from which the subjects' identities have been deduced, and finishing with a portrait of the composer himself.

enormous

Something **enormous** is out of the ordinary in terms of size, and this is the idea behind the word. It is from Latin *enormis*, from *e-* 'out of' and *norma* 'pattern, standard' (the root of **norm** and NORMAL). In early use it meant 'abnormal, unusual, extraordinary' and also 'abnormally bad, monstrous, shocking' as well as 'huge'. This bad sense is still found in **enormity**, which strictly means 'a grave crime or sin' or 'the extreme seriousness of something bad', although today people increasingly use it to mean simply 'great size or scale'.

enthusiasm

Until relatively recently **enthusiasm**, **enthusiast** and **enthusiastic** had stronger and less favourable meanings than they do today. Enthusiasm was originally, in the early 17th century, religious mania or divine inspiration, often involving 'speaking in tongues' and wild, uncontrollable behaviour. An enthusiast was a religious fanatic or fundamentalist. Over the next hundred years or so the force of enthusiasm and its related words weakened so that they arrived at something like our modern meanings. Some people do take their interests and hobbies rather seriously, though, and even today **enthusiast** can have a slightly disapproving feel.

The origin of **enthusiasm** is Greek *enthous* 'possessed by a god, inspired', from *theos* 'god', which is the root of many words including **atheist**, **pantheon** and THEOLOGY.

an Englishman's home is his castle

The patriotic proverb has been around since at least 1581. By 1837 Charles Dickens could safely mock the concept in *The Pickwick Papers*: 'Some people maintains that an Englishman's house is his castle. That's gammon [nonsense].'

envelope

An **envelope** was originally any kind of wrapper or covering, not just something to put a letter in. It is from the same word as **envelop**, 'to wrap up or surround', from Old French *envoluper*.

To **push the envelope** is to go up to, or beyond, the limits of what is possible, an idea that comes from aeronautics. Since the Second World War the envelope or flight envelope has been the set of combinations of speed, altitude and range within which a particular kind of aircraft can fly safely. If a test pilot is pushing the envelope he is flying the plane at the very limits of its performance. The phrase came into wider circulation after 1979 following its use in *The Right Stuff*, a book by the American author Tom Wolfe about the early days of the American space programme, which was later made into an Oscar-winning film.

ephemera

An **ephemera** or ephemeron was originally a fever lasting only one day, an insect with a very short lifespan, or a plant thought to last a day. Some ancient writers thought there were two plants of this name, one that sprang up and died in a day, the other that carried a poison causing death within a day. The word was then applied to a person or thing of short-lived interest. People started to use it in its current plural sense in the 1930s, to describe items like tickets, posters and greetings cards that were of no enduring value except to collectors. **Ephemera** and also **ephemeral**, 'lasting for a very short time', are from Greek *ephēmeros* 'lasting only a day', from *hēmera* 'day'.

epicure

In ancient times an **Epicure** was a follower of the Athenian philosopher Epicurus (341-270 BC). The Epicures or Epicureans were 'hedonists' who believed that pleasure was the highest good, although the pleasure they had in mind was of a restrained kind. They valued mental pleasure more highly than physical, and thought that the ultimate pleasure was freedom from anxiety and mental pain, especially that arising from needless fear of death and of the gods. In their view the gods did exist but did not concern themselves with human affairs.

So the ancient Epicures were pretty high-minded folk, but because they talked of 'pleasure' (*hēdonē* in Greek, as in HEDONIST) as the most desirable objective, people in later times thought of them as fun-loving party animals, and an epicure became someone dedicated to having a good time all of the time. Nowadays the word is restricted in meaning to someone with a particular interest in good food. See also CYNIC, STOIC.

equal

A word that came from Latin *aequus*, which is also at the root of **adequate**, **equanimity**, **equate**, **equity** and **iniquity**. George Orwell's satire on Communism *Animal Farm* (1945) is the source of the quotation 'All animals are equal but some animals are more equal than others.' Another historic use of **equal** is from the American Declaration of Independence (1776):

We hold these Truths to be self-evident, that all men are created equal, that they are endowed, by their creator, with certain unalienable rights, that among these are life, liberty and the pursuit of happiness.

See also FIRST.

equestrian

Both **equestrian** and **equine** (meaning 'like a horse') are from Latin *equus* 'horse', a word that goes right back to the earliest times – unsurprisingly, as horses would have been so important to ancient peoples. Its root was also the source of the Greek equivalent to *equus*, *hippos*, which is where we get HIPPOPOTAMUS or 'river horse'.

eradicate

The original meaning of **eradicate** was 'to pull up by the roots, to uproot', which reflects its source, Latin *eradicare*, from *radix* 'root'. *Radix* is the source of RADICAL, and is related to our word ROOT itself.

erotic

French, the language of love, gave us **erotic**, although the ultimate source was Greek *erōs* 'love'. **Eros** was the name of the Greek god of love, the son of Aphrodite and the equivalent of the Roman Cupid. He is usually pictured as a naked boy with wings, carrying a bow and arrow to wound his victims with the pains of love.

err

Like **error** and **erratic**, **err** comes to us from Latin *errare*, which meant 'to stray, wander' but could also mean 'to make a mistake'. The idea of straying or going off the correct course is still found in **erratic**, and also in the old term **knight errant**: medieval knights were so called not because they were constantly messing things up, but because they travelled far and wide in search of adventure.

The proverb **to err is human, to forgive, divine** is so old that it is found in Latin (*humanum est errare*, 'it is human to err'), and also in the work of Geoffrey Chaucer: 'The proverb says that to sin is human, but to carry on sinning is the devil's work.' The precise wording that we are familiar with comes from *An Essay on Criticism* (1711) by the poet Alexander Pope.

escalate

To **escalate** was originally 'to travel on an escalator'. The word came from **escalator** and was coined in the early 1920s, when escalators were still new and exciting. It is now so familiar that it is quite a surprise to realise that we have only been using it to mean 'increase rapidly' and 'become more intense or serious' since the 1950s.

Escalator started life in 1900, as a trade name in America. It was derived from the old word **escalade**, which meant 'to scale a fortified wall by ladder', and was suggested by **elevator**, the US word for 'lift', which had been around since the 1880s.

Eskimo

The traditional word for the indigenous people inhabiting northern Canada, Alaska, Greenland and eastern Siberia is **Eskimo**. The word is from a Native American language, Algonquian, and may have originally meant 'people speaking a different language'. It was formerly thought that the first meaning was 'person who eats raw meat', though, and because this was seen as insulting the word is now avoided by many. The peoples inhabiting the regions from the Canadian Arctic to western Greenland prefer to call themselves **Inuit**. There are comparatively few words in English from the Inuit language. **Kayak**, which came into English in the 18th century, is one of them, and **igloo** is the most notable other.

esquire

An **esquire** was originally, according to the *Oxford English Dictionary*, 'A young man of gentle birth, who . . . attended upon a knight, carried his shield, and rendered him other services'. **Esquire** comes from an Old French word which means 'shield bearer' and

A bit of how's your father

The flamboyant actor and writer Quentin Crisp called euphemisms 'unpleasant truths wearing diplomatic cologne'. His description captures perfectly the role of euphemism as a means of verbally sidestepping something objectionable or embarrassing by giving it another name – an art perfected by the sometimes reserved and squeamish British.

If the Victorians baulked at prostitution, childbirth and blasphemy, today the subjects requiring sensitivity are ethnicity, sexuality and disability. Some, though, such as bodily functions, sex, drink, madness and death, have remained remarkably constant over hundreds of years.

From the mid 18th century onwards many mild exclamations were coined to avoid profanity. Drat is a shortening of od rat, which is itself an alteration of God rot. Similarly, darn is a euphemism for 'damn', cripes and crumbs for 'Christ', Jiminy for 'Jesus', gosh and gum (in by gum!) for 'God' and heck for 'hell'.

There are innumerable expressions for sex, from plain intimacy or relations to the other, know in the biblical sense and get your oats. The music-hall comedian Harry Lauder coined how's your father, then popularised by servicemen in the First World War. A pregnant woman might be in trouble, in an interesting condition or in the family way, which sound more refined than up the duff, up the spout or up the stick.

The state of being drunk has been equally productive. Three sheets to the wind (see SHEET) is a nautical metaphor, while to have had one over the eight, 'to have had more than eight pints of beer', was first used by the British armed forces in the 1920s, when servicemen felt that a drinker should be able to manage eight beers without getting drunk. Tired and emotional, 'drunk', is

particularly associated with the British satirical magazine *Private Eye*, and first appeared as tired and overwrought in September 1967 with reference to the Labour MP and Cabinet minister George Brown: 'Mr Brown had been tired and overwrought on many occasions.' Its motivation was the avoidance of describing someone in the public eye as being drunk, which could potentially provoke a libel charge.

Mental illness has long been the subject of euphemism. As early as the 13th century a LUNATIC was someone whose madness was associated with changes in the moon, from Latin *luna* 'moon'. Some 600 years later doolally became a slang term for 'mad' in the British army. It originated in India and the military sanatorium at Deolali, which also doubled as a transit camp where soldiers waited for their boat home. As boats only left between November and March, some soldiers were there for many months, so boredom set in and behaviour deteriorated. Men could then go doolally, the Englishman's pronunciation of 'Deolali'.

If someone is round the bend they are a successor to mentally ill patients in Victorian hospitals, who were confined to areas invisible from the end of the long hospital driveways. Today's euphemisms for madness are often injected with black humour, as in variations on the formula three cards short of a deck, one sandwich short of a picnic and one bit short of a byte.

To be Upminster is to be completely mad. On the railway line from London the town is the stop after Barking, itself a euphemism influenced by the craziness of dogs.

one over the eight

Comic relief is a useful defence against unpleasantness or fear, and gallows humour features in many modern terms for death and dying. Idioms such as pop your clogs (see POP), kick the bucket (see KICK) and snuff it (from the image of extinguishing a candle) are all examples of comic disguise which sit alongside more reverent expressions such as passed away, no longer with us and gone to their reward.

See also ECONOMY, KNOW, OAT, POLITICS, WASH.

comes from Latin *scutum* 'shield'. SQUIRE is really the same word. **Esquire** later came to refer to a man belonging to the higher order of English gentry, below a knight, and from there became a polite title added to the name of a man, at first only one regarded as a 'gentleman'.

etiquette

A French word which means literally 'label or ticket' and also 'list of ceremonial observances at a royal court'. **Etiquette**, or its Old French root, is the source of our word TICKET. It is not completely clear why the word moved from meaning 'ticket or label' to 'code of correct behaviour', but people probably started thinking of an *étiquette* as a list of correct forms of behaviour. We have been using the word in English since around 1750.

euphemism

This word is from Greek *eu* 'well' and *phēmï* 'speaking' – the root is *phēnai* 'to speak', which is also where PROPHET came from. See feature on EUPHEMISMS.

Several other English words start with *eu* meaning 'well'. The **eucalyptus** tree is literally 'well covered': it is so called because the unopened flower is protected by a sort of cap. If you give a **eulogy** you praise, or speak well of, someone: the *-logy* part, found in a great many English words, comes from Greek *logos* 'speech, word, reason'. If something is **euphonious** it is pleasing to the ear – *phōnē* 'sound' is the Greek root. Finally, **euthanasia** is literally 'an easy death': *thanatos* is 'death' in Greek.

The *euro-* in **Europe** and related words is unconnected. **Europe** comes from *Europa*, the name of a princess of Tyre, in modern-day Lebanon, who was admired by the god Zeus. He turned himself into a bull and swam across the sea to Crete with the princess on his back. Once in Crete Europa bore Zeus three sons, and eventually gave her name to the continent of Europe.

eureka

In the 3rd century BC the Greek mathematician and inventor Archimedes, of Syracuse in Sicily, was asked by the king, Hiero, to test his new crown to find out whether it was really solid gold, as the maker claimed. The story goes that the solution eluded Archimedes until he overfilled his bath, which overflowed as he got in. Suddenly the solution to the problem hit him. He realised that he could test whether or not the crown was pure gold by putting it in water and seeing whether it made the water overflow as much as a similar amount of genuine gold did. He is said then to have run through

the streets shouting 'Eureka!', or rather *heurēka*, which means 'I have found it' in Greek.

Archimedes had discovered a way of determining the specific gravity, or relative density, of a substance. The name **Archimedes' principle** is given to the law stating that a body immersed in a fluid is subject to an upward force equal to the weight of fluid it displaces.

even

In the sense 'flat and smooth' **even** is an Old English word. **Even** as in **evening** is from a different Old English word, one that is related to German *Abend* 'afternoon'.

An even break, meaning 'a fair chance', was popularised by the American comedian W.C. Fields in his catchphrase, 'Never give a sucker an even break', which itself went on to become the title of one of his best-known films.

There does not seem to have been a real Stephen behind the phrase **even Stephen** or **even Stephens**, meaning 'completely even or equal'. It probably comes from *Journal to Stella* by Jonathan Swift: 'Now we are even, quoth Stephen' (1711).

If a ship is **on an even keel** it is not tilting to the side. The keel is the lengthwise supporting structure along the base of a ship; **even** is in the old sense 'in a level position, horizontal'.

every

An Old English word that is related to **ever** and **each**. **Every** occurs in two well-known proverbs. **Every little helps** has a rather rude, but funny, origin. It appears to be from a 1590 work by the French writer Meurier, which translates as 'Every little helps, said the ant, pissing into the sea.' In the first English example, ten years later, the ant is replaced by a wren. **Every man for himself and the devil take the hindmost** alludes to a chase by the Devil, in which the slowest will be caught.

evil

Like GOOD and BAD, **evil** goes back to the earliest times, and many have been the reflections on its nature over the centuries. 'The evil that men do lives after them', wrote Shakespeare in *Julius Caesar*. The car-maker Henry Ford, the coiner of several memorable phrases (see also BLACK, HISTORY), said in 1930: 'What we call evil is simply ignorance bumping its head in the dark.' The proverb **See no evil, hear no evil, speak no evil** is often represented by the image of 'three wise monkeys', who are pictured covering their eyes, ears and mouth with their hands. The carving of the original monkeys is found on a shrine at Nikko in Japan.

The idea of **a necessary evil** goes back to Greek. The first necessary evil was marriage, and the first example in English refers to a woman. This *was* in 1547, remember.

In his State of the Union address of February 2002 US President George W. Bush said of Iraq, Iran and North Korea that they constituted 'an axis of evil, arming to threaten the peace of this world'. The phrase is now used to encapsulate the Bush administration's stance in foreign relations, much as **the evil empire** summed up Ronald Reagan's view of the Soviet Union.

The 'three wise monkeys' at the Nikko shrine in Japan avoid all evil.

exaggerate

To **exaggerate** was originally 'to pile up, accumulate', and later 'to make much of, emphasise'. It comes from Latin *exaggerare* 'to heap up', from *agger* 'heap'.

Mark Twain is usually credited with saying, in response to an incorrect story that he had died, 'Reports of my death have been greatly exaggerated'. In fact, he said 'The report of my death was an exaggeration' – in the *New York Journal*, on June 2, 1897.

exchequer

In around 1300 an **exchequer** was 'a chessboard'. The word came into English from Old French *eschequier*, which was based on medieval Latin *scaccus* 'check' – the origin of our word CHECK. It took on its current, very different sense from the department of state that dealt with the revenues of the Norman kings of England. In those days they kept the accounts by placing counters on a chequered tablecloth, which was called the Exchequer. The Chancellor of the Exchequer, now the chief finance minister of the United Kingdom, was originally an officer appointed in the reign of Henry III (1216-72) as assistant to the treasurer.

excruciating

The source of **excruciate** is Latin *excruciare* 'to torment or torture', which was based on crux. This meant 'a cross', of the kind used to crucify someone, and is the root not only of CROSS but also of CRUCIAL, **cruise**, **crusade** and **crux**. In English to **excruciate** someone was originally to torture them.

exit

As an English word **exit** was used during the time of Shakespeare, as a stage direction meaning 'he or she goes out', which is the word's literal meaning in Latin. (The plural equivalent, 'they go out', is **exeunt**.) One of the best-known uses of the word is in a speech from Shakespeare's *As You Like It*:

All the world's a stage,
And all the men and women merely players:
They have their exits and their entrances;
And one man in his time plays many parts,
His acts being seven ages.

Shakespeare is also responsible for what must be the must famous of all stage directions, from *The Winter's Tale*: 'Exit, pursued by a bear'. People started using **exit** to mean 'a way out' at the end of the 17th century.

expect

First meaning 'to wait for', **expect** entered English from Latin *exspectare* 'to look out for', from *ex-* 'out' and *spectare* 'to look'. *Spectare* is also the source of SPECTACLE and **spectator**, and is related to many other English words.

'England expects that every man will do his duty' was the British admiral Lord Nelson's memorable last signal to his fleet before the Battle of Trafalgar, on October 21, 1805. See also BLIND and KISS for more about Nelson.

explode

In Roman days bad performers were exploded, but it was not as bad as it sounds. **Explode** comes from

Latin *explodere* 'to drive off with hissing or clapping, to boo off the stage', from *ex-* 'out' and *plaudere* 'to clap' (as in **applaud**, **plausible** and PLAUDIT). Early meanings of **explode** were 'to reject scornfully' and 'to show to be false' (still used in phrases like **explode a theory**). The modern sense appeared in the late 18th century via the sense 'to force out violently and noisily'.

express

In the sense 'to convey in words or by behaviour' **express** originally meant 'to press out, obtain by squeezing', and its root is Latin *pressare* 'to press'. **Express** meaning 'intended for a particular purpose' is from another Latin word meaning 'to press', *primere*, and is the source of **express train** and other uses that involve high speed. As early as 1845 an express train went 'expressly' or specifically to one particular place, not stopping at intermediate stations. This would have been a relatively fast train, and led to the word being interpreted as meaning 'fast, rapid'.

extraordinary

This odd word looks as though it is from **extra** and **ordinary**, but something extraordinary is far from ordinary. It actually comes from Latin *extra ordinem*, meaning 'outside the normal course of events'. In English **extra** means 'beyond, outside' in many words such as **extramarital**, **extracurricular** and **extraterrestrial**. When it means 'additional' or 'especially', as in **extra-special**, it is really a shortened version of **extraordinary**, which in the 17th and 18th centuries often meant 'additional, extra', as in an extract from the diary of the traveller Celia Fiennes, written in 1710: 'You pay a penny extraordinary for being brought from Tunbridge town.'

extravagant

Extravagant came to us from medieval Latin *extravagari*, from *extra-* 'outside' and *vagari* 'to wander' (the source of VAGABOND and VAGRANT). It first meant 'unusual, unsuitable' and 'diverging greatly', then 'excessive or elaborate', and did not come to mean 'spending or costing a great deal' until the early 18th century.

An **extravaganza** is an elaborate and spectacular entertainment or production. It is basically the same word as **extravagance**, but came into English from Italian *estravaganza* in the 1750s, when it meant 'extravagance in language or behaviour'.

eye

An Old English word that has given rise to a huge number of phrases in English. **The eyes are the window of the soul** is a proverb that goes back at least until 1545, when it is found in the form 'The eyes . . . are the windows of the mind, for both joy and anger . . . are seen through them'. The same idea was expressed by the Roman orator Cicero in the 1st century BC: 'The face is a picture of the mind as the eyes are its interpreter.'

An eye for an eye and a tooth for a tooth refers to the law set out in the Old Testament book of Exodus: 'Thou shalt give life for life, eye for eye, tooth for tooth, hand for hand, foot for foot, wound for wound.' In the Sermon on the Mount in the Gospel of Matthew, Jesus turned this on its head by saying: 'Ye have heard that it hath been said, An eye for an eye and a tooth for a tooth: But I say unto you, That ye resist not evil: but whosoever shall smite thee on thy right cheek, turn to him the other also.' A more recent take on the idea, credited to Mahatma Gandhi, is 'An eye for an eye makes the whole world blind.'

The eye of a needle is a tiny opening through which it would seem impossible to pass. The reference is again to the Gospel of Matthew, where Jesus said, 'It is easier for a camel to go through the eye of a needle, than for a rich man to enter into the kingdom of God.'

A person who has **an eye for the main chance** is on the lookout for an opportunity to profit. The origins of this expression lie in the gambling game of hazard, in which the person about to throw the dice calls out a number between five and nine. This number is called the **main** or the **main chance**, and if they roll it they have won.

If you would **give your eye teeth for** something you would do anything in order to have it. The eye teeth are the two pointed teeth in the upper jaw, so called because they are more or less immediately below the eyes, and are essential for tearing off chunks of food. They are more usually called canine teeth, and in dogs (and other meat-eating animals) are particularly distinctive.

To **give someone the hairy eyeball** is to stare at them coldly or contemptuously. The image behind this American expression is of someone glaring with their eyes narrowed and partly closed: the **hairy eyeball** is the effect of seeing the eyeball through the eyelashes.

Keep your eyes peeled, or remain very vigilant, comes from the idea of 'peeling' the covering from your eyes to see as clearly as possible. It goes back to the 1850s in the USA, but now is particularly associated with *Police 5*, a long-running British TV show that appealed to the public for information to solve crimes. The catchphrase of the presenter, Shaw Taylor, at the end of each programme was 'Keep 'em peeled!'

fabric

Part of the 'fabric' of the language since the late 15th century, **fabric** comes from Latin *fabrica* 'something skilfully produced'. A fabric was originally 'a building', and then 'a machine or appliance' and 'something made', which led to the main current meaning 'cloth, textile'. The related verb **fabricate** originally just meant 'to manufacture, construct', but towards the end of the 18th century it began to be used in the sense 'make up facts that are not true'.

fabulous

The Latin word *fabula* 'story', ultimately from *fari*, meaning 'to speak', is the source of both **fabulous** and **fable**. A **fable** is a short story which conveys a moral, and is particularly associated with the legendary Greek storyteller Aesop. See feature on THE CLASSICAL WORLD. In early use **fabulous** meant 'known through fable' or 'not based on fact' – writers would tell of 'fabulous animals' such as the unicorn. The idea of 'astonishing' led to it being understood as both 'beyond belief' and 'wonderful, marvellous'. As the Sixties started to swing, **fabulous** was shortened to **fab**, and the Beatles were nicknamed **the fab four**, while in the 1990s TV comedy *Absolutely Fabulous*, 'Fabulous, sweetie!' was the standard encouragement of PR guru Edina (Jennifer Saunders) and her best friend Patsy (Joanna Lumley). See also FATE, GROOVE.

face

The word **face**, from Latin *facies* 'form, appearance, face', is used in many expressions. To **fly in the face of**, meaning 'to do the opposite of', is recorded from the 16th century. It is taken literally from the notion of a dog attacking someone by springing directly at them.

To **lose face**, meaning to be humiliated, is a direct translation of a Chinese phrase. An article in *The Times* of February 10, 1893, describing imperial China in relation to foreign countries, notes that in Canton 'No official of any standing would spontaneously associate with a European. Even the Chinese *employés* of the various Legations would lose "face" if observed speaking with their masters in the streets.' The 16th-century dramatist Christopher Marlowe coined the phrase **the face that launched a thousand ships** to describe the great beauty of Helen, whose abduction by Paris caused the Trojan War.

factory

Factories are associated with the Industrial Revolution and mass production, but the first factories were far from any European urban area, in India and Southeast Asia. A **factory** in the late 16th century was a trading company's foreign base or station. The first use of the word in something like the modern sense came in the early 17th century, but until the Victorian era a building where goods were produced was more usually called a **manufactory**. The root of **factory** is Latin *facere* 'to make or do', the source of a great many English words such as **fact**, **factor**, **feat** and **feature**. The sense 'a place where things are made' probably came from Latin *factorium* 'oil press'.

faint

The adjective **faint** was an Old French word that the English started using in the 13th century. It is related to **feign**, and an early meaning was 'feigned, simulated'. Another early meaning was 'cowardly', a sense now preserved only in the proverb **faint heart never won fair lady**, which warns that being timid will prevent you from achieving your objectives.

fair

The word **fair** is recorded from Old English in the sense 'pleasing, attractive'. In early uses its opposite is often given as FOUL, as in the phrase **by foul means or fair**, meaning 'using whatever means are necessary'. This opposition remains in the phrases **fair play** and **foul play**, both of which first appeared in the late 16th century.

    Fair applied to handwriting to mean 'neat, legible' dates from the late 17th century. From this we get **fair copy**, the final corrected copy of a document.

    People have been saying **all's fair in love and war** to justify what they are doing since the early 17th century. **The fair** (or **fairer**) **sex**, a term for women, is recorded from the 17th century. By the early 20th century it was being reworked – the American humorist Ambrose Bierce entitled a 1909 poem about a woman at a railway ticket office who was calmly holding up a desperate queue while she searched for her money 'One of the Unfair Sex'.

The kind of **fair** with stalls and amusements is a completely different word. It comes via Old French from Latin *feria* 'holy day', as fairs were often held on religious holidays. See also COPPER, DINKUM.

fairy

Although we now think of fairies as small, delicate creatures they come from a powerful source – Latin *fata* 'the Fates' (see FATE). The old spelling *faerie* is first recorded in *The Faerie Queene*, the title of a poem by Edmund Spenser in celebration of Queen Elizabeth I (the figure of the 'Faerie Queene' herself was taken to stand for Elizabeth).

In some traditional stories the magical powers of a **fairy godmother** bring unexpected good fortune. The term is now used for any notably generous benefactor. An article in *The Guardian* of January 15, 2006, discussing arts funding in Scotland, gave the view that the First Minister Jack McConnell 'will never be the fairy godmother the arts community want him to be'.

faith

Both **faith** and **fidelity** come from the Latin word *fides*. **Fido**, a common name for a dog, is also related – it represents the Latin for 'I trust'. See also INFIDEL.

fall

When we say of a disappointed person that **his face fell**, we are using an expression which was originally a translation from Hebrew: 'And Cain was very wroth [angry], and his countenance fell.' If we say of someone who has given up an attempt that they have **fallen by the wayside**, we are echoing the parable of the sower, told by Jesus to his disciples in St Matthew's Gospel. The person who has stopped trying to achieve something is compared with seed which 'fell by the way side' and was eaten by birds, and therefore produced no crop. The same story gives us an expression for a suggestion which is badly received or ignored: it is said to **fall on stony ground**. This refers to the seed in the parable which 'fell on stony places' and withered.

In Christian, Jewish and Muslim tradition a **fallen angel** is an angel who rebelled against God and was cast out of heaven. The devil was the head of the fallen angels.

These are largely negative senses, but a more positive expression is found in **fall on your feet**, used to indicate that you emerge unhurt from a difficult or damaging situation. The reference is to cats, which always seem to land elegantly after a fall or jump. See also AUTUMN, FELL.

false

Along with **default**, **fail** and **fault**, **false** comes from Latin *fallere* 'to deceive'. A **false dawn** is a light which in Eastern countries is briefly seen about an hour before sunrise. The expression, the translation of an Arabic phrase, is often used to describe a promising situation which has, or is likely to, come to nothing.

fame

In early use **fame** could mean not only 'celebrity' but 'reputation', a sense that survives in the old term for a brothel, a **house of ill fame**. The word comes from Latin *fama* 'report, fame'. The desire to win fame has often been seen as a positive force to stir somebody up to action: in the 17th century John Milton wrote 'Fame is the spur that the clear spirit doth raise . . . To scorn delights, and live laborious days.' The writer Howard Spring borrowed *Fame is the Spur* as the title of a novel that was made into a film in 1947.

Famous is from the same root. To be **famous for 15 minutes** is to enjoy a brief period in the limelight before fading back into obscurity. The expression comes from the prediction by the American artist Andy Warhol in 1968 that 'In the future everybody will be world famous for 15 minutes.' A few years later **famous for being famous** is recorded to describe someone whose only real distinction is their celebrity status.

Everybody will be world famous for 15 minutes.

Andy Warhol

family

A person's **family** was originally the servants of their household. It then came to be 'all the people who live in one house, including parents, children and servants', before it settled on its modern meaning. The word is from Latin *famulus* 'household servant', as is **familiar**.

The former British Prime Minister Harold Macmillan made a speech in 1985 where he opposed the government's policy of privatising state assets and supposedly accused them of **selling the family silver**. What he actually said was: 'First of all the Georgian silver goes, and then all that nice furniture that used to be in the saloon. Then the Canalettos go.'

fan

The spelling **fan** can represent two quite different words. The first, meaning 'a device to create a current of air', goes back to the Old English noun *fann*, a word of Latin origin. It was a device for blowing air through harvested grain to winnow it, removing the husks or chaff from the seed.

The second **fan**, meaning 'an enthusiast or supporter', is short for **fanatic**. Its earliest uses are recorded from the end of the 17th century, but it became particularly established in American English during the 19th century. In Latin *fanaticus* meant 'inspired by a god' and came from *fanum* meaning 'a temple'. In its first English appearances **fanatic** was used as an adjective to describe the kind of frenzied speech or behaviour typical of someone possessed by a god or demon. As a noun it originally meant 'a mad person' and then 'a religious maniac'.

Fanzine was coined in the 1940s in the US for a magazine produced by amateur enthusiasts of science fiction, though fanzines are now often about music, film or sport. The word is a blend of **fan** and **magazine**.

fantastic

A word originally meaning 'existing only in the imagination, unreal' that comes from Greek *phantastikos*. **Fantasy** is of similar origin, and both words are related to PHANTOM – from the 16th to the 19th centuries the Latin-style spelling *phantastic* was also used. Another related word is **fancy**, which is a contracted version of **fantasy** that also used to be spelled with a *ph*.

The modern use of **fantastic** to mean 'wonderful, excellent' dates from the 1930s. The playful phrase **trip the light fantastic**, meaning 'to dance', goes back to the work of a serious literary figure. In John Milton's 1645 poem *L'Allegro*, the Nymph is invited to 'Come, and trip it as you go / On the light fantastic toe.'

farce

In 1796 the cookery writer Hannah Glasse wrote, 'Make a farce with the livers minced small.' **Farce** was an adoption of a French word meaning 'stuffing', its first sense in English. It took on its modern English meaning when applied to comic interludes which were 'stuffed' into the texts of religious plays. From this the term was used for a complete comic play, these days one that involves a lot of slapstick. In the 20th century two London theatres were associated particularly with farces. **Aldwych farces**, written in particular by Ben Travers, were presented at the Aldwych Theatre in the 1920s and 1930s, whereas **Whitehall farces** were produced at the Whitehall Theatre, especially between 1950 and 1967 by Brian Rix. See also INTERLUDE.

fascism

The term **fascism** was first used of the right-wing nationalist regime of Mussolini in Italy (1922-43), the *partito nazionale fascista* ('national fascist party'), and later applied to the regimes of Franco in Spain and of the Nazis in Germany. It comes from Latin *fascis* 'bundle'. In ancient Rome the *fasces* were the bundle of rods, with an axe through them, carried in front of a magistrate as a symbol of his power to punish people.

fashion

If you were **out of fashion** in the early 1500s you were not outmoded, you were 'out of shape'. **Fashion** originally meant 'make, shape, or appearance' as well as 'a particular style', and it was not until the mid 16th century that it developed the sense of 'a popular style of clothes or way of behaving'. **In fashion** and **out of fashion** were both used by Shakespeare to mean 'in vogue' and 'out of vogue'. In *Julius Caesar*, when the defeated Brutus plans to kill himself, he says, 'Slaying is the word. It is a deed in fashion.'

fast

The two meanings of **fast**, 'at high speed' and 'abstain from food', are different words, both Old English. The first originally meant 'firmly fixed in place', a meaning which survives in such uses as 'colour-fast' and 'make a rope fast'.

Fast and loose was an old fairground gambling game in which the player put a finger into one of the two figure-of-eight loops of a twisted belt or rope so that it caught in a loop when the belt or rope was pulled away. If it was not held, or 'fast', the punter lost the money. The person organising the game could easily make sure the loops always came free by twisting them in a particular way, which is where we get the expression **play fast and loose**, 'behave irresponsibly or immorally'.

Fast food has been eaten since the beginning of the 1950s in the USA. The first McDonald's restaurant opened there in 1940, but it was in 1948 that it was reorganised to offer a simple menu of speedily served burgers, fries and drinks which has spread worldwide. The first British McDonald's restaurant appeared in 1974. See also feature on US WORDS.

fat

People have been described as **fat** since Anglo-Saxon times. Weight has become a contentious issue, with media alarm about overweight children snacking on junk food and sitting in front of TV or computer games all day instead of taking exercise, but in the days when food was scarcer to be fat was not seen as such a bad thing. Shakespeare's Julius Caesar said:

Let me have men about me that are fat;
Sleek-headed men and such as sleep o'nights;
Yond' Cassius has a lean and hungry look;
He thinks too much: such men are dangerous.

More recently, the English writer George Orwell said in 1939, 'I'm fat, but I'm thin inside. Has it ever struck you that there's a thin man inside every fat man, just as they say there's a statue inside every block of stone?' Cyril Connolly echoed this in 1944 when he said that 'Imprisoned in every fat man a thin one is wildly signalling to be let out.'

For some women fat is a feminist issue – the title of a 1978 book by Susie Orbach.

In the biblical story of the Prodigal Son, the father is so relieved at the safe return of his errant son that he tells his servants to prepare a celebratory feast of meat from a calf that is being fattened up. When the dutiful elder brother, who has stayed at home to work for his father, comes in from the fields and asks what is happening, a servant explains 'Thy brother is come; and thy father hath killed the fatted calf.' From this we get the expression **kill the fatted calf**, meaning to celebrate something by laying on the best possible food.

The Bible also gives us **live on the fat of the land** as a way of saying that we have the best of everything. It comes from the Book of Genesis, in Pharaoh's promise to Joseph and his family, 'Ye shall eat the fat of the land'. **Fat** here represents an old sense of the noun meaning 'the richest or choicest part of something', which now survives only in this phrase.

The fat is in the fire, meaning that something has happened that will inevitably cause trouble, uses the image of a cookery disaster, and the smell and smoke of burnt fat from an overturned pan. Recorded from the mid 16th century, it originally referred to the complete failure of a plan.

People spending time chatting in a leisurely way can be said to be **chewing the fat**. The origin of the expression is not entirely clear – it may have first been used in the Indian Army – but the most likely explanation is that it derives from the similarity between the movements of the jaw in chewing through fat or gristle and those involved in talking animatedly. See also OBESE, OPERA.

fate

This comes from Latin *fatum* 'what has been said', from *fari* 'to speak' (see also FABULOUS). The main sense of *fatum* was 'the judgement or sentence of the gods', but it came to mean a person's 'lot', or what would happen to them.

The Fates were the three goddesses of Greek and Roman mythology who presided over the birth and life of humans. Each person was thought of as a spindle, around which the three Fates (Clotho, the spinner, Lachesis, who measured the thread, and Atropos, who cut it off) would spin the thread of human destiny.

father

The Old English word **father** is related to Dutch *vader* and German *Vater*. All these words go back to an ancient root which is also shared by Latin *pater*, from which we get PATERNAL.

The proverb **like father, like son** means that a son's character and behaviour can be expected to resemble that of his father. In this exact form it is recorded from the early 17th century, but the idea with slightly different wording goes back to the Middle Ages.

faun

In Roman mythology a **faun** was a lustful rural deity represented as a man with a goat's horns, ears, legs and tail. The word comes from the name of *Faunus*, a god of flocks and herds, who was associated with wooded places. He had a sister, *Fauna*, whose name in turn gives us **fauna**, which since the late 18th century has been used to mean 'the animals of a particular region or period'. **Flora**, 'the plants of a particular region or period' comes from the name of *Flora*, an ancient Italian goddess of fertility and flowers. See also FLOWER.

Fawn meaning 'a young deer' comes from Old French *faon* and is based on Latin *fetus* 'offspring'. The word did not mean 'a light brown colour' until much later, in the late 19th century. The verb **fawn** is earlier, and is a quite different word. In Old English *fagnian* meant 'make or be glad', often used of a dog showing delight by wagging its tail, grovelling or whining. **Fawn** was then used to convey the idea of a person giving a servile display of exaggerated flattery or affection, particularly in order to gain favour.

feast

People have been celebrating special occasions with a **feast** since the Middle Ages, and appropriately the word goes back to Latin *festus* meaning 'joyous'. **Festival** derives from the closely related Latin word *festivus*. In the Christian Church the date of some festivals like Easter, known as **movable feasts**, varies from year to year.

A **skeleton at the feast** is someone or something who casts gloom on what should be a happy occasion. This goes back to a story told in the 5th century BC by the Greek historian Herodotus. In ancient Egypt a painted carving of a body in a coffin was carried round the room at parties, and shown to guests with the warning that this was how they would be one day.

fee

A word bound up with the medieval feudal system, in which the nobles held Crown land in exchange for military service while the peasants were obliged to work their lord's land and give him a share of the produce. A **fee** was originally a **fief** or feudal estate, from which it developed through the meanings 'the right to an office or pension', 'a tribute to a superior' and 'a benefit or reward' to the modern sense. The word comes from Old French *feu* or *fief*, and is related to **feudal**.

feisty

A small farting dog is the surprising idea behind the word **feisty**, meaning 'spirited and exuberant'. It comes from the earlier and now obsolete word *feist* or *fist* meaning 'small dog', from *fisting cur* or *fisting hound*. This was a derogatory term for a lapdog, deriving from the old verb *fist*, meaning 'to break wind'. *Fist* may also be the source of **fizzle**, which in the 16th century meant 'to break wind quietly'. **Fart** itself goes back to Old English times and was formerly a more respectable word than it is now – Geoffrey Chaucer used it in *The Canterbury Tales*.

fell

The verb **fell** meaning 'to cut down' is recorded from Old English, and is related to FALL. **Fell** as a noun meaning 'hill' is a different word, not found until the Middle Ages. It comes from the Old Norse word for a hill, *fjall*.

Fell as an adjective meaning 'wicked' comes from an Old French word meaning 'wicked' or 'a wicked person', the same root as **felon** and **felony**. Today it is probably most familiar in the phrase **at one fell swoop**. This originally referred to the sudden descent of a bird of prey in deadly pursuit of its quarry, but came to be used to mean 'at a single blow' or 'all at one go'. In Shakespeare's *Macbeth*, when Macduff hears that his wife and children have been killed at Macbeth's orders, he cries out, 'What! All my pretty chickens and their dam / At one fell swoop?'

female

The spelling of **female** changed in the Middle Ages to match **male**, which is a quite different word. **Female** came via Old French *femelle* from Latin *femella*, which was a diminutive form of *femina* 'woman', whereas **male** is based on Latin *masculus*, also the source of **maculine**, from *mas* 'a male person'.

The saying **the female of the species is more deadly than the male** comes from the 1911 poem 'The Female of the Species' by Rudyard Kipling. Whether the animal in question is a cobra, a she-bear or a woman, the warning of where the greatest danger lies is the same, 'For the female of the species is more deadly than the male'. See also CHAUVINISM, MACHO.

ferret

Ferrets are furry, and **fur** is the basis for the word, although it is not the kind of fur we are familiar with. In Latin *fur* meant 'thief', and is the root of **ferret**, which entered English from Old French *fuiret*. Ferrets are known for stealing birds' eggs, and this was probably why they got their name.

fetish

Before its modern sense of 'an obsession' or 'an unusual form of sexual desire', a **fetish** was an object worshipped in West Africa for its supposed magical powers, or used as an amulet or charm. Early European visitors used the Portuguese word *feitiço* 'charm, sorcery' for it.

fever

People have suffered from **fever** since Anglo-Saxon times, when we borrowed the word from Latin *febris*. A fever makes you hot and bothered, and the word may ultimately go back to a root meaning 'to be restless'.

In herbal medicine the plant **feverfew** was traditionally seen as a cure for fever. In Latin the name was *febrifugia*, from *febris* 'fever' and *fugare* 'drive away', from which we get the medical term **febrifuge** for a drug that reduces fever.

few

The ancient root of **few** is shared by Latin *paucus* 'small', which gives us the later English word **paucity**. The name **the Few** for the RAF pilots who took part in the Battle of Britain in 1940 comes from a speech by Winston Churchill in August of that year: 'Never in the field of human conflict was so much owed by so many to so few.'

fiasco

A **fiasco** is a ridiculous or humiliating failure. The word was borrowed from Italian in the 19th century. In that language it meant originally 'a bottle', but the phrase *far fiasco*, literally 'make a bottle', was used in the theatre to mean 'fail in a performance'. In medieval English a **flask** was a cask or skin for holding liquor. The word came from medieval Latin **flasca**, but the 17th-century sense 'glass container' was influenced by Italian *fiasco*.

fiddle

In Old English **fiddle** was the usual word for a stringed instrument like a violin. It has relations in modern Dutch and German, and all three are based on Latin *vitulari* 'to celebrate, be joyful', which may come from *Vitula*, a Roman goddess of joy and victory.

In the sense 'to swindle' **fiddle** was first used in the 1630s. The connection with violin playing probably came from the idea that the 'fiddler' or player could make people 'dance to his tune'. Expressions like **fiddle-de-dee** and **fiddle-faddle**, meaning 'nonsense', come from the idea of violin playing being a trivial or pointless exercise, and in turn **fiddle-faddle** is the origin of **fad**.

When we criticise someone for concerning themselves with trivial affairs while ignoring serious matters, we may say that they are **fiddling while Rome burns**. This looks back to a story about the Roman emperor Nero. According to one historian, when Rome suffered from a disastrous fire Nero reacted by singing a song about the fall of Troy and accompanying himself on some instrument – not a fiddle, which had not been invented then.

To **play second fiddle** is to take a less important role. The idea here is that you are there to support the person taking the leading part. In 19th-century Oxford, an undergraduates' rhyme about Dean Liddell, father of Lewis Carroll's Alice, ran, 'I am the Dean, and this is Mrs Liddell; She the first, and I the second fiddle.'

filibuster

A **filibuster** was an 18th-century pirate of the Caribbean. The word links a number of languages, reaching back through Spanish and French to a Dutch word from which we also get **freebooter** (see FREE). In the 19th century the name was given to American adventurers who stirred up revolution in Central and South America, and came to be used in the USA to describe behaviour in congressional debates intended to sabotage proceedings. From this we get the current sense, 'a very long speech made in Parliament to prevent the passing of a new law', which links the long-ago pirates with politicians of today.

fillip

Today you would probably be pleased to hear of 'a fillip to sales', knowing it meant that your figures had received a bit of a boost. Less so in the Middle Ages when **fillip** meant simply 'a flick of the finger'.

fire

In ancient and medieval philosophy **fire** was seen, along with water, air and earth, as one of the four elements. The word goes back to an ancient root that also gave us the Greek word for fire, *pur*, the source of **pyre** and **pyromaniac**. The phrase **fire and brimstone** is a traditional description of the torments of hell. In the biblical book of Revelation there is a reference to 'a lake of fire burning with brimstone'. **Brimstone** is an old word for sulphur, and literally means 'burning stone'. A fire-and-brimstone sermon is one that gives vivid warning of the dangers of going to hell if you misbehave.

To **set the world on fire** is to do something remarkable. An earlier British version was to **set the Thames on fire**, and a Scottish one is **set the heather on fire**. Whichever version is used, it tends to be with a negative implication. In Anthony Trollope's novel *The Eustace Diamonds* (1873) Lady Glencora is clear about the limitations of 'poor Lord Fawn' who 'will never set the Thames on fire'.

firm

Firm meaning 'not yielding to pressure' comes from Latin *firmus*, which is also the root of **farm**. **Firm** meaning 'a company or business' has the same root, but the immediate origin is different. The Latin word had also given rise to Italian *firma*, and in the late 16th century this was adopted into English to mean 'an autograph or signature'. Over time it came to mean the name under which business was transacted by an organisation, as in 'trading under the firm of "Grant & Co."'. Finally, in the late 18th century, **firm** became the term for a company.

first

The Old English word **first** goes back to an ancient root which is shared by Latin *primus* (as in **primary**), and Greek *prōtos* (as in **protein** and **prototype**). The expression **first come, first served** goes back to the Middle Ages and is found in the poetry of Geoffrey Chaucer. It was originally used in the context of milling, when a mill would serve the whole community. The first person to bring their corn to the mill would be the first person to have it ground.

The **first among equals** is the member of a group that has the highest status. It is a translation of the Latin phrase *primus inter pares*, which was used as a title by Roman emperors. Many will know it today as the title of a Jeffrey Archer novel published in 1984.

In Scotland to **first-foot** is to be the first person to cross the threshold of a house in the New Year. Traditionally, it is thought lucky for the person to be a dark-haired man.

fish

A **fish** was originally any animal living exclusively in water, as distinct from the 'birds of the air' and the 'beasts of the field'. In Christian art a fish is a symbol

of Christ, and is often found in paintings in the underground catacombs of ancient Rome – for this reason modern Christians sometimes have a stylised fish displayed on the rear of their car or its number plate. The connection may go back to the first letters of the Greek words for 'Jesus Christ, Son of God, Saviour', which were read as *ikhthus* 'fish'.

We have been eating **fish fingers** for more than 50 years. Their inventor Clarence Birdseye, founder of the Birds Eye food company, launched them in 1955, and now more than a million are eaten in Britain every day.

The idea of being a **fish out of water**, or a person in a completely unsuitable environment, is very old, going back to the days of Geoffrey Chaucer, who wrote that 'A monk when he is reckless [meaning 'neglectful of his duty'] is like a fish that is waterless'. In 1613 the English travel writer Samuel Purchas said: 'The Arabians out of the desarts are as Fishes out of the Water.' See also RED.

flag

The **flag** that means 'a stone slab' is recorded from medieval English, and may be one of the words given us by the Vikings. The **flag** which is used as the emblem of a country has been with us since the mid 16th century, and is a different word. It is likely to represent the sound of something flapping in the wind, although it

may also be connected with an obsolete word *flag* meaning 'hanging down'.

When we want to make clear our support for something we might say that we **show the flag**. Originally this was used of a naval vessel making an official visit to a foreign port.

Flag meaning 'become tired' is probably related to the 'emblem' flag. It first meant 'flap about loosely, hang down'. In June 1940, after Dunkirk and before the Battle of Britain, Winston Churchill rallied the House of Commons with the words:

> We shall not flag or fail . . . We shall fight on the beaches, we shall fight on the landing grounds, we shall fight in the fields and in the streets, we shall fight in the hills; we shall never surrender.

See also BLOOD, FEW, HOUR for more from Winston Churchill.

flagrant

A flagrant violation of the law, or a flagrant abuse, are things to be stamped out, but early senses of **flagrant** such as 'glorious' and 'blazing' were positive. The word comes from the Latin word *flagrare* 'to blaze', as in **conflagration**, and is recorded from the late 15th century.

flamingo

The tall wading bird may be connected with **flamenco**, a style of Spanish Gypsy music and dance. In Spanish *flamenco* means both 'flamingo' and 'flamenco', and also 'like a Gypsy', 'strong and healthy-looking' and 'Flemish'. How 'Flemish' is related to the other meanings is not clear: it may be from the pink cheeks of north Europeans, or because of an apparent reputation that the people of Flanders had in the Middle Ages for flamboyant clothing. The name of the bird was probably influenced by Latin *flamma* 'flame', on account of its bright pink colour.

flannel

Ever since the Middle Ages we have worn **flannel**, which probably comes from Welsh, from the word *gwlân* 'wool'. In the 1920s the sense of 'bland, vague talk used to avoid a difficult subject' developed from the central idea of a soft, warm fabric – it seems to have started as military slang. See also CORGI, OAF.

flash

We think of **flash** in terms of fire and light, but in the Middle Ages it originally meant 'splash water about', and like **plash** and **splash** probably came from the sound of the word. The association with fire may have developed from the resemblance of the word to **flame**. The idea of 'ostentatious stylishness or display of wealth' goes back to the 17th century.

When calling a sudden, brief success **a flash in the pan** we are referring to early firearms. Sometimes the gunpowder would burn fiercely but ineffectually in the 'pan', the part that held the priming charge, without igniting the main charge. The result was a flash and some smoke, but the gun did not fire, and the ball did not go anywhere.

flavour

Originally **flavour** was associated with smell rather than taste, and meant 'fragrance'. Linked in English with **savour**, it comes from an Old French word which might be a combination of Latin *flatus* 'blowing' and *foetor* 'unpleasant smell'. The current meaning of 'a distinctive taste' dates from the 17th century. In the 1930s American ice-cream parlours ran campaigns to promote a particular **flavour of the month**, giving us the phrase we use today to mean 'person or thing that is currently very popular.'

flea

We have called **fleas** by that name since Anglo-Saxon times, with the first use of the word recorded as early as the 8th century. Fleas are jumping insects, and since the late 19th century an active, healthy person has been as **fit as a flea**. People have been sent away with **a flea in their ear** since the 15th century, and the idea dates back earlier in France. The telling-off is so 'sharp' that it is likened to the pain of a flea bite. **Flea markets** and **fleapits**, or scruffy cinemas, get their names from the idea that they are musty places which harbour fleas.

flesh

The most tangible part of the human body is **flesh**, and since the Middle Ages people have described their children, brothers, sisters, and other family members as **their own flesh and blood**. In the Book of Genesis God took out one of Adam's ribs when he was sleeping, and made it into a woman, Eve. Adam said, 'This is now bone of my bones, and flesh of my flesh: she shall be called Woman, because she was taken out of Man.'

To **go the way of all flesh** is to die. It is from a 17th-century English translation of the Bible, of what in most bibles is rendered as 'Go the way of all the earth'.

fleshpots

The first **fleshpots** 'places providing luxurious living', are in the book of Exodus, where they are literally pots for boiling meat. As the Israelites struggle in the desert after escaping from Egypt, they lament, 'Would to God that we had died by the hand of the Lord in the land of Egypt, when we sat by the flesh pots, and when we did eat bread to the full.'

flirt

Like words such as **biff**, **bounce**, **flick** and **spurt**, **flirt** apparently arose because it somehow 'sounded right' to convey the idea it represented. In the case of **flirt** the elements *fl-* and *-irt* probably suggest sudden movement – the original verb senses were 'to give someone a sharp blow', 'to move or propel suddenly' and 'to sneer at'. As a noun it first meant 'joke, gibe' and 'flighty girl', with a notion originally of cheekiness rather than of playfully amorous behaviour.

flog

This was first a slang word, which might be from Latin *flagellare* 'to whip', or could just have been formed in imitation of the 'whoosh-crack!' noise of a whip being wielded. **Flog** meaning 'to sell' started life as military slang, probably during the First World War. See also HORSE.

floozy

These days **floozy** has a dated feel, and is only really used in jokey contexts. It is not that old a word, though, and does not seem to have been used before the 20th century. It might come from the English dialect word **floosy**, meaning 'fluffy, soft', or from **flossy**, which is literally 'like silk, silky' but can mean 'saucy, cheeky' or 'showy, flashy' in the USA.

flora see FAUN.

flotsam

This legal term for wreckage found floating on the sea or washed up on the beach comes ultimately from French, from the verb *floter* 'to float'. **Flotsam and jetsam** is useless or discarded objects – JETSAM is specifically goods or material thrown overboard and washed ashore.

flout

Flout, which appeared in the 16th century and means 'to openly disregard a rule or convention', may come from a Dutch word *fluiten* meaning 'whistle, play the flute, hiss derisively'. There is a German dialect expression *pfeifen auf*, literally 'pipe at', which is used in a similar way. **Flout** is often confused with **flaunt**, 'to display something ostentatiously', but there is no connection – the origin of **flaunt** is unknown.

flower

Despite the big difference in meaning, **flower** and **flour** are the same word. In Middle English **flower** was spelt 'flour', but by the 17th century this spelling was limited to the specialised sense of 'ground grain'. **Flour** developed from the meaning the 'flower' or 'best part of something'. It was then used for 'the finest quality of ground wheat', and from this developed the sense we have today. The word comes through French from a Latin root which also gives us **flora** (see FAUN) and **flourish**.

flunkey

This has been part of the language since the mid 18th century, and was originally Scots. In Robert Burns's poem *The Twa Dogs* (1786), the laird's dog tries to impress the ploughman's collie with a grand description of his master's house: 'His flunkies answer at the bell.' It may come from *flank*, in the sense 'a person who stands at one's side'.

fly

In Old English a **fly** was any winged insect – the word is closely related to the verb 'to fly'. In the 17th century the clergyman Edward Topsell wrote of 'the black flies called beetles'.

A **fly in the ointment** is a minor irritation that spoils the success or enjoyment of something. The phrase goes back to a verse in the biblical book of Ecclesiastes, 'Dead flies cause the ointment of the apothecary to send forth a stinking savour.'

A **fly** or **flies** is a trouser zip, and also the flap of material that covers it. As with **flap** itself, the link is the idea of something being attached by only one edge and 'flapping' freely.

To **fly a kite** has had various incarnations in slang. It now means 'to try something out to test public opinion', but in the 19th century it was to raise money on credit. In the USA telling someone to **go fly a kite** is to tell them to go away.

fob

To **fob someone off** meant 'to cheat, deceive' in medieval days. Although the origin is uncertain, it may be related to German *foppen* 'deceive, cheat, banter', or to **fop**.

In the mid 17th century a **fob** was a small pocket in the waistband of a pair of breeches, for carrying a watch or other valuables. The use of the word to mean a chain attached to a watch developed from this. Again the origin is uncertain, but there may be a link with the earlier English verb, or there could be a connection with the idea of 'deceive', because the pocket was 'secret'.

focus

In Latin *focus* meant 'hearth, fireplace', and the optical sense of 'the burning point of a lens', the point at which rays meet after reflection or refraction, may have developed from this. It was first used in Latin in this sense by the German astronomer Johannes Kepler in 1604. By the beginning of the 18th century the word was established in English, and had appeared in the writings of such eminent figures as the philosopher Thomas Hobbes, the scientist Robert Boyle and the mathematician and physicist Isaac Newton. The **focus groups** of modern marketing are unsurprisingly much more recent, dating from the early 1960s. See also FUEL.

fog

In medieval English **fog** was a name for 'coarse grass'. Its origin is uncertain, but it may be related to Norwegian *fogg*. It gave rise to the adjective **foggy**, 'covered with fog', which also had the meaning 'thick, murky'. The weather term **fog** is probably linked with the earlier word, but at one remove, since it is likely to be from **foggy**.

fogey

This word for an old-fashioned or narrow-minded person is first found in the late 18th century, in Scots use. It is related to an earlier slang term *fogram*, and may be connected with *foggy* in the senses 'flabby, bloated' or 'moss-grown'. In the 1980s **young fogeys** appeared – young people noticeable for their conservative tastes and ideas. The phrase is first recorded in 1909, but became popular with the rise of the YUPPIE in the early 1980s, and in 1985 *The Young Fogey Handbook* was published.

fond

It is perfectly natural to be **fond of** someone, or to like having **fun**, but the root of both words is the medieval word **fon**, which meant 'a fool'. **Fond** originally meant 'foolish, silly' or 'mad', and did not acquire the modern sense 'affectionate' until the end of the 16th century – Shakespeare appears to have been the first to use **fond of**, in *A Midsummer Night's Dream*.

Fun first meant 'to cheat or trick'. The original sense of the noun was 'a cheat, trick or hoax', and when people started using it to mean 'enjoyment, amusement' in the 18th century it was regarded as a low slang word.

food

Recorded since the beginning of the 11th century, the Old English word **food** is related to **fodder** and **foster**. It can refer to mental as well as physical nourishment – the expression **food for thought** to indicate something that deserves serious consideration has been in the language since the early 19th century.

British food does not have the best reputation in the rest of the world. In his 1946 book *How to be an Alien* the Hungarian-born humorist George Mikes quipped, 'On the Continent people have good food; in England people have good table manners.' He also said that 'Continental people have sex life; the English have hot-water bottles.'

fool

The root of **fool** is Latin *follis*, which originally meant 'bellows, windbag' and came to mean 'an empty-headed person', in the same way that **windbag** does in English. The use of **fool** to mean a jester or clown also goes back to the Middle Ages.

People in the 16th century seem to have been particularly aware of the ways in which someone may come to grief through lack of wisdom, especially in their dealings with others. **A fool and his money are soon parted**, a **fool at forty is a fool indeed**, and **there's no fool like an old fool** all come from this period. Two centuries later foolish behaviour was still a matter for concern – in 1711 the poet Alexander Pope published the line which has in turn become proverbial, 'Fools rush in where angels fear to tread.' Eager prospectors have been mistaking worthless minerals such as iron pyrites, or **fool's gold**, for gold since the late 19th century.

The term **foolscap** for a paper size dates from the late 17th century, and is said to be named after a former watermark representing a fool's cap. Sadly, a traditional story that after the Civil War Parliament gave orders that a fool's cap should replace the royal arms in the watermark of the paper used for the Journals of the House of Commons apparently has no basis in fact.

foot

An Old English word that appears as far back as the epic poem *Beowulf*, probably written in the 700s, **foot** comes from an ancient root which also gives us Greek *pous*, the root of words as varied as ANTIPODES, OCTOPUS and **podium**, and Latin *pes* 'foot', as in PEDESTRIAN. The measure equal to 12 inches was originally based on the length of a man's foot.

When we use **feet of clay** to suggest that a respected person has a fundamental flaw, we are reaching back to a story from biblical times. In the book of Daniel, Nebuchadnezzar, the king of Babylon, dreamed about a magnificent idol which had feet 'part of iron and part of clay', and which was broken into pieces. The prophet Daniel interpreted this to mean that the kingdom would eventually fall.

To **have one foot in the grave** is to be near death. Although the idea dates back to the 17th century, it is now particularly associated with the British TV comedy *One Foot in the Grave*, starring Richard Wilson as the unlucky but defiant Victor Meldrew, who had been forced into early retirement. See also FIRST.

football

Football is truly the world sport, but it means different things in different places. In Britain it is Association football or SOCCER, or to some people RUGBY football. In the USA it is American football, and in Australia Australian Rules.

In most forms of football the ball is handled as well as kicked, and this seems to have been the case when similar games were played in ancient Greece, Rome and China. In medieval Europe it was a rowdy game with vague rules and large numbers of participants. Edward II banned it in 1314 because of the disruption and violence it brought – it then consisted of vast mobs attempting to kick, carry or throw the ball between opposing villages. During the Hundred Years War it was again banned because it was thought to interfere with archery practice. The first written evidence of the term football comes in 1424, when James I of Scotland decreed that 'na man play at the fut ball under the payne of 4d' (meaning that there was a fine of fourpence for anyone playing football).

In Britain a **political football** is a controversial or much-debated issue – one that is 'kicked around' in discussion – whereas in the USA a football is a briefcase containing the codes the President would use to launch a nuclear attack, carried by an aide and kept available at all times. The comparison was made because in American football players hold on to the ball tightly, letting go only to pass to a colleague.

forest

You would not necessarily link **forest** and **foreign**, but the two words have the same Latin root. **Forest** came via French from the Latin phrase *forestis silva*, literally 'wood outside', from *foris* 'outdoors, outside' and *silva* 'a wood'. It was the first of these words which then moved into English and became our 'forest'.

In early use **forest** had a special legal sense. It was an area, usually belonging to the King, that was intended for hunting, a mixture of woodland, heath, scrub and farmland not as thickly wooded as forests today. It had its own **forest laws**, and officers appointed to enforce them. The New Forest in Hampshire was reserved as Crown property by William the Conqueror in 1079 as a royal hunting area, and still has its own rules and officers, or **verderers** (a word that comes from Latin *viridis*, 'green').

Another word derived from Latin *foris* 'outside' is **forfeit**. It originally meant 'a crime or offence', the meaning of a fine or penalty developing from this.

fork

Rather than things to eat your dinner with, **forks** were originally agricultural implements. The fork used for holding food dates from medieval times, when Anglo-Saxon table manners were presumably affected by Norman ways. The word is from Latin *furca* 'pitchfork, forked stick'.

A snake's divided tongue is often described as forked, and snakes have been symbols of deceit since the serpent that tempted Adam and Eve in the Garden of Eden. So to speak **with forked tongue** is to speak untruthfully.

People have been **forking out**, or reluctantly paying money, since the 1830s or maybe before that. The phrase comes from the earlier literal meaning, 'to divide or move with a fork'.

forlorn

In Old English **forlorn** meant 'morally corrupted', but the core idea was 'lost', from the verb *forlese* 'to lose'. In the 16th century the current sense of 'pitifully sad' developed.

A **forlorn hope** is a persistent or desperate hope that is unlikely to be fulfilled. The phrase came into the language as a mistranslation of Dutch *verloren hoop* 'lost troop'. It originally referred to a band of soldiers picked to begin an attack, many of who would not survive. The current sense, based on a misunderstanding of 'forlorn', is recorded from the mid 17th century.

fortune

The Roman goddess *Fortuna*, who personified luck or chance, gave us the English word **fortune**. The saying **fortune favours the brave**, meaning that a person who acts boldly and decisively is likely to be successful, is found in English from the late 14th century, but the same idea can be traced back to classical times. The Roman poet Virgil included the line *audentes fortuna iuvat* 'fortune favours the brave' in his epic poem the *Aeneid*. See also HOSTAGE.

fossil

Fossils are the petrified remains of ancient or prehistoric creatures that are dug up – so it is unsurprising that **fossil** comes from Latin *fodere* 'to dig'. The word dates from the mid 16th century, and was originally used for a fossilised fish which was found in the earth. In those days before the theory of evolution people believed that it had lived underground too.

The use of the word for a person or organisation seen as outdated or resistant to change is found from the mid 19th century. In *The Innocents Abroad* (1869), the American writer Mark Twain refers to 'that poor, useless, innocent, mildewed old fossil, the Smithsonian Institute'. See also DINOSAUR.

Environmental concerns today often prompt the discussion of **fossil fuels**, fuel such as coal and gas formed from the remains of animals and plants. The phrase itself goes back to the mid 19th century.

foul

The Old English word **foul** comes from an ancient root shared by Latin *pus* and Greek *puos* 'pus' and Latin *putere* 'to stink', and the original sense was 'stinking or disgusting'. **Foul play** indicating unfair conduct or treachery is recorded from the late 16th century, and sports players have been able to complain of 'a foul' since the 1750s. The first examples of sporting fouls were in rowing and riding. See also FAIR.

fox

An Old English word that is related to German *Fuchs*. The **fox** is a common figure of folklore, long associated with artfulness and cunning, and is a character in a number of animal fables, such as that of the Fox and Grapes, the origin of the phrase **sour grapes** (see GRAPE). It is also a traditional quarry of hunters. Oscar Wilde described 'The English country gentleman galloping after a fox – the unspeakable in full pursuit of the uneatable'.

Today the fox is as much an urban animal as a rural one, and its meaning has also shifted significantly. The US sense 'an attractive woman' is first recorded in the early 1960s, but the related adjective **foxy** was used before the First World War.

fraction

Medieval mathematicians called numbers that were not whole numbers **fractions**. The name came from Latin *frangere* 'to break', also the root of **fracture**. People who struggled to learn about fractions may not be surprised to learn that the word is also linked to **fractious**, or 'bad-tempered'.

frank

In medieval English **frank** meant 'free', and our modern sense of 'open, direct' did not develop until the 16th century. It comes from the name of the **Franks**, an ancient Germanic people who conquered Gaul in the 6th century and established a kingdom in which they were the only free people. See also FRENCH.

If you wanted to send a letter without paying for it in the 18th century you could ask a Member of Parliament to **frank** it. This meant signing the outside of the letter to show that it was free of charge.

fraught

Something **fraught** is now usually filled with danger or anxiety, but at first the word simply meant 'laden' or 'equipped'. It comes from medieval Dutch *vracht* 'ship's cargo'.

fray

The spelling **fray** represents two distinct words. The verb meaning 'to unravel' comes from Latin *fricare* 'to rub'. A person eager to fight might 'plunge into the fray'. This comes from the same root as the old legal term **affray** 'a breach of the peace by fighting in a public place', Old French *afrayer* 'to disturb, startle'. Someone **frazzled** with exhaustion might not be surprised to hear that the word is probably linked with **fray** meaning 'to unravel'.

free

The adjective **free** appears in the writings of the Anglo-Saxon King Alfred, who reigned 871-99, and comes from an ancient root meaning 'to love', from which we also get FRIEND. **Freedom** is the wish of all who feel oppressed or downtrodden. The French philosopher Jean-Jacques Rousseau (1712-78) summed up the situation with 'Man was born free, and everywhere he is in chains', while in the cult 1960s TV series *The Prisoner* Patrick McGoohan cried 'I am not a number, I am a free man!'

Freebooter, a name for a lawless adventurer, comes from Dutch *vrijbuiter*. The second part of the word refers not to the boots worn by the **freebooter**, but to the booty he might hope to carry off.

We now use **freelance** as a term for a self-employed person working for a number of different companies. Back in the early 19th century it was written as two words, and used in a literary context to describe a medieval knight who offered his services – his 'lance' – as a mercenary. In Sir Walter Scott's novel *Ivanhoe* a knight whose help has been rejected by Richard the Lionheart says resentfully, 'I offered Richard the service of my Free Lances, and he refused.'

Freemasons were originally skilled workers in stone who travelled to find employment and had a system of secret signs and passwords that gained them access to work on important building projects. In the 17th century they began to admit honorary members, and membership of their societies or 'lodges' became a fashionable status symbol.

French

The Anglo-Saxons were using **French** to describe people from across the Channel at the beginning of the 11th century. The word represents the name of the earlier conquerors of Gaul, the Franks (see FRANK).

Unceremonious guests have been ready to take **French leave** since the 18th century. It is said to come from the custom of the French to leave a dinner or ball without saying goodbye to their host or hostess. The first record of the expression dates from just after the Seven Years War (1756-63), when France and Britain were struggling for supremacy overseas. It is perhaps not entirely surprising to find that the French themselves take a different view: the equivalent French expression is *filer à l'Anglaise* 'to escape in the style of the English'.

The British also regard the French as rather naughty, as the terms **French kiss**, **French knickers** and **French letter** (for a condom) indicate. This idea is far from new, as the following phrase from *Tom Jones* (1749) by Henry Fielding indicates: 'I would wish to draw a Curtain over . . . certain *French* novels.' As early as 1500 sexually transmitted disease was known in England as the **French pox** or **French disease**.

Ooh-la-la!

When they invaded England in 1066 the Normans brought over their language, and for the next 300 years kings and nobility spoke French. More recently, French has given English many expressions that can imply sophistication or a certain naughtiness.

The English view of the French as immoral or sexy goes back a long way (see FRENCH). Since the 1860s we have called something mildly indecent risqué, literally 'risked', whereas a word or phrase open to two interpretations, one of which is less innocent than the other, is a double entendre or 'double understanding'. A seductive woman who is likely to cause distress to any man who becomes involved with her is a femme fatale, or 'fatal woman'.

By the Victorian era the British upper classes had adopted French cooking, and French cooks were de rigueur (literally 'in strictness') or obligatory, with the result that French became the language of good eating. Someone who wants to produce food to the standard of haute cuisine or 'high cookery' might follow a cordon bleu course. The name refers back to the 'blue ribbon' which since the 1820s has marked a first-class cook but before the French Revolution indicated the highest order of chivalry. Ordering à la carte is choosing dishes as separate items rather than as a set meal, literally 'according to the menu card'. You may prefer the prix fixe, a set meal of several courses served at a 'fixed price', or make do with an hors d'oeuvre, a small savoury dish which is literally 'outside the work'. Or you could simply eat an éclair, which in French is not only a cream cake but also 'a flash of lightning', 'a flash or glint' or 'a moment' – un repas éclair is a quick meal. The cake's name could have been suggested by the

fact that its light texture makes it very quick to eat – the word is defined by the Chambers Dictionary as 'a cake, long in shape but short in duration'.

The traditional English prejudice against the French, who were not only their nearest rivals but were Catholics to boot, moderated after the fall of Napoleon in 1815, and people took up several French expressions. The best example of a particular type might be described as the crème de la crème or 'cream of the cream'. Someone who likes to leave things to follow their own course without interfering follows a policy of laissez-faire, from the French for 'allow to do'. If things do not turn out as you hope, you might console yourself with shrugging your shoulders and saying c'est la vie, the equivalent of 'that's life', or plus ça change – short for plus ça change, plus c'est la même chose, 'the more it changes, the more it stays the same', an 1849 quotation by the French novelist and journalist Alphonse Karr.

If you give someone complete freedom to act as they wish, you give them carte blanche. The literal meaning 'blank paper' carried the idea of a blank sheet on which to write anything desired, originally the terms of a peace treaty. You would probably not give the opportunity to your bête noire – an expression, literally 'black beast', for someone you greatly dislike. Originally an enfant terrible was, as the name suggests, a 'terrible child' who embarrassed its parents with untimely remarks, but it is now a person who behaves in an unconventional or controversial way.

That mainstay of corny sitcoms the au pair is a young foreign girl who helps with housework or childcare in exchange for food and accommodation. She has been around since 1960 or so, but in the 19th century an au pair arrangement was one in which each party paid the other in kind, by performing services. The phrase means 'on equal terms'.

Entrepreneur has been used in English since the 1820s. It first meant 'a director of a musical institution' and 'a person who organises entertainments', but later in the 19th century broadened to refer to somebody who runs a business and takes the risks it entails. The US President George W. Bush is said to have proclaimed, 'The problem with the French is that they don't have a word for entrepreneur' – a good story but one with no evidence to back it up.

haute cuisine

fresh

In Anglo-Saxon times, when meat was salted to last through winter, **fresh** meant 'not salt'. The sense of 'newly made, not faded or worn' developed in the Middle Ages. Fresh meaning 'cheeky' or 'impudent' popped up in the 19th century, and may have been influenced by German *frech* 'saucy'.

A desire for new areas of activity may be expressed as wanting **fresh fields and pastures new**. The phrase is a misquotation from a poem by the 17th-century poet John Milton, 'Tomorrow to fresh woods, and pastures new'.

fret

If we tell an anxious person not to **fret**, we are telling them not to worry, but in Old English the word meant 'devour, consume'. It is from the same root as EAT. The **fret** in **fretsaw** and **fretwork** is a different word, from Old French *freté*, while the **fret** on a guitar neck is yet another word, of unknown origin.

friend

In the Old English poem *Beowulf* the king's great hall is described as being filled with **friends**. This is the first recorded use of the word, which is from an ancient root meaning 'to love' that is shared by FREE.

The proverb **a friend in need is a friend indeed**, meaning that a real friend is someone who helps when you are in difficulty, can be traced back in English to the 11th century. More recent is **your flexible friend**, that faithful plastic companion on shopping trips. The slogan was used for the credit card Access from 1981.

fritter

Cooks have been frying **fritters** since medieval times, and the word comes from the same Latin root as FRY. When we say disapprovingly that someone likes to **fritter** their time or money away we are using a quite different word. It is based on an old verb *fitter* meaning 'to break into fragments, shred', and may be related to German *Fetzen* 'rag, scrap'.

frog

In the Middle Ages to call someone a **frog** was a general term of abuse. In the 17th century it was used particularly for a Dutchman, but by the late 18th century it was being applied to the French: this was probably partly due to alliteration, and partly to the reputation of the French for eating frogs' legs.

In July 2004 Britney Spears was quoted as saying of her second marriage, 'I kissed a bunch of frogs and finally found my prince.' The allusion was to the traditional fairy story of the **frog prince**. A frog in a pool returns a princess's lost golden ball in return for her promise that he may live with and be loved by her. When he claims the promise, she reluctantly kisses him, and he is restored to his true shape of a handsome prince. Sadly for Britney, her marriage to husband number two, Kevin Federline, ended in divorce, but at least it lasted longer than the first: in 2004 she married her childhood friend Jason Alexander in Las Vegas, but the marriage was annulled two days later.

Someone who is finding it hard to speak because they are hoarse may be described as having **a frog in the throat**. The expression dates from the late 19th century, but 'frog' here goes back to an earlier meaning of a soreness or swelling in the mouth or throat.

frost

This is one of our earliest English words, recorded from the 8th century and related to **freeze**. By the 19th century we start to hear of **Jack Frost**. The *Sporting Magazine* of 1826 recorded ruefully of the effects of frozen ground, 'Jack Frost, however, put a veto on our morning's sport.'

fruit

We can trace **fruit** back to medieval English. It comes ultimately from the Latin word *frui* 'to enjoy', and the central idea is one of enjoying the produce of harvest.

In America **fruit** is a term for a gay man. It could come from the US slang sense 'a dupe, an easy victim', with the idea of a fruit that is easily 'picked', or with the derogatory implication of homosexuals being 'soft' like fruit. **Fruitcake** meaning 'a mad person' is a play on **nutty** in **as nutty as a fruitcake**, with the double meaning 'full of nuts' and 'mad'. And **fruity** in the sense 'sexually suggestive' draws on the idea of being 'ripe and juicy'. See also NUT.

Forbidden fruit is something regarded as particularly enticing just because it is not allowed. The phrase looks back to the biblical account of the fruit of the tree of knowledge of good and evil, which was forbidden to Adam in the Garden of Eden, and which he was disastrously tempted to eat. See also APPLE.

fry

This word meaning 'to cook in hot fat or oil' comes from the Latin verb *frigere*, and is connected with FRITTER. **Fry** as a term for 'young fish' is a quite different word, which comes from Old Norse.

If you move from a bad situation to one that is worse you have moved **out of the frying pan into the fire**. You are in good company – the phrase was used by the scholar and statesman Sir Thomas More in the mid 16th century.

fudge

Today we think of **fudge** as primarily a sweet, and maybe also as a word thrown around as an insult by politicians, who are always accusing each other of 'fudging' facts or figures, or of twisting them to present a desired picture. But the first use of the word, in the late 17th century, was in the sense 'to turn out as expected' and also 'to merge together'. It then came to mean 'to fit together in a clumsy or underhand manner', or 'to manipulate facts and figures'. The word probably came from the old term **fadge**, which meant 'to fit'.

People have been enjoying the sweet since the 1890s or so, originally in America. The meaning was probably suggested by the old sense 'to merge together', because of the way in which you mix up the sugar, butter and milk or cream to make the fudge.

People started exclaiming 'fudge!' to express scorn or annoyance in the 18th century.

fuel

We have been burning **fuel** for warmth since the Middle Ages. The word comes ultimately from Latin *focus* 'hearth', which means that there has been a shift in meaning – the roots of the word go back not to what was being burned, but to where the fire was laid. See also FOCUS, FOSSIL.

fumigate

We would **fumigate** a room today if we wanted to disinfect it, but the earliest use of the word, dating from the mid 16th century, was 'to perfume'. It comes ultimately from Latin *fumus* 'smoke', which also gives us **fume**. See also FUNK.

fun

It is hard today to think of life without **fun**, but the word is a comparative newcomer. The earliest sense of 'trick' or 'hoax' is found in the 17th century. It seems to come ultimately from a dialect pronunciation of Middle English *fon* 'a fool'. Our current sense dates only from the 18th century, and in 1755 Dr Johnson described it disapprovingly as 'a low cant [slang] word'. He would probably have sympathised with the view given in the humorist A.P. Herbert's *Uncommon Law* (1935): 'People must not have fun. We are not here for fun. There is no reference to fun in any Act of Parliament.'

Things can be 'funny' in several different ways. The expressions **funny ha-ha** and **funny peculiar**, encapsulating the distinctions in meaning between what is amusing and what is strange, were coined by the writer Ian Hay in his novel *The Housemaster* (1936).

When withdrawing from the contest for leadership of the British Conservative Party in 1990, Margaret Thatcher remarked ruefully 'It's a funny old world'. She was echoing a line spoken by the American comedian W.C. Fields in the film *You're Telling Me* (1934), 'It's a funny old world – a man's lucky if he gets out of it alive'. The English soccer player Jimmy Greaves made 'It's a funny old game' his catchphrase when appearing regularly as a TV pundit during the 1980s.

funk

Funk can be defined as 'a kind of dance music having a strong rhythm that stresses the first beat in the bar', but if you really want to know what it is, listen to a James Brown record such as 'Sex Machine'. People started using **funk** and **funky** in musical contexts during the 1950s: before that, **funky** was a black English expression that meant 'worthless, bad', which reversed its meaning in the same way as BAD and WICKED to mean 'excellent'.

In the early 17th century, though, **funk** meant 'a musty smell', a sense which is still used in North American English. It may come from French dialect *funkier* 'blow smoke on', which was based on Latin *fumus* 'smoke' (the root of FUMIGATE).

Funk meaning 'a state of panic or anxiety' was Oxford University slang in the mid 18th century, in the phrase **in a blue funk**. It could refer to the slang sense of **funk** as 'tobacco smoke', or it could be from an old Flemish word *fonck*, 'disturbance, agitation'.

furphy

In Australia a **furphy** is a rumour or untrue story, a meaning that goes back to the First World War. Water and sanitary carts manufactured by the Furphy family of Shepparton, Victoria, had the maker's name painted on their sides. The term became associated with the spreading of unfounded stories, seemingly the military equivalent of water-cooler chat.

fuzz

If you are 'caught by the fuzz' you are arrested by the police. This **fuzz** is a different word from the one that means 'a frizzy mass', and may be a form of fuss, from the idea of the police 'making a fuss'. It has been used since the 1920s and originated in the USA.

The other **fuzz** entered English in the late 17th century, probably from Dutch or German, although **fuzzy** is recorded earlier, around 1600, when it meant 'spongy'. **Fuzzy logic** does not refer to the thought processes of a person with a hangover, but is a form of logic in which a statement can be partially true or false rather than having to be absolutely one or the other.

gadget

Sailors were the first people to talk about **gadgets**. The word started out in nautical slang as a general term for any small device or mechanism or part of a ship. This is the earliest recorded use, dated 1886: 'Then the names of all the other things on board a ship! I don't know half of them yet; even the sailors forget at times, and if the exact name of anything they want happens to slip from their memory, they call it a chicken-fixing, or a gadjet, or a gill-guy, or a timmey-noggy, or a wim-wom.' The word is probably from French *gâchette* 'a lock mechanism' or *gagée* 'tool'. See also WIDGET.

gaff

While to **blow the gaff** is a common phrase for revealing a plot or secret, the identity of **gaff** itself may be a mystery. One type of gaff is a stick with a metal hook used for landing large fish: it comes from Provençal *gaf* 'a hook'. In British slang a gaff can also be someone's home, a use dating from the 1930s and probably derived from an old term for a fair or music hall. The gaff in **blow the gaff**, though, may be linked to an early 19th-century sense, 'noise or pretence'. Letting out a secret indiscreetly could also be regarded as a **gaffe**, an embarrassing blunder or *faux pas*, which brings us back to metal hooks. In French *gaffe* means 'a boat hook' and, informally, 'a blunder', in which sense it came into English in the early 20th century.

galaxy

If you look into the sky on a dark moonless night you can see a band of pale light crossing the sky, made up of vast numbers of faint stars that appear to be packed closely together. This is the Milky Way, a direct translation of what the Romans called *via lactea*.

The Greeks were also reminded of milk and named it *galaxias kuklos* 'the milky vault', from *gala* 'milk', which is the origin of our word **galaxy**. It was adopted into medieval English and at first referred specifically to the Milky Way, though later it applied to any system of millions or billions of stars.

In current sporting usage, especially in football, **galactico** is a term for one of a team's superstar players. A Spanish word, it is chiefly associated with the club Real Madrid, whose high-profile signings Luis Figo, Zinedine Zidane, Ronaldo and David Beckham were collectively dubbed *Los Galácticos*, literally 'the galactics', because they were 'bigger than stars'.

gallant

A word normally associated with men, **gallant** at one time could also describe an attractive woman. Here is the poet John Lyly writing in 1579: 'This gallant girl, more fair than fortunate, and yet more fortunate than faithful'. The word first came into English in the Middle Ages in the sense 'finely dressed', from Old French *galant* 'celebrating', from *gale* 'pleasure or rejoicing', also the source of **gala**. It was also once used to mean 'excellent, splendid or noble', as in 'A more gallant and beautiful armada never before quitted the shores of Spain' (William H. Prescott, 1838), while the modern sense 'politely attentive to women' came into English from French in the 17th century. **Gallivant**, meaning 'to go from place to place in pursuit of pleasure', may be a playful alteration of **gallant**.

gallery

Galilee, the northern region of ancient Palestine where Jesus lived and travelled during his ministry, may be the ultimate source of **gallery**, which entered English from Italian *galleria* 'gallery' or 'church porch'. Its medieval Latin source was perhaps an alteration of *Galilea* 'Galilee', which was used as the name for a porch or chapel at the church entrance. The idea behind this was probably that the porch was at the end of the church furthest away from the altar, just as Galilee, an outlying portion of the Holy Land, was far from Jerusalem.

From the mid 17th century the highest seating in a theatre was called the gallery, and this was where the cheapest seats – and the least refined members of the audience – were found. Hence, to **play to the gallery**, an expression dating from the late 19th century, is to act in a showy or exaggerated way to appeal to popular taste.

galore

When the Scottish writer Sir Walter Scott wrote in his journal in 1826, 'Sent off proofs and copy galore before breakfast', he was using a word that originated in Ireland. **Galore** 'in abundance' comes from Irish *go leor*, which means 'to sufficiency, enough'.

galvanise

If something galvanises you it stimulates or shocks you into activity. And 'shocks' is the key to the origin of **galvanise**, which was first used to mean 'to stimulate a muscle or nerve by electricity'. It was based on the name of the Italian scientist Luigi Galvani (1737-98), who discovered that frogs' legs twitched violently when he ran electricity through them. Galvani believed that such convulsions were caused by 'animal electricity' found in the body, an idea that inspired Mary Shelley to write *Frankenstein* in 1818. To **galvanise** iron or steel is to coat it with a layer of zinc to stop it from rusting, originally done by means of an electrical current.

game

The original meaning of **game**, dating back to Old English, was 'amusement, fun or pleasure'. Shakespeare uses it in this sense in *Love's Labour's Lost*: 'We have had pastimes here and pleasant game'. Other early meanings included 'a jest or joke' and 'a laughing stock'. The adjective sense 'full of fight, spirited' (now used also to mean 'ready and willing') comes from a use of the noun as a term for a fighting cock. Australians say that a brave person is **as game as Ned Kelly**, referring to the 19th-century outlaw and folk hero who led a band of horse and cattle thieves and bank raiders.

To be **on the game** is to be involved in prostitution. Although the expression dates from the late 19th century, the use of **game** to mean 'sexual activity' is much older, as in Shakespeare's reference to 'daughters of the game' in *Troilus and Cressida*. At one time, being **on the game** was also thieves' slang for thieving or housebreaking.

Rather different, then, to **playing the game**, behaving in a fair or honourable way or abiding by the rules. The expression is recorded from the late 19th century and memorably used in Henry Newbolt's poem 'Vitaï Lampada' (1897), celebrating public school values:

> And it's not for the sake of a ribboned coat,
> Or the selfish hope of a season's fame,
> But his Captain's hand on his shoulder smote –
> 'Play up! play up! And play the game!'

People say **game on!** in situations, especially in sport, when one side has suddenly got themselves back into a contest and anyone can still win. The expression comes from darts, where it signals the start of play.

gamut

To **run the gamut** is to experience or display the complete range of something. In medieval music **gamut** was originally the name of the lowest note in the scale, but the term also came to be applied to the full range of notes which a voice or instrument can produce. In time it started to be used outside musical contexts. According to the acerbic American critic and humorist Dorothy Parker, the film actress Katharine Hepburn 'ran the whole gamut of emotions from A to B'.

gang

To understand its origin the best way to think of a **gang** is as a group of people who 'go about' together. The word comes from Old Norse *gangr* or *ganga*, 'gait, course or going', and is related to Scots *gang* 'to go'. In early use **gang** meant 'a journey', and later developed the senses 'way or passage' and 'a set of things which go together'. In the early 17th century it started to be applied to people too, specifically a ship's crew or a group of workmen, and soon any band of people going about together, especially when involved in some disreputable or criminal activity, could be described disapprovingly as a **gang**, as in 'Nutt the pirate . . . with all his gang of varlets'.

Both **gangway** and **gangplank** are based on the original 'going' sense of the word. **Gangster**, dating from the late 19th century, was altered in US black English in the 1980s to **gangsta**, and applied both to a member of a gang and to a type of rap music.

garbage

A word probably borrowed from Old French that originally meant 'offal or giblets'. These days its main modern use of 'rubbish, refuse' is commoner in American than in British English, but this sense goes back to the 16th century. In computing the saying **garbage in, garbage out** (often abbreviated as **GIGO**) is used to state the inescapable fact that incorrect or poor-quality input is bound to produce faulty output.

garden

Our word **garden** comes from Old French *jardin*. Going back even further, it has an ancient root that is also the ancestor of YARD.

You can say **everything in the garden is lovely** (or **rosy**) when all is well. This early 20th-century catchphrase originated in a song made popular by the English music hall star Marie Lloyd (1870-1922). If someone makes you believe something that is not true by giving you misleading clues or signals, they can be said to be **leading you up the garden path**. The phrase was first used in the early 20th century in the form **lead you up the garden**, suggesting that the original idea was of someone enticing a person they wanted to seduce or flirt with into a garden, away from the safety of the house.

gargle

The words **gargle** and **gargoyle** are closely related, linked by the idea of throats. **Gargle** comes from French *gargouiller* 'to gurgle or bubble', from *gargouille* 'throat'. A **gargoyle** is a grotesque figure of a human or animal carved on a building, especially one that acts as a waterspout, with water passing through its throat and mouth. In Old French *gargouille* meant not only 'throat' but also 'gargoyle', and this is the source of the English word.

garnish

Nowadays you might garnish a plate of food with a sprig of parsley or a spoon of coleslaw, which seems a far cry from what the word meant in the Middle Ages, 'to equip or arm yourself'. Over time the sequence of meanings evolved like this: 'to equip or arm yourself', 'to fit out with something', 'to decorate or embellish' and finally 'to decorate a dish of food for the table'. The source is Old French *garnir* (also the root of **garment**), which meant both 'to fortify or defend' and 'to provide or prepare'.

gas

This is an invented word. **Gas** was coined in the 17th century by the Belgian chemist and physician Joannes Baptista van Helmont (1577-1644), who was the first scientist to realise that there are gases other than air and who discovered carbon dioxide. Van Helmont based the word on Greek *khaos* CHAOS. It did not really catch on, though, until the 19th century, with earlier scientists like Robert Boyle preferring to think of gases as different types of AIR.

gauntlet

To **throw down the gauntlet** and **run the gauntlet** are two different expressions and two different gauntlets. If someone **throws down** (or **takes up**) **the gauntlet**, they issue (or accept) a challenge. In medieval times a gauntlet (from Old

French) was a glove worn as part of a medieval suit of armour. The custom was for a knight to challenge another to a fight or duel by throwing his gauntlet to the ground. The other knight would pick it up to show that he accepted the challenge. To **run the gauntlet** is to go through an intimidating crowd or experience in order to reach a goal. This expression has nothing to do with gloves, but refers to a former military form of punishment recorded from the mid 17th century. A soldier found guilty of an offence was stripped to the waist and forced to run between two lines of men armed with sticks, who beat him as he went past. **Gauntlet** here is a version of an earlier word **gantlope**, from Swedish *gatlopp*, from *gata* 'lane' and *lopp* 'course'. **Run the gantlope** was first recorded in English in 1646, but **gantlope** was soon replaced by **gauntlet**, which was a more familiar word.

gargantuan

A large-mouthed giant with a huge and insatiable appetite, called Gargantua, gave us **gargantuan**, meaning 'enormous or gigantic'. He appeared in the satirical tale *Gargantua*, published in 1534 by the French writer François Rabelais. In one memorable episode the colossal guzzler accidentally swallows six pilgrims while eating a salad.

gay

In its original sense of 'light-hearted and carefree, exuberantly cheerful', **gay** goes back to the 14th century and derives from Old French *gai*. By the 17th century the meaning had extended to 'addicted to social pleasures', often with an implication of loose morality, as in, for example, the expression 'gay dog' (a man fond of revelry) or these lines from William Cowper's poem 'To a Young Lady' (1782): 'Silent and chaste she steal along / Far from the world's gay busy throng'. In slang use the word could describe a prostitute.

The use of **gay** to mean 'homosexual', now the main meaning, is unambiguously found in examples from the 1930s, though there is evidence that it may have been used in this sense earlier.

gazump

These days we associate **gazumping** with the buying and selling of houses, a use that dates from the 1970s. It now means specifically 'to raise the price of a house after accepting an offer from a prospective buyer', but in the early 20th century it simply meant 'to swindle', deriving from Yiddish *gezumph* 'to overcharge'. In the late 1980s the opposite term **gazunder** (a combination of **gazump** and **under**) was coined to describe the practice of lowering the amount of an offer that the seller has already accepted while threatening to withdraw if the new offer is not accepted.

Überbabes and spritzers

War inevitably influenced Germany's 20th-century contributions to our language. But German has given us many other terms, including some that handily fill in where there is no English equivalent.

Take dogs, for example. The poodle is now generally a cute, pampered little thing, but it was bred to jump into water and retrieve waterfowl shot by its master, and its name is from German *Pudelhund* 'puddle dog'. The dachshund is often called a 'sausage dog' because of its long body, but it is literally a 'badger dog' – the breed was originally used to dig badgers out of their setts.

Since the 1920s we have criticised objects regarded as garish or sentimental as kitsch. At times this may be seen as a type of intellectual snobbery – in May 1961 *The Times* made a reference to 'highbrows ... who consider that the quality of the pure entertainment as such is generally *kitsch* or trash'. We might feel that this sort of thing was ersatz, or 'artificial', and add that it should be verboten, or 'forbidden'.

But there is no avoiding the language of war. Flak or 'anti-aircraft fire', borrowed directly from German in the 1930s, is an abbreviation of *Fliegerabwehrkanone*, literally 'aviator-defence-gun'. By the 1960s it was sufficiently established in English for the extended sense 'strong criticism' to develop.

In September 1940 blitz appeared in *Daily Express* reports of the heavy air raids made by the Luftwaffe (the German air force, a combination of 'air' and 'weapon') on London. Blitz is a shortening of blitzkrieg, which had been used the previous year as a description of the German invasion of Poland. In German *Blitzkrieg* means 'lightning war'. The metaphorical use 'a sudden concerted effort to deal with something' came up in *The Guardian* in 1960: 'The women did only the bare essentials of housework during the week, with a "blitz" at weekends.'

A spritzer is a mixture of wine and soda water named after the German word for 'a splash'. In the 1980s this drink was certainly in tune with the zeitgeist, or 'spirit of the time'. Since the 1990s we have used the German word for 'over', *über*, to form words expressing the idea of the ultimate form of something – supermodels are sometimes referred to as überbabes.

German was the language used by the Austrian psychotherapist Sigmund Freud (1856-1939) and his Swiss collaborator Carl Jung (1875-1961), and has given us several words for feelings. Angst, vague worry about the human condition or the world in general, entered English in the 1940s. Weltanschauung, from *Welt* 'world' and *Anschauung* 'perception', means 'individual philosophy, world view'. Until the 1890s English had no word for the regrettably familiar feeling of pleasure derived from another person's misfortune, and so imported one from Germany – schadenfreude combines 'harm' and 'joy'.

See also DUDE, HAM, HEROIN, LAGER, QUEER, TRADE.

gentle

The root word shared by **genteel**, **Gentile** (meaning 'not Jewish') and **gentle** is Latin *gentilis* 'of a family or nation, of the same clan', which came from *gens* 'family, race'. **Genteel** and **gentle** originally had similar meanings. **Genteel** first meant 'stylish, fashionable' and 'well bred' – the ironic or derogatory implications that it now tends to have date from the 19th century. The original sense of **gentle** was 'nobly born', from which came 'courteous, chivalrous', the idea behind **gentleman**. See also BLONDE.

genuine

'I rather choose to keep to the Language of the Sea, which is more genuine, and natural for a mariner.' So wrote Woodes Rogers, the English privateer, in 1712. **Genuine** is used here in its original sense, 'natural or proper'. The source of the word is Latin *genuinus*, from *genu* 'knee', with reference to the Roman custom of a father formally acknowledging that a newborn child was his by placing the baby on his knee.

gerrymander

Half-man, half-lizard – that is **gerrymander**. In political contexts gerrymandering is manipulating the boundaries of electoral districts to give an advantage to a particular party or class. The term was coined when Elbridge Gerry, governor of Massachusetts in 1812, created a new voting district that appeared to favour his party. Because the shape of this new district resembled –

with a bit of imagination – the outline of a salamander, a map, embellished with claws, wings and fangs, was published in the Boston *Weekly Messenger*, with the title *The Gerry-Mander*.

ghastly

This is one of those words that has weakened its meaning over the centuries. In medieval times **ghastly** described something that caused real terror or horror. Its source was the obsolete word *gast* 'to terrify', from Old English *gaestan*, which had the same meaning. GHOST is a related word, and it was the *gh* of **ghost** that influenced the spelling of **ghastly**. The usual modern sense 'very bad or objectionable' dates from the mid 19th century.

ghetto

Italian *getto* 'a foundry' is probably the source of this word for a part of a city, especially a slum area, occupied by a minority group. The first ghetto was established in 1516 on the site of a foundry in Venice. Alternatively, it may come from Italian *borghetto*, meaning 'a little borough'. In Italy the word referred to the quarter of a city to which Jews were restricted, a use which became used elsewhere, as in the Warsaw ghetto.

ghost

In Old English **ghost** meant 'a person's spirit or soul'. This sense is preserved in to **give up the ghost**, which originally meant 'to die', the idea being that the soul is the source of life, but now often refers to equipment that has finally broken down beyond repair. **The ghost in the machine** refers to the mind viewed as distinct from the body. It was coined by the British philosopher Gilbert Ryle in *The Concept of the Mind* (1949). See also GHASTLY.

giddy

If you are **giddy** now you feel dizzy, not the most pleasant of feelings but one which swiftly passes. Up until the 14th century, though, a giddy person was at best foolish, and at worse mad or insane. **Giddy** is an Old English word which probably came from the same root as GOD – the idea was presumably that the mad person was possessed by a god.

gift

A word related to **give** and deriving from Old Norse *gipt*. **Don't look a gift horse in the mouth**, people say, to advise someone to make the most of an opportunity or gift without finding fault with it or being ungrateful. This old proverb goes back to the 16th century (in the form **do not look a given horse in**

the mouth), but it can be found even earlier in a 5th-century Latin version in the writings of St Jerome. A common way of estimating a horse's age is to look at the state of its teeth, so if you were buying a horse you might want to have a good look into its mouth first. But if someone gave you a horse as a present, it might seem ungrateful to start quibbling about how old it was.

ginger

The English word **ginger** can be traced back to a word in Sanskrit (the ancient language of India), which became *zingiberis* in Greek and eventually made its way into English around AD 1000. There is no connection between this and the adverb **gingerly**. In early usage this was used to describe the way a person danced or walked, and meant 'with small elegant steps' or 'daintily'. Later it developed a more negative meaning, 'mincingly'. The modern meaning, 'carefully or cautiously', dates from the 17th century. **Gingerly** may come from Old French *gensor* 'delicate', and ultimately from Latin *genitus* 'born' or 'well born'.

A **ginger group** is an active or radical group within a political party or movement that presses for stronger action on an issue. The reason for the term is enough to make your eyes water. It comes from the old practice of unscrupulous horse dealers of putting a piece of ginger up the bottom of a worn-out horse in order to make it look more lively and frisky. This led to the metaphorical use of **ginger up** to mean 'to make more lively', and **ginger group** developed from this.

In the past gingerbread was traditionally decorated with gold leaf. This is why **take the gilt off the gingerbread** means 'to make something no longer appealing or to spoil the illusion'. **Gilt** is the old past participle of **gild** – these days we use **gilded**.

giraffe

The **giraffe** was known in Europe in the medieval period, but people then called it the **camelopard**. This name was from the Greek word for camel, *kamēlos*, and *pardalis*, which gave us the second part of LEOPARD. The modern name, which was used from the 16th century, is from Arabic *zarāfa*.

girl

For such a common word, it may come as a surprise to find that the exact origin of **girl** is not known for certain. What is perhaps also surprising is that it could once refer to a child or young person of either sex – not until the 16th century was a female child specified.

The phrase **the girl next door**, describing an ordinary and likeable young woman, was popularised by a film of that name in 1953. A **girl Friday** is a female assistant or secretary – it derives from the name of Man Friday in Daniel Defoe's *Robinson Crusoe* (1719), who helped the shipwrecked Crusoe.

glad

The meaning of **glad** has weakened over time – it originally had the sense 'delighted and rejoicing', but nowadays just means 'pleased'. If you are in your **glad rags**, you are dressed in your smartest clothes. The expression was first used in American English at the end of the 19th century, about the same time that **glad eye**, 'a look intending to attract the opposite sex', first appeared in British English. See also HAPPY.

glamour

Although rarely associated, **glamour** and **grammar** are in fact related. **Glamour** was originally a Scots word meaning 'enchantment or magic' or 'a magic spell or charm' – if someone **cast the glamour** over you, they enchanted or bewitched you – and was an altered form of **grammar**. Greek *gramma* 'a letter of the alphabet, something written down' was the source of **grammar**, which in medieval times had the sense 'scholarship or learning'. Learning and the study of books was popularly associated with astrology and occult practices, hence the connection with magic. The idea of 'magical beauty' became associated with **glamour** in the mid 19th century, and from the 1930s the word was particularly used of attractive women. In the early 1970s, though, a new kind of glamour was unveiled, and one displayed largely by men – **glam rock**, in which acts such as the Sweet, Gary Glitter and David Bowie wore exaggeratedly flamboyant clothes and glittery make-up. See also PRESTIGE.

glass

The substance **glass** goes back to ancient Mesopotamia or Phoenicia (modern Lebanon and Syria), and the word existed in Old English. The sense 'spectacles' dates from the late 18th century, although before that people would use a single glass or 'an eye glass'.

The proverb **those who live in glass houses shouldn't throw stones**, used to advise people against criticising or slandering others if they are vulnerable to retaliation, dates from the 17th century. People started complaining of the existence of a **glass ceiling**, meaning an unofficial barrier to advancement at work, especially for a woman, in the early 1980s.

The American wit Dorothy Parker (1893-1967) can lay claim to 'Men seldom make passes / At girls who wear glasses.'

glib

There are a number of words, such as **greasy**, **oily** and **slimy**, that link the ideas of smoothness and slipperiness, on the one hand, and insincere speech or behaviour on the other. **Glib** falls into this category, too. To give a glib answer is to speak fluently but in an insincere and shallow way, but one of its first meanings, back in the late 16th century, was 'smooth or unimpeded'.

glitch

Although nowadays a **glitch** can be any kind of hitch or snag, the word was originally used by US electronic engineers in the 1960s to mean 'a sudden surge of electrical current'. Astronauts began using the word to talk about any sudden malfunction of equipment. It may derive from Yiddish *glitsh* 'a slippery place'.

glitter

Things have glittered since the 14th century, and the word comes from Old Norse *glitra*. You can say **all that glitters is not gold** to warn someone not to be deceived by the attractive external appearance of something, which may not be a reliable indication of its true nature. This saying dates back at least to the early 13th century: Shakespeare uses it, in the form **all that glisters is not gold**, in *The Merchant of Venice*.

Glitzy, meaning 'showily attractive', first appeared in the USA in the 1960s. It was based on **glitter**, and probably influenced by **ritzy** and perhaps also by German *glitzerig* 'glittering'.

gnome

You would not really confuse a gnome with a pygmy, but the terms are closely related. It was probably the Swiss physician Paracelsus (*c.*1493-1541) who coined **gnome** as a synonym of *Pygmaeus*, the name given to a member of a mythical race of very small people believed to live in parts of Ethiopia and India. See also NAFF.

The **gnomes of Zurich** are Swiss financiers or bankers, thought of as having a sinister influence over international monetary funds. Former British Prime Minister Harold Wilson popularised the phrase in 1956: 'All these financiers, all the little gnomes in Zurich and other financial centres about whom we keep on hearing'.

Gnomic meaning 'clever but hard to understand', as in 'gnomic utterances', is a different word. It comes from Greek *gnōmē* 'thought, judgement', which was related to *gignōskein* 'to know' (see KNOW).

go

Words do not get much shorter, more common or more important than **go**. **What goes around comes around** is a modern proverb first used in the USA, suggesting that the consequences of a person's actions will have to be dealt with eventually. Also originating in the USA is **when the going gets tough, the tough get going**, a favourite family saying of President John F. Kennedy's father Joseph Kennedy. It is not certain, though, whether he actually coined it. This was later used as a slogan for the 1985 film *The Jewel of the Nile* and as the title of a hit pop song (and the theme song to the film) sung by Billy Ocean.

Another film-related expression is **go ahead, make my day,** originally uttered by Clint Eastwood's character Harry Callaghan in *Sudden Impact* (1983), as he aimed his .44 Magnum gun at a gunman, daring him to shoot. The phrase was appropriated by Ronald Reagan in 1985, when the President was threatening to veto legislation raising taxes. See also PEAR-SHAPED.

goblin

The word for the ugly dwarf-like creature of folklore is from Old French *gobelin*. *Gobelinus* was the name of a mischievous spirit said to haunt the region of Évreux in northern France in the 12th century. The term may be related to German *Kobold*, the name of a German spirit that haunted houses or lived underground in caves and mines, although another possible source is Greek *kobalos* 'goblin'. See also COBALT, GREMLIN, HOBBY.

gobsmacked

The first gobs were smacked in the 1980s. The word **gobsmacked** presumably refers either to the shock of being hit in the mouth or to the action of clapping your hand to your mouth in astonishment. **Gob**, an informal word for 'mouth', may come from Scottish Gaelic *gob* 'beak or mouth'. There is another **gob**, 'a lump of something', that came into English from Old French *gobe* 'mouthful or lump': **gobble** is probably based on this **gob**.

God

The Old English word **God** is related to similar words in German and in Scandinavian languages, but not to the Latin and Greek words, which were *deus* and *theos* (as in **theology**) respectively. The top gallery in a theatre is known as **the gods** – the original term in the 1750s was **the regions of the gods**, because the seats were high up and therefore close to the gods.

The person who presents the child at baptism and promises to take responsibility for its religious education has been its **godfather** or **godmother**

since around AD 1000. **Godfather** meaning 'a leader of the American Mafia' has been a familiar term since Mario Puzo's novel *The Godfather* (1969) and the film version by Francis Ford Coppola (1972), but was first recorded in the early 1960s.

The origins of the British national anthem **God save the Queen** (or **King**) are not known for sure, but the song was definitely sung in London theatres in 1745, when the country was threatened by the Jacobite uprising led by the Young Pretender, Bonnie Prince Charlie, and the words and tune probably date from the previous century. 'God save the king' was a password in the navy as early as 1545 – 'long to reign over us' was the correct response. See also LAP.

golden

Our word **gold** is Old English, from an ancient root meaning 'yellow'. **Golden** is medieval, and replaced the earlier word *gilden*.

People first used **golden age** in the mid 16th century to refer to an idyllic period in the past. It is a translation of the Greek and Roman poets' name for the first period of history, a time when the human race was believed to live in an ideal state.

In business contexts a **golden handshake**, dating from the late 1950s, is a sum of money paid by an employer to a retiring or redundant employee, usually a senior one. This has led to a number of other 'golden' terms, including **golden hello** (a substantial payment in advance offered to a senior executive to induce them to leave one company and join another) and **golden handcuffs** (a series of payments made over a period to encourage someone to stay with a company and not work for a competitor).

In September 2001 the former Spice Girl Victoria Beckham revealed on the *Parkinson* TV chat show that her own nickname for her husband, the footballer David Beckham, was **Goldenballs**. Victoria may not have been aware that the similar name *gyldin ballokes* ('golden bollocks') was recorded in the 11th century in the Domesday Book.

golf

The first recorded mention of **golf** is in 1457, in a Scottish edict that banned certain games (football was another one) because King James II thought they were distracting his people from archery practice. It does seem to have been a Scottish game originally, although the word may be related to Dutch *kolf* 'a club or bat'. It is now popular around the world, but according to the American writer Mark Twain, golf is 'A good walk spoiled'. See also PAR.

good

The ancient root of the Old English word **good** probably meant 'to bring together, unite' and was also the source of **gather**. Good and evil are the two most fundamental moral concepts, and for thousands of years great minds have striven to define them and give guidance on how to be good. The biblical book of Isaiah delivered the maxim 'Woe unto them that call evil good, and good evil', while the Koran stated 'Good and evil shall not be held equal. Turn away evil with that which is better.'

Goodbye is short for God be with you. Over time good replaced God to match good morning, goodnight and similar phrases.

In 1957 British Prime Minister Harold Macmillan said, 'Let us be frank about it: most of our people have never had it so good' – 'You Never Had It So Good' was the US Democratic Party slogan during the 1952 election campaign. Also in 1952, Kentucky Fried Chicken opened its first outlet, and for many years its slogan has been 'It's finger-lickin' good'.

Good Friday, the Friday before Easter Day, on which Christ was crucified, is not so called because it was regarded as a 'good' day. **Good** here is in the old sense 'observed as holy'.

Sweets and cakes have been called **goodies** since the mid 18th century, and the childish exclamation **goody** is first recorded not much later. **Goody goody gumdrops** was the catchphrase of Humphrey Lestocq, the host of the British children's TV show *Whirligig* from the 1950s.

googly

One way to bowl a maiden over in cricket is to deliver a **googly**, a deceptive ball which bounces in the opposite direction from the expected one. The word is first recorded in 1903, but beyond that nothing is known about its origin. The Australian term for a googly, **bosie**, comes from the name of the English cricketer Bernard Bosanquet (1877-1936).

goolies

In Britain **goolies** are testicles, but in Australia they are stones. The two are probably different words – the first was probably picked up by British soldiers in India from Hindi *golī* 'ball, pill, bullet', whereas the second may be from the Aboriginal word *goolie*, 'a stone'.

goon

To most people a **goon** is either Peter Sellers, Spike Milligan, Harry Secombe or Michael Bentine, creators of the crazy radio comedy series *The Goon Show* in 1951. The original sense of the word was 'a stupid or hapless person' – it came from the name of the US cartoon character Alice the Goon, created by the cartoonist E.C. Segar (1894-1938) and appearing in the *Popeye* strips that also introduced Eugene the Jeep (see JEEP). Segar probably took the name from the dialect term **gooney** 'a simpleton'. In the USA a goon also became a thug hired to terrorise people, and in the Second World War the term was given by British and US prisoners of war to their German guards. See also LURGY.

goose

Geese have long been a mainstay of the farmyard, and the Old English word **goose** is found in several idioms. If someone **kills the goose that lays the golden eggs** they destroy a reliable and valuable source of income. In one of Aesop's fables a man finds that one of his geese lays eggs of pure gold, which he sells and so becomes rich. But he grows dissatisfied with just one egg a day, and kills the goose in the mistaken belief that it will be filled with golden eggs. There is no gold inside it and, what is more, no longer any prospect of even a single golden egg. The US film producer Sam Goldwyn, famous for idiosyncratic expressions like 'include me out', said: 'That's the way with these directors, they're always biting the hand that lays the golden egg.'

In American usage a **goose egg** is a score of zero in baseball and other sports. This derives from the egg shape of the number, in just the same way as does the cricketing term DUCK (originally 'a duck's egg').

Today we associate the military marching step known as the **goose-step** with the Nazis, but the term was recorded much earlier than the 1930s, at the beginning of the 19th century. Goose-stepping soldiers advance by swinging each leg stiffly forward without bending it at the knee, in a way likened to geese.

To **goose** someone is to poke their bottom as a joke. This meaning probably comes from the way that geese can be aggressive and ready to peck at people unexpectedly.

Why a **gooseberry** is so called is a bit of a mystery. This 16th-century word may be a modified version of German *Krausebeere* or the French dialect *gozelle*, or it may simply have been created by combining the existing words **goose** and **berry**. The 'unwanted third party' sense, as in 'playing gooseberry', dates from the 19th century. See also GOSSAMER, SAUCE.

gorge

The Old French word *gorge* meant 'throat' and was adopted into English with the same meaning. In medieval times it referred to the pouch in a hawk's throat where food is stored for digestion, now called the 'crop', and it could also mean 'a meal for a hawk'. Hence it came to mean 'the contents of the stomach', and when we talk about **someone's gorge rising** in disgust it is in this sense that the word is being used. A gorge is also a narrow valley between hills, a sense that emerged in the middle of the 18th century from the idea of its being narrow like a throat.

gorilla
In the 5th or 6th century BC the Carthaginian explorer Hanno wrote an account of his voyage along the northwest coast of Africa. In the Greek translation of Hanno's account there appears a supposedly African word *gorillai*, the name of a wild or hairy people. This was adopted in 1847 by the US missionary Thomas Savage as the name of the large ape. See also GUERRILLA.

gospel
The Good News Bible is an English translation of the Bible, published in 1976, whose name refers to the root meaning of **gospel** itself. The word is not related to GOD, but was formed from Old English *gōd* 'good' and *spel* 'news, a story', and was a translation of Greek *euangelion* 'good news', the source of our words **evangelism** and **evangelist**. The four Gospels in the New Testament are credited to St Matthew, St Mark, St Luke and St John. All give an account of the teachings, crucifixion and resurrection of Christ, though the Gospel of John differs greatly from the other three. The rock musical *Godspell*, based on the Gospel of St Matthew and first produced in 1971, took its title from the original spelling of the word.

gossamer
Gossamer has a delightful origin. The word literally means 'goose summer', another name for St Martin's Summer, in early November, when geese were eaten. This is also the time of the year when you are likely to see cobwebs spun by small spiders, floating in the air or spread over a grassy surface, and so these cobwebs came to be called gossamer.

gossip
In Old English *godsibb* or **gossip** was the word for a godparent. It literally meant 'a person related to one in God' and came from *god* 'God' and *sibb* 'a relative', the latter word surviving in **sibling**. **Gossip** came to be applied to a close friend, especially a female friend invited to be present at a birth. From this developed the idea of a person who enjoys indulging in idle talk, and by the 19th century idle talk or tittle-tattle itself.

graffiti
Although we think of **graffiti** as being scribbled, painted or sprayed on a wall, it was originally scratched on. The word first appeared in English in the mid 19th century and was applied to ancient wall drawings or inscriptions found in ruins in Rome or Pompeii. This was an adoption of an Italian word in the plural form (the singular being *graffito*), from *graffio* 'a scratch'.

graft
A **graft** is a shoot from one plant fixed into a slit in another to form a new growth. Originally spelled *graff*,

Political graffiti covers a wall in the ancient Roman city of Pompeii.

it derives from Greek *graphion* 'stylus, pointed writing implement', from *graphein* 'to write'. The tapered tip of the shoot was thought to resemble a stylus. The other **graft**, 'hard work', may be related to the phrase *spade's graft* 'the amount of earth that one stroke of a spade will move', based on Old Norse *groftr* 'digging'.

grain

The first meaning of **grain**, which is from Latin *granum* 'seed', was 'a single seed of a plant'. From this developed the idea not only of a seed-like particle such as a grain of sand, salt or gold but also of an arrangement of fibres that resembles small seeds or grains side by side, such as the 'grain' of a piece of wood. If something **goes against the grain** it is contrary to your natural inclination. The phrase, dating from the mid 17th century, comes from carpentry. On a piece of wood the grain is the way the fibres in the wood are arranged lengthways. If you are smoothing a piece of timber it is much more difficult to plane across or against the line of these fibres than along them.

grape

A **grape** was originally not an individual berry but the whole bunch. It can be traced back to Old French *grap* 'hook', specifically a vine hook used for harvesting grapes. **Grapple**, first used to refer to a grappling hook, has a similar origin, and a **grapefruit** is so called because it grows in clusters, like grapes.

To **hear something on the grapevine** is to get information by rumour or by unofficial communication. The expression comes from the American Civil War, when news was said to be passed 'by grapevine telegraph'. **Bush telegraph**, originally an Australian term, is based on a similar idea.

The phrase **sour grapes** describes an attitude of pretending to despise something because you cannot have it yourself. The source is Aesop's fable of the fox and the grapes. In the story a fox tries to reach a bunch of juicy grapes hanging from a vine high above his head. After several attempts he gives up and stalks off, comforting himself with the thought that they were probably sour anyway and therefore no loss.

grass

The Old English word **grass** is descended from the same root word as both GREEN and GROW. According to the well-known saying, **the grass is always greener on the other side of the fence**, a sentiment echoed in the works of the Roman poet Ovid: 'The harvest is always more fruitful in another man's fields.'

A woman whose husband is often away for long periods can be referred to as a **grass widow**. In the

early 16th century, though, this was a term for an unmarried woman with a child, probably from the idea of the couple having lain on the grass together instead of in bed.

People have been smoking grass, or cannabis, since the 1940s, originally in the USA. The word has meant 'an informer' or 'to inform' since the decade before that. In this sense it is probably short for **grasshopper**, rhyming slang for **shopper**, a person who 'shops' someone. See also NARK.

gravy

In medieval cookbooks **gravy** describes a spicy sauce, usually consisting of broth, milk of almonds, spices and wine or ale. Only in the late 16th century did it start to refer to a sauce made out of meat juices. The most likely explanation for the word's origin is that someone misread Old French *grané* as *gravé*, which is quite possible given that the letter *u* was used to represent *v* in medieval manuscripts. *Grané* probably derived from *grain* 'spice', from Latin *granum* 'grain'.

Gravy can also mean 'money that is easily acquired', and to **board the gravy train** is to obtain access to an easy source of financial gain. Here 'gravy train' is perhaps an alteration of 'gravy boat', a long, narrow jug used for serving gravy.

grease

The ultimate source of **grease** is Latin *crassus* 'thick or fat', and in medieval English the word meant 'the fat part of the body of an animal' and 'fatness'. To **grease someone's palm**, a phrase that dates from the early 16th century, is to bribe them. The metaphor comes from the idea of applying grease to a machine to make it run smoothly. The idea behind **like greased lightning**, 'very quickly', is that lightning, the fastest thing imaginable, would presumably be even faster if greased.

Greek

The word **Greek** comes from Latin *Graeci*, which was the name the Romans gave to the people who called themselves the Hellenes. If you cannot understand something at all, you can say **it's all Greek to me** – the use of **Greek** to mean 'unintelligible language or gibberish' dates from around 1600. In Shakespeare's *Julius Caesar* the conspirator Casca, noting that Cicero speaks Greek, adds 'for mine own part, it was Greek to me'.

Greek also has a negative connotation in the proverb **beware** (or **fear**) **the Greeks bearing gifts**. In other words, if rivals or enemies show apparent generosity or kindness, you should be suspicious of their motives. This is a reference to the Trojan priest Laocoon's words in Virgil's *Aeneid*, 'I fear the Greeks even when they bring gifts', with which he warns his fellow Trojans not to take into their city the gigantic wooden horse that the Greeks have left behind on their apparent departure. He is right – the horse is hollow and conceals Greek warriors, who are able to enter and capture Troy.

green

The defining characteristic of **green** is that it is the colour of living plants. So it should come as no surprise that the word shares an earlier ancestor with GRASS and GROW. The colour has also long been associated with a sickly complexion, and phrases such as **green and wan** and **green and pale** were once common. To be **green around the gills** is to look or feel ill or nauseous – a person's gills are the fleshy parts between the jaw and the ears, by analogy with the gills of a fish.

Thriving plants are tended by green fingers, or, in the USA, a green thumb. The 'fingers' phrase originated as the title of a 1934 book of garden verse by the British comic writer Reginald Arkell.

An inexperienced person has been called **green** since the Middle Ages, in reference to the colour of unripe corn, and naïve or gullible people have been green since the beginning of the 17th century. Traditionally green has also been the colour of jealousy and envy. In *Othello* Shakespeare gave us a memorable term for jealousy, **the green-eyed monster**:

> O! Beware my lord of jealousy
> It is the green-eyed monster which doth mock
> The meat it feeds on.

The association of the colour with the environmentalist lobby dates from the early 1970s in West Germany.

British Conservative MP Norman Lamont is widely credited with introducing the phrase **the green shoots of recovery**, in relation to the performance of the economy after a recession, but what he said at the Tory Party conference of 1991 was 'The green shoots of economic spring are appearing once again'. See also SALAD, YELLOW.

gregarious

The Latin word *grex* meant 'a flock'. This is the source of **gregarious**, which can describe not only animals that live in flocks or communities but also people who are sociable and enjoy company. Other words sharing this idea of gathering together or assembling, like **aggregate** and CONGREGATE, also derive from *grex*.

gremlin

It was pilots who first talked about **gremlins**, mischievous sprites who they thought were responsible for any unexplained mechanical problems suffered by their planes. The earliest mention of the little pixies comes from the USA in the 1920s, but they are particularly associated with the Second World War. The word may be a combination of GOBLIN and *Fremlins*, a type of beer – so these were the sort of creatures you see when you have had one too many.

The US horror comedy films *Gremlins* (1984) and *Gremlins 2: The New Batch* (1990) featured mogwai, small furry creatures which looked cute as long as you obeyed certain rules, the most important of which was never to feed them after midnight. If you disobeyed the rules they changed into small but dangerous gremlins.

grenade

The Old French word *grenate*, the root of **grenade**, is a shortened form of *pome grenate* 'pomegranate', literally 'many-seeded apple'. The connection is the supposed resemblance between the shape of the bomb and that of the fruit. Early on in its history **grenade** could also refer to the fruit. Continuing the fruity theme, a hand grenade is informally known as a **pineapple**.

grey

An Old English word that since the Middle Ages has been used to describe the weather when the sky is overcast. The extension of this to mean 'dismal or sad' dates from the early 18th century. The following 1969 quotation from *The Times* appears to be one of the earliest instances of the word carrying connotations of 'faceless or anonymous': 'The identity of these grey men of politics should be revealed.'

A **grey area** is an ill-defined situation which does not readily fit into an existing category. It is so called because it is 'not black or white', and cannot be simply analysed or put into a single category. The expression was first used in the late 1940s in reference to countries that had Communist sympathies but were not completely pro or anti-Communist.

The name of the **greyhound** has nothing to do with the colour grey. It comes from Old English *grighund*, which meant 'bitch hound'. In the late 19th century an **ocean greyhound** was a steamship specially built for great speed.

grim

The meaning of **grim** has weakened over the centuries from its first appearance in Old English as 'fierce or cruel'. To **hang** (or **cling**) **on like grim death**, or with intense determination, dates from the mid 19th century, but the use of the adjective to suggest the forbidding appearance of the figure of Death is recorded much earlier. In the same vein, the **Grim Reaper** is a representation of Death in the form of a cloaked skeleton wielding a long scythe.

grin

When **grin** entered the English language in the 11th century it meant 'to bare the teeth in pain or anger', far from the happy expression the word suggests nowadays. This former sense of drawing your lips back in a grimace of pain is the one preserved in the expression **grin and bear it**, 'to suffer pain or misfortune stoically'. An earlier version of the phrase is **grin and abide**. Not until the late 15th century did **grin** begin to be used for various sorts of smile, from a forced, unnatural one, through a rather vacant, silly one, to eventually the cheerful and broad smile we associate with the word today.

grindstone

A **grindstone** is a thick revolving disc of stone on which knives and tools are sharpened. If someone got control over you and treated your harshly, for example by forcing you to work without a break, they were said to be **keeping your nose to the grindstone**. Nowadays the expression means 'to work hard and continuously'.

A word related to **grind** is **grist**, 'corn that is to be ground'. You can describe something which can be turned to good use, such as experience or knowledge, as being **grist to the mill**. The phrase comes from the 17th-century proverb **all is grist that comes to the mill**.

Groovy, baby!

Austin Powers

grizzly

A **grizzly** is a large North American bear which has brown fur with white-tipped hairs. Fearsome though the bear's appearance is, its name has nothing to do with the word **grisly**. In fact **grizzly**, dating from the early 19th century, is a variant of the much older word **grizzled**, 'streaked with grey hair'. This comes from Old French *gris* 'grey', whereas **grisly** is from Old English *grislic*, meaning 'terrifying'.

Grizzle meaning 'to cry or whine' is a different word. It started life in the dialect of Devon and Cornwall, and originally meant 'to grin or laugh'.

grocer

The Company of Grocers, incorporated in 1344, consisted of wholesale dealers in spices and foreign produce. The key word here is 'wholesale', as the term **grocer** originally referred to someone who sold things to shopkeepers 'in the gross', or in large quantities. By the middle of the 15th century grocers were selling all manner of household provisions directly to the public. The source is Old French *grossier*, which ultimately derives from Latin *grossus* 'large, bulky, gross'.

groove

In early use a **groove** was a mine, shaft or pit. The word comes from Dutch *groeve* 'furrow or pit', and is related to **grave**. From the 17th century it was used to refer to a channel or furrow cut in something and, in the 20th century, a spiral track cut into a record into which the stylus used to play it fits. The latter sense lies behind the phrase **in the groove**, 'performing consistently well or confidently', which was first used of jazz musicians and dates back to the 1930s. This phrase is also where we get the adjective **groovy** from, first recorded meaning 'excellent' in the 1930s, specifically in the context of playing jazz well. **Groovy** was a teenage slang term by the 1940s and became an era-defining word in the 1960s. It was revived by Mike Myers in the *Austin Powers* film spoofs – 'Groovy, baby!' See also FABULOUS.

grotesque

We think of something **grotesque** as being ugly or distorted, either in a comic or a repulsive way, but when the word first appeared in English in the 16th century it simply described the style of painting found in a grotto, specifically the murals discovered by excavation in the chambers of ancient Roman ruins. These decorative wall paintings involved interweaving human and animal forms with flowers and foliage. **Grotesque** comes from Italian *grottesca*, which was used in the phrases *opera grottesca* 'work resembling that found in a grotto' and *pittura grottesca* 'painting resembling one found in a grotto'. **Grotty**, meaning 'unpleasant or unwell', comes from **grotesque**. **Grotto** itself ultimately comes from Greek *kruptos* 'hidden', which is also the source of **crypt**.

gruesome

You can describe something horrific or disgusting as **gruesome**. Though it first appeared in English in the late 16th century, based on Scots *grue* 'to feel horror, shudder', it was rare before the late 18th century. It was popularised in the novels of Sir Walter Scott: 'He's as grave and grewsome an auld Dutchman as e'er I saw' (*Old Mortality,* 1816). *Grewsome* was the more common spelling until around 1850.

grunge

Before it became associated with rock music **grunge** was generally used to mean 'grime or dirt'. It was formed from **grungy**, a word that was coined in the 1960s, probably by blending **grubby** and **dingy**. In the 1990s **grunge** became the term for a style of rock music in which the guitar is played raucously and the lyrics delivered in a lazy vocal style. Among well-known practitioners of grunge were Seattle-based groups such as Nirvana and Pearl Jam.

guerrilla

A Spanish word that has nothing to do with GORILLA. **Guerrilla** means literally 'little war', and when it was first used in reports of the Peninsular War, fought between the French and the British in Spain and Portugal from 1808 to 1814, it meant 'irregular war carried on by small bodies of men' as well as 'a member of an independent group of fighters'.

guest

Although the immediate source of **guest** is Old Norse *gestr*, the history of the word can be traced back to an ancient root shared by Latin *hostis* 'enemy, stranger'. Faced with a stranger, your response can either be a positive or a negative one. On the one hand a stranger is a person who you might feel duty-bound to welcome into your home and extend hospitality to, or they are a person who you might view with suspicion or even hostility. Looked at this way, it is possible to see why **guest** and **hostile** have a common ancestry.

guinea pig

The **guinea pig**, a tailless rodent familiar as a child's pet, comes from South America – not Guinea, which is in Africa, or New Guinea, in the South Pacific. Guinea pigs are chubby little things that can squeal like pigs, but why Guinea was chosen nobody is really sure. The word could have been confused with Guyana, which *is* in South America, or was possibly used as an example of a far-off, exotic country that no one knew much about. Guinea pigs have been bred by humans for some 3,000 years, and are no longer found in the wild. Their use in animal testing led to the word's acquiring the sense 'a person or thing used as a subject for experiment' in the 1920s.

gulf

The Greek word *kolpos* had a number of meanings relating to a curved shape, including 'bosom', 'the trough between waves', 'the fold of a piece of clothing' and 'gulf or bay'. This is where our word **gulf** came from, via Italian and Old French. We can talk about a gulf between two groups, meaning a great division or difference between them. This was probably influenced by a biblical passage in the Gospel of Luke: 'Between you and us there is a great gulf set.'

gullible

A **gullible** person was originally someone who could be 'gulled', or deceived. **Gull** is now rare, but was a very common word from the 16th to the 19th centuries, and was used by Shakespeare. It may have come from **gull**, an old dialect term for an unfledged bird, which had nothing to do with **gull** as in **seagull**: this was a medieval word that probably came from a Celtic language such as Welsh or Cornish.

gum

In the sense 'a sticky secretion produced by some trees and shrubs', **gum** can be traced way back to an ancient Egyptian word. Among its more recent meanings it has been applied to a type of sweet pastille (as in 'fruit gum') since the early 19th century, and to **chewing gum** from the mid 19th century in the US. The **gum** as part of your mouth comes from an Old English word meaning 'the inside of the mouth or throat'.

Gumshoe is an American term for a detective. It dates from the early 20th century and relates to rubber-soled shoes, called gumshoes, suitable for doing something stealthily. The 1971 film *Gumshoe* starred Albert Finney as a Liverpool bingo caller who decides to turn private detective.

gun

The first device to be called a **gun** in English may have been a kind of catapult used in medieval warfare to hurl rocks or arrows at the enemy. It is possible that the term may have derived from a pet form of the Scandinavian name Gunnhildr (from *gunnr* and *hildr*, both meaning 'war'). Giving female personal names to weapons has been a common practice over the centuries. Examples include Mons Meg, a 15th-century cannon in Edinburgh Castle; Brown Bess, the nickname for a musket used by the British army in the 18th century; and Big Bertha, a large German gun used in the First World War.

If someone refuses to compromise or change, despite criticism, we can say that they are **sticking to their guns**. The expression comes from the battlefield, where sticking to your guns meant remaining at your post, loading and firing a cannon despite being under constant bombardment.

To **be gunning for** someone is to be looking for a chance to attack them. In the 17th century, though, to go gunning was to go hunting.

Gunboat diplomacy is foreign policy supported by the use or threat of military force. It is first mentioned in the 1920s, in reference to US policy in China.

gusto

If you do something with **gusto**, you do it with real relish or enjoyment. The word is borrowed from Italian, and came from Latin *gustus* 'taste'. One of its early meanings was 'a particular liking for something', as in this line from William Wycherley's play *Love in a Wood* (1672): 'Why should you force wine upon us? We are not all of your gusto.' This sense eventually dropped out of use, with the 'keen enjoyment' sense becoming common from the beginning of the 19th century.

gutter

'We are all in the gutter, but some of us are looking at the stars,' said Oscar Wilde in the play *Lady Windermere's Fan* (1892). A **gutter** was originally a watercourse, either a natural or an artificial one, and the word comes via Old French *gotiere* from Latin *gutta* 'a drop'. In the 16th century this became 'a furrow or track made by running water', from which developed the main modern meaning, 'a hollowed channel running at the side of a street, to carry away surface water'. The

gutter became the habitat of destitute people in the mid 19th century, and newspapers that pursue sensational stories about the private lives of public figures have been known as **the gutter press** since the end of that century.

guy

Expressions such as **fall guy**, **wise guy** and **tough guy** are all American in origin, and it used only to be Americans who called men **guys** at all. This use of the word dates from the late 19th century, as a development of an earlier sense applied to a person of grotesque appearance. Before it came to be applied to people, though, the word was used – as it still is today – to describe an effigy of Guy Fawkes, one of the Gunpowder Plot conspirators and Catholic extremists who intended to blow up James I and his parliament in 1605. People traditionally burn a **guy** on a BONFIRE each year on the 5th of November, the anniversary of the plot. To **guy** someone is now to make fun of them, but it was previously to carry an effigy of them around the streets. It came from the practice of **guying**, or carrying a guy around on the 5th of November. The **guy rope** on a tent is unconnected, and probably from a German word.

gymnasium

Ancient Greek men exercised naked. This fact is preserved in the origin of the word **gymnasium**, which came into English from Latin but is ultimately from Greek *gumnazein* 'to exercise or train naked', *gumnos* being the Greek word for 'naked'. The shortened form **gym** first appeared in the late 19th century.

gyp

If something **gives you gyp**, it causes you pain or discomfort. No one knows for certain where **gyp** comes from, but one theory holds that it is a dialect alteration of **gee-up**, an instruction to a horse to urge it to move faster. This is certainly plausible, as an earlier meaning of the expression was 'to scold or punish someone severely'.

Gypsy

When Gypsies first appeared in Britain in the 16th century no one was quite sure where they had come from. Their dark skin and hair led people to believe that they were from Egypt, and they were called *Gipcyans*, short for **Egyptians**. In fact Gypsies probably originated in the Indian subcontinent, and their language, Romany, is related to Hindi. See also BOHEMIAN and feature on ROMANY WORDS.

hack

The word **hack** meaning 'to cut with rough or heavy blows' goes back to ancient times. Modern computer enthusiasts have used it in the sense 'to gain unauthorised access to computer systems and data' since the 1980s, although the **hacker** appeared earlier, in the 1970s. It has no relation to **hack** 'a writer or journalist producing dull, uninteresting work'. This word originally referred to a horse for everyday riding, especially one let out for hire and consequently often tired and overworked. It is a shortening of **hackney**, probably taken from Hackney in East London, where horses were once pastured. This gave us the **hackney carriage**, originally a horse-drawn vehicle plying for hire and still the official term for a taxi. The idea of tiredness and overwork continues in **hackneyed**, 'overused, unoriginal and trite'. See also JADE, NAG, TAXI.

hackle

Hackles are the long feathers on the neck of a fighting cock or the hairs on the top of a dog's neck, which stand up when the animal is aggressive or excited. So if you **make someone's hackles rise** you make them angry or indignant. The word goes back to an ancient root related to HOOK. See also HECKLE.

haggard

A word from falconry, where it is a technical term for an adult hawk caught for training. Unlike hawks bred or raised in captivity, haggards are wild and untamed. Wild-looking people, or their wild-looking eyes, began to be described as **haggard** in the 17th century, and from there the word developed to the sense best known today, 'looking exhausted or unwell'. The word may be related to HEDGE. See also HAWK.

hair

The state of people's **hair** has a considerable effect on how they feel and behave – if you have a **bad hair day** you have a day when everything seems to go wrong, and if you **let your hair down** you become uninhibited. This idea started in the mid 19th century as to **let down the back hair**, with the notion of relaxing and becoming less formal.

The expression **the hair of the dog**, 'a small amount of alcoholic drink taken as a cure for a hangover', is a shortened version of **a hair of the dog that bit you**. It comes from an old belief that someone bitten by a rabid dog could be cured of rabies by taking a potion containing some of the dog's hair.

halcyon

The **halcyon** was a bird that in medieval times was thought to breed in a nest floating on the sea, and to charm the wind and waves so that the sea was calm. It was sometimes identified as a kingfisher, most of which actually nest in riverbanks, and the word comes from the Greek term for a kingfisher, *alkuōn*. The **halcyon days** were originally 14 days of calm weather which were supposed to occur when the halcyon was breeding. Today the phrase refers to a period of time in the past that was idyllically happy and peaceful, as in 'those halcyon days when students received full government grants'.

half

The ancient root of **half** meant 'side', and this was the first meaning in English – a half of something was one of its two sides.

The phrase **at half cock**, 'when only partly ready', comes from the days of old-fashioned firearms, and describes a flintlock pistol misfiring. The cock was the lever which was raised into position ready to be released when the trigger was pulled. A pistol at half cock had the lever raised halfway and held by the catch, which in theory ensured that it could not be fired even if the trigger was pulled. Inevitably the occasional pistol would be faulty and go off early, at half cock, and this gave rise to the extended meaning of doing something before you are fully prepared for it. See also HANG. After the farthing the **halfpenny** was the smallest unit of the old British currency, and from 1961 until decimalisation the smallest. A **halfpennyworth**, also spelled **ha'p'orth** to represent a common pronunciation, was a small or negligible amount, and so the proverb **don't spoil the ship for a ha'p'orth**

of tar, 'don't risk the failure of a large project trying to economise on trivial things', reflects on its paltry value. Contrary to appearances, the saying does not have a nautical origin, but referred to the use of tar to keep flies off sores on sheep: *ship* reflects a dialect pronunciation of **sheep**.

hallmark

Articles made of gold, silver or platinum have been taken to Goldsmiths' Hall in London to be tested since the Middle Ages, and then stamped with a mark if they reached the required standard of purity. This was the original **hallmark**. Goldsmiths' Hall is the home of the Worshipful Company of Goldsmiths, one of the traditional Livery Companies of the City of London.

ham

It is unlikely that **ham** actors get their name from smoked or salt meat. The word meaning 'an excessively theatrical actor' arose in the USA in the late 19th century and may be based on AMATEUR, although **hamfatter** was also used at this time to mean 'an inexpert performer' – the 'ham' connection could be from the idea of being 'ham-fisted'. The **radio ham** or amateur radio enthusiast appeared in the early 20th century.

The word **ham** goes back to an ancient root meaning 'to be crooked'. The earliest sense was 'the back of the knee', but in the 15th century people began to apply it to the back of the thigh, or the thigh and buttocks, and from there to the thigh and hock of an animal used as food. See also PIG.

There is no **ham** in **hamster**. This is a German word – odd, as the hamster is found from central Europe through Asia to China, but not in Germany. Odder still is the fact that the German word's origin means 'corn weevil', a kind of beetle.

hand

An Old English word first recorded around AD 800. Since the Middle Ages **hand** has had the meaning 'a person', as in **farmhand** or **deckhand**. **All hands** is the entire crew of a ship – the orders **all hands on deck** and **all hands to the pump** call upon all members of the crew, and now of any team, to assist. The phrase **hand over fist** also came from the world of sailing. Originally it had the form **hand over hand**, describing the action of a sailor climbing a rope or hauling it in, with each hand being brought over the other in rapid succession. By the 1820s the idea of speed had been extended to other contexts such as the rapid progress of a ship in pursuit of another, and soon after it was being used much more generally of any action

done quickly. Nowadays it is almost always the making of money that is done **hand over fist**.

Horse racing gave us **hands down**. A jockey who won hands down was so certain of victory in the closing stages of a race that he could lower his hands, relax his grip on the reins and stop urging on his horse.

handbag

The Conservative MP Julian Critchley was the first to use **handbag** to mean 'to attack or crush verbally'. In 1982 he said of Margaret Thatcher, then British prime minister, that 'she can't look at a British institution without hitting it with her handbag'. The article in *The Economist* that reported his comment went on to say that 'Treasury figures published last week show how good she has proved at handbagging the civil service'.

Football managers or commentators sometimes describe a minor fight or scuffle between players as being **handbags**, or sometimes **handbags at three** (or **ten**) **paces**. The idea is that the players are no more likely to inflict serious harm than two women hitting each other with their handbags. The expression seems to have originated in the mid to late 1980s.

handicap

This word derives from a popular old pastime that involved one person claiming an article belonging to another and offering something in exchange. The participants then appointed an umpire to adjudicate the difference in value, and then all three deposited forfeit money in a cap, the two opponents showing their agreement or disagreement with the valuation by putting in their hands and then bringing them out either full or empty. This sport was called **hand in cap**, later reduced to **handicap**. The word is first recorded

'She can't look at a British institution without hitting it with her handbag' in the mid 17th century, but the practice appears in the 14th century poem *Piers the Plowman*, and is known elsewhere in continental Europe from an early date. The **handicap race** (originally **handicap match**), in which an umpire determines what weight each horse carries in order to equalise their chances, dates from the mid 18th century.

handsome

The original sense of **handsome**, showing that the root word was HAND, was 'easy to handle or use'. In the mid 16th century this developed to 'suitable' and 'apt, clever'. The current senses 'good-looking' and 'striking, of fine quality' followed soon after. In the proverb **handsome is as handsome does**, 'character and behaviour are more important than appearance', the original reference was to chivalrous or genteel behaviour, though most people now take it to refer to good looks.

hang

To **hang** someone as a punishment was originally to crucify them. Later it came to involve tying a rope round their neck and removing the support from beneath them. This is now the only sense in which the past form **hanged** is used, but in early times it was the only possibility: **hung** did not appear until the 16th century.

The phrase to **hang fire** originates with the complex firing mechanism of the old flintlock pistol. A small quantity of gunpowder would be loaded into a metal hollow above the trigger, and when the trigger was released a spark from a flint would ignite the gunpowder, which in turn would ignite the main charge, causing it to explode and propel the shot out of the barrel. Sometimes the powder in the pan would fail to explode immediately, perhaps because it was damp, and merely smoulder, causing a delay in the firearm going off. When this happened it was said to **hang fire**. See also HALF.

happy

Before the 14th century you could be GLAD but not **happy**. The word depends on **hap** 'fortune, chance', which entered English a century or more earlier and which, except in **hapless** meaning 'unfortunate', is no longer used in everyday English. To be happy was at first to have good luck, be favoured by fortune – the

word came to refer to feelings of pleasure in the early 16th century.

To some the epitome of happiness is to be **as happy as a sandboy**. Apparently sandboys (who would have been grown men as well as boys) were 'happy' or 'jolly' because they were habitually drunk. A dictionary of slang terms published in 1823 explains that **jolly as a sandboy** referred to 'a merry fellow who has tasted a drop'. This association is reflected in a reference to a pub in Charles Dickens's *The Old Curiosity Shop*, published in 1840: 'The Jolly Sandboys was a small road-side inn . . . with a sign, representing three Sandboys increasing their jollity.' Sandboys were traders who sold sand for use in building, for household chores such as cleaning pots and pans and to spread on floors to soak up spillages, especially in pubs. In Australia you can also be **as happy as Larry**, which may be connected with the renowned 19th-century boxer Larry Foley, or owe something to **larry**, a dialect word meaning 'a state of excitement' that appears in the novels of Thomas Hardy. A North American equivalent is **as happy as a clam** or **as happy as a clam at high water**: when the tide is high, the clams are covered by seawater and are able to feed to their hearts' content, away from predators.

hanky-panky

People have been up to **hanky-panky** since the 1830s. Then it meant 'trickery' or 'dishonest behaviour', but since the Second World War it has referred to sexual indiscretions. The word could be a play on **hocus-pocus**, said by conjurors as they performed tricks, rather like 'abracadabra!'.

harass

Harassing someone may originally have involved setting dogs on them. The word came from French in the early 17th century and is probably from *harer* 'to set a dog on'. The notion of intimidation of people arose during the 19th century, with **sexual harassment** acquiring particular prominence in the 1970s. The sound and sense of **harass** may be similar to those of **harry**, but the two are unrelated: **harry** goes back to an ancient root meaning 'army, host'.

harlot

Harlots are definitely women these days, but in the 13th century a **harlot** was a term of abuse for a male beggar or villain. It then came to refer to a jester or comedian and to a male servant before it started to mean 'a promiscuous woman' in the mid 15th century. It was much used in early English versions of the Bible as a less offensive word than 'whore'.

harvest

The meaning of **harvest** in Old English was 'autumn'. Since early autumn was the season for the cutting and gathering in of ripened crops, this passed during the Middle Ages into 'the process of gathering in crops' and 'the season's yield or crop'. The word **harvest** itself has ancient roots: it is related to Latin *carpere* 'to pluck' (the origin of CARPET and **excerpt**) and Greek *karpos* 'fruit'. See also AUTUMN.

hash

A **hash** is a dish of cooked meat cut into small pieces and then reheated in gravy. To some it may sound horribly typical of old-fashioned school dinners, and however delicious it might taste, it probably does not look very appetising. Its 16th-century origin is a French word meaning 'an axe', from which HATCHET and the use of **hatch** meaning 'to mark a surface with close parallel lines to represent shading' also derive. The **hash sign** (the sign #) is probably also from this use of **hatch**. In the 18th century **hash** developed the sense of 'a jumble of mismatched parts', which forms the basis of the modern expression to **make a hash of**. See also HOTCHPOTCH.

hatchet

English took over French *hachette* in the Middle Ages. It derives from *hache* 'an axe' – see HASH. To **bury the hatchet**, 'end a quarrel or conflict', refers to a Native American custom which involved burying a hatchet or tomahawk to mark the conclusion of a peace treaty between warring groups. The custom is described as early as 1680; the current sense of the phrase emerged around 70 years later. In 1974 the then British Prime Minister Harold Wilson observed wryly of his Cabinet: 'I've buried all the hatchets. But I know where I've buried them and I can dig them up if necessary.'

Since the 1940s a **hatchet man** has been somebody employed to carry out controversial or disagreeable tasks, such as dismissing people from their jobs or writing journalistic pieces to destroy a person's reputation. The original hatchet man, in the USA during the late 19th century, was a hired Chinese assassin who carried a hatchet with the handle cut off.

hat-trick

If a bowler in a 19th-century cricket match took three wickets with three consecutive balls, his club was expected to present him with a new hat, or some equivalent. This is the origin of **hat-trick**, a term first used in the 1870s. From the beginning of the 20th century threefold achievements in other sporting activities also acquired the name, and since it is easier for a footballer to score three goals in a match than for a bowler to take three consecutive wickets, soccer is now the usual context of scoring a hat-trick.

havoc

A victorious army commander would once have given his soldiers a signal to start plundering: he would **cry havoc**. The sense of plunder gradually passed into destructive devastation, and the army itself would **make havoc**. Outside the battlefield other people and other circumstances eventually began to **work havoc** or, from the 20th century, to **create** or **wreak havoc** and to **play havoc with something**. The word **havoc** itself is a medieval alteration of French *havot*. The word was memorably used by Shakespeare in *Julius Caesar*: 'Cry, "Havoc!", and let slip the dogs of war.' See also MAYHEM.

hawk

In politics a **hawk**, a person who advocates hardline or warlike policies, contrasts with a DOVE, a peacemaker. The terms emerged in the early 1960s at the time of the Cuban missile crisis, when the Soviet Union threatened to install missiles in Cuba within striking distance of the USA.

To **hawk** meaning 'to carry about and offer goods for sale' was formed in the late 15th century, probably by removing the ending from **hawker**, 'a person who travels around selling goods'. The latter word is not recorded until the early 16th century, when hawkers came to legal notice as something of a nuisance to be suppressed, but was most likely in use long before it was written down. It is related to **huckster**, from a root meaning 'to haggle, bargain'. See also HAGGARD.

hay

An ancient word that goes back to around AD 800 in Old English. The phrase to **make hay**, 'to make good use of an opportunity while it lasts', is a shortening of the proverbial recommendation **make hay while the sun shines**, which has been in use since the 16th century. See also STRAW.

Since the late 19th century North American farmers have employed **haywire** to bind bales of hay and corn. Others found less suitable uses for it, so that haywire came to describe anything patched together or poorly equipped. By the 1920s to **go haywire** meant 'to go wrong', and in the 1930s it extended to cover people who were mentally disturbed or out of control.

hazard

Hazard was first a gambling game played with two dice in which the chances are complicated by arbitrary rules. It reached English in the Middle Ages through Arabic, Spanish and French, but goes back to Persian *zār* or Turkish *zar* 'dice'. In the 16th century **hazard** came also to mean 'a chance' and 'a risk of loss or harm'.

head

English **head** – in Old English *hēafod* – has parallels in numerous related languages, including Dutch *hoofd* and German *Haupt*. The earlier, more logical, version of **head over heels**, 'turning over completely in forward motion', was **heels over head**. The modern form dates from the late 18th century. It often describes an extreme condition, as in **head over heels in love** or **head over heels in debt**. A variant is **head over ears**, which is an alteration of earlier, and much more logical, **over head and ears**. The playwright and critic George Bernard Shaw wrote in 1912: 'I plunged in head over ears and . . . wrote off my 56 years'.

The expression to **give someone their head** comes from horse riding. Giving a horse its head meant allowing it to gallop freely rather than checking its pace by pulling on the reins. The idea of giving a horse freedom was readily extended to people, and the same image and meaning is to be found in the phrase to **give someone free rein** (see REIN), which these days people sometimes wrongly write as **free reign**, as if the idea was allowing someone to rule freely.

hearse

In English a **hearse** has always been a part of a funeral, but its origin is agricultural. The word derives from Old French *herce*, which meant 'a harrow' and goes back to Latin *hirpex*, a name for a kind of large rake. This came from Oscan, an extinct language of southern Italy known only from early inscriptions, where *hirpus* meant 'wolf': people were making a comparison between a wolf's teeth and the teeth of a rake. The earliest uses of **hearse** in medieval English were for a triangular frame, shaped like an ancient harrow, used for carrying candles at certain church services, and a canopy placed over the coffin of a distinguished person while it was in church. The modern meaning, 'a vehicle for conveying the coffin at a funeral', appeared in the mid 17th century.

heart

The Greek word *kardia*, from which English took **cardiac**, is directly related to **heart**. The shared root existed before their ancestor developed into different language families in Europe, Asia and northern India.

Since Anglo-Saxon times people have regarded the heart as the centre of emotions and feelings. If you **wear your heart on your sleeve**, you make your feelings clear for all to see. The British have traditionally frowned on such openness, regarding it as a sign of weakness. In a television interview in 1987 the former British Prime Minister Margaret Thatcher advised against it, saying: 'To wear your heart on your sleeve isn't a very good plan; you should wear it inside, where it functions best.' Nevertheless the phrase has its origins in courage and chivalry. In the Middle Ages, when jousting was a popular form of entertainment, it was the custom for a knight to tie a favour from a lady to his sleeve. A favour was a ribbon, glove or other small item belonging to the lady which she presented to her chosen knight as a sign of her love or support.

heat

The words **heat** and HOT go back to the same ancestor. The popular saying **if you can't stand the heat, get out of the kitchen** is associated with the Democratic statesman Harry S Truman, who was President of the USA between 1945 and 1953. When he announced his retirement in 1952 he did express the sentiment, in the form **if you don't like the heat . . .**, but attributed it to one of his military advisers, Major General Harry Vaughan.

heaven

The ultimate origin of **heaven** is unknown, although parallel forms exist in related languages, such as Dutch *hemel* and German *Himmel*. From the very beginning in English the word referred both to the sky which we can see and to the abode of God, usually regarded as beyond the sky. In Christian theology there is only one heaven, but some Jewish and Muslim people considered there to be seven, of which the seventh was the highest. There souls enjoyed a state of eternal bliss, and so **in seventh heaven** came to mean 'very happy, ecstatic'. See also MOVE, PARADISE.

heckle

Aggressive questioners have interrupted and abused public speakers from the dawn of democracy. Since the early 19th century the practice has had a name: heckling. The original meaning of **heckle**, in the Middle Ages, was 'to dress flax or hemp in order to split and straighten the fibres for spinning'. This was done with a **heckle** or **hackle**, an instrument with parallel steel pins. This is the same word as the hackles or long feathers on the neck of a fighting cock (see HACKLE). See also TEASE.

hedge

Hedges mark boundaries, but are also a means of protection or defence. The idea of protecting yourself is strong in to **hedge your bets**, 'to try to minimise the risk of being wrong or of making a loss by pursuing two courses of action at the same time'. In strict betting terms this means putting money on more than one horse in a race, but you can also hedge other financial liabilities, including speculative investments. Originally people would **hedge in** a bet. This is related to an earlier application of **hedge in**, in which debts were 'hedged in' by incorporating them into a larger debt for which better security was available. Much more recently, in the 1960s, **hedge fund** became the term for an offshore investment fund that engages in speculation using credit or borrowed capital.

helicopter

The first **helicopter** did not appear until the 1920s, but the word had already been invented by then, first of all in French – the science fiction writer Jules Verne wrote of a helicopter in *The Clipper of the Clouds* (1886). The French word was based on Greek *helix* 'spiral' and *pteron* 'wing', which is related to FEATHER and gave us the name of the flying reptile the PTERODACTYL.

hell

The traditional idea of **hell** as a place beneath the earth fits in with the word's origins. It descends from a form lost in the mists of time that meant 'to cover, hide' and also gave rise to Latin *celare* (root of **conceal** and OCCULT) and to English HOLE and **heel** 'to set a plant in the ground and cover its roots'.

The infernal regions are regarded as a place of torment or punishment, and many curses and exclamations, such as **a hell of a** — or **one hell of a** — , depend on this. These expressions used to be shocking, and until the early 20th century were usually printed as h—l or h—. Alterations such as **heck** served the same softening purpose in speech as well as in writing.

The saying **hell hath no fury like a woman scorned** is a virtual quotation from a 1697 play by William Congreve: 'Heaven has no rage like love to hatred turned, Nor Hell a fury like a woman scorned.' The dramatist Colley Cibber had used very similar words just a year earlier, and the idea was a commonplace in the Renaissance. It can be traced back to the Greek dramatist Euripides of the 5th century BC. Strictly the 'fury' is one of the Furies of Greek mythology, frightening goddesses who avenged

Hell is other people.

Jean-Paul Sartre

wrong and punished crime, but most people now use and interpret it in the sense 'wild or violent anger'.

The proverb **the road to hell is paved with good intentions** dates from the late 16th century, but earlier forms existed which omitted the first three words. Grumpy and misanthropic people everywhere will agree with the French philosopher Jean-Paul Sartre. He said in 1944: 'Hell is other people.'

hen

Ultimately the word **hen** is related to Latin *canere* 'to sing'. Apart from singing hens, what could be rarer than hen's teeth? Hens do not have teeth, so to describe something as **as rare as hen's teeth** is tantamount to saying that it is non-existent. The phrase was originally used in the USA during the mid 19th century.

The **henpecked** husband has long been a staple of comedies and seaside postcards, and the word goes back to *The Genuine Remains* (1680) by Samuel Butler. The expression comes from the way that hens will sometimes peck at the feathers of the cock bird.

henchman

The original sense of **henchman** was probably 'a groom'. It is a compound of Old English *hengest* 'male horse' and MAN. The first part also features in the names of the semi-mythological leaders Hengist and Horsa, who came to Britain at the invitation of the British king

Vortigern in 449 to assist in defeating the Picts. From the Middle Ages a henchman was a squire or page of honour to a person of great rank; in Scotland he was the principal attendant of a Highland chief. The word was taken up by Sir Walter Scott, whose novels were hugely popular throughout the 19th century, and Scott gave **henchman** to the wider world. The current sense, 'a criminal's follower', began in the mid 19th century in the USA.

heroin

The similarity in spelling between **heroin** and **hero** is not accidental. The name of the drug is a German word formed in the late 1890s from Latin *heros* 'hero', in reference to its effects. The dangerously addictive drug, intended as a painkiller, produces feelings of euphoria, and in early tests users reported that they felt 'heroic'.

hide

The **hide** meaning 'the skin of an animal' goes back far in prehistory to a root that also developed into Latin *cutis* 'skin' (the source of **cuticle**) and Greek *kutos*. A person who is **hidebound** is unable or unwilling to change because of tradition or convention. The word originally referred to physical condition, first of cattle who were so badly fed or so sick that their skin clung close to their back and ribs, and then of emaciated people. The **hide** meaning 'to put or keep out of sight' is unrelated. See also BUSHEL.

Someone who is **on a hiding to nothing** is unlikely to succeed, or at least unlikely to gain much advantage if they do. The term apparently arose in the world of horse racing, when a trainer, owner or jockey was expected to win easily and so could gain no credit from success but would be disgraced by failure. The word is the same as that in a **good hiding**, and means 'a beating' – the idea is one of beating the hide or skin off someone.

high

High is one of those small words that play a part in a large number of expressions. To begin on a high note, there is **high days and holidays**. In the calendar of the Christian Church there used to be two sorts of special day: a **high day** and a **holiday**. Holiday was originally **holy day** and was a day set apart for religious observance. A high day was a much more important religious festival commemorating a particular sacred person or event. Today holiday has lost all its religious significance and is any day off from work or school, and high days and holidays are just special occasions in general.

Being **high** on drugs is associated with the 1960s, but the expression goes back at least to the 1930s. Alcohol can also be classed as a drug, and you can read of a man being 'high with wine' as early as 1627.

The first records of **high, wide and handsome**, 'expansive and impressive', are from US newspapers in the 1880s. In 1932 a book on *Yankee Slang* comments that it is a common shout at rodeos: 'Ride him, Cowboy, high, wide and handsome.'

The expression to **be for the high jump** might conjure up pictures of shivering schoolchildren reluctantly lining up for various events on sports day, but behind it lies a much grimmer scene. The phrase dates from the early 20th century, when it was a slang term used by soldiers to mean 'to be put on trial before your commanding officer'. The image is actually of a person being executed by hanging, with the jump being the effect of the gallows trapdoor being suddenly opened beneath their feet. See also HOG.

heyday

To shout **hey-day!** in the early 16th century was to express joy, surprise or other intense emotion. It may have come from German *heida!* or *heidi!*, 'hurrah!'. By the end of the same century **heyday** meant 'a state of high spirits or passion'. Perhaps through a false association with day, it began to refer to the period of someone's greatest success or activity.

hill

The root of **hill** is also the source of Latin *collis* and Greek *kolōnos* 'hill'. The Bible uses hills as a symbol of permanence, but the comparison **as old as the hills** is not recorded until the 19th century. If you are **over the hill** you are old and past your best: the phrase first appeared in print in the USA in the mid 20th century.

hippopotamus

The huge, ungainly **hippopotamus** does not look much like a horse, but the animal was seen in that way by the ancient Greeks. Its name comes from Greek *hippopotamos* 'river horse'.

history

The history of **history** is long and involved indeed. The word goes back to a very ancient root that is also the source of Latin *videre* 'to see' and of the old English word **wit** 'to have knowledge'. More immediately it came from Greek *historia* 'finding out, narrative, history'. In its earliest use, in the Middle Ages, a history was not necessarily assumed to be true: it could be any narrative or story, an idea echoed by the American motor manufacturer Henry Ford (1863-1947) when he said 'History is more or less bunk.'

To **make history**, 'to do something that is remembered in or influences the course of history', dates from the mid 19th century. A less positive view of history appears in the phrase to **be history**, 'to be dead or no longer relevant to the present', which is recorded from the 1930s.

hit

The earliest sense of **hit**, in the Old English period, was 'to come upon, meet with, find'. Popular successes, first of all plays and then songs, have been called hits since the beginning of the 19th century – in 1927 *Melody Maker* ran an advert for 'The sensational hit – Sweeping the country like a cyclone – The Doll Dance'.

In the 1990s the phrase to **hit the ground running** became something of a cliché. It seems to refer to soldiers disembarking rapidly from a helicopter, though no one has been able to trace it back to any particular conflict. Marksmanship and shooting are behind a number of phrases, including to **hit the mark**, 'to be successful in an attempt or accurate in a guess' and **hit-and-miss** 'done or occurring at random', which is more understandable in its earlier form **hit-or-miss**.

hitch

The earliest sense of **hitch** was 'to move or lift up with a jerk'. The meaning 'to fasten or tether' dates from the early 17th century, and is the one that features in such expressions as to **get hitched** or get married and to **hitch your wagon to a star**. The US philosopher and poet Ralph Waldo Emerson introduced this second phrase in 1870 in the sense 'to have high aspirations', but it now tends to mean 'to form a relationship with a successful person'. **A hitch** meaning 'an obstacle' is probably from the word's use to mean 'a knot in a rope'.

hobby

In medieval times men and boys given the name Robin were sometimes known as Hobin or Hobby. A **hobby** then became a small horse, from which came the **hobby horse**, a figure of a horse made of wickerwork and worn over the head in a **morris dance** or PANTOMIME. Later it became a stick with a horse's head, for a child to ride when playing. The connection with pleasure or play led to the use of **hobby horse** for what we now call a **hobby**. Since the early 19th century **hobby** has taken over this sense and **hobby horse** now usually means 'a preoccupation or favourite topic'. The *hob* in **hobgoblin** is also from a pet form of Robin or Robert, as is **dobbin** as a name for a carthorse.

hobnob

In the 18th century drinkers would toast each other alternately with the words 'hob or nob' or 'hob and nob', probably meaning 'give or take' or 'have or have not'. Toasting each other in this way was to **drink hob or nob**, or, from the early 19th century, simply to **hobnob**. The image of convivial companionship led to the sense 'to be on familiar terms, to talk informally', which during the 20th century acquired negative associations of mixing socially with those thought to be of higher social status. It was the convivial connotations that probably persuaded McVitie's to come up with the name HobNobs for their new biscuit in 1985.

hog

This may be one of the small number of English words that comes from the language of the Celts, who lived in Britain before the Romans and Saxons. It is probably related to Welsh *hwch* and Cornish *hoch* 'pig, sow'. See also PIG.

A number of explanations have been offered for the expression to **go the whole hog**, which was first used in the USA in the early 19th century. The earliest examples are in a political context, prompting the idea that the phrase's origins might lie in the large political rallies which were then common. At these rallies various ploys were used to woo potential voters, notably the provision of vast quantities of free food: a whole pig – or hog, in American English – was typically the favoured roast. Another idea is that the phrase comes from a fable about Muslims in *The Love of the World: Hypocrisy Detected*, published in 1779 and composed by William Cowper (an English poet and hardly an expert on Islam). According to this fable certain Muslims, forbidden to eat pork by their religion but strongly tempted to have just a little, suggested that

hoi polloi

In Greek **hoi polloi** means 'the many'. It has been used since the mid 17th century as a snooty way of referring to ordinary people, 'the masses'. Strictly, as *hoi* means 'the' you should not say 'the hoi polloi', as this is equivalent to 'the the many'. But writers as renowned as Byron have said 'the hoi polloi', so you would be in good company.

Muhammad had meant to ban only one particular part of the pig. But they could not agree which part that was, and between them they ate the whole animal, each one telling himself that his own portion did not contain the part that was forbidden.

To **live high on the hog** is to have a luxurious lifestyle. The phrase probably comes from the idea of eating the best bits of a pig, which were higher up on the animal, as opposed to the offal and hoofs.

The verb use, 'to take all of something in a greedy way', comes from the proverbial greed of the pig. It was first used in the USA, in the 1880s.

hold

The ancient root of **hold** probably meant 'to watch over'. **Hold** meaning 'a large compartment in the lower part of a ship or aircraft' has a different origin, derived from **hole**.

The phrase **no holds barred**, 'with no rules or restrictions', comes from the sport of wrestling, where a hold is a particular way of grasping or restraining an opponent. Certain kinds of hold, such as gripping round the throat, are classed as unlawful because they are too dangerous. Sometimes, though, no-holds-barred contests would be set up where participants could do almost anything they liked.

holocaust

A **holocaust** was originally a sacrificial offering burned completely on an altar. This is reflected in its origin, Greek *holokauston*, from *holos* 'whole' and *kaustos* 'burned'. But from the 18th century it could also mean 'a great slaughter or massacre', and this is the sense most widely known today. **The Holocaust** was the mass murder of more than six million Jews and other persecuted groups under the German Nazi regime between 1941 and 1945, in concentration camps such as Auschwitz and Belsen. The term was introduced by historians during the 1950s, but as early as 1942 newspapers were referring to the killing of Jews by the Germans as 'a holocaust'. The Hebrew equivalent is *sō'āh* or **Shoah**, literally 'catastrophe', which is sometimes used in English.

holy

English **holy** is related to Dutch and German *heilig*, and all derive from the same root as WHOLE. You might describe a place as a **holy of holies** without realising that the phrase originally referred to the inner chamber of the sanctuary of the Jewish temple in Jerusalem, which was separated by a veil from the outer chamber and entered only by the High Priest on the Day of Atonement. The attitude of self-conscious virtue or piety that is **holier than thou** has a biblical source, in Isaiah, which deplores 'a rebellious people . . . Which say, Stand by thyself, come not near to me; for I am holier than thou'. See also HIGH, SACRED.

home

Many generations have reflected on **home**, an ancient word related to a Sanskrit term meaning 'safe dwelling'. The Greek poet Hesiod, who lived around 700 BC, expressed the same sentiment as **there's no place like home**, although its best-known expression is in the sentimental song 'Home Sweet Home' by John Howard Payne, first sung in the opera *Clari, the Maid of Milan* in 1823: 'Mid pleasures and palaces though we may roam, / Be it ever so humble, there's no place like home.' The saying **home is where the heart is** dates from the late 19th century.

A woman's place is in the home has been asserted since the 19th century, though best avoided in the 21st.

honeymoon

In the 16th century the first month of a couple's marriage was their **honeymoon** whether or not they went away on holiday – very few then did. The original reference was not to a 'moon' or month at all, but to 'sweet' affection changing like the moon.

honour

Latin *honor* is the source of **honour, honourable** and also of **honest**. The idea that **there is honour among thieves** was expressed even in the early 17th century. The English philosopher Jeremy Bentham was the first to put it in print in its modern form when he wrote in 1802: 'A sort of honour may be found (according to a proverbial saying) even among thieves.'

hoof

If a government makes policy **on the hoof**, it does so without proper thought and preparation. The original reference was to livestock that was alive and not yet slaughtered; the earliest example in print dates from 1818. The human foot is also treated like a cow's or horse's in the phrase to **hoof it** 'to walk as opposed to ride', which dates from as far back as the mid 17th century. To **hoof** meaning 'to dance' and **hoofer** 'a dancer' both arose in US slang in the 1920s.

hook

Hooks have many uses: for catching hold of things, for hanging things on, for controlling sheep, for carrying bait and others. The angler's hook features in **hook, line and sinker**, used to emphasise that someone has been completely deceived or tricked. The items all form part of fishing tackle, where a sinker is a weight used to sink the fishing line in the water. The image behind the expression is of a hungry fish deceived by the bait into gulping everything down off the hook. The expression **off the hook**, 'no longer in trouble or difficulty', is almost the opposite: the idea here is of a fish managing to wriggle off the hook that lodged in its mouth when it took the bait.

The type of hook referred to in **by hook or by crook**, 'by any possible means', is not certain. The expression dates back to the 14th century and most likely has a farming background, with the crook being a shepherd's hooked staff and the hook being a 'billhook', a type of heavy curved pruning knife. One indication as to how these implements might be used together comes from the writer and political reformer William Cobbett, who in 1822 described an ancient English forest law. According to this law, people living near a woodland were allowed to gather dead tree branches for fuel, using the hook to cut them off or the crook to pull them down.

To play hookey, or play truant, is a 19th-century US expression. It probably comes from hook off or hook it, meaning 'to go away'.

hooligan

The Hooligans were a fictional rowdy Irish family in a music hall song of the 1890s, and a comic Irish character called Hooligan appeared in a series of adventures in the magazine *Funny Folks*. One or other may have given their name to the **hooligan**, a phenomenon who made his debut in newspaper reports of cases in police courts in 1898. The **football hooligan** is first mentioned in the mid 1960s. See also THUG, VANDAL.

Hooray Henry see SLOANE.

hoot

This word probably imitates the sound that it represents. It was not originally the call of an owl, but a human cry of derision or disapproval. Why people should **not care a hoot** or **two hoots**, 'not care at all', is not clear. An earlier form of the phrase, recorded in the USA in the late 19th century, was **not care a hooter**, and it may be a corruption of **iota** (see JOT).

The nose has been the **hooter** since the 1950s. The idea is of a person blowing their nose loudly.

hope

People always need **hope**, and the word certainly goes back to ancient times. That **hope springs eternal** is thanks to the poet Alexander Pope, who wrote in his *Essay on Man* in 1732: 'Hope springs eternal in the human breast. Man never is, but always to be blessed.' See also PANDORA'S BOX.

horde

A **horde** was originally a tribe or troop of nomads, such as the Tartars led by Genghis Khan, who lived in tents or wagons and migrated from place to place in search of new pasture or to plunder and wage war. The word comes from Polish *horda*, which is itself from Turkish *ordu* 'royal camp', from which the language name **Urdu** also derives.

horn

The word **horn** is related to CORN 'a painful area of thickened skin', **cornea** 'the transparent layer forming the front of the eye' and the brass instrument the CORNET. This is because it shares its ancestor with Latin *cornu* 'horn'.

In to **draw** (or **pull**) **in your horns**, 'to become less assertive or ambitious', the image is of a snail drawing in its eyestalks and retreating into its shell when disturbed. The idea behind **on the horns of a dilemma**, 'faced with a decision involving equally unfavourable alternatives', is of a charging bull: if you avoid one horn you will still be impaled on the other. The alternatives of a dilemma were traditionally called 'horns', translating the term used in Latin, the international language of European scholars in the 16th century. See DILEMMA.

horror

The Latin word *horror* was formed from *horrere*, meaning 'to stand on end' (referring to hair) and 'to tremble, shudder'. This is the source of our word **horror** and of related words such as **horrible** and **horrify**. See also ABHOR.

horse

An ancient word that has related forms in most other northern European languages. The root may also be the source of Latin *currere* 'to run'.

The sport of horse racing has given numerous expressions to the language. The saying **horses for courses** is based on the idea that each racehorse is suited to one particular racecourse and will do better on that than on any other. A.E.T. Watson's *The Turf* in 1891 was the first to record this observation, which he describes as 'a familiar phrase on the turf'. The wider public took it up to mean that just because something suits one person, this does not mean that it will necessarily suit another. The underlying idea of **straight from the horse's mouth** is that the best way to get racing tips is to ask a horse directly. One of the first examples comes from a 1913 edition of the *Syracuse Herald*: 'Lionel hesitated, then went on quickly. "I got a tip yesterday, and if it wasn't straight from the horse's mouth it was jolly well the next thing to it."'

People often say something like, 'Oh, wild horses wouldn't . . .', meaning that nothing could persuade them to do that particular thing. They say it quite calmly, not realising the horrific reference – it comes from the old custom of executing criminals by tying each limb to the tail of a horse and then urging the horses on, so tearing the poor person into four pieces.

To **flog a dead horse** is to waste energy on a lost cause or a situation that cannot be altered. **Dead horse** used to be workmen's slang for work that was charged for before it was done: to **work** or **work for a dead horse** was to do work that you had already been paid for, and which felt rather pointless.

An early form of the proverb **you can lead a horse to water but you can't make him drink** was 'They can but bring horse to the water brinke, But horse may choose whether that horse will drinke' (1602).

The **horse chestnut** was formerly said to be a remedy for chest diseases in horses, and its name is a translation of Latin *Castanea equina*. In **horsefly**,

horseradish and similar terms **horse** implies 'large of its kind'. See also EQUESTRIAN, GIFT.

hospital

Latin *hospis* meant both 'host' and 'guest'. This hospitable word has sent out into the world **host** itself (in the meaning 'a person who entertains other people as guests'), **hostel** and HOTEL, as well as **hospice**, **hospital** and **hospitality**. In the Middle Ages, when **hospital** entered English from French, a hospital was a place where pilgrims and travellers could spend the night. It also came to describe a charitable institution for the housing of the needy. From the mid 16th century benefactors established hospitals for the education of the young, a use that survives in names such as Christ's Hospital, now a public school. The usual modern sense also dates from that time.

hostage

The word **hostage** has no connection with **host** in any of its uses – it goes back to Latin *ob* 'towards, against' and *sedere* 'to sit'. Originally an ally or enemy would hand over a hostage as security for the fulfilment of an undertaking. Now hostages are 'taken' as well as 'held', and are very seldom handed over voluntarily.

In a **hostage to fortune**, 'an undertaking or remark that invites trouble or could prove difficult to live up to', the word fortune means 'fate', with the idea being that future events are no longer under a person's control but in the hands of fate. The first recorded hostages to fortune were a man's family. In a rather jaundiced reflection on marriage the English philosopher Francis Bacon wrote in 1625: 'He that hath wife and children, hath given hostages to fortune; for they are impediments to great enterprises, either of virtue, or of mischief.'

hot

Hot shares an ancestor with HEAT. It has been used to describe sexual arousal since the Middle Ages, but a dictionary of US slang published in 1947 is the first to record **the hots** for desire, which may have originated in **hot pants**, first recorded in the 1920s and revived in Britain in the early 1970s to describe the fashion for incredibly skimpy shorts. People have used **hot air** for empty talk intended to impress since the late 19th century. See also BLOW.

hotchpotch

In the late Middle Ages English acquired the word **hotchpot** for 'a confused mixture'. It came from French *hochepot*, which was formed from *hocher* 'to shake' and *pot* 'pot'. **Hotchpot** is still used in

English law in the context of joining together all of a dead person's property so that it can be divided equally. In its everyday sense, though, people quickly changed it to **hotchpotch**, so that the elements rhymed for emphasis. The same rhyming impulses then gave rise to **hodgepodge**, now mainly used in North America. See also HASH.

hotel

English adopted the French word *hôtel* in the mid 17th century. For the first century of its life people used it only in French phrases and for the town mansions of French aristocrats. But since the mid 18th century the modern sense, 'a place providing accommodation and meals for paying guests', has prevailed.

The French word was originally spelled *hostel*, and this older form came into English in the Middle Ages, in the general sense 'a place to stay'. It was also used for an inn or what we would now call a hotel. The name **hostel** has since become resticted to places for specific groups of people such as students and migrant workers. The word goes back to Latin *hospis* (see HOSPITAL).

hour

The Anglo-Saxons did not have the word **hour**: it came in the Middle Ages from French, and goes back to Greek *hōra* 'season, hour', as in **horoscope** (YEAR is a more distant relation). The Old English equivalent was TIDE.

The eleventh hour, meaning 'the latest possible moment', comes from the parable of the labourers in the Gospel of Matthew. A man went out to the marketplace first thing in the morning and hired some labourers to work in his vineyard, promising them each a penny for the day's work. He went out four more times and took on more men, undertaking to pay each of them what was right. At the end of the day he paid the workers, giving those hired last, at the eleventh hour, a penny each, even though they had only done an hour's work. The people who had been hired first were understandably fed up about this, but the man told them to take what was theirs and go: he had done nothing wrong, because he had kept to their agreement. The phrase **their finest hour** was part of Winston Churchill's speech in the House of Commons on June 18, 1940, before the Battle of Britain began:

> Let us therefore brace ourselves to our duty, and so bear ourselves that, if the British Empire and its Commonwealth lasts for a thousand years, men will still say, 'This was their finest hour.'

See also BLOOD, FEW, FLAG.

house

The word **house** is related to Dutch *huis* and German *Haus*, and their ancient ancestor may have meant 'to hide'. It was used to mean 'a building for people to live in' in the Old English poem *Beowulf*.

The British Parliament emerged in medieval times as the assembly of the king and his Lords. From the 13th century representatives of the shires and boroughs were occasionally summoned to these assemblies, and under Edward III (1327-77) these 'Commons' began to meet separately from the Lords, although they did not get their own meeting chamber until the 16th century. The **House of Commons** was first called by that name in the early 17th century, quickly followed by the **Houses of Parliament** and the **House of Lords**.

The **house** music heard in clubs from 1986 onwards was probably named after the Warehouse, a club in Chicago where the music was first popular.

hub

The word **hub** is recorded from the early 16th century, but appeared in no dictionary until the 19th. It seems to have been an English dialect term that first meant 'hob', which before the days of electric or gas cookers was a surface behind or beside a fireplace used for heating pans. The sense 'the central part of a wheel' dates from the mid 17th century and was probably suggested by the shape of the original 'hub'.

hubbub

The sound of **hubbub** suggests the murmuring or chattering of a crowd, but this is not the origin of the word. It probably comes from Ireland, and may be based on the old Irish battle cry *abú* or *ababú* – in the mid 16th century, when it was first used in English, people talked of **an Irish hubbub**, meaning 'the confused noise of a crowd'.

hue and cry

In early times any person witnessing or surprising a criminal committing a crime could **raise a hue and cry**, calling for others to join in their pursuit and capture. In law the cry had to be raised by the inhabitants of the district in which the crime was committed, or otherwise the pursuers were liable for any damages suffered by the victim. The origin of the expression is in legal French *hu e cri* 'outcry and cry'. The first element has no connection with **hue** 'colour', which is a native English word related to Swedish *hy* 'skin, complexion'.

Hunting, shooting and fishing

'The game is afoot', cries Sherlock Holmes to Dr Watson at the start of one of their adventures. **Hunting** and other field sports have long been part of British life, leaving clear linguistic tracks behind.

Someone who cannot be found may be said to have gone to earth or gone to ground like a hunted fox seeking the safety of an underground burrow. If you are in possession of a useful clue you are on the scent, like a hound tracking its prey. You may be following a red herring (see RED) or a false scent, or even find that the trail has gone cold. The hunting connection is less clear when we draw a blank, but the literal sense of the words refer to an unsuccessful search for game made through a wood or thicket.

For some people August 12 is the Glorious Twelfth, because that is the day on which the grouse-shooting season starts. A good 'bag' of grouse shot on the twelfth is the source of the familiar bags of, as in 'Oh, there's bags of time'. Incidentally, the name of the grouse is nothing to do with complaining – it is thought to be from Latin *grus* 'crane', despite the difference in the sizes of the birds, whereas grouse meaning 'to moan or whinge' is related to grouch and probably goes back to Old French *grouchier* 'to grumble'.

Hunting itself is the source of venison, the meat of a DEER. The word was brought over by those keen hunters the Normans, who took it from Latin *venatio* 'hunting'.

The 18th-century satirist Jonathan Swift compared fishing with 'a stick and a string, with a worm at one end and a fool at the other', but some expressions from the world of angling suggest a degree of cunning. We speak of someone angling for advantage, or fishing for compliments or information. On the other hand, if you are too ready to accept a tempting offer you may be the one who swallows the bait.

See also BAY, CROPPER, FOREST, HOOK, QUARRY, SCENT, WHIP.

hulk

A **hulk** was originally a large cargo or transport ship. The word is probably of Mediterranean origin and related to Greek *holkas* 'cargo ship'. In the late 17th century it came to apply to an old ship stripped of fittings and permanently moored, especially one used for storage or as a prison.

Large, clumsy people began to be described as hulks in the late Middle Ages. In 1962 the comic superhero **the Incredible Hulk** appeared. He was born when the nuclear physicist Dr Robert Banner was caught in the explosion of a new kind of bomb that he had been working on, and was transformed into a huge, superhumanly strong creature with green skin.

human

In the beginning **human** and **humane** were the same word. The forms were used interchangeably until the 18th century, when **human** took over the scientific and general senses relating to people and **humane** became restricted to the meanings 'showing compassion' and 'without inflicting pain'. Both derive from Latin *humanus*, from *homo* 'man, human being'.

humble

A word that goes back to Latin *humilis* 'low, lowly, base', which was formed from *humus* 'earth'. English adopted it from French in the Middle Ages.

Before the mid 19th century there was no humility involved in eating **humble pie**. Humble pie was more correctly **umble pie**, made from the 'umbles' or innards of a deer of other animal. People considered offal to be inferior food, so began to pun on the similar-sounding **humble**. The first recorded example of to **eat humble pie**, 'to make a humble apology and accept humiliation', is from a collection of the dialect of East Anglia, published in 1830.

humour

In the Middle Ages scientists and doctors believed that there were four main fluids in the body and that the relative proportions of these determined an individual's temperament. Blood gave a cheerful or SANGUINE disposition; phlegm made somebody stolidly calm or PHLEGMATIC; choler or yellow bile gave a peevish and irascible, or CHOLERIC, character; and MELANCHOLY or black bile caused depression. These substances were the four humours, or **cardinal humours**. From this notion **humour** acquired the sense 'mental disposition', then 'state of mind, mood' and 'whim, fancy' (hence to **humour someone**, 'to indulge a person's whim'). The association with amusement arose in the late 17th century. The origin of **humour** directly refers to fluids – it derives from Latin *humor* 'moisture', from *humere* 'to be moist'.

hump

If something annoying makes you **get the hump** the word is being used in something like its original sense. **Hump** arrived in English in the mid 17th century and is probably related to German *humpe* 'hump' and to Dutch *homp* 'lump, hunk of bread'. Its earliest use was to mean 'a complaint', especially in the rhyming phrase **humps and grumps**, the ancestor of **get the hump**. With reference to a personal deformity it dates from the early 18th century.

hundred

Old English had two words for this number. One was **hund**, which came from an ancient root shared by Latin *centum* (as in **cent**, CENTURY and many other *cent-* words) and Greek *hekaton* (the source of **hectare**), and the other was **hundred**, which was formed from the same element plus another meaning 'number'. **Hundred** was also then used to refer to a division of a county or shire that had its own court. This unit may originally have been equivalent to a hundred hides of land – a **hide** is an ancient measure typically equal to between 60 and 100 acres, regarded as the growing area which would feed a family and its dependants. If a British MP wants to resign from the House of Commons they apply for the nominal office of the **Chiltern Hundreds**. Being steward of this district is legally an office of profit under the Crown, and holding it disqualifies a person from being an MP.

hunky dory

If everything is **hunky dory** it is going well, with no problems. To many people the expression is now most familiar as the title of a 1971 album by David Bowie. It is American, and comes from the old slang word **hunky**, meaning 'all right, safe and sound', from Dutch *honk* 'home, base': the reason for the *dory* bit is unknown. **Hunky** here has nothing to do with **hunky** meaning 'strong and fit', as in a hunky fireman or actor – this is from **hunk**, 'chunk or lump'.

hurricane

When Christopher Columbus arrived in the Caribbean in 1492 he encountered the Arawak. These peaceful people did not long survive the coming of the Spanish, and are thought to have died out as a result of the diseases carried by the Europeans and attacks by their aggressive neighbours the Carib. One part of their culture that lives on, though, is the term **hurricane** for a violent storm, specifically a tropical cyclone in the Caribbean. The word came into English via Spanish *huracán* from the name of the Arawak god of the storm, Hurakan. See also TORNADO, TSUNAMI, TYPHOON.

husband

In Old English a WIFE was simply 'a woman', and a **husband** was 'a male head of a household' or 'a manager or steward'. The word is from Old Norse *húsbondi* 'master of a house'. Not until the 13th century or so did a husband become the married partner of a woman. Around then the word also took on the meaning 'a farmer or cultivator' and also the verb use 'to cultivate', which are no longer used but are preserved in **husbandry**, 'the cultivation and care of crops and farm animals'. The modern verb sense, 'to manage resources', is also medieval.

husky

If you say that a hoarse-sounding person has a **husky** voice it has nothing to do with the barking of an Arctic husky dog. The two words are unconnected. The first comes from **husk** meaning 'the dry outer covering of a fruit or seed', a medieval word from Dutch *hūskjin* 'little house' – the husk was pictured as the 'house' of the seed that it contained. The name of the powerful dog used for pulling sledges probably comes from a Native American language, and meant 'an Eskimo' when it was first used in English in around 1830. Our use is from the shortening of **husky dog** or 'Eskimo dog'. See also ESKIMO.

hussy

'You brazen hussy!' is now the sort of thing a girl might call a female friend as a joke, but until the mid 20th century **hussy** was a serious term for an immoral woman. The original hussy, up until at least the mid 16th century, was far more respectable, though – she was a housewife. By the end of 17th century, **hussy** had become a rude or playful way of addressing a woman, and also a derogatory term implying a lack of morals.

hysteria

In ancient times doctors (all male) regarded hysteria as a disease of women caused by a disturbance of the uterus or womb. In the early 19th century English pathologists (also male) formed the English name from Greek *hustera* 'uterus, womb'. Earlier terms for the condition had been **hysteric** or **hysterical passion**, reflecting the same view, and **the vapours**. See also PANIC.

ice

The primary purpose of **breaking the ice** was to allow the passage of boats through frozen water, but by the end of the 16th century people were using the phrase to mean 'to begin an undertaking'. The modern sense, 'to do or say something to relieve tension or get conversation going', began in the 17th century. Ice has represented a person's cold nature or unfriendly manner since at least the time of Shakespeare. In the early 19th century the poet Lord Byron wrote in his *Don Juan*: 'And your cold people are beyond all price, When once you've broken their confounded ice.'

Ice cream has been around longer than you might think. The term first appeared in the mid 18th century, but the earlier equivalent **iced cream** is known from the late 17th. In 1848 the novelist William Makepeace Thackeray could use the shortened form **ice** in *Vanity Fair*: 'He went out and ate ices at a pastry-cook's shop.' See also SORBET, SUNDAE.

Since the early 18th century both **icing** and ice have been names for sugar paste for cakes. The American equivalent is **frosting**.

The icing on the cake, 'an attractive but inessential addition or enhancement', has been spread since the 1920s.

iceberg

The earliest meaning of **iceberg** in English was for a glacier which is seen from the sea as a hill. The term came in the late 18th century from Dutch *ijsberg*, from *ijs* 'ice' and *berg* 'hill'.

The expression **the tip of the iceberg**, 'the small visible part of a larger problem that remains hidden', is surprisingly recent, being recorded only from the 1950s.

The deceptive appearance of icebergs has been familiar to voyagers for much longer, most memorably the unfortunate passengers on SS *Titanic*, which sank after colliding with an iceberg in the Atlantic on April 14, 1912.

icicle

Before a hanging, tapering piece of ice was an **icicle** it was an **ickle**. In the early Middle Ages people put **ice** and **ickle** together to form a compound; writers spelled the term as two words into the 17th century, but then speakers lost sight of its origins and **icicle** emerged as the standard term. See also STALACTITE, STALAGMITE.

icon

Greek *eikōn*, the source of **icon**, meant 'a likeness, image'. The earliest use in English was for a simile, a figure of speech in which two things are compared, for example 'as white as snow'. Later it meant 'a portrait, a picture' and especially a plate or illustration in a natural history book. The 'portrait' sense partly continues in the modern use for 'a devotional painting of Christ or another holy figure'. The use to mean a celebrated figure such as a sporting or pop star dates from the early 1950s. Icons in computing, those symbols or graphic representations on VDU screens, appeared with the release of the Apple Macintosh computer in 1984.

At various times in the history of the Christian Church reformers, among them English Puritans in the 16th and 17th centuries, have condemned and destroyed religious images. Such a zealot is an **iconoclast**, a breaker of images – the -*clast* bit is from Greek *klan*, 'to break'. An iconoclast is now also a person who attacks a cherished belief or respected institution.

idol

Both **idyll** and **idol** go back to Greek *eidos* 'form, shape, picture'. Its earliest uses in English were for false gods, images that people revered as objects of worship and that Jewish and Christian tradition condemned. Outside religion, any object of excessive devotion has been called an idol since the mid 16th century, mainly in a condemnatory way. No one wanted to be a **pop idol** until the end of the 20th century, but in the 21st it is such a common ambition that the reality TV contest *Pop Idol* has been an outstanding success.

It is the 'picture' element that is prominent in **idyll** – a picture in words. When English adopted the word it meant 'a short description of a picturesque scene or incident', which is the sense in the title of Lord Tennyson's series of poems based on Arthurian legend, *The Idylls of the King*. Tennyson's popularisation of the term in the mid 19th century allowed creation of the word **idyllic** and the development of the usual modern sense, 'an extremely happy, peaceful or picturesque period or situation'.

ignorance

The word **ignorance** is from Latin *ignorare* 'not to know', the source of **ignore** and **ignoramus**. The poet Thomas Gray first expressed the thought that **ignorance is bliss** in 1742:

> Thought would destroy their paradise.
> No more; where ignorance is bliss,
> 'Tis folly to be wise.

In 1615 King James I attended a production of a farcical play by George Ruggle, a fellow of Clare College, Cambridge. Its title was *Ignoramus*, the name of a character in the play, and it satirised lawyers and their ignorance. The use of **ignoramus** for 'an ignorant person' appeared almost immediately afterwards. In Latin *ignoramus* means 'we do not know', which in legal Latin became 'we take no notice (of it)'. The original use of **ignoramus** in English was as the judgment that grand juries made on indictments that they considered to be backed by too little evidence: they would 'find an ignoramus', 'return an ignoramus' or 'bring in an ignoramus'.

ill

Anglo-Saxons were never **ill**. The word arrived in the early Middle Ages from Old Norse *illr* 'evil', and the modern sense, 'suffering from an illness or feeling unwell', came in the later medieval period. Before then a person would be SICK, as they still are in the USA.

The idea of harm and evil is prominent in many English proverbs, such as **it's an ill wind that blows nobody any good**. This refers to the days of sailing ships. The wind might be blowing in the wrong direction for you, but it was sure to be blowing the right way for someone, somewhere – it would be a very bad or 'ill' wind that was of no help to anyone.

imbecile

Originally a person described as **imbecile** was physically weak. The root meaning may be 'without a supporting staff', from Latin *baculum* 'stick, staff'. The current sense conveying stupidity dates from the early 19th century.

immaculate

For centuries Christian theologians had argued over whether God had preserved the Virgin Mary from the taint of original sin from the moment she was conceived. In 1854 the Vatican declared in favour of **the Immaculate Conception** and it became a dogma of the Roman Catholic Church. The term involves the earliest, medieval sense of **immaculate**, 'free from moral stain'. The physical sense, 'spotlessly clean or neat', dates only from the early 19th century. Similarly, **impeccable** originally meant 'incapable of sin', and is still used in this sense in theology, where it has an opposite, **peccable** 'liable to sin'.

imp

Plants and not mischievous children or imaginary devils were the original **imps**. The word goes right back to Greek *phuein* 'to plant'. The Old English sense 'a young shoot of a plant' became 'a descendant, especially of a noble family' in the late Middle Ages, and from there developed into 'a child of the devil'. Mischievous children began to be called imps in the mid 17th century. The Hillman company gave the name Imp to its new small car in

The Hillman Imp gets the 1960s advertising treatment.

1963 – it never matched the success of its rival, the Mini. See also SCAMP.

impudent

In the Middle Ages people who were **impudent** were lacking in shame or modesty rather than presumptuous or cheeky. The original meaning reflects the word's origin in the Latin word *pudere* 'to be ashamed'. The modern sense developed in the mid 16th century.

incentive

Modern management gurus may not realise it, but when they advocate incentives they are invoking magic. The word **incentive** is closely related to **incantation**, 'a series of words said as a magic spell or charm'. The root of both is Latin *incantare* 'to chant, charm', from *cantare* 'to sing', the source also of **chant**. In the general sense 'a thing that motivates or encourages someone to do something', **incentive** entered English in the Middle Ages, but it took until the 1940s for incentives to be offered to workers. The first **incentive payments** were proposed in early 1940 as a way to encourage US farmers to plant new crops.

inch

The **inch** and the OUNCE have the same ultimate origin, both going back to Latin *uncia* 'twelfth part'. The observation that **give someone an inch and they will take a mile**, that once concessions have been made to someone they will demand a lot more, dates from the mid 16th century. Originally people often took an **ell** rather than a **mile** (an ell is an old measure equal to just over a metre, used especially for cloth). The **inch** in the name of some Scottish islands, such as Inchcolm, is a completely different word, deriving from Scottish Gaelic *innis* 'island, land by a river'.

incognito

The word **incognito**, meaning 'having your true identity concealed', came from Italian in the mid 17th century. The Latin root is *cognoscere* 'to know', which is behind such English words as **acquaint** and **recognise**. At first **incognito** could mean simply 'unknown', without any implication of disguise or concealment, and was used mainly of royals or dignitaries who did not want to be recognised. In the 20th century the critic Kenneth Tynan wrote, 'The disguise . . . renders him as effectively incognito as a walrus in a ballet-skirt'.

indent

Although their meanings have in common an idea of a gap or notch, there are two completely unrelated words **indent** in English. One, meaning 'to make a dent or impression in', is formed directly from **dent** 'a hollow made by a blow or pressure', which is a variant form of **dint**. The other goes back to Latin *dens* 'tooth', the source of **dental** and related words. Its first meaning was 'to give a zigzag outline to', like a set of sharp teeth. The legal term **indenture**, 'a legal document, contract or agreement', is related to this. Before the days of easy duplication, lawyers would write out the same contract twice on a single piece of parchment or paper. They would then separate the two sections with a serrated or wavy edge and give one to each of the interested parties. If ever there was a dispute, the fact that the two edges fitted together was proof that they were part of the same agreement.

index

In Latin *index* meant 'forefinger, informer, sign', with its second part related to *dicere* 'to say' and *dicare* 'to make known', also the source of **indicate** and related words. The earliest uses in English refer to the finger that we would now usually call the **index finger**. Because this finger is used for pointing, **index** came to mean 'a pointer', either a physical one or some piece of knowledge that points to a fact or conclusion. And because a list of topics in a book points to their location in the text, publishers and scholars gave such a list the name **index**.

Indian

Christopher Columbus set sail from Europe in 1492 with the main object of reaching Asia and proving that the world was round. When his ships reached the New World – in fact some Caribbean islands – he initially believed that he had reached India, and so it seemed natural to give the name **Indian** to the indigenous inhabitants of the Americas. The name of the West Indies arose from the same mistake. People felt the need to make clearer this double use of **Indian**, for the peoples of the Indian subcontinent and those inhabiting the Americas before the arrival of Europeans. At first the latter were often called Red Indians, but this is now considered offensive. **American Indian** was another solution, but many now prefer to avoid the term **Indian** altogether, and use **Native American**.

  Indian summer, a period of unusually dry, warm weather in late autumn, refers to North America rather than Asia. The phenomenon is first mentioned towards the end of the 18th century in the USA, and was not adopted in Britain until the late Victorian period.

  India itself is named after the mighty River Indus, which flows from Tibet through Kashmir and Pakistan into the Arabian Sea, and the word is related to **Hindi** and **Hindu**. India gives its name to **indigo**, originally 'Indian dye' but now a colour between blue and violet generally regarded as one of the colours of the rainbow.

indolent

It now means 'lazy', but **indolent** was originally a medical term, referring to an ulcer or tumour that caused no pain to the patient. This reflects its root, Latin *dolere* 'to suffer or give pain'.

indoors

Before the 18th century people lived or remained **within doors** rather than **indoors**, and they worked or played **without doors** (meaning 'out of doors') before they did so **outdoors**. It was Arthur Daley, the leading character of the British TV series *Minder* (1979-93), who first referred to his wife as **her indoors**. Mrs Daley was a formidable-sounding woman whose reputation was enhanced by the fact that we never actually saw her on screen. Apparently the original writer of the series, Leon Griffiths, first heard the expression used by a taxi driver.

infant

To go by the origins of the word, which is from Latin *in-* 'not' and *fari* 'to speak', an **infant** is a child unable to speak. According to law, an infant is a person who has not reached the age of legal majority. The Italian equivalent *infante* meant 'youth' and also 'foot soldier', from which arose *infanteria*, a body of foot soldiers. English adopted this as **infantry** in the late 16th century. See also BABY, FATE.

inferno

In the early 14th century the Italian poet Dante Alighieri wrote *The Divine Comedy*, an epic poem describing his spiritual journey through hell and purgatory and finally to paradise. The description of hell in particular, the 'Inferno', had a lasting impact on the European imagination. The word came to mean 'hell' and then 'any raging fire that is out of control'. In the 1974 film *The Towering Inferno* a fire breaks out at the opening of a badly constructed office building and threatens to destroy the tower and everyone in it. Italian *inferno* comes from Latin *infernus* 'below, subterranean', which is also the source of **infernal** and is related to **inferior**.

infidel

An **infidel** is a person who is 'not faithful'. The word goes back to Latin *infidelis* (the source too of **infidelity**), from *fides* FAITH, and originally referred to a person of a religion other than your own. To a

Christian an infidel was usually a Muslim, who would consider a Christian an infidel in return, and to a Jew an infidel would be a Gentile. In the late 15th century Sir Thomas Malory's *Le Morte d'Arthur*, a translation of the legends of King Arthur, refers to 'two hundred Saracens or infidels'. **Fiancée** and **heathen** are related words.

influenza

Italy saw an outbreak of a severe respiratory ailment in 1743. The English minister to Tuscany, Sir Horace Mann, wrote of Rome that 'Everybody is ill of the *Influenza*, and many die'. The epidemic spread throughout Europe, and in English **influenza** became the general term for this type of contagious viral infection. The English shortened **influenza** to the more familiar **flu** in the mid 19th century – self-pity and exaggeration being common human characteristics, the word is also used for a severe cold. Italian *influenza* means 'influence' and derives from Latin *fluere* 'to flow'. The Italian word also had the sense 'an outbreak of an epidemic', and so 'an epidemic'.

ink

Roman emperors used a purple fluid for writing their signatures, which was called in Latin *encautum* or *encaustum*, from Greek *enkaiein* 'to burn in'. The word **ink** reached English through French in the Middle Ages. The black liquid ejected by a cuttlefish, octopus or squid to confuse predators has been called ink since the late 16th century.

inkling

From the 1930s to the 1960s the novelists and scholars C.S. Lewis and J.R.R. Tolkien met, with other friends, in Lewis's Oxford rooms to read their works aloud and to discuss them. They would also gather regularly in the pub the Eagle and Child in Oxford. The writers were dubbed the Inklings. There was a pun on the ink expended by writers, but also perhaps an implicit slighting of their endeavours. An **inkling** is 'a slight knowledge or suspicion, a hint', and originally 'a mentioning of something in an undertone, a faint rumour'. The word was formed in the late Middle Ages from **inkle** 'to give a hint of', which was never itself much used.

inn

An **inn** was originally any dwelling place or lodging. The word is related to **in** – an inn is a place you live or stay *in*. Medieval translators used it for Latin *hospitium*, meaning 'a residence for students'. This survives in the **Inns of Court**, the buildings of the four legal societies with the exclusive right of admitting people to the English bar. The usual modern sense of 'a public house' dates from the late Middle Ages – an inn specialised in providing accommodation and refreshment for travellers, as opposed to a TAVERN, which was just for drinking. See also HOTEL, PUBLIC.

innings

In cricket a team or batsman has an **innings** or turn at batting, but in baseball a batter has an **inning**. The word **inning** itself goes back to Old English, when it meant 'putting or getting in', and derives from **in**. Cricket has given many expressions to English, among them to **have had a good innings**, 'to have had a long and fulfilling life or career'. The first example of this extended meaning is in Charles Dickens's *The Pickwick Papers*, published in 1836, where it means someone's turn or opportunity to do something: 'It's my innings now, gov'rnor, and as soon as I catches hold o' this here Trotter, I'll have a good 'un.'

innuendo

Early legal documents would introduce an explanation of a word with **innuendo**, meaning 'that is to say, to wit', as in 'he (*innuendo* the plaintiff) is a thief' from a mid 17th-century glossary. **Innuendo** comes from a Latin word meaning 'by nodding at, by pointing to', from *in* 'towards' and *nuere* 'to nod'. In the late 17th century it became possible to have an innuendo, 'an explanation' and also, the modern sense, 'an oblique remark or hint'.

inoculate

Originally inoculation was a task of gardeners rather than of doctors and nurses. To **inoculate** something was to graft a bud or shoot into a plant of a different type. This corresponds to its Latin source *inoculare* 'to graft', from *in-* 'into' and *oculus* 'eye, bud' (as in **binoculars** and **ocular**). The horticultural sense dates from the late Middle Ages. As a medical procedure people could inoculate an infective agent and inoculate a person from the early 18th century – its first uses referred to the treatment of smallpox. See also VACCINE.

inquest

English words that come from Latin *inquirere* 'to ask for information' often have spellings with either *en-* or *in-*, with *en-* representing the older form acquired through French and *in-* a return to the Latin root. This is the case, for instance, with **enquire** or **inquire**, **enquiry** or **inquiry**, and used to apply to **inquest**, although the spelling **enquest** has not been used since the 18th century. In Britain an inquest is now usually an inquiry by a coroner's court into the cause of a death; formerly it could be any official inquiry into a matter of public interest.

Another word from Latin *inquirere* is **inquisition**. In the mid 13th century Pope Gregory IX established a tribunal for the suppression of heresy. This was the first Inquisition, which was active chiefly in northern Italy and southern France and became notorious for the use of torture. In 1478 **the Spanish Inquisition** began to target converts from Judaism and Islam, later extending its reach to Protestants. It operated with great severity and was not suppressed until the early 19th century. Mention the word to many people, and they will immediately cry, 'No one expects the Spanish Inquisition!' The classic Monty Python skit features Michael Palin as Cardinal Ximinez, who appears suddenly with two junior cardinals when anyone innocently says, 'I didn't expect a kind of Spanish Inquisition.'

insect

Insects have bodies that are divided into segments, and segments are the basic idea behind the word. **Insect** was formed in the 17th century from Latin *animal insectum* 'segmented animal', and originally referred o any small cold-blooded creature with a segmented body, for example a spider, not just what we would call insects. The root word is *secare* 'to cut', which gave us **dissect**, **section** and **segment**.

insular

The earliest use of **insular**, in the mid 16th century, was as a noun meaning 'an islander'. Islanders were popularly regarded as narrow-minded and ignorant of people and cultures outside their own experience, and the adjective **insular** later developed this meaning. The word itself goes back to Latin *insula* 'island', the source also of **isle** (see ISLAND) and of **insulate** and **insulin**. The hormone insulin, produced by the pancreas, gets its name from the islets of Langerhans, the group of pancreatic cells that secrete it. Paul Langerhans was the 19th-century German anatomist who first described them.

insult

An **insult** was originally an attack or assault, especially a military one. Sir Walter Scott in his poem *Marmion* wrote: 'Many a rude tower and rampart there / Repelled the insult of the air.' The word goes back to Latin *insultare* 'to jump or leap upon'. The phrase to **add insult to injury** comes from the 1748 play *The Foundling* by Edmund Moore: 'This is adding insult to injuries.'

interim

The chaos caused by the Reformation in 16th-century Europe was nowhere more acute than in Germany. The Holy Roman Emperor Charles V tried to tackle differences between the German Protestants and the Roman Catholic Church through provisional arrangements pending a settlement by a general council. This was called **the Interim**, and was reported in English in a diplomatic letter of July 1548. In Latin *interim* meant 'meanwhile'. Quickly people started using **interim** for other provisional arrangements, and then for 'an intervening time, the meantime'.

interloper

An **interloper** was originally an unauthorised trader trespassing on the rights of a trade monopoly. The word was coined in the late 16th century, and is a true hybrid. The first element derives from Latin *inter* 'between, among', while the second comes from **landloper**, an old word for a vagabond or tramp taken from Dutch.

interlude

Medieval miracle plays could last all day, so to provide variety and relieve tension performers would introduce short and often funny dramatic pieces between the acts – the original interludes. The word derives from Latin *inter* 'between, among' and *ludus* 'a play'. By the 17th century people were using **interlude** for the interval of

time between the acts of a play, and by the 18th for any intervening time, space or event. See also FARCE.

intrigue

The link between **intrigue** and **intricate** is intriguing. Both ultimately derive from Latin *intricare* 'to entangle, perplex'. **Intricate** came directly from Latin in the late Middle Ages, whereas **intrigue** lived an independent life, developing into Italian *intrigare*, which passed through French into English in the 17th century. The original English meaning was 'to trick, deceive, perplex'. The modern sense 'to arouse the curiosity or interest of' dates only from the late 19th century and shows the influence of a later development in French.

invest

The root of **invest** is Latin *vestis* 'clothes', which is also the source of **vest**, **transvestite** and **wear**. Latin *investire* meant 'to put clothes on someone', and that was the sense of **invest** when it entered English in the mid 16th century. Someone being formally installed in a new job or office would once have been ceremonially dressed in special clothing, and this is behind **invest** in the sense 'to formally confer a rank or office on someone'. The main modern financial use of the word came into English under the influence of a related Italian word in the early 17th century, apparently through a comparison between putting money into enterprises and dressing it in a variety of clothing.

iris

In classical mythology Iris was the goddess of the rainbow and a messenger of the gods. People saw the rainbow as a bridge or road let down from heaven for her to carry her messages along. The Latin and Greek word *iris*, taken from her name and meaning 'rainbow', is also in **iridescent** and the name of the chemical element **iridium**, which forms compounds of various colours. The name **iris** for the membrane behind the cornea of the eye appears to derive from the variety of its colours. As a name for a flowering plant **iris** dates from the late Middle Ages.

irk

Work irks many people, and the activity may even be related to **irk**, which possibly derives from Old Norse *yrkja* 'to work, take effect upon'. Its earliest sense in English was 'to be annoyed or disgusted'; things began to irk or annoy people in the later Middle Ages, at the same time as people and things became **irksome**.

Iris, Goddess of the Rainbow painted by John Atkinson Grimshaw in 1886.

iron

The English **iron** probably came from Celtic and was related to Latin *aes* 'bronze' and English **ore** as well as to a word in Sanskrit, the ancient language of India.

Many tools and implements are described as irons because they are or were originally made of iron, such as branding irons and fire irons. The expression to **have many irons in the fire**, 'to have a range of options or commitments', comes from the way such tools are made. Blacksmiths heat iron objects in a fire until they reach the critical temperature for shaping. If they have several items in the forge they can remove one and hammer it until it has cooled, then return it to the fire to heat up again while working on another one.

In a speech made in March 1946 Winston Churchill observed that 'an iron curtain has descended across the Continent [of Europe]'. This is often cited as the origin of **the Iron Curtain**, the notional barrier separating the former Soviet bloc and the West before the decline of communism after 1989, but the phrase had been used in reference to the Soviet Union in the 1920s, and had the more general meaning of 'an impenetrable barrier' as far back as the early 19th century. Its origins lie in the theatre. Today's theatres use a flame-resistant safety device called a fire curtain, which in the late 18th century would have been of metal – an iron curtain.

Margaret Thatcher was given the nickname **the Iron Lady** in January 1976 by the Soviet newspaper *Red Star*, which accused her of trying to revive the Cold War. Another iron lady was the **iron maiden**, an instrument of torture consisting of an upright box lined with iron spikes, in which the victim was forced to stand while the door was shut. The most notorious iron maiden was one at Nuremberg Castle, although this may have been created as a frightening hoax in the 18th or 19th century and never used. Nevertheless, the gruesome concept appealed to the heavy metal fans who founded the band Iron Maiden in 1975.

Irony has no connection with iron. It came from Greek *eirōneia* 'pretended ignorance'. See also VELVET.

island

In spite of their similarity of form and meaning, **island** and **isle** are completely unrelated. The first is an Old English word, with parallels in early forms of other north European languages, whereas the second came through French from Latin in medieval times. The first part of Old English *īegland* is *īeg* 'island', from a root meaning 'watery'. People wrongly associated it with **isle**, and in the 16th century changed the spelling accordingly. In fact there was no *s* in **isle** in the Middle Ages either: it was spelled **ile**, as it was in French at the time of its adoption. In the 15th century both French

and English people connected the word – this time correctly – with Latin *insula*, and added the *s*. See also INSULAR, PENINSULA.

The English poet and preacher John Donne memorably expressed the view that the lives and fates of humans are interconnected in *Devotions upon Emergent Occasions* (1624):

> No man is an island, entire of itself; every man is a piece of the Continent, a part of the main; . . . any man's death diminishes me, because I am involved in mankind; And therefore never send to know for whom the bell tolls; it tolls for thee.

italic

In 1501 Aldus Manutius, a printer based in Venice, published an edition of the Latin poet Virgil which he dedicated to Italy. It was printed in a typeface in which the letters sloped towards the right and which people gave the name **italic**. Before that **italic** had been used in the general sense 'Italian'. It came from Greek *Italikos*, from *Italia* 'Italy'. See also ROME.

item

Originally **item** was used to introduce each new article or particular in a list or document. In Shakespeare's *Twelfth Night* Olivia mocks attempts to shower her with exaggerated praise: '[My beauty] shall be inventoried and every particle and utensil labelled to my will, as, *item*, two lips, indifferent red; *item*, two grey eyes, with lids to them; *item*, one neck, one chin, and so forth.' This use for 'likewise, also' reflects its source, Latin *item* 'just so, similarly, moreover'. From there **item** started to refer to a statement or maxim of the type often introduced by the word 'item', then to an individual article or unit. A couple have been **an item** since around 1970, at first in the USA.

ivory

The Latin word *ebur*, from which **ivory** derives, is related to ancient Egyptian *āb* or *ābu* 'elephant'. Before poachers reduced elephant numbers, ivory was an important item of commerce, used for functional items as well as ornaments. The 'white' piano keys were made of ivory, and to **tickle** or **tinkle the ivories** is a familiar expression for 'to play the piano'. An **ivory tower**, the state of privileged seclusion from the real world, is an early 20th-century translation of French *tour d'ivoire*, used in 1837 by the critic and writer Charles Augustin Sainte-Beuve.

Make mine a cappuccino

The Italian loves of food, music and the good life have injected many bright colours into English usage. At the other extreme, the Italian language of crime, captured on film and TV, has infiltrated talk of murkier areas of life.

If you want pasta cooked so that it is still firm when you bite into it, you should ask for it to be **al dente**, literally 'to the tooth'. Varieties of pasta include **fusilli** or 'little spirals' and **penne** or 'quills' – most were unknown in English until the 20th century, but **vermicelli** or 'little worms' and MACARONI date back to the 17th century. A determined meat-eater might ask for **carpaccio**. This name for thin slices of raw meat comes from the surname of the medieval Italian painter Vittore *Carpaccio*, because of his characteristic use of red pigments, resembling raw meat.

Baroness Frances Bunsen (1791-1876) was a diplomat's wife who travelled widely. A letter about one of her trips has given us the first mention of the **pizza**, in 1825: 'They gave us ham, and cheese, and *frittata* [a kind of omelette] and *pizza*.' The Italian word simply means 'pie'.

Some kinds of Italian food suggest their appeal rather than their look or shape, such as the veal dish **saltimbocca**, whose name means literally 'leap into the mouth'. The dessert **tiramisu** was unknown to English until the 1980s, since when the combination of coffee-and-brandy-soaked sponge and mascarpone cheese has become irresistible. The name comes from *tira mi sù* 'pick me up'.

After the meal you might have the strong black **espresso**, whose name comes from *caffe espresso* 'pressed-out coffee', or the milder **latte**, from *caffe latte* 'milk coffee'. A **macchiato**, espresso with a dash of frothy steamed milk, is short for *caffe macchiato*, literally 'stained or marked coffee'. In Italian **cappuccino** means 'Capuchin monk', probably because the drink's colour resembles a Capuchin's brown habit. The Capuchins are a branch of the Franciscan order that takes their name from the sharp-pointed hood that the monks wear – *cappuccio* in Italian, which is from the same root as **cape**. It is now found on every high street, but cappuccino has been known in English only since the 1940s.

A life of heedless pleasure and luxury is a **dolce vita**, or 'sweet life', a phrase brought into English by the 1960 film *La Dolce Vita*, directed by Federico Fellini. A lazy person who likes the idea of pleasant idleness is attracted to **dolce far niente**, literally 'sweet doing nothing'.

The term **fresco** for a painting done rapidly on wet plaster on a wall or ceiling means in Italian 'cool, fresh'. The same word is part of **al fresco**, meaning 'in the open air' – in English this phrase tends to refer to eating outdoors, as in this example from *GQ* magazine: 'Open 7 days a week … with al fresco dining in fine weather'. The phrase dates back to the 1750s in English and was used by Jane Austen.

Sheet music was first printed during the Renaissance by Italians, which is why Italian is the language of musical terms, a number of which have moved into the wider language. We might talk of excitement reaching a **crescendo**, a word originally used to indicate gradually increasing loudness in a piece of music. Someone might be speaking **fortissimo**, 'very loudly', or **sotto voce**, 'in a quiet voice' – literally 'under the voice'. Italian has also given us the names for different ranges of singing voice, including **alto** 'high', **soprano**, from *sopra* 'above' and **baritone**, which is ultimately from Greek *barus* 'heavy' and *tonos* 'tone'. Many of the great opera singers have been Italian, and OPERA itself is the Italian word for 'work'.

Films like the *The Godfather* (1972) and *Goodfellas* (1990), and the more recent television series *The Sopranos*, have familiarised us with some of the enigmatic vocabulary associated with the MAFIA. Members practise **omertà**, or a code of silence, which is a dialect form of **umità** 'humility'. Within the group the adviser to the leader, who resolves internal disputes, is known as the **consigliere**, literally 'member of a council'. Presumably it is only after his arts have failed that someone may reach for his **lupara**, or sawn-off shotgun, a slang term that comes from *lupa* 'she-wolf'. A high-ranking member of the Mafia is a **don**, a word also used for a British university teacher, which comes from Latin *dominus* 'master'.

See also CONFETTI, FIASCO, GHETTO, GRAFFITI, INFERNO, INFLUENZA, MALARIA, PANTALOONS, PAPARAZZI, TENOR.

jack

In the Middle Ages **Jack** as a pet form of 'John' was used to refer to any ordinary man. By the 16th century it also meant a young man, and from this we get an alternative name for the **knave** in cards. In the 18th century a jack was a labourer, which gives us the second part of words like **lumberjack** and **steeplejack**. A jack was also an unskilled worker as contrasted with the master of a trade who had completed an apprenticeship, from which we get the saying **jack of all trades and master of none**. On the other hand, the apprentice could assert his equality with the words **Jack is as good as his master**. See also JOCKEY.

A **jack** can also be a thing of smaller than normal size. Examples include the jack in bowls – a smaller bowl placed as a mark for the players to aim at – and jack as in UNION JACK, which is a small version of the national flag flown on board ship.

Jack-o-lantern as a name for a pumpkin lantern made at Halloween looks back to an earlier use of the phrase. In the 17th century it was a name for a **will-o'-the-wisp**, a light seen hovering at night over marshy ground – exchanging the idea of Jack with a lantern for Will with a 'wisp', or handful of lighted hay. **I'm all right, Jack** is an early 20th-century catchphrase used to express selfish complacency, which became the title of a film starring Peter Sellers in 1959.

A 19th-century clergyman, known as 'the Sporting Parson', gave his name to the Jack Russell terrier. He was famed in hunting circles for breeding fox terriers.

Today a **jackpot** is a large cash prize in a game or lottery. The term was originally used in a form of poker, where the pool or pot accumulated until a player could open the bidding with two jacks or better. See also UNION JACK.

jade

Since the Middle Ages a worn-out horse has been described as a **jade**, although the origin of the word is unknown. When a tired person describes themselves as **jaded**, they are looking back to this use, rather than to the sense of **jade** as 'a headstrong or disreputable woman', which developed in the mid 16th century. See also HACK, NAG.

Jade as a name for a hard bluish-green precious stone is a quite different word. It comes from Spanish *piedra de ijada*, literally 'stone of the side or flank', which referred to the belief that it was a cure for colic.

jail

When you think of being 'behind bars', it may not be entirely surprising that **jail** comes from the same Latin root as **cage**. It arrived in medieval English in two forms, from Old French *jaiole* and Anglo-Norman *gaole*, which survives in the alternative British spelling of **gaol**.

jam

The British have been eating a preserve called **jam** since the 18th century. The best jam is packed with fruit, and its name probably comes from the verb meaning 'cram' or 'squeeze'.

When we want to express our regret that wished-for events never happen we may say resignedly **jam tomorrow and jam yesterday, but never jam today**. The saying comes from Lewis Carroll's *Through the Looking-Glass* (1872), where the White Queen explains to Alice that, 'The rule is, jam tomorrow and jam yesterday – but never jam today.'

In Britain if you are **jammy** you are lucky, but in Australia you are rather posh or affected. In Victorian slang the word first simply meant 'excellent'.

Traffic jams are an everyday reality, but the first jams were on rivers, not roads. From the beginning of the 19th century loggers talked of jams of logs being floated downriver – the original **logjam**. By the 1850s references to 'carriage jams' can be found. See also MONEY.

janitor

A caretaker or doorkeeper in North America is referred to as a **janitor**, a word that was borrowed into English from Latin in the mid 16th century. It comes from

How do you sudoku?

From the ancient culture of the samurai to modern electronic gadgets, cutting-edge business terms and novel pastimes, Japanese has provided English with distinctive Far Eastern touches.

The samurai were a powerful military class in feudal Japan, from the 7th to the 19th century, who carried the katana, a long, single-edged sword. Samurai warriors expert in ninjutsu, or stealthy spying, were known as ninja, from *nin* 'stealth, invisibility' and *sha* 'person, agent'. The term became well known from the Teenage Mutant Ninja Turtles, four cartoon turtles who first appeared in a US comic book in 1984. They were skilled ninja warriors, with a battle cry of 'Cowabunga!' (originally surfers' slang), who battled criminals and alien invaders from their home in the sewers of Manhattan.

According to the bushido, or code of honour, a disgraced samurai was expected to commit suicide by the gruesome method of hara-kiri or seppuku. As the literal meaning of hara-kiri ('belly-cutting') implies, the samurai had to disembowel himself with a single stroke of a knife or short sword across the belly. As soon as he had made the cut his head was severed by a friend or 'second' to spare him further suffering.

Japanese martial arts, or forms of unarmed combat, were first known in Europe in the late 19th century. The name aikido is literally 'spirit way', karate means 'empty hand', judo is 'gentle way' and ju-jitsu, from which judo evolved, means 'gentle skill'.

By no means all Japanese terms used in English are aggressive. A geisha, or 'performing arts person', is a hostess trained to entertain men with conversation or dance and song – the geisha has been known in English since the end of the 19th century, as has the unsprung mattress the futon. Bonsai, the practice of cultivating artificially dwarfed potted plants or small trees, is literally 'tray planting', and came into English in the early 20th century, while origami, the art of folding paper, is a still more recent import, recorded only from the 1950s.

As the Second World War turned against them Japanese pilots in the Pacific became suicide bombers, loading their aircraft with explosives and deliberately crashing on to enemy targets. These were known as kamikaze attacks. The word kamikaze means literally 'divine wind', and referred originally to a supposedly divine wind which blew up in 1281 and destroyed the navy of the invading Mongols.

Today the term is used of any reckless or apparently self-destructive behaviour, as in 'A wonderfully exhilarating night of gung-ho attacking and kamikaze defending' (*The Guardian*, 2006).

After the war America occupied Japan, and many of its servicemen were stationed there. They brought back the word honcho, 'the person in charge', from Japanese *honchÿ* 'group leader'. It first appeared in print in 1947.

It was only at the end of the 1970s that British people first became aware of the often excruciating possibilities of karaoke. Both the word and the entertainment were borrowed from Japanese, where its literal meaning is 'empty orchestra'.

In the 1990s manga cartoons and anime cartoon films became popular in the West. Anime was taken by the Japanese from French and just means 'animated', whereas manga is from *man* 'indiscriminate' and *ga* 'picture'.

The beginning of the 21st century saw many people become obsessed with Japanese number puzzles, in particular sudoku, which involves filling in a 9 x 9 grid of squares with the numbers 1 to 9. Its name is based on *su* 'number' and *doku* 'single', and is a shortening of its original Japanese name *Sūji wa dokushin ni kagiru*, which can be translated as 'only single numbers allowed' or 'numbers can only occur once'.

Since the 1980s an increasing number of Japanese business terms have become known in the West. In the kanban or just-in-time system the supply of components in a factory is regulated by the use of a card or sheet sent along the production line and to suppliers, ensuring that parts arrive exactly when they are required. Kaizen is a business philosophy of continuous improvement in working practices and personal efficiency. All this striving for improvement can be a strain for the salarymen and office ladies, as male and female workers are known – the term karoshi, 'death caused by overwork', was coined in the late 1980s.

See also MARCH, TSUNAMI, TYCOON.

Janus, the name of an ancient Italian god regarded as the doorkeeper of heaven, and the guardian of doors and gates. He was traditionally represented with two faces, so that he could look both backwards and forwards. **January** comes from a Latin word meaning 'month of Janus', and marks the entrance to the year.

jargon

Modern life is full of **jargon**, language used by a particular group that is difficult for other people to understand. Some technical jargon is so obscure that it might as well be gibberish, which is one of the word's early meanings. It comes from Old French *jargoun* 'the warbling of birds', and in medieval English meant 'twittering, chattering' and also 'gibberish'. Our current sense had developed by the 17th century.

jazz

We have been enjoying **jazz** since the early years of the 20th century, but no one is completely sure about the word's origin, although an enormous number of suggestions have been made. It seems that the original meaning may have been something like 'liveliness, energy, spirit' – in 1912 a baseball player said of his new way of pitching: 'I call it the Jazz ball because it wobbles and you simply can't do anything with it.' The first known musical use came in 1915 in Chicago. **Jazz** was also used with sexual connotations, and its source could be the slang word **jism** 'semen'. **And all that jazz**, meaning 'and all that stuff, etcetera', has been around since the 1950s, but is particularly known as a song from the 1975 musical *Chicago*.

jeans

Designer **jeans** in a 21st-century wardrobe look back as far as the late 16th century, when the name *jean fustian* was used for a kind of heavy cotton cloth. It meant literally 'fustian [a type of cloth] from Genoa', a city in Italy. **Jeans** as we know them date from the 1860s, when Levi Strauss (1829-1902), founder of the **Levi's** company, started to make durable denim work trousers which became popular with cowboys in the Wild West. **Denim** was

originally **serge denim**, from French *serge de Nîmes* 'serge of Nîmes', a city in the south of France. Serge is a woollen cloth, but modern denim is made of cotton.

Jeep

The name of the Second World War **Jeep** originally came, in American English, from the initials *GP*, standing for *general purpose*. It was probably also influenced by the name of 'Eugene the Jeep', a resourceful creature with superhuman powers that first appeared in the *Popeye* comic strip in 1936. See also GOON.

jelly

In the Middle Ages **jelly** was a savoury dish of meat or fish set in a mould of aspic. The first references to fruit-flavoured jellies are not found until the late 18th century. The word comes ultimately from the Latin word *gelare* 'to freeze'.

    Jelly Babies, the soft baby-shaped sweet, began life in 1918 as Peace Babies, launched by the Bassett's company to celebrate the end of the First World War. They were named Jelly Babies in 1953.

jeopardy

The early spelling of **jeopardy** was *iuparti*. The word comes from Old French *ieu parti* 'an evenly divided game' and was originally used in chess and similar games to mean a problem or position in which the chances of winning or losing were evenly balanced. This led to the modern sense 'a dangerous situation'

A Levi's advertisement from the 1880s.

and the legal use 'danger arising from being on trial for a criminal offence'.

jerry-built

Poorly built houses have been described as **jerry-built** since the mid 19th century. The term is nothing to do with **Jerry**, a derogatory name for a German that came out of the First World War. One suggestion is that it is from the name of a firm of builders in Liverpool, or it may allude to the walls of Jericho, which in the biblical story fell down at the sound of Joshua's trumpet. The **jerrycan** *does* come from **Jerry** – it was originally used by Germans, but was adopted by the Allies in the Second World War.

jet

The name **jet** for a hard black semi-precious mineral comes ultimately from the Greek word *gagatēs* 'from Gagai', a town in Asia Minor. When we refer to a jet of water or gas, or a jet aircraft, we are using a quite different word. It comes from a late 16th-century verb meaning 'to jut out', from French *jeter* 'to throw', which shares the same Latin root as **jettison**.

Especially if you use budget airlines, air travel today is far from glamorous, but in the 1950s the idea of flying abroad by jet aircraft was new and sophisticated. At the start of that decade people who flew for pleasure came to be known as the **jet set**.

jetsam

Originally **jettison** was a term for the throwing of goods overboard to lighten a ship in distress, which came from Old French *getaison* and ultimately from the Latin verb *jactare* 'to throw'. In the 16th century it was shortened to give us first the spelling *jetson* and then our modern word **jetsam**, for goods thrown overboard and washed ashore. FLOTSAM is wreckage found floating on the sea or washed up by it. The use of **jettison** as a verb meaning 'to throw something away' dates from the mid 19th century.

jewel

A richly dressed person has had the choice of adding to their finery with a **jewel** since the Middle Ages. Originally the term meant a decorative piece worn for personal adornment, but later it came to specify an ornament containing a precious stone, or the stone itself. The origin suggests that adornment was linked with entertainment, as the word comes from French

jeu 'game, play', and perhaps ultimately from Latin *jocus* 'jest'. See also JOKE, JUGGLE.

The jewel in the crown is the most valuable or successful part of something. It is the title of a 1966 novel by Paul Scott, and of a 1980s BBC TV series that was based on this and other novels by Scott. The phrase was used in the early 1900s as a name for the colonies of the British Empire.

jest

A **jest** was no joke in the Middle Ages. It was a notable exploit, spelled *gest*, from the Latin *gesta* 'actions, exploits'. Jest developed into a story of someone's deeds, then a word for 'an idle story' and finally 'a joke'.

jib

Since the mid 17th century the triangular sail in front of the mast on a sailing boat has been known as the **jib**. Its prominence and characteristic form provided a sailor's figure of speech **the cut of a person's jib**, which we now use to comment on a person's look or appearance.

The **jib** which is a projecting arm of a crane appears a century later, and is a different word. It is probably an abbreviation of **gibbet**, an upright post with an arm on which the bodies of executed criminals were left hanging as a warning or deterrent to others.

When we **jib** at doing something we are using yet another word. It may be related to a French word *regimber* or *regiber*, 'to buck, rear', and to **jibe**, 'to make insulting or mocking remarks'.

jiggery-pokery

This late 19th-century expression means 'deceitful or dishonest behaviour'. It is probably a variant of Scots *joukery-pawkery*, from *jouk* 'to skulk'.

jingo

Originally a word said by conjurors when performing a magic trick, rather like ABRACADABRA, **jingo** became used more widely in the expression 'by jingo!' to show how much in earnest a person was. In 1878 the British Prime Minister Benjamin Disraeli was determined to send a fleet into Turkish waters to resist Russia. Popular support for his policy included a music-hall song with the chorus: 'We don't want to fight, yet by Jingo! If we do, We've got the ships, we've got the men, and got the money too.' **Jingoism** as a word for an aggressive patriotism associated with vociferous support for a policy favouring war appeared in the language in the same year.

jockey

A diminutive form of the man's name *Jock*, **jockey** was originally used, rather like JACK, for any ordinary man,

Dictionary man

That dedicated wordsmith Samuel Johnson, known as Dr Johnson, worked for nine years on his *Dictionary* before publication on April 15, 1755. It was an important step in the development of English, doing much to standardise the spellings we use today.

Johnson's huge labour was not the first English dictionary, but none of its predecessors had been so large or so comprehensive – they were mainly concerned with covering 'hard' words rather than giving a systematic account of the whole English language. Johnson's work allowed ordinary people to check the spellings and meanings of everyday words for the first time, and is also responsible for the form of many modern words, for example ACHE, BONFIRE and CENTRE.

The nine years of toil clearly had an effect on Johnson's weary definition for lexicographer: 'a writer of dictionaries; a harmless drudge'. He was a formidable and outspoken personality, not afraid to inject definitions with his own prejudices. England's northern neighbour was one target. Look up the word oats and you find: 'a grain, which in England is generally given to horses, but in Scotland supports the people'. Johnson also said on another occasion that 'the noblest prospect which a Scotchman ever sees, is the high road that leads him to England'.

One of the pleasures of the book is the discovery of evocative terms that have now sadly passed out of use. Particularly good are disdainful examples such as a backfriend, 'a friend backwards; that is, an enemy in secret'; a bellygod, 'a glutton, one who makes a god of his belly'; and a garlickeater, 'a mean fellow'.

It is also interesting to see how different the meanings of some modern words were in 1755. Pencil is defined as 'a small brush of hair which painters dip in their colours', ENTHUSIASM as 'a vain confidence of divine favour or communication' and urinal 'a bottle, in which water is kept for inspection'.

Dr Johnson and his *Dictionary* appear in the third series of the 1980s British TV comedy *Blackadder*, with Dr Johnson presenting the manuscript of his great work to the Prince Regent. When it appears that the precious sheets have been used to kindle a fire, Blackadder and Baldrick are left trying to rewrite the book. Baldrick claims later to be pleased with his coverage of C – 'big blue wobbly thing that mermaids swim in'.

boy or underling. From this came a specialised sense of a servant as a mounted courier, which in the 17th century gave rise to today's meaning.

In American slang a **jockey** was a specific kind of worker – so a **beer jockey** was a barmaid, a **garage jockey** a garage attendant and a **typewriter jockey** a typist. From there it was natural to call someone who played records a **disc jockey**, in the 1940s. See also JUKEBOX.

jog

One of the most visible changes in society over the last 20 or 30 years has been the number of joggers pounding round the streets or through the park. As they run, few joggers will be aware that the original meaning of **jog** was 'to stab'. The word is related to **jag**, as in **jagged**, and in Scotland and northern England to **jag** is still 'to prick'. The 'stab' sense was medieval; after that **jog** meant 'to shake or push' or 'to give a gentle nudge', and also 'to walk or ride in a heavy or jolting way, trudge'. The modern sense of running for exercise came up only in the 1960s.

joke

There must have been reasons for laughing in earlier times, but **joke** does not appear in the language until the late 17th century. It seems to have been a slang use, but its origins are probably more respectable – it may well come from Latin *jocus* 'jest, wordplay'. See also JEWEL, JUGGLE.

jolly

Christmas celebrations are traditionally **jolly**, and this word, from Old French *jolif* 'merry, handsome, lively', may come ultimately from the Old Norse root of YULE. Shakespeare used it in a very Christmassy way, in *As You Like It*: 'Then heigh-ho! the holly! / This life is most jolly.'

keep up with the Joneses

The first Joneses were in the title of a comic strip, 'Keeping up with the Joneses – by Pop', which appeared in the New York *Globe* in 1913. 'Jones' was used simply because it is one of the commonest British and American family names.

jot

Greek *iōta* (ι), the smallest letter of the Greek alphabet, gave us **jot** as a word for a very small amount. To stress that someone cannot have any part of something, we might use the phrase **not one jot** or **not one iota**, which reflects the warning given by Jesus in St Matthew's Gospel that 'Till heaven and earth pass, one jot or tittle shall in no wise pass from the law' (a *tittle* here is a small stroke or accent).

Three gigantic chariots dominate the festival of Ratha Yatra in Puri, India. One carries the image of the Hindu god Jagannath, or Juggernaut.

journal

In the Middle Ages a **journal** was a book listing the times of daily prayers. It comes ultimately from the late Latin word *diurnalis* 'belonging to a day'. The use of the word to mean a personal diary, which in theory you filled in every day, comes in at the beginning of the 17th century. Journal meaning 'a daily newspaper' dates from the early 18th century, giving us our current uses of **journalist** and **journalism**.

The earliest senses of **journey** in medieval English were 'a day, a day's travel, a day's work'. Like **journal**, the word comes ultimately from the Latin root of *dies* 'day'. Today we use **journeyman** as a term for a worker or sports player who is reliable but not outstanding. This goes back to the Middle Ages and the name for someone who had served his apprenticeship but was not yet a master of his craft. He still worked for someone else, and was paid by the day.

jovial

When we describe a cheerful person as **jovial**, we are looking back to the Latin word *jovialis* 'of Jupiter'. This refers to the supposed influence of the planet Jupiter on those born under it. *Jove* is a poetical equivalent of Jupiter, the name of the most important god of the ancient Romans. See also SATURNINE.

jubilee

British people have celebrated **jubilees** since the Middle Ages. The word comes from Latin *jubilaeus annus*, meaning 'year of jubilee', based on the Hebrew name for a special year, celebrated in Jewish history every 50 years, when slaves were freed and the fields were not cultivated. The original sense of the Hebrew word was 'ram's-horn trumpet', with which the jubilee year was proclaimed. So in its strictest sense a jubilee is a 50th anniversary, although we celebrate **silver jubilees** (25 years) or **diamond jubilees** (60 years), with the 50 year jubilee described as a **golden jubilee**.

judge

The word **judge**, recorded in English since the Middle Ages, looks back to a Latin word based on *jus* 'law' (the source also of **just** and **justice**) and *dicere* 'to say'. Judges are often thought of as solemn and impressive figures, and the expression **sober as a judge** goes back to the 17th century.

juggernaut

If you are stuck behind an articulated lorry, or **juggernaut**, on the motorway, a beach resort on the Bay of Bengal is probably not what springs to mind. But Juggernaut (in Sanskrit *Jagannātha*, 'Lord of the

World') is the name given to the form of the Hindu god Krishna worshipped in Puri, eastern India, where at a festival each year his huge image is dragged through the streets in a heavy chariot. The use of the word for a large, heavy vehicle came into English, along with many other Hindi words, in the mid 19th century.

juggle

In the Middle Ages **juggle** meant 'to entertain with tricks and jokes'. It comes ultimately from Latin *jocus* 'joke'. The current senses of the word did not develop until the late 19th century. See also JEWEL, JOKE.

jukebox

The first **jukeboxes** appeared in the 1930s. In the USA a **juke** was a nightclub or bar that provided food, drinks and music for dancing. The word was based on a term from the Creole language of the Gullah, a black people living on the coast of South Carolina and nearby islands. In their language *juke* meant 'disorderly'. See also JOCKEY.

jumbo

In the early 19th century **jumbo** was applied to a large and clumsy person, which may represent the second bit of MUMBO-JUMBO. The term became well known when it was given as a name to an elephant at London Zoo, from where it was sold to the Barnum and Bailey circus in 1882. Since 1964 it has referred to a large jet airliner, in particular the Boeing 747.

jump

Like **bump** and **thump**, **jump** was probably formed because it 'sounded right', and seemed to express the sound of feet hitting the ground. It was first used around 1500. To **jump the gun**, or act too soon, comes from the idea of an athlete starting a race a split-second before they hear the starting gun.

Jumper, which in the 19th century was a loose outer jacket worn by sailors and is now a woollen jersey, probably travelled through other times and cultures to reach English. It may come from Scots *jupe*, 'a loose jacket or tunic', which in turn came through French from Arabic *jubba*. **Jumpers for goalposts** was the dreamy refrain of Ron Manager in the BBC TV comedy *The Fast Show*. He was a veteran soccer coach whose analysis of games inevitably broke down into reminiscence about the days when kids played football in the street, using jumpers for improvised goalposts.

jungle

It was not until the late 18th century that **jungle** was added to the language from Hindi. Its root was a Sanskrit word meaning 'rough and arid', and in Indian use **jungle** first meant simply 'rough and uncultivated ground, wasteland' rather than 'land overgrown with dense forest and tangled vegetation'.

The law of the jungle, the principle that only those who are strong and ruthlessly selfish will succeed, is from *The Jungle Book* (1894) by Rudyard Kipling. In Kipling's book, though, the law of the jungle is not necessarily selfish: 'Now this is the Law of the Jungle – as old and as true as the sky . . . the strength of the Pack is the Wolf, and the strength of the Wolf is the Pack.'

Since the 1920s a **concrete jungle** has been an unattractive urban area perceived as a harsh, unpleasant environment, where the 'law of the jungle' prevails. *Blackboard Jungle* was the title of 1954 novel by Evan Hunter about an undisciplined school; the soundtrack of the film, made the following year, featured the song 'Rock Around the Clock' by Bill Haley and the Comets.

junk

In the Middle Ages **junk** was a name for old or inferior rope. By the mid 19th century the current sense of 'old and discarded articles, rubbish' had developed. From there came the slang sense 'heroin or other narcotic drugs' in the 1920s, the source of **junkie** 'a drug addict'. **Junk food** has been making us OBESE since the early 1970s.

The **junk** which is a flat-bottomed sailing boat used in China and the East Indies is a quite different word. Dating from the mid 16th century, it comes through French or Portuguese from the Malay word *jong*.

junket

Today a **junket** is a dish of sweetened curds of milk. Originally, though, it was a rush basket, and the word goes back to Latin *juncus* 'a rush'. In early translations of the Bible it was the word used for the little boat of bulrushes in which the infant Moses was placed by his mother, and from there came to mean 'cream cheese' or 'dish of sweetened curds', which at one time was made in a rush basket or served on a rush mat. Junkets might be served at a feast, and by the 16th century the sense 'a feast, a party' arose, from which came the meaning 'a trip or excursion made by government officials and paid for by public funds'.

jury

Reflecting its origin, **jury** comes from the Latin word *jurare* 'to swear'. Early juries, composed of men only, had to swear to give true answers to questions asked of them which related to their personal knowledge of an event they had witnessed or experienced.

kaleidoscope

Sir David Brewster, the 19th-century inventor of the **kaleidoscope**, also coined the name for his invention. It is made up of elements from the Greek words *kalos* 'beautiful', *eidos* 'form' and *skopein* 'to look at'.

kettle

When we say that something is **a pretty kettle of fish** we are describing it as an awkward or muddled state of affairs. The idea of fitting a fish into a modern kettle seems bizarre, but originally a kettle was any container used to heat water over a fire. There may be a clue as to how this particular phrase developed in a travel book of the 1790s. This describes 'a kettle of fish' as a term used in Berwick-upon-Tweed for a high-society picnic where freshly caught salmon were cooked in kettles on the banks of the River Tweed. Perhaps the presentation of the cooked fish fell short of what the guests expected – as was then indicated by the ironical use of 'pretty'. **Kettle** is an Old English word which ultimately goes back to Latin *catinus* 'a deep container for cooking or serving food'.

The first example of **the pot calling the kettle black**, meaning that a person's criticisms of another could equally well apply to themselves, dates from 1693. In *Some Fruits of Solitude* William Penn, the founder of Pennsylvania, wrote: 'For a Covetous Man to inveigh against Prodigality . . . is for the Pot to call the Kettle black.'

kick

Although it is such a common word, nobody seems to know the origin of **kick**. If you **kick against the pricks** you are likely to hurt yourself by continuing to resist something that cannot be changed. The image is that of an ox fruitlessly kicking out at a whip or spur: the more it kicks, the more the driver goads it. The expression comes from the Bible story of Saul of Tarsus. He was an opponent of the followers of Jesus, and was going to Damascus to arrest any Christians in the city. On his journey he had a vision and heard the question, 'Saul, Saul, why persecutest thou me?' When he asked who the speaker was he was told, 'I am Jesus who thou persecutest: it is hard for thee to kick against the pricks.' After seeing the vision Saul became a Christian convert, under the new name Paul.

If you **kick over the traces** you refuse to accept discipline or control. The 'traces' in this expression are the two side straps by which a draught horse is attached to the vehicle it is pulling. If the animal is uncooperative or skittish and kicks out over these straps, the driver has difficulty in trying to regain control.

To **kick the bucket** meaning 'to die' has been in use since the late 18th century, although its exact origins are not clear. One gruesome suggestion is that a person who wanted to commit suicide by hanging themselves might stand on a bucket while putting the noose round their neck and then kick the bucket away. Another idea looks back to an old sense of 'bucket' meaning 'a beam used for hanging something on'. This meaning was also found in Norfolk dialect, in which it referred specifically to a beam from which a pig about to be slaughtered was suspended by its heels.

kid

Young goats, which have been called **kids** since the Middle Ages, are traditionally a source of soft pliable leather for fine gloves. In the 19th century this gave us the expression **handle with kid gloves** to mean 'to deal very tactfully and gently with'.

Our use of **kid** for a child or young person developed in the 19th century, but probably looks back to a much earlier slang use to mean a baby or young child. The verb **kidnap** – its second syllable is a slang word, *nap*, meaning 'to take or seize' – originally referred to the 17th-century practice of stealing children to provide servants or labourers for the new American plantations.

Since the 19th century **kid** has been used as a verb to mean 'to deceive playfully'. The idea behind it is probably 'to make a child or goat of' someone.

kill

Like **kick**, **kill** is of unknown origin, although it may be related to QUELL and has been in the language since the 13th century.

To **be in at the kill** is to be present at or benefit from the successful conclusion of an enterprise. The image comes from the idea of the climax of a hunt.

In 1814 the future William IV, contemplating the defeat of Napoleon, wrote triumphantly, 'The game is up with Bonaparte, and I shall be in at the kill.'

Medicine in the 18th century was a risky business, and people then vowed to take a particular remedy whatever its effect – **kill or cure**. This gave us our current use of the phrase for a course of action which is likely either to work well or to fail catastrophically.

The thought of achieving two goals at once is always an attractive one. Since the 17th century one way of expressing the idea has been to refer to the hope of bird scarers in farm fields that we can **kill two birds with one stone**.

The film *The Killing Fields*, released in 1984, dealt with the horrific events in Cambodia during the Khmer Rouge dictatorship of 1975-9, when thousands of people were executed in **killing fields** and many more died of starvation. The term is first recorded in the early years of the 20th century and is a variation of **killing ground**, a place where seals were slaughtered.

kilter

The word **kilter**, meaning 'good condition or order', emerges in English dialect use in the 17th century, and is recorded in areas from Northumberland to Cornwall. It survives in mainstream language only in the phrase **out of kilter**, meaning 'out of balance'.

kind

In Old English the original senses of **kind** were 'nature, the natural order' and 'innate character', which led to our use of the word for 'a class or type of similar people or things'. **Kind** is also related to **kin** and through it to KING. In medieval times it was used as an adjective to mean 'well born, well bred', and the association of good breeding with good manners in turn gave us the familiar meaning of 'considerate and generous'.

In the film comedy *Kind Hearts and Coronets* (1949) an upper-class but impoverished young man seeks to murder all the heirs to the family fortune, all of whom are played by Alec Guinness. The title was taken from lines from 'Lady Clara Vere de Vere' by Lord Tennyson, written in 1842:

Kind hearts are more than coronets,
And simple faith than Norman blood.

kill with kindness

People have been **killed with kindness** – spoiled by overindulgence – since at least the mid 16th century. The expression appeared in the title of a play of the early 17th century, Thomas Heywood's *A Woman Killed with Kindness*.

king

The first kings in England were the chiefs of various tribes of Angles and Saxons who invaded the country and established their own small states. The Old English word was also applied to the British chiefs who tried to resist them, and became **king**. See also KIND.

To say that something expensive costs **a king's ransom** is to hark back to feudal times, though the expression itself is not recorded before the 16th century. In the Middle Ages prisoners of war could be freed on payment of a ransom. The ransom varied according to the rank of the prisoner, and so a king, as holder of the highest rank, would require a vast sum of money to be paid to secure his release.

kiss

In Anglo-Saxon times people would **kiss** just as they do now. An action or event causing certain failure for an enterprise may be described as **the kiss of death**. Although the phrase is relatively recent it is thought to refer to a story in the Bible. In the biblical account of the arrest of Jesus in the Garden of Gethsemane, Judas Iscariot identified Jesus to the soldiers who would arrest him by greeting him with a kiss. The expression is often used of apparently beneficial or well-meaning actions which somehow tempt fate, and have the opposite result to that intended. A much earlier traditional expression for an act of betrayal, a **Judas kiss**, refers to the same story.

The last words of Lord Nelson, fatally wounded at the Battle of Trafalgar in 1805, are usually quoted as **Kiss me, Hardy**, spoken to Thomas Hardy, the captain of Nelson's ship, HMS *Victory*. According to eyewitnesses he did say this, but it was not his final speech. His last words were either 'Drink, drink. Fan, fan. Rub, rub', asking the doctor to give him a drink, fan him and rub him to relieve his pain, or 'Thank God I have done my duty'. See also BLIND, EXPECT.

In 1968 the American film critic Pauline Kael wrote a book called *Kiss Kiss Bang Bang*. She said about the title, 'The words "Kiss Kiss Bang Bang", which I saw on an Italian movie poster, are perhaps the briefest statement imaginable of the basic appeal of movies.'

kit

If you were told in the Middle Ages to **get your kit off** it would be a wooden tub you removed, not your clothes. **Kit** comes from Dutch *kitte*, meaning 'wooden vessel', later applied to other containers. Its use for a soldier's equipment, dating from the late 18th century, probably comes from the idea of a set of such articles packed in one container. See also CABOODLE.

kitchen

An Old English word based on Latin *coquere* 'to cook'. **Everything but the kitchen sink**, meaning 'everything imaginable', seems to have started life in the Second World War. A 1948 dictionary of forces' slang says that it was used in the context of a heavy bombardment: 'They chucked everything they'd got at us except, or including, the kitchen sink.'

Kitchen-sink drama depicts drab or sordid subjects in a realistic way. The term refers in particular to post-war British drama, such as John Osborne's *Look Back in Anger* (1956) and Arnold Wesker's *Roots* (1959), which used working-class domestic settings rather than the drawing rooms of conventional middle-class theatre.

The knickerbocker style is all the rage in 1922.

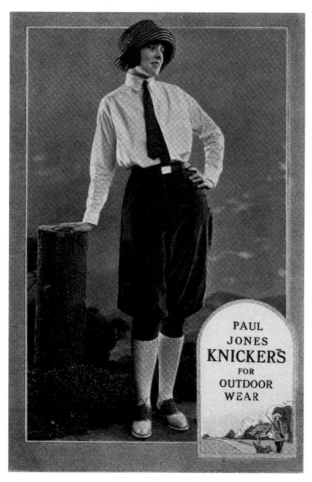

PAUL JONES
KNICKERS
FOR
OUTDOOR
WEAR

kith

An Old English word meaning 'native land' or 'countrymen' that is now only used in the phrase **kith and kin**, 'family or relations'. The 20th-century American poet Ogden Nash made neat use of it when he suggested that 'the wiles of a stranger' would be less dangerously appealing 'If one's own kin and kith / Were more fun to be with'.

kitty

This 18th-century pet name for a cat is a shortening of the earlier word **kitten**. Both ultimately go back to *chitoun*, an Old French diminutive for *chat* 'cat'. When a successful person is said to **scoop the kitty** their success has nothing to do with cats, but looks back to the use of **kitty** in northern English as a word for a prison. By the end of the 19th century it was being used generally in gambling as a name for the pool of money that is staked – to be scooped up by the luckiest player.

knickers

A writer for the magazine *Queen* offered some good advice on warm underwear in 1882: 'I recommend . . . flannel knickers in preference to flannel petticoat.' At that time **knickers**, then Bridget Jones-style big pants rather than thongs, were becoming part of every woman's wardrobe and part of the vocabulary. The word, originally meaning 'short trousers', comes from an abbreviation of **knickerbockers**. The use of **knickerbockers** for loose-fitting breeches arose from the resemblance of these garments to the knee breeches worn by Dutch men in the illustrations to Washington Irving's book *History of New York* (1809), which was supposedly by 'Dietrich Knickerbocker'. By the 1970s somebody who was becoming upset and angry might be warned against **getting their knickers in a twist**.

knight

To Anglo-Saxons **knight** meant 'boy, youth or servant', but in medieval times this developed into a name for a man of honourable military rank. Knights in traditional stories are rescuers of people in danger or distress, and a **knight in shining armour** is an idealised or heroic person, especially a man who comes to the rescue of a woman. While a **white knight** is also a saviour of distressed damsels, in stock exchange language it is a person or company that makes an acceptable counter-offer for a company facing a hostile takeover bid from a **black knight**.

A 17th-century highwayman might be called ironically a **knight of the road**. The phrase has survived into the modern language as a jokey term for someone like a sales representative or a lorry driver who habitually travels the roads. See also DAMSEL, ERR, PAGE, SQUIRE.

knock

The sound of a knock gave us **knock** in Old English. When you decide to finish an idea or plan you may say that you are going to **knock it on the head**, a phrase well established in English – a source from 1584 notes that 'Witchcraft . . . is knocked on the head'.

To **knock spots off** someone is to outdo them easily. The expression probably comes from the world of competitive shooting. Contestants keen to show off their skilled marksmanship would be required to shoot out the pips or spots on a playing card. The winner would be the person who shot out the most pips – and who might then be described as having 'knocked spots off' their rivals.

knot

Something travelling fast might be described as going **at a rate of knots**. A **knot** here is a measure of speed, equivalent to one nautical mile an hour, and the expression gives a clue as to how the word was adopted as a nautical unit of speed. In the days of sailing ships a line with knots tied at fixed intervals and a float at the end was run out into the sea over a certain time to gauge the ship's speed. If the line unwound very rapidly, with each knot appearing in quick succession, then the ship was going 'at a rate of knots'.

know

The ancient root of **know** is shared by **can** and **ken** ('to know' in Scots), and also by Latin *noscere* and Greek *gignōskein* 'to know'. To **know in the biblical sense**, meaning 'to have sex with', comes from an early sense of **know** particularly associated with the Bible. A verse in the book of Genesis runs: 'And Adam knew Eve his wife; and she conceived, and bare Cain.'

To **know the ropes** is to be thoroughly acquainted with the way in which something is done. The phrase comes from the days of sailing ships, when skill in handling ropes was essential for any sailor – people more familiar with their fields than the seven seas might be said to **know their onions**. The ancients valued self-knowledge as the way to wisdom – inscribed on the Greek temple of Apollo at Delphi were the words **know thyself**.

The line 'It's life, Jim, but not as we know it' is the mainstay of anyone trying to do an impression of Dr Spock from the TV series *Star Trek*, but he never said it in the programme. He did say that there was 'no life as we know it', but the quoted phrase is from the 1987 song 'Star Trekkin'' by the Firm.

knuckle

In medieval times a **knuckle** was the rounded shape made by a joint like the elbow or knee when bent, but over the years it became limited to the joints of the fingers. The word may ultimately be related to KNEE.

Someone prepared to **knuckle down** is ready to concentrate on a task, but the phrase originally comes from a game. People playing marbles in the 18th century set their knuckles down on the ground before shooting or casting the 'taw', a large marble.

The knuckle might be thought of as marking a particular point, and something which threatens to go beyond the limits of decency can be described as being **near the knuckle**. This was originally used more generally to mean 'close to the permitted limits of behaviour'.

kop

The Taylor Report after the Hillsborough disaster of 1989, in which 96 Liverpool fans were killed in a crush at the ground of Sheffield Wednesday, recommended that major soccer grounds in England should become all-seated, and spelled the end for the traditional terrace or **kop**. The original and best-known kop was the one at Anfield, home of Liverpool FC, which was known in full as Spion Kop. The name came from the site of a battle in 1900 during the Boer War, in which troops from Lancashire, including many from Liverpool, led the assault. In Afrikaans *kop* means 'hill', and so was an appropriate name for a high bank of terracing.

kosher

Only **kosher** food may be eaten by Orthodox Jews. Animals must be slaughtered and prepared in the prescribed way, meat and milk must not be cooked or consumed together, and certain creatures, notably pigs and shellfish, are forbidden. The word is from Hebrew *kāsēr* 'right, proper', and was first used in English in the mid 19th century – the slang sense, 'genuine and legitimate', is almost as old, going back to the 1880s.

labour

The people of Anglo-Saxon England worked but did not **labour**: the latter word came into English during the early Middle Ages, through French from Latin *labor* 'toil, distress, trouble'. In the late 18th century the Scottish economist Adam Smith used the word more technically for work directed towards providing the needs of a community, and paved the way for the use of **labour** in political contexts. The British **Labour Party** was formed in 1906 to represent ordinary working people. See also TORY.

A task requiring enormous strength or effort is a **labour of Hercules** or a **Herculean labour**. In Greek mythology Hercules was a man of superhuman strength and courage who performed 12 tasks or 'labours' imposed on him as a penance for killing his children in a fit of madness. After his death he was ranked among the gods.

laconic

The Spartans or Laconians of ancient Greece were known for their austere lifestyle and pithy speech. When Philip of Macedon threatened to invade Laconia in the 4th century BC, he wrote to its governing magistrates in an attempt to frighten them into submission, saying that if he entered Laconia he would raze it to the ground. They are reported to have sent a one-word reply – 'If'. Since the 16th century **laconic** has meant 'using very few words'. See also SPARTAN.

lad

Like BOY, the word **lad** appeared from nowhere in the early Middle Ages. By the mid 16th century it was being used for 'a boisterously spirited young man', and **laddism** was first mentioned in the 1840s. It was in the early 1990s, though, that laddism and **new lads** became a social phenomenon, driven by the rise of the rock group Oasis and the launch of the **lad's mag** *Loaded* in 1994. A young woman who is **a bit of a lad** has been a **ladette** since around 1995.

lady

The root meaning of **lady** was 'kneader of bread'. Old English *hlafdige*, from which the modern word developed, comes from an early form of LOAF and a word meaning 'knead' from which DOUGH also derives. The corresponding male form is LORD, in Old English *hlafweard* 'keeper of bread'. In spite of the humble associations of baking, a lady in Anglo-Saxon times was a powerful woman who ruled over a household and made its staple food – bread.

These days a certain type of lady meets during the day in expensive restaurants – they are the **ladies who lunch**. The source of this expression is the title of a 1970 song by Stephen Sondheim from the musical *Company*, which pokes fun at members of the affluent charity fund-raising set.

lager

The fuller name for **lager**, no longer much used, is **lager beer**. It comes from German *Lagerbier* 'beer brewed for keeping', from *Lager* 'storehouse', which shares its root with an animal's **lair** and also with **lie**. Modern brewing techiques have often resulted in a product of lower quality than the word's origin would suggest, and since the 1980s we have had the **lager lout**, the young man who drinks too much and then behaves in an unpleasant or violent way. See also BEER.

lairy

For a century or more **lairy** has been Australian and New Zealand slang for 'ostentatious, flashy'. British English has adopted this use, to join an earlier, originally Cockney sense 'cunning or conceited', as well as the meaning 'aggressive, rowdy'. The word is a form of **leery**, which means 'cautious or wary' and is related to **leer** 'to look at in a lecherous way', from Old English *hleor* 'a cheek'.

land

Celtic words such as Irish *lann* 'enclosure' and Welsh *llan* 'enclosure, church' are related to **land**, as well as the closer Dutch *land* and German *Land*. **In the land of the living** is now a jokey way of saying that someone is alive or awake. The expression is biblical, occurring for example in the Book of Job: 'Man knoweth not the price thereof; neither is it found in the land of the living.' **The land of Nod** is also biblical,

What the Romans did for us

As well as education, wine, roads, underfloor heating and the fresh water system, the Romans gave us words and phrases. Far from being a dead language, Latin is alive and well and can be found in a sentence near you.

English is full of words of Latin origin that came into the language by way of the French spoken by the Norman invaders of 1066. But we also use many phrases that came into English later, typically in the 17th and 18th centuries, and remain in their original Latin form.

In Latin index referred to the 'forefinger' or 'index finger', with which you point. From this we got our term for a list of topics in a book which 'point' to the right page. When we decide to leave by a door marked exit, we may not know that in Latin this meant 'he or she goes out'.

The phrase in flagrante delicto, literally 'in blazing crime', means in English 'in the very act of wrongdoing', and particularly refers to sexual misconduct. If someone is caught in flagrante delicto they are generally found in bed with someone else's partner.

If we want to say that someone really knows about something we might say that they are bona fide, Latin words meaning 'with good faith'. A remark that has no logical connection with a previous statement is a non sequitur – literally, 'it does not follow'. A particular stipulation or condition is a caveat, a word which means literally 'let a person beware'. If a person is preparing to buy something, you might say caveat emptor, 'let the buyer beware', to remind them that it is the buyer alone who is responsible for checking the quality of the goods before the purchase is made.

Someone who dislikes sailing might be very glad to find themselves back on terra firma or 'firm land'. If they had heard too much of the delights of the sea, they might say that they had been lectured about it ad nauseam, or 'to sickness'. They might be wary of decisions taken on an ad hoc basis, Latin for 'to this', used in English to mean 'created or done for a particular purpose'. Sometimes you have no chance to influence what happens, as things may be done in your absence, or in absentia.

In 1992, following the marital troubles of her children and a disastrous fire at Windsor Castle, the Queen said in a speech that it had turned out to be an annus horribilis. This term for a year of disaster or misfortune is an alteration of an established Latin phrase annus mirabilis 'wonderful year'.

Changes are often received with apprehension, especially by people who would prefer to preserve the existing state of affairs or status quo – literally 'the state in which'. The band Status Quo had their first hit, 'Pictures of Matchstick Men', in 1968 and are still going strong. Another band with a Latin name are Procol Harum, who released the enigmatic 'A Whiter Shade of Pale' in 1967. The band's name is a misspelled version of a Latin phrase meaning 'far from these things' – it should really be procul his.

The legal world is full of Latin. If someone is not of sound mind they are said to be non compos mentis, literally 'not having control of the mind'. Journalists may sometimes feel frustrated at not being able to report freely on a case because it is sub judice 'under a judge' – under judicial consideration and so prohibited from public discussion.

Latin had supplied a number of well-known mottoes. E pluribus unum, or 'one out of many', is the motto of the United States. In 1913 King George V approved per ardua ad astra, 'through struggle to the stars', as the motto of the Royal Air Force.

Some Latin phrases lie behind our most familiar abbreviations. If we want to emphasise the importance of something, we may say or write NB – short for nota bene, or 'note well'. QED, pointing out that a fact or situation demonstrates the truth of what you are saying, stands for quod erat demonstrandum, 'which was to be demonstrated'. A long list of items may finish with etc., standing for et cetera 'and the rest'. Advancing age may be referred to jokingly as Anno Domini, Latin for 'in the year of the Lord', which also gives us the abbreviation AD. The passage of time inevitably leads to RIP, short for requiescat in pace, 'rest in peace', although the same cannot be said to apply to Latin itself.

CTIVS · C · F · V CIVS

first used for the state of sleep by Jonathan Swift, who based it on the place name **Nod** in Genesis: 'And Cain went out from the presence of the Lord, and dwelt in the land of Nod, on the east of Eden'. See also EAST.

lap

Originally a **lap** was a fold or flap of a garment, which gave rise to **lapel** in the 17th century. By the Middle Ages it was also the front of a skirt when held up to catch or carry something, and from there the area between the waist and the knees as a place where a child can be nursed or an object held. Since the 1980s erotic dancers or striptease artists have also performed a **lap dance** while sitting on the laps of – or at least dancing close to – paying customers.

The expression **in the lap of the gods**, referring to the success of a plan or event that is outside your control, can be traced back to several passages in the works of the Greek epic poet Homer, thought to have been written during the 8th century BC. The idea is that the course of events is determined by the gods, and so is completely outside human control. The phrase probably comes from the image of someone trying to placate or influence a person in authority by placing gifts in their lap as they sit ready to pass judgement.

larder

In the past, and in peasant societies in general, the pig has been a vital source of food for winter: it can be salted and preserved, and traditionally you can eat every part of it except its squeak. This is reflected in the word **larder**, which in origin is a place for storing bacon. It comes from the French word meaning 'bacon' that also gave us **lard** and the **lardon**, the cube or chunk of bacon inserted in meat before cooking. See also PANTRY.

lark

Old English *laferce* developed into Scottish and northern English **laverock**, and in the Middle Ages was contracted to **lark**, which become the standard name for this songbird. References to the early morning singing of the lark date back to the 16th century. People often refer to an early riser as a lark, while a late-to-bed counterpart is an OWL. The phrase **up with the lark**, 'up very early in the morning', also plays on the word **up**, since the lark sings on the wing while flying high above its nest. In to **lark about** or **around**, and in the sense 'something done for fun', **lark** may be a shortening of **skylark**, which was formerly used in the same way, or it may be from dialect **lake** 'to play', from a Scandinavian word.

launder

In the sense 'to wash clothes or linen' **launder** was originally a contracted form of *lavender*, a medieval word meaning 'a person who washes clothes'. It goes back to Latin *lavare* to wash, the source of **lava**, **lavatory** and **lavish**. The Watergate scandal in the USA in the early 1970s, in which an attempt to bug the national headquarters of the Democratic Party led to the resignation of President Richard Nixon, gave the world **money laundering**, concealing the origins of money obtained illegally by transfers involving foreign banks or legitimate businesses.

Before bathrooms, pedestal sinks and running water, people washed from a basin or bowl. This is what a **lavatory** originally was – a vessel for washing. In the mid 17th century the word came to refer to a room with washing facilities, from which developed the modern sense of a toilet. See also TOILET.

law

The words **legal, legitimate** and **loyal** all descend from Latin *lex* 'law', the source also of **law**. It was Charles Dickens who first said **the law is an ass**, or rather his character Mr Bumble did in *Oliver Twist*: '"If the law supposes that," said Mr Bumble . . . "the law is a ass . . . a idiot."' See also JUNGLE.

lead

Two entirely different strands come together in the spelling **lead**, with different pronunciations. The **lead** that rhymes with *bead* shares an ancient root with LOAD; the **lead** that rhymes with *bed* and means 'a metal' is related to Dutch *lood* 'lead' and German *Lot* 'plumb line, solder'.

The image in to **lead someone by the nose**, 'to control someone totally', is of an animal being led by a ring in its nose. Boxing gave us to **lead with your chin** 'to behave or talk incautiously'. It refers to a boxer's stance that leaves his chin unprotected. See also BALLOON.

lean

The two words spelled **lean** are of different origins. Both are Old English, but the one meaning 'be in a sloping position' shares a root with Latin *inclinare*, as in **incline**.

We sometimes talk of **lean years** or **a lean period**. This expression comes from the story of Joseph in the Bible. Joseph is in prison in Egypt, where he successfully interprets the dreams of two officials who are imprisoned with him. Pharaoh then has a disturbing dream, in which seven plump, healthy cattle come out of the river and begin to feed. Seven lean, malnourished animals then leave the river and proceed to eat the plump cattle. No one can interpret this until Joseph, having earned something of a reputation, is brought out of prison to do so. According to Joseph's interpretation, there will be seven years of plenty in Egypt followed by seven lean years. Pharaoh, impressed by Joseph's take on the situation, appoints him vice-regent to prepare the country for the ordeal of the seven lean years, and Joseph rises to a position of great power. See also FAT.

The active and alert-looking **lean and hungry** is from Shakespeare's *Julius Caesar* – 'Yond' Cassius has a lean and hungry look.'

left

The original core sense of **left** is 'weak' – the majority of people are right-handed, and the left-hand side was regarded as the weaker side of the body. The political application of **left** originated in the French National Assembly of 1789, in which the nobles as a body took the position of honour on the president's right, and the Third Estate – the French bourgeoisie and working class – sat on his left. See also AMBIDEXTROUS, SINISTER.

In baseball **left field** is the part of the outfield that is to the left from the perspective of the batter. In US English something that is **left-field** or **out of left field** is surprising or unconventional, or possibly ignorant or mistaken. The connection with baseball probably came from the fact that in many early ball parks the left field was larger than the right, making it more difficult to retrieve balls hit there and sometimes leading to delay and general confusion.

In some places, particularly Scotland and Ireland, **left-footer** is a derogatory name for a Catholic. The term is said to come from the tradition that in Northern Ireland Catholic farm workers used spades that required them to push with their left foot when digging, while Protestants used the right foot.

lemon

The root of **lemon** and also **lime** is an Arabic word that was a collective term for citrus fruit. On fruit machines the lemon is the least valuable symbol, and this may be behind uses representing bad or disappointing things, such as **the answer is a lemon** 'the response or outcome is unsatisfactory'. Especially in the USA, a **lemon** may be a substandard or defective car, of the type all too often bought from shady used-car dealers.

leopard

Two Greek words combine in the root of **leopard**: *leōn*, the source of LION, and *pardos*, the source of

pard, an old word for a leopard. The saying **the leopard does not change his spots** is inspired by the Book of Jeremiah in the Bible: 'Can the Ethiopian change his skin, or the leopard his spots?' See also GIRAFFE.

leprechaun

The name of the small, mischievous sprite of Irish folklore is based on old Irish words meaning 'small body'. The spelling of Irish has always been a mystery to the uninitiated: when the **leprechaun** first appeared in English literature in the 17th century, it was named **lubrican**. The modern form dates from the 19th century.

lesbian

Sappho was a Greek lyric poet of the early 7th century BC who lived on the island of Lesbos in the eastern Aegean Sea. Many of her poems express her affection and love for women, and so people came to associate her with female homosexuality. In the late 19th century she inspired two descriptive terms, **lesbian**, from her island home of Lesbos, and **sapphic**.

lethal

When the souls of the dead in Greek mythology drank the water of Lethe, a river in Hades, the underworld, they forgot their life on Earth, and so in Greek the word *Lēthē* meant 'forgetfulness'. Many ancient Romans were familiar with this, and along the line they altered their Latin word *letum* 'death' to *lethum*, to be closer to the Greek. The altered Latin form is the source of English **lethal** 'deadly'.

letter

English adopted **letter** from Old French in the 13th century. Its ultimate source is Latin *litera* or *littera*, from which **literal** and **literature** also derive – the Latin word meant 'written communication or message' as well as 'letter of the alphabet', and both senses came over into English. The phrase **to the letter** 'to the last detail' has a parallel in French *au pied de la lettre*, which people of a literary bent have also used in English. See also ALPHABET.

lettuce

Lettuces and milk could hardly be more different, but they are related by the history of the word **lettuce**. It came into English from Old French *letues* or *laitues*, from Latin *lactuca*, whose root was *lac* 'milk' – the connection was the milky juice that lettuce produces when it is crushed. Latin *lac* also gave us **lactic**, 'relating to milk'.

level

The ultimate root of **level** is Latin *libra* 'scales, balance', also the source of the sign of the zodiac **Libra**. It has many senses in English, the earliest being 'an instrument used to determine whether a surface is horizontal', as in **spirit level**. Since the 1980s the image of **a level playing field** has been a cliché of business and politics to signify a situation in which everyone has a fair and equal chance of succeeding. In games an uneven playing surface will favour the home side, who will be more familiar with its hazards.

leviathan

In the Bible Leviathan is a sea monster, sometimes identified with a whale, sometimes with a crocodile, sometimes with the Devil. In 1651 Thomas Hobbes published a treatise of political philosophy called *The Leviathan*, in which the monster in question is sovereign power. Modern uses of **leviathan** for 'an autocratic monarch or state' derive from this. Hobbes himself considered that a monarch with absolute power was essential to maintain an ordered state in a world in which 'the life of man is solitary, poor, nasty, brutish and short'.

liberty

The root of **liberty** is Latin *liber* 'free', the source also of **liberal**, **libertine** and **livery** and an element in **deliver**. During the French Revolution the rallying cry was **liberty, equality, fraternity**. Supporters of change and opponents of the monarchy wore the **cap of liberty**, a red conical cap of a type that had originally been given to Roman slaves when they were freed.

The figure of Liberty in French revolutionary costume (1793-4).

In the 1880s the French state made a gift to the USA of **the Statue of Liberty** to commemorate their alliance during the War of American Independence from 1775 to 1783. The statue, designed by Frédéric-Auguste Bartholdi, represents a draped female figure carrying a book of laws in her left hand and holding aloft a torch in her right. It stands at the entrance to New York harbour. For the use of **liberty** in the American Declaration of Independence see EQUAL.

life

The English word **life** is related to Dutch *lijf* and German *Leib* 'body', and also to **leave** and LIVE. The expression **as large as life**, 'conspicuously present', goes back to the days before photography when portrait painting was common, being almost the only way of capturing a person's likeness. Professional artists did not come cheap, and a good way of showing off your wealth would be to have a portrait painted which was life-size. Early versions of the expression, dating from the mid 17th century, are **greater** or **bigger than the life**, with the modern form first recorded in the early 19th century.

When someone lives **the life of Riley** they are enjoying a luxurious and carefree existence. *Reilly* or *Riley* is a common Irish surname, and the phrase may come from a popular song of the early 20th century called 'My Name is Kelly'. This included the lines: 'Faith and my name is Kelly Michael Kelly,/ But I'm living the life of Reilly just the same.' It is possible that the songwriter, H. Pease, was using an already existing catchphrase, but the song would anyway have made it more widely known.

light

There are two main sources for the various words spelled **light**. The **light** referring to the rays that stimulate sight shares an ancestor with Greek *leukos* 'white' (seen in **leukaemia** and similar words) and Latin *lux* (source of **lucid**). The **light** referring to weight comes from the same ancient root as **lung** – the lightness of the lungs distinguishes them from other internal organs. This sense of **light** survives in **lights**, the lungs of sheep, pigs or bullocks, used as food, especially for pets.

If someone does something that creates a tense or exciting situation, people might say that they **light the blue touchpaper**. A touchpaper is a type of fuse consisting of a twist of paper impregnated with saltpetre, potassium nitrate, so that it will burn slowly when touched by a spark. It is now only used with fireworks, but in the past would also have been a means for igniting gunpowder.

likely

The earliest English sense of **likely** was 'liable to, probable', but in the later Middle Ages the word developed the sense 'apparently suitable' and then 'promising'. This last meaning is seen in *The Likely Lads*, the title of a BBC TV comedy written by Dick Clement and Ian La Frenais that took to the screen in 1964. It featured James Bolam and Rodney Bewes as young working-class friends in the northeast of

England. The programme ran for several series, and in 1973 returned with a sequel, *Whatever Happened to the Likely Lads?*

limb

There was no *b* in **limb** meaning 'an arm or leg, etc.' until the 16th century: the Old English word was *lim*. Old English *thuma* similarly became **thumb** in the 13th century. Words such as **comb** and **dumb** that always ended in -*b* in English may have influenced the new spelling.

The **limb** in the expression **out on a limb**, 'without support from anyone', is the branch of a tree. The image conjured up is of someone clinging precariously to the end of a projecting branch, with nothing or no one to assist them in their difficult situation.

limbo

In some versions of Christian theology **limbo** is the abode, on the border of hell, of the souls of unbaptised infants and of just people who died before Christ's coming. The word represents a form of Latin *limbus* 'edge, hem, border'. From the late 16th century it developed extended uses such as 'an uncertain period of awaiting a decision or resolution' and 'a state of neglect or oblivion'.

Doing the West Indian dance the **limbo**, bending backwards to pass under a horizontal bar, may be some people's idea of hell or purgatory, but there is no linguistic connection. The name of the dance, recorded from the 1950s, is an alteration of **limber** 'lithe, supple'. See also HEAVEN, HELL, INFERNO, PARADISE, PURGATORY.

limelight

Before electricity and gas supplies and strong spotlights, the managers and stagehands of theatres lit up important actors and scenes using **limelight**. This was an intense white light produced by heating up a piece of lime in a flame of combined oxygen and hydrogen, a process invented around 1825 by Captain T. Drummond of the Royal Engineers. From the end of the 19th century, as modern lighting ended the need for real limelight, the word came to be more common in the sense 'the focus of public attention'.

limerick

Limerick is on the River Shannon in the west of the Irish province of Munster, and is the principal town of a county of the same name. In a country famous for its CRACK, or enjoyable sociability, tradition has it that in some convivial gatherings it was the custom for each person to improvise a piece of nonsense verse. The audience would then follow every performance with a chorus containing the words 'Will you come up to Limerick?' Through this the town gave its name to the humorous five-line poem the **limerick**, made particularly popular by Edward Lear in *A Book of Nonsense* (1845), for example:

> There was an Old Man of Coblenz,
> The length of whose legs was immense;
> He went with one prance
> From Turkey to France,
> That surprising Old Man of Coblenz.

Edward Lear brings to life the amazing 'Old Man of Coblenz'.

limousine

In French a *limousine* was a cloak with a cape, of a type worn in Limousin, a region and former province of central France. People saw a resemblance between this distinctive garment and early forms of motor car in which the driver's seat was outside in a separate compartment covered with a canopy. The name **limousine**, first recorded shortly after 1900, passed to large, luxurious cars driven by a chauffeur separated from the passengers by a partition. The word was abbreviated to **limo** in the 1960s, while in the 1980s the **stretch limo**, the must-have transport for hen nights, made its appearance.

lingerie

Women may prefer their underwear to be light, silky and slinky, but the root of the word **lingerie** is much more homespun and practical. It comes from French *linge* 'linen', and originally referred to articles made out of linen.

lion

The lions known in parts of Europe and around the Mediterranean in early times were not African but Asiatic lions, which are extremely rare animals in the 21st century. The name **lion** came into English from French and ultimately from Greek *leōn*, in the Middle Ages. The Anglo-Saxons had used the Latin form **Leo**, which was overtaken by **lion** for the animal, but which is still the name of a constellation and of the fifth sign of the zodiac.

In ancient Rome lions and other wild beasts provided entertainment in the Colosseum and similar amphitheatres. Christians and other religious and political dissidents were left at their mercy in the arena, a practice behind our phrase **throw someone to the lions**, 'to cause someone to be in an extremely dangerous or unpleasant situation'.

After the terrible slaughter of British soldiers during the First World War, the phrase **lions led by donkeys** became popular as a way of encapsulating the idea that the men had been brave but had been let down by their incompetent officers. It is not clear who first came up with the description, but in 1871 the French troops defeated by the Prussians were described as 'lions led by packasses'.

From medieval times until the opening of London Zoo in the 19th century the Tower of London contained a menagerie or collection of unusual animals, among which were lions. Not surprisingly, they were a great attraction for visitors to the city, and the phrase to **see the lions** sprang up with the meaning 'to see the sights or attractions of a place'. From there a lion became a

celebrity or noted person, a sense which gave us **lionise**, 'to treat as a celebrity', in the 1830s. See also BEARD.

liquorice

Contrary to appearances, **liquorice** has no connection with **liquor**. The word goes back to a Greek compound formed from *glukus* 'sweet' (source of **glucose**) and *rhiza* 'root' (as in **rhizome**). Liquorice is made by evaporating the juice of the root of certain members of the pea family.

Liquorice allsorts have been a favourite sweet of many since they were introduced in 1899. The story behind their invention is that a salesman from the company Bassett's was visiting a client and showing him samples of the various liquorice sweets that the company made. The client was unimpressed by any of them until the salesman gathered up his samples to leave and in doing so dropped them all, creating a mix of sweets that the client liked.

list

In the sense 'a number of connected items or names', **list** came from French in the late 16th century. The origin of the French word appears to be the root of another **list** that already existed in English, with the meaning 'a border, edge or strip' – presumably from the strip of paper on which a list would have been written. Its main use now is in sewing, to refer to the selvedge or sewn edge of a piece of fabric.

The origins of to **enter the lists** 'to issue or accept a challenge' have nothing to do with signing up for some risky undertaking, but go back to the days of knights and jousting tournaments. In medieval times the **lists** were the enclosed area where jousts took place. The lists were actually the barriers surrounding this area, but the meaning was extended to refer to the yard itself. If you chose to **enter the lists** you were formally agreeing to take part in combat.

litter

The earliest, medieval meaning of **litter** was 'a bed', which was also that of its source, Latin *lectus*. Its journey to the modern sense 'rubbish lying in a public place' took until the mid 18th century. The link is bedding made of straw or rushes, once used by poorer people, who put it down on the floor and then discarded it when soiled. A **litter** of animals such as kittens probably gets its name from the mother giving birth in a sheltered sleeping place.

little

Like SMALL, this is an Old English word, recorded from the earliest times. The proverb **a little learning is a dangerous thing** quotes a line from Alexander Pope's *Essay on Man* of 1711; nowadays people often substitute 'knowledge' for 'learning'.

live

In the sense 'to remain alive', **live** goes back to the same root as LIFE and **leave**. The other **live**, with a different pronunciation, is a mid 16th-century shortening of **alive**.

The proverb **live and let live**, 'you should tolerate the opinions and behaviour of others', is identified as Dutch in the earliest known reference, from 1622 – *Live and Let Die*, the 1954 James Bond book, made into a film in 1973 starring Roger Moore, subverted it. The rhyme 'He who fights and runs away / Lives to fight another day' gives us the phrase **live to fight another day**. The idea is found in the works of the Greek comic playwright Menander, who lived from around 342 to 292 BC.

load

The ancient root of **load** is related to that of the metal LEAD. The word **lode** meaning 'a vein of ore' and found also in **lodestone** was originally just a different spelling of **load**. In earlier use **load** and **lode** were used interchangeably for both sets of meanings.

The expression **loads of** 'lots, heaps' goes back as far as Shakespeare's *Troilus and Cressida*, where the original spelling was 'loades a'. In the 20th century **loadsa** started appearing in print as one word, and in the late 1980s the comedian Harry Enfield created the character Loadsamoney, a flash Tory plasterer who boasted about the money he had made and threw wads of cash around. Loadsamoney was seen as epitomising the 'get-rich-quick' ethos of the Thatcher years.

loaf

Originally **loaf** meant 'bread' as well as 'a shaped quantity of bread'. Like the basic foodstuff it refers to, the word goes back to ancient times. In the British expression to **use your loaf**, 'to use your common sense', **loaf** most probably comes from the rhyming slang phrase **loaf of bread** meaning 'head'. It is first recorded in a 1920s dictionary of army and navy slang as '*Loaf*, head, e.g., Duck your loaf, i.e., keep your head below the parapet'. To **loaf** or spend time in an aimless, idle way is not connected with bread, but comes from **loafer**, which itself is probably based on German *Landläufer* 'a tramp'. See also BREAD, LADY, LORD.

lobby

Both **lobby** and **lodge** go back to medieval Latin *lobia* 'covered walk, portico'. The earliest uses of the word, in the mid 16th century, refer to monastic cloisters, but after Henry VIII dissolved the monasteries it moved into the secular world of the rich subjects who turned them into houses. A **lobby** became an antechamber or entrance hall, and is now often the foyer of a hotel. The British Houses of Parliament, and other parliaments, have a central lobby where MPs can meet constituents and members of pressure groups, and two division lobbies where MPs assemble to vote. To **lobby** meaning 'to try to influence a legislator on an issue' originated from this arrangement in the USA.

lobster

The **lobster** and **locust** are linguistically the same. Latin *locusta*, from which both derive, had both meanings. Look at close-up pictures of the two and you will see some similarities. See also OYSTER.

lock

They seem like very different words, but the **lock** that is a fastening mechanism and the **lock** of hair may be related. Both are Old English, and possibly derive from a root that meant 'to bend'.

All the elements in **lock, stock and barrel**, 'including everything', are parts of an old-fashioned firearm, with only the stock and barrel found in modern guns. The lock was the mechanism for exploding the charge, the stock is the part to which the firing mechanism and barrel are attached, and the barrel is the cylindrical tube out of which the shot or bullet is fired. The expression first appears in the early 19th century in the alternative version **stock, lock and barrel**, used by the novelist Sir Walter Scott. A vivid expansion of the phrase was used as the title of the 1998 British gangster film *Lock, Stock and Two Smoking Barrels*.

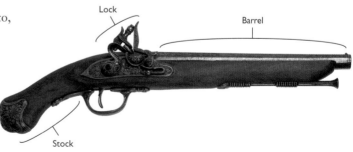

Lock

Barrel

Stock

log

The word **log** is first recorded in the Middle Ages in the sense 'a bulky mass of wood'. The ship's log or official record of events during the voyage got its name from a device used to find out the rate of a ship's motion, a thin quarter-circle of wood loaded so as to float upright in the water and fastened to a line wound on a reel. The captain would record the information obtained from this in a journal, or log. See also JAM, KNOT, SLEEP.

at loggerheads

The origins of this expression, meaning 'in violent dispute or disagreement', are obscure. The earliest meanings of **loggerhead**, dating from the late 16th century, were 'a disproportionately large head' and 'a stupid person' (similar to **blockhead**). Around half a century later the word was applied to various animals with very large heads, notably the **loggerhead turtle**. Finally, in the 1680s, it described a long-handled iron instrument with a bulbous end, used for heating liquids. The last sense is probably the source for the modern expression, as it arose at the same time and the implement may also have been a weapon.

logo

A 1930s shortening of either **logogram**, 'a sign or character representing a word or phrase, such as those used in shorthand', or the printing term **logotype**, 'a single piece of type that prints a word, phrase or symbol'. Both go back to Greek *logos* 'word'.

Lolita

In Vladimir Nabokov's novel *Lolita* (1958), Humbert Humbert, a man in his late 30s, becomes sexually obsessed with Dolores Haze, a 12-year-old girl whom he dubs Lolita. The book's controversial and disturbing subject matter created a scandal when it was published in the USA, but it gave the world two words for 'a sexually precocious young girl', **Lolita** itself and **nymphet**.

lollipop

Late 18th-century children enjoyed a particular kind of sweet that dissolved easily in the mouth. Its dialect name was a **lollipop**, which may derive from another dialect word, **lolly** meaning 'tongue', though there is no written record of this until a century later. Lollipops are now flat rounded boiled sweets on a stick. The shortened form **lolly** appeared in the mid 19th century, and is still a general word for a sweet in Australia and New Zealand.

long

The **long** referring to length and the **long** meaning 'to desire' are unrelated, though both have ancient roots. The phrase **long in the tooth** was first used to describe horses, and comes from the way you can estimate a horse's age by looking at its teeth: if the gums have receded and the teeth consequently look very long, you know the animal is rather old. The same idea is behind the old proverb **don't look a gift horse in**

How long have you got?

People often wonder what the longest word is in English. Few contenders are used in everyday speech, and some have been made up simply for fun or to create what might be the longest.

'Supercalifragilisticexpialidocious', sang Julie Andrews in the 1964 film *Mary Poppins*. The 'atrocious'-sounding children's nonsense word would certainly be a contender, but most dictionaries ignore it. The title was not invented by the

Sherman brothers, who wrote the film score, but first occurred with a slightly different spelling as the title of a song called 'Supercalafajalistickespialadojus' in 1949.

The longest words in most dictionaries are deinstitutionalisation, 'the discharge of long-term inmates from institutions such as psychiatric hospitals or prisons', electroencephalograph, a machine for measuring electrical activity in the brain, and antidisestablishmentarianism, meaning 'belief that the Church of England should not be disestablished'

pneumonoultramicros

the mouth, meaning 'don't find fault with something that you have been given'.

The background to **long time no see**, 'it's a long time since we last met', would nowadays probably be seen as politically incorrect. It was originally an American expression and arose in the early 20th century as a supposedly humorous imitation of the broken English spoken by a Native American. This dubious past is long forgotten and the phrase is now freely used on both sides of the Atlantic. See also ARM.

loo

The upper-class author Nancy Mitford first put **loo**, meaning 'toilet', into print in her 1940 novel *Pigeon Pie*. People have put forward different theories about its origin, but none is conclusive. Perhaps the most plausible suggests the source as **Waterloo**, a trade name for iron cisterns in the early 20th century. A popular but unlikely one, not least because of the discrepancy in dates, refers it to **gardyloo**, a cry used in 18th-century Edinburgh to warn passers-by that someone was about to throw dirty water or slops out of a window into the street. It is based on pseudo-French *gar de l'eau* 'mind the water' (real French would be *gare l'eau*). Another French phrase is behind a third suggestion, that British servicemen in France during the First World War picked up *lieux d'aisances* 'places of ease', used for 'a toilet'.

loose

The medieval word **loose** is related to **lose** and **loss** and also to the ending **-less**, signifying 'without'. The sense 'immoral, promiscuous' dates from around 1470. The term **a loose cannon** for someone unpredictable or likely to cause unintentional trouble sounds as though it could be centuries old, perhaps deriving from the days of warships in Napoleonic battles. In fact, the first recorded uses are from the late 19th century, and the phrase only really gained currency in the 1970s. That said, it does originate from the idea that a cannon which has broken loose from its mounting would be a particularly dangerous hazard on any ship, but especially a wooden one. See also FAST.

loot

Like THUG, the word **loot** has its origins in the experience of the British in India. Soldiers picked it up for 'valuables plundered from an enemy' from their Hindi-speaking counterparts – it goes back to a word meaning 'to rob' in Sanskrit, the ancient language of northern India. The slang sense 'money' developed in the 1940s, and was used by Joe Orton as the title of his play *Loot* in 1965.

lord

The root meaning of **lord** was 'keeper of bread'. Old English *hlafweard*, from which the modern word developed, comes from early forms of LOAF and WARD.

antidisestablishmentarianism

(deprived of its official status). The latter, used since around 1900, is occasionally found in genuine use, but it is most often cited simply as an example of a very long word.

Other similar curiosities are floccinaucinihilipilification, 'the action or habit of estimating something as worthless', and pneumonoultramicroscopicsilicovolcanoconiosis (the longest word in the *Oxford English Dictionary*), which is said to mean a lung disease caused by inhaling fine ash and sand dust, but has never been a real medical term. The formal systematic names of chemicals are almost unlimited in length, but the longer examples are often sprinkled with numerals, Greek letters and other non-alphabetic symbols.

The longest word that you might encounter in Britain is the Welsh place name Llanfairpwllgwyngyllgogerychwyrndrobwllllantysiliogogogoch, generally abbreviated to *Llanfair PG*, which translates as 'The church of St Mary in the hollow of white hazel trees near the rapid whirlpool by St Tysilio's of the red cave'. It was created in the 19th century in an attempt to get publicity for the Anglesey village.

icsilicovolcanoconiosis

Straight from the heart

The great lovers of history and literature always seem to be male, and their names have often become bywords for amorous behaviour. Women are more likely to have been portrayed as dangerous temptresses.

A passionate lover or seducer can be a Romeo but not a Juliet. The saint of lovers is also a man. Valentine was the name of two early Italian martyrs, who may have been the same person – a Roman priest martyred in around 269, and a bishop of Terni, Umbria, who died around the same time. St Valentine's Day, February 14, became associated with lovers in the Middle Ages, perhaps because of an old belief that birds mate on that day. The chosen or allotted person has been someone's valentine since the late Middle Ages.

Probably the most famous seducer was the Italian writer, soldier, spy, musician and diplomat Giovanni Jacopo Casanova (1725-98), whose memoirs described his sexual exploits and led to an amorous man being called a Casanova. Other great lovers were fictional characters. Don Juan was a legendary Spanish nobleman who first appeared in a story written in the early 17th century, but who is best known from Lord Byron's poetic romance *Don Juan* (1819-24).

The Fair Penitent was a tragedy in blank verse by Nicholas Rowe, produced in 1703. It was a great success, and the name of one of its characters, 'the haughty, gallant, gay Lothario', became proverbial. The dramatist Sir William Davenant had used the name Lothario for a similar character in *The Cruel Brother* of 1630, but it is Rowe's Lothario who entered the language.

A man with many lovers may be called a philanderer. In Greek *philandros* meant 'loving or fond of men', and often appeared as a name for a lover in stories, perhaps because people wrongly thought it signified 'a loving man'. From the 17th century Philander was used in English as a name for a lover and later for a male flirt or seducer, and flirtatious behaviour or seduction by men became philandering in the mid 18th century.

Famous female lovers tend to be seductive femmes fatales like Mata Hari, a Dutch exotic dancer and secret agent born Margaretha Zelle. In the First World War she probably worked as an agent for both sides, and in 1917 she was arrested and shot by the French. After her death she became a legend, largely on account of the film *Mata Hari* (1931), starring Greta Garbo.

In the Old Testament Jezebel was a princess from Phoenicia (modern-day Lebanon and Syria) who married Ahab, King of Israel, and persuaded him to worship her god, Baal. She is described as 'painting her face' or putting on make-up, which was regarded as shocking in 16th-century England and led to a shameless or immoral woman being known as a Jezebel. In the 1938 film *Jezebel*, Bette Davis plays an 1850s Southern Belle whose unconventional and provocative behaviour, including wearing a red dress to a society ball, earns her the epithet of the title.

See also SIREN.

The corresponding female form is LADY, in Old English *hlafdige* 'kneader of bread'.

The Devil has many names, among them **Lord of the Flies**, the literal meaning of the Hebrew form **Beelzebub**. In 1954 William Golding published his first novel, *Lord of the Flies*, in which a group of schoolboys marooned on an uninhabited tropical island revert to savagery and primitive ritualistic behaviour.

lottery
In Britain the National Lottery was introduced in 1994, with the slogan 'It could be you!' Cynics pointed out that the odds against winning a significant prize were so high that the lottery was in effect a tax on stupidity, in

which they were echoing the novelist Henry Fielding, who said in 1732: 'A lottery is a taxation / Upon all the fools in creation.' In his gloomy forecast of the future *Nineteen Eighty-four*, written in 1948, George Orwell said: 'The Lottery, with its weekly pay-out of enormous prizes, was the one public event to which the proles paid serious attention . . . It was their delight, their folly, their anodyne [painkiller], their intellectual stimulant.' **Lottery** probably came into English from Dutch *loterij*, but it is related to the Old English word **lot**.

lotus
The works of the ancient Greek poet Homer gave us **lotus**. It appears as a type of clover which Homer

described as food for horses, and also as a plant whose fruit sent all who ate it into a state of dreamy forgetfulness, with no desire to return home. People who succumbed to its temptation were the **lotus-eaters** (or more closely following the Greek, the **lotos-eaters**). 'The Lotos-Eaters', based on the Homeric story, is one of the best-known poems of Lord Tennyson.

Two large water lilies are also called **lotus**, the red-flowered **sacred lotus** of Asia, and the white or blue-flowered **Egyptian lotus**. The former gives its name to the **lotus position** for meditation, with the legs crossed and the feet resting on the thighs.

love

As you might expect, **love** is almost as old as time. The word's ancient root is also the source of Latin *lubido* 'desire' (which gave us **libido**) and of *lubhyati* 'desires' in Sanskrit, the ancient language of India.

Reflections on love could fill a book. That **love is blind** goes back to classical times, but first appeared in 14th-century English in Geoffrey Chaucer's *Canterbury Tales*. Lewis Carroll seems to have been the first to use **love makes the world go round**, in *Alice's Adventures in Wonderland* (1865) – he may have based it on a French folk song with the lines *c'est lamour, l'amour, l'amour, Qui fait la monde à la ronde*, 'it is love, love, love that makes the world go round'. In 1967 the Beatles sang 'All You Need is Love', and a slogan associated with the weepie film *Love Story* (1970) was 'Love means never having to say you're sorry'.

The love that dare not speak its name is homosexuality. The description is by the poet Lord Alfred Douglas, whose association with Oscar Wilde led to Wilde being imprisoned in Reading gaol for homosexual activity.

The use of **love** in tennis and squash for a score of zero apparently derives from the phrase to **play for love**, that is for the love of the game, not for money. A popular explanation connects it with French *l'oeuf* 'egg', from the resemblance in shape between an egg and a zero. See also DUCK, LUVVY.

lovely jubbly

In the BBC television series *Only Fools and Horses* Del Boy, played by David Jason, expresses pleasure or approval by uttering the words **lovely jubbly**. The writer of the series, John Sullivan, adopted the phrase from **lubbly Jubbly**, a 1950s advertising slogan for Jubbly, a frozen orange-flavoured soft drink.

I WAS UNLUCKY IN CARDS AND IN LOVE... I GOT THE JOKER BOTH TIMES!

luck

The native English word for the power or agency which determines events was WEIRD. **Destiny** came later from French, FATE from Italian and **luck** in the late Middle Ages from German. As soon as you had **luck**, you could be **lucky** – and unlucky. The idea of **lucky at cards, unlucky in love** is already commonplace in Jonathan Swift's *Polite Conversation* in 1738: 'Well, Miss, you'll have a sad husband, you have such good luck at cards.'

Luddite

In the second decade of the 19th century workers in English cotton and woollen mills believed that the use of machinery was threatening their jobs. Bands of men joined to destroy machinery, and it was said that their leader was a Captain Ludd. Another story described how Ned Lud smashed up a weaver's frames in a Leicestershire village around 1779. Whoever Ludd or Lud was, if indeed he existed, the opponents of mechanisation had the name **Luddite** by 1811.

lumber

The earliest **lumber** in English meant 'to move in a slow, heavy, awkward way'. Its origin is not known, but its form may have been intended to suggest clumsiness or heaviness, rather like **lump**. This may have been the origin of **lumber** in the sense 'disused furniture and articles that take up space', but people also associated the term with the old word **lumber** meaning 'a pawnbroker's shop', which was an alteration of **Lombard** or 'person from Lombardy in northern Italy'. The mainly North American sense 'timber sawn into rough planks' appears to be a development of the 'disused furniture' meaning, as is the verb to **be lumbered** or burdened with something unwanted. The slang phrase **in lumber**, 'in trouble', originally meant 'in pawn, pawned'.

lunatic

It was once believed that the changes of the moon brought on intermittent insanity in some people. Such an unfortunate was called a **lunatic**, from Latin *luna* 'moon'. Medical and legal professionals no longer use the term, but ordinary people may well still call someone extremely foolish or eccentric a lunatic. See also MAD.

lunch

Until the 19th century a light midday meal was a **luncheon**, and when the shortened form **lunch** appeared in the 1820s people regarded it as either lower-class or a fashionable affectation. Nowadays it is **luncheon** that sounds formal or affected, and **lunch** that is the standard term. **Luncheon** was probably derived from Spanish *lonja* 'slice'. See also LADY, SUPPER.

The modern proverb **there's no such thing as a free lunch**, 'you never get something for nothing', was first used in the 1960s among US economists. It was probably suggested by the practice, dating from the mid 19th century, of some bars providing free lunch if you bought a drink. **Lunch is for wimps** was a saying favoured by the ruthless Gordon Gekko, played by Michael Douglas, in the 1987 film *Wall Street*. Gekko also said 'Greed – for lack of a better word – is good. Greed is right. Greed works', which is now often rendered as **greed is good**.

lurch

The **lurch** in **leave someone in the lurch**, 'to leave an associate without support when they need it', derives from French *lourche*, the name of a 16th-century game resembling backgammon. As well as a game, **lurch** then was a score or state of play in which one player was enormously ahead of the other. The unsteady, uncontrolled **lurch** is a different word – it was originally a sailors' term which described the sudden leaning of a ship to one side.

lurgy

In the 1950s and 1960s the crazy radio comedy series *The Goon Show* introduced the world to **the dreaded lurgy**, a fictitious highly infectious disease. The Goons themselves spelled it **lurgi**. It is not clear whether they invented it or not – one theory holds that it was taken from **allergy**, but there are words in English dialect which may have inspired it. In Derbyshire **the lurgies** were a feeling of depression experienced after having drunk too much, while in northern England to be **lurgy** was to be lazy – 'lurgy fever' was laziness or idleness. See also GOON.

luvvy

One caricature of actors is that they all gushingly call each other 'love'. In the late 20th century an actor, or anyone actively involved in entertainment, came to be a **luvvie**. 'Luvvies', featuring over-the-top quotations from theatrical types mainly sent in by readers, is a regular feature of the British satirical magazine *Private Eye*. The word itself is a respelling of **lovey**, an affectionate term of address used since the mid 18th century. See also THESPIAN.

luxury

Nowadays most people would love to live a life of luxury, but originally they would have condemned it. From the Middle Ages to the early 19th century **luxury** was 'lust, lasciviousness' – the Latin source *luxuria* also implied indulgence as a vice – and the modern English sense 'great comfort or elegance' was not used until the mid 17th century.

lynch

During the War of American Independence (1775-83) a Captain William Lynch of Pittsville, Virginia, headed a self-constituted court with no legal authority which persecuted 'Tories', or people who supported the British side. People called this illegal punishment **Lynch's law** or **lynch law**. The penalties handed out were beatings or tarring and feathering, but by the mid 19th century to **lynch** a supposed offender was generally to hang him.

macabre

One of the medieval miracle plays presented the slaughter of the Maccabees, family members and supporters of Judus Maccabaeus, who led a religious revolt in Judaea in 165 BC. This gruesome event probably gave rise to **macabre**, 'disturbing, horrifying', originally in the phrase **dance of macabre**, a term for the dance of death (see DEATH). The name Maccabaeus, where all this started, may come from a Hebrew word meaning 'hammer'.

macaroni

When 'Yankee Doodle went to town a-riding on a pony' and 'stuck a feather in his hat and called it macaroni', he was not confusing his headgear with pasta. He was presenting himself as a dandy – completely unconvincingly, and deliberately referring to the English view of Americans, then still under British colonial rule, as lacking sophistication. In 18th-century Britain the macaronis were a group of young men who had travelled abroad and exaggeratedly imitated continental fashions. The pasta dish pre-dated and outlived this trend. Its name also survives in **macaroon**, which came through French, changing its recipe on the way. Italian *macaroni* goes back to Greek *makaria* 'food made from barley'. See also PASTE.

Machiavellian

Niccolò di Bernardo dei Machiavelli was an Italian statesman and scholar who lived from 1469 to 1527. His best-known work is *The Prince*, translated into English in 1532 and highly influential in Tudor and Elizabethan politics. *The Prince* advises rulers that the acquisition and effective use of power may necessitate unethical methods that are undesirable in themselves. People simplified and exaggerated his ideas, and his name became a byword for unscrupulous, deceitful and cunning methods. The word **Machiavellian** immortalises him.

macho

To Mexicans a *macho* man was originally one admired for his vigour and virility. But when English-speaking Americans adopted the word from Mexican Spanish in the 1920s it acquired overtones of 'masculine in an overly assertive or aggressive way'. The Spanish word *macho* derives from Latin *masculus* 'male', the source of **masculine**.

mad

In English **mad** has always meant 'insane'. In extreme cases a person can be **as mad as a hatter** or **as mad as a March hare**. The comparison with hatters has a sound scientific basis: in the past some hatters, or hat-makers, really did become mentally ill. Felt hats were made from fur, and one of the processes in their manufacture involved brushing a solution of mercurous nitrate on to the fur to make the fibres mat together. As a result of inhaling the mercury fumes some hat-makers suffered from mercury poisoning, a nasty condition which can produce symptoms such as confused speech, hallucination and loss of memory. The phrase **as mad as a hatter** was around in the 1830s, but from 1865 it was popularised by one of the characters in Lewis Carroll's *Alice's Adventures in Wonderland*, the Mad Hatter. The equivalent comparison **as mad as a March hare** arose from the excitable behaviour of hares at the beginning of the breeding season

'Mad Dogs and Englishmen / Go out in the midday sun' is the beginning of the 1931 song 'Mad Dogs and Englishmen' by the English dramatist, actor and composer Noël Coward. He also wrote the song 'Mad about the Boy'.

The word **madding** is a rather poetic way of saying 'acting madly'. It is most familiar through the phrase **far from the madding crowd**, 'private or secluded'. Many will associate it with the title of one of Thomas Hardy's classic novels, but Hardy took the title from a line in Thomas Gray's poem 'Elegy Written in a Country Church-Yard', published in 1751: 'Far from the madding crowd's ignoble strife'.

When Lady Caroline Lamb met Lord Byron at a ball in 1812 she called him **'Mad, bad and dangerous to know'**. The poet is one of the few people to have an adjective to themselves – a **Byronic** man is alluringly dark, moody and mysterious.

madonna

In Italian *madonna* means 'my lady' – the second element goes back to Latin *domina* 'mistress', the root of which also gave us DAME, DANGER, **dominate**, DOMINION and DUNGEON. At first in English it was used as a title or mock title for an Italian woman, but in the 17th century **the Madonna** began to refer to the Virgin Mary. Madonna is the actual given name of the equally famous pop star and actress: her full name is Madonna Louise Ciccone.

maelstrom

Maelstrom was a mythical whirlpool supposed to exist in the Arctic Ocean, west of Norway, and to suck in all ships from a wide radius. Although it was just a traveller's tale, the name, which came from Dutch *maalen* 'to grind, whirl' and *stroom* 'stream', appeared on maps, and now a **maelstrom** is a powerful whirlpool or a situation of violent turmoil.

mafia

The first printed reference to the **Mafia** dates from 1866. The secret criminal society originated in Sicily – in Sicilian dialect *mafia* meant 'bragging'. Other communities harboured similar organisations: a **Chinese mafia** is reported in California in 1891 and a **Russian mafia** in 1903, and by the 1940s any group regarded as exerting a secret and sinister influence could be given the name. See also GOD.

magazine

The first **magazines** were storehouses, often for arms, ammunition and provisions for war. The word comes from Italian *magazzino* and goes back to Arabic. From the mid 17th century books providing information useful to particular groups of people often had **magazine** in their title. The use for a periodical publication providing a range of stories and articles developed from this: the first was *The Gentleman's magazine; or, Monthly Intelligencer*, launched in 1731.

Military uses of the word developed alongside the cultural strand. A container for holding a supply of cartridges to be fed automatically into the breech of a gun came to be called a magazine in the 1860s.

maggot

Around 2003 a photograph circulated on the internet purporting to show a man with **maggots in the brain**. The maggots were just an urban myth – one story said that the condition resulted from eating the Japanese raw-fish dish sashimi; another that it resulted from swimming in water where parasitic fish could enter the urinary tract (the candiru, a small catfish of the Amazon basin, does occasionally do this). The scare was new, but not the idea. When the Gothic novelist Charlotte Dacre published *Zofloya, or the Moor* in 1806, with its plot of murder and a Satanic lover, a reviewer pronounced that she must be 'afflicted with the dismal malady of maggots in the brain'. **Maggot** is probably an alteration of the earlier word **maddock**, meaning 'maggot' or 'earthworm', influenced by *Maggot* or *Magot*, pet forms of the names Margery or Margaret.

magic

The Magi were the 'wise men' from the East who visited the infant Jesus soon after his birth. They were said to have been kings named Caspar, Melchior and Balthasar who brought gifts of gold, frankincense and myrrh. A **magus** was a member of a priestly caste of ancient Persia, and the word, filtered through Greek and Latin, is the origin of our **magic** and **magician**.

magpie see PIE.

maiden

The ancient root of **maiden** is also that of Scottish and Irish Gaelic *mac* 'son', the element in surnames beginning **Mac-** or **Mc-**, and seems to have referred to a young person of either sex. In the Middle Ages **maiden** was also shortened to **maid**, and the two continued alongside each other, both meaning 'a young female' and 'a virgin of any age', and also 'a female servant', for which **maid** is now the usual term. This ambiguity led to words and phrases such as GIRL or **young lady** replacing **maiden** and **maid** in the 'young female' sense.

Cricketers trying to bowl a **maiden over** are hoping to ensure that no runs are scored from the six balls they are bowling. The idea, dating from the 1850s, is that the over is 'virgin' or 'unproductive'.

mail

Modern English has two different words spelled **mail**, both dating from the Middle Ages. The **mail** that refers to the postal system came immediately from French, but is related to Dutch *maal* meaning 'wallet, bag'. This is also the oldest sense in English, and **mails** in the USA and Scotland is still a term for baggage. The use of a postal service arose in the mid 17th century from the bag in which letters and packages were carried. From there it developed to the contents of the bag – 'an item delivered' is the origin of newspaper titles such as the *Daily Mail*. At the same time **mail** also came to apply to a person or vehicle delivering letters and packages, and then to the postal system itself. British usage favours POST for both the system and the material delivered, while **mail** is dominant in North America and Australia. For electronic messages, though, **mail** and **email** are universal – the ordinary post is **snail mail**.

In **coat of mail** the word came from Latin *macula* 'stain, blemish, mesh of a net', seen also in IMMACULATE. Originally it referred to the individual metal rings or plates that make up the armour, so a knight would have worn a **coat of mails**. See also BLACKMAIL.

malapropism

'As headstrong as an allegory [alligator] on the banks of the Nile' and 'He is the very pineapple [pinnacle] of politeness' are some of the confused words of Mrs Malaprop, a character in *The Rivals*, a comedy by Richard Sheridan produced in 1775. Her most notable characteristic is an aptitude to misapply long words. The play was a great success, and the character clearly memorable, giving English the **malapropism**. See also SPOONERISM.

malaria

Before people understood that **malaria** was transmitted by mosquitoes, they attributed the disease to an unwholesome condition of the atmosphere in marshy districts. It was particularly prevalent in Italy, and especially near Rome. In a letter of 1740 the writer and statesman Horace Walpole wrote of 'A horrid thing called the mal'aria, that comes to Rome every summer and kills one'. Italian *mal'aria* is a contraction of *mala aria* 'bad air'.

male see FEMALE.

malice

Some people undoubtedly harboured a desire to harm each other before the 14th century, but it was not called **malice**. The word is an Old French one that is first found in English around 1320 and goes back to Latin *malus* 'bad', the source also of **malign** and **malaise**. Since the 15th century **malice** has been a legal term, found especially in **malice aforethought**, the intention to kill or harm which distinguishes murder from manslaughter.

mall

The game pall-mall was popular in the 17th century. Players used a mallet to drive a boxwood ball through an iron ring suspended at the end of a long alley, itself also called a pall-mall. Pall Mall, a street in central London known for its large number of private clubs and formerly a fashionable place to promenade, was originally a pall-mall for the game. From the 18th century other sheltered places for walking came to be called malls – the first reference to a **mall** for shopping dates from 1950 in the USA.

mammoth

In Siberia people used to dig up fossil remains and frozen carcasses of a large elephant-like hairy mammal with long curved tusks. They called this in Russian the *mamont*, which probably came from a Siberian word meaning 'earth horn'. In the early 18th century English acquired this as **mammoth**. The word began to refer to anything of a huge size in the early 19th century. See also COLOSSAL.

man of the cloth

A **man of the cloth** has not always been a clergyman. Before the mid 17th century he could work in other occupations, notably the law and the military, with a special dress code or uniform – the person's 'cloth'. The writer Jonathan Swift first used 'the cloth' to refer only to the clergy in 1710.

man

The English word **man** goes back to an age-old root that also gave *manu*, 'humankind', in Sanskrit, the ancient language of India. From Anglo-Saxon times **man** meant both 'a person of either sex' and 'an adult male', as well as referring to the human race in general.

Shakespeare's *Hamlet* provided the phrase **man and boy**, 'throughout life from youth', when the gravedigger says, 'I have been sexton here, man and boy, for thirty years.' The original **man for all seasons** was Sir Thomas More, the scholar and statesman who wrote *Utopia* and was beheaded for opposing Henry VIII's marriage to Anne Boleyn. The name came into prominence in 1960 as the title of a play about More by Robert Bolt.

The use of **man** for humans in general survives in proverbs and in phrases such as **the man in the street**. The judge Lord Bowen, who died in 1894, used **the man on the Clapham omnibus** (Clapham is a district of south London) to refer to any ordinary reasonable person, such as a juror is expected to be.

Man cannot live by bread alone is found in two passages of the Bible, one from the Old Testament, in Deuteronomy, and the other from the New, in the Gospel of Matthew. The proverb **man proposes,**

God disposes goes back to the 15th century, but also reflects a 14th-century French saying. The ancient Greek philosopher Plato provided a precedent for **man is the measure of all things**, recorded in English from the mid 16th century.

As a way of addressing someone, **man** goes right back to the Anglo-Saxons and was common in the 18th and 19th centuries, although the old uses tended to sound impatient or encouraging – 'Pick up your feet, man!' The modern use of **man!**, often expressing surprise, admiration or delight, came from the speech of black Americans. See also MOUSE.

manage

Managers now manage businesses, organisations and staff, but the first things to be managed were horses. The earliest sense of **manage** in English was 'to handle or train a horse', or put it through the exercises of the **manège**. This French word, used in English to mean 'an area in which horses and riders are trained' and 'horsemanship', is at root the same word as **manage** – both go back through Italian to Latin *manus* 'hand', the source also of **manicure, manipulate**, MANNER, MANOEUVRE, **manual** and **manuscript**.

mandarin

Few words can claim such different meanings as a language, a fruit, and a civil servant, but **mandarin** can. A mandarin was an official in a senior grade of the former imperial Chinese civil service. The word is not Chinese, though, but came into English from Portuguese in the late 16th century, and goes back to a term meaning 'counsellor, minister' in Sanskrit. The use of **mandarin** for a leading civil servant in Britain, as in 'Whitehall mandarins', dates from the early 19th century.

In 1703 Francisco Varo published his *Arte de la Lengua Mandarina*, the first grammar of any spoken form of Chinese, which described the Chinese used by officials and educated people in general. In 1728 **Mandarin** first appeared in English, and it is now the name for the standard and official form of Chinese.

Mandarin was first applied to a citrus fruit in Swedish. The reason for the name is not certain – it might refer to the colour of Chinese officials' silk robes, or to the high quality of the delicious little oranges. A translation of a Swedish travelogue introduced the **mandarin orange** to English in 1771.

manger

In Christianity the **manger** is a symbol for the birth of Jesus, as told in the Gospel of Luke: 'And she brought forth her firstborn son, and wrapped him in swaddling clothes, and laid him in a manger; because there was no room for them in the inn.' This word for an animal's feeding trough goes back through Old French *manger* 'to eat' (seen also in **mangetout** and BLANCMANGE) to Latin *manducare* 'to chew'. The name of the skin disease **mange** has a very similar origin. It causes intense itching, and another meaning of *manger* was 'to itch'. See also DOG.

manner

Latin *manus* 'hand' is ultimately the source of **manner**, as it is of MANAGE and many other words. The first sense was 'sort, kind', followed by 'usual practice or behaviour' and then 'customary rules of behaviour in society' and (in the plural) 'polite or well-bred social behaviour' – the kind of **manners** that parents try to teach their children.

The phrase **as if to the manner born**, 'naturally at ease in a particular job or situation', derives from a passage in Shakespeare's *Hamlet*. The British television series *To the Manor Born*, starring Penelope Keith, played on this to refer to someone with aristocratic origins, contrasting with a member of the nouveau riche, and was so popular that this is now often mistaken for the correct form of the phrase.

manoeuvre

Soldiers, sailors and farmers come together in the words **manoeuvre** and **manure**, which share the Latin origin *manu operari* 'to work with the hand', from *manus* 'hand' (see MANAGE). The earliest sense of **manoeuvre**, which came from modern French in the mid 18th century, was 'a planned movement of military or naval forces'. An earlier form of French gave us **manure** in the late Middle Ages. Then it had the senses 'to till or cultivate land' and 'to administer or manage land or property' – the use for dung or compost dates from the mid 16th century.

mansion

The rich person's **mansion** and the minister's **manse** have the same origin. They both derive from Latin *mansio* 'place where someone stays', from *manere* 'to stay' (the source of **remain**). A mansion was originally the home of a medieval lord of the manor, but the word later extended to any large, impressive house. 'The principal house of an estate' was also the original sense of **manse**; it became increasingly restricted to an ecclesiastical residence, and is now a house occupied by a Church of Scotland or other Nonconformist minister. A **son** or **daughter of the manse** (like the Labour politician Gordon Brown) is a child of a Church of Scotland minister. See also PALACE.

marathon

In 490 BC the Athenians won a victory over an invading Persian army at Marathon on the coast of Attica in eastern Greece. The Greek historian Herodotus described how the herald Pheidippides ran the 150 miles from Athens to Sparta to get help before the battle. According to a later tradition a messenger ran from Marathon to Athens, a distance of 22 miles, with news of the victory, but fell dead on arrival. The first modern Olympic games in 1896 instituted the **marathon** as a long-distance race – fortunately for competitors, based on the shorter version of the story. The present standardised distance of 26 miles 385yd (42.195km) dates from 1924.

marble

The name **marble** goes back to Greek *marmaros* 'shining stone', a limestone used for building and sculpture. The small balls of the children's game have been called marbles since the late 17th century, though they are now mostly made of glass. In the game players take turns at shooting their own marble, with finger and thumb, at marbles inside a ring, trying to knock the marbles out of the ring to win them. Some players lose some or all of their marbles – the idea behind **marbles** as a term for someone's mental faculties.

march

There are three English words **march**, if you include **March**. The **march** with the sense 'to walk in a military manner' came from French *marcher* 'to walk' in the late Middle Ages. If you **march to a different tune** you consciously adopt a different approach or attitude to the majority of people. The variant **march to a different drummer** was inspired by an observation from the 19th-century US essayist and poet Henry David Thoreau: 'If a man does not keep pace with his companions, perhaps it is because he hears a different drummer.'

Another **march** means 'the border or frontier of a country', now found mainly in the geographical term **the Marches**, used for the area of land on the border of England and Wales, such as the counties of Shropshire and Monmouthshire. It too came from French, but is probably related to **mark**, from the idea of 'marking' boundaries.

The month is named after Mars, the Roman god of war, and was originally the first month of the Roman calendar. Weather lore tells us that **March comes in like a lion, and goes out like a lamb** – traditionally the weather is wild at the beginning of March, but fair and settled by the end. The name of the god Mars is also the source of **martial**, 'relating to fighting or war', which entered English in the late Middle Ages. The **martial arts**, sports such as judo, karate and kendo, originated in Japan, China and Korea and first came to European attention in the late 19th century, though the general term **martial arts** is not recorded until 1920. See also MAD.

marine

The root of **marine** is Latin *mare* 'sea', the source also of **mariner**, **maritime** and **mermaid**. Marines were originally any men serving on board a ship, but later the meaning was restricted to troops who were trained to serve on land or sea, now particularly the Royal Marines or, in the USA, the Marine Corps.

These facts shed little light on the likely source of **tell that to the marines**, used to express disbelief. It may have begun with a remark made by Charles II. He advised that implausible tales should be checked out with sailors, who, being familiar with distant lands, might be the people best qualified to judge whether they were true or not. Another idea picks up a clue left in the longer version **tell that to the horse marines**. The horse marines were an imaginary troop of cavalry soldiers serving on board a ship, used as an image of total ineptitude or of people completely out of their natural element. The idea is that such people are so clueless that they will believe anything they are told.

marmalade

Oranges were not the original fruit in **marmalade**. Early marmalade was a solid quince jelly that was cut into squares for eating, rather than spread on toast – in 1524 King Henry VIII was given 'a box of marmalade'. The word is recorded in English in the late 15th century, and comes from Portuguese *marmelada* 'quince jam'. The Scots are generally credited with inventing the kind of marmalade we are familiar with, and the first marmalade factory was built in Dundee in 1797, by the Keiller family.

maroon

The Maroons were descendants of runaway slaves who lived in the mountains and forests of Suriname and the West Indies. Their name came from French *marron* 'feral', from Spanish *cimarrón* 'wild'. In the 18th century to **maroon** someone

The colour maroon began with the reddish-brown fruit of the chestnut.

became to put them down on a desolate island or coast and to leave them there, especially as a punishment. None of this has anything to do with the colour **maroon**, which derives from French *marron* 'chestnut'. The earliest examples of **maroon** in English, from the late 16th century, refer to this lustrous reddish-brown nut, with the colour dating from the late 18th century. The noise of a chestnut bursting in a fire accounts for **maroon** as the name of a firework that makes a loud bang, often with a bright flash of light, used as a signal or warning.

marry

Both **marry** and **marriage** derive from Old French *marier* 'to marry', which goes back to Latin *maritus* 'a husband', source also of **marital**. Traditional advice on marriage includes **marry in haste and repent at leisure**, from the late 16th century, and **never marry for money, but marry where money is**, first formulated in Lord Tennyson's poem 'Northern Farmer, New Style' (1870).

A **marriage of convenience** is one concluded to achieve a practical purpose. The essayist Joseph Addison used the expression in the early 18th century, translating French *mariage de convenance*. Whatever

the married state, we have been assured since the mid 16th century that **marriages are made in heaven**, and since the mid 17th that **marriage is a lottery**.

marzipan

The sugary paste used on cakes has taken an exotic journey starting at the port of Martaban on the coast of southeast Burma (Myanmar), once famous for exporting glazed jars containing preserves and sweets. In the course of a long trek through Persian and Arabic into European languages, the name Martaban emerged as Italian *marzapane*, with a shift of meaning from the container to its contents. From the 16th to the 19th centuries the usual form in English was **marchpane**. Only in the 19th century, when English reborrowed the Italian word, did **marzipan** become established.

mascara

Acting and clowning are indirectly linked in **mascara**, from Italian *maschera*, which goes back to an Arabic word meaning 'buffoon'. Most of the earliest English uses refer to theatrical make-up, though the first known, from 1886, suggests a more discreet use by gentlemen: 'For darkening the eyebrows and moustaches without greasing them and making them prominent'. Through Italian *maschera* **mascara** is also linked to **mask** and **masquerade**.

mascot

The French operetta *La Mascotte* by Edmond Audran had its première on December 29, 1880. The following year the word made its first appearance in English. French *mascotte* derives from *masco* 'witch' in the language of southern France. At first **mascot** meant simply 'a person or thing supposed to bring good luck' and did not have to be carried or displayed, as now. See also TALISMAN.

mash

Brewing provides the earliest context of **mash**. The mash is a mixture of ground malt and hot water which is left to stand until the sugars from the malt dissolve to form the infusion called 'wort'. The first example of **mash** meaning 'mashed potatoes' is from 1904, by the British novelist and MP A.E.W. Mason: 'I . . . go into a public-house . . . and have a sausage and mash and a pot of beer.' The word may ultimately be related to **mix**.

As an abbreviation for 'mobile army surgical hospital' **MASH** goes back to 1950. The term was made famous in the 1970 film *M*A*S*H*, directed by Robert Altman and set in a field hospital during the Korean War. The film gave rise to a long-running TV series (1972-83) featuring Alan Alda.

masochism

Sexual pleasure derived from pain features in several of the stories by the 19th-century Austrian writer Leopold von Sacher-Masoch. The German term *Masochismus* was used in 1890, and by 1892 English had adopted it as **masochism**. See also SADISM.

mason see FREE.

mass

There is no relation at all between **mass** 'a large body with no definite shape' and **Mass** 'the celebration of the Christian Eucharist'. The first goes back to Greek *maza* 'barley cake' and is related to **magma**, the hot fluid or semi-fluid material below the Earth's crust. The other derives ultimately from Latin *mittere* 'to dismiss, send', and so is connected with MESSAGE and **missive** as well as with words such as **admit** and **permit**. The use for the religious service may come from its last words in Latin, *Ite, missa est* 'Go, it is the dismissal'. Ordinary people have been called **the masses** since at least 1837, and they have been supplied with goods by **mass production** since 1893.

maudlin

St Mary Magdalene was a follower of Jesus, who cured her of evil spirits and appeared to her after his resurrection. Medieval artists traditionally depicted her weeping. **Maudlin** was the early English equivalent of her French name Madeleine, and from the early 16th century people applied **maudlin drunk** to the stage of drunkenness characterised by tearful sentimentality and effusive displays of affection. In the early 17th century they shortened this to simple **maudlin**, and soon applied it to tearful sentimentality with any cause.

maverick

In the middle of the 19th century Samuel Augustus Maverick owned such a large herd of cattle in Texas that he left the calves unbranded. People in the USA noted this unusual practice and began to use **maverick** for any unbranded calf or yearling. From the 1880s the word came to signify 'individualistic, unorthodox or independent-minded'.

May

Maia was one of the seven daughters of the Titan Atlas in Greek mythology. In Roman mythology she came to be identified with Maia Majesta, a goddess of fertility and of the spring, who is said to have given her name to the month of **May**. Since the late Middle Ages **may** has also been a name for hawthorn blossom or the hawthorn, which in Britain typically flowers in May.

Many people believe that the proverb warning us not to leave off old or warm clothes until the end of May, **ne'er cast a clout till May be out**, refers to hawthorn blossom, but the first recorded example makes it clear that the word applies to the month.

May Day has been known since the 13th century as a time for springtime festivities and the election of a pretty girl as **May queen** or **Queen of the May** to preside over them. In some countries it is now a holiday in honour of working people.

> **The international radio distress signal Mayday is a version of the French *m'aider*, short for *venez m'aider* 'come and help me'.**

mayhem

Between the 15th and 19th centuries **mayhem** was a crime which involved maiming a person so that they could no longer defend themselves. In origin the word is a form of **maim**, which came through French but whose ultimate origin is unknown. The modern sense 'violent or extreme disorder' originated in the USA in the 19th century.

mayonnaise

Most books say that **mayonnaise** comes via French *mahonnais* from Port *Mahon*, the capital of Minorca, which was taken by the French in 1756. The first reference is not found until 1808, though, when the success was hardly fresh in the French mind, and the spelling was with *-y-* rather than *-h-* from the beginning. The chef M.A. Carême, who lived from 1784 to 1833, explained the word as being from French *manier* 'to handle' and so referring to the method of preparation. It could also be a corruption of French *bayonnaise*, meaning 'from the town of Bayonne'.

the real McCoy

The source of this expression is far from clear. The trouble is that **McCoy** is a relatively common surname and so there are numerous candidates for the post of the original McCoy. The earliest example of the phrase, dating from 1856, is Scottish, uses the form **Mackay**, and describes a brand of whisky: 'a drappie [drop] o' the real McKay'. The distillers G. Mackay and Co. apparently adopted 'the Real Mackay' as an advertising slogan in 1870, and this was the form familiar to Robert Louis Stevenson, who used it to mean 'the genuine article' in a letter in 1883.

It seems clear that the expression was well established as **the real McKay** by the end of the 19th century, but in the early part of the next century most examples have

The boxer Charles 'Kid' McCoy – the real McCoy.

the **McCoy** spelling and are American. Possibly the most likely reason for this spelling change is one Norman Selby, also known as Charles 'Kid' McCoy. He was an American boxer who became welterweight champion in 1896 after knocking out Tommy Ryan, his sparring partner, to whom he had previously pretended to be ill and unfit. Apparently he often used this trick of feigning illness, only to appear fighting fit on the day itself, prompting commentators to wonder whether this was **the real McCoy**.

meal

Eating a meal of meal involves two distinct words. The **meal** meaning 'the edible part of any grain or pulse' goes back to an ancient root shared with Latin *molere* 'to grind', while the **meal** at which food is eaten has a root meaning 'to measure'. In Old English **meal** also meant 'a measure', a use which survives in **piecemeal** 'characterised by unsystematic partial measures taken over a period of time'. The expression to **make a meal of** dates from the early 17th century in the sense 'to take advantage of', but the notion 'to make something unduly laborious' goes back only to the 1960s.

The idea behind **mealy-mouthed**, 'afraid to speak frankly or straightforwardly', is of a person having their mouth full of meal and so being afraid to open it fully. It is first recorded in the 1570s, and probably comes from an old German proverb.

mean

The word **mean** means many things in English, and it would be mean not to say something about it, having the means to do so. The ancient root of **mean** 'to intend to convey' is related to MIND. The original meaning of **mean** 'not generous, small-minded' was 'common to two or more people', reflecting its ancient root, shared with Latin *communis* 'common' (see COMMON). Modern uses developed from 'low on the social scale' through 'inferior', while a complete reversal comes in the informal sense 'excellent', dating from the early 20th century. Use as a term of approval has a precursor in expressions involving a negative, **no mean . . .**: in the Bible St Paul declared 'I am . . . a Jew of Tarsus . . . a citizen of no mean city.' The mathematical use of **mean**, 'an average', goes back to Latin *medianus* 'middle', source also of **median**. This is the **mean** behind **means** 'a method', as in a **means to an end**, a thing that is not valued or important in itself but is useful in achieving an aim. See also END.

meander

The River Menderes in southwest Turkey rises in the Anatolian plateau and winds some 384km (240 miles) to the Aegean Sea. It was known in ancient times as the Maeander, and its winding course gave its name to **meander**.

meat

Meat is related to **mete**, an old word meaning 'to measure', and both go back to a ancient root shared with **meditate**. The earliest sense of **meat** was simply 'food'. This survives in the proverb **one man's meat is another man's poison**, which is recorded in English from the late 16th century but has a parallel in the work of the Roman poet and philosopher Lucretius of the 1st century BC. Other early meanings include 'an item of food', now found only in **sweetmeat**. See also FLESH.

mechanical

Both **mechanical** and **machine** go back to Greek *mēkhanikē* 'machine'. Originally **mechanical** and **mechanic** were more or less interchangeable, but nowadays the first primarily means 'operated by or relating to a machine' or 'done without thought, automatic', and the second refers to a skilled worker. An old meaning of both is 'a manual labourer or artisan', as in 'A crew of patches, rude mechanicals, / That work for bread, upon Athenian stalls' from Shakespeare's *A Midsummer Night's Dream* (**rude** here means 'unsophisticated' rather than 'bad-mannered').

medley

A **medley** was originally a fight, and is the same word as **melee**, 'a confused fight or scuffle'. The source is French, and goes back to Latin *misculare* 'to mix', the source of **mix** and related to **meddle**. The mixing and mingling of combatants in hand-to-hand fighting led to **medley** having a variety of uses that involve a mixture of parts: it was applied to a collection of songs or tunes performed as a continuous piece in the 17th century, and the swimming event with each part involving a different stroke appeared in the 1920s.

melancholy

According to the medieval theory of the four humours (see HUMOUR), **melancholy** or black bile caused depression. The word goes back to Greek *melankholia*, from *melas* 'black', the source of **melanin** and **melanoma**, and *kholē* 'bile', which is the source of **cholera**, **choleric** and **cholesterol**. Today it tends to refer to a pensive or moody sadness rather than deep depression.

Melba

We have all seen entertainers retire and make a comeback, or do numerous farewell performances. In Australia and New Zealand they would be said to **do a Melba**. At the beginning of the 20th century Dame Nellie Melba was one of the most famous opera singers in the world, and she continued to perform long after her official retirement. Melba was not her real name – she was born Helen Porter Mitchell near Melbourne in Australia, and took her stage name from that city.

Outside her native country many associate Dame Nellie's name with a number of dishes created in her honour by the French chef Georges-Auguste Escoffier. He is said to have devised the dish of ice cream and peaches with raspberry sauce that he called **peach Melba** in London around 1892, although the first known record is from 1909; in 1897, when Dame Nellie was ill and took to a plain diet, he apparently recommended very thin crisp toast, promptly dubbed **Melba toast** or **toast Melba**.

memory

English adopted the Latin word *memoria* twice, first directly from Latin in the Middle Ages as **memory**, then a little later through French as **memoir**. The earliest sense of **memoir** was 'a memorandum'; people's **memoirs**, either recording historical events or recounting their own lives, first appeared in the 17th century. Latin *memoria* is formed from *memor* 'mindful', which is also the source of **memorable** and **memorandum**. A 1903 song introduced the world to **Memory Lane**, while another song took the same title in 1924. In both lyrics people 'wandered', whereas nowadays we **take a trip down memory lane** when we indulge in pleasant or sentimental memories.

In medieval times and later, merchants, lawyers and diplomats would write **memorandum that . . .** at the head of a note of something to be remembered or a record of what had been done. In Latin *memorandum* means 'it is to be remembered', and is a form of *memorare* 'to bring to mind', which is also from *memor* 'mindful'. From the late 15th century people could also refer to a **memorandum**, a note recording something for future use or a written message in business or diplomacy.

menace

The root of **menace** is Latin *minae* 'threats'. The original English sense, which survives mainly in legal contexts, was also 'a threat' – the Larceny Act of 1861 made it a criminal offence to demand **money with menaces**, and the phrase has been used in subsequent Acts dealing with similar offences. In the sense 'a person or thing that threatens danger or catastrophe', **menace** is recorded from the mid 19th century, but has since progressively weakened to mean 'an inconvenience, an annoyance, a nuisance'.

Dennis the Menace made his first appearance in issue 452 of the comic *The Beano* on March 17, 1951. He has been causing trouble ever since.

menu

When people first used **menu** in English they treated it as a foreign word, printing it in italic type and perhaps pronouncing it in a 'French' way. The word means 'detailed list' in French, and is a use of *menu* 'small, detailed' from Latin *minutus* 'small', the source of MINUTE in the same sense and also of MINCE, **minutiae** 'small, precise or trivial details' and **diminish**. The application to a list of dishes available in a restaurant dates from the mid 19th century; by the 20th it was fully anglicised, and by the 1960s **menu** could also mean 'a list of facilities or commands displayed on a computer screen'.

mercury

Mercury was the Roman god of eloquence, skill, trading and thieving, and was the messenger of the gods. His name came from Latin *merx* 'merchandise', the source also of **market** and **merchant**. The Romans called a planet after him, and in later Latin *mercurius* was also the name of a silvery-white metal, liquid at room temperature. The use probably arose from the fluidity of the metal being likened to the rapid motion associated with the god. In English the metallic element was first called **mercury** in the Middle Ages – its earlier name was **quicksilver** (see QUICK).

mercy

In the Latin of the early Christian Church, *merces*, which had meant simply 'reward' in classical times, came to be used for 'heavenly reward' and also 'pity, favour'. These are the senses in which **mercy** first appears in the Middle Ages. The phrase to **be thankful for small mercies** is first recorded in Sir Walter Scott's novel *The Heart of Midlothian*, published in 1818.

mesmerise

The Austrian doctor Friedrich Anton Mesmer developed a therapeutic system for hypnotising patients by the exercise of a force which he called **animal magnetism**. Eventually the Austrian authorities accused him of fraud, and he left for France in 1778. His claims were still controversial, but his techniques had great popular appeal, and other practitioners developed them until ultimately they formed the basis of the modern practice of hypnosis. The American statesman and scientist Benjamin Franklin introduced the word **mesmerism** into English in 1784. In the sense 'to hypnotise', **mesmerise** appeared in the 1820s; it now has a less technical use, 'to capture the complete attention of someone'.

mess

Current senses of **mess**, 'a dirty or untidy state' and 'a confused situation full of problems', date only from the 19th century. Back in the Middle Ages a mess was 'a portion of food', and especially 'a portion of liquid or pulpy food'. This is the meaning in the phrase to **sell for a mess of pottage** (pottage is soup or stew), 'to sell something for a ridiculously small amount', which refers to the biblical story, told in Genesis, in which Esau sells his birthright to his brother Jacob.

At medieval banquets diners were divided into small groups, usually of four people, who sat together and were served from the same dishes. Such a group was also called a **mess**, which is still the case on board ship and in military canteens. From this developed the sense 'a place providing meals and recreational facilities for members of the armed forces', as in **the officers' mess**.

message

The root of **message** is a form of Latin *mittere* 'to send' that is the source of **Mass** (see MASS) and **missile** as well as of **messenger** and **dismiss**. The phrase to **shoot** (or **kill**) **the messenger**, 'to treat the bearer of bad news as if they were personally to blame for it', is recorded only from the 1960s, but breaking bad news has always been a thankless task. The idea occurs at least twice in Shakespeare – in *Coriolanus* there is reference to beating the messenger – and the ancient Greek dramatist Sophocles expressed it as 'No one loves the messenger who brings bad news.'

Messiah

In the Hebrew Bible the **Messiah** was the person who, it was promised, would be sent by God to usher in a new era of peace and harmony on Earth. The early Christians regarded Jesus as being the Messiah of the Hebrew prophecies and the saviour of humankind. The word Messiah comes ultimately from Hebrew *māsīah*, which literally meant 'anointed' – **Christ** was originally a Greek translation of this.

Monty Python's film *Life of Brian* caused a great deal of controversy when released in 1979, although it was intended to satirise politics and organised religion rather than poke fun at faith. In the film the Three Wise Men turn up at the wrong stable, and rather than hailing Jesus as the Son of God acclaim one Brian Cohen instead. Brian, played by Graham Chapman, never claims to be divine, but spends his life being pestered by people who think he is the Messiah. In an attempt to disperse a crowd of would-be worshippers his mother (Terry Jones) cries, 'He's not the Messiah, he's a very naughty boy!'

metal

The words **metal** and **mettle** were once the same. Both could refer to a physical material and to a quality. In the 17th century the quality came to be particularly 'vigour, spiritedness', originally of horses but later also referring to people. By the mid 18th century the form **mettle** was being restricted to this, and **metal** to the solid material. Their ultimate origin is Greek *metallon* 'mine, quarry, metal'.

metre

The French Revolution brought France the metric system, of which the **metre** is the fundamental unit. The French word *mètre* was taken from Greek *metron* 'measure' in 1791, and by 1797 the **metre** was mentioned in English. The word **metre** already existed for the rhythm of a piece of poetry – it also went back to Greek *metron*, but this time came through Latin in the Old English period.

mews

Nowadays if a person in Britain lives in a **mews** they are likely to have a fairly exclusive address, but before the 19th century they would have been in a stables, and originally in a cage or prison. In the Middle Ages a **mew** was a cage for a hawk, especially one that was moulting. The word comes ultimately from Latin *mutare* 'to change', source of **moult** and **mutation**. In the 14th century stables were built on the site of the royal hawk mews at Charing Cross in London, and from the 17th people also applied the name **mews** to other sets of stables built round an open space or alley, providing accommodation for carriages as well as horses. Developers then converted some of these stables and outhouses into living accommodation, and from the turn of the 19th century **mews** became an address.

the Midas touch

Midas was a legendary king of ancient Phrygia (modern-day Turkey). According to Greek legend he captured Silenus, the companion of the god Dionysus, but treated him well. Because he had treated his captive so kindly, Dionysus granted him one wish, and Midas asked to have the power of turning everything he touched into gold – **the Midas touch**. At first this seemed a marvellous gift to have, but Midas very soon realised that he would starve to death, as even his food and drink turned to gold. He prayed to have the gift taken away, and Dionysus, taking pity on him, told him that if he bathed in the River Pactolus the power would be washed away. The story may have originated as a way of accounting for the presence of gold particles in this river.

midriff

Bare midriffs are fashionable among many young women around Britain. The girls might not be too pleased to know that the second part of **midriff**, Old English *hrif* 'belly', goes back to the same root as Latin *corpus* 'body', the source of many English words, including **corporation**, one of whose meanings is 'a protruding abdomen'.

midwife

The original sense of **midwife** seems to have been 'a woman who is with the mother'. *Mid-* here is not connected to **middle**, but is an old word meaning 'with' that is related to Greek *meta* 'with', which appears in English words beginning **meta-**, such as **metabolism**, **metaphorical** and **metaphysics**. 'A woman' (rather than 'a married woman') is the oldest sense of WIFE, and still used in Scotland.

migraine

People unfortunate enough to suffer from **migraine** know that this sort of throbbing headache usually affects one side of the head – exactly reflected in the origin of the word. It goes back to Greek *hemi-* 'half' and *kranion* 'skull', the source of English **cranium**. Until the 20th century the form **megrim** was more common than **migraine**.

mile

Where Roman legions marched they left roads, bridges and other works of civil engineering. One thousand paces (or two thousand steps) marched by disciplined troops became a fixed unit of measurement of distance – in Latin this was *mille passus* or *mille passuum* 'one thousand paces', later shortened to simple *mille*. The word entered most of the languages of Europe, and the precise distance of a mile was adapted to local practices, especially to measurements used in agriculture. In Britain it was brought into relation with the FURLONG: an Act of Elizabeth I in 1592 fixed the mile at 8 furlongs (equal to 1,760yd, approximately 1.609km).

When you urge someone to **go the extra mile**, 'to make a special effort to achieve something', you are echoing the Bible. In the Sermon on the Mount, recorded in the Gospel of Matthew, Jesus says, 'And whosoever shall compel thee to go a mile, go with him twain' (two). See also INCH, MISS, MILLION.

The mile-high club is the imaginary association of people who have had sex on an aircraft. The phrase is not found in print until 1972, in *Come Fly With Us* by J.W. Wells, but must have been in circulation before that.

militant

The root of **militant**, Latin *miles* 'soldier', is shared by **military**, **militate** and **militia**. For most of its history the main sense of **militant** has been 'engaged in warfare', but from the late 19th century it has meant in particular 'aggressively active in pursuing a political or social cause'. In Britain the **Militant tendency** was a Trotskyite political organisation which published a weekly newspaper, *Militant*, between 1964 and 1997.

A shufti in mufti

Military life has always left its mark on the language, but it was the mass conflicts of the 20th century that laid down the richest seam of expressions. Modern warfare continues to drum up new linguistic recruits.

Events in Iraq since 2003 have reminded the civilian world of military terminology. Sadly, one of these has been friendly fire, weapon fire from your own side causing death or injury. This expression has been used since the mid 1970s. A more recent alternative is blue on blue, from the use of the colour blue to indicate friendly forces in military exercises. Journalists attached to military units during the course of a conflict are embedded, and may travel in a Humvee, a high-mobility multi-purpose vehicle.

Camouflage is a First World War word, first recorded in 1917, that comes from French *camoufler* 'to disguise'. If a serving soldier is wearing civilian clothes rather than camouflage he is in mufti, an expression which goes back to the early 19th century and may be a use of mufti meaning a Muslim legal expert – the connection could be the resemblance between an officer's former off-duty clothing of dressing gown, tasselled smoking cap and slippers and the costume of a mufti. Someone taking a quick and cautious look round is taking a shufti, another Arabic word that means 'to try to see'.

camouflage

The British Ministry of Defence is in Whitehall, London, and a military officer employed there rather than on active service is sometimes referred to derisively as a Whitehall Warrior. Since the end of the 19th century a senior officer has been described as top brass or a brass hat, because of the gilt insignia on his cap, whereas in the 1920s and 1930s a soldier leaving the army was said to be getting his bowler hat, then an obligatory item of male civilian wear.

There have always been people who find service life difficult. They may be seen as members of the awkward squad, originally a group of recruits and soldiers who needed further training. The expression is recorded in a saying by the Scottish poet Robert Burns shortly before his death in 1796: 'Don't let the awkward squad fire over my grave.' In more extreme cases a soldier tired of square-bashing on the parade ground might go 'absent without leave', or AWOL – a First World War expression. They might eventually be found in the NAAFI, a canteen run by members of the Navy, Army and Air Force Institutes.

See also BUFF, DRUM, NAME, RANK, TANK, YOMP.

milk

The ancient root of **milk** may have meant 'to rub', and so would refer to the method of hand-milking cows or goats by pulling on their teats. It is connected with the Latin word *mulgere* 'to milk', the source also of EMULSION.

The phrase **the milk of human kindness** comes from Shakespeare's *Macbeth*. Lady Macbeth expresses to herself her suspicion that her husband might not use violent methods to seize the Scottish throne: 'Yet I do fear thy nature; it is too full o' the milk of human kindness / To catch the nearest way.'

In the Book of Exodus in the Bible the Promised Land of Israel is described as 'a land flowing with milk and honey'. The phrase **milk and honey** is proverbial for prosperity and abundance – for example, in 1998 the sports section of the *Sunday Telegraph* reported: 'Promotion back to English football's land of milk and honey is his priority this season.'

mill

Early mills ground corn into flour using water or wind power. The root of **mill** is Latin *molere* 'to grind', also the source of MEAL 'the edible part of any grain or pulse' and **molar** (the 'grinding tooth'). Since the early 19th century people have been able to **put someone through the mill**, or cause them to have a difficult experience.

A **millstone** is the large circular stone used to grind corn. The origins of the phrase **a millstone around your neck**, 'a heavy burden of responsibility', lie in a far more unpleasant practice. The expression is thought to come from an ancient method of execution which involved throwing a person into deep water with a heavy stone attached to their neck.

milliner

In the 16th century the city of Milan in northern Italy was renowned for making small articles of women's dress, accessories and other fancy goods. Those who sold them were the original **milliners** (or 'milaners'). In time the word became restricted to 'a person who makes or sells women's hats'.

million

In Latin *mille* means 'a thousand' – this is the sense reflected in MILE and **millennium**. In **million** the thousand got multiplied by itself. This seems to have happened in Italian, where the word *millione* (now *milione*) was formed.

In 1956 Frank Sinatra and Celeste Holm enjoyed great success with the duet 'Who wants to be a millionaire?' from Cole Porter's *High Society*. The answer in the song is 'I don't', but the television company ITV found that they were in a small minority when they introduced the quiz show *Who Wants To Be A Millionaire?* in September 1998. Thousands have applied to be contestants and millions have been won; the show has given several catchphrases to the language, including 'phone a friend' and 'is that your final answer?' The top prize in the British show is £1m, but the first millionaires had a thousand French francs. The poet Lord Byron wrote in a letter in 1816: 'He is still worth at least 50-000 pds – being what is called here a "Millionaire" that is in Francs and such Lilliputian coinage.'

mince

The words **mince**, **minutiae** 'small, precise or trivial details', MINUTE 'small', MENU and DIMINISH all derive ultimately from Latin *minutus* 'small'. The use of **mince** in the context of expressing yourself candidly, now found mainly in **not mince your words**, goes back to Shakespeare: in *Henry V* King Henry says to the French princess he is courting, 'I know no ways to mince it in love, but directly to say, I love you.' This use produced 'to say in an affectedly refined way' and then 'to walk with in an effeminately dainty way', as early as the 1560s.

In the sense 'ground meat' **mince** was earlier **mincemeat** and even earlier **minced meat**. The mincemeat put in pies at Christmas originally contained meat as well as fruit. To **make mincemeat of**, to defeat easily in a fight or contest, dates from the late 17th century.

mind

English **mind** shares its ancient root with Latin *mens* 'mind', from which **demented**, **mental** and **mention** derive. The mind can do many wonderful things, including 'boggling'. The phrase **the mind boggles**, meaning that someone becomes astonished or overwhelmed at the thought of something, is first recorded in the 1890s. **Boggle** itself is probably a dialect word related to **bogle** 'a phantom or goblin' and **bogey** 'an evil or mischievous spirit'.

Someone may have warned you to **mind your Ps and Qs**, 'be careful to behave well and avoid giving offence'. The expression has been known since the 1770s, but its exact origins are uncertain. One obvious suggestion is that it comes from a child's early days of learning to read and write, when they might find it difficult to distinguish between the two tailed letters *p* and *q*. Another idea suggests that printers had to be very careful to avoid confusing the two letters when setting metal type.

Mind how you go!, meaning 'be careful, look after yourself', has been common in Britain since the 1940s. It was popularised by the long-running BBC TV series *Dixon of Dock Green* (1955-76), in which it was a catchphrase of the avuncular PC George Dixon, along with **evening all**.

miniature

When monks and scribes decorated the initial letters of chapters in illuminated manuscripts, they inevitably painted small images. It was not the smallness that the sources of **miniature** originally referred to, though, but the colour of the paint. Latin *minium* was a word for the red pigment VERMILION. It is the source of Italian *miniatura*, which originally referred to the illuminating of manuscript letters but came to be used for small portraits, and gave us **miniature** in the late 16th century.

Mini is an abbreviation of **miniature** that became popular in the early 20th century. The **Mini** car, originally known as the Mini Minor, was launched by the British Motor Corporation in 1959, and became an iconic vehicle of the swinging 60s that was immortalised in the film *The Italian Job* (1969).

The other mini of the sixties was the **miniskirt**, which symbolised the decade's sexual permissiveness. The French fashion designer André Courrèges is credited with its invention, although it was popularised by Mary Quant. The word is first recorded in 1965, the year when the fashion was first seen.

minstrel

Originally a **minstrel** would be employed to provide a variety of entertainment. Minstrels sang, played music, told stories, juggled – whatever their employer demanded. A minstrel could be closer to a jester or buffoon than the singer of heroic and lyrical poetry that later writers romantically portrayed. Sir Walter Scott's poem *The Lay of the Last Minstrel*, published in 1805, has a lot to answer for here. It is a romance based on an old Border ballad, put into the mouth of an ancient minstrel, the last of his race. The Irish poet Thomas Moore, who died in 1852, also played his part: in the song 'The Minstrel Boy' he wrote of 'the warrior bard' with 'his wild harp slung behind him'. The original meaning of **minstrel** was simply 'a servant'. It goes back to Latin *minister* 'servant', the source also of **minister**. See also TROUBADOUR.

mint

In Anglo-Saxon times there were often many, competing mints, but with improved communications and increased state centralisation in the Middle Ages the right to mint coins was restricted. For 500 years the Royal Mint was based in the Tower of London, but in the 18th century it moved to Tower Hill to cope with the demands of mechanisation, and finally in the 1960s and 1970s it was transferred to Llantrisant, near Cardiff. The phrase **in mint condition**, 'new or as new', refers to a newly minted coin, and people have **made a mint**, or a great deal of money, since the late 16th century. Latin *moneta* is the source of both this **mint** and of MONEY; the **mint** that refers to the plant used in cooking and as a flavouring for sweets is an entirely different word.

minute

English words spelled **minute** have two different pronunciations and entered English by different routes, but share an origin in Latin *minutus* 'small', the source also of MINCE, MENU and many other words. The closest to the original Latin is **minute** 'small'. The **minute** referring to a period of 60 seconds comes through medieval Latin *pars minuta prima* 'first minute part'. The use of **minute** in the minutes of a meeting goes back to the times before printing, when a scribe would make a rough version of a record or memorandum in 'small writing' (Latin *scriptura minuta*) before the fair copy was made in the more formal style of writing called 'book hand'. See also HOUR, SECOND.

The BBC radio programme *Just a Minute* has been broadcast for more than 35 years. In it panellists have to talk on a given subject without hesitation, repetition or deviation for a minute. The theme tune is Chopin's 'Minute Waltz'.

miss

To **miss**, meaning 'to fail to hit', goes back to the Old English period. On the surface of it the proverb **a miss is as good as a mile** is puzzling. The original longer form, from the early 17th century, is clearer: **an inch in a miss is as good as an ell** (an ell is an old measure of distance equal to about 1.1m). As a title for a young girl or an unmarried woman **miss** is a shortening of **mistress**, which itself is from the same Old French root as **master**.

missile

The root of **missile** is a form of Latin *mittere* 'to send', found also in words such as **dismiss**, MESSAGE and **messenger**. The earliest missiles were gifts, such as sweets, thrown to crowds by Roman emperors. From there the word came to mean any object which is forcibly propelled at a target, in the 1650s – the modern sense of a rocket or similar self-propelled weapon is first found in 1945.

Mission is also from Latin *mittere*. *Mission: Impossible* was an American TV series that was first shown between 1966 and 1973, and in 1996 the director Brian De Palma used it as the basis of a film of the same name, starring Tom Cruise. The original series featured stories about the Impossible Mission Force (IMF), a team of secret agents employed by the US government.

mistletoe

The words **mistle** and **mistletoe** originally meant exactly the same thing. The second element of the longer form represents Old English *tān* 'twig', a word that people did not understand and so changed to the more familiar **toe**. The shorter word **mistle** did not survive the 17th century as a name for the tree, but it continues in **mistle thrush**, a large thrush with a spotted breast and a fondness for mistletoe berries.

mitten

Mittens often used to be made of fur, and the name may derive from French *mite*, a pet name for a cat which probably imitated its mewing. This implies that the fur in question was cat's fur – the medieval world could not afford to be sentimental about its animals. The word **mitten** was shortened to **mitt** in the mid 18th century, in the sense 'fingerless glove'.

From the late 19th century **mitt** was also used for 'a person's hand', as in to **get your mitts on**. See also GAUNTLET, GLOVE.

mobile

In the 21st century the first thing that comes to mind when you hear the word **mobile** is probably a portable phone. At least that is the case in Britain – in the USA and elsewhere people are more likely to say **cellphone**. The term **mobile phone** was first recorded in the USA in 1945, but it was not until the 1980s that the mobile or cellphone became more widely available, and even then it was out of reach of the ordinary person. A 1984 source refers to one 'available now with a suggested price of $1,995'.

The word **mobile** itself dates in English to the late 15th century and goes back to Latin *movere* 'to move', the source of MOVE. It started to be used of people's ability to move between social levels at the beginning of the 20th century, and a person can now be **upwardly mobile** or **downwardly mobile**.

In Latin *mobile vulgus* meant 'the common people, the fickle crowd'. English adopted the phrase in the late 16th century, and two centuries later shortened it to **mobile** and then even further to simple **mob**. This became a term for a gang of criminals in the early 19th century, and in 20th-century America **the Mob** is an alternative name for the Mafia.

mocker

The phrase to **put the mockers on**, 'to put an end to, thwart', is originally Australian. It may come from Yiddish *make* 'sore, plague', or be the same word as **mocker** meaning 'someone who mocks'.

Another Antipodean **mocker**, meaning 'clothes, dress', was brought back from Egypt by New Zealand troops after the First World War. It is based on Egyptian Arabic *makwagi* 'presser of clothes' – in Egypt and other Middle Eastern countries there are clothes-pressing establishments with changing rooms where people can shed the outfits they are wearing and have them pressed.

Mock meaning 'to make fun of' is a quite different word, from Old French *mocquer* 'to ridicule'.

mogul

If you are a skier you are probably familiar with the **mogul**, the hump or bump that disrupts your progress. You may also have wondered what snow bumps have to do with the movie mogul or any other such important person. The answer is nothing. The skier's **mogul** comes from Austrian German *Mugel* 'hillock'. The media **mogul** is a use of **Mogul**, a member of the Muslim dynasty of Mongolian origin which ruled much of India from the 16th to the 19th centuries. This historical term is now more usually spelled **Mughal**. It is originally from Persian *mugul* 'Mongol'.

Mohican

The villain of James Fenimore Cooper's novel *The Last of the Mohicans*, published in 1826, is Magua, a Native American Huron warrior whose aim is to prevent the few remaining Mohicans from safely escorting an English colonel's daughters to the safety of his fort. The Huron were allies of the French against the English, and the name **Huron** comes from French, meaning 'having hair standing in bristles on the head'. There have been several illustrated editions of the novel, and the character of Magua, with his distinctive hair, is the most memorable. The Mohicans never had a Mohican, nor did the **Mohawk**, another Native American people whose name is used for the hairstyle, especially in the USA. The style is particularly associated with the PUNK movement of the 1970s, though some Teddy boys had

Babur, the first emperor of the Mughal, or Mogul, empire.

adopted it in the 1950s. The Mohican was correctly seen on a Huron when *The Last of the Mohicans* was made into a film starring Daniel Day Lewis in 1992. See also TEDDY.

mole

English has several unrelated words spelled **mole**. The oldest refers to a small blemish on the skin; in Old English this meant 'a discoloured spot on cloth'. Next to appear was the **mole** that now means 'a structure serving as a pier, breakwater or causeway', which goes back to Latin *moles* 'mass' (the earliest sense in English). The **mole** that is a burrowing animal stayed underground until the later Middle Ages, and went under other names before then – in Old English it was a **want**, and then also a **mouldwarp**. The novels of John le Carré popularised the term **mole** for a spy who gradually achieves an important position within the security defences of a country: it first appeared in *Tinker, Tailor, Soldier, Spy* in 1974. The world of espionage seems to have adopted the use from le Carré, rather than vice versa. See also MOUNTAIN.

moment

The Latin word *momentum* is the source of our words **moment** and **momentum**. Its root is *movere*, 'to move'.

At the end of a bullfight the matador faces the bull and prepares to make the final sword thrust. In Spanish this is *la hora de la verdad*, translated into English as **the moment of truth**. The first recorded use was by the writer Ernest Hemingway in his 1932 book *Death in the Afternoon*.

money

In ancient Rome money was coined in a temple to the goddess Juno, where she was identified with a pre-Roman goddess called Moneta. Latin *moneta* has come down to English as **money**, and also as MINT.

Many proverbs reflect on the place of money in human lives. That **money is the root of all evil** derives from the Bible, in the Book of Timothy, where it is stated more carefully that 'the love of money is the root of all evil'. People down the ages have agreed that **money can't buy happiness**, though this exact formulation appeared only in the 19th century. In 1964 the Beatles sang that 'Money can't buy me love', although they had earlier recorded the song 'Money (That's What I Want)'.

In Britain money or a reward gained with little effort is **money for jam** or **money for old rope**. These expressions, which date back to the early 20th century, probably originated in military slang. In 1919 *The Athenaeum* stated that **money for jam** arose as the result of the 'great use of jam in the Army'. See also COLOUR, LOAD, MUCK.

monitor

Today's familiar uses of **monitor**, for a computer or TV screen and for checking the progress or quality of something over a period of time, date only from the mid 20th century. A much earlier sense was 'a reminder or warning', reflecting its origin in Latin *monere* 'to warn', which is the source also of **admonish**, **monster** and **monument**. A **monitor lizard** is a large tropical lizard, in Australia also called a **goanna**, whose name derives from the way its reactions can warn people of the approach or presence of a venomous creature. In schools from the 16th century a monitor was a pupil with responsibility for supervising and disciplining other pupils, who in the past might have done some teaching.

monkey

The origin of **monkey** is unknown. Historically, APE was used as the general term for all apes and monkeys, and appears much earlier in English. People often associate monkeys with mischief and mimicry. British **monkey tricks** 'mischievous behaviour' are **monkeyshines** in the USA. The use of **monkey business** for 'mischievous or deceitful behaviour' seems to have come from India.

If you **don't give a monkey's** you do not care at all. This phrase, recorded from the late 19th century, is a shortening of something ruder, such as **don't give a monkey's ass** or **f—**. See also BRASS, CHEEK.

The slang sense of **a monkey**, meaning £500 (or, in Australia, $500), goes all the way back to the 1830s, while **a pony**, or £25, is from the late 18th century.

month

A month corresponds to the period of time of the moon's revolution, and the words **month** and MOON are indeed related. Their ancient ancestor is also the source of Greek *mēn* 'month', from which English took **menstruate**, **menopause** and similar words.

Shops and entertainments now open on Sundays, but in the past this was not necessarily so. Where Christianity was the dominant religion, restrictions on pleasure and activity meant that Sundays were quiet, private days. This may be behind the expression **a month of Sundays**, 'a very long, seemingly endless period of time'. The expression is known from 1836 in *The Clockmaker* by Thomas Chandler Haliburton: 'Mr. Slick . . . told him all the little girls there would fall in love with him, for they didn't see such a beautiful face once in a month of Sundays.'

the full monty

In the 1997 film *The Full Monty*, a group of Sheffield steelworkers become male strippers after being made redundant. The film popularised the phrase and highlighted a specific sense, 'a full strip or total nudity'. It may come from **the full Montague Burton**, which was a complete three-piece suit named after a tailor producing made-to-measure clothing in the early 20th century – **the full monty** in this case was the complete opposite of total nudity. Another suggested source is the full English breakfast that Field Marshal Montgomery (nicknamed 'Monty') used to insist on each morning. The trouble with these stories is that the expression is only recorded since the 1980s, and none of the other suggested theories as to its origin are supported by reliable evidence. As with many phrases, we will probably never know the truth.

moon

The words **moon**, MONTH and **measure** all go back to the same ancient root. Since the earliest times people have looked at the full moon and seen a face or figure there, which has been identified as **the man in the moon** since the Middle Ages. The patterns on the moon's disc were formerly also seen as a man leaning on a fork and carrying a bundle of sticks or as a man with his dog and a thorn bush, while other cultures have seen a rabbit, hare, frog or other animal.

The distance and unattainability of the moon is behind such phrases as to **cry for the moon** 'to ask for what is impossible or unattainable' and to **promise someone the moon**. For a dog to **bark at the moon** is a singularly pointless act, and people have used the phrase to express futility since the mid 17th century.

The third of Ian Fleming's James Bond books was published in 1955 under the title *Moonraker*, and in 1979 it inspired a film of the same name starring Roger Moore. A **moonraker** is a small square sail set above a skysail on a sailing ship – the ship's highest sail. The title also refers to an old Wiltshire story of men caught raking a pond for kegs of smuggled brandy, who feigned madness to fool the revenue men by saying that they were raking out the moon. A native of the county of Wiltshire is still a **moonraker**. See also BLUE.

moot

Groups of law students are sometimes given the exercise of discussing an imaginary doubtful law case for practice. This is an old training method, which died out in the 19th century but has since been reintroduced into university law courses. A discussion of this kind is a **moot**, and in the USA a **moot court** is a mock court at which law students argue imaginary cases. These legal assemblies are behind a **moot point**, one which is subject to debate or is no longer of any practical purpose. Originally **moot** was used more widely, of any meeting or assembly. The word derives from the same root as **meet**.

morning

The word for the beginning of the day in Old English was *morgen*, which survives in the literary words **morn** and **morrow**. Then in the Middle Ages **morn** was exended to **morning** on the model of **evening**. Excessive drinking has resulted in **the morning after** (more fully **the morning after the night before**) since the late 19th century, although the symptoms must have been all-too-familiar since people learned to make and drink alcohol.

over the moon

No post-match appraisal would be complete without an **over the moon**, 'extremely happy', from a victorious footballer or football manager. The phrase can be traced back to the early 18th century, its origins lying in the nursery rhyme that begins 'Hey diddle diddle, The cat and the fiddle, The cow jumped over the moon'.

morris dance

Since the Middle Ages groups of dancers in a distinctive costume, usually wearing bells and ribbons and carrying handkerchiefs or sticks, have been performing the **morris dance**. Nothing could seem more traditionally English, but this was originally the **Moorish dance**. No one is now sure how the association with the Moors of North Africa came about, although there are dances with similar names elsewhere in Europe, and the name could go back to a memory of fights between Christians and Moors in Spain – some dancers blacken their faces to make them look Moorish. See also TRY.

mortuary

In the Middle Ages a **mortuary** was a gift claimed by a parish priest from a deceased person's estate. The word derives from Latin *mortuus* 'dead', the source also of **mortgage** and **mortify** and related to MURDER. The current sense, 'a room or building in which dead bodies are kept', dates from the mid 19th century. In Paris the bodies of people found dead formerly were taken to a building at the eastern end of the Île de la Cité, where they were kept until identified. It was called the Morgue. By the 1830s **morgue** was being used in English for other mortuaries; the parallel use of French *morgue* is not recorded until the 1940s and was borrowed back from English.

moth

In Anglo-Saxon times a **moth** was any parasitic pest such as a maggot or worm, especially the larva of the clothes moth. The name eventually extended to the adult clothes moth, and then to other similar insects. People have been able to use a **mothball** to protect stored clothes since the 1890s; shortly after that **in mothballs** came to mean 'unused but kept in good condition for future use'. See also BUTTERFLY.

mother

English **mother**, Dutch *moeder* and German *Mutter* share their ancient ancestor with Latin *mater* (source of **maternal**, **matriarch**, **matrimony**, **matrix** and **matter**) and Greek *mētēr*. The root probably first arose from the use of the sound *ma* made by babies, eagerly identified by mothers everywhere as a reference to themselves.

The British expression **some mothers do 'ave 'em**, commenting on a person's clumsy or foolish behaviour, was apparently originally a Lancashire saying. The comic Jimmy Clitheroe popularised it, as *don't some mothers 'ave 'em*, in his BBC radio programme *The Clitheroe Kid*, which ran from 1958 to 1972. The phrase gained further currency as the title of the 1970s BBC television comedy series *Some Mothers Do 'Ave 'Em*, in which Michael Crawford starred as the clumsy, accident-prone Frank Spencer.

The female equivalent of **like father, like son** (see FATHER) is **like mother, like daughter**. The saying was apparently proverbial even in biblical times: 'Behold, every one that useth proverbs shall use this proverb against thee, saying, As is the mother, so is her daughter' (Ezekiel).

The former Iraqi dictator Saddam Hussein is remembered as having promised **the mother of all battles** on the eve of the first Gulf War. On January 7, 1991 *The Times* reported that he had no intention of relinquishing Kuwait and was ready for the 'mother of all wars'.

The proverb **necessity is the mother of invention** is first recorded in 1658, in *Northern Memoirs* by R. Franck: 'Art imitates Nature, and Necessity is the Mother of Invention.' The idea can be traced back further to classical times, to the Roman satirist Persius, who stated that 'The belly is the teacher of art and giver of wit'.

motley

The word **motley** originally described a fabric woven from different-coloured threads, and was later extended to refer to the multicoloured costume traditionally worn by a court jester in the Middle Ages. To **wear motley** is to play the fool, and a **motley fool** is a professional jester. By the early 17th century the image of starkly contrasting colours and distinctive appearance had developed so that **motley** could apply to any group consisting of a rather incongruous assortment of people or things.

mould

The root of **mould** 'a hollow container used to give shape to hot material when it cools' is Latin *modulus*, source of **model** and **module**. The **mould** that is a furry growth of fungi is unconnected, and came from an old Scandinavian word.

The origins of the expression to **break the mould**, 'to change to a markedly different way of doing things', can be traced back to the manufacture of objects cast in moulds. Destroying a mould afterwards ensured that no further copies could be made. The phrase dates back to the 1560s and probably comes from a translation of the Italian epic poem *Orlando Furioso*, written by Ludovico Ariosto in 1532: 'Nature made him and then broke the mould.' In 1980 one of the founders of the Social Democratic Party, Roy Jenkins, promoted the newly formed party as breaking the 'out-of-date mould' of British politics.

mountain

The Latin word *mons* 'mountain' was extended in French to create the ancestor of **mountain**. It is also the source of **mount**, which is now found mainly in proper names such as **Mount Everest** in the Himalayas. The **Sermon on the Mount**, delivered by Christ and recorded in the Gospel of Matthew, includes the Lord's Prayer.

The story behind the proverb **if the mountain won't come to Muhammad, Muhammad must go to the mountain**, 'if one party refuses to compromise, the other party will have to make the extra effort', was told in 1625 by the philosopher Francis Bacon. Muhammad was once challenged to prove his credentials as a prophet by summoning Mount Safa to come to him. Inevitably, the mountain did not move a centimetre in response to his summons, but Muhammad had a ready answer for this. He observed that if the mountain had moved it clearly would have crushed him and all his followers to death. Therefore it was only right that now he should go to the mountain and give thanks to God for his mercy in sparing them all from this disaster.

The phrase to **move mountains** means both 'to achieve spectacular and apparently impossible results' and 'to make every possible effort'. In the first sense it goes back to Paul's First Epistle to the Corinthians in the Bible: 'And though I have the gift of prophecy, and understand all mysteries, and all knowledge; and though I have all faith, so that I could remove mountains, and have not charity, I am nothing.'

The contrast of size between mountains and molehills has been exploited since the late 16th century. People who exaggerate the importance of something trivial are still said to **make a mountain out of a molehill**.

mouse

English **mouse**, Dutch *muis* and German *Maus* share their ancient ancestor with Latin and Greek *mus*. The essential meaning of the word, that of a small rodent, has remained unchanged. See also MUSCLE.

The shared initial *m* sound, as well as differences of size and character, has prompted contrasts with MAN. A person might mock another's timidity by asking, 'Are you a man or a mouse?' Robert Burns's poem *To a Mouse* reminded people in 1786, as it does today, that 'The best laid schemes o' Mice an' Men, Gang aft agley' ('often go awry'). John Steinbeck's *Of Mice and Men*, published in 1937, told the story of two farm labourers, one of huge strength but low intelligence, the other who both exploited and protected him.

The computer mouse appeared in the 1960s. The choice of the term, from its small size and cord suggesting the tail, was a happy one.

People began setting mousetraps in the 15th century: before that the usual word was **mousefall**, still used in Scots dialect. The phrase **a better mousetrap**, 'an improved version of a well-known article', comes from an observation attributed to the US philosopher and poet Ralph Waldo Emerson in 1889, though it is also claimed by Elbert Hubbard: 'If a man write a better book, preach a better sermon, or make a better mousetrap then his neighbour, tho' he build his house in the woods, the world will make a beaten path to his door.' Agatha Christie took *The Mousetrap* as the title for her most successful play, a murder mystery premiered in London in 1952 and still going strong as the longest continuously running play of all time.

> A person who spent most of their time sitting at a computer or surfing the internet got the name **mouse potato** in the 1990s, in imitation of **couch potato**.

move

Latin *movere* 'to move' is the source of MOBILE and MOMENT as well as of **move**. People have **moved with the times** since 1875, and were prepared to **move heaven and earth** to get what they wanted in the 1790s.

In 1873 the English poet Arthur O'Shaughnessy wrote, 'Yet we are the movers and shakers / Of the world for ever, it seems.' In the 1950s **mover and shaker** was borrowed for 'a powerful person who initiates events and influences people'. See also MOUNTAIN.

muck

English **muck** is from an early Scandinavian word that goes back to an ancient root meaning 'slippery, slimy' from which **mucus** also descends. The verb first meant 'to clean muck from' and 'to spread manure', from which we get **muck up** or make a mess of and **muck around**, 'to behave in a silly or aimless way'.

Down-to-earth northerners might often comment that **where there's muck there's brass**, 'dirty or unpleasant activities are also lucrative'. This form of the proverb, using BRASS in the sense 'money', is recorded in print only from the 1960s, but an earlier version was **where there's muck there's money**. Another plain-speaking people, the Australians, introduced **Lady Muck** and **Lord Muck** at the beginning of the 20th century as names for a socially pretentious woman or man.

The first **muckraking** was done by poor people, who would collect manure from the filthy streets of the city in the hope of selling it or finding something valuable. Since the start of the 20th century, though, it has been searching out and publicising scandal about people, which can be a far more profitable business than selling horse dung.

Mucker or 'friend' was originally military slang, first recorded in the 1940s. It probably comes from the idea of a friend being a person who 'mucks in' or shares tasks cheerfully.

mud

German probably gave **mud** to English, in the Middle Ages. The expression **someone's name is mud**, 'someone is in disgrace or unpopular', draws on an 18th and 19th-century slang use of **mud** meaning 'a stupid or foolish person'.

mug

A **mug** was first of all a measure of salt, then a large earthenware vessel or bowl. In the 18th century drinking mugs commonly represented a grotesque human face. This may be the origin of **mug** in the sense 'a face', which in turn probably gave rise to **mug** as an insult for a stupid or gullible person, from their blank or unintelligent expression. In 19th-century slang **mug** was particularly a term for someone who has been duped by a card sharp or confidence trickster – this is behind **a mug's game**. People were robbed and attacked in public places before the 1860s, but before then the words **mug** and **mugger** would not have been used. They go back to the 'face' sense: **mug** was originally a boxing term meaning 'to punch an opponent in the face' or 'a blow to the face'.

mule

A **mule** results from crossing a donkey and a horse, strictly a male donkey and a female horse (the technical name for the offspring of a female donkey and a stallion is **hinny**). Mules have traditionally been used as beasts of burden, and are also traditionally regarded as stubborn. Someone stubborn, stupid or physically tough has been called a mule since the 15th century. As a name for a courier for illicit drugs, **mule** dates from the 1920s in US slang.

The name of the animal goes back to Latin *mulus*. It has no connection with **mule** in the sense 'a slipper or light shoe without a back'. This comes from a term for the reddish shoes worn by magistrates in ancient Rome, Latin *mulleus calceus*.

mull

People have put forward several theories for the origin of the **mull** in **mulled wine**. One unlikely suggestion is that **mulled ale** is a corruption of **mouldale** 'funeral banquet', and another is that the original sense may have been 'to soften, make mild'. The earliest examples seem to imply that the primary sense is 'to heat'. The **mull** in to **mull over** may come from mulling wine, but this is by no means certain. As a Scottish place name, as in **the Mull of Kintyre**, celebrated in the 1977 hit song by Paul McCartney's group Wings, **mull** means 'a promontory or headland' and comes from Gaelic.

mum

Like **ma** and **mama**, **mum** and **mummy** go back eventually to the first semi-articulate sounds made by children, which tend to be 'ma, ma'. MOTHER itself probably has the same origin.

The expressions **mum's the word** and to **keep mum** are perhaps most associated with life during the Second World War, conjuring up warnings about careless talk costing lives – for example, 'Be like dad. Keep mum.' Both phrases are much older, being recorded as far back as the early 16th century. The word **mum** itself was used on its own in medieval times to mean 'hush!' or 'shh!', and probably originated as a representation of the sound you make when you close your lips firmly together and try to speak.

Ancient Egyptian mummies are named after the substance in which the dead person's body was enbalmed. **Mummy** in this sense goes back to Arabic *mūmiyā* 'bitumen' – bitumen is found in Egypt and the ancient Greeks used it for embalming. For 'the body of an embalmed person or animal' **mummy** is recorded in English from the early 17th century.

A wartime poster of 1942 warns the public to 'keep mum'.

Keep mum she's not so dumb!

CARELESS TALK COSTS LIVES

murder

The ancient root of **murder** is shared by Latin *mors* 'death', from which **mortal** also derives, as do **mortgage**, **mortify** and MORTUARY. In his *Canterbury Tales* Geoffrey Chaucer wrote 'Murder will out'. The idea is older, but his concise way of expressing it ensured that it became proverbial.

From the 18th century BLUE was thought of as the colour of plagues and of harmful things in general, and someone being attacked would **cry** or **scream blue murder** to emphasise their plight. The phrase now refers to making a noisy protest.

muscle

The ancient Romans saw a resemblance between a flexing muscle in the upper arm and the movements of a mouse. Latin *musculus*, from *mus* 'mouse', meant 'little mouse' and also 'muscle'. It entered English as **muscle** through French in the 14th century. The edible mollusc the **mussel** is the same word, and the accepted spellings of both words remained variable into the 19th century.

muse

People who **muse** look thoughtful and reflective, and the word probably originally referred to facial expression, as it is related to **muzzle**. It has no connection with the Muses of classical mythology, the nine goddesses regarded as inspiring learning and the arts. The Greek word for a Muse, *mousa*, is also the source of **music** and **museum**. An institute called **the Museum** was established at Alexandria in about 280 BC by Ptolemy I of Egypt, and became the most renowned of the museums in the ancient world. Ptolemy was a Macedonian general of Alexander the Great who founded the Ptolemaic dynasty, of which Cleopatra was the last representative. The word **museum** derived from Greek *mouseion* 'seat of the Muses'.

In origin **music** is 'the art of the Muses'. Old astronomers imagined the Universe to consist of transparent hollow globes that revolved round the Earth carrying the heavenly bodies and making a harmonious sound known as the **music of the spheres**. Many other things have been regarded as making music, such as birds, running brooks and packs of hounds – since the 1930s a man and woman making love have been said to **make beautiful music together**.

musket

A **musket** is literally a hawk. The name of the old type of long-barrelled gun comes from Italian, and is probably a use of *moschetto* 'sparrowhawk'. It was not uncommon for ballistic weapons to take their names from birds of prey, and arrows and crossbows had previously been called sparrowhawks.

The soldier armed with a musket was immortalised in *The Three Musketeers* by the 19th-century French novelist Alexandre Dumas, though film versions of the story are more memorable for their sword fights. In the 17th and 18th centuries the musketeers formed part of the household troops of the French king.

muster

The word **muster** has a military swagger to it, conjuring up a picture of troops gathering for inspection or in preparation for battle. In Australia and New Zealand, though, the things most often mustered are cattle, sheep and other livestock that are scattered and need to be rounded up. The phrase to **pass muster**, 'to be accepted as adequate or satisfactory', was originally to **pass the musters** and referred to soldiers undergoing inspection without getting into trouble with senior officers. The word itself goes back to Latin *monstrare* 'to show', the source also of **demonstrate**.

mutton

A word that came from French but is probably related to Scottish Gaelic *mult* and Welsh *mollt*. Mutton – the meat of sheep more than a year old – is not much eaten in Britain now, where diners prefer the meat of younger animals, lamb. The insult **mutton dressed as lamb** describes a middle-aged or old woman dressed in a style suitable for somebody much younger, and there is a long tradition of using **mutton** of women in a derogatory way. It was used as a slang term for prostitutes from the early 16th century, and the phrase to **hawk your mutton** meant 'to flaunt your sexual attractiveness' or, of a prostitute, 'to solicit for clients'. See also BEEF.

mystery

There is no mystery to **mystery** – it goes back to Greek *mustērion*, which is related to **mystic** and **mystify**. In ancient Greece mysteries were secret religious ceremonies witnessed only by the initiated, who were sworn never to disclose their nature. In Christianity the word means either a truth long kept secret but now revealed through Christ, or something of symbolic significance. The first English uses of **mystery** were in religious contexts, but it soon spread into wider use for something inexplicable or beyond human comprehension, and then for simply a puzzle or conundrum.

nachos

A Mexican chef called Ignacio Anaya is thought to have invented **nachos**, a snack consisting of small pieces of tortilla topped with melted cheese and spices, in the 1940s – people named Ignacio are sometimes called Nacho by their family and friends. An alternative origin could be the Spanish word *nacho*, which means 'flat-nosed'.

nadir see ZENITH.

naff

The first recorded example of **naff**, meaning 'lacking taste or style', is from the script of the BBC radio programme *Round the Horne* by Barry Took and Marty Feldman (1966): 'I couldn't be doing with a garden like this. I mean all them horrible little naff gnomes.' One of the most popular theories about its origin is the suggestion that the word was formed from the initial letters of *Normal As F—* or *Not Available For F—ing*, but more likely is the idea that it is from Polari (a form of theatrical slang incorporating Italian words, rhyming slang and Romany, used especially by gay people), and that it comes ultimately from Italian *gnaffa* 'despicable person'.

Naff off, meaning 'go away!', is probably a different word, which may be a variant of **eff**, as in 'eff off!' Its first recorded use is from Keith Waterhouse's novel *Billy Liar* (1959): 'Naff off, Stamp, for Christ sake!' It was often used in the script of the BBC comedy series *Porridge* as an acceptable substitute for the bad language characteristically used in prison, and in 1982 Princess Anne was famously supposed to have told reporters to 'Naff off!' when they photographed her after she had fallen from her horse. See also GNOME.

nag

In the sense 'to find fault persistently', **nag** was originally a northern English expression meaning 'to gnaw or nibble' that probably came from Scandinavia or Germany. The first written evidence is from the early 18th century, but may well be earlier, as dialect expressions are often used for a long time before they appear in print.

Nag meaning 'an old or worn-out horse' is a different word. It may be from early Dutch, or it could be related to **neigh**. See also HACK, JADE.

nail

When the word **nail** emerged in the Old English period it already had its main modern meanings of 'small metal spike' and 'fingernail'. To **nail a lie** is to expose a falsehood, an idiom known from the early 19th century. The reference is most likely to shopkeepers nailing forged coins to their shop counter to expose them and put them out of circulation, or to farmers pinning dead vermin to a barn door as a deterrent to others.

If money is paid **on the nail** it is paid without delay, immediately. The phrase may come from the *Satires* of the Roman poet Horace, who used *ad ungulum*, 'on the nail', to mean 'to perfection' or 'to the utmost'. This referred either to Roman sculptors making the finishing touches to their work with a fingernail, or to carpenters using a fingernail to test the accuracy of a joint. An American equivalent was **on the barrelhead**, an upturned barrel being a simple shop counter.

Gordon Bennett! Bloomers!

Amelia Bloomer, Charles Mackintosh and Gordon Bennett have something in common – they are all in the dictionary. These people are part of a select band who have given their names to everyday items and expressions.

As underwear bloomers are deeply unfashionable, but they had a much more progressive beginning. In the 1850s, when women wore long elaborate skirts and dresses, the social reformer Amelia Jenks Bloomer of New York advocated more practical dress, known as 'Bloomer costume', consisting of a short skirt and long loose trousers gathered closely round the ankles. The trousers themselves, worn for active pursuits such as cycling, were then dubbed bloomers, although the style was also called 'rational dress'.

The cardigan takes its name from James Thomas Brundenell, 7th Earl of Cardigan (1797-1868), who led the Charge of the Light Brigade during the Crimean War in 1854. His troops are thought to have first worn this type of garment under their coats to keep warm in the bitterly cold winter. Another item of clothing originating in the Crimean War is the balaclava, a type of woollen covering for the head and neck worn by soldiers and named after a village in the Crimea, now part of Ukraine.

The British have always needed help in keeping out the rain. In June 1823 the Scottish inventor Charles Mackintosh patented a waterproof material consisting of two or more layers of cloth stuck together with rubber. From the 1830s raincoats made of this material sold in considerable numbers, and the mackintosh became an essential part of the British wardrobe. The wellington boot is named after Arthur Wellesley, the first Duke of Wellington, whose army defeated Napoleon at the Battle of Waterloo in 1815. The first wellington boots were long leather ones, as worn by the great general – rubber wellies do not seem to have caught on until the beginning of the 20th century.

In the 18th century John Montagu, the 4th Earl of Sandwich, was a notorious gambler. So that he did not have to leave the gaming table to eat, he had cold beef put between slices of bread and brought to him. This was the first sandwich, whose earliest mention comes in 1762, although it is hard to believe that no one had eaten them before this.

Several of the people whose names have entered the dictionary are French. The trapeze artist Jules Léotard developed a style of costume suited to his profession, and 50 years after his death in 1870 the appearance of the word leotard guaranteed his continuing fame. The physician Joseph-Ignace Guillotin (1738-1814) gave his name to the guillotine, whose use he recommended for executions in 1789, at the time of the French Revolution. And praline, made by boiling nuts in sugar and used as a filling for chocolates, was named after Marshal de Plessis-Praslin (1598-1675), the French soldier whose cook invented it.

Thomas Hobson (1554-1631) delivered mail and hired out horses in the university town of Cambridge. When customers came to him they were told they could take the horse nearest the door or none at all. His fame spread, and since the mid 17th century Hobson's choice has been 'no choice at all'.

The Gordon in the exclamation Gordon Bennett was probably James Gordon Bennett (1841-1918), an American publisher who sponsored a number of sporting events, especially an international motor race called the Gordon Bennett Cup, which was in the news when the expression was first used in the 1890s. His name was chosen because it made a good euphemistic alteration of gorblimey, 'God blind me'.

A Mickey Finn is a drink given surreptitiously to someone to make them unconscious. Mickey Finn was a notorious Chicago bartender who drugged and robbed his customers on a regular basis – his Lone Star saloon had its licence removed in 1903, and Finn promptly left town.

The English cartoonist and illustrator William Heath Robinson (1872-1944) lampooned the machine age by drawing scenes featuring absurdly complicated contraptions designed to perform simple tasks such as peeling potatoes or scaring cats. Today any rickety-looking and overcomplicated apparatus can be described as Heath Robinson. The American equivalent is Rube Goldberg – Reuben Goldberg (1883-1970) was a cartoonist who depicted similarly convoluted devices.

See also JACK, SIDEBURNS, SPOONERISM.

naked

The Old English word **naked** comes from the same ultimate root as NUDE, Latin *nudus*. The sense of 'blatant, clear, unashamed', as in **naked ambition**, dates from the 13th century.

First recorded as early as 1530, stark naked developed into starkers in the 1920s.

The naked truth, meaning 'the plain truth, without concealment or embellishment', dates back to the 14th century. It may originally have developed as a translation of the Latin phrase *nudaque veritas* in the *Odes* of the Roman writer Horace, or have come from fables personifying Truth as a naked woman, in contrast to Falsehood, who is elaborately dressed.

Stark naked is an alteration of **start naked**, which probably meant 'naked even to the tail', as a **start** was an animal's tail.

namby-pamby

This began as a play on the name of the English writer Ambrose Philips, who died in 1749. His poems were ridiculed as insipid and over-sentimental by writers including the poet and essayist Alexander Pope. See also WIMP.

name

The Latin word *nomen* is the source of **name** and also of other words in English, such as **denominate**, **misnomer**, **nominate** and **noun**. **What's in a name?** expresses the view that names are arbitrary labels. It alludes to Shakespeare's *Romeo and Juliet*. Juliet is saying the fact that Romeo belongs to the rival Montague family is irrelevant: 'What's in a name? That which we call a rose / By any other name would smell as sweet.'

nano-

Placing **nano-** before a word shows that the thing referred to is submicroscopically small; technically, it refers to a factor of a thousandth of a million (10^{-9}), approaching the dimensions of individual atoms or molecules. A **nanosecond** is one thousand millionth of a second, while **nanotechnology** deals with the manipulation of individual atoms and molecules.

Nano- comes from the Greek word *nanos*, meaning 'dwarf'. It was adopted in English as early as 1947, athough *nano-* words only entered most people's consciousness in the 1990s, when technology using tiny components had been developed. By 2005 the concept was familiar enough for the Apple company to call its new slimline iPod music player the iPod Nano.

narcissus

The flower **narcissus**, a kind of daffodil, takes its name from a handsome youth in Greek mythology. Narcissus fell so deeply in love with his own reflection in a pool that he pined away and died, whereupon the narcissus flower sprang up at the spot. **Narcissism**, 'excessive admiration of your own physical appearance', comes from the infatuation of Narcissus with his own beauty, and seems to have been invented by the poet Samuel Taylor Coleridge in 1822. As a technical term in psychology, referring to a personality type characterised by extreme selfishness, an inflated view of your own talents and a craving for admiration, it is particularly associated with the theories of the psychotherapist Sigmund Freud.

no names, no pack drill

The phrase, first used in army circles in the First World War, means that punishment for a misdeed cannot be meted out if everyone involved keeps quiet. Pack drill is a military punishment in which an offender has to perform parade-ground exercises while carrying a heavy pack.

nark

The original meaning of **nark** was 'an annoying or troublesome person', a sense which survives in Australia and New Zealand and in the verb **nark**, meaning 'to annoy'. The word is from Romany *nok* or *nak*, 'nose'. SNOUT and SNITCH are other words that mean both 'nose' and 'informer', and the word NOSY itself implies an inappropriate interest in other people's business. See also GRASS, QUISLING, STOOL, TURNCOAT.

nasty

The origins of **nasty**, which was first recorded in the Middle Ages, are uncertain, although it is probably related to Dutch and Swedish words with similar meaning. It originally meant 'filthy, offensively dirty', but its force has been gradually toned down over the centuries, although in America it remains a more strongly negative term than it is in Britain.

The phrase **something nasty in the woodshed**, used in connection with something shocking or distasteful that has been kept secret, comes from the comic novel *Cold Comfort Farm* (1932) by Stella Gibbons: Aunt Ada Doom's peculiarities are explained by the fact that when she was small she had seen something nasty in the woodshed. See COLD.

Nasty piece of work or **nasty bit of work**, 'an unpleasant person', is a slang term first found in a 1923 book by the author 'Bartimeus' (the pseudonym for Lewis Anselm da Costa Ricci). 'Bartimeus' wrote books on a nautical theme, such as *Naval Occasions* and *Seaways*, and it is possible that the expression originated as naval slang.

In informal English **nasty** can also be a noun, meaning 'a nasty person' or 'an unpleasant or harmful thing'. Today it is most often found in connection with gratuitously violent or pornographic films or **video nasties**, a use first recorded in the early 1980s.

nation

The word **nation** first appeared in English during the mid 14th century, via Old French from Latin *natio*, which came from *nasci*, meaning 'to be born'. The link between 'country' and 'birth' was the idea of a people sharing a common ancestry or culture. The Latin verb *nasci* is the source of many familiar English words connected with birth, among them **innate** (inborn or natural), **native**, **nativity** (birth), **nature** and RENAISSANCE (literally 'rebirth'). Also related is the name of the former province of **Natal** in South Africa, which was first sighted by the explorer Vasco da Gama on Christmas Day 1497. He called it **Terra Natalis** or 'land of the day of birth', in recognition of Christ's birth. A similar idea lies behind **Noel**, 'Christmas', which is a French word that comes ultimately from Latin *natalis*.

England is a nation of shopkeepers is supposed to have been Napoleon's scornful dismissal of the enemy across the Channel. Napoleon was not the first person to use the phrase, though, and the economist Adam Smith and possibly also the American revolutionary Samuel Adams referred to 'a nation of shopkeepers' in 1776. Another of Napoleon's notable phrases, **An army marches on its stomach**, may also be doubtful and has been attributed to Frederick the Great. **Not tonight, Josephine** was Napoleon's legendary rejection of his wife, the Empress Josephine. He is said to have been cold to her when he returned from battle in 1809, and the couple were divorced later that year. Again, it is doubtful whether Napoleon actually said these words (or, rather, their French equivalent). See also SCRATCH, SUBLIME.

natty

The informal word **natty**, 'smart or stylish', probably comes from **neat**. It was first recorded in 1785, in *The Classical Dictionary of the Vulgar Tongue* by Francis Grose, which was a collection of slang terms that Dr Johnson had deliberately left out of his dictionary of

Powwow time

The 'cowboys and Indians' of the western have had a big influence on our use of Native American words in English. But it goes back much further than that.

The team game lacrosse is played chiefly in girls' schools in Britain, but to North Americans it is a man's sport. French missionaries in the 17th century saw Native Americans playing the game, and gave it its name, from French *jeu de la crosse*, 'game of the hooked stick'.

In westerns Indians always greet people with how! This is nothing to do with the English word how – it seems to be based on an expression used by northeastern American peoples, possibly *háo* or *hou* in the Sioux or Omaha languages. A powwow is now a conference or discussion, but was originally a ceremony involving feasting and dancing. The word, first used during the 1620s, is from *powah* or *powwaw*, meaning 'priest or healer' in the Narragansett language of New England.

Although scalp is a Scandinavian word, it is strongly associated with the American Indian practice of cutting or tearing the scalp from an enemy's head as a battle trophy. This was first recorded in the 17th century, and since around 1750 scalp has also meant 'a trophy or symbol of victory', as in 'Home games against France and Wales will give them a chance to take a scalp' (*Scottish Rugby*, 1991).

Wigwam, a word which means 'their house' in Ojibwa (a language of central Canada), was first used in English in the 1620s. A wigwam is a dome-shaped hut or tent, whereas a tepee, from Sioux *típí* 'dwelling', is conical. A totem is an object or animal believed to have spiritual significance, and Indians of the northwest USA hang or carve totems on a totem pole. Totem is from Ojibwa *nindoodem* 'my totem', and was first recorded in the mid 18th century.

The names of many US and Canadian animals and plants are Native American – moose and skunk are from Abnaki (a language of Maine and Quebec) *mos* and *segankw*, raccoon and terrapin are from Algonquian *aroughcun* and *turepé*. A moccasin is a dangerous kind of viper, and also a soft-soled leather shoe based on a Native American style of footwear. The word comes from the Powhatan language of Virginia.

See also HATCHET, INDIAN, LONG, POSSUM, WAR, WEST.

1755. **Natty lads** in those days were young thieves or pickpockets. A quotation from the poet Shelley (1812) shows the modern meaning: 'As natty a beau, As Bond Street ever saw.' See also SPICK AND SPAN, SPRUCE.

Among Rastafarians **natty** is used to describe hair that is uncombed or matted, as in dreadlocks; in this context it is a form of **knotty**. A **natty dread** is a Rastafarian. See also DREAD.

naughty

Today **naughty** generally refers to children or animals that misbehave in a fairly harmless way, but from the late medieval period until quite recently it was a stronger word meaning 'wicked' or 'morally bad', as in 'An Oxe of mine being a naughty beast, through ye default of mine owne fence hath goared a Cow of your Worships' (1592) or ''Tis a villanous Error of some naughty Men' (1699). **Naughty** comes from the English word **naught**, 'nothing', and originally meant 'possessing nothing, poor, needy'. The sense 'mildly rude or indecent', found in expressions such as 'naughty bits', dates from the mid 16th century.

nausea

Nausea is a feeling that some people unfortunately experience when at sea. It will probably be of little consolation for them to know that **nausea** originally meant 'seasickness' and is based on the Greek word *naus*, 'ship'. It entered English in the Middle Ages via Latin from Greek *nausia*, 'seasickness, nausea'. *Naus* is the source of the English word **nautical** and of *-naut*, as in **astronaut** or **aeronaut**. **Noise** also comes from *nausea* – as it developed through Latin and early French, *nausea* took on a series of meanings that went from 'seasickness' to 'upset, malaise' and 'disturbance, uproar' and so to 'noise', which was the word's spelling and meaning when it first appeared in medieval English.

navvy

A **navvy** is a labourer employed in building a road or railway. The word is a 19th-century shortening of **navigator**, which in the 18th century was a term for a labourer employed in the rapidly expanding enterprise of canal construction (in parts of England a canal is known as a **navigation**). **Navigate** derives from the Latin word for ship, *navis*, which gave rise to **navy**

and also, because of its shape, to the **nave** or long central part of a church or cathedral. The ultimate root of *navis* is the Greek word for ship, *naus*. See also NAUSEA and NOISE.

neat

The word **neat** came into English in the Middle Ages, via French *net*, from Latin *nitere*, meaning 'to shine'. It was first used in a sense quite similar to its main modern meaning, but with a greater emphasis on the handsome appearance of the thing described, as in this quotation from the 16th century, 'O thou Jerusalem full faire . . . much like a Citie neat'. The sense 'undiluted', as in 'neat whisky', derives from the old use 'free from impurities, clean', which was first found in the late 15th century. The slang sense 'excellent' has always been American, and goes back much further than you might expect, to the beginning of the 19th century.

neck

In Old English the word **neck** (then spelled *hnecca*) was quite rare, and actually referred to the back of the neck. Our idea of 'neck' was expressed by the words **halse** and **swire,** which today survive only as Scottish and northern English dialect terms.

A number of common phrases involve necks. **Neck and neck**, meaning 'level in a race or contest', is older than you might expect, dating back to 1672: it refers to two horses struggling to establish the lead in a race. Horses have been winning races **by a neck** since at least 1791. **The same neck of the woods**, 'the same small area or community', derives from the sense 'narrow strip of woodland', which is recorded from the mid 17th century, originally in the USA. People have used **necking** to mean 'kissing and cuddling' since the early 19th century, presumably from the idea of clasping someone affectionately around the neck. See also SAVE.

nectar

In Greek and Roman mythology **nectar** was the drink of the gods. Today you might sometimes hear a delicious drink being described as 'nectar', and in America it is the usual term for a thick fruit drink. The word took on its usual modern meaning 'a sugary fluid secreted in flowers' in the early 17th century.

---

naughty but nice

An advertising campaign for cream cakes in the 1970s popularised the phrase **naughty but nice**. The idea to use it as an advertising slogan came from the novelist Salman Rushdie, who worked at the time as a copywriter. It goes back to the 19th century, and can be found in a hit song of 1871, 'It's Naughty But It's Nice'.

All at sea

As Britain is an island, with a renowned navy and a long history of exploration by sea, it is unsurprising that so many words and phrases in English are of nautical origin.

The weather was of prime importance in the days of sail. To make heavy weather of a task is to find it unnecessarily difficult, from the nautical expression make good or bad weather of it, which refers to a ship's ability to weather a storm. Heavy weather is a strong wind accompanied by driving rain and rough sea. To keep a weather eye on something, or observe its progress carefully, could simply refer to keeping an eye on the weather, or may be from the idea of looking through a telescope to observe coming weather when at sea. To batten down the hatches is to fix tarpaulins across a ship's hatches with wooden strips called battens in expectation of a storm.

The weather side of a ship is the side from which the wind is blowing (and from which the next weather would come), the opposite side from the sheltered lee or lee side. Leeway is the sideways drift of a ship to the leeward (pronounced by sailing folk *loo-uhrd*) of the desired course, away from the wind – this deviation from course had to be corrected, hence our idea of making up leeway or struggling out of a bad position, or of having leeway or opportunity to move or change.

Edward Vernon (1684-1757) was a British admiral who was nicknamed Old Grog because he wore a cloak made from grogram, a type of coarse fabric. In 1740 he is said to have ordered diluted rum to be served out to sailors instead of the traditional neat rum. The word grog came to be applied to the watered-down rum itself, and later to any alcoholic drink, and is the source of groggy, now meaning 'dazed or woozy' but originally 'drunk'. A related expresssion is splice the main brace, which in the Royal Navy formerly meant 'to serve out an extra tot of rum'. It perhaps arose from the issue of a tot of rum as a reward for the actual splicing of the main brace (attaching a rope to the main spar), which would be a rare and difficult operation.

Get under way was originally a nautical way of saying 'to leave': it was a translation of the Dutch word *onderweg*. To up sticks is also to leave a place, a reference to the process whereby sailors erected the ship's masts before setting off on a voyage.

If you cut and run you make a rather hastier departure, originally by cutting the anchor cable to save time – to run is to sail swiftly or easily, especially with the wind.

When we say an impending event is in the offing we are reaching back to seagoing usage. Offing is a term for the more distant part of the sea visible from a harbour or anchoring ground.

A person who swings the lead is shirking a duty or being lazy. Swinging the lead was the job of slowly lowering a lump of lead suspended by a string to ascertain the depth of water, a task which in itself was quite important but which sailors perhaps sometimes deliberately did as slowly as possible to avoid being assigned a more strenuous duty.

To sail close to the wind now generally means 'to behave in a risky way', but at sea is a term for sailing as nearly against the wind as possible. There is a similar connection with the direction of the wind in by and large, which originally referred to the handling of a ship against the wind and with it: if you sailed 'by the wind' you sailed almost directly into it, whereas a 'large' wind was a favourable one blowing from behind or the side.

If a person is taken aback they are shocked or surprised. A ship, though, is taken aback when the wind blows directly against its square sails from the front and forces them against the masts, stopping forward motion in a very dangerous way.

See also ALOOF, BERTH, BOARD, BUSK, DAVY JONES'S LOCKER, GADGET, PLAIN, PORT, STARBOARD, SUN, YARD.

swing the lead

Nectarine, now the name of a smooth-skinned kind of peach, was originally an adjective meaning 'like nectar'.

negotiate

You often **negotiate** or take part in **negotiations** during business dealings, and it is business that lies at the heart of these words. They both came into English from the Latin verb *negotiari*, which was made up of the two parts *neg-*, meaning 'not', and *otium*, 'leisure'. So negotiation is 'not leisure'. *Otium* is also the root of the English word **otiose**, 'serving no practical purpose, pointless'.

neighbour see BOOR.

neon

This gas, used in fluorescent lamps and illuminated advertising signs, was named in 1898 by its discoverers, the scientists Sir William Ramsay and M.W. Travers. **Neon** is simply the Greek word for 'new thing'. The same Greek word is the source of the many English words that start with *neo-* and refer to a new or revived form of something, such as **neoclassical**, **neocolonialism** and **neo-Nazi**.

nephew

A nephew could originally also be a grandson – the word **nephew** entered medieval English from Old French *neveu*, which came from Latin *nepos* 'nephew, grandson'. **Nepotism**, or favouritism towards friends or relations, also comes from *nepos*. The reference is to privileged treatment formerly given to the 'nephews' of popes, who were in many cases their illegitimate sons.

nerd

Originally an American term, **nerd in the sense of** 'boring, unfashionable person' was first recorded in 1951. The word itself appeared the previous year in *If I Ran the Zoo* by Dr Seuss, who seems to have invented it:

> I'll sail to Ka-Tro
> And Bring Back an It-Kutch, a Preep and a Proo
> A Nerkle, a Nerd, and a Seersucker, too!

Some think that this is the origin of **nerd**, but Dr Seuss used the word in nonsense verse as the name of a kind of animal, and there is no connection with the obsessive computer fan we are familiar with. Another theory links the word with Mortimer Snerd, a dummy used by the American ventriloquist Edgar Bergen in the 1930s.

nest

A **nest** was originally a 'sitting-down place'. The Old English word comes from the same ancient roots as **nether** and **sit**. The related word **nestle** first meant 'build a nest', and did not take on its modern meaning until the 16th century. **Niche**, 'a shallow recess' or 'a comfortable or suitable position', is another related word.

Never-Never Land

Although **Never-Never Land** is now usually associated with the imaginary perfect country in J.M. Barrie's *Peter Pan* (1904), the name was used at the end of the previous century to refer to the remote outback, in particular to the unpopulated northern part of the Northern Territory and Queensland in Australia, from which a person might never return. Barrie's imaginary country was first called **Neverland** or **Never Land**, but in *When Wendy Grew Up* (1908) the longer name was introduced.

The **never-never** is an informal term for hire purchase or, today, for buying by credit card. It originated in the 1890s, also in Australia.

new

The Old English word **new** comes from the same root as Latin *novus*, which is the source of the English words **innovate**, NOVEL, **novice** and **renovate**. The noun **news** is simply the plural of **new**. It came into use as a translation of Old French *noveles* or medieval Latin *nova*, meaning 'new things'.

The proverb **no news is good news**, although modern-sounding, can be traced back at least as far as the time of King James I, who wrote in 1616 that 'No newis is bettir then evill newis'. It may be based on the Italian phrase *Nulla nuova, buona nova* ('No news, good news').

newt

Like NICKNAME, the name of the **newt** is an example of the phenomenon known as 'wrong division' or 'metanalysis', whereby people came to attach the last letter of one word to the beginning of the next. Originally the animal was **an ewt**. **Ewt** was an Old English word which has given us the dialect term for a newt, an **eft**. See also ADDER, APRON, UMPIRE.

his nibs

The origin of this odd expression, a mock title used to refer to a self-important man, is uncertain. It is first found in 1821, although the form **his nabs** was around before that time. It may be from the slang word **nob**, meaning 'a wealthy or titled person', which was formerly also spelled **nib**. The rhyming sound of 'his' with 'nibs' may be the reason for the favouring of that form.

nice

In medieval English **nice** meant 'foolish, silly, ignorant', and the word comes from Latin *nescius* 'ignorant'. It developed a range of largely negative senses which are now obsolete, from 'wanton, dissolute', 'ostentatious, showy', 'unmanly, cowardly' and 'delicate, fragile' to 'strange, rare' and 'coy, reserved'. In *Love's Labour Lost* Shakespeare talks of 'nice wenches', meaning 'disreputable women'. The word was first used in the more positive sense 'fine or subtle' (as in **a nice distinction**) in the 16th century, and the current main meanings, 'pleasant' and 'kind', seem to have been in common use from the mid 18th century. This example from a letter written in 1769 sounds very contemporary: 'I intend to dine with Mrs. Borgrave, and in the evening to take a nice walk.' The development of the word's senses from negative to positive is similar to that of PRETTY.

Nice guys finish last, suggesting that you need to be ruthless in sport to succeed, is credited to Leo Durocher, manager of the Brooklyn Dodgers baseball team between 1951 and 1954. In his 1975 autobiography *Nice Guys Finish Last* he is quoted as saying of a rival team: 'Take a look at them. All nice guys. They'll finish last. Nice guys. Finish last.'

Nice one Cyril will be remembered by many as a catchphrase from the 1970s. It started life as part of a song in a television advert for bread, but was taken up by the crowd at Tottenham Hotspur football club, who used the song to celebrate the popular player Cyril Knowles.

The song was recorded by the Tottenham players in 1973 and became one of the more successful recordings made by a football team. The 1970s gave British TV viewers two other 'nice' catchphrases. **Nice to see you, to see you nice** was how the host Bruce

Forsyth introduced each episode of the game show *The Generation Game*. A **nice little earner**, or a profitable, if perhaps slightly shady, activity, was what Arthur Daley was constantly seeking in the British TV series *Minder* (1979-93). See also INDOORS, OYSTER.

nick

These days to **nick** something is to steal or pinch it, but the verb has a great many meanings that are apparently unrelated. The first, most basic meaning is 'make a nick or notch in', from which developed various senses to do with striking something or hitting a target. The meaning 'to apprehend, take into custody', as in 'You're nicked!', is first found in the play *The Prophetesse* (1640) by John Fletcher and Philip Massinger: 'We must be sometimes witty, to nick a knave.' The sense 'to steal' is more recent, dating from the 1820s.

The noun **nick** first meant 'notch, cut, or groove'; the sense 'condition' ('you've kept the car in good nick') seems to come from Worcestershire and Gloucestershire dialect, and was first recorded at the end of the 19th century. **In the nick of time** developed from an old meaning 'the precise or critical time or moment', and was in the mid 16th century simply **in the nick** or **the very nick**. The slang sense 'prison' or 'police station' was originally Australian, with the first written evidence in the *Sydney Slang Dictionary* of 1882.

Old Nick, a name for the devil, is probably a shortening of the man's name Nicholas. One theory as to why this familiar name was adopted links it with the Italian politician and philosopher Niccolò Machiavelli (see MACHIAVELLIAN), although he is reputed to have been unscrupulous and scheming rather than downright evil. Another is that it is short for **Iniquity**, which was the name for the character symbolising Vice in old morality plays – **Old Iniquity** is found as a name for the devil in the 19th century. Other names for the devil in parts of Britain are Old Harry, Old Horny, Old Ned and Old Scratch, so maybe there is no particular reason why **Nick** should have been chosen.

night

Although an Old English word, **night** comes ultimately from the same root as Latin *nox*, the source of **equinox** and **nocturnal**. **Fortnight**

Nice one Cyril
Nice one son
Nice one Cyril
Let's have another one!

is an Old English contraction of '14 nights', and reflects an ancient Germanic custom of reckoning time by nights rather than days.

The original **night of the long knives** was the legendary massacre of the Britons by the Saxon leader Hengist in 472. According to the 12th-century Welsh chronicler Geoffrey of Monmouth, the Saxons attended a meeting armed with long knives, and when a prearranged signal was given each Saxon drew his weapon and killed the Briton seated next to him. The phrase is now more commonly associated with the brutal suppression of the Brownshirts (a Nazi militia replaced by the SS) on Hitler's orders in 1934. It is also used of any decisive or ruthless sacking, in particular the occasion in 1962 when British Prime Minister Harold Macmillan dismissed a third of his Cabinet in one go.

Contrary to what you might expect, nightmares are nothing to do with horses. In the Middle Ages a **nightmare** was thought of as an evil female spirit or monster that lay on sleeping people and suffocated them: the -*mare* part comes from Old English and meant 'suffocating evil spirit'.

Nimby

A **nimby**, short for *Not In My Back Yard*, is a person who objects to the siting of something unpleasant in their own neighbourhood while not objecting to similar developments elsewhere. Although first recorded in 1980, in the USA, it is associated by most people with the British politician Nicholas Ridley, who in 1988 attacked country dwellers as selfish for opposing development, calling their attitude 'pure Nimbyism'. It was later discovered that he himself was opposing the building of new houses near his own country home.

nincompoop

Used since the late 17th century, **nincompoop** perhaps came from **Nicodemus**, the name of a Jewish Pharisee in the New Testament who became something of a byword for slow-wittedness. Nicodemus secretly visited Jesus one night to hear about his teachings. Jesus explained, 'Except a man be born again, he cannot see the Kingdom of God', which puzzled the Pharisee, who took Jesus literally and said 'How can a man be born when he is old?'. The -*poop* part of the word may have come from the old verb **poop**, which meant 'to deceive or cheat'.

nickname

In the Middle Ages a nickname was an **eke-name**, or 'an additional name' – eke meant 'additional'. People misinterpreted an **eke-name** as a **neke nam** or, later, a nickname. See also NEWT.

nine

All of our main number words go back to the most ancient times. **Nine** is Old English but can be traced back to a root that was shared by Latin *novem* and Greek *ennea*.

The phrase **dressed up to the nines**, 'dressed very smartly or elaborately', dates from the early 18th century. At first it meant 'to perfection, to the greatest degree', but by the mid 19th century was particularly associated with smart dress, as in 'When she's dressed up to the nines for some grand party' (Thomas Hardy, 1896). One theory is that it comes from the name of the 99th Wiltshire Regiment, known as **the Nines**, which was famous for its smart appearance. But their reputation seems to have dated from the 1850s, which means that it is unlikely to account for this much earlier phrase.

The reason that a **99**, an ice-cream cone with a stick of flaky chocolate in it, is so called is not straightforward. It seems that Italian ice-cream sellers in the north of England were cutting Cadbury's chocolate flakes in half and sticking them in cones as early as the 1920s. A Cadbury's sales manager had the theory that the name came from the elite bodyguard of 99 soldiers who surrounded Italian kings, and that the number 99 signified the finest quality. The trouble is that the bodyguard he had in mind was probably the Vatican's Swiss Guard, which traditionally had 105 members and now has 100. Another theory comes from the Edinburgh ice-cream maker Rudi Arcari, who claimed that her grandfather invented the 99 in the 1920s and named it after the address of the family's shop at 99 Portobello High St. See also TALK.

nit

A **nit** is the egg of a human head louse. The word's use to mean 'stupid person' is first found in *Love's Labour's Lost* by Shakespeare: 'And his Page, . . . Ah heavens, it is a most patheticall nit.' **Nitwit** is much more recent, not being recorded until the 1920s.

Nit-picking or pedantic fault-finding did not come into the language until the 1950s. The idea here is of painstakingly searching through someone's hair for nits.

In Australia children shout 'nit!' to warn their friends when a teacher is approaching. The person who is keeping watch is said to **keep nit**. **Nit** in this context is probably an alteration of **nix**, which comes from German *nichts*, 'not'.

nod

The proverb **a nod's as good as a wink to a blind horse**, meaning that only the slightest indication is needed to get across a suggestion, is first recorded in a letter written in 1793. The phrase is puzzling, as such a horse would be unable to understand whatever signal the nodder or winker was attempting to convey. The use of **a nod and a wink** to mean 'a hint or suggestion' is first found in 1710, several decades earlier than the proverb: it seems that the 'blind horse' was tacked on to the original phrase as a surreal piece of fun.

noise see NAUSEA.

noon

The Old English word **noon** originally meant 'the ninth hour from sunrise', or approximately 3pm. It came from the Latin phrase *nona hora* 'ninth hour'. The time change appears to have occurred in the Middle Ages: examples of **noon** meaning 'midday' are found from around 1225, and by the 14th century it seems to be the ordinary sense of the word. The Church service of **nones** could give a clue as to why its meaning shifted. Nones – a word from the same root as **noon**, *nona* – are prayers generally said at 3pm, but among Benedictine monks in Italy the service was held closer to midday. See also LUNCH.

Norman

Contrary to what many people think, the Normans who invaded England in 1066 were not simply Frenchmen. They were a people of mixed Germanic and Scandinavian origin who settled in Normandy from about AD 910 under their chief, Rollo, and became dominant in western Europe and the Mediterranean. Their name is a form of **Northman**, which was first used in Old English in reference to Scandinavians, especially Norwegians (the related form **Norseman** comes from the Dutch word for 'north'). The form **Norman** first arose in the late 13th century, by which time it referred specifically to the people from Normandy.

nose

The Latin root of **nose** is *nasus*, which is the source of our word **nasal**, and is also related to **ness**, meaning a headland or promontory. A **nostril** is literally a 'nose hole'. In Old English the word was spelled *nosterl* or *nosthyrl*, and came from *nosu* 'nose' and *thyrl* or *thyrel* 'hole'.

To **cut off your nose to spite your face** is to disadvantage yourself while trying to harm someone else. This idea was proverbial in both medieval Latin and French, and has been found in English since the mid 16th century.

Since the 1780s a **nose** has been a spy or police informer. The idea of such a person being a 'nose', or 'sticking their nose in', is also found in words such as NARK and SNOUT, and in **nosy**. The first **nosy parker** appeared in a postcard caption from 1907, 'The Adventures of Nosey Parker', which referred to a peeping Tom in Hyde Park. **Nosy** itself goes back to 1620, in the sense 'having a big nose', and to at least the 1820s in the sense 'inquisitive'. The common surname **Parker** was originally a name for the caretaker of a park or large enclosure of land.

nostalgia

As the saying goes, 'Nostalgia isn't what it used to be'. In English **nostalgia** first meant 'acute homesickness', coined in the 18th century from the Greek words *nostos*, 'return home', and *algos*, 'pain', as a translation of the German word *Heimweh* or 'homesickness'. The familiar modern meaning, 'longing for the past', had become established by the early 20th century. There are a number of medical terms also derived from *algos*, all relating to physical pain, such as **neuralgia**, 'pain in a nerve', and **analgesia**, 'relief of pain'.

not on your nelly

Nobody knows who Nelly was, if indeed she was ever a real person. The phrase was originally **not on your Nelly Duff** – in the 19th century **Nelly Duff** was rhyming slang for 'puff' (meaning 'breath of life'), and so the expression is roughly equivalent to **not on your life**.

notorious

When it appeared in the late 15th century **notorious** first meant just 'commonly or generally known, famous', as, for example, in the 1588 quotation 'Manie of you . . . are men verie notorious for their learning and preaching.' The modern, negative meaning did not emerge until 1549, in the *Book of Common Prayer*: 'Suche persones as were notorious synners.' The word comes from Latin *notus* 'known', which is also the root of the English words **notice**, **notify** and **notion**.

novel

As an adjective **novel** first meant 'recent'. It entered English in the 15th century via Old French from the Latin word *novellus*, which came from *novus*, 'new'.

Novel meaning 'a book' is at root the same word, deriving from Italian *novella* (*storia*) 'new (story)', which was also from *novellus*. People first started speaking of a literary novel when referring to *The Decameron* by Boccaccio. This medieval Italian work contains 100 tales that were supposedly told in ten days by a party of ten young people who had fled from the Black Death in Florence. It was not really what we would think of as a novel, though. **Novel** meaning 'a fictitious prose narrative of book length' first started being used in the 1630s. At first the term was contrasted with ROMANCE, novels being shorter and having more connection to real life.

nubile

A **nubile** girl is today young and sexy, but originally she was simply old enough to marry, with no implication of attractiveness. The word comes from Latin *nubilis*, from the verb *nubere*, 'to put on a veil, get married'. In English **nubile** first, in the mid 17th century, had the same meaning as the Latin word, but this use is now only found in anthropology and other technical contexts. *Nubere* is also the source of the English word **nuptial**, 'to do with weddings', and ultimately derives from the Latin word for a cloud, *nubes*, which is the root also of **nuance**.

nucleus

The **nucleus** of something is literally its 'little nut'. In Latin *nucleus* meant 'kernel, inner part' and was a diminutive of *nux* 'nut'. First used in English in the mid 17th century, **nucleus** originally referred to the bright core at the centre of a comet's head, and then to the central part of the Earth. Today its main technical meaning is 'the positively charged central core of an atom'. This was identified by Sir Ernest Rutherford (1871-1937), who is regarded as the founder of nuclear physics, in 1911.

number

The source of **number**, and of **enumerate** and **numerous**, is the Latin word *numerus*.

The first written use of **your number is up**, meaning 'the time has come when you are doomed to die or suffer some other disaster', was by the English essayist Charles Lamb in a letter written in 1806, in which the reference is to someone drawing a winning ticket in the 'lottery of despair'. Other suggestions have been made as to the phrase's origins. One links it to various passages in the Bible that refer to the 'number of your days', meaning the length of your life. Another proposes that the number in question is a soldier's army number, associated with identifying casualties on the battlefield and the fatalistic expectation of a bullet with 'your name and number' on it.

nut

The Old English word **nut** is related to the Latin root *nux*, also meaning 'nut', and so also to NUCLEUS. The informal meanings 'crazy or eccentric person' and 'person who is excessively interested in a particular thing', as in 'They'll just think I'm some old nut' or 'He's a football nut', both date from the early 20th century. They come either from the idea of a nut being an example of something small and cheap or from the informal sense 'a person's head'. This latter sense is the one behind phrases like **do your nut**, or get very cross, and is the root of **nutty** meaning 'mad or crazy'. It is also the source of the verb 'to nut', or butt with the head, which is first found in the 1930s. See also FRUIT.

A **nutshell** has been used since the late 16th century to symbolise compactness or shortness. Shakespeare's Hamlet says, 'I could be bounded in a nutshell, and count myself a king of infinite space, were it not that I have bad dreams.' The idea is thought to have arisen from the supposed existence of a copy of Homer's epic poem the *Iliad* which was small enough to fit into an actual nutshell, mentioned by the Roman statesman and scholar Pliny (AD 23-79) in his work *Natural History*.

nutmeg

A **nutmeg** is not technically a nut, but its name comes from the Latin root of NUT, *nux*, and *muscus*, 'musk'. It is used in sport to describe the action of a footballer cleverly playing the ball through the legs of an opponent. This probably comes from an old use of the noun to mean 'testicle' (also shared by NUT), which was first recorded in the 1690s. Players have been 'nutmegged' since at least 1979. As a noun the term dates from slightly earlier, cropping up in Rodney Marsh's 1968 book *Shooting to the Top*. In this the former Fulham, Queens Park Rangers and Manchester City footballer describes performing the trick and then compounding the humiliation for the opposing defender by shouting 'Nutmeg!', which he says was traditional in the circumstances.

oaf

You would not associate the splendid elves of J.R.R. Tolkien's *The Lord of the Rings* with someone stupid, rude or clumsy, but the word **oaf** goes back to Old Norse *alfr* 'an elf'. It originally meant 'an elf's child, a changeling', and from this came to be used for 'an idiot child', and then 'fool' or 'halfwit'. Finally, in the early 20th century, it acquired the general sense of 'large clumsy man', a sense used by Rudyard Kipling in *The Islanders* (1903) when he referred to cricketers and footballers as 'flannelled fools at the wicket' and 'muddied oafs at the goals'.

oak

The name of the **oak** goes back to Old English and is related to Latin *aesculus*, a word for a species of oak sacred to the Roman god Jupiter. Oak timber was traditionally used in shipbuilding, which gave the 18th-century actor David Garrick the line for a song about the British Navy, 'Heart of oak are our ships'.

The Oaks is the name of an annual flat horse race for three-year-old fillies run on Epsom Downs, over the same course as the Derby. It was first run in 1779. It was named after a nearby estate, presumably distinguished for its oak trees.

The oak features in some traditional weather rhymes. One from the mid 19th century suggests that we can predict the weather for the coming summer by observing whether the oak or the ash comes into leaf first:

> When the oak is before the ash, then you will only
>   get a splash;
> When the ash is before the oak, then you may
>   expect a soak.

See also ACORN.

oasis

In the classical world **Oasis** was the name of a particular fertile spot in the Libyan desert, noted by English travel writers in the 17th century. It came ultimately from an ancient Egyptian word for 'dwelling place'. By the early 19th century the word was being used for a place of calm in the midst of trouble or bustle. In Sir Arthur Conan Doyle's *The Sign of Four* (1890), a character describes his richly furnished house as being 'an oasis of art in the howling desert of South London'.

oats

Oats are used as feed for horses, making them friskier and more energetic, and if you show signs of being lively and buoyant you may be said to be **feeling your oats**. To be **off your oats**, on the other hand, means that you have no appetite for food. **Wild oats** are weeds found in cornfields which resemble cultivated oats. They have no value as a crop, so you would be wasting your time sowing them instead of good grain. Since the 16th century **sowing your wild oats** has been a term for behaving wildly or promiscuously when young, while to **get your oats** is to have sex. See also feature on DR JOHNSON'S DICTIONARY.

obey

A word based on Latin *audire* 'to hear' (see AUDIENCE), via Old French *obeir*. In the traditional Church of England wedding vows, derived from the *Book of Common Prayer*, the husband promises 'to love and cherish' his wife 'till death us do part', while the wife promises to 'love, cherish, and obey' her husband. Since the 1980s, though, many wives have chosen not to 'obey' their husbands. One woman who would certainly have opted out of this declaration was Hilda, the wife of the ageing barrister Horace Rumpole in John Mortimer's long-running television series *Rumpole of the Bailey*. Rumpole called her **She who must be obeyed**, which was the title of the beautiful sorceress Ayesha in the adventure story *She* (1887) by Sir H. Rider Haggard.

object

It may seem surprising that **object** as a noun meaning 'a thing you can see and touch' and as a verb meaning 'to say that you disagree with something' are related, but they both go back to the same Latin word, *obicere*. This meant 'to throw at something else'. The earliest meaning in English was 'put something in the way of something else', and from this we get the idea of 'oppose'. An obstacle placed in the path is something that can be seen, and this gives us the noun sense.

occult

Today **occult** describes the world of supernatural beliefs and practices, but when it was formed in the early 16th century the word simply meant 'secret, hidden'. By the end of that century it had taken on something more like its modern meaning, and was being used in reference to alchemy, magic and other arts of a secret or mysterious nature. It comes from Latin *occulere* 'to cover over'.

ocean

The first mention of **ocean** in English is found in the Middle Ages, but it looks back to classical times. The ancient Greeks believed that the world was surrounded by a great river, which they called *okeanos*. **The ocean** originally described the body of water ('the Great Outer Sea' as contrasted with the Mediterranean and other inland seas) regarded as enclosing the Earth's single land mass, that of Europe and Asia, which at the time was the only land known. The **Mediterranean** was literally the sea 'in the middle of the Earth' or 'enclosed by land', combining Latin *medius* 'middle' and *terra* 'land'. See also ATLAS, PACIFIC.

octopus

The name of the **octopus** is from Greek *oktōpous*, from *oktÿ* meaning EIGHT and *pous* 'foot'. The prefix *oktÿ* gives us words like **octagon** for an eight-sided figure and **octogenarian** for someone aged between 80 and 89. In the modern world **October** is the tenth month, but the word comes from Latin *octo* 'eight', because it was the eighth month in the Roman calendar. It became the tenth month after the addition of July (named after Julius Caesar) and August (named after the Emperor Augustus) in the 1st century BC. See also CALENDAR, MONTH.

odds

The first meaning of **odd**, an Old Norse word used in English since the Middle Ages, was 'having one left when divided by two', as in 'odd numbers'. This led to 'single, solitary' and then 'strange, unusual'. In the betting sense **odds** have been around since the end of the 16th century. If you **lay odds** or **give odds** you are offering a bet with odds favourable to the other person betting. The opposite is to **take odds**, where you offer a bet with odds unfavourable to the other person betting. A person who talks loudly and opinionatedly is sometimes said to be **shouting the odds** – the idea here is of someone calling out the odds on a racecourse, encouraging punters to bet. When we say of something that **it makes no odds** we mean that it will not alter things in any way. This is not the gambling sense of **odds**, but an old use of the word with the sense 'difference in advantage or effect'.

odour

Today an **odour** (from Latin *odor*) tends to be an unpleasant smell, but in medieval times it was a sweet smell or perfume. This gives us the expression **an odour of sanctity** for a state of holiness – literally a sweet scent supposedly given off by the bodies of saints when they are at or near death. To be **in good odour** (or **in bad odour**) with someone is to be in (or out of) favour with them, a use that has been around since the end of the 17th century.

offal

Liver, kidney and other **offal** is now the internal organs of an animal used as food, the bits 'left over' when the meat is cut up by the butcher. This idea of being 'left over' is close to the original sense, as the word referred to waste material, such as husks from milling grain or chips of wood from carpentry. It probably comes from old Dutch *afval*, from *af* 'off' and *vallen* 'to fall'.

LOOK DADDY AN OCTOPUS

office

In the Middle Ages **office** meant a duty that went with someone's position or employment. It goes back ultimately to Latin *officium* 'performance of a task', which in turn comes from the combined elements of *opus* 'work' and *facere* 'to do'. The sense of 'a room or building for business' is recorded from the later Middle Ages. Today many people feel that they spend most of their life in the office, working. Some had their pain alleviated by the pleasure they got from the BBC TV comedy *The Office*, created by Ricky Gervais and Stephen Merchant and first broadcast in 2001. Such was it success that an American version was created, and there is also a French one, *Le Bureau*, and a French Canadian version called *La Job*. See also OPERA.

oil

The English word **oil** goes back to Latin *oleum*, which referred especially to olive oil. We have a number of phrases that testify to the different uses to which oil has been put. If someone sits up writing or reading until very late they are **burning the midnight oil**, an expression looking back to the days when the main source of artificial light would be an oil lamp. Oil paints are traditionally used for portraits, and since the early 20th century the unkind verdict that someone is **no oil painting** has been a way of saying that they have little physical attraction.

Water and oil are two liquid substances that repel each other and cannot be mixed. People who are incompatible may be described as being like **oil and water** together. In classical times, there was a belief among seamen – recorded by the Roman statesman and scholar Pliny the Elder – that pouring oil into a stormy sea could calm the waves. This is probably what lies behind the proverbial expression **pour oil on troubled waters**, meaning to try to settle a disagreement by soothing those involved.

OK

The use of **OK** to reassure someone that all is well has been part of the language since the mid 19th century. The expression came from the USA, and is probably an abbreviation of *orl korrect*, a jokey spelling of 'all correct', used as a slogan during the presidential re-election campaign of Martin Van Buren in 1840. It was reinforced by the initials of his nickname Old Kinderhook, derived from his birthplace.

old

Appropriately, **old** is one of the oldest English words. It shares an ancient root with Latin *alere* 'to nourish', which links it with **alimentary** and **alimony**.

Networking may be thought of as a modern business practice, but the idea of **the old boy network** as providing mutual assistance (and often career advancement) among people from the same social and educational background goes back to the 1950s. Members of such a group might well refer to ideas of group loyalty and tradition in terms of **the old school tie** – values seen as associated with the wearing the tie of a particular public school. The first writers to use the phrase were those astute social commentators Rudyard Kipling, in 1932, and George Orwell.

An old wives' tale is a widely held traditional belief now thought to be unscientific or incorrect. This phrase, with its earlier variant **an old wives' fable**, has been part of the language since the 16th century. It is first found in William Tyndale's translation of the Bible, where the faithful are instructed to 'cast away' such stories.

Some behaviour becomes inappropriate as you get older, and there is a risk for some of being considered a **dirty old man**. First recorded in the 1930s, the phrase was Harold Steptoe's familiar rebuke to his father in the TV comedy *Steptoe and Son* (1962-74).

olive

Olives are particularly associated with the countries around the Mediterranean, and the word **olive** comes from Greek *elaion* 'oil'. **Extra-virgin** olive oil is made from the first pressing of the olives.

To **hold out an olive branch** is to make an offer of peace and reconciliation. A branch of an olive tree is a traditional emblem of peace and goodwill, featuring in both classical mythology and biblical tradition. In ancient Greece olive crowns were presented to winners in the Olympic Games and to worthy civic dignitaries, and brides would wear olive garlands. Probably the most familiar occurrence of the olive branch is in the story of Noah and the Ark in the Bible, in which a dove returns to Noah with an olive branch (or more likely, given the size of a dove, an olive twig) to indicate that God is no longer angry and that the waters of the flood have begun to recede. See also DOVE.

ombudsman

There are not many words in English that come directly from Swedish, but **ombudsman** is one of them. In the 1950s we adopted the Swedish word for 'legal representative' as a term for an official appointed to investigate individual complaints against companies or the government, though the British Parliamentary Commissioner for Administration, as the office is formally known, dates from 1967.

omelette

People have been cooking and eating **omelettes** since the early 17th century, when the word was borrowed from French. It goes back ultimately to the Latin word *lamella* 'thin plate', which was presumably suggested by the shape of an omelette. By the 19th century the familiar actions of breaking and beating eggs to make the dish had led to the saying **you cannot make an omelette without breaking eggs**.

omnibus

The 1820s saw the introduction in Paris of a horse-drawn vehicle that carried passengers along a fixed route for a fare. This was called a *voiture omnibus*, a 'vehicle for everybody'. When it came to London the vehicle was called simply an **omnibus**. Though 'omnibus' was taken from French, its origin is a Latin form meaning 'for all', based on *omnis* 'all', and people very quickly shortened this rather pompous, learned word to **bus**.

In the 1830s an **omnibus** came to be a volume containing several works previously published separately. *Omnis* also gives us words such as **omnivorous**, literally 'all-eating', and **omniscient**, 'knowing everything'.

one

Like the other main number words, **one** goes back to Old English. It shares an ancient root with Latin *unus*, and so is linked with such words as **unique** and **unity**.

The **one that got away** is a term for something desirable that has eluded capture. The phrase comes from the angler's traditional way of trying to impress by boasting about the large fish that managed to escape after almost being caught, 'You should have seen the one that got away'.

A **one-horse town** is a small town with hardly any facilities, particularly in the USA. Such towns are associated with the Wild West, and the term is first recorded in a US magazine of 1855. The previous year, though, there is a record of a specific place of that name: 'The principal mining localities are . . . Whiskey Creek, One Horse Town, One Mule Town, Clear Creek [etc.].' Also American is the **one-trick pony**, a person with only one talent or area of expertise. This goes back to the days of travelling circuses in the early 20th century, when animals that could do tricks were an attraction. It would be a poor circus whose pony had only one trick.

Once and future refers to someone or something that is eternal, enduring or constant. It probably comes from T.H. White's *The Once and Future King* (1958), a series of novels about King Arthur. In White's story the enchanter Merlyn says to Arthur: 'Do you know what is going to be written on your tombstone? *Hic jacet Arthurus Rex quondam Rexque futurus.* Do you remember your Latin? It means, the once and future king.'

A bad experience can make you wary of the same thing happening again, a feeling which might be summed up concisely with the words **once bitten, twice shy**. The expression has been around since the late 19th century, although in the USA you might say instead **once burned, twice shy**.

onion

Onions have been part of the vegetable garden since medieval times, and the name comes ultimately from Latin. To **know your onions** is to be very knowledgeable about something. The phrase was first used in the USA in the 1920s, when there were a number of similar phrases that involved knowing a lot about foodstuffs, and onions may simply have been chosen as the most popular vegetable or the easiest to grow. Another idea is that **onions** is short for 'onion rings', rhyming slang for 'things', but this does not fit with an American origin. The same is true of another theory, that there is a link with the lexicographer C.T. Onions, one of the first editors of the *Oxford English Dictionary*. Despite his eminence as a scholar it seems unlikely that his name would have been widely known on both sides of the Atlantic.

opera

A mid 17th-century adoption from Italian which goes back to Latin *opus*, meaning literally 'labour, work'. In mid 1970s America the saying **the opera isn't over till the fat lady sings** became a way of warning that something had not been finally settled, and that an outcome could still change. The reference is probably to the final solo of an operatic heroine, often played by a large woman.

opium

The name of this addictive drug is found in medieval English and comes ultimately from the Greek word *opion* 'poppy juice'. The **opium of the people** is something regarded as giving people a false sense of security and contentment. The phrase originated as a direct translation of the German *Opium des Volks*, as used by the founder of modern Communism, Karl Marx, in 1843-4.

opportune

Since medieval times we have used **opportune** of something that has happened at a good or convenient time. Originally, though, the word was associated with a much more specific meaning. It comes from Latin *opportunus*, from *ob-* 'in the direction of' and *portus* 'harbour', referring to the favourable wind which brought ships into the harbour.

Opportunity comes from the same root. The phrase **opportunity knocks** is used to mean that a chance of success might happen, often with the implication that every person has a chance to succeed. It was the title of a hugely popular TV talent show broadcast from the late 1950s to 1978, with a revival in the late 1980s, and originally hosted by Hughie Green. The programme was a predecessor of *Pop Idol* and *The X Factor*, in which the performances of a variety of unknown acts were judged by the public. People wrote in with their choices – no texting or phone votes in those days – although there was also a 'clapometer' in the studio that measured the audience's applause for each act.

optimism

Philosophers in the 18th century coined **optimism** for the theory that this WORLD is the best of all possible worlds. The word goes back to Latin *optimum* 'best thing'. By the early 19th century it had gained wider currency, and was being used to mean a general tendency to hope for the best. The opposite, **pessimism** (from Latin *pessimus* 'worst'), was also coined in the 18th century, when it meant 'the worst possible state or condition'.

orange

The name of the **orange**, first recorded in English in medieval times, goes back through Arabic to Persian, although the native home of the fruit may have been Southeast Asia. The Arabs brought what we now call the **Seville orange**, or **bitter orange**, to Sicily in the Middle Ages, and from Sicily it was introduced to the rest of Europe. In the 16th century the Portuguese brought the **sweet orange** from China, and gave us the fruit which we now know simply as the orange.

The children's game of **oranges and lemons**, in which two players make an arch with their joined hands and the rest pass underneath while the song beginning with these words is chanted, is recorded from the early 19th century but is probably a lot older. The song lists the bells of a number of London churches, beginning with St Clement's, and the final line runs 'Here comes a chopper to chop off your head.' This has led to the theory that the song looks back to the days of public executions, when the condemned person was taken in procession to execution while the church bells were tolled. There may also be an association with the marriages of King Henry VIII, and the beheading of two of his wives.

The **Orangemen** of Northern Ireland are members or supporters of the Orange Order, a Protestant political society in favour of continued union with Britain. Their name comes from the wearing of orange badges as a symbol of adherence to King William III, who defeated the Catholic James II at the Battle of the Boyne in 1690. William was also known as William of Orange, a town in southern France which was the home of the ancestors of the Dutch royal house.

orang-utan

The Malay language has made few contributions to English, but a large ape with long reddish hair provides one of them. The **orang-utan**, first recorded in the late 17th century, comes from Malay *orang huan* meaning 'forest person'.

orb

The Latin word *orbis* 'ring' is the ancestor of **orb** and **orbit**. During the Middle Ages an orb was a sphere or circle. In the early 17th century it developed the particular sense of a golden globe surmounted by a cross, forming part of the royal regalia, and held by the monarch at their coronation. **Orbit** was originally a term for the eye socket, but the astronomical sense of the regular course of a celestial object was used as early as 1670.

orc

In J.R.R. Tolkien's *The Lord of the Rings* the **orcs** are ugly, malevolent goblin-like creatures that attack in hordes and sometimes ride wolves. The word was not invented by Tolkien, and had been used by the Anglo-Saxons, to whom an *orc* was 'a demon'. It had died out by AD 1000, but came back into English in the 17th century from Italian *orco* 'man-eating giant'. The source in both cases was *Orcus*, the name of a Roman god of the underworld which was also the root of **ogre**, 'man-eating giant'. By the time that Tolkien was writing in the 1930s **orc** had become rare, and he revived the word – as a noted scholar he would have been aware of the earlier Old English use.

orchard

In Old English **orchard** was simply a name for a garden. The most likely explanation of its origin is that the first part of the word comes from Latin *hortus* 'garden'. The second part represents YARD, so an orchard would originally have been a 'garden yard'.

order

One early meaning of **order**, which comes from Latin *ordo* 'row, series, rank', was an institution founded by a ruler to honour people. The **Order of the Garter**, the highest order of English knighthood, was established by Edward III in around 1344. According to tradition, the

The coat of arms of the 1st Duke of Marlborough, incorporating his Order of the Garter.

garter was that of the Countess of Salisbury, which fell off while she was dancing with the king. To spare her blushes he promptly picked up the garter and put it on his own leg, saying 'Honi soit qui mal y pense' (shame be to him who thinks evil of it), which was adopted as the motto of the order. **Order** was also used to mean a rank, such as priest or bishop, in the Christian Church, which gave us the expression **take orders** for someone who becomes a priest.

In the 16th century **out of order** meant 'not in normal sequence'. The meaning was gradually extended to mean 'not in a settled condition', and by the 18th century to 'not in good health'. Finally it came to be used of machinery that was not working, or behaviour that was seen as unacceptable.

The sense of the word to mean 'a statement telling someone to do something' is found from the 16th century. By the 18th century **doctor's orders** had established itself as a term for an instruction from your doctor that had to be obeyed. Charles Dickens, in a letter of January 1841, wrote that: 'I have been obliged to make up my mind – on the doctor's orders – to stay at home this evening.'

The Latin word *ordo* also gave us **ordain**, **ordinance** 'an authoritative order' and **ordnance**.

In the army now ordnance refers to mounted guns or artillery, but in earlier days it was also used for the official body responsible for the supply of military equipment. In 1791 the official in charge, known as the **Master-General of the Ordnance**, was told to organise an official survey of the south coast of England to the scale of an inch to a mile, in anticipation of a French invasion. This grew into a series covering the whole of Great Britain and Ireland and was the origin of the **Ordnance Survey**, which today prepares large-scale detailed maps of the United Kingdom.

orgy

Determined party-goers were no doubt enjoying **orgies** long before the 16th century, when the word entered the language. It goes back to Greek *orgia* 'secret rites or revels'. In the classical world these were part of the worship of Bacchus, the god of fertility and wine, in the annual festivals held in his honour, which were celebrated with extravagant dancing, singing and drinking.

Orient

Since the Middle Ages the countries of the East have been referred to as the **Orient** – the first recorded use of the term appears in Geoffrey Chaucer's *Canterbury Tales*. The name goes back to Latin *oriri* 'to rise', and refers to the rising of the sun. The opposite is **Occident**, a name for the countries of the West which comes from Latin *occidere* 'to go down, set', and refers to the setting of the sun.

The English football club Orient (later known as Clapton Orient, and now as Leyton Orient) was founded in 1881. The name was suggested by a player who worked for the Orient shipping line, and was appropriate, as the club is based in the East End of London.

Oscar

An **Oscar** is a gold statuette given by the Academy of Motion Picture Arts and Sciences for achievement in the film industry – its proper name is an **Academy Award** (see ACADEMY). In 1931 Margaret Herrick, librarian and later executive director of the Academy, is said to have remarked that the statuette reminded her of 'uncle Oscar', the name by which she called her cousin Oscar Pierce. The term **Oscar** was first used officially by the Academy in 1939.

ostracise

In ancient Athens the people of the city would gather together every year to vote on whether an unpopular citizen should be expelled for ten years. They wrote

An *ostrakon* bearing the name of Themistocles, 'ostracised' in the 5th century BC.

the name of the person they wanted to send into exile on an *ostrakon*, a shell or fragment of pottery, and somebody who was exiled in this way was said to have been **ostracised**. Today a person who is ostracised is excluded from a society or group. See also OYSTER.

ostrich

The first mention of the **ostrich** in English is medieval, and one early source is John Wycliffe's 14th-century translation of the Bible. The first part of the word comes from Latin *avis* 'bird', but the second part goes back to the Greek name for a very different bird – *strouthos* 'sparrow'. The fuller term in ancient Greek was *megas strouthos* 'large sparrow'. It was also called *strouthokamelos* or 'sparrow camel', perhaps in recognition of its long neck.

There was a traditional belief that hunted ostriches would bury their heads in the sand, thinking that this would hide them from view. From this we get the use of 'ostrich' to mean a person who refuses to face reality or accept facts, and also the phrase to **bury your head in the sand**.

ounce

The unit of weight goes back to Latin *uncia*, where it meant 'twelfth part'. In imperial measurement this would have been the twelfth part of a pound, but it is also the basis of INCH as the twelfth part of a foot.

Ounce is also another name for the snow leopard. This is a quite different word, which originally had an extra letter. In medieval French it was *lonce,* but the 'l' was misunderstood as representing *le*, the French for 'the'. The word actually goes back to Latin *lynx*, the root of **lynx**.

oval

When we say that something is **oval**, we are calling it 'egg-shaped'. The word goes back to Latin *ovum* 'egg', which is used in English as the term for a female reproductive cell. **The Oval** is an oval cricket ground in Kennington, south London, opened in 1846, the home ground of Surrey County Cricket Club. The **Oval Office** is the informal name for the oval-shaped private office of the President of the United States.

owl

The name of the **owl** probably comes from an imitation of its call. The bird was traditionally taken as a symbol of wisdom – in classical times it was associated with the Greek goddess Athene – and to call someone **owlish** suggests that they look solemn or wise. It is a nocturnal bird, and its name is also used for someone, a 'night owl', who habitually goes to bed late and feels more lively in the evening. The opposite is a LARK.

In the 17th century **owling** was the term for smuggling wool or sheep out of England, to avoid paying tax. Although possibly a different word, it may also come from the bird's nocturnal habits, since such smuggling would have been done at night.

oyster

A medieval word that goes back ultimately to Greek *ostreon*, which was related to *ostrakon* 'shell or tile' and is linked to OSTRACISE. The proverbial warning **don't eat oysters unless there is an R in the month** probably comes from the tradition that oysters were likely to be unsafe to eat in the warmer months between May and August.

The possibility that on opening an oyster you might find a pearl has given us an expression that goes back to Shakespeare. In *The Merry Wives of Windsor* the boastful Pistol brags to Falstaff, 'Why then, the world's mine oyster, which I with sword will open.' To say that **the world is your oyster** is to assert that you are in a position to take all the opportunities that life has to offer. The wide-boy character Arthur Daley in the TV comedy drama *Minder* was apt to get the quotation wrong and say, 'The world is your lobster, my son.'

ozone

Today the usual association of **ozone** is with the **ozone layer**, a layer in the Earth's stratosphere that absorbs most of the harmful ultraviolet radiation reaching the Earth from the sun, and which is under threat from atmospheric pollutants. Ozone is a strong-smelling, poisonous form of oxygen whose name is recorded from the mid 19th century and goes back to Greek *ozein* 'to smell'. It was originally believed to have a tonic effect and to be present in fresh air, especially at the seaside. In Penelope Mortimer's autobiographical *About Time* (1987) she writes: 'An important part of our middle-class Englishness was the seaside holiday – no baking on a Mediterranean beach, but lungfuls of ozone, gales, hard sand.'

pacific

In 1520 the Portuguese explorer Ferdinand Magellan passed through the stormy waters of the strait between what is now Tierra Del Fuego and mainland Chile. To his relief he emerged to calm seas, and dubbed the welcome ocean *Mar Pacifico* 'tranquil sea'. The explorer's name is no longer applied to the Pacific Ocean, but the treacherous sound he passed through is still the Strait of Magellan. The word **pacific**, meaning 'peaceful in character or intention', goes back to Latin *pax* 'peace'. See also ATLAS, PAY.

pad

Well-heeled bankers or financial traders may well now have a posh **pad** in the city to complement their home in the country, but the word's origins are humble and even disreputable. A pad was originally a bundle of straw for lying or sitting on – in the early 18th century the slang sense 'a bed' developed, and by the 20th century criminals were using the term for a room or apartment, especially one where people could take drugs or where a prostitute could entertain a client. The origin of the word is not known.

pagan

In Latin *paganus* meant 'of the country, rustic' and also 'civilian, non-military' until, probably around the 4th century AD, it developed the sense 'non-Christian, heathen'. One theory is that belief in the ancient gods lingered on in the rural villages after Christianity had been generally accepted in the towns and cities of the Roman Empire; another refers to the 'civilian' sense, and points out that early Christians called themselves 'soldiers of Christ', making non-Christians into 'civilians', while a third likens heathens to people outside the civilised world of towns and cities, belonging to the countryside. Whatever the development, **pagan** entered English in the Middle Ages. The Latin root *paganus* came from *pagus* 'country district', which is also the source of **peasant**. **Heathen** is similar in meaning and development, coming from a word meaning 'inhabiting open country' which is related to **heath.**

page

English has two words spelled **page**. One originally meant 'a boy or youth employed as a servant or messenger' and now usually refers to a uniformed hotel employee or to a young boy attending a bride at her wedding. It may be related to Greek *pais* 'boy', from which English gets **paediatrics**, **paedophile** and similar words. Until the 1930s to **page** someone was to send a pageboy to look for them.

The **page** found in a book comes from Latin *pagina*, which goes back to *pangere* 'to fasten'. Originally a page was just one side of the piece of paper, as it still is in technical discussions of books and printing: the physical object with two sides that you can turn was a LEAF.

pain

There was no **pain** in the Old English period: Anglo-Saxons suffered **sore**. The usual modern term arrived around 1300, from Latin *poena* 'penalty, punishment', the source also of **penal** and **penalty**. Originally it referred to punishment for a crime or offence and to the suffering of hell as well as to physical pain from any cause.

no pain, no gain

The phrase took off in the 1980s as an exercise class slogan. But pain and gain have been linked since the late 16th century. 'No Pains, No Gains' is the title of a 1648 poem by Robert Herrick.

paint

The English words **paint** and **pigment** both derive from Latin *pingere* 'to paint', another form of which gave PICTURE. You can paint many things beside landscapes, portraits and walls. Americans first went out to enjoy themselves and **paint the town red** in the 1880s. This expression is something of a mystery. The traditional story takes it back to 1837, when an aristocratic yob called the Marquis of Waterford and some hooray Henry friends ran riot in the Leicestershire town of Melton Mowbray and painted some of the buildings red. If this is the source, though, it is surprising that the phrase first appears in the USA. Another idea is that revellers were thought of as having such a wild time that they treated the entire town like a red light district (see RED).

In Britain people with a never-ending task are compared to those who **paint the Forth Bridge**. The Forth Railway Bridge spanning the Firth of Forth in Scotland was built during the 1880s. Not only was it one of the first cantilever bridges ever constructed, it was also, for a time, the longest bridge in the world. The steel structure, with its gigantic girders, has required continuous repainting ever since: by the time the painters reach one end the other end needs another coat. See also OIL.

palace

The Roman emperors had their imperial residence on the Palatine hill, one of the seven hills on which the city of Rome is built. In Latin the name of the hill was *Palatium*, which came to refer to the emperor's home and then to any vast and luxurious building housing royal officials or bishops. Our word **palace** derives from this, as does Italian *palazzo*, a large mansion of an Italian noble family. From the 1830s lavish places of entertainment were also called palaces, from the **gin palace**, a gaudily decorated pub, to the **palace of varieties**, a variety theatre. See also MANSION.

palaver

The first **palaver** was a talk between Africans and European traders. When early Portuguese traders in West Africa had disputes or misunderstandings with the locals they used the Portuguese word *palavra*, literally 'word, speech', to mean 'a talk between local people and traders'. The Africans picked up the term from them, and in time passed it on to English sailors. In English **palaver** first meant a prolonged and tedious discussion, then in the late 19th century a fuss, commotion or rigmarole. The Portuguese source *palavra* developed from Latin *parabola* (see PARABLE).

pale

A **pale** is a pointed wooden post used in making a fence, and it can also mean 'a fence' and formerly 'a fenced or enclosed area'. In this sense **pale** comes from Latin *palus*. **The Pale** was a name given to the part of Ireland under English jurisdiction before the 16th century. The earliest reference to the Pale in Ireland, from the modestly titled *Introduction to Knowledge* of 1547, stated that Ireland was divided into two parts, one being the English Pale and the other being 'the wild Irish'. Many people believe that this enclosed English

part of Ireland was the source of **beyond the pale**, 'outside the bounds of acceptable behaviour', but this is extremely unlikely, as the phrase is not recorded until the 18th century, and its origin remains something of a mystery. A modern example of its use can be found in *Debrett's New Guide to Etiquette and Modern Manners*, published in 1996: 'Traditionally it is beyond the pale to light up before the Loyal Toast.'

The more familiar **pale**, meaning 'light in colour', goes back to a different Latin word, *pallidus*, the source also of **pallid**. People who are pallid in a romantic or poetic way have been described as **pale and interesting** since the early 19th century – appropriately, the earliest example found is from a letter by Lord Byron in 1817. A US newspaper of 1837 includes 'Sentimental young ladies would call him pale and interesting looking', which suggests the phrase had by then already become something of a cliché.

palm

Although most dictionaries regard them as separate English words, **palm** meaning 'a tropical tree' and **palm** 'the inner surface of the hand' are from the same root, Latin *palma* 'palm of the hand', which is related to *planus* 'flat' (see PLAIN). In ancient Rome a leaf or branch of a palm tree would be placed in the hands of the victor in a contest, from which the tree got its name.

pamphlet

The 12th-century Latin love poem *Pamphilus, seu de Amore* was popular in the Middle Ages and was translated into French, English and other languages. Its popular name was *Pamphilet*, which became **pamphlet**, meaning 'a short handwritten work of several pages fastened together', and lived on long after the original poem was forgotten. Pamphlets have been associated with political theories or campaigns since as early as the end of the 16th century.

panache

Soldiers in the 16th century would often wear a tuft or plume of feathers in their helmets. This tuft or plume was the original **panache**, a word that goes back to Latin *pinnaculum* (source of **pinnacle**) and so to *pinna* 'feather'. Men trying to give an impression of elegance or swagger would imitate the fashion, whose stylish associations gave rise to the modern sense, 'flamboyant confidence', in the late 19th century.

pandemonium

John Milton's epic poem *Paradise Lost*, first printed in 1667, tells the story of the Fall of Man. In Book I the angels who rebelled against God build Satan's new palace and capital, Pandemonium. Milton coined the name, meaning 'the place of all the demons', from Greek *pan* 'all' (see PANORAMA) and *daimōn* 'demon' (see DEMON). From the mid 18th century the word came to refer to other places that were centres of wickedness or haunts of evil and then to noisy, disorderly places. In the early 19th century **pandemonium** developed its usual modern sense of 'noisy disorder, chaos'. See also BEDLAM, CHAOS.

pander

Medieval legends elaborated some of the stories of the Trojan War told in Homer's *Iliad*. Among later developments was the tale of Troilus and Cressida, two lovers who were brought together by Pandarus. Homer did have a character Pandarus in the *Iliad*, but his role was breaking the truce with the Greeks rather than acting as a go-between in a clandestine love affair. The 14th-century Italian writer Giovanni Boccaccio invented the later version, and Geoffrey Chaucer adapted it and introduced the character of Pander into English in his *Troilus and Criseyde*. Less than a century later **pander** had become a general name for a pimp. The sense 'to act as a pimp' appeared in the 17th century, and developed into the weaker modern use to **pander to**, meaning 'to indulge an unreasonable desire or bad habit'.

Pandora's box

In Greek mythology Pandora was the first mortal woman. According to one version of the story she was created and sent to Earth by the gods in revenge for Prometheus having given the forbidden gift of fire to the world. The gods had given her a box containing all human ills, which she foolishly opened, allowing them all to fly out. An alternative account has the box containing all the blessings of the gods, which would have been preserved for the world had she not allowed them to escape: the only blessing that remained was HOPE. The Labour statesman and trade unionist Ernest Bevin once issued a memorable warning about the Council of Europe: 'If you open that Pandora's Box, you never know what Trojan 'orses will jump out.'

panel

The word **panel** goes back to Latin *pannus* 'piece of cloth', from which **pane** also derives. It applied to various pieces, divisions and sections, including the slip or roll of parchment on which the names of jurors were listed. The sense 'a jury' led to the modern use 'a small group of people brought together to decide on a matter'.

panic

Pan was the Greek god of flocks and herds, usually represented with the horns, ears and legs of a goat on a man's body. His sudden appearance was supposed to cause terror similar to that of a frightened and stampeding herd. Before **panic** meant 'sudden uncontrollable fear or anxiety' it appeared in phrases such as **panic terror** and **panic dread**, referring to the effect of an encounter with Pan. See also HYSTERIA.

The **panic button** originated in the US Air Force. Second World War bombers had an emergency bell system that was used if the aircraft was so badly damaged by fighters or flak that it had to be abandoned – the pilot gave a 'prepare-to-abandon' ring and then a ring meaning 'jump'. To **hit the panic button** and similar phrases meaning 'to respond to an emergency by panicking or taking emergency measures' date from the early 1950s. See also feature on CATCHPHRASES.

panorama

In 1787 the painter Robert Barker invented the **panorama**, a spectacular method for presenting a large painting of a landscape or other scene. It could either be arranged on the inside of a cylinder and viewed from the inside or be unrolled and made to pass in front of the viewer to show the various parts in succession. By the early 1800s **panorama** had come into wider use as 'a complete and comprehensive survey or presentation of a subject' and 'an unbroken view of the whole region surrounding an observer'. Barker formed the word from Greek *pan* 'all' and *horama* 'view' – *pan* is an element in numerous other English words including **panacea**, **pandemic** and PANDEMONIUM.

pantaloons

Pantaloon was one of the stock characters in the Italian theatre called the commedia dell'arte, which was popular from the 16th to the 18th centuries, and later in English pantomime. In the Italian tradition he was a foolish old man in a predominantly red costume that included long close-fitting trousers that covered the feet. These trousers must have made an impression, as from the 17th century the name **pantaloons** was given to a succession of styles, including that worn by Pantaloon himself. In the USA from the mid 19th century **pantaloons** was a name for any trousers, hence the modern term PANTS. See also ZANY.

pantomime

The first pantomimes in Britain were a kind of mime, which later developed into a comic dramatisation with the stock characters of Clown, Pantaloon (see

PANTALOONS), Harlequin and Columbine. The familiar **pantomime** or **panto** based on fairy tales such as Mother Goose or Cinderella and involving music, topical jokes and slapstick comedy developed in the 19th century, with a new set of conventional characters including the **dame**, the principal boy and the pantomime horse.

The word itself originally referred to classical Greece: a pantomime was an actor who represented mythological stories through gestures and actions. It comes from Greek *pan* 'all' (see PANORAMA) and *mimos*, the source of **mime** and **mimic**.

pantry

In origin a **pantry** is a place where you keep bread. The word goes back to Latin *panis* 'bread', from which we also get COMPANION and **pannier**. See also LARDER.

pants

In the USA **pants** is the usual word for trousers, whereas in Britain it normally means 'underpants'. The word is a shortening of PANTALOONS, and was first recorded in the 1830s in the USA. Since the early 1990s people in Britain have also used **pants** to mean 'nonsense, rubbish', rather like KNICKERS – as in 'A Liberal Democrat stunned his fellow peers when he dismissed a landmark report on the future of the historic environment as "a load of pants"' (*The Independent*, 2000).

paparazzi

Most celebrities have a love-hate relationship with the **paparazzi**. Originally, Paparazzo was the name of a society photographer in Frederico Fellini's 1960 film *La Dolce Vita*. By the following year **paparazzo** was appearing as a general name in English for a press photographer, and it had acquired a plural **paparazzi**, which is how it most commonly appears nowadays. See also feature on ITALIAN words.

paper

The words **paper** and **papyrus** are ultimately the same: their origin is Greek *papuros*. Papyrus is a material that the ancient Egyptians prepared from the pithy stems of a water plant, which was used in sheets throughout the ancient Mediterranean world for writing or painting on.

We have the German statesman Otto von Bismarck to thank for the expression **paper over the cracks**, 'to disguise a problem rather than try to resolve it'. Bismarck used the German equivalent of the phrase in a letter written in 1865, referring to a convention held at Gastein in Austria between Austria and Prussia. Tension had been rising between the two countries since their combined victory over Denmark in the previous year had given control of the duchy of Schleswig to Austria and that of Holstein to Prussia, but neither was quite ready to go to war. The Gastein deal gave a semblance of order to the situation, while in fact giving time for both to make preparations for an inevitable conflict.

To call a person or thing that appears threatening but is ineffectual a **paper tiger** is to use a Chinese expression first found in an English translation in 1836. It came to wider attention through a 1946 interview with the Chinese Communist leader Mao Zedong, in which he expressed the view that 'all reactionaries are paper tigers'.

Anita Ekberg, playing the film star Sylvia, poses for photographers – the 'paparazzi' – in *La Dolce Vita*.

par

Latin *par* means 'equal' or 'equality', and English **par** and **parity** both derive from it. In golf **par** refers to the number of strokes a good player should require for a particular hole. The game provides phrases such as **par for the course** 'what is normal or expected in a particular circumstance' and **above par**, **below par** and **under par**, 'better or worse than is usual or expected'. A score of one under par for a hole is a **birdie**, two under par is an **eagle**, three under par is an **albatross** or **double eagle** and one over par is a **bogey** (see BOGUS). This scoring terminology is said to have originated at the end of the 19th century when an American golfer hit a bird with his drive yet still managed to score one under par at the hole – this bird suggested **birdie**, and the other bird names were added to continue the theme. In the USA something exceptional has been a **bird** since the 1830s, though, so the story may be an unnecessary complication.

parable

The **parables** of Jesus were simple stories told to illustrate a moral or spiritual lesson. The Latin source of **parable**, *parabola* 'comparison, speech, word', not only gave us the curve known as the **parabola** but also PALAVER, **parley** and **parole**, and is related to PARLIAMENT.

paradise

The word **paradise** goes back to the ancient Iranian language in which the sacred texts of the Zoroastrian religion were written in the 4th century AD. *Pairidaēza* then meant 'an enclosure, park'. Via Greek and Latin it entered Old English, where it meant 'the Garden of Eden' before coming to refer to the heaven of Judaism, Christianity and Islam.

paraphernalia

Until the Married Women's Property Acts in the late 19th century a husband became the owner of all his wife's property when the couple got married. A partial exception to this was her purely personal belongings such as clothes and jewellery, which she could keep after her husband's death. These were her **paraphernalia** – the word derives from Greek *parapherna* 'property apart from a dowry'. Outside the strict confines of the law, the word came to refer to a person's bits and pieces, and then to the items needed for or associated with a particular activity.

parcel

Latin *particula* 'small part', from the same source as PART, has given us **particle** and **particular** as well as **parcel**. In early use **parcel** shared with these other words the notion of something forming a section of a larger whole, as in **a parcel of land**. This survives in contexts such as **part and parcel** and to **parcel out**. Early uses of the parcel wrapped up for sending by post concentrate on its contents, which would usually be a quantity of a substance or a number of goods wrapped up in a single package. Now a parcel often contains just a single item, and the emphasis is more on the wrapping.

pariah

The original pariahs were a people in southern India who acted as sorcerers and ceremonial drummers and also as labourers and servants. They were a tribal people outside the traditional Hindu caste system, and came to be regarded as 'untouchables' who did all the insanitary jobs. From there the sense 'a social outcast' developed in the early 19th century. The word **pariah** comes from the southern Indian languages Tamil and Malayalam, and means 'hereditary drummer'.

parish

In the Christian Church a **parish** is a district which generally has its own church and priest, and in British civil administration it is the smallest unit of local government, established only in rural areas. The word **parish** goes back through Latin *parochia* 'staying', from which **parochial** also derives, and eventually to Greek *oikos* 'house'.

park

Scholars do not agree about the ultimate origin of **park**, which came into English from French in the Middle Ages. It was originally a legal term for enclosed land held by royal grant for keeping game animals, as distinct from an open FOREST or chase. A military sense 'space occupied by artillery, wagons and stores in an encampment', known from the late 17th century, is the origin of the verb to **park**, as in parking a vehicle.

The British slang term **parky**, 'cold', dates from the 1890s. It probably comes either from **perky**, 'lively, sharp', or simply from **park**.

parliament

A **parliament** is historically just a talking shop. It originates from French *parler* 'to talk', which goes back to Latin *parabola* 'word' (see PARABLE). The first assembly called a parliament, around 1100, was French. The early Plantagenet kings used the term in

13th-century England for their great councils, and Parliament survived changes of monarchs, government and distribution of power to become the highest legislature of the United Kingdom. See also HOUSE.

parrot

The origin of **parrot** may lie in the tendency to give pet birds human names. The word, recorded in the early 16th century, could represent French *Pierrot*, a form of *Pierre* 'Peter'. People often address a pet bird as 'Pretty Polly', and the name **Polly** has been used to mean 'a parrot' since the early 19th century; it is a longer form of **Poll**, first recorded as a parrot's name in 1600. See also SICK.

parson   see PERSON.

part

Latin *pars* 'piece, share', from which **part** derives, is behind many English words, including PARCEL, **participate**, **partition** and **party**. Both parts (so to speak) of **be part and parcel of**, 'to be an essential element of', have fundamentally the same meaning, as one of the earliest senses of **parcel** was 'a part'. The phrase was first used in the mid 16th century in legal documents, but by the mid 19th century had crept into general use.

A **parting shot** is a final shot, or now a cutting remark, made by someone just as they are leaving. The phrase was probably influenced by **Parthian shot** – the Parthians were an ancient people from what is now Iran who were known for the trick of shooting arrows backwards while fleeing or pretending to flee.

paste

Italian **pasta** still retains a sophistication that the humble British **pasty** does not have, yet **pasta**, **pasty** and **paste** all go back through Latin to Greek *pastai* 'barley porridge'. The earliest use of **paste** in English was to mean 'pastry'; **pastry** took over the sense in the 15th century.

pasteurisation

Food poisoning can be a serious threat to health even today, but it was more of a hazard before the days of refrigeration. The 19th-century French scientist and bacteriologist Louis Pasteur devised a method of subjecting wine and beer to a high temperature for a set period of time, which destroyed most of the micro-organisms and enzymes present. This process, called **pasteurisation** after him, has made milk and other liquids and foods safer to consume and keep.

pat

The **pat** meaning 'readily' and in phrases such as to **have off pat**, 'to have memorised perfectly', is probably originally the same as **pat** meaning 'to touch gently with the flat of the hand'. In early use it often appears in to **hit pat**, as if with the hand, and the original word probably just imitated the sound of the action. In the Australian expression **on your pat**, 'on your own', **pat** is a shortening of rhyming slang **Pat Malone**.

patience

Hospital patients have to have patience, and they sometimes suffer, so it is not surprising that the Latin word *pati* 'to suffer' is the root of both **patience** and **patient**. People have maintained that **patience is a virtue** since the 14th century, though a Latin equivalent is recorded much earlier. As a card game **patience** dates from the early 19th century – the earlier name, still used in the USA, is **solitaire**.

pattern

Originally **pattern** and **patron** were the same word, **patron**, which came from French and went back to Latin *pater* FATHER. A patron was a protector or master, and the word **pattern** developed from the idea of a patron giving an example to be copied.

pavlova

Anna Pavlova was a Russian ballerina who became world famous for her solo dance *The Dying Swan*, created for her by the choreographer Michel Fokine in 1905. She later settled in Britain and formed her own ballet company, and in 1926, when well into her forties, toured Australia and New Zealand. This tour inspired chefs to commemorate her in a dessert. The first recorded **pavlova** was composed of coloured layers of jelly made in a mould resembling a ballerina's tutu, but by the time the recipe reached Britain it was a meringue dish. See also MELBA.

pawn

The **pawn** in chess came from Latin *pes* 'foot' (source of **pedal**, **pedestal** and **pedestrian**) via the sense 'foot soldier'. In the sense 'to deposit an object as security for money lent', **pawn** is a different word, which entered English from French *pan* 'pledge, security' in the 15th century.

pay

The original meaning of **pay** was 'to pacify', and it goes back to Latin *pax* 'peace'. The notion of 'payment' arose from the sense of 'pacifying' a creditor. A cartoon caption from the magazine *Punch* in 1846 was the source of **you pays your money and you takes your choice**, used to convey that there is little to choose between one alternative and another. See also CALL, PACIFIC.

pea

You could not eat a **pea** until the mid 17th century. The earlier form was **pease**, which people began to think was a plural, so that if you had a handful of peas you must be able to have one pea. The original is recorded in Old English, and goes back to Greek *pison*; it survives in **pease pudding**, a British dish of boiled split peas mashed to a pulp. The **pea** of **peacock** has no connection – it derives from Latin *pavo* 'peacock'.

A **pea-souper** was a very thick yellowish fog of the kind associated with the London of the late 19th century, the days of Jack the Ripper and Sherlock Holmes. Since the clean air legislation of the 1950s such fogs now belong largely to history.

pear

An Old English word related to French *poire* 'pear'. The expression **go pear-shaped**, 'to go wrong', does not come from the idea of a woman putting on weight around her hips, but rather from RAF slang. Although the first written examples are from the early 1980s, around the time of the Falklands War, it was probably in use several decades earlier. Some sources suggest that it may have arisen as a darkly humorous reference to the shape of a fighter plane after it has nosedived and crashed into the ground. A more cheerful alternative theory is that it describes a novice pilot's less than successful attempts to produce a perfect circle when performing a loop in the air.

peck

Hens and other birds have been seen to **peck** from the late 14th century. The word is probably related to **pick**. In the 1920s researchers in animal behaviour observed that hens have a social hierarchy in which some within the flock are able to attack or threaten others without retaliation. This is the **pecking order**, soon recognised in other animal groups and also in human society. Although the origins of the British expression **keep your pecker up**, 'stay cheerful', are quite innocuous, it will raise eyebrows in the USA. The phrase has been around since the 1850s, and is even used by Charles Dickens in a letter written in 1857. It most probably comes from the comparison of a bird's beak to a person's nose. Try to avoid using this phrase to an American acquaintance, though, as **pecker** is a slang word for the penis in the USA.

peculiar

The earliest senses of **peculiar** in English include 'unlike others' and 'specific to a person', with the development 'strange, odd' not emerging until the early 17th century. Latin *peculium*, from which **peculiar** derives, meant 'private property'. It came from *pecu* 'cattle, farm animals' – livestock formed the basis of many people's wealth.

pedigree

In medieval manuscripts a mark consisting of three curved lines was used to indicate a person's family descent or succession. People saw a resemblance between this mark and the claw or track of a crane, and called it 'a crane's foot' – *pé de grue* in the French spoken by the descendants of Norman settlers in England. The name, which became **pedigree**, then came to refer to a family tree, and from that to a person's or animal's lineage or descent.

peeping Tom

Lady Godiva was an 11th-century noblewoman, the wife of Leofric, Earl of Mercia. According to a

MAY I HAVE YOUR PECKING ORDER SIR?

13th-century legend her husband agreed to reduce unpopular taxes if she rode naked on horseback through the marketplace of Coventry. When she did this the grateful people of Coventry all stopped watching, except for a tailor named Tom, who was punished by being struck blind (or in some versions, dead). As a character **peeping Tom** appears to date from the 18th century: the name first appears in the Coventry city accounts on June 11, 1773, where it is noted that a new wig and fresh paint have been provided for his effigy.

pelican

The **pelican** has always been noted for its long bill and deep throat pouch for scooping up fish. This distinctive feature probably gave the bird its name, which came from Greek *pelekan*, probably based on *pelekus* 'axe'.

In Britain a **pelican crossing** is a road crossing with traffic lights operated by pedestrians. The name, first used in 1966, was taken from the initial letters of the formal title, *pe*destrian *li*ght *con*trolled *crossing*. Two other pedestrian crossings were given bird names by analogy with the pelican, the **puffin crossing** (from *pe*destrian *u*ser *f*riendly *in*telligent) and **toucan crossing**.

pell mell

People like words that combine two almost identical forms, like **helter-skelter**, **mishmash**, NAMBY-PAMBY and **wishy-washy** – and **pell-mell**. Its second element represents a form of French *mesler* 'to mix' (related to **meddle**). The first part might be from *pelle* 'shovel', giving the sense 'mixed together with a shovel', but the simple love of rhyme may be the only explanation needed.

pen

The earliest pens were made from a feather with its quill sharpened and split to form a nib which is dipped in ink. The origin of **pen** directly reflects this, going back to Latin *penna* 'feather', from which the pasta **penne** also derives. The idea that **the pen is mightier than the sword**, that writing is more effective than military power or violence, appeared in the works of the Latin author Cicero in the 2nd century BC.

penguin

Like CORGI, **penguin** is a rare example of a word that is probably from Welsh, in this case from *pen gwyn* 'white head'. Sailors and fishermen first gave the name **penguin** to the great auk of the seas around Newfoundland, which the penguin resembled closely, both birds being large, flightless waterfowl with black and white plumage adapted to life in freezing waters.

British sailors may have mistaken penguins for great auks, or simply applied a term they knew to a previously unseen bird. Penguins have fared rather better than great auks: penguins are popular and much studied, whereas great auks were hunted to extinction, the last killed on an islet off Iceland in 1844.

peninsula

A **peninsula** is a piece of land mostly surrounded by water or projecting out into the sea. It is *almost* an island, a fact reflected in its name. The word, first used in English during the mid 16th century, is from Latin *paeninsula*, from *paene* 'almost' and *insula* 'island'.

penny

The English word **penny** is related to Dutch *penning* and German *Pfennig*, but their ultimate origin is unknown. The penny, originally of pure silver, was first used in England in the 8th century. The origins of the phrase **the penny has dropped**, 'someone has finally realised or understood something', lie in gambling arcades. The idea is of a coin-operated slot machine whirring into action when you insert a small coin. The reference to **penny** gives a clue as to the age of the expression, as it goes back to the 1950s. You would probably have to say 'the pound has dropped' if you were inventing the phrase nowadays.

Inflation has also caught up with proverbial sayings such as **in for a penny, in for a pound**, used to express someone's intention to see an undertaking through – it dates from the late 17th century, when a penny would have been a significant investment to many.

*Inflation means you would need at least 20p now to **spend a penny** in a British public lavatory. The phrase dates from the days of coin-operated locks on the doors of public toilets.*

pension

In early use a **pension** was a payment, a tax or a regular sum paid to keep someone's loyalty. The word is derived from Latin *pendere* 'to pay', the source also of **stipend**. Use of the word to describe an annuity paid to a retired employee has developed since the early 16th century – since the Old Age Pensions Act of 1908 it has been paid to everybody of retirement age in Britain.

penthouse

A **penthouse** now suggests a luxurious apartment with extensive views, but originally was much more humble – a shed, outhouse or lean-to attached to the outside of a building, and called a **pentis**. The word

Caravanning in tiaras

What we now know as Iran was once Persia, a country whose ancient empire swallowed up much of the Middle East. It had a great language to match, which has given English many familiar terms.

To Persians a kiosk was not a small hut or cubicle where you can buy items such as newspapers, but a light open pavilion or summer house. The word came via French and Turkish from Persian *kus*. The original caravan was quite different from the white holiday trailers that fill our roads in summer. It was a group of traders or pilgrims travelling together across a desert in Asia or North Africa, from Persian *kārwān*. Because these people would travel heavily laden with baggage or merchandise, a caravan became a covered wagon or carriage in the late 17th century, then the travelling home of Gypsies or circus people and in the 1930s a vehicle towed by a car and used for holidays.

Persia is the source also of many words for fabrics. Seersucker, a light material with a crimped or puckered surface, often striped, derives from Persian *shīr o shakkar*, meaning 'milk and honey' and also 'striped cotton garment'. The first English record dates from the early 18th century. Another Persian fabric is taffeta, which in medieval times was a name for a kind of silk, from *tāftan* 'to shine'. A shawl was originally worn in the Indian subcontinent as a scarf, turban or belt – the word is from Persian *sāl*, probably based on the name of Shaliat, a town in India. Khaki takes its name from its colour, coming via Urdu (a language of northern India) *kākī* 'dust-coloured' from Persian *kāk* 'dust'. The dull brownish-yellow material was first used for uniforms by British troops in India during the 1840s.

The practice among women in certain Muslim and Hindu societies of keeping out of the sight of men or strangers is known as purdah, from Persian *parda*, meaning 'a veil or curtain'. Much more glamorous is a tiara, which was originally an ancient Persian headdress, in particular a kind of turban worn by kings. The word comes ultimately from Greek. In English the use of it to refer to a jewelled coronet or headband dates from the early 18th century.

See also ARSENIC, CHEESE, DIVAN, HAZARD, TURBAN.

---

came from a shortening of French *apentis*, which is from Latin *pendere* 'to hang ', the source of **appendage**, APPENDIX and **pendant**. In the 16th century people began to forget its origins and to associate it with French *pente* 'slope' and HOUSE. The modern use for a flat on the top floor of a tall building began during the 1890s in the USA. At first these penthouses were not necessarily exclusive – the first reference to one talks of it as accommodation for a janitor and his family.

people
The shared root of **people**, **popular** and PUBLIC was Latin *populus* 'the people'. All entered English in the Middle Ages from Old French. Diana, Princess of Wales is sometimes referred to as **the People's Princess**. After her death in 1997 Prime Minister Tony Blair said: 'She was the People's Princess, and that is how she will stay . . . in our hearts and in our memories forever.'

perish
To **perish** is literally to 'pass away' or 'go away' – that is the meaning of the source, Latin *perire*. A mischievous or awkward person, especially a child, has been a **perisher** since the end of the 19th century.

For many the word is particularly associated with the comic strip *The Perishers*, about a group of children and their sheepdog, Boot, which ran in the *Daily Mirror* newspaper from 1958 to 2006.

Shakespeare's plays have not always been popular. From the later 17th century people preferred them in updated form, often with wholly inappropriate happy endings. In 1700 the English comic actor, dramatist and theatre manager Colley Cibber brought out a rewritten version of Shakespeare's *Richard III*. Its only claim to fame is that it gave English **perish the thought**, used to show that the speaker finds a suggestion or idea completely ridiculous or unwelcome.

perk
The origin of **perk** in to **perk up**, 'to become more lively, cheerful or interesting', is not completely clear, although it may be related to **perch**. A **perk** meaning a benefit to which you are entitled because of your job is a shortening of **perquisite**, from medieval Latin *perquisitum* 'acquisition'. People began to **perk** coffee in a percolator around 1920. This comes from **percolate**, which is based on Latin *percolare* 'to strain through'.

person

When first used in English in the early Middle Ages, **person** meant 'a role or character assumed in real life or in a play' as well as 'an individual human being'. The first sense has largely been taken over by **persona**, which came directly in the mid 18th century from the source of **person**, Latin *persona* 'actor's mask, character in a play' and also 'human being'. The Latin term was also used by Christian writers as a term for the rector of a parish, what we would now call a **parson**.

pessimism   see OPTIMISM.

pet

The word **pet** was first used for 'a hand-reared lamb' in Scotland and northern England, where it also meant 'a spoilt or favourite child'. It came in the mid 16th century from Scottish Gaelic *peata* 'tame animal'. By the early 18th century it had spread south to apply to any domestic or tamed animal or bird kept for pleasure or companionship. The verb, meaning 'to stroke or pat affectionately', is found in the early 17th century, although the sense 'to engage in sexually stimulating caressing', as in **heavy petting**, is no older than the 1920s.

petrify

If something really petrified you, you would never move again. The original sense of **petrify** was 'to convert into stone', from the Latin and Greek root *petra* 'rock'. The sense 'to terrify, astonish' dates from the mid 17th century. **Petroleum**, an oil refined to produce fuels such as petrol and paraffin, is from the same source – it is found in rocks. The second part is Latin *oleum* 'oil'.

pheasant

An old name for the river Rion in Georgia in southeast Europe was the Phasis. People believed that the **pheasant** originated in that region before it spread westwards, and the geographical name is the basis of the word for the bird. It arrived in English at the end of the 13th century.

philately

This is one of the few words whose origin can be pinned down precisely. A Monsieur Herpin, a keen stamp collector, proposed the French word *philatélie* in the November 15, 1864, issue of *Le Collectionneur de Timbres-poste*. He formed it from Greek *philo-* 'loving' and *ateleia* 'exemption from payment', as a stamp shows that the price for delivery has already been paid. British stamp collectors quickly anglicised the French word to **philately**, which is recorded in an enthusiasts' magazine in December 1865.

philistine

There is no reason to believe that the Philistines were philistines. In biblical times, during the 11th and 12th centuries BC, they were a people who occupied the southern coast of Palestine and who frequently came into conflict with the Israelites. The first book of Samuel tells the story of David and Goliath, a Philistine giant, and Judges relates Delilah's betrayal of Samson to the Philistines. In the late 17th century students in the university town of Jena in Germany, bearing these passages in mind, started using *Philister* (German for 'Philistine') as an insulting name for a townsperson or non-student. By the 1820s English travellers had made this German university slang familiar, and people began to use **philistine** for 'an uncultured person'. The word itself goes back to the same root as **Palestine**.

phoney war

The **phoney war** was the period of comparative inaction at the beginning of the Second World War, between the German invasion of Poland in September 1939 and that of Norway in April 1940. The expression is now used of any coming confrontation, as in 'the debates on tax in the pre-election phoney war' (*Earth Matters*, 1997).

phlegmatic

According to the medieval doctrine of the four humours (see HUMOUR) phlegm made people stolidly calm. The root of **phlegm**, and so of **phlegmatic**, is Greek *phlegma* 'inflammation'.

phoney

The fraudulent practice of the **fawney-rig** is probably the source of **phoney** 'not genuine, fraudulent', which was first recorded in the USA at the end of the 19th century. In 1823 Pierce Egan, a chronicler of popular pursuits and low life in England, described how the fawney-rig worked. 'A fellow drops a brass ring, double gilt, which he picks up before the party meant to be cheated, and to whom he disposes of it for less than its supposed, and ten times more than its real, value.' The word **fawney** came from Irish *fáinne* 'a ring'.

photograph

The words **photographic**, **photography** and **photograph** all appeared in 1839, hot on each other's heels. The original of them all was French *photographie* 'photography', first recorded in 1834. Both the French and English words were formed from Greek *photo-* 'light' (found in **photogenic** and numerous other words) and *graphē* 'writing, drawing', as in **autograph**, **seismograph** and **telegraph**. As early as 1860 Queen Victoria was using the short form **photo**, writing in a letter about someone 'waiting to know . . . about the photo'.

physician

The Old English word for a medical doctor was **leech** (nothing to do with the worm, but a word meaning 'a healer'). **Physician** arrived in the early Middle Ages, and goes back to Greek *phusis* 'nature', the root also of **physical**, **physics** and numerous other English words. A **doctor** was originally not a physician but any learned person able to give an authoritative opinion, especially one of the early Christian theologians. The word started referring specifically to a medical expert at the start of the 15th century.

piano

Before the mid 18th century the usual musical instrument in comfortable European households was the harpsichord. Its strings are plucked by quills, and the player has little or no control over the length of notes or volume. From the 18th century the **pianoforte** or **fortepiano** was developed, with strings struck by hammers, dampers to stop vibration when the keys are released and pedals to regulate the length and volume of notes. The names came from Italian *piano* 'soft' and *forte* 'loud', referring to the innovation of volume control. Soon the shortened form **piano** appeared, and nowadays **pianoforte** is a rather formal term for a piano, whereas **fortepiano** tends to refer to early forms of the instrument.

picture

The word **picture** goes back to a form of Latin *pingere* 'to paint', from which PAINT and **pigment** also derive. It entered English in the late medieval period.

Doan's Backache Kidney Pills, claiming to cure everything from rheumatism to diabetes, were promoted with the advertising slogan **every picture tells a story**. The first known advertisement using it appeared in the *Daily Mail* of February 26, 1904. The novelist Charlotte Brontë had anticipated the advertising copy, though: in 1847 she wrote in *Jane Eyre*, 'The letter-press . . . I cared little for . . . Each picture told a story'.

A caption in the magazine *Printer's Ink* for December 8, 1927, read: 'Chinese proverb. One picture is worth ten thousand words.' There is no evidence at all that it is Chinese, but **a picture is worth a thousand words** has certainly gone on to be a modern English proverb.

pidgin

A **pidgin** is nothing to do with a PIGEON, but is a simplified form of a language used for communication between people not sharing a language. It originally represented a Chinese pronunciation of the English word BUSINESS, and with the meanings 'business, occupation or affair' became part of the simple language used between European and Chinese traders from the 1820s. By the 1850s people were also using **pidgin** to describe the language itself, especially in the fuller form **pidgin English**.

pie

The **pie** that is a dish with a pastry crust is the same as the **pie** in names of birds such as the magpie, which until the late 16th century was simply called a **pie**. The various ingredients in a pie may have suggested the objects randomly collected by the

The magpie – the original 'pie'

'thieving magpie'. The word itself comes from Latin *pica* 'magpie'.

Originally **pied** meant 'black and white like a magpie' and referred to the robes of some friars. Now it chiefly refers to birds, such as the **pied wagtail**. Mammals such as horses are described as **piebald**, which also means 'black and white': the second part is BALD in the old sense 'streaked with white'.

The expression **pie in the sky**, 'something pleasant to contemplate but very unlikely to be realised', was originally American and comes from a song written in 1911 by Joe Hill, one of the leaders of an organisation called the Industrial Workers of the World (also known as the Wobblies). Along with their union card, each member would receive a songbook containing parodies of popular songs and hymns of the day, with the motto 'To Fan the Flames of Discontent' on the cover. The song from which this phrase comes is called 'The Preacher and the Slave'. It parodies a Salvation Army hymn, 'In the Sweet Bye and Bye', which promised those suffering on Earth a better life in heaven. In response to the slave asking the preacher for some food, the chorus of the parody goes: 'Work and pray, live on hay, / You'll get pie in the sky when you die.'

pig

The word **pig** appears in Old English only once, the usual word being SWINE, and in the Middle Ages first meant specifically 'a young pig', as it still does in North America. See also HOG.

Observations such as **pigs might fly** and **pigs have wings** are used to mock people's incredulity. A 17th-century parallel is **pigs fly with their tails forward**. Lewis Carroll used the idea in *Alice's Adventures in Wonderland*: '"I've a right to think," said Alice sharply . . . "Just about as much right," said the Duchess, "as pigs have to fly."'

In **a pig in a poke**, 'something that is bought or accepted without first being seen or assessed', **poke** means 'a small sack or bag', now found mainly in Scottish English. The British phrase to **make a pig's ear out of**, 'to handle ineptly', probably derives from the proverb **you can't make a silk purse out of a sow's ear**, recorded from the 16th century.

In the children's game **pig** (or **piggy**) **in the middle**, first recorded in the *Folk-Lore Journal* of 1887, two people throw a ball to each other while a third tries to intercept it. This is behind the use of **pig in the middle** for a person who is in an awkward situation between two others.

pigeon

The name of the **pigeon** comes from French *pijon*, a word for a young bird, especially a young dove. It is an alteration of Latin *pipio*, which imitates the piping or cheeping of a nestling. The phrase to **be someone's pigeon**, 'to be someone's concern or responsibility', has nothing to do with homing pigeons going astray, or indeed anything involving the bird: **pigeon** here is a respelling of PIDGIN. The pigeon's distinctive strutting walk gave us **pigeon-toed**, meaning 'having the toes or feet turned inwards', and **pigeon-chested** or **pigeon-breasted**, 'having a protruding chest', from the end of the 18th century.

pike

The freshwater fish the **pike** gets its name from the resemblance of its long pointed jaw to the old infantry weapon called a **pike**, which has a pointed steel or iron head on a long shaft. This came into English during the 16th century from French *piquer* 'to pierce'. The Australian and New Zealand expressions to **pike out**, 'to withdraw or go back on a plan or agreement', and to **pike on**, 'to let someone down', go back to the 15th and 16th-century use to **pike yourself**,

'to provide yourself with a pilgrim's pike or staff' and so 'to depart, leave'. See also PLAIN.

pilgrim

This is one of the earliest words that came into English from French just after the Norman Conquest in 1066. It goes back to Latin *peregrinus*, 'foreign, alien', the source of **peregrinate** 'to wander from place to place' and of **peregrine**. The peregrine falcon was called the 'pilgrim falcon' because falconers caught individuals fully grown on migration rather than taking them from the nest. The **Pilgrim Fathers** were the English Puritans who sailed across the Atlantic in the *Mayflower* and founded the colony of Plymouth, Massachusetts, in 1620.

pill

In the past physicians would cover bitter pills thinly with gold to make them easier to swallow. This gave rise to the early 17th-century phrase **gild the pill**, 'to make an unpleasant or painful necessity more palatable'. As the practice of sugar-coating superseded gilding pills, the more familiar version **sugar the pill** took over from the end of the 18th century. **Pill** itself goes back to Latin *pilula* 'little ball'.

pillar

The Latin word *pila* 'pillar, pier' is the source of **pillar** and also **pile**. People were shunted **from post to pillar**, 'from one place to another', back in the early 15th century, but for some reason the version **from pillar to post** came into use in the middle of the following century and soon became the favoured choice. Its origins lie in the sport of real tennis, played in an enclosed court (a bit like the one used for squash, only much larger) with sectioned walls and buttresses off which the ball can rebound. These are the 'posts' and 'pillars' of the expression. The game developed from one played by sporty 11th-century monks in the cloisters of monasteries.

pillion

The first people to ride **pillion** were on horses, not motorbikes, and they were not necessarily sharing their mount. In the 15th century a pillion was a light saddle, especially one used by women. **Pillion** is one of the earliest words to have entered English from Gaelic, coming from Scottish Gaelic *pillean* and Irish *pillín* 'small cushion', the root of which is Latin *pellis* 'skin', the source also of **pelt**. The sense 'seat behind a motorcyclist' dates from the late 19th century.

pilot

The earliest pilots steered ships rather than flew aircraft. As early as the 15th century a pilot is described as going on board a ship to guide it out of port. The aerial pilot is also earlier than expected, with the person flying a balloon being called a **pilot** in the 1830s. The ultimate root is Greek *pēdon* 'oar, rudder'.

To **drop the pilot** is to abandon a trustworthy adviser. 'Dropping the pilot' was the caption of a famous cartoon by John Tenniel, published in *Punch* on March 20, 1890. It depicted Kaiser Wilhelm II's dismissal of Otto von Bismarck as German Chancellor.

pink

A dianthus plant, or 'pink'

A **pink** is a plant (called a **dianthus** by botanists) with sweet-smelling flowers which are usually various shades of pink, purple or white. The use of **pink** for the colour beloved by little girls actually comes from the flower, rather than the other way round. Shakespeare uses the plant to signify the supreme example of something in *Romeo and Juliet*: 'I am the very pink of courtesy.' Here he was probably making a pun on the expression **the flower of**, meaning 'the finest part or example'. This Shakespearean phrase led to the development of the expression **in the pink of condition**, which in time was shortened to simply **in the pink** 'in very good health and spirits'.

The plant name appeared in the mid 16th century, but its origin is not known for certain. It may be short for **pink eye** 'small or half-shut eye', which would make the name like its French equivalent *oeillet*, which means 'little eye'.

pin money

The **pin** in **pin money** is the decorative kind that women use to fasten their hair or clothing. It now means 'a small sum of money for spending on inessentials', but the phrase, dating from the end of the 17th century, first referred to an allowance made to a woman by her husband for personal expenses such as clothing.

pip

The name for the small hard seed in a fruit is a shortening of **pippin**, an apple grown from seed. English adopted the word from French, but its ultimate origin is unknown.

The British politician Sir Eric Geddes was the first to use the expression **squeeze until the pips squeak**, 'to extract the maximum amount of money from', in a 1918 speech about the compensation to be paid by Germany after the First World War: 'The Germans . . . are going to pay every penny; they are going to be squeezed as a lemon is squeezed . . . until the pips squeak.' Extracting money has always been popular with Chancellors of the Exchequer, and the Labour Shadow Chancellor Denis Healey was no exception when in 1974 he promised taxes that would 'squeeze the rich until the pips squeaked' if Labour were to win the forthcoming election, which they then did.

Another **pip** is an unpleasant disease of chickens and other birds which is documented as far back as medieval times. From the late 15th century various human diseases and ailments also came to be called **the pip**, though the precise symptoms are rarely specified: today's equivalent would probably be **the dreaded lurgy** (see LURGY). Whatever the nature of the disease, the sufferer would probably be in a foul mood, hence **the pip** became 'bad temper' and to **give someone the pip** was to irritate or depress them. The name came from medieval Dutch *pippe*, which was probably based on Latin *pituita* 'slime, phlegm', found also in **pituitary gland**.

pipe

The Old English word **pipe** goes back to Latin *pipare* 'to chirp, squeak'. It first referred to a simple tube-shaped wind instrument, from which came the meanings 'a tube used to convey water or other fluid' and, when tobacco was first brought to Europe in the mid 16th century, 'a device for smoking tobacco'. People have been told to **put that in your pipe and smoke it**, or accept what has been done, since the 1820s, and Charles Dickens used the phrase in *The Pickwick Papers* (1837).

In **piping hot**, 'very hot', **piping** refers to the hissing and sizzling of food just taken from the oven or off a fire. This phenomenon has been remarked on down the centuries, with the earliest recorded example being in *The Miller's Tale* by Geoffrey Chaucer.

pit

The **pit** that is a large hole in the ground is based on Latin *puteus* 'well shaft'. As a North American term for the stone of a fruit, **pit** seems to have been taken from Dutch in the 19th century, and is related to **pith**.

Since the 1960s people have used **pits** as an informal shortened term for **armpits**. These often have a tendency to be damp and smelly and so it was but a small linguistic leap to have them symbolise the worst example of something. That is one explanation of to **be the pits**, 'to be extremely bad'. A more refined interpretation connects the bottom of a deep, dark hole with the lowest possible rank or class.

pit your wits

The old spectator sports of cock and dog fighting gave us **pit your wits**, 'to test in a conflict or competition'. The creatures were 'pitted' or put together in a pit or other enclosure (literally a **cockpit**), a sense used from the mid 18th century.

pitch

Of the two **pitch** words in English, one is simple in its meaning and history and the other complex and obscure. The name of the sticky dark substance is related to Dutch *pek* and German *Pech* and goes back to Latin *pix*. The other **pitch** has senses ranging from 'the quality of a sound' through 'an area of ground for a game' to 'to aim at a target'. The ultimate origin is unknown and historical development unclear.

In the original military sense a **pitched battle** is one fought between large formations of troops which is more or less confined to one location, as contrasted with a chance skirmish or a running battle carried on while one side flees and the other pursues. Today **pitched battle** tends to be used of football hooligans or violent protesters clashing with the police.

place

If you have been to Italy or Spain you have probably visited the **piazza** or **plaza** of a town. These words have the same origin as English **place** and French *place*, namely Latin *platea* 'open space', from Greek *plateia hodos* 'broad way'. From the early Middle Ages, when it was adopted from French, **place** superseded **stow** (found in place names such as Stow on the Wold and Padstow) and **stead**, as in Wanstead.

The orderly person's mantra **a place for everything and everything in its place** goes back to the 17th century, but the modern formulation first appears in the 1840s in Captain Frederick Marryat's nautical yarn *Masterman Ready*: 'In a well-conducted man-of-war . . . every thing in its place, and there is a place for every thing.'

In 1897 the German Chancellor, Prince Bernhard von Bülow, made a speech in the Reichstag in which he declared, 'we desire to throw no one into the shade [in East Asia], but we also demand our place in the sun'. As a result the expression **a place in the sun**, 'a position of favour or advantage', has been associated with German nationalism, but it is recorded much earlier, although it is traceable back to the writings of the 17th-century French mathematician and philosopher Blaise Pascal.

placebo

In Latin **placebo** means 'I shall be acceptable or pleasing'. Doctors have probably always prescribed some drugs just to keep a patient happy, and used the term **placebo** for these as far back as the late 18th century. Researchers testing new drugs give some participants substances with no therapeutic effect to compare their reactions to those who have genuinely been treated: such a substance is also a **placebo**. Results may be confused, though, by the **placebo effect**, first identified in the early 1950s, in which the person's belief in the treatment brings about beneficial effects that have nothing to do with the properties of the placebo they have taken.

plague

The late 14th-century translation of the Bible supervised by John Wyclif introduced the word **plague** to English. Its root is Latin *plaga* 'a stroke, wound', and 'a blow' was one of its first English senses. It was also used in reference to **the ten plagues of Egypt**, described in Exodus. Although these included boils and the death of cattle and, finally, firstborn children, they were mainly not medical conditions, but afflictions like hordes of frogs and swarms of locusts. Nevertheless, by the late 15th century people were applying **plague** specifically to infectious diseases and epidemics, such as **bubonic plague** (from the inflamed swellings in the armpit or groin called 'buboes'). The Black Death that reached England in 1348 is thought to have been bubonic plague. To **avoid like the plague** is not medieval, dating from the end of the 17th century, when the Great Plague of 1665-6 was fresh in people's memories.

plain

The source of both **plain** and **plane** is Latin *planus* 'flat'. Mathematicians introduced the spelling **plane** in the early 17th century to distinguish the geometrical uses of **plain** from senses such as 'ordinary' and 'simple'. **Plane** meaning 'an aircraft' is completely unconnected, and is a shortening of AEROPLANE. Also unconnected is the **plane tree**, which is not flat but 'broad', the meaning of its Greek source *platus*.

The earlier version of the expression **as plain as a pikestaff**, 'very obvious', was **as plain as a packstaff**, which gives a small clue as to its origins. A packstaff was a long stick which a pedlar used to carry his pack of goods for sale, and would probably have been obvious from a distance as the pedlar trudged along the road. By the end of the 16th century people had started to use the current version with **pikestaff**, and 100 years later it had more or less taken over. A pikestaff was a walking stick with a pointed metal tip, which possibly replaced **packstaff** because it sounded similar and pedlars were becoming a less familiar sight.

Plain Jane first appears in 1912, in the novel *Carnival* by Compton Mackenzie. There was probably no real Jane – she was simply a fortunate rhyme.

The phrase **plain sailing**, 'smooth and easy progress', probably represents a use of **plane sailing**. This refers to the practice of determining a ship's position on the theoretical assumption that it is moving on a plane.

planet

Early Greek astronomers observed certain heavenly bodies moving around the night sky in contrast to the stars, which stayed permanently in a fixed position in relation to one another. This is why they are called **planets**, from Greek *planētēs* 'wanderer'. The Sun and the Moon were once thought of as planets too. **Plankton**, the term for small and microscopic organisms floating in the sea, comes via German from the related Greek word *planktos*, 'wandering or drifting'. See also AEROPLANE.

plank

The medieval word **plank** ultimately comes from Latin *planca* 'a board or slab'. Britons have been calling less bright people **planks** since the early 1980s, from the phrase **as thick as two planks** or **two short planks**, recorded from the previous decade.

Walking the plank is a method of execution associated with pirates, who are supposed to have forced their prisoners to walk blindfold along a plank jutting out over the side of a ship to their death in the sea. There is little evidence that this was regularly done, though, and most pirates probably just threw their victims overboard.

plastic

The Greek word *plastikos* meant 'able to be moulded into different shapes', and came from *plassein* 'to mould'. When **plastic** entered English in the 17th century it had a similar meaning, but its main modern sense refers to the synthetic compounds developed in the early 20th century and now used for just about everything. This sense of **plastic** was first used in print in 1909 by the Belgian-born scientist Leo Baekeland, inventor of Bakelite.

Plastic surgery does not involve plastic, but refers to the shaping or transferring of tissue. Since the 1990s cosmetic plastic surgery has become very popular, but the term goes back much further – the first mention of the use of plastic surgery in treating injury was in 1837.

platoon

Cyclists not soldiers formed the original **platoon**. In a road race such as the Tour de France the main pack of riders is known as the *peleton*, a French word, as are many cycling terms, that means 'a little ball' (from *pelote* 'a ball', the source also of **pellet**). It can also be applied to a small detachment of foot soldiers acting as a closely organised unit, and it is from this use that we got the English word **platoon** in the 17th century.

plaudit

You receive **plaudits** when you are praised for something good you have done. The source is Latin *plaudite* 'applaud!', which is what Roman actors used to ask the audience to do at the end of a play. This comes from *plaudere* 'to applaud or clap', as does **applaud** itself. **Plausible**, also ultimately from *plaudere*, was at one time used to mean 'deserving applause or approval'. And what if the actors' performance wasn't worth applauding? Then you could simply add *ex* 'out' to *plaudere* to make *explaudere*, meaning 'to drive off the stage by clapping, hissing and booing'. This became EXPLODE in English and was first used to mean 'to reject scornfully' and 'to prove false'.

play

In Old English *plegan* or *plegian* meant 'to exercise', while *plega* meant 'brisk movement or activity', and could also be used to describe a dramatic performance on stage. These are the first uses of the verb and noun **play**. Today terms such as **swordplay** and **gunplay** preserve the old 'brisk movement' sense of the noun.

To **play with fire** is to take foolish risks with something potentially dangerous. The proverb **if you play with fire you get burned** dates from the late 19th century, though a similar sentiment is expressed by the poet Henry Vaughan in 1655: 'I played with fire, did counsel spurn . . . But never thought that fire would burn / Or that a soul could ache.'

Play it again, Sam is a popular misquotation from the film *Casablanca* (1942). Although these precise words are never actually spoken in the film, Humphrey Bogart does say 'If she can stand it, I can. Play it!', and earlier in the film Ingrid Bergman says 'Play it, Sam. Play "As Time Goes By".'

The US magazine *Playboy* was founded in 1953 by Hugh Hefner. The 'rabbit' logo appeared in the second issue, and when the first of a series of Playboy clubs opened in Chicago in 1960 the waitresses were dressed in skimpy rabbit costumes – the Playboy bunnies or **bunny girls**. A **playboy** was at first, back in 1616, a boy actor. The modern sense, 'an irresponsible pleasure-seeking man', started in Ireland, and is first recorded in the 1820s.

please

A word that comes via Old French *plaisir* 'to please' from Latin *placere*. In phrases like **yes, please** it was originally short for *may it please you* or *let it please you*. **Please** on its own was not known to Shakespeare, who used *please you*: 'Will you hear the letter? – So please you, for I never heard it yet' (*As You Like It*). The proverbs **you can't please everyone** and **little things please little minds** are both old – they can be traced back to the late 15th and late 16th centuries.

plight

In the traditional marriage ceremony the bride and groom each say 'I plight thee my troth', meaning 'I pledge my word'. Neither of the words **plight** and **troth** is commonly used outside this phrase. **Plight**, an Old English word, means 'to promise solemnly', and **troth** is an old variant of TRUTH, meaning 'giving your word' and still preserved in **betroth**. The other meaning of **plight**, 'a predicament', is from Old French *plit* 'fold', suggesting the idea of a difficult or complicated situation.

Play it, Sam. Play 'As Time Goes By'.

plonk

There are two different **plonks**. One, as in 'to plonk something down', was originally a northern English word meaning 'to hit or strike with a heavy thud'. The other **plonk**, describing cheap wine, started out in Australia. It is probably a corrupted form of *blanc* in the French phrase *vin blanc* 'white wine', though some suggest that it might be meant to imitate the sound of a cork being taken out of a bottle.

Plonker, meaning 'an idiot', dates from the 1960s but was popularised by the 1980s BBC television sitcom *Only Fool and Horses*. Del Boy Trotter tended to direct it at his hapless younger brother Rodney. It is based on the first **plonk** and was first used to mean 'something large or substantial' and also 'penis'.

plot

The first meaning of **plot** was 'a small piece of ground'. The sense 'secret plan' dates from the late 16th century and was probably influenced by Old French *complot* 'dense crowd, secret project'. Relating to another sense of **plot**, 'the main sequence of events in a play, novel or film', is the expression **the plot thickens** – something you hear people say when a situation is becoming more complicated and puzzling. The person to thank for it is George Villiers, the 2nd Duke of Buckingham, whose satirical drama *The Rehearsal* (1671) includes the line 'Ay, now the plot thickens very much upon us.'

plough

The spelling **plough** did not become common until the 18th century. Before that only the noun was normally spelled this way, and the verb was **plow**, which is still the US spelling for both noun and verb. The word was probably brought over from Old Norse *plógr* around the 12th century – the Old English equivalent was *sulh*.

A staple of the pub lunchtime menu is the **ploughman's lunch**, a cold meal consisting of bread and cheese usually served with pickle and salad. This is not the traditional rural snack it might seem. The first recorded use of the term can be traced back only to 1960, though two years before that the same kind of thing was being given a similar name in *The Times*: 'In a certain inn to-day you have only to say, "Ploughboy's Lunch, please," and for a shilling there is bread and cheese and pickled onions to go with your pint, and make a meal seasoned with gossip, and not solitary amid a multitude.' And over a century earlier we find this curious pre-echo: 'The surprised poet swung forth to join them, with an extemporized sandwich, that looked like a ploughman's luncheon, in his hand' (John Lockhart, *Memoirs of the Life of Sir Walter Scott*, 1837).

plum

Latin *prunum* is the source of both **plum** and **prune**, which is a plum preserved by drying. **Plum pudding** was originally made with plums, but even when these were replaced by raisins and currants in the recipe the name stuck. The use of **plum** to refer to something highly desirable, 'the pick of the bunch', probably arose from the idea of picking the tastiest bits out of a plum pudding.

Upper-class people are sometimes said to have **a plum in the mouth**, or to speak with a **plummy** voice. The idea of having a plum in the mouth goes right back to the 1530s, though at first it meant that the speech was indistinct rather than posh.

plumb

You can say that something that is not quite perpendicular is **out of plumb**. This draws on the original meaning of **plumb**, a ball of lead attached to a string to determine a vertical line, or a **plumb line**. Another early use was as a term for a sounding lead used for measuring the depth of water. To **plumb** a body of water was to measure its depth in this way, and, via the idea of getting to the bottom or lowest point of something, is the source of the phrase **plumb the depths**.

The source of **plumb** is Latin *plumbum* 'lead', also the root of **plumber**. Medieval plumbers dealt in and worked with lead, and it was not until the 19th century that the word was applied solely to people trained in fitting and repairing water pipes, which were initially all made of lead.

The Latin word *plumbum* is also the basis of **plummet**, which came into medieval English from Old French and then referred to a plumb line. The use of **plummet** as a verb meaning 'to drop straight down rapidly, to plunge' is more recent, first recorded in the 1850s. An early use of the verb was 'to let a vertical line fall by means of a plummet', and the modern sense developed from this. See also APLOMB.

plump

If you described someone as **plump** in the 15th century you meant that they were blunt or forthright. Our word is related to old Dutch and German words that meant 'blunt, stupid' and also 'clumsy, squat'. Pretty soon the sense of the English word had become more positive, describing someone who is slightly fat or fleshy, particularly in an attractive way. The other sense of **plump**, 'to choose', is related to an old German word *plumpen*, which meant 'to fall heavily into water'.

poach

Poaching eggs and poaching game may seem vastly different activities. but they are both probably connected with the Old French word *pochier* or French *pocher*, 'to enclose in a bag'. When you poach an egg you can think of the white of the egg as forming a pocket or bag for the yolk to cook in. The second **poach** first meant 'to push together in a heap', and acquired the 'steal game' sense in the early 17th century. The connection with the source word comes from the pocket or bag that a poacher would stuff his ill-gotten gains into.

poet

A **poet** is literally 'a maker'. The English word which replaced Old English *scop* in the Middle Ages can be traced back to Greek *poētēs* or *poiētēs*, 'maker, poet', which came from *poiein* 'to create'. When someone experiences a fitting or deserved retribution for their actions, you can say that it is **poetic justice**. Alexander Pope used the phrase in his satire *The Dunciad* (1742), where he depicts 'Poetic Justice, with her lifted scale'. See also LAUREL.

po-faced

The **po** in **po-faced**, 'humourless and disapproving', probably comes from the use of **po** to mean 'chamber pot', though it might also have been influenced by the exclamation '**poh!**', used to reject something contemptuously. In any event, the phrase, dating from the 1930s, is likely to be modelled on the expression **poker-faced**.

poignant

Something that makes you feel a keen sense of sadness or regret can be described as **poignant**. This comes from an Old French word that meant 'pricking' and derived from Latin *pungere*, 'to prick'. Back in the Middle Ages you could describe a weapon as **poignant**, meaning that it had a sharp point. Here is an example from Geoffrey Chaucer: 'The God of Love an arrow took / Full sharp it was and poignant'. The word could also be applied to sharp tastes or smells, as in 'a poignant sauce' or 'a poignant scent'. This sense is now covered by the related word **pungent**, which originally meant 'very painful or distressing' and at one time could also mean 'telling or convincing', as in Samuel Pepys's reference to 'a very good and pungent sermon'.

point

Most senses of **point** ultimately derive from Latin *punctum* 'a small hole made by pricking', from *pungere* 'to pierce or prick'. A boxer **wins on points** when he wins because the referee and judges have awarded him more points than his opponent, rather than by a knockout. The **point of no return** is the point in a flight at which it is impossible for an aircraft to return to its point of departure because of lack of fuel and so it has no choice but to continue. It can also be the point at which you are committed to a course of action and must continue to the end.

To refuse or ask about something **point-blank** is to do so directly or abruptly and without explanation. The phrase literally describes a shot or bullet fired from very close to its target, **blank** being used here in the old sense of 'the white spot in the centre of a target'. If you aim or point a gun directly at the centre of the target, you need to be sufficiently close for the bullet still to be travelling horizontally (rather than starting to follow a downward trajectory) as it hits the spot. The more general meaning arose as far back as the 1650s.

poise

The word **poise** originally meant 'weight', and came via Old French *pois* from Latin *pensum* 'a weight'. This gave rise to the idea of 'equal weight, balance, equilibrium', of something being equally weighted on both sides, from which developed the modern senses of 'composure' and 'elegant deportment'.

poison

A **poison** does not necessarily need to be in liquid form, but in early use the word meant a drink or medicine, specifically a potion with a harmful or dangerous ingredient. The source was Old French *poison* 'magic potion', from Latin *potio*, also the source of **potion**. The saying **one man's meat is another man's poison** has been around for centuries and was being described as long ago as 1604 as 'that old moth-eaten proverb'. A similar idea is found in the work of the Roman poet and philosopher Lucretius (*c*.94-55 BC): 'What is food to one person may be bitter poison to others.'

A **chalice** is a large cup or goblet, and a **poisoned chalice** something that seems attractive but is likely to be a source of problems. A poisoned chalice features in Shakespeare's *Macbeth*, and is the source of our expression.

pole

The Old English word from which we get **pole**, as in 'flag pole' or 'telegraph pole', meant 'stake'. To be **in pole position** is to be in a leading or dominant position, from motor racing, where it describes the first place on the starting grid, on the front row and on the

Sex and drugs and rock and roll

In their short history, pop lyrics have dealt with most subjects, from the taboo to the everyday. They have touched more people's lives in the past 50 years than poetry or drama and given the language some memorable phrases.

The most-quoted pop lyrics must be those penned by John Lennon and Paul McCartney for the Beatles. In 1964 they told us that 'It's been a hard day's night' and 'Money can't buy me love', and continued with 'Ticket to Ride' in 1965, 'Nowhere Man' in 1966, 'With a Little Help From My Friends' in 1967 and 'Let It Be' in 1970.

In his solo work John Lennon was just as memorable. His idealistic 'Imagine' (1971), with 'Imagine no possessions / I wonder if you can', was matched by 'Give Peace a Chance' (1969) until the latter's tune was adopted by soccer fans and the words changed to 'All we are saying / Is give us a goal.' The ultimate football song, and one particularly associated with Liverpool, home of the Beatles, is 'You'll Never Walk Alone'. This was written by Richard Rodgers and Oscar Hammerstein II for the 1945 musical *Carousel*,

but a version recorded in 1963 by the Merseyside group Gerry and the Pacemakers led to its use as the Liverpool FC club song.

Few have dealt with the subject of sex as thoroughly as Madonna, in songs such as 'Like a Virgin' (1984) and 'Erotica' (1992), although she has competition from the US soul singer Marvin Gaye, with 'Let's Get It On' (1971) and 'Sexual Healing' (1982). The Rolling Stones complained that '(I Can't Get No) Satisfaction' in 1965, while a more romantic approach was taken in the soul ballads 'Try a Little Tenderness', recorded by Otis Redding in 1967, and 'When a Man Loves a Woman' (1966) by Percy Sledge. Again, the Beatles had the most to say about love, with 'Love Me Do' (1962), 'She Loves You' (1963) and 'All You Need is Love' (1967), and the 2006 album of remixed versions of their songs was simply entitled *Love*.

inside of the first bend. But its origins actually lie in horse racing. On 19th-century racecourses a pole marked the starting position closest to the inside boundary rails, a favourable position in a race.

police

In the 15th century **police**, which came from medieval Latin *politia* 'citizenship, government', was another word for **policy**. Over time the word came to mean 'civil administration' and then 'the maintenance of public order'. The first body of officers to be named **police** in the current sense was the Marine Police, a force set up around 1798 to protect merchant shipping in the Port of London. The police force established for London in 1829 was for some time known as the New Police. See also CONSTABLE, COPPER.

politics

We have the ancient Greek philosopher Aristotle to thank for **politics**. Aristotle, a pupil of Plato and tutor to Alexander the Great, wrote a treatise called *ta politika*, or 'The Affairs of State', which gave us our word. His title was based on Greek *polis*, 'city', also the source of ACROPOLIS, **cosmopolitan** and **policy**.

The concept of **political correctness** originated in the USA during the 1980s as a term for the avoidance of words or actions that are perceived to insult disadvantaged groups, but it dates back a lot longer. **Political correctness** is recorded in 1840 in the USA, and **politically correct** goes back even further, to 1793, in the records of the US Supreme Court. Originally both terms referred to people conforming to the prevailing political views of the time – we might call them **onside** today.

poltroon

A **poltroon** is an utter coward. French *poltroon* came from Italian *poltrone*, a term for either a coward or a lazy person which was possibly based on the Italian word for a bed or couch, *poltro*. A story once widely believed was that the word related to archers shirking military service by cutting off their right thumbs, a self-inflicted wound which would make them incapable of drawing a longbow. **Poltroon** was supposed to be a corruption of *pollice truncus*, 'maimed or mutilated in the thumb'.

Drug references in songs became obligatory once musicians started experimenting with LSD in the mid 1960s, with lyrics as a result often becoming lost in obscurity. In 1967 the Beatles released 'Lucy in the Sky with Diamonds' (whose initial letters spell *LSD*) and 'I Am the Walrus', which alluded to the work of Lewis Carroll, as did 'White Rabbit' by the US band Jefferson Airplane, released in the same year. The link between popular music and drugs was nothing new, though, as Cole Porter was penning 'Some get a kick from cocaine' back in 1934 in his song 'I Get a Kick Out of You'.

Early rock and roll lyrics celebrated music itself, as in '(We're Gonna) Rock around the Clock' (1953) by Bill Haley and the Comets, 'Roll over, Beethoven' by Chuck Berry (1956) and 'Whole Lotta Shakin' Goin' On', recorded by Jerry Lee Lewis in 1957. Other subjects were usually cars or girls – Chuck Berry was a master of both, with 'No Particular Place to Go' and 'Sweet Little Sixteen'.

Wild living with no thought for the future is a recurring theme in lyrics, often summed up as 'Live fast, die young (and leave a beautiful corpse)', a line from the 1949 juvenile delinquent movie *Knock on Any Door*, starring Humphrey Bogart. 'My Generation' (1965) by the Who expressed this idea as 'Hope I die before I get old', which was parodied by Robbie Williams as 'I hope I'm old before I die' ('Old Before

I Die', 1997). Another classic in this vein is 'Born to be Wild' (1968) by the Canadian band Steppenwolf, which included the first musical use of the term heavy metal. Bruce Springsteen coined two memorable 'born' phrases, 'Born to Run' in 1974 and 'Born in the USA' in 1984.

With the appearance in Britain of punk in 1976 the established rock stars were suddenly old hat. The first album by the Sex Pistols, *Never Mind the Bollocks, Here's the Sex Pistols* (1977), was banned in places because of its 'obscene' title. This was based on the slogan 'Never mind the quality, feel the width', the title of a TV comedy series (1967-9) about a tailoring business in the East End of London and ultimately probably a reversal of a saying used in the cloth trade.

In 1996 the Spice Girls used their girl power and had a number one with their first single, 'Wannabe' – 'I'll tell you what I want, what I really really want.' The band did not invent girl power or wannabe, the former being recorded in 1986 and wannabe in 1981, in relation to surfing.

'Sex and Drugs and Rock and Roll' itself was the title of a 1977 song by Ian Dury, itself poking fun at rock clichés. Dury was one of the most literate of pop lyricists, fond of wordplay like 'Einstein can't be classed as witless / He claimed atoms were the littlest.'

pomegranate

Our name for this fruit comes from Old French *pome grenate*, from *pome* 'apple' and *grenate*, which meant 'pomegranate' but was based on Latin *granatum*, 'having many seeds'. See also GRENADE and feature on AUSTRALIAN WORDS.

pony

Different as they seem, **pony** and **poultry** have the same starting point. Latin *pullus* meant 'young animal', but it tended to be applied specifically to young horses and young chickens. The 'young horse' strand became Old French *poulain* 'a foal', and the diminutive form of this, *poulenet*, was adopted into Scots in the early 18th century as *powny*, coming into general English usage as **pony**. The 'young chicken' strand is the source of Old French *pouletrie*, from which we get **poultry**. See also MONKEY.

poor

The Latin word for 'poor', *pauper*, is the base of **pauper**, **poverty** and **poor**. The phrase **poor as a church mouse**, or 'extremely poor', comes from the notion that a church mouse must be particularly

deprived as it does not have the opportunity to find pickings from a kitchen or larder, and there are few crumbs to be found in a well-swept church. You sometimes hear a wealthy young person whose money appears to bring them no happiness described as **poor little rich girl** (or **boy**). Though he did not coin the phrase, Noël Coward certainly popularised it with his 1925 song 'Poor Little Rich Girl'.

pop

Like **splash**, **crack** and **bang**, **pop** imitates the sound it describes. It was first used to refer to a blow or knock, the 'abrupt explosive noise' meaning coming later. The phrase **pop the question**, meaning 'to propose marriage', is first recorded in the early 18th century. The fizzy **pop** that you can drink gets its name from the sound made when the cork is pulled out. It was first mentioned at the beginning of the 19th century.

To **pop your clogs** is to die. **Pop** here is used in the sense 'to pawn', the idea being that a person who has just died no longer has any need of their shoes or clogs and so they can be pawned. The phrase is recorded only from the 1970s, which is surprisingly recent – it may have been made up as an 'imitation' dialect expression, or be an example of a folk expression that existed for generations without being recorded in print.

In reference to music, **pop** is short for **popular**, which itself is from Latin *populus* 'the people'. The first mention of this **pop** was in 1910 – 'a pop vaudeville house' – and **pop songs** were mentioned in *Variety* magazine during 1921. A issue of *Melody Maker* from April 7, 1956, gives us the first recorded mention of **Top of the Pops**, the best-selling recorded song or piece of music at a given time, although the first British singles chart was published in the November 14, 1952, edition of the *New Musical Express*. The BBC pop music programme *Top of the Pops* ran for 42 years from 1964 to 2006.

poppycock

The English language has any number of curious words for 'nonsense', such as **balderdash**, **bosh**, **bunkum**, **claptrap**, **codswallop** and **piffle**. **Poppycock** is another one. It was originally Dutch, and comes from *pappekak*, which meant either 'soft dung' or 'doll's excrement' – nothing to do with poppies.

porcupine

An early form of **porcupine** was *porke despyne*, which possibly came from Latin *porcus spinosus* 'prickly pig'. Between the 15th and 17th centuries, the word appeared in many forms, including *portepyn*, *porkpen*, *porkenpick* and *porpoynt*. Shakespeare knew the animal as a **porpentine** and it appears in this form in his plays, often as the name of an inn. The ghost of Hamlet's father tells Hamlet that his story could make his son's hairs 'stand on end,/ Like quills upon the fretful porpentine'.

porridge

At first **porridge** was a soup thickened with barley. The word is a 16th-century alteration of **pottage**, which in turn comes from Old French *potage* 'something put in a pot'. The porridge we are familiar with, consisting of oatmeal boiled in water or milk, is mentioned in the 1640s.

The informal use of **porridge** to mean 'prison' dates from the 1950s. It probably derives from porridge as a typical prison food, though it might be based on a pun involving two meanings of **stir**, one as in 'stir the porridge' and the other a slang term for 'prison', which is perhaps from Romany *sturbin* 'jail'. The term was immortalised by the BBC comedy series *Porridge* of the 1970s, which starred Ronnie Barker as Norman Stanley Fletcher, a cynical but good-hearted old convict.

port

Latin *portus* 'haven or harbour' is the source of our word **port**. Its nautical use to refer to the left side of a ship, the opposite of STARBOARD, dates from the mid 16th century and probably comes from the idea that this was the side of the ship where the loading hatch was fitted and which was turned towards the quay when the ship was in port. It replaced an older word **larboard**, which was hardly surprising given the potential for confusion between the similar-sounding 'starboard!' and 'larboard!' when shouted into the teeth of a gale at sea.

The drink **port** was not so called because it was a favourite of sailors. The word is a shortened form of **Oporto** in Portugal, from which the wine is shipped.

porter

The **porter** who acts as a doorman at the entrance of a hotel and the one who carries luggage are completely different words. The former comes from *porta*, the Latin word for a gate or a door which is also the source of **portal**, meaning 'a doorway or entrance', and **porthole**. The latter comes from Latin *portare* 'to carry', and so is related to words like **portable** and **portfolio**, a large flat case used for carrying drawings or maps. The drink **porter**, a dark brown bitter beer, was originally made for porters and others whose work involved carrying loads.

posh

One of the more frequently repeated explanations of the origin of a word is the story that **posh**, meaning 'elegant or stylishly luxurious' or 'typical of the upper classes', comes from the initials of 'port out, starboard home'. This is supposed to refer to the location of the more desirable cabins – on the port side on the outward trip and on the starboard side on the return – on passenger ships between Britain and India in the 19th century. Such cabins would be sheltered from the heat of the sun or benefit from cooling breezes and so were reserved by wealthy passengers. Sadly, there is no evidence to support this neat and ingenious explanation. The P&O steamship company is supposed to have stamped tickets with the letters P.O.S.H., but no tickets like this have ever been found. A more likely explanation is that the word comes from a 19th-century slang term for a dandy, from thieves' slang for 'money'. The first recorded example of **posh** is from a 1915 issue of *Blackwood's Magazine*.

positive

At the core of **positive** is the idea of placing something firmly, and the ultimate source is Latin *ponere* 'to place'. In the 14th century the English word was used to refer to laws as being formally laid down. From this developed the more general meaning 'explicitly laid down and admitting no question' (the meaning preserved in 'proof positive'), and later 'very sure, convinced'.

posse

The word **posse** calls to mind the image, familiar from westerns, of a body of men being recruited by a sheriff and saddling up to pursue outlaws or other wrongdoers. The key element in its meaning is not the pursuing, though, but the fact that the sheriff has empowered this group of people to enforce the law. In medieval Latin *posse* meant 'power', and came from Latin *posse* 'to be able'. **Posse** pre-dated the widespread colonisation of the USA, and was first used in Britain during the mid 17th century to mean 'an assembled force or band' and specifically 'the population of local able-bodied men summoned by a sheriff to stop a riot or pursue criminals'. See also POWER.

possum

An informal American term for the **opossum**, a marsupial whose name comes from a Native American word meaning 'white dog'. The animal feigns death when it is threatened or attacked, which is why **playing possum**, an expression recorded from the early 19th century in the USA, is pretending to be asleep or unconscious. In Australia, to **stir the possum** is to stir up controversy or liven things up. The Australian possum is also a marsupial but a different animal from its American counterpart.

A possum, playing possum.

post

English has three words spelled **post**. The one meaning 'a long, sturdy piece of wood' and 'to display a notice in a public place' is from Latin *postis* 'doorpost'. The other two, 'the official service or system that delivers letters and parcels' and 'a position of paid employment, a job', are both derived from Latin *ponere* 'to place'. The 'delivering letters' sense arose from its application to each of a series of mounted couriers who were stationed at suitable places along a route and carried important letters and despatches on to the next post. A fourth **post** is the one found in expressions like POSTHUMOUS, **post mortem** and **post-war**. This comes from Latin *post* 'after'.

In American English to **go postal** is to become irrational and violent, especially as a result of stress. This expression, which dates from the 1990s, arose as a result of several reported cases that involved employees of the US postal service running amok and shooting down their colleagues. The phrase can also be used to mean 'to get very angry, to fly into a rage'. Cher, the main character in the 1995 high-school film *Clueless*, predicts that 'My father's going to go postal on me' when he reads her school report card.

posthumous

In English **posthumous** means 'happening after a person's death'. Latin *postumus*, on which it is based, meant 'last'. Think of a baby born posthumously, after the death of its father – it would be the father's last child. The *h* was added to the spelling of the English word because of the influence of *humus* 'ground, earth' or *humare* 'to bury', both words that relate to the idea of a person's death.

posy

A **posy** is a small bunch of flowers, but it was originally a short line of verse inscribed on something such as a ring or used as a motto. It comes from **poesy**, an old word meaning 'poetry'. See also ANTHOLOGY.

pot

An Old English word that originally referred to a cylindrical container. A number of words and expressions are based on the idea of a kitchen pot being used to cook food. A **potboiler** is so called because writers dash off such books, written to appeal to popular taste, simply to earn a living, to 'keep the pot boiling'. **Potshot** comes from the idea of shooting an animal 'for the pot', purely for food rather than for display, which would require skilled shooting.

You can say that something has **gone to pot** when it has deteriorated through neglect. This expression dates back to the 1530s and used to mean 'to be ruined or destroyed'. It is based on the image of chopping ingredients up into small pieces and putting them in a pot ready for cooking. So to go to pot is to go to pieces. You can talk about **the pot calling the kettle black** when someone makes criticisms about someone else which could equally well apply to themselves. A version of this saying, 'The pot calls the pan burnt-arse', is included in a 1639 collection of proverbs by John Clarke. Another saying, **a watched pot never boils**, meaning that time feels longer when you are waiting for something to happen, dates from the 19th century. According to a comic strip in the *Washington Post* in April 2002, 'Whoever said "A watched pot never boils" obviously didn't own a microwave.'

Pot meaning 'cannabis' is a different word, recorded from the 1930s in the USA. It is probably from Mexican Spanish *potiguaya* 'marijuana leaves'.

potato

'Let the sky rain potatoes', prays Falstaff in Shakespeare's play *The Merry Wives of Windsor*. A bizarre wish, you would think, until you know that he is referring to sweet potatoes, believed in the 16th and 17th centuries to have aphrodisiac qualities. Falstaff is in fact praying for erotic prowess. The first vegetables referred to as a **potato** in English was the sweet potato, introduced to Europe before the common white potato that we are most familiar with today. By the late 16th century, when white potatoes had appeared in England from America, the word was being applied to the new arrival. It comes from Spanish *patata*, a variant of an old Caribbean word *batata* 'sweet potato'.

pound

The Old English word **pound** goes back to Latin *libra pondo*, a Roman weight equivalent to 12oz – *libra* meant 'scales, balance' and *pondo* was 'by weight'. The 'money' sense, also Old English, arose because the first monetary unit called a pound was literally a pound of silver. **Pound** meaning 'to beat, strike heavily' is a different Old English word, as is **pound** in the sense 'an enclosure'.

In Shakespeare's play *The Merchant of Venice* the moneylender Shylock lends the merchant Antonio money on condition that if he fails to repay it on time he must forfeit a pound of his flesh. When Antonio is unable to pay, Shylock holds him to the agreement, but is foiled by the clever pleading of Portia, who argues that if the flesh is taken it must be exactly a pound and done without spilling any blood, as the deed specifies flesh only. To demand **your pound of flesh** has come to mean 'ruthlessly demand something you are owed'.

pour

It appeared in English in the Middle Ages, though the ultimate origin of **pour** is uncertain. Someone who **pours oil on troubled waters** is trying to settle a dispute with calming words. The phrase is based on a long-standing belief that oil can calm rough seas. According to an account given by the Roman scholar Pliny (AD 23-79), sailors poured oil into the sea to calm the waves in a storm.

powder

Latin *pulvis* 'dust' is the source of **pulverise** as well as **powder**, which came into English via Old French *poudre*. If someone tells you to **keep your powder dry** they mean that you should be ready for action. Popular tradition attributes the advice **put your trust in God, and keep your powder dry** to the English statesman and general Oliver Cromwell (1599-1658). The combination of spiritual encouragement and practical measures is typical of him, but the line did not appear until the mid 19th century, 300 years after his death, in an Irish ballad.

> The genteel and euphemistic toilet-related expression **powder your nose** has been recorded since the 1920s.

In American English to **take a powder** is to depart quickly, especially in order to avoid a difficult situation. This may be based on the idea of a person fleeing down a road and raising dust as they go. Another theory is that it relates to a person taking a laxative powder and so having to rush to the toilet.

power

Like POSSE, **power**, which came into English in the Middle Ages, can be traced back to Latin *posse* 'to be able'. 'We know that power does corrupt, and that we cannot trust kings to have loving hearts', wrote Anthony Trollope in *The Prime Minister* (1876). The saying **power corrupts** is usually used, though, with this slightly later quotation from Lord Acton in mind: 'Power tends to corrupt, and absolute power corrupts absolutely. Great men are almost always bad men, even when they exercise influence and not authority' (letter to Bishop Mandell Creighton, 1887). Whoever the authorities or people in control are in a particular situation can be referred to as **the powers that be**, a phrase that comes from the Bible: 'For there is no power but of God: the powers that be are ordained of God' (Epistle to the Romans).

prank

A **prank** was once more serious than it is now, indicating not a practical joke or piece of mischief but rather some wicked or malicious act. For example, the 17th-century biblical commentator John Trapp described a person's murder of their brother and sister as 'lewd pranks'.

precipice

The original meaning of **precipice** was 'a headlong fall'. It was not long, though, before **precipice** was being used in its modern sense, describing a steep cliff or mountainside from which you might fall. The ultimate source is Latin *praeceps* 'steep or headlong', which is also the origin of **precipitation**. In the early 17th century this referred to the action of falling or throwing down, but it now means rainfall or snow.

precocious

You can describe a child or young person as **precocious** if they are very advanced or developed for their age, but the word was first used in the 1650s to describe flowers or fruit that blossomed or ripened early. Its source is Latin *praecox*, from *praecoquere* 'to ripen early'. See also APRICOT.

preposterous

The Latin word *praeposterus*, from which we get **preposterous**, meant both 'reversed, back to front' and 'absurd', combining *prae* 'before' and *posterus* 'coming after'. When the English word entered the language in the mid 16th century it had a pair of meanings that mirrored those in the Latin. One of these, 'having last what should be first', is very rare now. But the other, describing anything that seems contrary to reason, nonsensical or absurd, is still going strong.

president

The idea at the heart of the word **president** is that this is the person who sits in front. Indeed, the related word **preside** originally meant 'to occupy the seat of authority in an assembly'. The Latin source of both is *praesidere* 'to sit before'. **President** was first used as a title for the elected head of the government in the USA during the 1780s, just before the establishment of George Washington as the first President of the USA in 1789 – it had been the title for the head of a British colony in America since the early 17th century, and was carried over into the new independent republic. The American sense 'the head of a company' dates from the mid 18th century.

press

Both **press** and **print** can be traced back to Latin *premere*, 'to press', as can **pressure**. Journalists and the newspaper industry have been known as **the press**, in reference to printing presses, since the late 18th century, although before that a press was a printing house or publisher's. Another name for journalists, used since the 1830s or 1840s, is **the fourth estate**. The three traditional estates of the realm are the three groups constituting Parliament, the Lords spiritual (the heads of the Church), the Lords temporal (the peerage) and the Commons – the fourth estate was originally the common people.

Press the flesh is a US slang expression from the 1920s meaning 'to shake hands'. These days it is generally used of celebrities or politicians greeting crowds by shaking hands with random people.

The heyday of the **press gang**, a group employed to force men to join the navy, was the 18th and early 19th century, but the first record of the term comes before 1500. Press-ganging people was really a form of arbitrary conscription, which was introduced in Britain in 1916.

prestige

The 2006 film *The Prestige* is about a rivalry between two stage magicians in Edwardian London, reviving an early meaning of the word, 'an illusion or conjuring trick'. **Prestige** came into English in the mid 17th century, borrowed from a French word meaning 'illusion, glamour' which came from Latin *praestigium* 'illusion'. The modern meaning, 'widespread respect and admiration', developed by way of the sense 'dazzling influence, glamour'. The idea is that the glamour of a person's past achievements can blind people to any possible faults they might have. The related adjective **prestigious** is an older word which originally described the skilful use of your hands when performing conjuring tricks. It only came to mean 'inspiring admiration' in the early 20th century.

presto

Magicians often say **hey presto!** to announce the climax of a trick. **Presto** is borrowed from Italian, in which it means 'quick or quickly', and comes ultimately from Latin *praestus*, 'ready'. **Presto, be gone** seems to have been a common feature of the patter of 17th-century conjurors and jugglers, and **hey presto** became popular in the following century. See also ABRACADABRA.

pretty

In his diary entry for May 11, 1660, Samuel Pepys mentions 'Dr Clerke, who I found to be a very pretty man and very knowing'. Pepys meant that the doctor was admirable, 'a fine fellow'. This is merely one of the many senses that **pretty**, an Old English word that comes from a root meaning 'trick', has had over the centuries. The first was 'cunning, crafty', which was followed by 'clever, skilful', 'brave' and 'admirable, pleasing, nice' before the main modern one, 'attractive', appeared in the 15th century. Around that time the meaning 'considerable, great' also developed, which is now only found in the expression **a pretty penny**, 'a large sum of money'.

Pretty has been used as an adverb in the sense 'fairly, moderately', since the mid 16th century. **Sitting pretty**, 'comfortably placed or well situated', is originally American, and is first recorded in 1915.

prevent

People originally used **prevent** to mean 'to act in anticipation of or in preparation for something', as in the 17th-century poet George Herbert's lines 'Thus we prevent the last great day,/ And judge our selves.' Similarly, you could once talk about preventing someone's wishes or desires, or anticipating them. The word comes from Latin *praevenire* 'to precede or hinder'. In time to **prevent** something was to thwart someone's plans, from which developed the idea of stopping something from happening. The saying **prevention is better than cure** dates from the 17th century. An early example comes from 1618: 'Prevention is so much better than healing, because it saves the labour of being sick.'

price

The medieval English word *pris*, which was from Old French, meant not only 'price' but also 'prize' and 'praise'. Over time these three meanings split off into three different words. *Pris* became **price**, and the meaning 'praise' started to be spelled *preise* and then **praise**. Originally simply an alternative way of spelling **price**, **prize** too became a separate word to cover this particular strand of meaning.

pride

In Old English *pryde* was 'excessive self-esteem', and from medieval times **pride** was regarded as the first of the Seven Deadly Sins. Also medieval is its use to mean 'a social group of lions'.

People say **pride goes** (or **comes**) **before a fall** as a warning to someone who is being too conceited or self-important that something is sure to happen to make them look foolish. The phrase is a reworded version of a sentence from the biblical Book of Proverbs: 'Pride goeth before destruction, and an haughty spirit before a fall.'

To have **pride of place** is to have the most prominent or important position among a group of things. The expression is associated with falconry, referring to the high position from which a falcon swoops down on its prey. It is first recorded in Shakespeare's play *Macbeth*, in a passage suggesting how the natural order of things has been reversed following the killing of Duncan: 'A falcon, tow'ring in her pride of place, / Was by a mousing owl hawk'd at and kill'd.'

Your **pride and joy** is the thing you are most proud of – maybe your car, or your garden. The expression is recorded only from the beginning of the 20th century, but since the Middle Ages something a person is very proud of has been their 'pride'. **Pride and joy** may have been suggested from the poem *Rokeby* (1813) by Sir Walter Scott: 'See yon pale stripling! when a boy, / A mother's pride, a father's joy!'

prig

A **prig** is a self-righteously moralistic person who behaves as if they are superior to others. Perhaps they would feel less superior if they knew that a **prig** in the 16th century was a tinker or a petty thief. As time went on the word came to be applied to anyone who was disliked, and by the end of the 17th century it was used specifically to describe someone who was affectedly and self-consciously precise.

prime

At the start of the 16th century to **prime** was 'to fill or load', especially in the context of preparing a gun for firing. It was probably based on Latin *primus* 'first', also the source of the adjective **prime**, since priming something is the first operation you perform before using it. Someone who stimulates or supports the growth or success of an enterprise, especially by supplying it with money, can be said to be **priming the pump**. This refers to pouring a small amount of water into a mechanical pump to establish suction so that it can begin to work properly.

prince

The Latin word *princeps*, 'first, chief, sovereign', is the source of **prince**, and also of both **principal** meaning 'chief' and **principle** 'a rule or theory on which something is based'. A prince was originally a ruler of a small state, as in the **Prince of Wales**, a title that since the reign of Edward III has been given to the eldest son of the King or Queen of England. At first this was the only 'prince' in England, but over the centuries the use of the term has been extended to include other members of the royal family. In the reign of James I it was applied to all the sons of the sovereign, and later, under Queen Victoria, to all the grandsons too.

Prince Charming is the traditional name of the young prince who marries the heroine in a pantomime or fairy tale such as *Cinderella* or *Sleeping Beauty*. He first appeared as *Le roi Charmant*, or 'King Charming', in the French fairy story *The Blue Bird* (1698), and made his English debut in a play of 1851.

private

Someone who is **private** has literally 'withdrawn from public life' – that is the meaning of the Latin root, from *privare* 'to bereave, deprive', the root also of **deprive** and **privation**. In the army privates are ordinary soldiers as opposed to officers. They were originally, from the 1570s, **private soldiers**. **Privates** meaning 'the genitals' is first recorded in around 1450.

Back in the 13th century **privy**, which is from the same root, meant 'belonging to your own private circle'. The sense 'sharing in a secret' developed from this later. The meaning 'a lavatory' is as old as the adjective and comes from the idea of this being a private place.

problem

A **problem** was initially a riddle or puzzle, or a question put forward for academic discussion. 'Put forward' are the key words here, as the ancestor of the English word is the Greek verb *proballein*, 'to throw out or put forth'. This Greek word is based on *pro* 'forward' and *ballein* 'to throw', also the source of **ballistic**.

procrastinate

To **procrastinate** is to put off doing something. The Latin word it comes from, *procrastinare*, had the sense 'to put off till the morning', with the *cras* part meaning 'tomorrow'. There is a similar idea behind the Spanish word *mañana*, meaning 'tomorrow' and often used to express, in a spirit of easy-going procrastination, an unspecified time in the future. The saying **procrastination is the thief of time** originates in the poem *Night Thoughts* (1742-5) by Edward Young: 'Procrastination is the Thief of Time / Year after year it steals, till all are fled.'

proof

A medieval word that came via Old French *proeve* from Latin *probare*, 'to test or prove'. **Proof** is a way of describing the alcohol content of spirits. **Proof spirit** or 100 per cent proof spirit was originally defined as a solution of alcohol that will ignite when mixed with gunpowder – in Britain this meant an alcohol content of 57.07 per cent.

In the expression **the proof of the pudding is in the eating**, **proof** is used in the sense 'test' rather than 'verification, proving to be true'. It is only by actually tasting food that you can be sure that it has been cooked properly. In other words, the real value of something can be judged only from practical experience or results and not from appearance or theory.

A word to the wise

All countries have their proverbs, observing sagely on the everyday. This homespun wisdom from around the world continues to find a place in the language.

The idea that you cannot achieve an aim without sacrificing something has been expressed since the 1850s as you cannot make an omelette without breaking eggs, and a modern saying suggesting that you should make the best of difficult circumstances runs if life hands you lemons, make lemonade. In snowbound parts of North America, where the dog sled is a familiar method of transport, an ambitious person who wants more independence may feel that if you are not the lead dog, the view never changes. Other countries might be less sympathetic to this kind of ambition – in Japan they say that the nail that sticks up must be hammered down.

To point out that you cannot change someone's essential nature you might say that the leopard cannot change his spots, or reach for the African warning that no matter how long a log floats in the river, it will never become a crocodile. The familiar let sleeping dogs lie can be matched by the Japanese poke a bush, a snake comes out.

Cats often feature in proverbs, especially in the role of mouser. We are told that when the cat's away the mice will play, and another traditional saying, which conjures up a picture worthy of Beatrix Potter, warns that a cat in gloves catches no mice. A Chinese saying takes a practical approach: it hardly matters if it is a white cat or a black cat that catches mice. Whatever their hunting prowess, though, cats cannot equal dogs for loyalty. A Japanese proverb makes the contrast: feed a dog for three days and he will remember your kindness for three years; feed a cat for three years and she will forget your kindness in three days.

Sometimes a saying may develop a modern extension. The reminder that the early bird catches the worm has been used since the 17th century, but we now also have the warning it's the second mouse that gets the cheese.

Inevitably, some proverbs have more modern relevance than others – but we should probably remember the Russian saying there is no proverb without a grain of truth.

propaganda

Today **propaganda** has negative connotations, with implications of bias and deception, but these date only from the mid 19th century. In 1622 Pope Gregory XV set up the *Congregatio de Propaganda Fide*, the 'Congregation for Propagation of the Faith', a committee of cardinals of the Roman Catholic Church responsible for spreading the word of Christianity by missions around the world. From the late 18th century a **propaganda** was a scheme or organisation for promoting a particular doctrine, but only since the 1830s has the word referred to biased or misleading information used to advance a cause or point of view.

prowess

Nowadays **prowess** refers to skill or expertise in some activity, but back in the 16th century the word was used in the sense 'bravery in battle'. It was based on the old word *prow*, 'valiant or brave'. The poet Edmund Spenser was fond of this word, referring in *The Faerie Queene* to 'the prowest knight that ever field did fight'.

prude

The old French word *prudefemme*, which was applied to a modest and respectable woman, was the source of **prude** in the early 18th century. This was the female equivalent of French *prud'homme* 'a good man and true'. The English word was used in a more negative sense than the French ones, though, describing an excessively prim and demure woman, and is now applied to either sex.

public

The root of **public**, Latin *publicus*, is shared by **publish** and **republic**, and is related to PEOPLE. People have been able to go to a **public house** for a drink since the 1650s, and to the abbreviated **pub** since around 1800. In Australia they could also stay the night – there a pub can also be a hotel.

The first **publicans** were collectors of taxes, not sellers of drinks. This explains the disparaging references to them in various biblical passages, such as: 'And when the Pharisees saw it, they said unto his disciples, Why eateth your Master with publicans and sinners?' (Gospel of Matthew). The use of the term to refer to a person who manages a pub dates from the early 18th century.

In North America and elsewhere **public schools** are schools supported by public funds and open to all, and people often wonder why English public schools, which are private, fee-paying and independent, are so called. In England a public school, a term first recorded in 1580, was originally a grammar school founded for the benefit of the public, as opposed to a **private school** run for the profit of its owner. Such schools were open to all and took resident students from beyond their local neighbourhood. The passing of the Public Schools Act in 1868 to regulate the large, long-established schools of Eton, Winchester, Westminster, Harrow, Rugby, Charterhouse, Shrewsbury, Merchant Taylors and St Paul's led to the term becoming a prestigious one which was also applied to newer schools.

The source of the adage **any publicity is good publicity** appears to be a passage by Raymond Chandler, in the *Black Mask* (1933): 'Rhonda Farr said: "Publicity, darling. Just publicity. Any kind is better than none at all."' An alternative form is **there's no such thing as bad publicity**. See also SALOON.

pudding

'Black pudding' preserves the original meaning of **pudding**, 'a kind of sausage'. The link between this and the modern meaning is the idea of putting a filling into a casing, as is done when making sausages. The word was subsequently applied to various dishes made by tying ingredients up in a bag and cooking them by boiling, steaming or later baking. Puddings could be savoury, like a steak and kidney pudding, or sweet, like a Christmas pudding, but by the end of the 19th century a sweet pudding was a popular way to end a meal, and had become the word's dominant meaning. **Pudding** comes from Old French *boudin* 'black pudding', from Latin *botellus* 'sausage, small intestine'.

When someone goes too far in doing or embellishing something, they are said to **over-egg the pudding**. The idea is of using too many eggs in making a pudding, so that it does not set or cook properly or is too rich. See also BOWEL, PROOF.

puerile

These days any childishly silly behaviour can be described as **puerile**, but the adjective started off meaning 'like a boy'. The root of the word is Latin *puer* 'boy'.

pull

An Old English word that originally expressed a short sharp action, more like **pluck** or **snatch**. To **pull the plug** is to prevent something from happening or continuing. Nowadays this probably brings to mind the image of someone disconnecting an electrical device by pulling out the plug from the socket in the wall, but the plug referred to here is one found in a forerunner of the flushing toilet, used from the mid 18th century. To flush it you had to pull a stopper or plug to flush the lavatory.

To **pull someone's leg**, or tease them, has been used since the late 19th century, but the idea probably goes back to the 16th century, when you might **pull someone by the ear**, **nose** or **sleeve** to insult or make fun of them.

If you **pull out all the stops** you make a huge effort to achieve something. The stops in this expression are the knobs or levers on a church organ which control each of the different sets of pipes. Pulling out a stop allows the air to flow through the pipes and produce the sound. Pulling out all the stops will result in the full range of pitch and the maximum volume possible.

pulse

The **pulse** you can feel in your wrist comes from Latin *pulsus* 'beating', from *pellere* 'to drive or beat'. Other words descended from *pellere* include **compel**, **expel**, **propel** and **repel**. The other kind of **pulse**, an edible seed, is a different word, which comes via Old French from Latin *puls* 'porridge of meal or pulse'.

punch

The **punch** that means 'to strike' was first used in the sense 'to puncture or prod', which is probably where the term for a tool for making holes comes from. A person doing something that might be thought to be beyond their capacity or ability can be said to be **punching above their weight**. This a boxing metaphor – contests are generally arranged between opponents of nearly equal weight.

The drink **punch**, first mentioned in English in 1632, has a completely different source. It seems to be based on Sanskrit *pañca* 'five, five kinds of'. The drink originally had five ingredients – strong alcohol, water, fruit juices, spices and sugar.

Finally, there is the **Punch** that appears in the early 19th-century expression **pleased as Punch** (or **proud as Punch**), meaning 'feeling great delight or pride' and referring to the gleeful self-satisfaction of the grotesque hook-nosed male character of the Punch and Judy Show. **Punch** was originally a dialect term for a short, fat person and is a short form of Punchinello, the name of a stout hook-nosed character in traditional Italian theatre.

Punchinello as illustrated in a 19th-century book of clowns.

punctual

Nowadays a **punctual** person is someone who arrives at a place or does something at the appointed time. In the past, though, the word had a number of other senses, such as 'sharp-pointed' (as in 'a punctual instrument'), 'made by a point' (as in 'a punctual mark'), 'to the point' (as in 'a punctual story') and 'accurate, precise, timely' (as in 'punctual time' or 'punctual revolt'). The common thread is POINT, and the English word is based on Latin *punctum* 'a point'.

pundit

A modern **pundit** is an expert in a particular subject called on to give their opinions about it to the public. The source of the word is Sanskrit *pandita* 'learned', used to describe a learned man versed in Sanskrit law, philosophy and religion. The 'learned expert or authority' sense dates from the early 19th century.

pungent see POIGNANT.

punk

Long before the days of Johnny Rotten and the Sex Pistols, all sorts of people found themselves labelled as **punks**. In the past the word has been used as a term for a prostitute, a male homosexual and, in show business, a youth or young animal. In American English it has been used since the early 20th century as a disparaging word for a person (as in 'stop right there, punk!') and in particular a young hooligan or petty criminal. In the film *Dirty Harry* (1971) Clint Eastwood says to a crook:

I know what you're thinking. 'Did he fire six shots or only five?' Well, to tell you the truth, in all this excitement I kind of lost track myself. . . . You've got to ask yourself a question: Do I feel lucky? Well, do ya, punk?

Since the 1970s the word has been applied to admirers or players of **punk rock**, a loud, fast-moving, aggressive form of rock music: the first US mention of punk rock comes in 1971, five years before the first British punk record, 'New Rose' by the Damned. The original punk was not a person at all, but, in 17th-century North America, a term for soft crumbly wood that has been attacked by fungus, used as tinder.

Its ultimate origin is not known, although it may be related to **spunk**, meaning 'semen' and 'courage and determination', which is itself of uncertain origin.

punt

A flat-bottomed boat, a long kick and a bet have little in common, and most dictionaries class **punt** as three separate words. The kind of boat you propel with a long pole is from Latin *ponto*, which meant 'flat-bottomed ferry boat' and is also the source of **pontoon**, a vessel used to support a temporary bridge or landing stage.

The **punt** that is a bet is a much later word, dating from the 18th century, from French *ponte* or Spanish *ponto* 'point'. In English it first referred to a person playing a card game. **Punter**, 'a person who gambles', comes from this word – the sense 'a customer or client' first appeared as recently as the 1960s.

Punt meaning 'a long kick' is first recorded in the rules of RUGBY football at Rugby School in 1845, only 20 or so years after the game was invented. It may be from the local dialect word **punt**, meaning 'to push or kick'.

puny

A **puny** person is small and weak, but originally they were simply younger or more junior. The word comes from *puisne*, a legal term for a junior judge, from an Old French word meaning 'born after'.

pup

The word **pup** is a shortening of **puppy**, from Old French *poupee* 'doll, plaything', which is related to **poppet** and **puppet**. To **sell someone a pup** is to swindle them, especially by selling them something that is worth far less than they expect. This dates from the early 20th century and was presumably based on the idea of dishonestly selling someone a young and inexperienced dog when they were expecting an older, trained animal.

pupil

The two words spelled **pupil** have entered English by different routes and acquired very different meanings, but they share a root, Latin *pupa*, which meant both 'doll' and 'girl'. The first **pupil** was originally an orphan or ward under the care of a guardian, from which emerged the idea of someone taught by another. It came into English via Old French *pupille* from Latin *pupus* 'boy' and *pupa* 'girl'. The other **pupil**, the round opening in the centre of your eye, comes from the 'doll' meaning of *pupa*. People must have noticed the tiny images of themselves reflected in another person's eyes

and thought they resembled little dolls (a similar idea is behind an old use of BABY). In the 18th century *pupa* was borrowed directly from Latin as a term for an insect in its inactive immature form, between larva and adult.

pure

We get our word **pure** from Latin *purus*. If you describe someone as **pure as the driven snow**, you mean that they are completely pure. 'Driven snow' is snow that has been piled into drifts or made smooth by the wind. The image is of spotless, immaculate whiteness. The phrase was memorably parodied by the American actress Tallulah Bankhead (1903-68) in 1947: 'I'm as pure as the driven slush.'

purple

Just as CRIMSON is named after an insect, so **purple** is named after a shellfish, and at one time these two words described the same colour. The first thing to be described as **purple** was a crimson dye obtained from some molluscs, called *porphyra* in Greek. The dye was rare and expensive and was used for colouring the robes of Roman emperors and magistrates. The actual colour of the dye varied widely, and over time the word came to mean the colour between red and blue that we now call **purple**.

From the late 16th century **purple** has been used to mean 'striking' or 'ornate' in phrases such as **purple prose** or **a purple patch**. The latter term, describing an overelaborate passage in a literary composition, is a translation of Latin *purpureus pannus* and comes from the Roman poet Horace's *Ars Poetica*: 'Works of serious purpose and grand promise often have a purple patch or two stitched on, to shine far and wide.'

purse

A **purse** gets its name from its traditional material, leather. The word came into English some time in the 11th or 12th centuries from Latin *bursa*, which meant 'money bag' and also 'leather, animal skin'. *Bursa* is the source of **bursar**, a person who manages the finances of a college or school, and **reimburse**, 'to repay'. Despite the difference in spelling, it is also the root of **sporran**, a small pouch worn around the waist by Scotsmen as part of Highland dress. The Latin *bursa* developed into Irish *sparán* 'purse' and then Scottish Gaelic *sporan*, and was first used in English by the Scottish novelist Sir Walter Scott in the early 19th century.

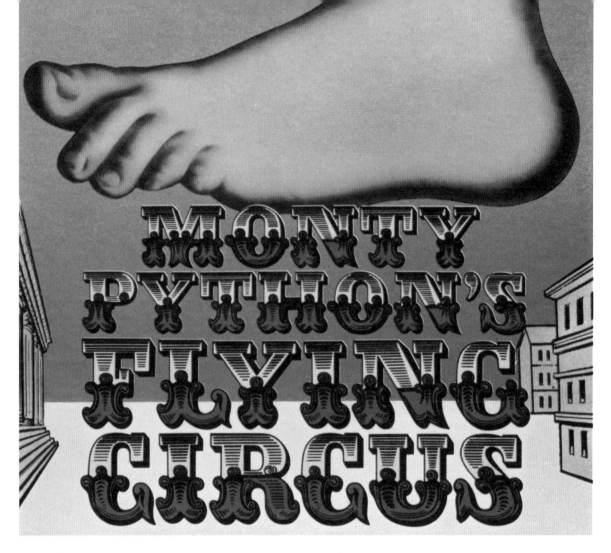

puzzle

The word **puzzle** is a puzzle. Some have suggested that it is derived from **pose**, just as **nuzzle** came from **nose**. Although **pose** did at one time mean 'to perplex someone or put them at a loss', the evidence for a connection between the two words is not strong and it is likely that they arose independently.

pygmy

The original **pygmies** were a mythological race of tiny people, reputed to inhabit parts of Ethiopia or India. In one story about them an army of pygmies found the mighty hero Hercules asleep and tried to tie him down, but when he woke he simply rolled them up in the lion's skin that he wore. The term comes from Greek *pugmaios* 'dwarf', from *pugmē*, 'the length from the elbow to the knuckles', which was said to be the height of these people. From the late 19th century the word was applied to members of certain peoples of very short stature in equatorial Africa and parts of Southeast Asia.

python

A **python** is a large snake that kills its prey by constriction rather than by poisoning. Its name comes from Greek *Puthÿn*, the name of a huge serpent or monster killed by Apollo in Greek legend. Poets in the 17th and 18th centuries sometimes described any monster or plague as a **Python**.

The BBC television comedy series **Monty Python's Flying Circus** was first shown on October 5, 1969. The name was deliberately chosen to have no real meaning – it was the winning candidate from a list of absurd titles such as *Gwen Dibley's Flying Circus*, *Vaseline Review* and *Owl-Stretching Time*. After a slow start the programme became so popular and influential that in 1975 it gave the language a new word, **Pythonesque**, to describe surreal humour.

quack

'If it looks like a duck, walks like a duck and quacks like a duck, then it just may be a duck' was the comment made by the US union leader Walter Reuther about the alleged communists investigated by Senator Joseph McCarthy in the early 1950s. The **quack** of a duck, recorded from the mid 16th century, is just an imitation of the bird's characteristic sound. The kind of **quack** who dishonestly claims to have medical skills was originally a **quacksalver**, a 17th-century word from Dutch *quacken* 'to talk foolishly' and *salf* 'ointment, salve'.

quaint

In the Middle Ages **quaint** meant 'wise, clever' and 'ingenious, cunningly designed or skilfully made'. Another early sense was 'beautiful or elegant'. Over time these meanings led to the more general notion of 'out of the ordinary'. The current use, describing something interestingly unusual or old-fashioned, is found from the late 18th century – before this revival in its usage the word had become quite rare. It comes from Old French *cointe*, from Latin *cognoscere* 'to know', which is the root of words such as **acquaint**, **cognoscenti**, INCOGNITO and **recognise**.

quantum leap

Although you will often come across a sentence like 'This product represents a quantum leap forward in telecommunications technology', the curious thing about the term **quantum leap** is that, strictly speaking, it does not describe a large change at all, but a tiny one. **Quantum** comes from Latin *quantus*, 'how big?' or 'how much?', and originally meant 'a quantity or amount'. In physics a quantum (a term introduced by the physicist Max Planck around 1900) is a very small amount of energy, the minimum amount of energy that can exist in a given situation, and a **quantum jump** is the abrupt change of an electron or atom from one energy state to another. Although this is a tiny jump in terms of size, it is an instantaneous and dramatic one, which explains why the term came into general usage from around 1970 to describe a sudden large increase or major advance.

quarantine

Literally meaning '40 days', **quarantine** comes from Italian *quarantina*, from *quaranta* '40'. In the early 16th century this was the number of days during which a widow had the right to remain in her deceased husband's house. A more familiar meaning to us, though, refers to a period of isolation imposed on a person or animal to test that they are not carrying a contagious disease that they might otherwise spread. This was first used in English in the mid 17th century, though the practice dates back to the 14th century, when the ports of Venice and Ragusa (now called Dubrovnik) required ships from plague-stricken countries to lay at anchor for a period of 40 days before they were allowed to enter the ports.

quark

In physics a **quark** is a type of subatomic particle believed to be one of the basic constituents of matter. The name was coined in the 1960s by the American physicist Murray Gell-Mann, who initially spelt it *quork* but changed this to **quark** after he came across the line 'Three quarks for Muster Mark' in James Joyce's *Finnegans Wake* (1939). Joyce's word is meant to suggest the cawing sound seagulls make. It appealed to Gell-Mann, as at the time only three varieties of quark (known as **up**, **down** and **strange** quarks) were believed to exist.

quarry

The **quarry** that yields stone, a meaning that dates from the early 17th century, comes ultimately from Latin *quadrum* 'a square'. This is based on the idea that a quarry is a place where stones are squared, or cut in regular shapes, to make them ready for use in building. The other **quarry**, 'a pursued animal', is from Old French *cuiree* and based on Latin *cor* 'heart' (see CORDIAL). In medieval deer-hunting the term referred to the deer's entrails, which were placed on the hide and given as a reward to the hounds. It could also be used to refer to a heap of deer carcasses piled up after a hunt, and so to a pile of dead bodies: 'Then went they in haste to the quarry of the dead, but by no means could find the body of the King' (John Speed, *The History of Great Britain*, 1611).

queen
The Old English spelling of **queen** was *cwēn*. This originally meant 'a wife', though not any wife but specifically that of a king or some other important man. Related to *cwēn* was Old English *cwene* 'woman', which became the now archaic **quean**, 'a bold or impudent woman', and in the 16th and 17th centuries also a term for a prostitute. The sense 'an effeminate gay man' dates from the beginning of the 20th century.

queer
There is some doubt as to the origin of **queer**, but it may come from German *quer* 'oblique, perverse'. 'Eccentric' and 'strange' were early senses, though there was also the notion 'of questionable character, dubious'. The meaning 'unwell, ill' dates from the late 18th century, although it is often avoided now because of the potential confusion with the derogatory sense 'homosexual', recorded from the late 19th century.

A rather old-fashioned way of saying that someone is in difficulty, especially by being in debt, is to say that they are **in Queer Street**. This was an imaginary street where people in difficulties were supposed to live. Since the early 19th century the phrase has suggested various kinds of misfortune, though mainly financial difficulty: 'Queer Street is full of lodgers just at present' (Charles Dickens, *Our Mutual Friend*, 1865). To **queer someone's pitch** is to spoil their chances of doing something, especially secretly or maliciously. This started out as 19th-century slang. The 'pitch' in question was probably the spot where a street performer stationed themselves or the site of a market trader's stall. **There's nowt so queer as folk** is first recorded in 1905, though it is described as an 'old saying'. **Nowt** is a northern English variant of **nought**, 'nothing'.

queue
Think of a long **queue** of people stretching back from a ticket office or bus stop. It looks a bit like an animal's tail, and this is the literal meaning of the word, which comes from French and was based on Latin *cauda* 'tail'. **Queue** was originally used as a heraldic term for the tail of an animal. In the 18th and 19th centuries it also referred to a pigtail, as in 'Old cocked-hats, and tied queues, still stalk about the town' (George Le Fevre, *Life of a Travelling Physician*, 1843), and it came to describe a line of people in the mid 19th century.

quibble
A **quibble** was originally a pun or play on words. It probably comes from Latin *quibus*, meaning 'for which' or 'for whom', a word that often appeared in legal documents and so was associated with subtle distinctions or verbal niceties. The idea of a pun led to that of basing an argument on some likeness or difference between words or their meanings, and from this arose the notion of a petty objection or a trivial point of criticism.

quick
The original meaning of **quick** in Old English was 'living' or 'alive', contrasting with something dead or inanimate. This early sense still survives in the expression **the quick and the dead**, meaning 'the living and the dead', which comes from the Apostles' Creed in the *Book of Common Prayer* (1662): 'From thence he shall come to judge the quick and the dead.'

Quicksand is so called because it moves – and swallows things up – as if it were alive. The original 'alive' sense of **quick** also led to the use of the word to refer to the soft, tender flesh below the growing part of a fingernail, toenail or, in animals, a hoof. Nervous people might bite their nails right down 'to the quick'. This area of flesh is well supplied with nerves and is very sensitive to touch or injury (and so seems more 'alive' than other parts of the skin). So **to cut someone to the quick** is to upset them very much by saying or doing something hurtful. It was a simple step in the word's history to go from 'alive' to senses such as 'lively' and 'vigorous' and, from the late 16th century, 'fast'.

MERCURY was formerly known as **quicksilver**. This name drew on the old sense 'living, alive' – the silver substance moves in such an unpredictable way that it seems to be alive.

quid
Nowadays **quid** is an informal word for £1, but it formerly referred specifically to a sovereign, a gold coin worth a pound. Its origin is unknown. In Australian English someone who is **not the full quid** is not very intelligent – in Britain the equivalent is **not the full shilling**. To be **quids in** is to be in luck or in a fortunate position, an expression that dates from the First World War.

quintessence
Classical and medieval philosophers believed that there were four elements – air, earth, fire and water – that made up everything that existed in the world. In addition, they thought that there was a fifth substance

hidden in all things, of which the heavenly bodies were composed. This they called the **quintessence**, from medieval Latin *quinta essentia* 'fifth essence'. Later the word came to mean 'the most typical or perfect example or form of something', as in Sir Walter Scott's remark in a letter written in 1823, 'You have escaped the quintessence of bores.'

quisling

A **quisling** is a traitor who collaborates with an enemy force occupying their country. The original quisling was Major Vidkun Quisling, an army officer who ruled Norway on behalf of the German occupying forces during the Second World War. After the war he was charged with treason and executed.

quit

An Old French word from the same root as **quiet**, Latin *quietus* 'quiet, still, resting'. The first meanings of **quit** were 'to pay off a debt', 'to repay a service or favour' and 'to set free'. It also meant 'to declare a person not guilty', a meaning for which we would now use the related word **acquit**. The modern meanings, 'to leave, go away' and 'to stop doing something', are from the 17th century.

To **call it quits** is to agree that terms are now equal, especially in the settlement of a debt, or to decide to abandon what you are doing in order to cut your losses. It dates back only to the 1890s and is a fairly informal expression, but an earlier version, **cry quits**, is recorded from the 1630s and comes from the world of officialdom. Church records of accounts from the late 15th century use the word **quits** to indicate that money owing to someone has been paid in full. Church business was then usually conducted in Latin, and so **quits** probably arose from a scribe's shortening of the medieval Latin word *quittus*, meaning 'discharged', written on receipts to indicate that the goods had been paid for.

quixotic

A **quixotic** person is idealistic, unrealistic and impractical, like the hero of the Spanish novel *Don Quixote* (1605-15) by Miguel de Cervantes. Don

Major Vidkun Quisling inspects Nazi troops in Germany in the mid 1930s.

Quixote is a middle-aged country gentleman obsessed with tales of chivalry who decides to become a knight and rides out with his squire Sancho Panza in search of adventure. See also TILT.

quiz

The credit for inventing the word **quiz** is sometimes given to a late 18th-century Dublin theatre proprietor called Daly. He is said to have made a bet that he could introduce a new word into the language within 48 hours, and to have hired a number of street urchins to chalk the nonsensical **quiz** on walls all over the city. The next day all Dublin was talking about this new word. Unfortunately there is no evidence to support this story. What we do know is that **quiz** was first used to mean either 'an odd or eccentric person' or 'an odd-looking thing', as in 'Where did you get that quiz of a hat?' (Jane Austen, *Northanger Abbey*, 1798). As a verb it originally meant 'to mock or make fun of someone'. The use of the word for a test of knowledge came later, in the 1860s, and might have been influenced by the word **inquisitive**. See also MILLION.

rabbit

We think of **rabbits** as being as much part of the language as of the countryside, but the rabbit was introduced to Britain by the Normans in the 12th century to provide meat and fur, and the name is not recorded until the late 14th century, when it meant particularly a young animal of this kind. Before that, the ancestors of Beatrix Potter's blue-coated hero Peter were known as **conies**.

To **breed like rabbits** is to reproduce prolifically, like the animal itself. This view of the rabbit is of quite long standing. In 1868 Queen Victoria explained why she could not be too excited by acquiring a 14th grandchild. 'It seems to me' she wrote to her eldest daughter 'to go on like the rabbits in Windsor Park!'

A person who chatters incessantly is sometimes said to 'rabbit on'. This expression comes from rhyming slang, in which **rabbit and pork** means 'talk'. See also BUNNY, PLAY.

race

The earliest sense of **race** was of rapid forward movement. It was originally a word from northern English, which entered the general language around the middle of the 16th century. It comes from Old Norse *rás* 'current'. Particular senses that developed at this period were 'contest of speed' and 'channel, path', as in **mill race** or 'mill stream'. **Race** with the meaning 'a division of humankind' dates from the 16th century, and is a quite different word. It probably comes from an Italian word, *razza*, of unknown origin.

In Australia and New Zealand, to **be in the race** is to have a chance of success – although it is usually found in the negative, implying that actually you have no chance at all. The idea of **a race against time** as a situation in which you try to do or complete something in a given time or before something else happens is found from the mid 19th century. See also RAT.

rack

The **rack** is the name of a medieval instrument of torture. It consisted of a frame on which a victim was stretched by turning rollers to which their wrists and ankles were tied. To rack someone was to torture them on this device, and from this we get **rack your brains** to mean 'to make a great effort to think of or remember something'. The **rack** that you stand things on is related, and both come from German *rek* 'horizontal bar or shelf'.

Another use of **rack** represents a different word. When something deteriorates through neglect we may say that it is **going to rack and ruin**. **Rack** here is a variant spelling of **wrack**, meaning 'destruction' and related to WRECK.

radar

This system for detecting aircraft, ships and other objects by sending out radio waves which are reflected back off the object was developed in the 1930s. The name comes from the opening letters of **radio detection and ranging**, and was coined in 1941. Police started using **radar traps** to detect speeding motorists in the early 1960s – a 1962 issue of the *Daily Telegraph* quotes an aggrieved driver saying that police radar speed traps were 'un-British' when he was fined £10 for doing 58 miles per hour.

radical

The earliest sense of **radical** is 'having to do with the basic nature of something, fundamental', and it goes back to Latin *radix* 'root', the source also of ERADICATE and **radish**. In political terms, a radical is someone who wants complete political or social reform – to be achieved by going to the root of the problem. In the 1970s, the American writer Tom Wolfe coined the term **radical chic** for a fashionable affectation of radical left-wing views.

raffle

The first **raffle** was a kind of dice game played with three dice, with the winner the player who threw a triple or the highest double. The dice game was simple gambling, but by the 18th century **raffle** was also being used for a sale of tickets to take part in a draw for prizes. From this we get the familiar fund-raiser of today. The word entered English from Old French. See also LOTTERY.

raft

A **raft** is a floating platform originally made of logs or beams bound together, and in the Middle Ages a **raft** was a beam or rafter. The source was Old Norse *raptr* 'rafter'.

Politicians of today often talk about their party having **a whole raft of** policies. **Raft** meaning 'a large amount' appears in the 19th century. It represents an alteration of a dialect word *raff* meaning 'abundance', probably by association with the earlier **raft** 'floating mass'.

rag

A Scandinavian word for 'tufted' probably lies behind **rag**. In **lose your rag**, 'to lose your temper', **rag** is probably an old slang term for the tongue – the phrase was originally **get your rag out**. This sense of **rag** may well be behind the student rag or prank, and the dated verb meaning 'to tease, play a joke on'.

A group of people regarded as disreputable or undesirable may be described as **ragtag and bobtail**. Almost every permutation of the main elements of this expression has been used over the centuries. It originally involved three words, and occurred in the versions **tag, rag and bobtail**, **rag, tag and bobtail** and **tagrag and bobtail** before the form with **ragtag** emerged as the favourite. **Bobtail** did not vary, as it was an established term for a horse or dog with a docked tail, but **rag** and **tag** were separate words conveying the same meaning of 'tattered or ragged clothes'. Putting them together in whatever way you fancy gives you the literal sense of 'people in ragged clothes together with their dogs and horses'.

In one traditional folk song a lady leaves her house, land and 'new-wedded lord' to run away with 'the raggle-taggle gypsies'. **Raggle-taggle** here is an elaboration of **ragtag**.

ragamuffin

Children in ragged, dirty clothes might be described disapprovingly as **ragamuffins**. The word has been around since medieval times, and probably comes from RAG with a made-up ending that has nothing to do with either English or American muffins. **Ragamuffin** in turn gave rise to the 1990s term **ragga** for a style of dance music originating in Jamaica and derived from reggae, because of the style of clothing worn by those who enjoyed it.

rage

In medieval times **rage** could also mean 'madness'. It goes back ultimately to Latin *rabere* 'to rave', and is related to **rabies**, a disease of dogs and other mammals that causes madness and convulsions.

Since the late 18th century something that is the subject of a widespread temporary enthusiasm or fashion has been described as **the rage** or **all the rage** to mean 'very popular or fashionable'. In 1811 the poet Lord Byron wrote that he was to hear his fellow poet Samuel Taylor Coleridge, 'who is a kind of rage at present'.

Bad drivers have always caused annoyance, but with increasing traffic and pace of life some people are now provoked into **road rage**. The phrase is first recorded in 1988, since when many other kinds of rage have been reported, among them **air rage** on a plane, **trolley rage** in a supermarket and even **golf rage** on a course.

from rags to riches

The concept of rising from extreme poverty to great wealth, like Cinderella in the fairy tale, is ancient. But this phrase was first recorded only in the late 19th century, when a play called *From Rags to Riches* was mentioned in a US newspaper.

rail

You might think that trains have no link to the classical world, but the word **rail** goes back to Latin *regula* 'straight stick', the source also of RULE. The first rails that vehicles ran along – pulled then by horses – are described in the account of an English colliery at the end of the 16th century. Before that a **rail** was a fixed bar forming part of a fence, which in due course gave us both **railings** and the rails of a racecourse.

The first references to **railways** begin in the late 17th century, followed a little later by **railroad**, now the American term but at first used in Britain interchangeably with **railway**. To **railroad** someone, meaning to rush or coerce them into doing something, comes from the use of the word to mean 'to transport by rail'.

Someone whose behaviour is out of control may be said to have **gone off the rails**. The phrase is first recorded in 1848, when railways and trains would have been a novelty.

Someone who complains bitterly is sometimes said to **rail**. This is a completely different word, and goes back ultimately to Latin *rugire* 'to roar' (see also RUT).

Proper pukka

Early in the 17th century Britain began to take an interest in India, and the impact of its languages on English goes back almost as far. But it was the Raj – the British colonial rule – that fixed many Indian words in everyday speech.

Some terms were consciously borrowed. In the 18th century a wealthy man who had made his fortune in India might be called a nabob, a word that came ultimately from Urdu (a language of northern India which took many words from Persian) and was originally the name for a Muslim official under the Mogul empire. Sahib was a polite title for a man in British India, and memsahib for a woman – sahib came via Urdu from Arabic sāhib 'friend, lord', while the mem- in memsahib was an Indian pronunciation of ma'am.

Other words have become so much part of the language that it is easy to forget their Indian origin. Living in a bungalow may seem completely part of the British scene, but the first 'bungalows' were cottages built in Bengal for early European settlers there, and the name comes from a Hindi word meaning 'belonging to Bengal'. If you make out a chit for someone's expenses you are using a term that comes from Hindi citthī 'a note or pass'.

British chef Jamie Oliver gleefully introduced pukka to millions of TV viewers in the slang sense 'excellent', but the word was being used in India as far back as the middle of the 17th century. Its first sense was 'of full weight', which gradually evolved into 'certain, reliable' and 'genuine, authentic' and then 'top-quality, impeccable' and 'socially acceptable, well brought up'. Jamie's sense is of early 1990s vintage. The word is from Hindi pakkā, meaning 'cooked, ripe or substantial'. And Indian cuisine has contributed other familiar terms, including curry, from a Tamil word adopted in the late 16th century, and kedgeree, from Hindi khichri, originally a dish of rice and pulses.

Things first got cushy during the First World War. It was originally an Anglo-Indian word from Urdu kushi 'pleasure', going back to Persian kus. As well as describing an easy job or post, cushy could also be used in connection with a wound that was not dangerous or serious.

Riders have been wearing jodhpurs since the late 19th century. The word comes from Jodhpur, a city in western India where similar garments are worn by men as a part of everyday dress. The gymkhana, a children's event with races and other competitions on horseback, is now a staple of every pony club, but in Victorian India it was a public place with facilities for sports. The English form of the word, which comes from the Urdu term gendkhāna, meaning 'racket court', has been influenced by the spelling of gymnastic.

The pyjamas we put on at night are literally 'leg clothing' – the word is from Urdu pāy 'leg' and jāma 'clothing'. They were originally loose silk or cotton trousers that both men and women wore in such countries as Turkey, Iran and India, until Europeans living in these places started wearing them for bed. A man might wear a cummerbund, a kind of sash, around his waist as part of evening dress for a smart party, but it was first worn in the Indian subcontinent by domestic staff and office workers of low status. The word is from Urdu kamar-band, from kamar 'waist or groin' and bandi 'band'.

Some Indian-based words may look misleadingly as though they come from familiar English words. Shampoo, for example, has nothing to do with sham, or with poo. English speakers first came across the term in the 18th century in Turkish baths, where the original use was 'to give a massage to'. The word itself is from Hindi cāmpo!, an instruction to a masseur to 'press!'. The 1930s slang word of approval, tickety-boo, has no association with tick or ticket, but probably comes from a Hindi expression thīk hai 'all right'.

The British rule of India as a Crown possession from 1858 to 1947 is known as the Raj, from the Hindi word rāj 'reign'. The Raj itself has long since passed into history, but the term is still with us. Evidence of its lasting impact on the language came in 2005, when the journalist Jeremy Paxman reached for it to describe the number of Scottish politicians at Westminster. 'We live', he said, 'under a sort of Scottish Raj.'

See also HORDE, INDIAN, JUGGERNAUT, JUNGLE, LOOT, THUG, VINDALOO.

cushy

rain

Such is the national obsession with the weather, it is hardly surprising that **rain** has been part of the English language for around 1,200 years. Rain features in a number of sayings and common expressions. The phrase **it is raining cats and dogs** is first found in the 18th century, but the alternative **rain dogs and polecats** goes back a further 100 years. In the past, gullible people might have believed that drowned dogs and cats seen floating in flooded streets had fallen from the skies during the previous heavy downpour.

Someone concerned about a future period of financial need might talk about saving for **a rainy day**. This may go back to the days when farm labourers working on a casual basis needed to save a proportion of their wages for times when bad weather stopped them working and earning money.

rainbow

The **bow** in **rainbow** is the kind used for shooting arrows, used here in the original sense 'curved line'. **Rainbow** first appears in a translation of the Book of Genesis by an Anglo-Saxon scholar, in which the reference is to the bow placed in the sky by God as a sign after the Flood.

A bewildering array of colours may be suggested by the phrase **all the colours of the rainbow**. In Shakespeare's *The Merry Wives of Windsor* Falstaff complains that he has not just been beaten black and blue but 'into all the colours of the rainbow'. In modern politics a **rainbow coalition** is an alliance of minority peoples and other disadvantaged groups. The expression goes back to a speech by the American politician Jesse Jackson, who said in 1988: 'When I look out at this convention, I see the face of America, red, yellow, brown, black, and white. We are all precious in God's sight – the real rainbow coalition.'

A rainbow can be associated with something both highly desirable and elusive. A thing much sought after but impossible to attain can be found **at the end of the rainbow**, and to **chase rainbows** is to pursue an illusory goal. The first of these comes from the old folk tale in which a person is promised that if they follow a rainbow to its end they would find a pot of gold.

---

take a rain check

You could read this text or **take a rain check**, implying that you might take it up at a later date. In the USA a **rain check** is a ticket given to spectators at a sporting event. If the event is cancelled because of rain – or 'rained off' – they can then claim a refund.

---

rake

The **rake** used by gardeners to smooth soil or gather leaves in autumn is an Old English word, from a root meaning 'heap up'. Concerns today about the ultra-slimness of fashionable models might be expressed by saying that someone is as **thin as a rake** – a comparison used since Geoffrey Chaucer's day. The phrases **rake over old coals** and **rake over the ashes** come from the idea of searching through a dead or dying fire to see if a spark remains, or trying to revive the memory of a past event which is better forgotten.

A fashionable, rich but immoral man can also be known as a **rake**. This is an abbreviation of the old word **rakehell**, which had the same meaning: the original idea was of the kind of sinful person likely to be found if you searched through Hell with a rake. A **rake's progress** is a progressive deterioration, especially through self-indulgence – *A Rake's Progress* was a series of engravings by the 18th-century artist William Hogarth, which depicted the progression of the rake from wealthy and privileged origins to debt, despair and death on the gallows.

rampant

Something **rampant** flourishes or spreads in an uncontrolled way. This is a development of the original use in heraldry, which described an animal, like the **lion rampant** of Scotland, rearing up on its left hind foot with its forefeet in the air. Its origins are much less vigorous, going back to French *ramper*, which means 'to creep, crawl' or 'to climb'.

ramshackle

A shaky building or a car with its bumper tied on with string might be called **ramshackle**, but it has nothing to do with rams or shackles. The word was originally a dialect term meaning 'irregular, disorderly' and is related to RANSACK.

ranch

The **ranch** featuring in many westerns appears in American sources from the early 19th century and comes from Spanish *rancho*, 'a group of people eating together'. The phrase **meanwhile, back at the ranch** was originally used in cowboy stories to introduce a subsidiary plot.

rank

In relation to position in a hierarchy **rank** has the same root as RING, and has been part of the language since medieval times, when it came into English from Old French. When we talk about the **rank and file** of an organisation we mean the ordinary members as distinct from the leaders. This goes back to the idea of rows and columns of soldiers in military formation, drawn up 'in rank and file', the ranks being the rows and the files the columns. If you fail to maintain solidarity with your fellows you **break ranks**, and if you unite to defend a common interest you **close ranks**. In the armed forces **the ranks** are those who are not commissioned officers: if you work your way up from a lowly position to one of seniority you may be said to have **risen from the ranks**.

Rank as an adjective is a different word, which dates back to Old English. Early senses included 'fully grown' and 'luxuriant', but later meanings involve the idea of disagreeable excess: a rank smell is extremely unpleasant, and rank grass grows too thickly.

ransack

This is a word which is still very close in meaning to its original 14th-century sense. If someone has **ransacked** a house, they have gone hurriedly through it to steal or search for things. The Old Norse word *rannsaka* from which it comes, made up of *rann* 'house' and a second element related to 'seek', was a legal term referring to the searching of property for stolen goods. See also RAMSHACKLE.

ransom

In medieval times a captured enemy might be released if a sum of money, or **ransom**, was paid, and if you held them captive and demanded such a payment you were said to **hold them to ransom**. Today the expression is used generally to express the idea of forcing someone to do something by threatening them. The word comes from the same Latin root as **redeem**, *emere* 'to buy'. See also KING.

rap

Since the end of the 18th century **rap** has been associated with rebuke and punishment, as in the phrase **a rap on the knuckles** for a sharp criticism. In early 20th-century American English the word developed the further meanings of 'a criminal charge' and 'a prison sentence'. If you were acquitted you were said to **beat the rap**. To **take the rap** was to be punished or blamed, especially for something where other people were wholly or partly responsible.

Performers of **rap** music tend to have a dangerous, bad-boy image, but the root of the term is not the 'criminal charge' or 'prison' senses but the old northern English sense 'conversation, chat'. This was carried over the Atlantic, and **rap** in the sense 'a talk or discussion' is now an American use. The first reference to rap music, in which words are recited rapidly and rhythmically over an instrumental backing, comes in 1979.

raspberry

A **raspberry** was originally a **rasp** or a **raspis**, but the ultimate origin of all these words is unknown. Most people *do* know that to **blow a raspberry** is to make a derisive or contemptuous sound with your lips. The expression comes from rhyming slang, where **raspberry tart** means 'fart'. See also CHEER.

rat

The **rat** has been part of our language since Anglo-Saxon times, and the ancient root of the word probably goes back to the time when the creature was first seen in Europe, having originated in Asia.

From the mid 20th century the term **rat race** has been used for a way of life in which people compete fiercely for money and power. The image behind this is of rats struggling with each other to move forward in a confined space, rather than of the ordered world of a race track.

Sailing ships would traditionally have been infested with rats, which would try to escape en masse from a vessel that was in trouble. This gave rise to a term for people hurrying to escape from a failing organisation, **rats deserting a sinking ship**. Such a person has been a **rat** since the 1760s, and 50 or so years later to **rat** started to mean 'to desert a cause, become a traitor' and then 'to inform on'.

smell a rat

We have been smelling rats for more than 200 years. The phrase appears in the 18th century as part of an elaborate mixed metaphor attributed to Boyle Roche, an Irish politician: 'Mr Speaker, I smell a rat; I see him forming in the air and darkening the sky; but I'll nip him in the bud.'

ration

The words **ratio**, **ration**, and **rational** all come from the same Latin root, *ratio* 'reckoning, reason', which is also related to REASON. The use of **ration** for 'a fixed allowance' became particularly associated with official control of scarce food supplies, or **rationing**, at the time of the First World War. Before that it was used in the armed forces for a soldier's daily share of the provisions.

rattle

Part of the language since medieval times, and probably a word which comes from the sound it makes. **Sabre-rattling** has meant 'the display or threat of military force' since the 1920s. A **sabre** is a heavy cavalry sword with a curved blade and a single cutting edge. If you rattled it in its scabbard you would be giving your opponent a wordless threat.

raw

This Old English word shares an ancient root with Greek *kreas* 'raw flesh'. In Australian English a stupid person can be referred to as a **prawn**, and to **come the raw prawn** is to attempt to deceive someone, presumably by pretending that you are too simple to cheat.

ray

The **ray** that means 'beam of light' is a medieval word going back to Latin *radius* 'spoke, ray', the source of **radiate** and **radius**. The term **ray of sunshine** for someone who brings happiness into the lives of others, dating back to the early 20th century, is often used ironically for someone who in fact spreads little cheer. **Ray** as a name for a fish is a different word, from Latin *raia*.

read

Alfred the Great, who was king of Wessex between 871 and 899, did much to promote education in his kingdom, and the word **read** is first found in his writings. He would certainly have been in favour of **the three Rs**, which since the early 19th century have been 'reading, (w)riting and (a)rithmetic', regarded as the fundamentals of elementary education. The expression is said to have originated as

Read my lips: no new taxes.

George H.W. Bush

a toast proposed by the banker and politician Sir William Curtis (1752-1829).

Read my lips is used to emphasise the importance of what you are going to say, by telling your hearers to listen carefully. The expression was most famously used by the first President Bush in 1998. In making a campaign pledge not to raise taxes, he said 'Read my lips: no new taxes.'

If you want to give someone a severe warning or reprimand, you may **read the riot act** to them. The Riot Act was passed by the British government in 1715, in the wake of the Jacobite rebellion of that year, to prevent civil disorder. The Act made it an offence for a group of 12 or more people to refuse to disperse within an hour of being ordered to do so, and after a magistrate had read a particular section of the Act to them. The last point created something of a problem, as reading legal language aloud is not the easiest thing to do in the middle of a genuine riot – and defendants might claim later that they had not heard the key words. The Act failed to prevent a number of major disturbances over the years, but was not repealed until 1967.

ream

The term **ream** for 500 sheets of paper is first found in medieval times, and goes back ultimately to Arabic *rizma* 'bundle'. It came to mean a large quantity of paper, without reference to the specific number of sheets – in 1814 Sir Walter Scott referred to 'whole reams of modern plays'. In turn this gave us the general use of **reams of** to mean 'a large quantity of', which is found from the beginning of the 20th century.

reap

We might think of gathering in the harvest as a key activity of early times, but the Old English word **reap** is something of a mystery. We do not know its origin, and it has no matching words in related languages.

A person who seems unwilling to face up to the consequences of their actions may be told that **you reap what you sow**. This proverbial saying goes back to a verse in the biblical Epistle to the Galatians: 'Be not deceived; God is not mocked: for whatsoever a man soweth, that shall he also reap.' See also GRIM.

reason

The ultimate source of **reason** is Latin *reri* 'to consider', which is also the root of RATION and associated words. **Theirs not to reason why**, a reluctant admission that it is not someone's place to question an order or system, comes from Lord Tennyson's poem 'The Charge of the Light Brigade' (1854). This describes a notorious incident in the Crimean War, when British cavalry unhesitatingly obeyed a suicidal order to ride straight at the Russian guns. See also RHYME.

rebel

Today **rebel** might be used generally for someone who opposes authority, but it goes back to a much more precise root. The Latin word *rebellis* was originally used in reference to someone making a fresh declaration of war after being defeated. The root was *bellum* 'war', as in **bellicose** or 'warlike'.

A person who is deeply dissatisfied by society in general but does not have a specific aim to fight for might be described as **a rebel without a cause**. The first such person was James Dean, star of the 1955 film *Rebel Without a Cause*.

rebuke

Someone who has been **rebuked** or told off may feel cut down to size – a link to the origins of the word. Its source is medieval French *rebuker*, which originally meant 'to cut down wood'.

red

An Old English word which shares an ancient root with Latin *rufus*, Greek *eruthros* and Sanskrit *rudhira* 'red'. The colour **red** has traditionally been associated with radical political views, and particularly Communists from the 19th century onwards. During the Cold War, when Americans feared **reds under the bed** or Communist sympathisers, the expression **better dead than red** was used to mean that the prospect of nuclear annihilation was preferable to that of a Communist society. The slogan was reversed by nuclear disarmament campaigners of the late 1950s as 'better red than dead'.

Something involving savage or merciless competition might be described as **red in tooth and claw**. The phrase originated as a quotation from Lord Tennyson's poem 'In Memoriam' (1854): 'Nature, red in tooth and claw'.

In Church calendars a saint's day or Church festival was distinguished by being written in red letters. This gives us a **red letter day** for a pleasantly memorable,

FOR THE LAST TIME RED MEANS STOP NOT CHARGE!

fortunate or happy day. A less cheering use of red ink was customarily made to enter debit items and balances in accounts – which gives us **in the red** to mean in debt or overdrawn.

The colour red is supposed to provoke a bull, and is the colour of the cape used by matadors in bullfighting. From this we say that something which is certain to provoke or anger somebody will be like a **red rag to a bull**.

A **red herring** is something, especially a clue, which misleads or distracts you. The pungent scent of a dried smoked herring (red in colour as a result of the curing process) was formerly used to lay a trail when training hounds to follow a scent.

The **red light district** of a town is one with a lot of brothels, strip clubs and other businesses concerned with sex. The phrase is from the red light traditionally used as the sign of a brothel. See also PAINT.

People have been complaining about **red tape**, or excessive bureaucracy, since the 1730s. Real red or pinkish-red tape is used to bind together legal and official documents.

reek

We think of a **reek** today as an unpleasant smell, but in Old English the word meant 'smoke'. This gave us the traditional name of **Auld Reekie** ('Old Smoky') for Edinburgh – a nickname showing an early awareness of the drawbacks of pollution.

regatta

In the Venetian dialect of Italian *regatta* meant literally 'a fight, a contest', not necessarily one between rowers. It was borrowed into English in the 17th century as a name for a boat race held on the Grand Canal in Venice. By the late 18th century the word was being used for home-grown enterprises, and the first English **regatta** was held on the Thames on June 23, 1775.

regency

Between 1811 and 1820 George, Prince of Wales was regent for his father King George III, who was suffering from a long-term mental illness. The Prince was known for his fun-loving lifestyle and support for the arts, and the period of **the Regency** was noted for its distinctive fashions and architecture – such as, for example, the wildly exotic Brighton Pavilion, designed by John Nash. The balls and parties held by the aristocracy of the time are imagined in the romantic historical novels set in this period and called **Regency romances**. The source of **regency** is Latin *regere* 'to rule', which means it is related to words like **regal**, **royal** and RULE.

remorse

The idea behind **remorse** is of regret or guilt that eats away at you, prompting you to repent. The word goes back to Latin *remorsus*, from *remordere* 'to annoy, trouble'. The first part of the word, *re-*, adds intensity, and the second comes from *mordere* 'to bite'.

Renaissance

The **Renaissance** of the 14th to 16th centuries was literally a 'rebirth' of culture after what was regarded as the uncivilised period of the Middle Ages. It began in Florence, Italy, where there was a revival of interest in classical antiquity, and spread to Venice, Rome and then throughout Europe. **Renaissance** is a French word derived from Latin *nasci* 'to be born' (see NATION), which was not used in English until the 1840s – before that it was known as the **Revival of Learning**. A **Renaissance man** has many talents and interests, like the great Renaissance figure Leonardo da Vinci, who was a notable painter, scientist, inventor and engineer. An ideal gentleman of the time was expected to have many accomplishments and a broad education in both the arts and the sciences.

repercussion

When medieval doctors talked about **repercussion**, they meant the forcing back or driving away of an infectious condition. The idea of repelling something reflects its Latin source, *repercutere* 'to push back'.

The idea of driving something back gave rise to 'a blow given in return', which resulted in the current use of **repercussions** for the consequences of an event or action.

reprieve

Some words have not just changed their meaning, but also reversed it. When **reprieve** came into English from Old French, based on Latin *reprehendere* 'to seize, take back', it meant 'to take back to prison'. In the mid 16th century it referred to postponing or delaying a legal process, before developing into the current sense of rescuing someone by cancelling an impending punishment.

reptile

A mention of **reptiles** today conjures up a picture of snakes and lizards, but in the 14th century the word included other creatures. It comes from Latin *repere* 'to crawl' and was originally used for any creeping or crawling animal.

rest

In the sense 'to stop working or moving' **rest** is an Old English word from a root meaning 'league' or 'mile'. The reference was to a distance after which a person rested.

The **rest** that means 'the remaining part' comes from Latin *restare* 'to remain', also the source of **restive**. Like REPRIEVE, **restive** is a word whose meaning has been reversed. Its original meaning was 'inclined to stay still, inert'. It was then applied particularly to a horse which remained stubbornly still or shifted from side to side instead of moving on. From this came the current meaning of 'restless, fidgety'.

revenge

'Revenge', said the 17th-century courtier and scholar Francis Bacon, 'is a kind of wild justice.' The idea that wrongs can be most successfully avenged by someone who has taken the time to plan their response is formulated in the proverb first recorded in the late 19th century, **revenge is a dish best eaten cold**. The word is from Old French *revencher*, from Latin *vindicare* 'to claim, avenge' – the root of **vindicate**.

rhapsody

A word which links classical poetry to cries of delight. **Rhapsody** comes from Greek *rhaptein* 'to stitch', and its earliest sense carries the idea of words woven together. In the 16th century a rhapsody was a long poem, like Homer's *Odyssey* or *Iliad*, suitable for recitation. From this developed first the idea of a

Would you Adam and Eve it?

You do not need to be a true Cockney, born within earshot of Bow Bells, to know some rhyming slang. Although associated with the East End of London, it has spread as far as Australia, and colourful new examples are still being created.

In rhyming slang words are replaced with rhyming words or phrases, so apples and pears means 'stairs' and boat race is 'face'. The rhyming word is often omitted – your china is your mate, from 'china plate', and your loaf or 'loaf of bread' is your head.

Rhyming slang is first mentioned in a slang dictionary of 1859 as having originated about 15 years previously – joanna, 'a piano', is recorded from 1846, and mince pies or 'eyes' from 1857. It was linked in the dictionary with Seven Dials, an infamous den of thieves in Holborn, London, and by the end of the century was associated with London street traders. Rhyming slang was particularly popular at the beginning of the 20th century, after which it seems to have declined. George Orwell, writing in *Down and Out in Paris and London* (1933), observed 'Twenty-five or thirty years ago … the "rhyming slang" was all the rage in London … It was so common that it was even reproduced in novels; now it is almost extinct.' But Orwell was wrong, and rhyming slang is alive and well, even if it is now mostly used for fun.

Thanks to London-based TV programmes such as *Minder*, *Only Fools and Horses* and *EastEnders*, and films like *Lock, Stock and Two Smoking Barrels*, most British people know the classic examples, such as dog and bone 'phone', tea leaf 'thief' and trouble and strife 'wife'. The 1970s TV police drama *The Sweeney* took its title from an example of 1930s rhyming slang – Sweeney is short for Sweeney Todd, an 18th-century barber who murdered his customers and whose name rhymes with 'Flying Squad', a division of the police force capable of reaching an incident quickly.

Some rhyming slang is incredibly convoluted. Your arris is your bottom – arris is an abbreviation of 'Aristotle', which rhymes with 'bottle' and so leads to 'bottle and glass' = 'arse'. Other examples are obscure. If you are boracic or brassic you have no money – boracic lint rhymes with 'skint'. Someone on their tod is alone, from the name of the US jockey Tod Sloan (1873-1933). One of the most ingenious examples is titfer, 'hat', from 'tit for tat'.

Barnet for 'hair' is obscure unless you know London – the full form is Barnet fair, a reference to the annual fair still held in Barnet, just north of the capital.

Mutt and Jeff, used since the 1930s for 'deaf', is from the names of two cartoon characters, one tall and the other short, who appeared in a strip created by the US cartoonist 'Bud' Fisher (1885-1954). Brahms and Liszt, 'drunk', rhymes with 'pissed' and comes from the 1920s. Also from the 1920s is Rosie Lee, 'tea' – although Rosie does not seem to have been a real person.

Not all rhyming slang is from London. Australians have a long tradition of using it – jimmygrant for 'immigrant', recorded as early as 1845, would have been brought over from England. More recent examples are strictly Antipodean – they include Joe Blake for 'snake', found from the 1920s, and noah (Noah's Ark) for 'shark', used since the 1940s.

Modern-day examples of rhyming slang include pork pie or porky for 'lie', from the early 1980s, and ruby or Ruby Murray, 'curry', which is from the name of the Northern Irish singer Ruby Murray (1935-96). The trend in the 2000s has been to rhyme on the name of a celebrity. 'Popney', as it is called, features such rhymes as Britney Spears for 'beers', Shania Twain for 'pain' and Tony Blairs for 'flares' or flared trousers. In Australia, too, rhyming slang is thriving, and draws on local culture. So mud and ooze is 'booze' and Reg Grundys are 'undies', after the successful media mogul Reg Grundy.

See also APPLE, BERK, BRISTOL, BUTCHER, COB, GRASS, RABBIT, RASPBERRY.

'apples and pears'

'Ruby Murray'

'dog and bone'

medley or collection, and then the sense of pleasure and approval expressed with enthusiasm rather than careful thought.

rheumatism

Doctors have been diagnosing **rheumatism** in their patients since the 17th century. The disease was originally supposed to be caused by watery fluids in the body, and the word comes from Greek *rheumatizein* 'to snuffle', from *rheuma* 'stream'.

rhinoceros

It is the look of the **rhinoceros** that provides its name, which comes from Greek *rhino-* 'nose' and *keras* 'horn'. The animal has been known in English since the end of the 14th century, but the first reference to it calls it a kind of unicorn.

rhubarb

English speakers have been eating **rhubarb** since medieval times. The fruit came originally from China and Tibet, and the name reflects its exotic origins. It goes back to Greek *rhabarbarum*, the second part of which comes from *barbaros* 'foreign' (see BARBARIAN). Actors who wanted to give the impression of indistinct background conversation on stage traditionally achieved this by repeating 'rhubarb, rhubarb'.

rhyme

Both **rhyme** and **rhythm** come from the same source, Greek *rhuthmos*, and before it referred to a musical beat **rhythm** originally meant 'rhyme'. Since the 16th century a person wanting to complain that something completely lacked logical explanation might say that there was no **rhyme or reason** to it.

rich

The Anglo-Saxons would probably have understood the US novelist F. Scott Fitzgerald's remark to Ernest Hemingway: 'Let me tell you about the very rich. They are different from you and me.' In Old English **rich** meant both 'powerful' and 'wealthy'. The idea of unlimited wealth led to an association of 'given without restraint', and in the 18th century **rich** began to mean 'outrageous, beyond acceptable limits', which gave us **a bit rich** in reference to something causing ironic amusement or exasperation.

riddle

In Anglo-Saxon times people were fond of asking each other **riddles**. One person would recite a poem describing features of a familiar object, such as a sword or a key, and end with the challenge 'What am I?'

Winston Churchill referred to a more modern kind of riddle at the beginning of the Second World War when he said: 'I cannot forecast to you the action of Russia. It is a riddle wrapped in a mystery inside an enigma.'

The word comes from the same root as READ. **Riddle** meaning 'to make many holes in something' is a different word, and ultimately goes back to the same root as Latin *cribrum* 'sieve' and *cernere* 'to separate', and Greek *krinein* 'to decide'.

ride

An Old English word related to ROAD, from a time when horses were the usual means of transport. When people in Yorkshire refer to the **East Riding**, **North Riding** or **West Riding** they are not making any reference to horses, though. The word for each of the county's three former administrative divisions goes back to Old Norse *thrithjungr* 'third part', from *thrithi* 'third'. Over the years the initial '*th*' was lost, so that the east, north or west 'third part' of the county became a **riding**.

A person who behaves in a reckless or arrogant way that invites defeat or failure is sometimes said to **ride for a fall**. The phrase comes from 19th-century descriptions of hunters riding in a way likely to lead to an accident.

To **ride herd on** someone is to keep watch over them. This North American expression comes from the idea of cowboys guarding or controlling a herd of cattle by riding round its edge. People who achieve a happy conclusion may be said to **ride off into the sunset**, a reference is to the traditional closing scene of a western, when the main characters ride off towards the setting sun after everything has been satisfactorily resolved.

The proverb **he who rides a tiger is afraid to dismount**, meaning that once a dangerous or troublesome venture is begun the best course is to carry it through to the end, is recorded from the 19th century. Winston Churchill used it with ominous effect in 1937: 'Dictators ride to and fro upon tigers which they dare not dismount. And the tigers are getting hungry.'

right

The root meaning of **right** is not a turn or side but movement in a straight line – the first senses were 'straight, not curved' and 'direct, straight to the destination' as well as 'morally good, just' and 'true, correct'. **Right** as in the opposite of LEFT is a later meaning that dates from the 13th century.

The political application originated in the French National Assembly of 1789, in which the nobles as a body took the position of honour on the president's right, and the Third Estate – the French bourgeoisie and working class – sat on his left. A person who holds right-wing views of the most extreme kind can be described as being **somewhere to the right of Genghis Khan**. This expression uses Genghis Khan (1162-1227), the founder of the Mongol Empire, as a supreme example of a repressive and tyrannical ruler. The name of the early 5th-century warlord Attila the Hun, seen as an equally dominant and brutal figure, is sometimes substituted for Genghis. See also DEXTER, SINISTER.

ring

In Anglo-Saxon times a gold **ring** was worn as an indication of wealth and status – the word comes from the same root as RANK. In some traditional legends, such as the one told in Wagner's opera cycle *The Ring of the Nibelungen*, a ring is also an object of power, an idea reinforced by J.R.R. Tolkien's fantasy *The Lord of the Rings*.

Ring-a-ring o'roses is a singing game played by children, in which players hold hands and dance in a circle, falling down at the end of the song. The song is commonly interpreted as referring to the bubonic plague which swept through England in 1665-6, with the 'ring o'roses' the rash symptomatic of the disease, the 'pocketful of posies' herbs carried to ward off infection and the final 'falling down' part symbolising death. This is now considered unlikely, though, as the song first appeared in print only in 1881. The 'all fall down' may have been a curtsy or similar gesture.

The use of **ring** to mean 'give out a clear sound' is also recorded from Old English, but is a quite different word, probably representing an imitation of the sound. The idea that something vaguely remembered might **ring a bell** in your head is a common one, but the expression goes back only to the 1930s.

rink

In medieval Scotland jousting knights not skaters took to a **rink**. It was only in the 18th century that a rink became a stretch of ice set aside for the sport of curling, and the word remained a Scottish one until the end of the following century.

rival

A **rival** was originally someone you had to share your water supply with. Recorded in English from the late 16th century, the word goes back to Latin *rivalis*, which originally meant 'person living on the opposite bank

and using the same stream as another'. It comes ultimately from the same root as RIVER.

river

Rivers have been part of the English language since medieval times. The word goes back to Latin *ripa* 'bank of a river' and is related to RIVAL.

To **sell someone down the river** is to betray them, especially to benefit yourself. The expression refers to the slave-owning period of American history. It was the custom to sell troublesome slaves to owners of sugar-cane plantations on the lower Mississippi, where conditions where harsher than those in the more northerly slave-owning states. The first recorded use is in 1851 by the American writer Harriet Beecher Stowe, whose best-known work is the anti-slavery novel *Uncle Tom's Cabin* (1852). The 'betray' sense did not emerge until much later, in the 1920s, perhaps because the subject was too sensitive to be used casually. In the USA someone who has been sent **up the river** is in prison. The phrase originally referred to Sing Sing prison, situated up the Hudson River from the city of New York.

ring the changes

The 'changes' you ring to vary ways of doing something come from bell-ringing. They are the different sequences in which a peal of church bells can be rung.

road

In Old English **road** meant 'a journey on horseback', and the word is related to RIDE. The sense of 'a wide track to travel on', the equivalent of STREET, did not appear until the end of the 16th century. The **middle of the road** has been the place for moderate views since the 1890s, originally in the context of US politics. The phrase has referred to easy-listening music since the late 1950s.

People sometimes use **the road less travelled** to refer to an unconventional or unusual course of action. The phrase alludes to the poem 'The Road Not Taken' (1916) by Robert Frost:

Two roads diverged in a wood, and I—
I took the one less travelled by,
And that has made all the difference.

See also HELL, RAGE.

rob

The words **rob** and **robe** come from the same ancient root, a word meaning 'booty' – clothing would have been the kind of property stolen in a raid. To **rob Peter to pay Paul** is to take something away from one person to pay another. The expression probably refers to the apostles St Peter and St Paul, who in Christian art are often shown together as equals. Although the earliest examples feature robbery, other versions have cropped up over the centuries, such as **unclothe Peter to pay Paul** and **borrow from Peter to pay Paul**. The last example probably helped in the additional meaning 'to pay off one debt only to incur another'.

robot

This is one of the few English words to have come from Czech – from *robota* 'forced labour'. The term was coined in Karel Čapek's play *R.U.R.*, or 'Rossum's Universal Robots' (1920), when it described an artificial man or woman.

rock

The hard **rock** that makes up much of the Earth came into medieval English from Old French *rocque*, which can be traced back to medieval Latin *rocca*. The classical Latin word was *petra*, the source of PETRIFY. People have been **caught between a rock and a hard place** since the 1920s, first of all in Arizona and California. Also American is **on the rocks** meaning 'on ice', first recorded in 1946.

Rock meaning 'to move to and fro' is an Old English word. **Rock music** was originally **rock and roll**, which is first found in 1951, although a song called 'Rock and Roll' came out in 1934. Rock and roll combined black rhythm and blues and white country or 'hillbilly' music. Elvis Presley's first single, 'That's All Right Mama' and Bill Haley's 'Rock Around the Clock', both released in 1954, are often considered the first rock and roll records, but similar-sounding music was produced in the 1930s and 1940s by black performers like Big Joe Turner and Fats Domino.

If you are **off your rocker** you are mad or crazy. A **rocker** here is a concave piece of wood or metal placed under a chair or cradle so that it can rock backwards and forwards. In the early 1960s rockers were also youths who liked rock music, leather clothing and motorcycles and were the sworn enemies of the **mods** (short for **modernists**), who were noted for their smart appearance, motor scooters and fondness for soul music.

rocket

Recorded in English from the early 17th century, **rocket** comes ultimately from Italian *rocca* 'a distaff', the stick or spindle on which wool was wound for spinning. Like the firework, it was cylindrical in shape. The development of rockets for space travel after the Second World War gave rise to the expression **not rocket science** to suggest that something is not really very difficult. Rocket meaning 'a reprimand', as in to **give** or **get a rocket**, is Second World War military slang – the first recorded example is **stop a rocket**. The salad vegetable **rocket** is a totally different word, which came via French *roquette* from Latin *eruca*, meaning a kind of cabbage.

rod

In Old English **rod** meant 'slender shoot growing on or cut from a tree' but also 'straight stick or bundle of twigs used to inflict punishment', and phrases linked with it tend to evoke traditional, and severe, ideas of discipline. If you exert control over someone strictly or harshly you may be said to **rule them with a rod of iron**. The expression goes back to the Bible, to Psalms: 'Thou shalt break them with a rod of iron; thou shalt dash them in pieces like a potter's vessel.' The proverb **spare the rod and spoil the child**, meaning that if children are not physically punished when they do wrong their personal development will suffer, is found from Anglo-Saxon times. It too has a biblical origin, from Proverbs: 'He that spareth his rod, hateth his son.' See also KISS.

rodent

The teeth of rodents such as rats and mice grow continuously and must be kept worn down by gnawing – a clue about the origin of the term **rodent**. The word comes from Latin *rodere* 'to gnaw', which is related to CORRODE, ERODE, ROOT and ROSTRUM.

roll

Recorded from medieval times, **roll** goes back to Latin *rotula* 'little wheel' and is related to an actor's part or **role** in a play or film. **Role** entered English from French *roule* 'roll', which referred to the roll of paper on which the part would originally have been written.

If you **roll with the punches** you adapt yourself to difficult circumstances. The image here is of a boxer moving their body away from an opponent's blows so as to lessen their impact.

A **rolling stone** is someone who does not settle in one place for long. The expression comes from the proverb **a rolling stone gathers no moss** – meaning that a person who is always moving on is not likely to acquire property, status or responsibilities. Led by vocalist Mick Jagger and guitarists Keith Richards and Brian Jones, the Rolling Stones played their first gig in 1962 at the Marquee Club in London. They took their name not directly from the proverb but from a song by the US blues musician Muddy Waters.

romance

It now conjures up images of love, mystery and excitement, but **romance** was originally the language spoken by the ordinary people of a country such as France, as opposed to Latin. The **Romance languages** are the European languages descended from Latin, and the word **romance** came via Old French from Latin *Romanicus* 'Roman'. A romance became a medieval narrative in the local language that described the adventures of a hero of chivalry. These adventures tended to be so wild and improbable that the word came to be associated with any work of fiction depicting events remote from everyday life or, because love was often a subject of the medieval romances, dealing with love. The senses 'idealised or sentimental love' and 'a love affair' are Victorian.

Romantic is a more recent word, which entered English only in the mid 17th century. At the end of the 18th century the **Romantic movement** arose, exemplified by the writers Wordsworth, Coleridge, Byron, Shelley and Keats and painters like William Blake, J.M.W. Turner and Goya. The term was revived by the flamboyant but rather less highbrow **New Romantics** in the early 1980s, which featured bands such as Spandau Ballet, Culture Club and Duran Duran wearing make-up and dressing in extravagant costumes.

Rome

For centuries **Rome**, known as **the Eternal City**, was the heart of a great empire. It became a byword for power and features in a number of common phrases. The proverb **all roads lead to Rome**, meaning that different routes will be drawn to a powerful centre, echoes a Latin saying which reflected the power and prestige of Rome. The city was built up gradually from humble beginnings, a fact which gave us the practical warning against expecting results too quickly, **Rome was not built in a day**.

Adjusting to the unfamiliar customs of another country or organisation require tact and care – as the reminder **when in Rome** indicates. The full proverb, **when in Rome do as the Romans do**, refers to a comment by St Ambrose, 4th-century Bishop of Milan. He wrote to St Augustine that when he was in Rome he followed the local custom of fasting on a Saturday, although in Milan he did not do this. See also FIDDLE.

Fill your mush with cushty words

Romany, the language of the Gypsies, is related to the Hindi and Sanskrit tongues of India, where these wandering people originated. It has given English some colourful slang words.

The word Romany itself comes from *Rom*, which means 'a male Gypsy' in Romany – the plural of Rom, *Roma*, is another name for the Gypsy people. A rye is 'a man or gentleman', while a Romany rye is a man who is not a Gypsy but who associates with them. You might find him in a vardo, 'a caravan', but that would be no place for a gorgio, 'a non-Gypsy'.

Probably the best-known English expression to come from Romany is pal, which is first recorded in the late 17th century and can be traced back through Turkish and Transylvanian Romany to ancient Sanskrit. Pals were originally accomplices in crime, but now they are simply friends. Older people might refer to a pal as a decent cove, a word meaning 'a man' which is probably from Romany *kova* 'thing or person' and goes back as far as the 1560s. Another friendly word from Romany is mush (pronounced like *push*), which is British slang for a person's mouth or face, and is also a form of address. In Romany the word simply means 'man'.

Cushty, meaning 'very good', has been around since the 1920s, but was popularised by the TV comedy *Only Fools and Horses* in the 1980s. It derives from Romany *kushto* or *kushti* 'good' – the spelling was probably influenced by cushy, meaning 'easy, undemanding'. Another word familiar to Del Boy and Rodney in *Only Fools and Horses* is wonga, 'money', from Romany *wongar*, which means 'coal' as well as 'money'.

Some Romany terms reflect the traditionally marginalised status of Gypsies. Dick meaning 'detective' may be from the old slang word *dick*, 'look', which was a Romany expression. Stir or 'jail' dates from around 1850 and is probably from Romany *sturbin*, also meaning 'jail', and a chiv or shiv is a knife or razor used as a weapon, from *chiv* 'blade'.

See also BLOW, CHAV, NARK.

room

In Old English **room** meant 'the amount of space occupied by something', and did not mean 'an interior division of a building' until the 14th century. The majority of houses then would have had only one room. Sometimes political negotiation is described as having taken place **in a smoke-filled room**, meaning that it has been conducted privately rather than more openly. The expression comes from a 1920s news report about the selection of the Republican presidential candidate, Warren Harding, who in 1921 became the 29th President of the United States. According to the report he was 'chosen by a group of men in a smoke-filled room'. Harding was at the time something of a dark horse, and a lack of openness and democracy was associated with his selection.

Room at the top is a way of describing the opportunity to join the higher ranks of an organisation. The phrase is attributed to the American politician Daniel Webster (1782-1852), who was warned against attempting to enter the overcrowded legal profession. He is said to have replied, 'There is always room at the top.' The phrase was taken up in the early 20th century and was used as the title of John Braine's first novel, published in 1957, about an ambitious young man in an industrial town in the north of England. It was filmed in 1959 with Laurence Harvey taking the lead.

An **elephant in the room** is an obvious, major problem or controversial issue that is being studiously avoided as a subject for discussion. The phrase was originally American, and seems to have been first used in the early 1980s, in the language of therapists treating people addicted to drink or drugs. An alternative is a **moose on the table**. See also CAT.

root

An Old English word related to Latin *radix* (see RADICAL) and **wort**, which is used in the names of plants such as St John's wort. **Root and branch**, used to emphasise how thoroughly something is dealt with, goes back to the biblical book of Malachi: 'The day cometh that shall burn them up . . . that it shall leave them neither root nor branch.' See also MONEY.

Root used of an animal turning up the ground with its snout in search of food is a completely different word, that may ultimately be linked to Latin *rodere* 'gnaw' (see RODENT). Someone backing a candidate for a post may be said to be **rooting for** them – perhaps with the idea of trying to find further support through their efforts.

rope

One of the oldest English words, recorded as early as AD 725. A way of dealing with a person who is causing problems is to **give them enough rope** – give them enough freedom of action that they bring about their own downfall. The phrase comes from a proverb which makes the grim origins of the saying clear: **give a man enough rope and he will hang himself**.

Someone who is in a desperate position, or a state of near collapse, may be described as being **on the ropes**. This is an expression from boxing, and conjures up the picture of a losing contestant forced back by his opponent against the ropes that mark the sides of the ring.

To **show someone the ropes** is to teach them the established way of doing things. The origins of this expression go back to the mid 19th century and the days of sailing ships. Skill in handling ropes and tying knots was essential for any sailor, and the idea was soon extended to other walks of life. A range of variations on the theme developed, including **learn the ropes** and the more familiar **know the ropes**. **Ropy** meaning 'not very good' is RAF slang, dating from the early 1940s. It probably derives from the phrase **money for old rope** (see MONEY), although another idea links it to the old biplanes, festooned with 'ropes' or supporting wires, that were then being replaced by modern Spitfires and Hurricanes.

rose-coloured spectacles

The Victorians wore the first over-optimistic **rose-coloured spectacles**. Dickens talked of living 'in a rose-colored mist' in *Little Dorrit* (1857), but the full phrase first appears in *Tom Brown at Oxford* (1861) by Thomas Hughes.

rose

The **rose** (from Latin *rosa*) is beautiful but prickly, and the proverbial saying **no rose without a thorn**, meaning that even the pleasantest things have their drawbacks, goes back to medieval times. There is nothing spiky about an **English rose**, an attractive, fair-skinned English girl. Elton John's reworking of his song 'Candle in the Wind', sung at the funeral of Diana, Princess of Wales on September 7, 1997, was called 'Goodbye England's rose'.

The importance of a name, especially as it affects how we see something, may be dismissed with the phrase **a rose by any other name**. This alludes to a line in Shakespeare's *Romeo and Juliet*: 'That which we call a rose / By any other name would smell as sweet.' See also RING.

rostrum

A **rostrum** is now a raised platform on which a person stands to make a speech, but it was originally part of a ship. It is an English use of a Latin word meaning 'beak', which came from *rodere* 'to gnaw'. In the days of the Roman Empire the part of the Forum in Rome which was used as a platform for public speakers was decorated with the 'beaks' or pointed prows of captured enemy warships. See also RODENT, ROOT.

row

There are enough versions of **row** to form a row. The one meaning 'an orderly line' is recorded from Old English. **Row** meaning 'to propel with oars' is also Old English, but is a different word that goes back to a root shared also by Latin *remus* 'oar'. The kind of **row** that results from a heated argument is a different word again, with a different pronunciation. It turned up in English from an unknown source in the middle of the 18th century, when it was considered to be slang or 'low' speech.

rub

If you want to impress the consequences of a mistake on someone you may be tempted to **rub their nose in it**. This comes from a misguided way of house-training puppies or kittens: literally rubbing their noses in any deposit they may make in the house in an attempt to dissuade them from repeating the offence. To **rub someone up the wrong way**, or irritate them, is another pet-related image, from the idea of stroking a cat against the lie of its fur.

Someone pointing out a particular difficulty may say **there's the rub**. The expression comes from Shakespeare's *Hamlet*, when Hamlet says: 'To sleep: perchance to dream: ay, there's the rub.' In the game of bowls a **rub** is an impediment that prevents a bowl running smoothly. The same idea is found in **the rub of the green**, which in golf is an accidental interference with the flight or roll of the ball, such as hitting a tree. More broadly it is also luck or fortune, especially in sport.

rude

Many a schoolchild has sniggered at old books or hymns that mention 'rude dwellings'. Especially for children, the dominant sense of **rude** is now 'referring to a subject such as sex in an embarrassing or offensive way', yet this is a recent development, being recorded only from the early 1960s. The word came via Old French from Latin *rudis*, 'unfinished, roughly made, uncultivated', and in medieval times meant 'uneducated, ignorant, uncultivated' and 'roughly made' as well as 'impolite'. See also MECHANICAL.

In Jamaica a **rude boy** is a poor, lawless urban youth. The expression became more widely known in the late 1970s with the popularity of bands playing 'ska' (a kind of speeded-up reggae) such as Madness and the Specials, many of whose songs mentioned rude boys.

rugby

The game of **rugby** is named after Rugby School in Warwickshire, England, the public school where it was first played. According to tradition, in a school football match in 1823 a boy named William Webb Ellis first took the ball in his arms and ran with it, so originating the game. The informal name **rugger** was invented at Oxford University in, it seems, 1893. At the time

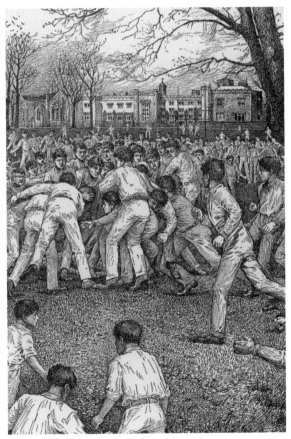

Rugby schoolboys get stuck into a game of rugby in the 19th century.

there was a student craze for adding -er to the end of words, which gave us words such as SOCCER, **brekker** (for 'breakfast') and **preggers** (for 'pregnant'), as well as some that lasted only for a year or so, like **Pragger-Wagger** for the Prince of Wales, and even **wagger-pagger-bagger** for 'wastepaper basket'. Ironically, the craze began at Rugby School.

rule

We think of **rules** as giving us lines to follow, and the word goes back to Latin *regula* 'straight stick', and beyond that to *regere* 'to rule', the source of **regal** and **royal**. To **rule the roost** is to be in complete control. The original form of the phrase was **rule the roast**, from the end of the 15th century, which may imply that it referred to the most important person at a banquet or feast. **Roast** changed to **roost** in the 18th century when people started thinking about a cockerel asserting itself over the other roosting birds in the farmyard.

The **rule** in **run the rule over**, 'to examine quickly', is a measuring stick or ruler. It has the same meaning in **rule of thumb**, 'a broadly accurate guide based on practice rather than theory'. This expression, recorded from 1692, is probably from the ancient use of parts of the body, such as the FOOT and the **hand**, as units of measurement. The first joint of a man's thumb is about an inch long, and so is useful for making rough measurements when you have mislaid your ruler. See also RAIL.

ruminate

A person who **ruminates** might be said to 'chew over' a particular problem or idea, and this is where the word originally comes from. It goes back to Latin *ruminari* 'to chew over', and has also given us a name for an animal like a cow or sheep which chews the cud – a **ruminant**.

rummage

When we **rummage** for a lost article in a drawer we are using a word originally associated with the sea. It comes ultimately from Old French *arrumer* 'to stow away', from medieval Dutch *ruim* 'room'. At first, in the late 15th century, to rummage was to arrange items such as casks in the hold of a ship, but by the early 17th century it was someone searching a ship, perhaps for contraband cargo, who was said to 'rummage' it.

run

An important little Anglo-Saxon word found in many common phrases. If you come into conflict with someone you have **run foul** of them. This nautical expression refers to a ship which had collided or become entangled with another vessel or with an obstacle. If people are angry public feeling may **run high**, which is another nautical phrase, from waves or tides rising about their normal height, especially in stormy conditions. Both of these phrases appeared around 1700.

An ordinary or undistinguished person might be described as a **run of the mill** type. Here the **run** is the material produced from a mill before it has been sorted or inspected for quality.

When you find someone after a long search you may feel that at last you have **run them to earth**. The earth is a fox's home, and the literal meaning is 'to chase a hunted animal to its lair and corner it there'.

A confrontation that has gone on for a long time is sometimes called a **running battle**. The idea reaches back into the history of warfare. Literally, a **running** battle is one that constantly changes its location, the opposite of a **pitched battle** (see PITCH). The expression is first recorded in the late 17th century as **running fight** and described a naval engagement that continued even as one side was fleeing. The current version was not recorded until the 20th century, but is now the more common. See also GAUNTLET.

ruse

In hunting terminology a **ruse** was a turn or detour made by a hunted animal to escape the hounds. The word came from Old French *ruser*, which meant 'to use trickery' and which in another sense, 'to drive back', was also the origin of **rush**.

rut

In the days of horse-drawn vehicles a cartwheel travelling many times along the same track would carve out a deep groove or **rut**. The deeper the rut became, the more difficult it would be to follow any other route. Someone following a fixed, and probably rather tedious, pattern of behaviour is **in a rut**. **Rut** in this sense is probably from Old French *rute*, the source of **route**.

The **rut** of male deer is quite a different word. In the breeding season stags challenge one another by roaring calls, when they are said to be **in rut**: here **rut** probably comes from Latin *rugire* 'to roar' (see also RAIL).

ruthless

A **ruthless** competitor or criminal has no compassion for their rival or victim, and compassion is at the root of the word. In medieval times **ruth** was another word for compassion, which is now dated or poetic.

sabbath

The **sabbath** is the traditional day of rest – Saturday for Jews, Sunday for Christians. The Hebrew word *sabat*, 'to rest', is the ultimate source of our word **sabbath**.

The Law of Moses dictated that every seventh year should be observed as a 'sabbath', during which the land lay fallow. In the late 19th century US universities extended the idea of this **sabbatical year** to give professors and other academic staff every seventh year free to research or travel. Nowadays a **sabbatical** may come at other intervals of time, and members of other occupations also use the term for paid leave for professional development.

sabotage

French peasants and other workers traditionally wore *sabots*, simple shoes shaped and hollowed out from a single block of wood. When French workmen took action against the introduction of new technology by destroying machines and tools, people looked at them and called the action **sabotage**. The word first appeared in English the first decade of the 20th century, referring to a court case in Paris. By 1916 the *Sydney Morning Herald* could report a labourer on an Australian sheep farm threatening sabotage against politicians and employers.

sack

When it refers to a bag, **sack** is related to Dutch *zak* and German *Sack* and goes back to Semitic, the family of languages that includes Hebrew and Arabic. The **sack** meaning 'to plunder or pillage a town or city' came in the mid 16th century from French, where the phrase was *mettre à sac*, 'to put to the sack'. This may have originally referred to filling a sack with plunder, so the two words would ultimately be the same.

People in employment have been given **the sack** since the early 19th century, probably echoing a French phrase. In ancient Rome **the sack** was much more serious than losing a job – it was being sewn in a sack and drowned as a punishment for killing a parent or other near relative.

Sacks were made of a coarse rough fabric woven from flax and hemp, called **sackcloth**. The Gospel of St Matthew describes the wearing of sackcloth and the sprinkling of ashes on your head as signs of repentance and mourning, and people experiencing these emotions can still be **in sackcloth and ashes**.

sad

The original meaning of **sad** in Old English was 'having no more appetite, weary'. The word comes from the same root as Latin *satis* 'enough', the source of **sated**, **satisfactory** and **satisfy**, and the idea was similar to our expression **fed up** – of being unhappy through being too 'full' of something. The word then developed through 'firm, constant' and 'dignified, sober' to our modern sense of 'unhappy' in the medieval period. In the 1990s 'You're so sad!' became the refrain of every teenager in the land, often to their parents. This use, meaning 'pathetically inadequate or unfashionable', was not completely new, and had been around since the 1930s. See also MELANCHOLY.

sadism

During several periods of imprisonment in the later 18th and early 19th centuries, the Marquis de Sade wrote pornographic books. One sexual perversion in particular fascinated him, arousal from inflicting pain on others. The French named it *sadisme* after him, and English adopted the word as **sadism** in the 1880s. See also MASOCHISM.

safety

Like **safe**, this ultimately comes from Latin *salvus* 'uninjured, safe', also the source of **salvage**, SALVER, **salvation** and SAVE. The proverb **there is safety in numbers** has echoes in the biblical Proverbs: 'In the multitude of counsellors there is safety'. The first to use the modern phrasing was Jane Austen in her novel *Emma*, published in 1814: 'She determined to call upon them and seek safety in numbers.'

saga

The original medieval sagas told traditional stories of the families of Iceland and the kings of Norway. No one in Britain paid much attention to them until the 18th century, at the same time as the word **saga** entered the language. Its old Icelandic original is the equivalent of

English **saw** in **old saw**, an old proverb or maxim, and meant 'a narrative, a story'. From the mid 19th century **saga** came also to apply to stories of heroic achievement and then to novels tracing families through several generations.

The 1990s gave us the **Aga saga**, a novel by a writer such as Joanna Trollope set in a rural location and concerning the emotional lives of characters who set great store by their Aga, a kind of stove invented in Sweden – a link back to the Scandinavian **saga** itself.

salad

One of many words that go back to Latin *sal* SALT. The root implies that it was the dressing or seasoning that originally characterised a **salad**, and not the lettuce or other vegetables.

The expression **your salad days**, 'the time when you are young and inexperienced', is one of Shakespeare's inventions, occurring in *Antony and Cleopatra*. The idea behind the phrase becomes clearer when you read the full line spoken by Cleopatra: 'My salad days, When I was green in judgement'. Shakespeare used the word **salad** in a play on GREEN, which is still used today in the sense 'inexperienced or naive'.

saloon

Along with gunfights between goodies in white Stetsons and baddies in black ones, the **saloon** or bar is an important feature of westerns. Like many an outlaw in the American West, people may sometimes have to **drink at the last chance saloon**, 'take one final chance to get something right'. The name, sometimes expanded to First and Last Chance Saloon, was used in the US from about 1890 for the name of a saloon on the edge of town. Saloons (the word comes via French from Italian, from *sala* 'hall') were originally much more genteel than those on the wild frontier – the word at first applied to a large reception room or an elegant drawing room, as did **salon**, which has exactly the same source. Until many pubs were remodelled in the 1980s, most had a **saloon bar**, a separate area that was more luxuriously furnished and where drinks were more expensive than in the **public bar**.

During the 19th century a **saloon** was a luxurious railway carriage used as a lounge or restaurant or for a private party. As the age of the car followed that of the train, a closed car with a separate boot came to be a **saloon car** in Britain. The American name is **sedan**, which was an Italian dialect word from Latin *sella* 'seat', the root of **saddle**.

salt

The root of **salt** is Latin *sal*, from which words such as SALAD, **salami**, **saline** and SAUCE derive. A person who is **the salt of the earth** is kind, reliable and honest. The phrase comes from St Matthew's Gospel: 'Ye are the salt of the earth: but if the salt have lost his savour, wherewith shall it be salted?'

The expression **sit below the salt**, 'to be of lower social standing', goes back to the days when formal dinners were more common and when a person's rank determined where they sat at the table. Long dining tables running the length of the room were the norm, and those of the highest rank sat at the top end of the table, with the others arranged in descending order of status along the remaining length. The salt cellar was usually placed halfway down, and so anyone sitting below it knew they had a long way to climb before they made it to the A-list.

Salt cellar itself has nothing to do with dark underground storage places. The second element was originally **saler**, which meant 'salt cellar' on its own. It came through Old French from Latin *salarium*, which also gave us **salary** – a *salarium* was originally a Roman soldier's allowance of money to buy salt. As early as the 15th century people did not fully understand **saler** and added **salt** in front of it. Finally it became a complete mystery, and they substituted the familiar **cellar**.

Before the invention of the fridge food was salted, or treated with salt, to preserve it. This is the idea behind **salting away** money for future use, an expression that dates from the 1840s.

salary

Few things show the importance of salt to human life more than the word **salary**, which is literally 'salt money'. Before the Latin root *salarium* referred more generally to pay, it specifically meant a Roman soldier's allowance to buy rations of *sal*, salt.

salver

Early Spanish kings were afraid of being poisoned, so they employed servants to taste their food and drink before touching it themselves. The taster would put items that had been checked on a tray or **salver** for presenting to the monarch – anything on the tray was free from danger. Spanish *salva* 'the sampling of food' came from *salvar* 'to make safe' and goes back to Latin *salvus* 'uninjured, safe', the root also of SAFETY.

sandalwood

The name of this Indian tree and its fragrant timber and oil has no connection with sweaty feet and sandals. It is based on *candana*, a word in Sanskrit, the ancient language okf India, which passed into Latin as *sandalum*. Our word **sandal** came instead from Greek *sandalon* 'wooden shoe'.

sanguine

According to the medieval doctrine of the four humours (see HUMOUR), having a constitution in which blood predominated over the other three gave people a cheerfully optimistic or **sanguine** disposition, as well as a florid complexion. The root of **sanguine** is Latin *sanguis* 'blood'.

sarcasm

The words of a sarcastic person are 'biting', and it is the idea of biting into the flesh that is behind **sarcasm**. The word came into English in the mid 16th century from French, and is based on Greek *sarkazein* 'to tear flesh', which also came to mean 'to gnash the teeth, speak bitterly'.

sarcophagus

An ancient **sarcophagus** or stone coffin with inscriptions is often seen in museums, but the origin of the name seems more appropriate to horror movies. Its Greek original meant 'flesh-eating', and was formed from *sarx* 'flesh', the root also of SARCASM and **sarcoma**, and *-phagos* 'eating'. Sarcophagi were originally made of a type of stone that the ancient Greeks believed consumed the flesh of any dead body in contact with it.

sardonic

The Greek epic poet Homer, of the 8th century BC, used the word *sardanios* to describe bitter, scornful laughter. Later Greeks and Romans did not really understand the reason for this word and decided it must be *sardonios* 'Sardinian' and refer to a 'Sardinian plant' which produced facial convulsions resembling horrible laughter, usually followed by death. English adopted **sardonic** in the mid 17th century to refer to grimly mocking or cynical smiles, grins and looks as well as to laughter. The island of Sardinia also gave us the name of the **sardine**, the small fish which was once common off its shores – the Latin source of the word, *sarda*, is probably from the Greek name for the island, *Sardÿ*.

sash

A **sash** is now worn over one shoulder or around the waist, but it was originally wrapped round the head.

Between the late 16th and early 18th centuries a sash was a length of fine fabric twisted round the head as a turban, as in some Middle Eastern countries – the word is Arabic.

The **sash** in **sash window** is an alteration of **chassis**, which means 'frame' in French. Originally both French and English people pronounced the final *-s* of **chassis**. English-speakers then took this as a plural form and shortened it to form a new singular. **Chassis** was readopted from French in the early 20th century to mean 'the base frame of a vehicle'.

Satan

This has been used as a name for the Devil since Anglo-Saxon times, and goes back to Hebrew *sātān*, which literally meant 'adversary'. William Blake's great poem 'Jerusalem', which is part of *Milton* (1804-8) and later became a popular hymn, is the source of the phrase **dark satanic mills**. 'Jerusalem' also gave us 'England's green and pleasant land'.

satellite

In 1611 the German astronomer Johannes Kepler, writing in Latin, gave the name *satellites* to the moons of Jupiter, which Galileo had recently discovered. An English publication referred to 'a Satellite of Jupiter' in 1665. In Latin *satelles*, of which *satellites* is the plural, meant 'an attendant or guard', a use occasionally found

The first official picture of Sputnik I, the world's first artificial satellite.

in English from the mid 16th century, usually with overtones of subservience or fawning attentiveness. Until the 1930s the only satellites in space were natural bodies like planets and moons, but in 1936 the word was first applied to a man-made object (at that point just a theoretical one) put into orbit around the Earth. The first artificial satellite to be launched was the Russian Sputnik 1, in 1957, and in 1962 the Telstar satellite relayed the first satellite television signal.

saturnine

In medieval astrology the planet Saturn represented lead, and those born under its influence could expect to be gloomy, sluggish and cold. Belief in planetary influence may no longer be scientific, but the description **saturnine** lives on. The planet takes its name from the Roman god Saturn, the equivalent of Greek Cronus or Kronos, who had been the supreme god until Zeus dethroned him. **Saturday** is 'the day of Saturn'. See also JOVIAL.

sauce

Another word that goes back to Latin *sal* SALT, along with **sausage** and **salsa**, which is simply the Spanish word for 'sauce'. The popularity of Mexican and Tex-Mex cookery has given us the spicy tomato sauce **salsa**, whereas the Latin American dance the **salsa** is so named because it is 'saucy'.

The expression **what's sauce for the goose is sauce for the gander** implies that both sexes should be able to behave in the same way. John Ray, who recorded the saying in his *English Proverbs* of 1670, remarked that 'This is a woman's Proverb'.

Cups now sit on saucers, but in the Middle Ages a **saucer** was used for holding condiments or sauces, and was usually made of metal. The description **saucy** originally simply meant 'savoury, flavoured with a sauce'. In the early 16th century it began to refer to people and behaviour, meaning at first 'impudent, presumptuous', mellowing into 'cheeky', then taking on suggestive overtones.

savage

According to the origin of the name, savages live in woods. **Savage** derives from Latin *silva* 'a wood', the source also of the literary word **sylvan** and perhaps of **sylph**, an imaginary spirit of the air. The overtones of **savage** are usually negative, suggesting violence and cruelty, but in the later 18th century the French writer and philosopher Jean-Jacques Rousseau conceived the idea of the **noble savage**, an idealised being without the corrupting influence of civilisation and showing the natural goodness of humankind.

save

A medieval word that is based on Latin *salvus* 'uninjured, safe' (see SAFETY), the source also of **salvage**, SALVER and **salvation**. The idea of **saving someone's skin** goes back to the late 16th century, a century before **save someone's neck** is recorded. See also BACON.

A boxer in imminent danger of being knocked or counted out may be **saved by the bell** for the end of the round and go back to his corner for a rest, a drink and the patching up of cuts and bruises. People outside the world of boxing can now also be **saved by the bell** by an unexpected intervention that gets them out of a difficulty. Goalkeepers in soccer have saved shots since the 1880s, but before that the word was used in cricket when a fielder prevented a run being scored.

scale

English has three main words **scale**, two of which share an ancestry. The **scale** of fishes and reptiles has the same root as the **scale** used for weighing, and both are related to **shell**. The first **scale** is the one in **the scales fall from someone's eyes**, 'someone is no longer deceived'. In the biblical Acts of the Apostles the expression describes how St Paul, blinded by his vision on the road to Damascus, was given his sight back by God. The **scale** in music and measuring derives from Latin *scala* 'ladder', from the root of *scandere* 'to climb', an element in **ascend** and **descend**.

scamp

Nowadays most scamps are children, regarded indulgently by parents and other adults for being mischievous in a likeable or amusing way. But in the 18th century a scamp was a much more serious proposition – a highwayman, who might well have ordered you to 'stand and deliver'. In the 19th century the original sense moderated into 'a swindler, cheat', a derogatory use still in existence in Caribbean English. The word probably derives from early Dutch *schampen* 'to slip away'. See also IMP.

scandal

The words **scandal** and **slander** are closely related. Both go back to Latin *scandalum* 'cause of offence', from Greek *skandalon* 'snare, stumbling block'. Originally **scandal** was a term restricted to the Christian Church. It referred to behaviour by a religious person that might bring discredit on their beliefs, and then, going back to the idea of a 'stumbling block', something that hinders faith. Our modern sense of an event causing general public outrage dates from the late 16th century.

scapegoat

In the biblical Book of Leviticus God tells Moses that the Jewish people should take two goats and cast lots to determine their fate – the chief priest is to lay the sins of the people on one before driving it out into the wilderness, while the other is to be sacrificed. The animal driven away is the **scapegoat**. This was the only context in which the word appeared until the early 19th century, when it extended its meaning to 'a person who is blamed for the wrongdoings of others'. The first part, **scape**, is a shortening of **escape**.

scavenger

The earliest form of **scavenger** was **scavager**, an official who collected **scavage**, a toll on foreign merchants' goods, from the 15th century. Scavagers eventually also acquired the duty of keeping the streets of their town clean. In the mid 16th century people began to insert an *n* in the word and **scavenger** was born, in the same way as **messenger** and **passenger**, both also words that started out life without an -*n*-. In time the municipal officials lost their more important duties and a **scavenger** became just a street cleaner and then a person who collects anything usable from discarded waste.

scene

The scenes in **behind the scenes**, 'in private', are the pieces of scenery on a theatre stage. This reflects the origin of **scene**, which is ultimately from Greek *skēnē* 'tent, stage', source also of **scenario**, **scenery** and **scenic**. The area behind the 'scenes' or pieces of scenery is where the actors wait to go on stage and where the means of moving various props are located, all of which should remain hidden from the audience. The theatrical associations of **scene** gave us the meaning 'a public display of emotion or anger', which is from the middle of the 18th century.

scent

Before it was perfume, **scent** was a hunting term for a hound's sense of smell. From there it became an odour picked up by a hound, and then in the 15th century a pleasant smell. The word came into medieval English through Old French from Latin *sentire* 'to feel or perceive', from which **sensation**, **sense**, **sensible**, **sensitive**, **sensory** and numerous other words without a *c* derive. People started spelling **scent** with a *c* in the 17th century, but no one knows exactly why.

sceptre

The **sceptre** carried by modern rulers on ceremonial occasions as a symbol of sovereignty is generally a short ornamented stick, but the word's origin shows that it was originally longer. Sceptre came into medieval English from Old French *ceptron,* but goes back to Greek *skēptron*, from *skēptein* 'to lean on'. Ancient Greek vase paintings show kings holding tall sceptres long enough to lean on.

sceptred isle

Britain is the poetic **sceptred isle**. The name comes from John of Gaunt's description of the island in Shakespeare's *Richard II*: 'This royal throne of kings, this sceptred isle ... This precious stone set in the silver sea.'

school

The **school** that children go to derives from Greek *skholē* 'leisure, philosophy, place for lectures', the source also of **scholar**. Many ancient Greeks clearly spent their leisure time in intellectual pursuits rather than physical recreation. English children have attended schools for more than a thousand years, as the word is first recorded in Old English around AD 1000, although education for all between the ages of 5 and 13 in England and Wales was not compulsory until the passing of the Education Act of 1870.

This is not the same **school** that large groups of fish or sea mammals congregate in. Here the word comes from early German and Dutch *schōle*, 'a troop, multitude', and is essentially the same as **shoal**.

science

Originally **science** was knowledge in general, or any branch of knowledge, including the arts, and the word is from Latin *scire* 'to know'. The restricted modern sense of **science**, concentrating on the physical and natural world, dates from the 18th century.

Science fiction was first mentioned in 1851, but this was an isolated use, and the term did not become common until the end of the 1920s, when US 'pulp' magazines (so called because of the cheap paper they were printed on) like *Astounding Stories* carried tales of space adventure. Before **science fiction** was coined the stories of writers such as Jules Verne were called **scientific fiction** or **scientifiction**.

For auld lang syne

Scotland has given English many words – some from the Gaelic language, some from Scots and others reflecting links to further shores. The 18th-century Scots poet Robert Burns has also weighed in with memorable expressions.

After a history marked by conflict the Scottish and English nations were joined by the Act of Union in 1707, but tensions still sometimes surface. When a Scot calls an Englishman a Sassenach he is reaching back into history, as the word is a Gaelic version of Latin *Saxones* 'Saxons'.

Anyone who has ever been to a New Year's Eve party will have linked arms to the song 'Auld Lang Syne', but probably not known what the expression means. Auld lang syne is literally 'times long past', and for auld lang syne is 'for old times' sake'. The phrase was popularised as the title and refrain of a 1788 song by Robert Burns. Syne is an old Scottish and northern English spelling of since.

Wee, 'small', was originally a noun meaning 'a little or young thing, a child' and 'a small quantity'. It is from Old English *wēg* or *wēge*, which was connected with WEIGH. The word is particularly associated with the opening of Burns's poem 'To a Mouse' (1786): 'Wee, sleekit, cowrin', tim'rous beastie /

O what a panic's in thy breastie!' Sleekit or sleeked means 'having smooth, glossy skin or fur'.

Scotland is known as the Land of Cakes, but the phrase refers to oatcakes rather than to sweet treats. It is also famous for a dish addressed by Burns as 'Great chieftain o'the puddin'-race'. This was not a dessert, though, but the haggis. Scots have been eating a dish called haggis, consisting of chopped offal with suet and oatmeal boiled in a casing (traditionally a sheep's stomach), since the late Middle Ages. The word probably comes from hag 'to hack, cut', a Scottish and northern English equivalent of hew.

Robert Burns is also responsible for the name of the tam-o-shanter, a woollen cap of a kind originally worn by ploughmen and other workers in Scotland. It is named after the hero of the poem 'Tam o'Shanter' (1790), a farmer who, returning home late after a long evening in the pub, came upon witches dancing in a churchyard and was

scone

There would now be nothing unusual about going into an English tea shop and ordering tea and scones, and a cream tea demands them, but until the 19th century the **scone** was known only in Scotland. The novels of Sir Walter Scott probably helped bring the word to wider notice, and Robert Louis Stevenson wrote in 1886 in *Kidnapped*: 'We lay on the bare top of a rock, like scones upon a girdle.' The first scones were large round cakes made of wheat or barley and often cut into four quarters. The word is probably from early Dutch *scoon broot*, 'fine bread'.

Scone can be pronounced to rhyme with either *gone* or *tone*. In the US the pronunciation rhyming with *tone* is more common, whereas in British English the two pronunciations traditionally have different regional and class associations. The first tends to be associated with the north of England, while the second is associated with the south and is thought of as more 'refined'.

scotch

To **scotch** or decisively put an end to something derives from an old use of the word for a wedge placed under a wheel to prevent it moving or slipping. Another use of **scotch**, 'to make something

temporarily harmless', goes back to a line from Shakespeare's *Macbeth*: 'We have scotched the snake, not killed it.' This is not what originally appeared in Shakespeare's text, where the word first used was 'scorched', meaning 'slashed with a knife'. This was an alteration of **score** but was short-lived, and later editors wondered what on earth burning the skin of a snake had to do with it, assuming that 'scorched' must be a printer's error. The origin of **scotch** itself is unknown, though it may be related to **skate**.

scot-free

The people of Scotland are fond of freedom, but they play no part in this expression, which means 'without suffering any punishment or injury'. The **scot** here is a payment corresponding to a modern tax or property rate, so **scot-free** was 'tax-free'. The word came from old Scandinavian in the Anglo-Saxon period, and is the equivalent of Old English **shot**.

The first **Scots** were an ancient Gaelic-speaking people that migrated from Ireland to the northwest of Britain around the end of the 5th century. The name appears in Latin around AD 400, and then in Old English, originally referring to Irishmen, then to the Scots in northern Britain.

chased by them over a bridge, escaping only because his horse's tail came off as the leading witch grasped it. Contemporary illustrations of the poem often showed Tam in this kind of cap.

Many Scots words refer to distinctive clothing. Nothing could be more Scottish than tartan, a woollen cloth woven in a pattern of coloured checks and intersecting lines, but the word is probably from Old French *tertaine*, a kind of cloth that may have got its name because it was imported from the distant East through Tartary, a region that included what are now Siberia, Turkestan and Mongolia.

The origins of the kilt are less distant. In medieval English kilt was a verb meaning 'to tuck up the skirt around the body' that came from Scandinavia. As an item of male Highland dress it is not recorded until around 1750.

You are most likely to see a plaid as part of the ceremonial dress of the pipe band of a Scottish regiment

– it is a piece of tartan worn over the shoulder. Although people now associate it with the Scottish Highlands, the plaid was formerly also worn as a shawl or cloak in other parts of Scotland and in the north of England. In the Highlands it was often a person's principal – if not only – garment. The word may come from Scottish Gaelic *plaide* 'blanket', though it is possible that plaid is an early form of plied: to ply originally meant 'to fold'.

A brogue was originally a crude kind of shoe worn by the inhabitants of the wilder parts of Ireland and the Scottish Highlands. The word comes from Gaelic, though in origin it is Scandinavian and related to breeches. In the early 20th century the brogue emerged as a stout shoe for outdoor pursuits. The use of brogue to mean an Irish or Scottish accent may come from the way that those who wore brogues spoke.

See also MULL, PILLION, SLOGAN, TROUSERS, WHISKY.

'Wee, sleekit, cowrin', tim'rous beastie'

There is no original person called Scott in the exclamation **Great Scott!**, which is recorded from the 1880s. It was simply a way to avoid saying 'God'. Other similar expressions of the time were **Great Caesar!** and **Great Sun!** See also feature on EUPHEMISMS.

Scouse
The success of the Beatles and other Liverpool groups and singers in the 1960s focused attention on their native city, and the words **Scouse** and **Scouser** became widely familiar in Britain. They represent shortenings of **lobscouse**, a stew made with meat, vegetables and ship's biscuit formerly eaten by sailors and so a staple food in the thriving port of Liverpool. **Lobscouse** is recorded from the early 18th century, but its origin is unknown. Before the 1960s **Scouse** meaning 'Liverpudlian' appeared in print only in a 1945 report of a trial, where a witness used the word and a puzzled judge asked for an explanation.

scout
Scouts go ahead of a main force to gather information about an enemy's position and strength. The root of the word **scout** implies that the first scouts used their ears

to pick up clues rather than making visual observations, as it is Latin *auscultare* 'to listen to'. The English soldier Lord Baden-Powell admired the skills and resilience of these military scouts, and had also seen the successful use of boys as scouts by the Boers in southern Africa. In the summer of 1907 he organised a camp for boys on Brownsea Island in Dorset, and the following year founded **the Scout Association** to develop boys' characters by training them in self-sufficiency and survival techniques. The organisation now exists worldwide, and has admitted girls since 1990. **Scout's honour** is the oath members take, and even people outside the movement use **Scout's honour** to indicate that they will stand by a promise or tell the truth.

scrabble
In the game **Scrabble** players build up words from small lettered squares or tiles. The name was registered as a trademark in January 1950, but the word **scrabble** dates from the mid 16th century, and came from early Dutch *schrabben* 'to scrape'. The original meaning was 'to scrawl or scribble', followed by 'to scratch or grope about' in the late 16th century.

scratch

Two English dialect words with the same meaning, **scrat** and **cratch**, probably combined in the medieval period to form **scratch**. The origins of **from scratch**, 'from the very beginning, without making use of any previous work', lie in the sporting world. In the past certain sports such as cycling and running sometimes used a particular handicap system. A line or mark, known as the scratch, was drawn to indicate the starting position for all competitors except those who had been awarded an advantage: they were allowed to start a little way in front. So a competitor starting from scratch would start from a position without any advantage. The expression **up to scratch**, meaning 'up to the required standard', also comes from this practice, as originally it referred to someone who was good enough to start from the scratch line.

Napoleon had bad experiences in Russia. In 1812 the severity of the Russian winter and the resistance of her people forced his retreat from Moscow, a defeat celebrated in Tchaikovsky's *1812 Overture*. Of the Russians Napoleon is reported to have said 'scratch the Russian and you will find the Tartar'. Whether or not this is true, from 1823 the saying is referred to in English, and people began to use the formula **scratch X and find Y** of other nationalities and persons. George Bernard Shaw wrote in *St Joan* in 1924: 'Scratch an Englishman, and find a Protestant.' See also NATION.

screw

Pigs have curly tails like corkscrews, and the ultimate source of **screw** is Latin *scrofa* 'a sow', source also of **scrofula**, a disease that people thought breeding sows were particularly susceptible to. Scrofula was also called the **King's Evil**, because kings were traditionally thought to be able to cure it. The word changed its meaning to 'screw' in Latin, and then altered its form as it passed through French and arrived in English in the late medieval period.

The obscene slang sense 'to have sex', dating from the early 18th century, is probably the source of **screw up** meaning 'to mess up', which started off in the Second World War. It was a US euphemism for **f— up**.

Scrooge

The transformation of the bad-tempered, miserly Ebenezer Scrooge into a kind and philanthropic old gentleman is the theme of Charles Dickens's *A Christmas Carol*, published in 1843. On Christmas Eve the ghost of Marley, his former business partner, shows him visions of the past, present and future, including one of what his own death will be like if he does not mend his ways. On Christmas Day Scrooge sends a turkey to his abused clerk Bob Cratchit, subscribes willingly to charities and is generally genial to all. The book became an instant Christmas classic, and since the mid 20th century any miserly killjoy has been a **Scrooge**.

scruff

The **scruff of the neck** was originally the **scuff** – the word is recorded from the late 18th century, but its origin is obscure. As an insult for a person with a dirty or untidy appearance, **scruff** is an alteration of **scurf**, meaning dandruff or a similar skin condition. The reversal of letters from **scurf** to **scruff** is also seen in BIRD and DIRT, originally *brid* and *drit*.

sea

An Old English word, related to Dutch *zee* and German *See*. A person who is **at sea** or **all at sea** is confused or unable to decide what to do – they are being likened to a ship out of the sight of land which has lost its bearings. The term **sea change** for a profound or notable transformation comes from the song 'Full fathom five' in Shakespeare's *The Tempest*:

> Nothing of him that doth fade,
> But doth suffer a sea change
> Into something rich and strange.

seal

Rather than signing their name, people formerly stamped a personal seal in wax on a completed letter or other document. The expressions **put the seal on**, 'to put the finishing touch to something', and **set your seal to**, 'to mark something with your own distinctive character', both derive from this. To **seal something off** reflects the use of seals to check that something has not been opened or disturbed. In these and related uses, **seal** goes back to Latin *sigillum* 'small picture',

The tail of a sow – the origin of screw.

from *signum* 'a sign', the source of **design**, **sign**, **signal** and numerous other English words. The name of the animal **seal** derives from Old English *seolh*.

seat

An old Scandinavian word from the same root as **sit**, which goes back even further to the same source as Latin *sedere* 'to sit'. The Latin word is also the origin of **sedentary**, **sedate**, **sediment** and **sedition**. The sense 'a place where a government is based', as in **seat of government** or **power**, comes from the throne or 'seat' of a king or governor.

American pilots in the 1940s were the first to use **by the seat of the pants**, meaning that they flew the plane using their instinct and experience rather than relying on the aircraft's instrument panel. An experienced pilot could tell by a change in the vibrations of the seat if, for example, the plane was about to stall, and so take early action to rescue the situation.

see

The **see** meaning 'to perceive with the eyes' perhaps comes from the same ancient root as Latin *sequi* 'to follow', seen in **consequence**, SEQUEL and **sequence**. Referring to the district of a bishop or archbishop, **see** goes back to Latin *sedere* 'to sit' (see SEAT).

In the 1927 film *The Jazz Singer* Al Jolson uttered the aside 'You ain't heard nothing yet'. This became the model for similar phrases, notably **you ain't seen nothing yet**. 'The Best is Yet to Come' by Cy Coleman and Carolyn Leigh, recorded by Frank Sinatra in 1964, includes the lines 'And wait till you see that sunshine day / You ain't seen nothin' yet'. More recently, after the mid-term US elections in 2006, the Democratic Party adopted as one of its theme songs 'You Ain't Seen Nothing Yet' by Bachman-Turner Overdrive, originally a hit for the band in 1974.

The computer slogan **what you see is what you get** – abbreviated as **WYSIWYG** – began life in the USA; the first recorded example is from the *New York Times* in 1971. It refers to the representation of text on screen in a form exactly corresponding to its appearance on a printout.

'Why don't you come up and see me sometime?' will be forever associated with the vampish actress Mae West. What she actually said, though, in the film *She Done Him Wrong* (1933) was 'Why don't you come up sometime, and see me?' Steve Harley and Cockney Rebel took the idea one step further with their song 'Make Me Smile (Come Up and See Me)' in 1975. Mae West is remembered for a number of saucy quips, among them 'Is that a gun in your pocket, or are you just glad to see me?' and 'It's not the men in my life that counts – it's the life in my men', while her buxom figure led to the inflatable life jacket issued to RAF personnel during the Second World War being called a **Mae West**. See also EVIL.

sell

An Old English word that originally meant 'to give, hand over in response to a request'. The longer version of the expression **sell your soul**, 'to do absolutely anything to achieve your objective', is **sell your soul to the devil**, and refers to tales of deals supposedly struck with the devil. Over the centuries various people reputedly agreed to give their soul to the devil if in return he would grant them all their heart's desires in this life. The most famous person alleged to have made such a pact was the 16th-century German astronomer and necromancer Faust, whose story inspired Christopher Marlowe's play *Doctor Faustus*.

senior see SIR.

sequel

The earliest use of **sequel** was 'a band of followers'. Latin *sequi* 'to follow' is the source, seen also in **consequence** and **sequence** and perhaps the root of SEE. **Sequel** developed the senses 'what happens afterwards' and 'the remaining part of a story' in the early 16th century. In the 1970s the **sequel** that takes up the narrative of an earlier book or film inspired the **prequel**, which portrays events which precede those of an existing completed work (see STAR).

serenade

A **serenade** conjures up an image of a young man singing or playing to his beloved under her window or balcony at night. The word's origins imply none of these things, requiring only that the performance be 'serene'. It goes back through French and Italian to Latin *serenus* 'calm, clear, fair'. The idea of serenading by night may derive from association with *sera*, the Italian word for 'night'.

serendipity

The delightful word **serendipity**, meaning 'the occurrence of events by chance in a beneficial way', was invented by the writer and politician Horace Walpole before or at the beginning of 1754, from **Serendip**, an old name for Sri Lanka. Walpole was a prolific letter writer, and he explained to one of his main correspondents that he had based the word on the title of a fairy tale, *The Three Princes of Serendip*, the heroes of which 'were always making discoveries, by accidents and sagacity, of things they were not in quest of'.

sesame

One of the stories told in the *Arabian Nights* is that of Ali Baba and the Forty Thieves. Ali Baba gains access to the robbers' cave by saying the magic words 'open sesame!', at which the door flies open. This and the other Arabic tales in the collection were published in French in the early 18th century and were quickly translated into English. This gave a new lease of life to, and fixed the form of, **sesame** as the name of a plant with oil-rich seeds, which had appeared occasionally since the later Middle Ages in a variety of spellings. The word itself is recorded in Greek as *sēsamon* or *sēsamē*, but is probably connected to Arabic *simsim*. Since the early 19th century **an open sesame** has meant an easy way of securing access to what would normally be inaccessible.

seven

Seven days of the week, seven deadly sins, seven dwarfs, seven wonders of the world, the Magnificent Seven . . . the number **seven** crops up again and again in history and culture. The word comes from the same ancient root as Latin *septem* and Greek *hepta* 'seven' – *septem* is the source of **September**, originally the seventh month of the Roman year, and of **septet**, whereas *hepta* is found in other seven-related words such as **heptagon** and **heptathlon**. The **seven-year itch** was originally a semi-proverbial medical condition, dating from the middle of the 19th century, but these days is a supposed tendency to infidelity after seven years of marriage. The phrase originated in the USA, but *The Seven Year Itch*, a 1955 comedy directed by Billy Wilder and starring Marilyn Monroe, introduced it to a wider audience.

sex

A tiny word, but what an important one. **Sex** is not Old English, but entered the language in medieval times from Latin *sexus*, and first referred to the two genders. Women have been **the fair** or **the fairer sex** since the middle of the 17th century, when men were sometimes called **the better** or **the sterner sex**. In reference to hanky-panky **sex** has only been used since the early part of the 20th century, with that lusty writer D.H. Lawrence being among the first to talk of 'having sex'. The American film director and writer Woody Allen is known for his witty lines about sex, such as 'That was the most fun I ever had without laughing', from the 1977 film *Annie Hall*.

To **sex up** has been around as an expression since the 1940s, meaning 'to make more sexy'. A new use hit the headlines in 2003 when a BBC journalist claimed that the British Labour government had knowingly 'sexed up' a report on whether Iraq possessed weapons of mass destruction. Dr David Kelly, a civil servant named as the source of the quotes, committed suicide, and a judicial inquiry criticised the BBC while clearing the government of wrongdoing.

People or things have been **sexy** in the literal sense since the 1920s. The sense 'very exciting or appealing' appeared in the 1950s, and has led to some odd phrases, like this from the *New York Magazine* in 2003: 'Sexy flat-panel screen, woofer, and remote control included'.

shade

The Old English word **shade** is related to **shadow**. The origins of **shades of —**, used to suggest that one thing is reminiscent of another, have nothing to do with colour, but go back to an old use of **shade** to mean 'a ghost'. The idea behind the phrase is that the person or event either resembles or calls to mind someone or something from the past. By the late 19th century the meaning 'ghost' was more or less restricted to works of literature, so it is odd that it should have been revived in this phrase in the mid 20th century. An example from the American magazine *Town & Country* reflects its popularity: 'Shades of Jackie O, the Duke and Duchess, Capote, and an era when classic French cuisine, spacious luxury, and swizzle sticks were de rigueur.'

No great shakes, meaning 'not very good', dates from the early 19th century. It probably comes from the shaking of dice, where an unlucky throw would be 'no great shakes'.

shake

Early examples of **shake**, an Old English word, include not only the senses 'to tremble' and 'to make something vibrate' but also the poetical sense 'to depart or flee'. The **Shakers** are members of a US religious sect, properly called the United Society of Believers in Christ's Second Coming, which split off from the Quakers (properly called the Religious Society of Friends) in the mid 18th century. Participants in the group's services engaged in wild ecstatic movements, and people called them the **Shaking Quakers**. They were persecuted for their radicalism, and in 1774 left for America, where they now live frugally in celibate communities and make furniture noted for its simplicity and elegance.

People sometimes think of the spy James Bond as being **shaken not stirred**, but the phrase refers to his

As the Bard once said

At the turn of the 17th century Londoners flocked to the Globe Theatre to see 'the latest Shakespeare'. Ever since, William Shakespeare has had a huge influence on English, his legacy a remarkable number of phrases in everyday use.

We may often be unaware that we have Shakespeare to thank for familiar expressions. Someone made of sterner stuff is better able to overcome problems than others. In *Julius Caesar* Mark Antony commented that Caesar had wept when the poor cried, adding 'Ambition should be made of sterner stuff.'

hoist with your own petard

Shakespeare was writing more than 400 years ago, using many terms unfamiliar to us today. Despite this we still talk about being hoist with your own petard – a phrase from *Hamlet* that means your plans to cause trouble for others end up backfiring. A 'petard' was a small bomb in the form of a metal or wooden box filled with gunpowder, and 'hoist' here means 'lifted and removed'. Someone 'hoist with their own petard' was blown into the air by their own bomb.

Hamlet is probably Shakespeare's most-quoted play, and contains the famous 'To be or not to be' speech. In this soliloquy Hamlet muses on the nature of life, and whether it is ever justifiable to commit suicide. He talks of 'the slings and arrows of outrageous fortune' (see SLING), and observes there's the rub (see RUB). The passage has also given us shuffle off this mortal coil, meaning 'to die'. Coil in this sense is a different word from the modern one, of unknown origin, which meant 'fuss, confusion or turmoil'.

Someone who has treated another person harshly may justify themselves by saying that it was for the person's own good – they were being cruel to be kind. Hamlet was the first person to use this line of reasoning, explaining why he had criticised his mother so bitterly for making her second marriage only a month after his father's death.

Shakespeare seems to have been pleased with his invention to your heart's content, as it features in two of his plays, *Henry VI, Part 2* and *The Merchant of Venice*, with the meaning 'complete inward satisfaction'. Nowadays we use it to mean 'as much as you want to'.

To gild the lily is to try to improve something that is already beautiful or excellent and does not really need improving. The phrase is a slightly mangled version of a quotation from *King John*: 'To gild refined gold, to paint the lily … Is wasteful and ridiculous excess.'

Sometimes we probably *are* aware that we are quoting Shakespeare – asking the question 'When shall we three meet again' is likely to bring up the memory of the witches in *Macbeth*, and people reluctant to say goodbye might think of Romeo and Juliet, those star-crossed lovers, when lamenting 'Parting is such sweet sorrow.' Many can quote the first line of Sonnet 18, but fewer know more than that:

> Shall I compare thee to a summer's day?
> Thou art more lovely and more temperate:
> Rough winds do shake the darling buds of May,
> And summer's lease hath all too short a date.

This gave H.E. Bates the title of his novel *The Darling Buds of May* (1958), dramatised on British TV in 1990-2.

Whether we are commenting on a brave new world of technological advances, or explaining away quirks in our filing system by saying there is method in our madness, Shakespeare often has just the right words. Ben Jonson, his contemporary, addressed him as 'Sweet Swan of Avon', and the admiration for the Bard of Avon continues to this day. 'Fantastic! And it was all written with a feather!', as the US film producer Sam Goldwyn is supposed to have said.

See also CAKE, DARK, FELL, GREEN, HEART, MANNER, MILK, NAME, POISON, POUND, RUB, SALAD, SEA, SLING, THUMB, WELL, WINTER, WITCH.

drink, not to his temperament. In *Dr No* (1958) by Ian Fleming, Bond gave instructions on how he wanted his favourite tipple: 'A medium Vodka dry Martini – with a slice of lemon peel. Shaken and not stirred.' Although Bond is usually described as being **licensed to kill**, the phrase does not occur in any of the original novels by Ian Fleming. 'The licence to kill for the Secret Service, the double-0 prefix, was a great honour', again from *Dr No*, was the closest approximation. In the 1962 film version it became 'If you carry a 00 number it means you're licensed to kill, not get killed.'

shambles

'He was felled like an ox in the butcher's shambles', writes Charles Dickens in *Barnaby Rudge* (1841). The writer is referring not to a state of chaos but to a slaughterhouse. Over the period of a thousand years **shambles**, from Latin *scamnum* 'a bench', has moved from being 'a stool' and 'a counter for displaying goods for sale' to 'a state of total disorder'. The link lies in covered butchers' stalls in market places, a use which in Britain survives in street names, notably the Shambles in York, a narrow winding medieval street. In the mid 16th century a **shambles** became also 'a place for slaughtering animals for meat', and later in the same century 'a place of carnage'. The less bloody modern sense did not appear until the 20th century, in the USA. As a description of ungainly movement, to **shamble** may derive from **shamble legs**, a description of misshapen legs that probably refers to the splayed legs of the trestles of a butcher's stall.

shanty

The **sea shanty**, the song with alternating solo and chorus to which sailors can haul ropes, probably comes from French *chantez!*, an order to 'sing!' It is recorded from the mid 19th century. A slightly earlier **shanty** appeared in North America for a small, crudely built shack and may come from Canadian French *chantier* 'lumberjack's cabin, logging camp'. This **shanty** gave the world the **shanty town**, such as the **favela** in Rio de Janeiro and other Brazilian cities.

shape

An Old English word related to **scoop** that originally meant 'to create'. The origins of to **lick into shape**, 'to bring into a better state', go back to early medieval times when books called bestiaries were popular. A bestiary was an early sort of reference book giving information and observations on different kinds of animal. Some of these bestiaries described how bear cubs were supposedly born as formless lumps and were licked into shape by their mother. This belief seems to have persisted for some time, as the current use does not appear until the early 17th century. Since then other versions including to **knock** and **whip someone into shape** have come into use, possibly reflecting the former popularity of corporal punishment as a parenting tool.

on Shanks's pony

This strange expression for going somewhere on foot is based on a pun with the surname Shanks and **shanks** meaning 'legs', which came from an Old English word for 'shin bone'. It was first used by the Scottish poet Robert Fergusson in 1785 as **shanks-nag**. In North America another common alternative is **on Shanks's mare**.

sheep

We have had **sheep** in the language since Anglo-Saxon times, but perhaps surprisingly people did not start using the word to mean 'someone too easily influenced or led' until the 16th century. The expression to **separate the sheep from the goats**, 'to divide people or things into superior and inferior groups', is a biblical reference to the account of the Last Judgement in the Gospel of Matthew. There the apostle describes how all the nations of the world will be gathered before God and how 'He shall separate them one from another, as a shepherd divideth his sheep from the goats: And he shall set the sheep on his right hand, but the goats on his left.'

sheet

English dictionaries usually recognise two words spelled **sheet**. The first, referring to items including bed coverings, paper and glass, shares an ancient root with **shoot**, one sense of which was 'to project'. The second is nautical, and was distinct from the first in Old English, though they are ultimately related. Sheets are the ropes attached to the corners of a ship's sail, used for controlling the extent and direction of the sail. If they are hanging loose in the wind, the vessel is likely to be out of control or taking an erratic course. This is the situation referred to in **three sheets to the wind**, meaning 'very drunk'.

sherbet

The words **sherbet** and **sorbet** are essentially the same, and are closely related to **syrup** and **shrub**, a drink made with sweetened fruit juice and rum or brandy. All go back to a group of words centring on Arabic *sariba* 'to drink'. The sharp-tasting powdered sweet **sherbet** was originally used to make a fizzy drink, from the 1850s.

shibboleth

The people of Gilead, east of the river Jordan, and members of the Hebrew tribe of Ephraim did not speak the same dialect, and neither were they the best of friends. The Book of Judges recounts a battle between them, in which Jephthah told his men, the Gileadites, to identify defeated Ephraimites by asking them to say 'shibboleth', a Hebrew word meaning 'ear of corn' or 'stream in flood'. Ephraimites had difficulty in pronouncing *sh*, and if a soldier said 'sibboleth' then he was killed as an enemy. Since the mid 17th century English speakers have used **shibboleth** for 'a word used to detect foreigners or strangers', and in the early 19th century extended this to 'a custom, principle or belief that distinguishes a particular class or group'. It now especially refers to a long-standing belief regarded as outmoded or no longer important.

shilling

Before decimalisation of the British currency in 1971 a **shilling** was a coin and monetary unit equal to one-twentieth of a pound or 12 old pence. **Shilling** is an Old English word of ancient German origin, and the coin was used before the Norman Conquest. It was the Normans who made it equal to 12 pence – before them its value varied, being 5 pence in Wessex and 4 pence in Mercia.

It was once the practice for a recruiting officer to pay a shilling to a man enlisting as a soldier, so to **take the King's shilling** was to join the army. Someone who is **not the full shilling** is not very intelligent – in Australia the equivalent is **not the full quid**.

shilly-shally

People unable to make up their minds whether to do something are likely to ask themselves 'Shall I?' repeatedly. With the rhyming impulse also seen in **dilly-dally** and WILLY-NILLY, people in the 18th century mocked this tendency by expanding it to 'shill I, shall I?', and so **shilly-shally** was born. The earliest use was in to **stand** or **go shilly-shally**, which had the same meaning as simple **shilly-shally**, 'to fail to act resolutely or decisively'.

shingle

With the meaning 'a rectangular wooden tile used on walls or roofs', **shingle** probably goes back to Latin *scandula* 'split piece of wood'. In the early 19th century the word developed the meaning 'a piece of board', and in the USA in particular 'a small signboard'. To **hang out your shingle**, an American expression for 'to begin to practise a profession', refers to a doctor or lawyer hanging up a sign outside their office advertising their professional services. The **shingle** on a seashore is a different word, whose origin is unknown, and the painful medical condition **shingles** is different again. Its origin is medieval Latin *cingulus* 'belt, girdle', a reference to the rash of blisters that appear in a band around the body.

ship

An Old English word related to Dutch *schip* and German *Schiff*. The expression **when someone's ship comes in**, 'when someone's fortune is made', is recorded from the mid 19th century. The safe arrival of a ship carrying a valuable cargo meant an instant financial reward for the owner and any others with shares in the enterprise. See also BRISTOL, HALF.

shirt

Macho men will be horrified to realise that the garments **shirt** and **skirt** share an ancient root, which is also that of **short**. The idea behind **shirty**, 'bad-tempered or annoyed', is the same as that behind **keep your shirt on**, 'don't lose your temper, stay calm'. The offended or riled person is about to take his shirt off ready for a fight. In **lose your shirt** or **put your shirt on** the shirt is seen as the very last possession that you could use to bet with.

shock

The **shock** that now means 'a sudden upsetting event or experience' came from French *choc* in the mid 16th century with the sense 'an encounter between two charging forces or jousters', and in English it started life as a military term. **Shocking** meaning 'very bad' is first found at the end of the 18th century, in a collection of letters called *The Paget Papers*: 'Shocking Weather since you left'.

A modern **short, sharp shock** is likely to be a brief but harsh custodial sentence imposed on offenders in an attempt to discouraging them from committing further offences. At the Conservative Party Conference in

1979 the then Home Secretary William Whitelaw had proposed this as a form of corrective treatment for young offenders. He was quoting from *The Mikado* (1885) by Gilbert and Sullivan: 'Awaiting the sensation of a short, sharp shock, / From a cheap and chippy chopper on a big black block.'

An unkempt or thick **shock** of hair probably did not get its name from its shock value. The word originally referred to a dog with long shaggy hair – the poodle was a typical **shock dog**, though the term is long obsolete. It may be the same as earlier **shough**, a lapdog said to have originated in Iceland. Shakespeare in *Macbeth* wrote of 'spaniels, curs, shoughs'.

shop

The earliest shops were small stalls or booths, like the ones you might see today in a market or used by a pavement trader. **Shop** came into English as a medieval shortening of early French *eschoppe* 'lean-to booth'. The slang sense 'to inform on' is earlier, dating from 1583 – the original implication was of causing someone to be locked up.

> Shopping, the most popular hobby for many people, has been known by that name since the 1760s.

A slang dictionary of 1874 first recorded **all over the shop** as 'pugilistic [boxing] slang' – to inflict severe punishment on an opponent was 'to knock him all over the shop'. Nowadays it means 'everywhere, in all directions', 'in a state of disorder or confusion' or 'wildly or erratically'.

show

The ancient root of **show** meant 'to look', and in Old English the first meaning was 'to look at, inspect'. **Show** as in 'an elaborate public display or performance' comes from the 16th century, and **show business** from the 1850s. 'There's No Business like Show Business' is the title of a song from *Annie Get Your Gun* (1946) by Irving Berlin.

In **show your hand**, 'to disclose your plans', the image is of players revealing their cards in a card game. The determination that **the show must go on**, recorded from the 1890s, is now associated with the theatre, but may actually derive from the circus.

shrapnel

During the Peninsular War in Spain and Portugal (1808-14), General Henry Shrapnel invented a shell that contained bullets and a small bursting charge, which, when fired by the time fuse, burst the shell and scattered the bullets in a shower. Those firing the projectile gave it the name **Shrapnel shell** – the bullets were **Shrapnel shot**, or simply **shrapnel**. During the Second World War **shrapnel** acquired its modern sense, 'fragments of a bomb, shell or other object thrown out by an explosion'. The sense 'coins, loose change' started life as New Zealand military slang around the time of the First World War.

shrew

No one knows for certain whether a bad-tempered woman is a **shrew** because people compared her to the mouse-like animal or whether the animal is a **shrew** because it was considered venomous and dangerous, like an aggressively assertive woman. It is a chicken-and-egg situation. When **shrewd** first appeared it shared these negative associations, but as connection with the shrew and belief in the shrew's evil nature weakened, it developed the sense 'cunning' and then the modern positive meaning 'having sharp powers of judgement, astute'. The word **shrew** appears in Old English, but its origin is unknown.

shrift

To give someone **short shrift** is to treat them in a curt and dismissive way. The phrase originally referred to the short time that a condemned criminal was allowed to make their confession to a priest and be **shriven**, prescribed a penance and absolved of their sins, before being executed. Its first use in the literal sense comes in Shakespeare's *Richard III*: 'Make a short shrift, he longs to see your head.'

The **Shrove** in **Shrove Tuesday** is a form of **shrive**. Although the day has religious significance as the one preceding Ash Wednesday and the start of Lent, it is marked by feasting and celebration before the Lent fast begins. In Britain people eat pancakes on the day, giving the alternative name **Pancake Day** or **Pancake Tuesday**. Other countries celebrate it as the carnival of **Mardi Gras**, French for 'Fat Tuesday'. See also CARNIVAL.

shrink

In the informal sense 'a psychiatrist' **shrink** is a shortening of **headshrinker**. The longer form appeared in print in 1950, and **shrink** itself in 1966. A headshrinker was originally a head-hunter who preserved and shrank human heads.

shyster

An American story goes that there was once an unscrupulous lawyer called Scheuster who gave his name to the **shyster**, but no record of him has ever been found. It is much more likely that German *Scheisser* 'worthless person' is the word's origin, since it first appeared in New York, home to many German-speaking immigrants, as a name for an unqualified lawyer who preyed on inmates of the notorious prison called the Tombs. **Shyster** was first recorded in 1843, and soon took on the sense of an unscrupulous lawyer rather than a fake one. See also CHARLATAN.

Siamese twins

Chang and Eng from Siam, now Thailand, were born in 1811 physically joined at the waist, but led an active life for more than 60 years. They were not the first such babies to survive – Kentish twins Eliza and Mary Chalkhurst, for example, died in 1734 at the age of 34 – but they were the first to have modern communications to spread their fame. *The Times* is the earliest-known English source to refer to them in print as **the Siamese twins**, in 1829. Doctors and specialists use the term **conjoined twins**.

sick

The Old English word **sick** was the usual way of referring to someone physically unwell before ILL arrived in the Middle Ages. A variety of animals have cropped up over the centuries in phrases emphasising how ill someone is feeling. The first was the DOG, back in the early 18th century. Other comparisons include the HORSE, the PIG and the CAT, the latter well known for its problems with hairballs. All these phrases refer to physical sickness, whereas being **as sick as a**

Chang and Eng – the Siamese twins

parrot is a mental state, to do with feeling depressed. This version goes back to the 1970s and is particularly associated with despondent footballers and managers being interviewed after a crushing defeat. The phrase may have been suggested by the Dead Parrot sketch in the television comedy series *Monty Python's Flying Circus*. The opposite is **over the moon** – see MOON.

Tsar Nicholas I of Russia reportedly said of the Sultan of Turkey in 1853: 'I am not so eager about what shall be done when the sick man dies, as I am to determine with England what shall not be done upon that event taking place.' His remarks reflected the precarious state of the Ottoman Empire and its slow but inevitable disintegration. Political commentators exploited this view and started to refer to Turkey as **the sick man of Europe**. The expression **the sick man of —** was applied to other countries over the following decades, and now often refers to factors other than economics or politics. An example from *The Scotsman* exploits the literal meaning of the phrase: 'Scotland remains the "sick man of Europe" in terms of smoking-related diseases, with some 13,000 deaths and 33,500 hospital admissions each year.'

sideburns

The 19th-century American general Ambrose E. Burnside sported muttonchop whiskers and a moustache, with a clean-shaven chin. By the 1870s people were calling this style a **Burnside**; then changing fashion did away with the moustache and **burnsides** became the strips of hair down the face in front of a man's ears. Fame fades fast, and the general's name must have puzzled many, though they understood the 'side' part. In the 1880s the elements reversed order to form **sideburns**, though this still left 'burns' as a puzzle, and the more familiar **sideboards** was occasionally substituted as an alternative.

sight

An Old English word related to SEE. The sport of shooting has given us the expression **in your sights**, 'within the scope of your ambition or expectations', with the sights in question being a device on a gun which helps you to aim at the target more precisely. The implication is that you are firmly focused on achieving your ambition. The same idea is found in to **raise** (or **lower**) **your sights**, meaning 'to become more (or less) ambitious' and to **set your sights on**, meaning 'to have something as an ambition'.

silence

Both **silence** and **silent** came from Latin *silere*, 'to be silent', the former in the early Middle Ages, the latter towards the end of the 15th century. The fuller form of

silence is golden, 'it is often wise to say nothing', is **speech is silver but silence is golden**. Both are recorded from the 19th century. Originally **the silent majority** were the dead. In the 20th century they became those who hold moderate opinions but rarely express them. Richard Nixon brought the phrase to prominence by claiming to speak for this section of society in his 1968 presidential campaign.

silhouette

Étienne de Silhouette was an 18th-century French author and politician. Why he gave his name to the dark outline of something against a brighter background remains obscure. One account says that the word ridiculed the petty economies Silhouette introduced while holding the office of Controller General, while another refers to the shortness of his occupancy of that post. A scholarly French dictionary suggested that Silhouette himself made outline portraits with which he decorated the walls of his château. More than two centuries on, we shall probably never know the truth.

silk

In the ancient world **silk** came overland to Europe from China and Tibet. The Greeks and Romans called the inhabitants of these faraway and unknown lands **Seres**, and from this word **silk** developed.

The observation that **you can't make a silk purse out of a sow's ear**, 'you can't turn something inferior into something of top quality', has been proverbial since the late 16th century. There was an earlier version featuring 'a goat's fleece' rather than 'a sow's ear'. A **silk** is a senior lawyer who has been made a Queen's (or King's) Counsel. The name comes from the silk robes they are entitled to wear – they are also said to **take silk** when they reach this rank.

silly

A medieval Englishman would have been pleased if you described him as **silly** – you would have been saying he was happy or lucky. The word is an alteration of earlier **seely**, from an ancient root meaning 'luck, happiness'. The Old English sense of **seely** was 'happy, fortunate, blessed by God'. This subsequently developed into 'holy', then 'innocent, defenceless, deserving of pity', at which point, in the later Middle

Ages, **silly** largely took over. Cynical people often regard goodness and simplicity as showing a lack of intelligence, and since the late 16th century the primary sense has been 'foolish'.

In cricket **silly** is used in the names of fielding positions such as **silly mid-off** and **silly point**, to indicate that the fielder is positioned closer than usual to the batsman. What makes such positions 'silly' is that the fielder is required to stand perilously close to the bat.

In high summer wealthy and important people deserted Victorian London while Parliament and the law courts were in recess. Since the mid 19th century the months of July and August have been **the silly season**, when British newspapers often print trivia because of a lack of important news. See also CRAZY, DAFT, INNOCENT.

silly billy

The first **silly billy** was either William Frederick, the Duke of Gloucester (1776-1834), or King William IV (1765-1837). William IV, the predecessor of Queen Victoria, became unpopular when he intervened in politics by imposing the Conservative Robert Peel as Prime Minister, despite a Whig majority in Parliament.

silver

The metal **silver** is an Old English word that may ultimately be of Eastern origin. As a term for the film industry **the silver screen** goes back to the early days of film-making and is recorded from the early 20th century. A real silver screen was a projection screen covered with metallic paint to give it a highly reflective surface. Nowadays people tend to use **the silver screen** to refer to the golden age of Hollywood films in the 1930s and 1940s. See also CLOUD.

sinister

In Latin *sinister* meant 'left' or 'left-hand', but apart from terms in heraldry such as **bend sinister**, a broad diagonal stripe from top right to bottom left of a shield which is a supposed sign of illegitimacy, **sinister** in English has never meant the physical left-hand side. Instead it reflects deep-rooted prejudices against left-handedness, suggesting evil, malice or dishonesty. See also AMBIDEXTROUS, DEXTEROUS.

sir

A shortened form of **sire** that has been a title for a knight since the Middle Ages. Kings were formerly addressed as **sire**, though now the term is more often used for the male parent of an animal. **Sire** is from Latin *senior* 'older, older man', related to *senex* 'old, old man', from which **senile** also derives. In languages descended from Latin, words based on *senior* often became the way of addressing a man, for example

señor in Spanish, **signor** in Italian and the second element of **monsieur** in French.

siren

In classical mythology the Sirens were sea nymphs whose beautiful singing lured sailors to their doom on submerged rocks. People hear a **siren song** or **siren call** when they are attracted to something that is both alluring and potentially harmful or dangerous. In 1819 the French engineer and physicist Charles Cagniard de la Tour used **siren** as the name for his invention of an acoustic instrument for producing musical tones. Later in the century steamships began to use a much larger instrument on the same lines as a foghorn or warning device, and in the Second World War sirens sent people scurrying to their cellars or shelters for protection from air raids.

sirloin

The name **sirloin** for a choice cut of beef dates from the late Middle Ages. It came from French, and the first element is from French *sur* 'above'. The later spelling with *sir-* has led to false associations with SIR and various accounts of a king knighting the roast for its excellence, dubbing it 'Sir Loin'. A mid 17th-century source mentions a tradition that the monarch in question was Henry VIII. Jonathan Swift, on the other hand, names James I, while yet another account attributes the action to Charles II. We can be reasonably certain that it was none of them.

six

The number **six** is Old English, but comes from the same ancient root as Latin *sex* and Greek *hexa* 'six'. These gave us **sextet**, **sextuple**, **hexagon** and similar words.

Those familiar with the game of cricket will know that a six is a hit that sends the ball clear over the boundary without first striking the ground, scoring six runs. The ball needs to be struck with a mighty whack to travel as far as that, and this is the image behind the expression to **knock for six**, 'to utterly surprise or overcome', recorded from the beginning of the 20th century. A form of the phrase also occurs as to **hit for six**, which tends to have the slightly different meaning of 'to affect very severely', as in 'The beef industry was hit for six by the BSE crisis'.

The origins of **at sixes and sevens**, 'in a state of total confusion and disarray', lie in gambling with dice. Betting on the fall of dice has been popular for centuries, and the phrase first occurs in Geoffrey Chaucer's poem *Troilus and Criseyde*, in the version to **set on six and seven**. It is most likely that the phrase

was an alteration of the Old French words for five and six, *cinque* and *sice*, these being the highest numbers on a dice. The 'inflation' of the numbers probably came about either because people who did not know French misheard the words, or a joky exaggeration. The idea was that risking all your worldly goods on the possibility of these two numbers coming up was the height of recklessness, and could result in your whole world falling apart.

A man's **six-pack** is his toned midriff – the abdominal muscle is crossed by three bands of fibre which look like a set of six separate muscles if the person is slim and fit. The original six-pack – a pack of six cans of beer held together with a plastic fastener – is associated more with couch-potato characters such as Homer Simpson.

skid

To **hit the skids**, 'to begin a rapid decline or deterioration', and the similar to **put the skids under someone or something**, meaning 'to hasten their decline or failure', both originated in the USA. **Skid** is a North American term for a wooden roller that is used as part of a set to move logs or other heavy objects. Once a log is on the skids it can be slid forward very easily, gathering momentum until it reaches the end of the rollers and comes to an abrupt halt. **Skid row**, meaning 'a run-down part of town frequented by tramps and alcoholics', is also connected with logging. It originated as **skid road** in the late 19th century, and at first simply described a part of town frequented by loggers, presumably notorious for being rough, tough hard drinkers.

skin

Old Scandinavian gave us **skin** in the later Old English period – the original word was **hide**. The expression **by the skin of your teeth**, 'by a very narrow margin, only just', arose from a misquotation from the biblical book of Job: 'I am escaped with the skin of my teeth.' The implication is 'and nothing else'. See also BEAUTY.

The **skinhead** is associated with the Britain of the 1970s, but the first skinheads were American. In the 1950s recruits to the US Marines were known as skinheads because of the severe way their hair was cropped when they joined up.

slap

When **slap** first came into medieval English it was probably meant to imitate the sound of a blow with the palm of the hand. **Slap and tickle** is playful sexual activity, which has gone on since time immemorial, though the phrase dates only from the early 20th century. To create the sound of a blow in the theatre or circus, pantomime actors and clowns use a device consisting of two flexible pieces of wood joined together at one end. This is a **slapstick**, so called since the late 19th century. Since then it has also been the term for comedy based on deliberately clumsy actions and embarrassing events.

Slaphead is British slang for a bald man, recorded from the late 1980s. It could be a reference to a long-running routine of the comedian Benny Hill, in which Hill slapped his short, bald sidekick Jackie Wright repeatedly on the head. Another 1980s British slang term of uncertain origin is **slapper**, 'an unattractive woman'. It may be from a woman 'slapping on' a large amount of make-up, or could be connected with Yiddish *schlepper* 'scruffy person'.

slate

Schoolchildren formerly used flat pieces of slate for writing on in chalk, and shops and bars used the same materials for keeping a record of what a customer owed. This is the origin of the British expression **on the slate**, 'to be paid for later, on credit'. The word comes from Old French *escalate*, meaning 'a piece broken off'.

In the sense 'to criticise', dating from the mid 19th century, **slate** is probably a different word. It might derive from the slightly earlier Irish sense 'to beat, beat up' and be related to a Scots use of **slate** meaning 'to set a dog on', which is from Old Norse.

slave

Our word **slave** was shortened from early French *esclave* in the Middle Ages. In Latin the equivalent form *sclavus* is identical with *Sclavus*, the source of **Slav**. The Slavic peoples of eastern and central Europe had been conquered and reduced to a servile state during the 9th century.

The slave trade was abolished on British ships in 1807, and slavery itself throughout the British Empire in 1833. When the American Civil War ended in 1865 slaves in the South were freed, and now we are left with **wage slaves**, a term used in the English translation of the *Communist Manifesto* by Karl Marx and Friedrich Engels.

sleazy

In the 17th century it was thin or flimsy fabrics that were **sleazy**, not nightclubs or bars. The familiar modern senses 'squalid and seedy' and 'sordid, corrupt or immoral' did not develop until the 1940s, from the idea of cloth being cheap and poor-quality. The corresponding noun **sleaze** was created from

sleazy in the 1960s, and usually refers to political scandal and corruption.

sledge

The **sledge** that is a vehicle used on snow and ice came in the late 16th century from Dutch and is related to **sled**, sleigh and **slide**. As a name for what we would now more usually call a **sledgehammer**, the other **sledge** is recorded in Old English and goes back to a root meaning 'to strike' and related to **slay**. A sledgehammer is a large, heavy hammer used for jobs such as breaking rocks and driving in fence posts, so to **take a sledgehammer to crack a nut** is to use a disproportionately forceful means to achieve a simple objective. The expression is recorded in the 1930s, but a decade earlier an American version **use a sledgehammer to kill a gnat** appears.

Sleigh is also from Dutch, but dates from the early 18th century and was originally North American. To **take for a sleigh ride** is a dated slang phrase meaning 'to mislead', from the use of **sleigh ride** for an implausible or false story or a hoax. A **sleigh ride** could also mean 'a drug-induced high' – this went with the use of **snow** for cocaine in white powder form.

In the 1970s Australian cricketers started **sledging**, or making offensive or needling remarks to opposing batsmen in an attempt to break their concentration. The idea behind the term is the crudity and lack of subtlety involved in using a sledge or sledgehammer.

sleep

An Old English word first recorded around AD 800. The modern-sounding phrase **sleep with**, meaning 'to have sex with', is almost as old, and was used by the Anglo-Saxons. **Sleep like a log**, meaning 'to sleep very soundly', is not recorded before the 1880s, but the earlier version **sleep like a top** was used in the 17th century – the **top** here was a wooden toy that spun when whipped by a child, but was otherwise still and lifeless.

The modern form of the proverb **let sleeping dogs lie**, 'avoid interfering in a situation that is currently causing no problems', appears first in Sir Walter Scott's 1824 novel *Redgauntlet*. Long before that, in the 14th century, Geoffrey Chaucer advised in *Troilus and Criseyde* that 'it is not good a sleeping hound to wake'.

sleuth

A **sleuth** was first a **sleuth-hound**, a type of bloodhound employed in medieval Scotland for pursuing game or tracking fugitives. A tracker or detective has been a **sleuth-hound** since the mid 19th century, and shortly after that in the USA a simple **sleuth**. The word **sleuth** itself derives from Scandinavian, and its earliest meaning was 'the track or trail of a person or animal'.

sling

When referring to a loop used as a support or weapon, **sling** dates from the medieval period and is probably from Dutch. The most famous sling was the one used by David in the Bible to fire the stone that killed the Philistine giant Goliath.

The expression **slings and arrows**, 'adverse factors or circumstances', comes from the 'To be or not to be' speech in Shakespeare's *Hamlet*:

Whether 'tis nobler in the mind to suffer
The slings and arrows of outrageous fortune,
Or to take arms against a sea of troubles,
And by opposing end them.

slip

English has several words spelled **slip**. The one meaning 'to lose your footing' or 'to move out of position or someone's grasp' is probably German, from a root that also gave us **slippery**. This is the **slip** in **slipper** and in **slipshod**, which originally meant 'wearing slippers or loose shoes'.

In phrases such as **a slip of a girl**, meaning a small, slim person, **slip** is the same word that means 'a small piece of paper' and 'a cutting taken from a plant'. It dates from the later medieval period and probably comes from early Dutch and German *slippe* 'a cut, strip'.

The saying **there's many a slip 'twixt cup and lip** – in other words, many things can go wrong between the start of something and its completion – dates back to the mid 16th century. A similar idea was expressed by the Roman statesman and orator Cato the Elder: 'I have often heard that many things can come between mouth and morsel'.

Sloane

We have one person to credit for calling upper-class young women **Sloanes** or **Sloane Rangers**. In 1975 Peter York, style editor on the magazine *Harpers & Queen*, identified the cultural stereotype of the wealthy, fashionable but conventional-minded London girls and began writing about them, eventually co-authoring the book *The Official Sloane Ranger Handbook* in 1982. He coined the name by combining Sloane Square in west London with the masked cowboy hero the Lone Ranger. Her male equivalent is the **Hooray Henry**, a loud but harmless young upper-class man. He is first mentioned in a story by the US writer Damon Runyon in 1936, as a Hoorah Henry.

slogan

The first **slogan** was not in the world of advertising or politics, but was the Scottish Gaelic word for a battle cry or war cry, *sluagh-ghairm* – from *sluagh* 'army' and *gairm* 'shout'. For Scottish Highlanders the slogan would often be someone's surname or a place name. For three centuries the word was confined to the work of Scottish writers but in the early 19th century it gained a wider popularity in the novels of Sir Walter Scott, and later in the century came to mean a short memorable motto or phrase.

slough

A **slough** is a swamp (*slōh* in Old English), and a **slough of despond** a condition of despondency, hopelessness and gloom. The phrase comes from John Bunyan's *The Pilgrim's Progress* (1678), where it is the name of a deep boggy place between the City of Destruction and the gate at the beginning of Christian's journey.

Slough in southern England also takes its name from Old English *slōh*, not the most appealing of origins. To add to the unglamorous town's image problems, the English poet John Betjeman wrote of it in 1937: 'Come, friendly bombs, and fall on Slough! / It isn't fit for humans now.'

Come, friendly bombs, and fall on Slough! It isn't fit for humans now.

John Betjeman

slug

In medieval times a **slug** was a slow-moving lazy person, and over time the word came to describe any slow-moving animal or vehicle. For example, the big-game hunter William Baldwin, writing in 1863, described one of his horses as 'an incorrigible slug'. It has been the term for a slimy snail-like creature since the early 18th century.

A **slug** of whisky, or of lead, is probably the same word, but to **slug** someone is not, and is related to **slog**. **Sluggard** is based on the rare verb **slug**, 'to be lazy or slow', which may be Scandinavian in origin and which is probably also the source of **sluggish**, 'slow and lazy'.

slur

The medieval English word *slur* meant 'thin, fluid mud'. This is the base of our word **slur**, though the connection is not immediately obvious. Early senses of the verb were 'to smear' and then 'to criticise' – you can see the same metaphor at work in the phrase 'mud-slinging' and in the history of the word ASPERSION. Later on it came to mean 'to gloss over a fault', and from this developed the idea of speaking indistinctly. **Slurry** also comes from medieval *slur*, and here the connection with mud is much clearer.

smack

English has many **smacks**. **Smack** as in 'it smacks of fish' is based on Old English *smaec* 'flavour or smell'. The one meaning both 'to part your lips noisily' and 'to strike someone' arrived from Dutch *smacken* in the mid 16th century. Initially people smacked their lips in the context of eating and drinking and, later, kissing, but by the early 19th century the word was being used in the sense of hitting someone. The **smack** that is a kind of sailing vessel is also Dutch, while the slang word for 'heroin' is probably from Yiddish *schmeck*, 'a sniff, a smell'.

small

A word recorded since around AD 700. In Old English it could refer to something slender or narrow as well as something more generally of less than usual size.

You can describe something insignificant or unimportant as **small beer** or. From the 16th century **small beer** was a term for weaker beer, the sort that people drank for breakfast in those days when water

supplies were unsafe. **Small potatoes** started out as a phrase in American English, usually in the fuller form **small potatoes and few in the hill**.

The phrase **small is beautiful**, suggesting that something small-scale is better than a large-scale equivalent, comes from the title of a book by E.F. Schumacher, published in 1973. It is perhaps best known as a slogan adopted by environmentalists.

smart alec

That irritating person who seems to know it all or have the right answer to every question is a **smart alec** – but who was 'alec'? He was probably Alex Hoag, a notorious thief and conman in New York in the 1840s, whose reputation for never getting caught earned him the nickname Smart Alex.

smart

The first English use of **smart** was as a verb meaning 'be painful', which survives in the verb meaning 'to feel a sharp, stinging pain in a part of the body' – its root is probably related to Latin *mordere* 'to bite'. The original meaning of the adjective was 'causing sharp pain', which led to 'keen or brisk' and developed into the current senses of 'mentally sharp, clever' and 'neat, well turned out'.

In the late 17th century **smart money** was money paid to sailors and soldiers to compensate them for wounds received while on duty. **Smart** here meant 'physical pain'. In modern usage from around 1900 the phrase refers to money bet by people with expert knowledge, with **smart** meaning 'quick-witted'.

The sugar-coated chocolate sweets called **Smarties** were launched in 1937. They were famous for the cardboard tube they were sold in until 2006, when this was replaced by a new six-sided 'hexatube'.

smell

No one is sure where **smell** comes from, though it has been used in English since the Middle Ages. To **come up smelling of roses** is to make a lucky escape from a difficult or unpleasant situation with your reputation intact. This is a shorter, and rather more polite, version of the full form of the expression, to **fall in the s— and come up smelling of roses**. Rose bushes thrive on plenty of manure, and the image here is of someone falling into a freshly fertilised rose bed. A similar-sounding expression, dating from the 1930s and American in origin, is **stop and smell the roses**, or take time to fully appreciate life's pleasures. If someone tells you to **wake up and smell the coffee**, on the other hand, they are urging you to be *less* relaxed, and to become more realistic or alert. The phrase was popularised by the US advice columnist Ann Landers from the mid 1950s.

smithereens

The tiny fragments into which something is broken or smashed were first recorded in the early 19th century. The word, often used in the phrase 'blown to smithereens', probably comes from Irish *smidirín*.

smock

In Old English *smūgan* meant 'to creep'. Just as today we can talk about, say, wriggling into a pair of jeans or slipping into a dress, so the Anglo-Saxons used the word as a way of describing putting on a piece of clothing. This is why the related word *smoc*, which became **smock**, was applied to a woman's loose-fitting undergarment. It was not until the 19th century that the word was used for a piece of clothing worn by agricultural workers, and only since the 20th that it has described a loose dress or blouse or the loose garment that artists wear to keep their clothes clean.

smoke

The Old English word **smoke** is around 1,000 years old, and people are first recorded as smoking tobacco at the start of the 17th century. A big city has been called **the Smoke** or **the Big Smoke** since the 1840s – the first examples refer not to London but to Australian towns.

A piece of indisputable and incriminating evidence can be described as **a smoking gun**. This conjures up the vivid image, familiar from detective novels and films, of someone standing holding a smoking gun next to a corpse with gunshot wounds. The natural assumption is that they are the guilty party. The phrase came to prominence during the Watergate scandal in the early 1970s. An incriminating tape revealed President Nixon's wish to limit the FBI's involvement in the investigation, prompting Republican congressman Barber T. Conable to observe: 'I guess we have found the smoking pistol, haven't we?'

When a rumour is being discussed, you often hear someone say **there's no smoke without fire**, suggesting that there is always some reason for a rumour. The English version dates back at least to the 15th century, though the same idea appears in the work of the Roman comic dramatist Plautus – 'the flame is right next to the smoke' – and in a 13th-century French proverb.

The phrase **smoke and mirrors** refers to the obscuring or embellishing of the truth of a situation with misleading or irrelevant information. The metaphor relates to the illusion created by conjuring tricks and can be traced back to the US political columnist Jimmy Breslin, writing in 1975:

All political power is primarily an illusion . . . Mirrors and blue smoke, beautiful blue smoke rolling over the surface of highly polished mirrors . . . If somebody tells you how to look, there can be seen in the smoke great, magnificent shapes, castles and kingdoms, and maybe they can be yours.

smug

No one likes a **smug** person, but in the mid 16th century they were popular. The word comes from German *smuk* 'pretty' and originally meant 'neat or spruce' when describing men. Not much later it was being applied to women and girls too, as in 'She is indeed a good smug lass', a line from a play by Thomas Otway in 1677. Another early meaning was 'smooth', hence Shakespeare's reference to 'the smug and silver Trent'. Exactly when **smug** began to suggest complacency is difficult to pinpoint.

snake

The fact that snakes have no legs and crawl along the ground gives them their name. The ancestor of **snake** is an ancient Germanic word that meant 'to crawl or creep'. **Serpent** has a similar origin – it comes from Latin *serpere*, which also meant 'to crawl or creep'.

You can describe a treacherous or deceitful person as **a snake in the grass**, with the idea of a danger that lurks just out of sight. Snakes have been associated with treachery since the 6th century BC and the fables of the Greek storyteller Aesop. In one of his tales a man finds a snake frozen with cold and puts it close to his chest to warm it up. As soon as the snake revives it bites him. Before the 17th century the equivalent phrase had featured toads, which were at one time thought to be poisonous – a treacherous person was called **a pad in the straw** (*pad* is an old dialect word for a toad). The current expression may have originated from a Latin poem by the Roman poet Virgil. See also ADDER.

The children's game **snakes and ladders**, called in the USA **chutes and ladders**, was first played at the end of the 19th century. It may be based on an ancient Indian game called Moksha Patamu, which was used to teach children about the Hindu religion – the good squares allowed a player to go to a higher level of life, whereas the evil 'snakes' sent them back through reincarnation to lower tiers of life.

sneeze

When we get a cold we should really start *fneezing* rather than **sneezing**. This is because the word comes from medieval English *fnese*. People were not used to seeing the *fn-* combination at the beginning of a word by then, and someone must have misread it and written it down as *sn-* instead.

snob

There is a long-standing belief that **snob** has some connection with Latin *sine nobilitate* 'without nobility', abbreviated to *s-nob*, which then became **snob**. It is an ingenious theory but highly unlikely, as a **snob** was first recorded in the late 18th century as a shoemaker or cobbler. The word soon came to be used for any person of humble status or rank – Cambridge undergraduates used the term to mean 'someone from the town, not a member of the university', and this in turn led to the broader sense 'a lower-class person or a person lacking in good breeding or good taste'. In time the word came to describe someone who seeks to imitate or give exaggerated respect to people they perceive as superior in social standing or wealth.

snook see COCK.

snooker

Snooker, both the game and the word, originated among British army officers serving in India in the 1870s. Colonel Sir Neville Chamberlain (not the future British Prime Minister) is said to have coined the name for a fast-moving version of billiards that he and his associates in the officers' mess had devised. **Snooker** was army slang for 'a newly joined cadet', and may have been intended to refer to the inept play of a fellow officer.

snout

Think how many words to do with noses begin with the letters *sn-*. Most are medieval. There is **snout**, which in early use could describe not only the projecting part of an animal's face but also an elephant's trunk and a bird's beak. A variant of **snout** was **snoot**, which is where **snooty** comes from – snooty people have their noses stuck in the air. **Snot** and **snotty** are also based on **snout**. **Snuff** used to mean 'to inhale through the nostrils' before it became a term for powdered tobacco that you inhale through your nostrils. **Snuffle** is related. **Snivel** originally referred to mucus. **Snore** and **snort** once had each other's meanings – **snore** meant 'a snort' and **snort** meant 'to snore'.

snug

The first use of **snug** was as a sailors' term, probably from German or Dutch, that meant 'shipshape, properly prepared for bad weather': 'Captain Read . . . ordered the Carpenters to cut down our Quarter Deck to make the Ship snug and the fitter for Sailing'

(William Dampier, *A New Voyage Around the World*, 1697). A small, comfortable room in a pub was known as a **snug** from the 1830s, but the original name was a **snuggery** – in *The Pickwick Papers* (1837) Charles Dickens refers to 'the snuggery inside the bar'. There also used to be a verb **snug** that meant 'to lie or nestle closely', and this is where we get **snuggle** from.

soap

Although **soap** would have been a much less common substance in Anglo-Saxon days, the word does date back to that period. It was probably brought to England by traders from the Middle East and Arabia, where people *did* bathe regularly.

A **soap opera** is so called because in the 1930s such serials, then broadcast on the radio in the USA, were sponsored by soap manufacturers. Americans say **no soap** as an equivalent of 'nothing doing', when there is no chance of something happening or occurring. This may be related to a mid 19th-century use of **soap** in informal American English to mean 'money'. Also American is **soft soap**, or persuasive flattery, first recorded in the 1830s.

soccer

A shortening of **Association football**, the official name given in the late 19th century to the game, to distinguish it from rugby football. The word was formed by the same process that gave us **rugger** for RUGBY.

soil

You might think that **soil** meaning 'earth' and **soil** meaning 'to make dirty' are linked, but they are quite distinct words. To take the noun first, when you refer to, for example, 'home soil' or 'foreign soil' you are using the word in its original sense. It came from Old French and once referred to a land or country: 'The man who with undaunted toils / Sails unknown seas, to unknown soils' (John Gay, 1727). It could also refer to the ground, and later to the layer of earth that plants grow in. The verb **soil**, 'to make dirty', comes from Old French *soiller*, which was based on Latin *sucula* 'a little pig'. Pigs are not as dirty as their reputation suggests, but there is presumably the idea of making a place into a pigsty behind the use of the English word. The related noun was first used in English as a term for 'a muddy place used by a wild boar to wallow in'.

soldier

Soldiers take their name not from the fact that they are trained to fight but because they are paid to do so. The word entered English in the 13th century, from Old

French *soldier*, from *soulde* 'pay, especially army pay'. The ultimate source is Latin *solidus*, the name of a gold coin that the Romans used.

Don't come (or **play**) **the old soldier** is something you might say to a person who tries to use their greater age or experience of life to deceive you or to shirk a duty. An old soldier, someone who has been around and knows all the tricks, has been a proverbial figure since the 1720s.

sombre

If you are in a **sombre** mood you can be thought of as being under a shadow, rather like those cartoons showing a dark cloud hanging over a person's head. The word came into English from French in the middle of the 18th century but was based on Latin *sub* 'under' and *umbra* 'shade or shadow'. **Sombrero**, the broad-brimmed hat, is a Spanish word with a similar origin. See also UMBRELLA.

son

An Old English word, but one which shares its root with Greek *huios* 'son'. When we affectionately call someone a **son of a gun** we are using a term that probably originated in naval history. The gun in question was one of the guns carried on board ships, and the phrase is supposed to have been applied to babies born at sea to women allowed to accompany their husbands. If the father was not known, the child was described in the ship's log as a 'son of a gun'.

Sonny Jim, now a slightly disparaging address for a man or boy, was originally **Sunny Jim**. Jim was an energetic boy used to advertise a brand of breakfast cereal called Force in the early years of the 20th century. He was the winning entry in a competition run by the company to find a suitable character to promote the cereal. One slogan ran: 'High o'er the fence leaps Sunny Jim / 'Force' is the food that raises him.'

song

The Old English words **sing** and **song** are from the same ancient root. The phrase to **sing for your supper**, 'to derive a benefit or favour by providing a service in return', derives from the nursery rhyme *Little Tommy Tucker*:

Little Tommy Tucker
Sings for his supper;
What shall we give him?
White bread and butter.

If something is on sale **for a song** it is being sold cheaply. This expression may come from the old practice of selling written copies of ballads at fairs. You could also say **for an old song**, perhaps because you would be likely to pay much less for an old ballad sheet than for a recent one. The phrase was popularised in the 1970s when *Going for a Song* was used as the title of a television quiz show in which teams had to guess the date and value of antiques.

If you **make a song and dance about** something you cause a fuss or commotion or, in American English, give a long explanation that is deliberately misleading or confusing. In 17th-century America a 'song and dance' referred to a form of entertainment consisting of singing and dancing, later applied to a vaudeville act. The modern senses developed around the turn of the 20th century. See also ALL.

soon

Over the centuries **soon** has become less urgent. In Anglo-Saxon times it meant 'immediately, without delay'. A similar case is **presently**, which also used to mean 'immediately' and now means 'soon'.

soothe

In Anglo-Saxon times to **soothe** was to show or prove that something is true. The first part of **soothsayer**, 'someone who can foresee the future', is based on the same word and originally described someone who speaks the truth. During the 16th century the meaning of **soothe** moved from 'to corroborate a statement, back someone up in what they are saying' to 'to humour or flatter someone by agreeing with them'. This finally led to the meaning 'to calm, comfort or placate' which we are familiar with today.

sop

The Old English word **sop** first meant 'to dip bread in liquid', but nowadays a sop is something you do or offer as a concession to appease someone. This was originally used in the phrase **a sop to Cerberus**, referring to the monstrous three-headed watchdog which, in Greek mythology, guarded the entrance of Hades. In the *Aeneid* Virgil describes how the witch guiding Aeneas to the underworld threw a drugged cake to Cerberus, which allowed the hero to pass the monster in safety.

When **soppy**, which comes from **sop**, first appeared in English in the early 19th century it meant 'soaked with water', not tears, as you might expect today from a feeble, sentimental soppy person. The writer H.G. Wells was one of the first to use the word in this sense.

sophisticated

If you describe someone as **sophisticated** you probably mean that they are worldly-wise, discriminating and cultured – all positive traits. But when the word was first used in the early 17th century it had a much more negative meaning, 'corrupted' or 'adulterated', especially referring to food and drink. Over time it shifted in sense and acquired associations of a lack of naturalness or simplicity, as in this example from Leslie Stephen's *The Playground of Europe* in 1871: 'The mountains . . . are a standing protest against the sophisticated modern taste.' This in turn led to the modern sense. The root was Greek *sophos*, 'wise'.

sorcerer

A **sorcerer** was originally a *sorser*. The word comes via Old French *sorcier* from Latin *sors* 'lot, fortune', the root of **sort**. The Latin source relates to the use of oracles and the casting of lots to foretell the future.

A **sorcerer's apprentice** is a person who starts a process but then cannot control it without help. This is the translation of the French *L'apprenti sorcier*, the title of an 1897 symphonic poem by Paul Dukas based on *Der Zauberlehrling*, a ballad written in 1797 by the German poet and dramatist Goethe. In the ballad the apprentice's use of magic spells when his master is away sets off a series of events which he cannot control.

sorry

In the Anglo-Saxon period to be **sorry** was to be pained or distressed, full of grief or sorrow – the meaning gradually weakened to become 'sad through sympathy with someone else's misfortune', 'full of regret' and then simply an expression of apology. The source was **sore**, which originally had the meaning 'causing intense pain, grievous'.

Sorrow is also Old English, but is not closely related to the other two words. The expression **more in sorrow than in anger** is taken from Shakespeare's *Hamlet*. When Hamlet asks Horatio to describe the expression on the face of his father's ghost, Horatio replies, 'a countenance more in sorrow than in anger'.

Meerkats on a tickey

South Africa, the 'Rainbow Nation', has 11 official languages. These include the native Zulu and Xhosa, and Afrikaans, spoken by the descendants of the Dutch who first settled the country in the 17th century and a generous donor of words to English.

First of those in any dictionary is the aardvark, a badger-sized burrowing mammal whose name comes from *aarde* 'earth' and *vark* 'pig'. The meerkat, star of natural history programmes, has a complex history. The word is Dutch and may come from *meer* 'sea' and *kat* 'cat', perhaps with the idea of a cat-like creature from overseas, or it could be an alteration of Hindi *markata* 'ape'.

Meerkats are agile creatures, able to turn on a tickey, or in a very small area. The expression goes back to the period before South African coinage was decimalised, when a tickey was a tiny silver coin worth three pennies. The equivalent British phrase is on a sixpence.

The most athletic person would not be able to emulate a meerkat, even when wearing tackies, or plimsolls. There may be a connection here with the English word tacky meaning 'slightly sticky', perhaps to do with the effect of extreme heat on the plimsolls' rubber soles. Wherever the name comes from, it has provided a number of phrases. The essential worthlessness of an old plimsoll gives us a piece of old tackie for an easy task that presents no problems, and to tread tackie is to drive or accelerate, with the idea of putting your foot down on the accelerator.

Dutch settlers in South Africa came to be known in English as Boers, from the Dutch word for 'farmer'. In 1835 many of them set out northwards on the Great Trek (see TREK) to find and settle new territory. On overnight stops they formed their wagons into a laager or circular encampment, which has given us laager mentality for an entrenched viewpoint.

In the TV comedy series *Fawlty Towers* Basil Fawlty crushes an expectant hotel guest by asking sarcastically if she was expecting to see 'herds of wildebeest sweeping majestically' out of a Torquay window. He was using the Afrikaans word for a creature better known as the gnu, a name from the indigenous African languages Khoikhoi and San which probably imitates the sound the animal makes.

See also BOOR, COMMANDO.

spade

Our word **spade**, meaning a tool that you dig with, is related to Greek *spathē* 'blade or paddle' and has been in the language since Anglo-Saxon times, while the spade that appears on a playing card dates from the 16th century. The latter is based on Italian *spada* 'a broad-bladed sword', though the design (a black upside-down heart shape with a stalk) looks more like a pointed spade than a sword.

To **call a spade a spade**, 'to speak plainly, without avoiding unpleasant or embarrassing issues', dates from the mid 16th century. A tongue-in-cheek variation, from the early 20th century, is **call a spade a shovel**. **In spades** means 'to a very high degree' or 'as much as or more than could be desired', and comes from the card game bridge, where spades are the highest-ranking suit.

spare

In the senses 'left over, extra' and 'to avoid harming' **spare** is an Old English word, but the **spare** in **spare ribs** is quite different. **Spare ribs** probably comes from the old German word *ribbesper*, which meant 'pickled pork ribs roasted on a spit'. Once English speakers started using the German term in the 16th century they soon swapped the two parts round to make it sound more like an English word. The title of the British feminist magazine *Spare Rib*, first published in 1972, is a pun on the 'spare' rib that God took from Adam's body to create the first woman, Eve.

spartan

A **spartan** place or lifestyle is one lacking comfort or luxury. The word is a tribute to the Spartans of ancient Greece, traditional foes of Athens, who left weak or sickly babies out on a cold mountain slope at night to die and forced all children to live in military 'boarding schools' from the age of about seven. Their terse speech also gave us the word LACONIC.

speak

You may not realise it at the time, but if you say 'I speak as I find', indicating that you base your opinion of someone purely on personal experience, you are quoting Shakespeare. The phrase first appeared in *The Taming of the Shrew*: 'Mistake me not; I speak but as I find.' **Never speak ill of the dead** has an even longer history. 'Speak no evil of the dead' is attributed to the Spartan magistrate Chilon, as far back as the 6th century BC, and a later Latin proverb, *de mortuis nil nisi bonum*, can be translated as 'say nothing of the dead but what is good'. The English version of the proverb is first recorded in the 16th century, originally in the form 'rail not upon him that is dead'.

Paella on the patio

Many of the Spanish words that have entered English are connected with relaxation and enjoyment. No wonder Spain is such a popular choice for Brits holidaying or moving abroad.

Spanish paella and tapas are perfect for outdoor dining on a patio, originally the name for an inner courtyard in a Spanish house. The dish of rice with chicken and shellfish, cooked in a large shallow pan, goes back to Latin *patella* 'a small shallow dish' – so the plate of food balanced on your knee has a close connection with patella as the anatomical name for the kneecap. Tapas, small savoury dishes served with drinks at a bar, used to come free, and were traditionally served on a dish balanced atop a glass. This was the origin of the name, since the word literally means 'cover' or 'lid'.

Sangria, a mixture of red wine and lemonade, would be just the drink for a patio meal. Its colour is the source of the name, which in Spanish means 'bleeding'. Although sherry feels typically British, the name comes from *vino de Xerez* or 'wine of Xerez' – the original name of Jerez in southern Spain, from which the drink came. After all this eating and drinking a siesta or nap might be welcome. This Spanish word for a rest taken in the heat of the day goes back to Latin *sexta hora* 'sixth hour of the day'.

Certainly *not* relaxing, but traditionally Spanish, is a bullfight. A mounted bullfighter is called a toreador, from *toro* 'bull', and the bullfighter whose task is to kill the bull is the matador, a word which means literally 'killer'. It goes back ultimately to Persian *māt* 'dead', the origin of the *-mate* part of checkmate (see CHECK).

An English proverb warns us not to put off till tomorrow what we can do today, but the relaxed Spanish have given us mañana, 'tomorrow', to express a more easy-going attitude to pressing schedules. You could respond to any protests about slackness with que sera sera, which indicates that you have no control over the future. The Spanish phrase, meaning 'what will be, will be', was popularised in English by the 1956 song 'Que Sera, Sera', sung by Doris Day.

See also AMATEUR, CASTLE, FLAMINGO, SOMBRE.

species

The connection may not be immediately obvious, but **species** is based on Latin *specere* 'to look'. The Latin root is reflected in some of the early uses of the word, such as 'the outward look or appearance of something' or 'an image or reflection'. Over time this idea of the visible form of something developed into the more general notion of a thing's 'type' or 'kind'. See also FEMALE.

Other English words based on Latin *specere* or the related verb *spectare* include **spectator**, **spectre** (literally 'an appearance') and **specimen**. Another is **spectacle** – a spectacle, originally used in the singular, was a term for a device to assist eyesight as far back as the 15th century. In one of his sermons written in 1628, the poet and preacher John Donne thanked the man 'that assists me with a Spectacle when my sight grows old'.

spick and span

'My Lady Batten walking through the dirty lane with new spick and span white shoes', writes Samuel Pepys in his diary in 1665. He was not saying that her shoes were clean or neat, but that they were brand new, which is what **spick and span** meant in the 17th century. It was based on the earlier phrase **spick and span new**, a more emphatic version of the dialect **span new**, which came from Old Norse *span-nýr*, 'as new as a freshly cut wooden chip'. The *spick* part was influenced by Dutch *spiksplinternieuw*, literally 'splinter new'.

spike

In the noun sense 'a sharp-pointed piece of metal or wood' **spike** is a medieval word that probably derived from Dutch or German. The verb came later, in the early 17th century. To **spike someone's guns** is to thwart their plans. This expression refers to the practice of disabling cannons captured from the enemy. A spike was driven into the small hole through which the charge was ignited, making it impossible to fire the gun. To **spike someone's drink**, first recorded in the late 19th century, is based on the idea of making a drink 'sharper'.

spin

An Old English word that originally meant 'to draw out and twist fibre'. The expression to **spin a yarn**, 'to tell a long, far-fetched story', is nautical in origin. An important job on board ship was making and repairing ropes, a task which involved twisting together a number of long threads or 'yarns'. The image of this process and the reputation sailors had for telling tall tales of fabulous far-flung lands combined to produce the phrase we know today.

spin doctor

Tony Blair's Labour government in Britain, elected in 1997, gained a reputation for its use of **spin** and **spin doctors**, but **spin** meaning 'the presentation of information in a particular way, a slant' started in the USA. It was first recorded in 1977 in the *Washington Post*, with **spin doctor** following in 1984.

spinster

A **spinster** was originally a woman who spun cotton or wool, something that many unmarried women used to do at home to earn their living. The word was often added after the name of a woman to describe her occupation, and in time became the official description of an unmarried woman. Today it has a dated feel and alludes to a stereotypical figure of an older woman who is unmarried, childless and prim or repressed. The word could also once refer to another kind of spinner, a spider, and **spider** itself is descended from Old English *spinnan* 'to spin'.

spirit

Our word **spirit** is based on Latin *spiritus* 'breath or spirit', from *spirare* 'to breathe' – the ancient Romans believed that the human soul had 'breathed' into the body. The sense 'strong distilled alcoholic drink' comes from the use in alchemy of **spirit** to mean 'a liquid essence extracted from some substance'.

People sometimes say **the spirit is willing but the flesh is weak** when they have good intentions but yield to temptation and fail to live up to them. The source is the New Testament, where Jesus uses the phrase after finding his disciples asleep in the Garden of Gethsemane despite telling them that they should stay awake.

spit

The root of the Old English word **spit** imitated the sound of someone spitting out saliva from their mouth. When we notice that someone looks exactly like someone else we can say that they are **the spit of** or **the spitting image** of the other person. This last phrase is an altered form of an earlier version, **spit and image**, early examples of which, from the 1600s, describe a man as being so like another that he could have been spat out of the latter's mouth. Another explanation is based on the idea of a person apparently being formed, perhaps by witchcraft, from the spit of another, so great is the similarity between them.

Easier to explain is the expression **spit and sawdust**, used to describe an old-fashioned or unpretentious pub. This recalls the former practice of sprinkling the floor of the pub with a layer of sawdust, to soak up spillages in general and customers' spit in particular.

splendid

Early 17th-century examples of **splendid**, which comes ultimately from Latin *splendere* 'to shine brightly', describe a grand place or occasion. The phrase **in splendid isolation** was first used at the end of the 19th century to refer to the diplomatic and commercial non-involvement of Great Britain in Europe.

spoke

In the sense 'a bar or rod connecting the centre of a wheel to its edge', **spoke** is an Old English word, related to SPIKE. It appears in the slightly puzzling expression **put a spoke in someone's wheel**. This means 'to prevent someone from carrying out a plan', but since wheels are supposed to have spokes it does not appear to make a lot of sense. It is probably a mistranslation of Dutch *een spaak in 'twiel steeken*, 'to put a bar in the wheel' – the image that should come to mind is of a bar being stuck into a wheel to stop it turning properly.

spoof

An example of a word made up by a specific person, the English comedian Arthur Roberts (1852-1933). He invented a card game involving bluff, which he called **spoof**. The word subsequently came to be applied to a hoax or swindle, and to a parody.

spoon

In Old English a **spoon** was a chip of wood or a splinter – the 'eating utensil' sense came in the Middle Ages. The team that comes last in a competition can be said to **win the wooden spoon**. The original winner, back in the early 19th century, was the candidate coming last in the final examination in mathematics at Cambridge University. As a symbol of his 'wooden-headedness' or stupidity he would be presented with a wooden spoon.

Spooning is an old slang word meaning 'to behave in an amorous way, kiss and cuddle', first recorded in the 1830s and in vogue until the middle of the next century. It probably comes from the use of **spoon** to

mean 'a foolish person', which developed into **being spoons about** someone, or **having the spoons for** them – being infatuated with them.

spoonerism

A **spoonerism** is a verbal error in which you accidentally swap round the initial parts of two words, as in 'Our queer old dean' instead of 'Our dear old queen'. The term comes from the name of the Reverend William Archibald Spooner (1844-1930), an Oxford academic who was apparently prone to such slips of the tongue. The classic 'spoonerisms' associated with him were 'You have tasted your worm, you have hissed my mystery lectures, and you must leave by the first town drain', said to an idle student.

spring

An Old English word that originally referred to the source of a well or stream, the place where a flow of water rises naturally from the earth. People soon started using **spring** in the context of the first sign or beginning of something – expressions such as 'the spring of the day', 'the spring of the dawn' and 'the spring of the year' were commonly used from around 1380 to 1600. From the middle of the 16th century the last of these expressions became shortened to **spring** as the name of the first season of the year, between winter and summer. Before that this season of new growth had been known as **Lent**, a word now only used in a religious context to refer to the period of fasting and repentance between Ash Wednesday and Easter.

Someone who is **no spring chicken** is not as young as they used to be, a phrase recorded from the early years of the 20th century. Spring chickens were birds born in spring and eaten when they were about 10-15 weeks old.

The kind of **spring** that is a metal coil is also the same word. This meaning was suggested by the verb sense 'to come out or jump up suddenly'.

spruce

Prussia was a former kingdom that covered much of modern northeast Germany and Poland. Between the 14th and 17th centuries it was also known in English as both **Pruce** and **Spruce**, and these words could also be used to mean 'Prussian'. **Spruce** was in time used as the name of a type of fir tree, grown in Prussia. It was also used in the phrase **spruce leather**, a fashionable type of leather imported in the 16th century from Prussia and used especially for jerkins. It is probably from this that the sense 'neat or smart in dress or appearance' developed.

spud

Nowadays a **spud** is a potato, but before that it was what you used to dig it out of the ground. The informal 'potato' sense dates from the mid 19th century, but some centuries before that it was used in a succession of other senses, mainly referring to various implements such as a short dagger or knife, a type of spade and a digging fork. It was also late 17th-century slang for a short stocky person.

square

A word that comes via Old French from Latin *quadra* 'square'. The rather odd term **a square meal** is sometimes said to derive from the square wooden platters on which meals were served on board ship. More likely, though, is that (as with 'square deal' and 'fair and square') **square** simply suggests something that is 'honest', 'straightforward' or 'right', with the additional idea that it has been solidly or properly constructed. The word was used since the 17th century to mean 'honorable, upright', which gave us the square person who is old-fashioned or boringly conventional. From the 1940s in the USA, squares were people who did not appreciate modern jazz, preferring the regular rhythms of more traditional music.

To **square the circle** is to do something that is considered to be impossible. The phrase refers to the mathematical problem of constructing a square equal in area to a given circle, a problem which cannot be solved by purely geometrical means, though this has not stopped mathematicians from the ancient Greeks onwards from trying to solve the puzzle.

The use of **square up** in reference to a person about to fight comes from the typical posture adopted, with the shoulders back and the fists held out at right angles. It is first found in the 1820s.

squirrel

A **squirrel** is literally a 'shadow-tail', an appropriate description if you picture the animal holding its long bushy tail over its back like a sunshade. The Greeks called it *skiouros*, based on *skia* 'a shadow' and *oura* 'a tail', and the English name evolved from this.

stable

The French word *estable*, from which we get **stable**, could refer to a shelter for pigs as well as one for horses, and in English a stable originally housed not only horses but cattle, goats and other domestic animals. **Stable** meaning 'firmly fixed' is a quite different word, that goes back to Latin *stare* 'to stand'.

The saying **shut** (or **lock**) **the stable door after the horse has bolted** – take preventive measures too late, once the damage has already been done – dates back to medieval times, though until the late 19th century it specifically referred to horse-stealing and was used in the form **shut the stable door after the steed is stolen**. Here is an example from Robert Louis Stevenson's novel *Kidnapped* (1886): 'A guinea-piece . . . fell . . . into the sea . . . I now saw there must be a hole, and clapped my hand to the place in a great hurry. But this was to lock the stable door after the steed was stolen.' See also CONSTABLE.

stake

In the sense 'a thick pointed stick driven into the ground' **stake** is related to **stick**. The gambling sense might relate to the idea of an object being placed as a wager on a post or stake, though there is no definite evidence of the existence of this custom.

If you **stake a claim** you declare or assert your right to something. This expression originated in America at the time of the California gold rush of 1849. Prospectors would register their claim to a particular plot of land by marking out the boundary with wooden stakes that they drove into the ground, a process known as 'staking a claim'. Also American in origin is the phrase **pull up stakes**, meaning 'to

move or go to live elsewhere'. The stakes being referred to here are pegs or posts for securing a tent or making a fence around a temporary settlement.

stalactite

Stalactites hang down from the roof of a cave. The name comes from Greek *stalaktos* 'dropping or dripping'. Stalagmites rise up from the floor of a cave. Greek *stalagma* 'a drop or drip' is the source this time.

stale

Stale ale may not sound terribly appealing, but beer is what **stale** originally described, back in the Middle Ages. Not beer that has gone off, but beer that has been standing long enough for it to clear and perhaps improve in strength.

stamina

At the heart of the word **stamina** is the idea of threads, from Latin *stamen* meaning 'a thread of woven cloth'. The botanical use of **stamen** comes from the Roman naturalist Pliny applying it to the male reproductive parts of a particular kind of lily, which he thought resembled threads. *Stamina* was the plural form of the Latin word, and could be used to refer to the threads of people's lives spun by the Fates. When the word was adopted into English in the late 17th century it was initially in the sense 'the essentials or rudiments of something', thought of as being like the threads of cloth. It was not long before the notion of threads was extended to the idea of a person's life force and vigour.

standard

A **standard**, from Old French *estendre* 'to extend', was originally a flag raised on a pole as a rallying point for soldiers, and typically carrying the distinctive badge of a sovereign, leader, nation or city. The word appears first in English with reference to the Battle of the Standard in 1138, between the English and the Scots. The 'standard' in question was apparently the mast of a ship with flags at the top, mounted on a wagon brought on to the battlefield. In later use the idea of the royal flag or 'standard' came to represent a source of authority, the centre from which commands are issued. This led to its modern use in connection with the setting of a fixed scale of weights and measures, and indeed of any established level of quality or quantity.

star

The Latin word *stella* 'star', which gave us **star** and **stellar**, was related to the two Greek equivalents, *astēr* and *astron*, the source of words such as ASTERISK and **astronomy**. **Star** referred to the twinkling heavenly

object as early as AD 800, but did not apply to famous or talented entertainers until the beginning of the 19th century. Eventually a star was not big or glittering enough, and **superstar** was coined around 1925, followed by **megastar** in 1976.

The US flag is known as **the Stars and Stripes**. When first adopted by Congress in 1777 it contained 13 stripes and 13 stars, representing the 13 States of the Union. It now contains 13 stripes and 50 stars.

The science fiction film *Star Wars* was released in 1977. Three films were initially produced in the series, but in 1999 a 'prequel' called *The Phantom Menace* came out, which covered events that happened before the time of the first film. This was followed by two further episodes, making the original film the fourth in terms of chronology. See also HITCH.

starboard

The side of a ship or aircraft that is on the right side when you are facing forward is **starboard**. The word comes from Old English *stēorbord* 'rudder side', because early vessels were steered with a paddle over the right side. See also PORT.

starve

Nowadays **starve** means 'to be very hungry', but in Anglo-Saxon times it was even more serious than that, because it meant 'to die', especially die a lingering death from hunger, cold, disease or grief. People continued to use the word in this way for many centuries, and in northern English dialect **starve** can still mean 'to die of cold'. The origin of the word is probably an ancient Germanic base that meant 'to be rigid'. This rigid/dead connection is preserved in the modern slang use of STIFF to refer to a dead body.

stationer

In the Middle Ages **stationers** sold not writing materials but books. The word comes from medieval Latin *stationarius*, referring to a tradesman who had a shop or stall at a fixed location, as opposed to one who travelled around selling their wares. The ultimate source is Latin *statio* 'standing', which is also the root of **stationary** with an *a*, 'not moving'. In medieval England selling parchment, paper, pens and ink was a branch of the bookseller's trade, and in due course booksellers became known as stationers.

staunch

'Our Ship was staunch, and our Crew all in good Health', wrote Jonathan Swift in *Gulliver's Travels* in 1726. The adjective **staunch** has meant 'loyal' since the early 17th century, but Swift is using an older sense of the word, 'watertight'. You can see the connection, via the idea of restricting the flow of water, with the verb **staunch** (also spelt **stanch**) meaning 'to stop blood flowing from a wound'.

steal

An Old English word related to **stealth**. If someone **steals your thunder** they win attention for themselves by pre-empting your attempt to impress. The source of this expression is surprisingly literal. The English dramatist John Dennis (1657-1734) invented a new method of simulating the sound of thunder as a theatrical sound effect and used it in his unsuccessful play *Appius and Virginia*. Shortly after his play came to the end of its disappointingly short run he heard the same thunder effects used at a performance of Shakespeare's *Macbeth*. Dennis was understandably furious. 'Damn them!', he fumed, 'they will not let my play run, but they steal my thunder!'

Stealth originally meant 'theft', and the phrase **by stealth** meant 'by theft' in late medieval English. The modern meaning of **stealth** evolved by homing in on all the furtiveness and secrecy associated with stealing.

steam

In Old English **steam** was any kind of hot vapour or gas, and did not settle into the modern meaning until the 15th century. The phrase **let off steam,** meaning 'to get rid of pent-up energy or strong emotion', originated in the context of steam engines in the early 19th century. The literal meaning is 'to release excess steam from a steam engine through a valve', vital in preventing the engine from blowing up. The meaning which is familiar today arose in the 1830s in the alternative version **blow off steam**. Just as steam engines need to release excess pressure so people sometimes need to give vent to feelings of tension or stress. There is a related image in **have steam coming out of your ears**, meaning 'to be very angry'. Other phrases that recall the days of steam engines include **get up** (or **pick up**) **steam**, **run out of steam** and **under your own steam**.

stew

When **stew** entered the language in the Middle Ages it referred to a cauldron or large cooking pot, not to what was being cooked in it. The source was Old French *estuve*, probably based on Greek *tuphos* 'smoke or steam', which is also where the fevers **typhus** and **typhoid** come from. The verb 'to stew' originally referred to bathing in a hot bath or steam bath. It was not long before the idea of heating people in a bath had changed to heating food in an oven, specifically cooking a dish of meat and vegetables by simmering it slowly in a closed vessel.

stick

The two English words spelled **stick** are both Old English. The noun, 'a thin piece of wood', and the verb, meaning 'to push something pointed into' and 'to cling, adhere', are probably connected, with the basic idea being one of piercing or pricking.

If a person **comes to a sticky end** they meet a nasty death or other fate. The phrase is first found in a 1904 account of a US baseball game, and by 1916 had made its way to Britain. In his book about the First World War, *With the Flying Squadron*, Harold Rosher, who died in the conflict, wrote: 'I wish we could get out to the front . . . I would much rather come to a sticky end out there than here.' See also WICKET, WRONG.

steeplechase

A cross-country race on horses over hedges, walls and ditches was the original **steeplechase**. The term dates from the late 18th century and comes from the idea of using a distant church steeple to mark the finishing point of the race, which you have to reach by clearing all intervening obstacles.

stickler

A **stickler** is a person who insists on a certain quality or type of behaviour. The first recorded sense, in the 1530s, was 'referee or umpire', and the word was based on the now obsolete term *stickle*, meaning 'to be an umpire': 'There had been blood-shed, if I had not stickled', wrote the English dramatist William Cartwright in 1643.

stiff

An Old English word that seems to be related to **constipate**. As a noun meaning 'a dead body' it dates back to the USA of the 1850s. **The stiffs**, meaning the reserve team of a sports club, is a 1950s use. See also STARVE.

The **stiff upper lip**, a quality of uncomplaining stoicism so often thought of as a peculiarly British characteristic, is apparently North American in origin. The earliest recorded example is from the US writer John Neal's novel *The Down Easters* (1833): 'What's the use o' boo-hooin'? . . . Keep a stiff upper lip; no bones broke.' P.G. Wodehouse used the phrase in the title of one of his best-loved books about Bertie Wooster and his butler, *Stiff Upper Lip, Jeeves* (1963).

still

In the sense 'not moving' **still** is Old English. The kind of **still** used to make whisky and other spirits is a different word, from **distil**, which itself is based on Latin *stilla* 'a drop'.

The **still small voice** is the voice of a person's conscience. The phrase is biblical in origin. The prophet Elijah is hiding out in a cave but is told to come out and hear the word of God. A great wind comes first, then an earthquake, and finally a fire: 'And after the earthquake a fire; but the Lord was not in the fire: and after the fire a still small voice.' Going back at least to the 15th century is the expression **still waters run deep**, suggesting that a quiet or placid manner may conceal a passionate or subtle nature. A 1616 version is 'Where rivers run most stilly, they are the deepest.'

stitch

In Anglo-Saxon times **stitch** was used to describe any sharp stabbing pain rather than just a pain in the side caused by strenuous exercise. Shakespeare seems to have been the first to mention a stitch brought on by laughing. In *Twelfth Night* Maria invites her fellow conspirators to observe the lovelorn Malvolio, saying: 'If you . . . will laugh yourselves into stitches, follow me.'

The sewing sense of **stitch** arose in the Middle Ages. According to the 18th-century proverb, **a stitch in time saves nine**. In other words, if you sort out a problem immediately, it may save a lot of extra work later. There does not seem to be any particular significance in the choice of the number nine aside from its similarity in sound to the word 'time'.

Stitch up, meaning 'to frame or betray someone', is recorded only from the 1970s. It was probably suggested by the betrayal being as neat and conclusive as an invisible repair to an item of clothing.

stoic

Today a child who falls over but does not cry might be described as **stoic** – a long way from the original Stoics of ancient Athens. They were the followers of a school of philosophy which taught that wise men should live in harmony with Fate or Providence, and be indifferent to the ups and downs of life and to pleasure and pain. From there **stoic** or **stoical** came to mean 'enduring pain and hardship without complaint'. The word is from the *Stoa Poikilē*, or 'Painted Porch', where the school's founder, Zeno, taught. See also CYNIC, EPICURE.

stomach

The ultimate source of our word **stomach** is Greek *stomakhos* 'gullet', from *stoma* 'mouth'. A common saying is **the way to a man's heart is through his stomach**. The earliest expression of these sentiments is by John Adams, the second American President, in a letter he wrote in 1814: 'The shortest road to men's hearts is down their throats'. The US comedian Roseanne Barr turned this round to 'The quickest way to a man's heart is through his chest', and her British counterpart Jo Brand went one step further with 'The quickest way to a man's heart is through his chest with a breadknife'. See also NATION.

stone

An Old English word first found in the writings of Alfred the Great, the Anglo-Saxon king. The imperial unit of weight, recorded from the 14th century, is now equivalent to 14lb but formerly varied, and would originally have been just the weight of a particular rock used as a local measure.

To **cast** (or **throw**) **the first stone** is to be the first to accuse or criticise. The phrase comes from an incident recorded in St John's Gospel. A group of men preparing to stone to death a woman who had committed adultery were addressed by Jesus with the words: 'He that is without sin among you, let him first cast a stone at her.' Drug takers have been **stoned** since the 1950s, originally in the USA – the image is of someone so dazed they seem to have been hit by a large stone.

If you say that something is **set** (or **carved**) **in stone** you mean that it is fixed and unchangeable, often in the context of rules or decisions that cannot be changed. This expression refers to another biblical story, of Moses and the Ten Commandments. According to the Book of Genesis God wrote the Commandments on tablets of stone and handed them down to Moses on Mount Sinai. See also KILL, ROLL.

stool

In Anglo-Saxon times a **stool** was any kind of seat for one person, and in particular a throne. Among the other types of seat it came to refer to was one enclosing a chamber pot, and so a privy or lavatory. Then the word was transferred to the act of going to the toilet itself, which is how it ended up as a term for faeces. The Groom of the Stool (or, more commonly, Groom of the Stole) was formerly a high officer of the royal household, in medieval times responsible for the royal commode or privy.

Nowadays a stool is generally a three or four-legged seat without a back or arms. To **fall between two**

stools is to fail to take either of two satisfactory alternatives. This comes from the proverb **between two stools one falls to the ground**, which was first referred to in English by the medieval writer John Gower around 1390: 'Thou farest as he between two stools / That would sit and goes to ground.'

The first **stool pigeon** is often said to have been a pigeon fixed to a stool as a decoy for wildfowl, but in reality it probably had nothing to do with a small chair. It is more likely to come from the old term **stale**, from Old French *estale*, applied to a pigeon used to entice a hawk into a net. In the mid 19th century it came to be applied to a person employed by gamblers or criminals as a decoy, and later (on the other side of the law) to a police informer. See also NARK.

story

What is the story – or the history – of **story**? Both **storey** and **story** (and indeed HISTORY) come from Latin *historia* 'history, story'. A **story** was initially a historical account or representation, usually involving passages of bible history and legends of the saints. From the 1500s the word was used in connection with fictitious events for the entertainment of people. As for **storey**, which is essentially the same word, there may have originally been a reference to tiers of painted windows or sculptures used to decorate the front of a building, each one representing a historical subject. So each tier was a different 'story' or, once the spelling changed, 'storey'. Eventually the word came to refer to a level or floor of a building.

At some time in the 1930s or before, someone told a long, rambling anecdote about a dog with shaggy hair. It must have caught the public imagination, as ever since then any long rambling story or joke that is only amusing because it is absurdly inconsequential or pointless has been a **shaggy-dog story**.

straight

The word **straight** is the archaic past form of **stretch**, and so originally meant 'extended at full length'. The sense relating to an alcoholic drink, 'undiluted', is the American equivalent of NEAT and dates from the middle of the 19th century.

The straight and narrow is the honest and morally acceptable way of living. The earliest examples of this expression were in the longer version **the straight and narrow path (or way)**. It arose through a misunderstanding of the meaning of a word in this passage from the Gospel of Matthew: 'Because strait is the gate, and narrow is the way, which leadeth unto life, and few there be that find it'. **Strait** here simply means 'narrow', an old sense which only really

survives today in the noun meaning 'a narrow passage of water connecting two seas', as in the Straits of Gibraltar or the Menai Strait. The confusion probably came about because **crooked**, the opposite of **straight**, had long been used to mean 'dishonest'.

straw

An Old English word related to **strew** that shares an ancient ancestor with Latin *sternere* 'to lay flat'. Straws crop up in various common English expressions. The person who ends up being chosen to perform an unpleasant task can be said to **draw the short straw**, which is based on the idea of drawing lots by holding several straws of varying lengths with one end concealed in your hand and then inviting other members of the group to take one each.

In the absence of a lifebelt, a person in danger of drowning would try to grab hold of anything to keep afloat, the source of the old proverb **a drowning man will clutch at a straw**, recorded in various forms since the mid 16th century. Nowadays you are more likely to come across the abbreviated version **to clutch (or grasp) at straws**.

Another phrase drawn from an old proverb is **the last (or final) straw**, referring to a final minor difficulty or annoyance that, coming on top of a whole series of others, makes a situation unbearable. The full version is **it is the last straw that breaks the camel's back**. Earlier variations included **the last feather breaks the horse's back**, which dates back to the mid 17th century.

No one is really sure what **strawberries** have got to do with straw. One possible explanation is that a strawberry's 'runners' – the long stems that a strawberry plant throws out from the base of its main stem in all directions – reminded people of straw strewn on floors. Or perhaps the name of the fruit refers to the small seeds scattered over its surface, which resemble tiny pieces of straw or chaff.

street

A **street** is literally a road with a paved surface, based on Latin *strata via* 'paved way'. Some ancient Roman roads in Britain preserve this usage in their names, such as Watling Street (from Dover to Wroxeter) and Ermine Street (from London to Lincoln and York). The modern use, referring to a public road in a city, town or village that runs between lines of houses and buildings, goes back to Anglo-Saxon times. We have used the phrase **the man on the street** to refer to an ordinary person in contrast to an expert since the early 19th century. See also MAN, QUEER.

The words on the street

Slang has always been used to mark group identities and exclude the uninitiated. As soon as outsiders scale the wall new terms are needed, and this high turnover makes street slang one of the most vibrant forms of English.

Many items of slang are so short-lived that they are already old-fashioned when they appear in the latest dictionaries – for example, the positive, 'reversed' meanings of WICKED and BAD that were so popular in the 1980s and 1990s have been pushed aside in favour of fresh terms of approval like nang, sick and fly. Other slang expressions are surprisingly long-lived, though, with COOL going back to the late 19th century and groovy to the 1940s.

Slang itself is much older than that, and examples of underworld slang are recorded from the 16th century. Then it was known as cant or rogues' cant, from Latin *cantare* 'to sing' – it first meant 'singing', and came to mean 'the slang of a particular group' by way of the sense 'a whining way of speaking', as associated with beggars. It was the language of thieves or prigs, as they were sometimes known. A prig is now a respectable, moralistic person, but in the 16th-18th centuries a prig was a tinker, a thief or a dandy. Today's rogues have an array of new terms at their disposal, from shoulder-surfing, spying on someone using a cash dispenser to get their PIN or password, to phishing, impersonating a reputable company and sending fake emails asking for personal information. This respelling of fishing dates from around 1996.

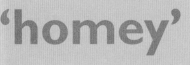

Teenagers may talk of hanging with their homies or friends. Homie or homey is short for homeboy or homegirl, a US and South African term recorded since the 1940s for an acquaintance from your own town or neighbourhood. Or they may be chilling (a rap term from the late 1970s) at their crib or home. In this sense crib dates from the early 19th century, when it was used among thieves as a term for a house they were set to burgle or 'crack'. It fell out of use in British English, but came back into the spotlight in the USA through *MTV Cribs*, a TV series featuring tours of celebrities' houses that was first shown in 2000. The word itself is Old English, and first meant 'a container for animal fodder, a manger'.

Black English is a significant influence on slang, much of which originates in the USA. Today's coinages from the streets of New York or Los Angeles are in the mouths of British youth within weeks, thanks to the internet and the worldwide popularity of rap culture. Rappers are behind one of the defining words of the late 1990s and early noughties, bling. The term, probably suggested either by the idea of light reflecting off a diamond or by the sound of jewellery clashing together, first appeared in a song by the US rapper B.G. ('Baby Gangsta') in 1999. From there it moved quickly into the mainstream to describe ostentatious jewellery and flashy clothes. Such has been the impact of the 'bling' phenomenon that black slang has been dubbed Blinglish.

Slang moves as quickly as fashion, and terms coined to describe the latest trends in clothes are often among the most colourful. What were once threads are now garms, short for 'garments'. There are even slang terms for underwear, such as chuddies or 'underpants', featured in the late 1990s TV comedy series *Goodness Gracious Me* and popular especially among British Asians. For women, the thing to avoid is the muffin top, the 'spare tyre' of flesh which protrudes between hipster trousers and a cropped top. Once the fashion choices are made and the result is BUFF or criss (a West Indian term derived from CRISP and meaning 'smart or fashionable'), then you may go out chirpsing or on the chirps (flirting) to find a new boo, meaning a girlfriend or boyfriend. This US term may be an alteration of French *beau* 'boyfriend, male admirer'. You would certainly hope not to end up with a minger or unattractive person, a word popular since the mid 1990s that comes from Scots ming 'excrement', as does minging, meaning 'very bad' or 'foul-smelling'.

See also BOOTY, CHAV, FABULOUS, GROOVE.

strict

People first used **strict** to mean 'restricted in space or extent'. The 17th-century philosopher Richard Burthogge wrote in 1675: 'I am apt to think that Hell is of a Vast Extent, and that the bounds and limits of it, are not so strict and narrow, as the most imagine.' Other early meanings included 'tight' (as in 'a strict embrace') and 'stretched taut' (as in 'rain falling on the strict canvas of the tents'), before the meaning 'imposing severe discipline' developed in the late 16th century. The source is Latin *strictus*, based on *stringere* 'to tighten or draw tight'.

strike

In Anglo-Saxon times to **strike** was 'to go or flow' or 'to rub lightly', close in meaning to the related word **stroke**. By the Middle Ages striking had become more forceful, and the word was being used in the familiar sense 'to deliver a blow'. To **strike while the iron is hot** is to make use of an opportunity immediately, a metaphor from the blacksmith's forge, where iron can only be hammered into shape while it is hot. The proverb is quoted by Geoffrey Chaucer in 1386 and used in a slightly modified form by Shakespeare in *Henry VI Part 3*: 'Strike now, or else the iron cools.'

The sort of **strike** that involves stopping work as a protest was first heard of in 1810, but the verb, meaning 'to go on strike', was earlier. This quote from the *Annual Register* of 1768 could be the source of the term:

> A body of sailors . . . proceeded . . . to Sunderland . . . and at the cross there read a paper, setting forth their grievances . . . After this they went on board the several ships in that harbour, and struck [lowered] their yards [spars], in order to prevent them from proceeding to sea.

In the 1980s legislation was passed in some states of the USA known as the **three strikes** law or rule. It makes an offender's third felony punishable by life imprisonment or other severe sentence. The term comes from baseball – if a batter has three 'strikes', or unsuccessful attempts to hit a pitched ball, they 'strike out' or are out.

string

The root of the Old English word **string** is related to **strong**, and in early use it could refer to a rope or cord of any thickness. If you **have many strings to your bow** you have a wide range of resources that you can make use of, just as an archer ought to have a spare string or two. A related expression is **have another** (or **a second**) **string to your bow**, meaning 'to have an alternative resource you can make use of'.

A different kind of string lies behind the expression **have someone on a string**, meaning 'to have someone under your control or influence'. The idea behind this 16th-century phrase is of a puppeteer manipulating a puppet by its strings. An opportunity or offer with **no strings attached** has no special conditions or restrictions that apply. This is a relatively recent expression, first used in the 1950s, though it is based on an earlier US use of **string** meaning 'a limitation or condition'.

stroll

'You had a foolish itch to be an actor,/ And may stroll where you please', wrote Philip Massinger in his play *The Picture* (1629). If you **strolled** in the early 17th century you were wandering from place to place, especially as a vagrant, a use now obsolete, although the phrases 'strolling player' and 'strolling actor' are still used. The sense of walking in a leisurely way only appeared towards the end of the 17th century. **Stroll** may come from a German word for 'a vagabond'.

stub

A **stub** was originally a tree stump. From this developed the general idea of a portion being left behind when something has been removed, such as a counterfoil in a chequebook or a cigarette butt. The verb was initially used in the sense 'to dig up a plant by the roots'. The meaning 'to accidentally strike', as in 'I stubbed my toe', was first used in the USA in the mid 19th century.

Stubborn may be based on **stub**, though this is by no means certain. It is true that a **stub** or tree stump is difficult to move, though, so there may be a connection. **Stubborn** originally meant 'untameable or ruthless' before the modern meaning, 'obstinate', emerged.

stuff

The word **stuff** may be vague now, but it started out with a more precise meaning in reference to material for making clothes. It is a medieval shortening of Old French *estoffe* 'material or furniture', which is related to *estoffer* 'to equip, furnish', the source of the verb **stuff**.

Do your stuff is an older phrase than you might think, first recorded in 1663 in the journal of George Fox, founder of the Quakers: 'A while after, when the priest had done his stuff, they came to the friends again.' **Stuff and nonsense**, first found in *Tom Jones* (1749) by Henry Fielding, is really 'nonsense and nonsense' – **stuff** is used in the 16th-century sense 'nonsense, rubbish'.

stump

One sense of **stump** refers to part of a limb remaining after an amputation, and this was the original meaning of the noun. The verb was initially 'to stumble over an obstacle', especially over a tree stump. Its current meaning, 'to baffle', was first used in American English in the early 19th century and probably arose from the idea of coming across stumps in ploughing which obstruct the progress of the plough.

The Australian phrase **beyond the black stump** means 'beyond the limits of settled, and therefore civilised, life'. It comes from the custom of using a fire-blackened stump of wood as a marker when giving directions to travellers.

To be **on the stump** is to go about the country making political speeches or canvassing, a usage that originated in rural America in the late 18th century, when a person making a speech would often use the stump of a felled tree as an impromptu platform. The Democratic politician Adlai Stevenson said of Richard Nixon that he was 'the kind of politician who would cut down a redwood tree, and then mount the stump and make a speech on conservation'.

To **stump up** a tree is to dig it up by the roots. This gives the meaning 'to pay up, especially reluctantly', from the image of digging deep into your pocket to find the necessary cash.

stupid

Our word **stupid** comes from French *stupide* or Latin *stupidus*, from *stupere* 'to be amazed or stunned', also the source of **stupor**. The original 16th-century sense suggested being dulled through shock. The poet John Dryden often used the word in the sense 'stunned': 'Men, Boys, and Women stupid with Surprise,/ Where ere she passes, fix their wond'ring Eyes.' The familiar 'slow-witted, foolish' sense dates from a similar period and eventually became established as the main meaning.

sturdy

'Reckless, violent' and 'rebellious, obstinate' were the early meanings of **sturdy**, which comes from Old French *esturdi* 'stunned or dazed'. This may be based on Latin *turdus* 'a thrush', a bird that used to be associated with drunkenness, probably because it was once common to see thrushes tottering around unsteadily after eating partly fermented grapes – there is a French expression *soûl comme une grive*, which means 'drunk as a thrush'.

stymie

Life for **stymie** began in golf, to describe the situation on the green where one player's ball lay between another's ball and the hole. In 1951 the rules were changed so that in these circumstances a player was allowed to pick up an obstructing ball and mark its position. In current usage to be **stymied** is to be hindered or thwarted. No one knows the origin of the word for certain, but it may be related to the Scottish word **stymie** for a person who does not see well.

sublime

Originally **sublime** meant 'dignified or aloof' – the source is Latin *sublimis* 'in a high position, lofty', probably from *sub-* 'up to' and *limen* 'threshold or lintel'. The modern sense of 'outstandingly beautiful or grand' arose in the 17th century.

The expression **from the sublime to the ridiculous** is a shortening of the saying **from the sublime to the ridiculous is only a step**, a remark attributed to Napoleon Bonaparte, following the retreat from Moscow in 1812. Napoleon was not the first to express such an idea, though. The English political writer Thomas Paine wrote in *The Age of Reason* (1794): 'The sublime and the ridiculous are often so nearly related, that it is difficult to class them separately. One step above the sublime, makes the ridiculous; and one step above the ridiculous, makes the sublime again.' See also NATION.

From the sublime to the ridiculous is only a step.

sucker

For many centuries a **sucker** was a young mammal before it was weaned, or a baby feeding at its mother's breast. The notion of a naïve and innocent baby led in the 19th century to that of a gullible person or an easy victim. See also EVEN.

suffer

The root of **suffer** is Latin *sufferre*, from *sub-* 'from below' and *ferre* 'to bear'. As well as 'to undergo or endure', it can mean 'to tolerate', and this is the sense you are using when you say that someone

Napoleon Bonaparte

323

does not suffer fools gladly. In other words, they are not patient or tolerant towards people they regard as incompetent or foolish. The expression is biblical, from the second Epistle to the Corinthians: 'For ye suffer fools gladly, seeing ye yourselves are wise.'

sullen

To be **sullen** originally related to the idea of being on your own. The source is Old French *sulein*, from *sol* 'sole, alone', which came ultimately from Latin *solus* 'alone'. Early meanings were 'single', 'solitary' and 'unusual'. There is obviously a link between being solitary and being averse to company or unsociable, and such associations led in the late 14th century to a shift in sense as the word came to describe someone who is silently gloomy, resentful and moody.

sun

An Old English word whose root was related to the Latin and Greek words for sun, *sol* and *hēlios*. People say **the sun is over the yardarm** when they think that the time of day has been reached when it is socially acceptable to drink alcohol. This is an old nautical expression which goes back to the late 19th century. A yardarm is the end section of a yard, a thick tapering pole slung across a ship's mast for a sail to hang from. At certain times of year the sun rises far enough up the sky to show above the topmost yardarm. In summer in the north Atlantic, where the phrase seems to have originated, this would have been at about 11am, which was the time of the first rum issue of the day – not 6pm in the evening, as is often thought. The earliest known example of the phrase comes from a series of travel articles by Rudyard Kipling, published under the title *From Sea to Sea* (1899): 'The American does not drink at meals as a sensible man should . . . Also he has no decent notions about the sun being over the yard-arm or below the horizon.'

A **sundowner** is a different matter. In colonial days, especially in South Africa, it was a drink taken at sunset, whereas in Australia it was a tramp who arrived at a sheep station around sundown and pretended to be seeking work, to get food and a night's lodging.

The phrase **there is nothing new under the sun** is biblical, from the Book of Ecclesiastes: 'The thing that hath been, it is that which shall be; and that which is done is that which shall be done: and there is no new thing under the sun.'

People have only **sunbathed** since the 1940s – before that the usual term was **sunbath** or, in Australia and New Zealand, **sunbake**. In ancient times a **sun worshipper** literally worshipped the sun: the meaning 'keen sunbather' began in the 1960s. See also SON.

sundae

The name for the ice-cream dessert, originating in the USA at the end of the 19th century, could be an alteration of **Sunday**. The reason for this is not certain, but it may be because the dish was made with ice cream left over from Sunday and sold cheaply on the Monday, or because it was sold only on Sundays to get round Sunday legislation. It may be that the spelling was changed out of deference to religious people's feelings about the word Sunday.

superb

The first things described as **superb** were buildings and monuments – grand, majestic and nobly proportioned ones. Later the word could describe a proud or haughty person, as in John Aubrey's 1697 assessment of William Oughtred, the English mathematician and inventor of the slide rule: 'Before he died he burned a world of papers, and said that the world was not worthy of them; he was so superb.' From the early 18th century people started using **superb** in the sense 'very fine, excellent'. It comes from Latin *superbus* 'proud, magnificent'.

supercilious

A **supercilious** person has an air of contemptuous superiority. One way they might show this is by raising their eyebrows in disdain – a clue to the word's origin. *Supercilium*, the Latin source of the English word, means 'eyebrow'.

superstition

The Latin word *superstitio* comes from *super-* 'over' and *stare* 'to stand', with the idea of 'standing over' something in amazement or awe. By the time **superstition** first appeared in English at the beginning of the 15th century it referred to an irrational religious belief based on fear or ignorance or to a religious belief considered false or pagan. The more general 'irrational or unfounded belief' sense is first recorded in the 1790s.

surgeon

The key thing about **surgeons** for word history is that they work with their hands, using manual skill to cure or treat people rather than giving them drugs. **Surgeon** is a shortening of Old French *serurgian*, which came via Latin *chirurgia* from Greek *kheirourgia* 'handiwork', from *kheir* 'hand' and *ergon* 'work'.

surprise

From the 15th century a **surprise** was a sudden unexpected attack or seizure of a place. You could also use the word to talk about simply taking a place by force, whether unexpected or not, as in 'the surprise of Troy', even after a siege of ten years. Over time the suggestion of force faded away and the sense of something being unexpected came to the fore. The source was medieval Latin *superprehendere* 'to seize'.

survive

Gloria Gaynor's song 'I Will Survive' has been a mainstay of club singers and karaoke performers since its release in 1979. The word itself has survived since the 15th century after entering English via Old French from Latin *supervivere*, based on *vivere* 'to live', as in **revive**, **vivacious** and **vivid**.

According to Charles Darwin's theory of evolution, those animals and plants which tend to survive and produce more offspring are the ones best adapted to their environment, while those less well adapted become extinct. The idea is summed up in the phrase **the survival of the fittest**, which was coined by the English philosopher and sociologist Herbert Spencer in *Principles of Biology* (1865). Darwin himself had originally used the term **natural selection**, but approved of Spencer's version. Beyond its technical use the phrase is often used loosely to suggest that the strongest or most ruthless will succeed at the expense of others, though this is a distortion of the original Darwinian notion.

swagger

A bulging bag is the link between **swagger** and **swag**. This is what **swag** first meant, and it later led to the word being used as a verb 'to make something sway or sag'. **Swagger** appears to have developed from this, expressing the idea of walking or behaving arrogantly or self-importantly. By the late 18th century the 'bulging bag' meaning of **swag** was used for a thief's booty. It also came to refer to a bundle of belongings carried by a traveller in the Australian bush.

swallow

A **swallow** is popularly regarded as a sign of summer. According to the proverb, though, **one swallow does not make a summer** – a single fortunate event does not mean that what follows will also be good. The proverb is recorded from the 16th century: 'It is not one swallow that bringeth in summer. It is not one good quality that maketh a man good.' Charles Dickens has

an expanded version in *Martin Chuzzlewit* (1844): 'One foul wind no more makes a winter, than one swallow makes a summer.' The bird's name and the verb meaning 'to allow food or drink to pass down the throat' are unrelated, though both are Old English.

swan

The bird's name and the verb **swan**, meaning 'to go about in a casual or ostentatious way', are the same word. The bird is Old English, while the verb originated as military slang as recently as the 1940s, referring to the free movement of armoured vehicles.

A **swansong** or final public performance or work is based on German *Schwanengesang*, which refers to a song resembling the one that, according to the old legend, a dying swan is supposed to sing just before its death. The legend is also behind the long association of bards and poets with swans, hence Shakespeare's title **the Swan of Avon**.

swashbuckler

Nowadays a **swashbuckler** is a film in period costume full of adventure and excitement and typically featuring thrilling sword fights. The term comes from the old word **swash**, meaning 'to make a noise like swords clashing or of a sword beating a shield' or 'to swagger about', and **buckler** 'a small round shield'. So a **swashbuckler** was literally someone who made a noise by striking his own or his opponent's shield with his sword. In the 16th century it was initially a term for a swaggering and noisy ruffian.

swear

The Old English word **swear** first meant 'to make a solemn declaration'. The use of **swear** in connection with bad language came later, around the 15th century, as an extension of the idea of using a sacred name in an oath. Someone who swears a lot can be said to **swear like a trooper**. A trooper was originally a private soldier in a cavalry unit. By the 18th century these soldiers had developed a terrible reputation for coarse behaviour and bad language. In his novel *Pamela* (1739-40), Samuel Richardson wrote: 'She curses and storms at me like a Trooper.'

sweet

A word that already meant 'having the pleasant taste of sugar or honey' in Anglo-Saxon times, though the

surly

Before people were **surly** they were *sirly* – a clue to its early meaning. In medieval times *sirly* meant 'in the manner of a Sir' or lord, and **surly** was originally used in the sense 'lordly, haughty, arrogant'. The 'bad-tempered and unfriendly' meaning emerged late in the 16th century.

'dessert' and 'confectionery' senses only date from the 19th century. The slang use **sweet on**, 'infatuated with', dates from the mid 18th century, while the meaning 'fine, good' is Australian, from the 1890s.

The phrase **sweetness and light** was first used by Jonathan Swift in *The Battle of the Books* (1704). Both are produced by bees: 'Instead of dirt and poison, we have rather chosen to fill our hives with honey and wax, thus furnishing mankind with the two noblest things, which are sweetness and light.' Later the phrase was taken up by Matthew Arnold in *Culture and Anarchy* (1869), where he used it with aesthetic and moral reference: 'The pursuit of perfection, then, is the pursuit of sweetness and light.'

swim

The Old English epic poem *Beowulf*, probably written in the 8th century, is the first recorded source of **swim**. To **sink or swim**, 'to fail or succeed entirely by your own efforts', refers to the ducking of a woman suspected of witchcraft. It was not an attractive choice – either the woman sank and was drowned or she floated on the surface of the water and was therefore proven to be a witch. **In the swim**, meaning 'in tune with the fashion', first appeared in the late 19th century.

swing

Our word **swing** meant both 'to beat or whip' and 'to rush, to fling yourself' in Old English. The 'playground swing' sense of the noun dates from the late 17th century. People sometimes mention **swings and roundabouts** to suggest that the disadvantages or losses in one quarter are balanced by advantages or gains in another. This comes from the saying **what you lose on the swings you gain on the roundabouts**, a metaphor not from the playground but from the fairground. See also feature on NAUTICAL WORDS.

Swing is an easy flowing but vigorous rhythm, especially in jazz, and is also the name of the sort of big-band music played by people such as Glenn Miller and popular in the 1930s and 1940s. 'It don't mean a thing / If it ain't got that swing' is from the song 'It Don't Mean a Thing' (1932), by Duke Ellington and Irving Mills.

In the 1930s a **swinger** was a jazz musician who played with 'swing'. The 1960s saw the swinger become a lively, fashionable person, and also someone who was into partner-swapping or group sex – known as **swinging**.

sword

As with SWIM, Beowulf gives us the first example of **sword**. The notion of devoting resources to peaceful rather than aggressive or warlike ends is sometimes expressed as **beating** (or **turning**) **swords into ploughshares**, a reference to the biblical image of God's peaceful rule: 'they shall beat their swords into ploughshares, and their spears into pruning hooks' (Book of Isaiah). Also biblical in origin is the expression **he who lives by the sword dies by the sword** – those people who commit violent acts must expect to suffer violence themselves. In the account of the Gospel of Matthew, when the men came to arrest Jesus in the Garden of Gethsemane one of his disciples drew his sword and cut off the ear of 'the servant of the high priest', earning a rebuke from Jesus: 'All they that take the sword shall perish with the sword.' See also THREAD.

swot

A 19th-century variation of **sweat** that started life as army slang. **Swot** was first 'studying, school or college work', and referred especially to mathematics. This led to its use to describe someone who studies hard or excessively.

sweet Fanny Adams

Fanny Adams was real, the victim of a brutal murder of 1867, her body mutilated and cut up by the killer. By the end of the century Royal Navy sailors were using her name, with gruesome black humour, as slang for a type of tinned meat or stew. The current meaning, 'absolutely nothing at all', arose in the early 20th century.

sycophant

This is a story of figs and flattery. The Greek word *sukophantēs* meant 'informer'. It was based on *sukon* 'fig' (also the root of **sycamore**) and *phainein* 'to show', and so literally meant 'a person who shows the fig'. Some people have suggested that this related to the practice of informing against people who illegally exported figs from ancient Athens, as recorded by the Greek biographer Plutarch. Another possible explanation is that the term referred to an obscene gesture known as 'showing (or making) the fig'. When **sycophant** entered the English language in the 1530s it meant 'an informer', and soon also 'a person who tells tales or spreads malicious reports about someone'. The modern sense of 'a servile flatterer' probably comes from the notion that you can ingratiate yourself with someone in authority either by slandering others or by flattering the person in question.

T

One way of saying that something is an exact fit is to say that it fits **To a t** (or **to a tee**). Various ideas as to what the **T** stands range from a golfer's tee to a builder's T-square, but none is totally convincing. It may have originated from the action of completing a letter T with the horizontal stroke, as in **dot the i's and cross the t's**, meaning 'to make sure all the details are correct'. The problem with all these explanations is that this 17th-century expression is found earlier than the proposed sources. One historically possible suggestion is that it is a shortened version of the early 17th-century phrase **to a tittle**, which has the same meaning as **to a T**. A **tittle** was a small stroke in writing or printing, such as the crossbar of a *T* or the dot of an *i*, which fits the idea perfectly. See also JOT.

The **T-shirt** is so called because it is shaped like a T when spread out flat. The term was first recorded in 1920.

tabby

A striped **tabby** cat is said to get its name from a kind of silk taffeta which was originally striped, although later the word was used for silk with a watered finish. The word goes back to the name of the quarter of the Iraq capital Baghdad where the material was manufactured, al-'Attābiyya.

table

The first **table** had no legs. The earliest examples of the word, which came into English around AD 900 from Latin *tabula*, referred to a flat board, slab or surface, and it did not grow legs until around 1300. One of the first meanings was the board used for games such as chess, draughts or backgammon – in the case of backgammon the plural **tables** was used, because its board has two folding halves. Although this meaning had died out by the mid 18th century it is preserved in the expression **turn the tables**, which arose from the common practice of turning the board round between games so that a player had to play from what had previously been their opponent's position. The idea of a reversal of positions is illustrated in this example from *Glamour* magazine: 'Penélope turned the tables on the paparazzi and took their photograph from the red carpet.' See also CARPET.

taboo

There are not many words in English which come from Tongan, the Polynesian language spoken in the South Pacific country of Tonga, but **taboo** is one of them. It was introduced into English by the explorer Captain James Cook in 1777 in the narrative of his voyages. He wrote: 'Not one of them would sit down, or eat a bit of any thing . . . they were all *taboo*.' He went on to explain that the word was generally used to mean 'forbidden'. See also TATTOO.

tail

The base of the Old English word **tail** meant 'hair'. The opposite side of a coin to **heads** has been **tails** since the 1680s or thereabouts – it is so called because it is the 'reverse' or 'rear' of the main or front side.

A dog's tail is a good indicator of its mood, and this has given us various expressions. Someone who appears ashamed or dejected has been described since the Middle Ages as having their **tail between their legs**. Alternatively, someone **with their tail up** is in a confident or cheerful mood. Sometimes the usual roles in an organisation are reversed, and a less important part dictates what is going to happen. When that occurs, someone may comment that **the tail is wagging the dog**.

tailor

A **tailor**'s work is indicated in the source of the word, which goes back to Latin *taliare* 'to cut'. The title of John Le Carré's 1974 spy novel *Tinker, Tailor, Soldier, Spy* comes from a child's traditional fortune-telling rhyme for counting out objects such as cherry stones or flower petals, 'Tinker, Tailor, Soldier, Sailor, Rich man, Poor man, Beggarman, Thief'.

talent

This Old English word came ultimately from Greek *talanton*, and referred originally to a unit of weight used by such ancient peoples as the Babylonians,

Assyrians, Romans and Greeks. The use of **talent** to mean 'natural aptitude or skill' comes from the biblical **parable of the talents** in the Gospel of Matthew. In this story a master gives one, two and ten talents of silver to each of three servants. Two of them use their talents well and double the value of what they have been given, but the third buries his coin and fails to benefit from it.

Talent scouts and **talent shows** have searched for new talent since the 1930s, and in recent times shows such as *The X Factor* have become an important part of reality television. Another kind of talent is the local **talent**, or the good-looking people of an area – an expression used since the 1940s, and probably originating among British servicemen.

talisman

You will often hear a sports commentator refer to a team's key player, who regularly produces match-winning performances that inspire the whole team, as their **talisman**. The term refers to an object that is thought to have magic powers and to bring good fortune, a lucky charm. The first reference to a **talisman** in English is found in the 17th century. It is based on an Arabic word, which in turn goes back ultimately to Greek *telesma* 'completion, religious rite'.

talk

A medieval word from the same root as **tale** and TELL. A person who talks incessantly is sometimes said to be able to **talk the hind leg off a donkey.** Versions of this expression go back to the 19th century but the animal may vary – *Cobbett's Weekly Political Register* for 1808 has 'talking a horse's hind leg off', and in 1879 the novelist Anthony Trollope mentioned **talk the hind legs off a dog** as an Australian variant.

The rock band Talking Heads, formed in 1974, took their name from the term **talking head** for a television reporter who is viewed in close-up addressing the camera, first recorded in 1968. Also American, and from slightly earlier in the 1960s, is **talk show**, a programme in which the presenter talks informally to celebrities.

talk nineteen to the dozen

Another way of saying that someone chatters constantly is to accuse them of **talking nineteen to the dozen**. Presumably the idea is that the person is talking so quickly that they get in 19 words in the time it would take someone else to say a dozen. Nobody has the slightest clue why 19 is the traditional number, but the phrase has been with us ever since it was first written down in the late 18th century.

tall

Some words have undergone remarkable changes in meaning over the centuries. One such word is **tall**. In medieval times it was used in such senses as 'quick', 'handsome' and 'good at fighting', as in Sir Walter Scott's reference to 'the "tall men", or champions, of Wales'. Only in the 16th century did the sense 'of more than average height' appear.

A privileged or distinguished person may be referred to as **a tall poppy**. This goes back to a story about the Roman tyrant Tarquin, who is said to have struck off the heads of a row of poppies in a gruesomely graphic demonstration of how the important men of a captured city should be treated. Since the early 1980s, originally in Australia, the expression **tall poppy syndrome** has been used for the tendency to criticise people who have become rich, famous or socially prominent.

tally

A **tally** has always been a record of an amount or score, but its nature has changed since the Middle Ages. Originally it was a stick that was cut with notches to indicate the amount of a debt, and then split lengthways so that both parties had a record of the agreement. The word goes back to Latin *talea* 'twig'.

tamper

An alteration of TEMPER whose origin may lie in the idea of working with or 'tempering' clay. **Tamper** was first used in the mid 16th century to mean 'to busy yourself for a particular purpose', but quickly developed the negative associations of meddling or interfering damagingly with something.

tan

Today a **tan** is mainly the brown colour that the skin acquires after exposure to the sun, but this dates only to the middle of the 18th century. As a term for converting skin or hide into leather the word goes back to medieval times. It probably comes directly from Latin *tannare*, but may go back to a Celtic word for an oak tree. This reflects the process of **tanning**, whereby the crushed bark of an oak was steeped in water in which skins and hides were then immersed. The related word **tawny**, which also refers to the golden-brown colour given to tanned leather, is also medieval.

tandem

In Latin *tandem* means 'after a long time' or 'at length'. It came into English in the late 18th century as a slang term for a carriage drawn by two horses harnessed one behind the other – a 'long' set-up which inspired a pun on 'at length'. A tandem is now most familiar as a bicycle for two riders, one behind the other – the 'bicycle built for two' of the music-hall song 'Daisy, Daisy'. The expression **in tandem** is still used today to mean 'one behind another', but is more common in the sense 'together as a team'.

tang

In medieval times a **tang** was the forked tongue of a snake, which was believed to be its 'sting'. The word goes back to Old Norse *tangi* 'the point of a knife'. The idea of a piercing point lies behind the modern sense of 'a penetrating flavour'.

tangle

Scandinavia is probably the origin of **tangle**, which is probably related to Swedish *taggla* 'to disarrange'. A **tangled web** is a complex and difficult situation. The expression comes directly from Sir Walter Scott's epic poem *Marmion* (1808): 'Oh what a tangled web we weave / When first we practise to deceive.' The 20th-century American humorist Ogden Nash was one of many to pick up the phrase in his observation on parenthood, 'Oh, what a tangled web do parents weave / When they think their children are naïve.'

tango

In Latin *tango* means 'I touch', which would seem to be an appropriate origin for the sensual South American dance the **tango**, but the word has quite a different origin. It is from Latin American Spanish, and is perhaps ultimately of African origin. **It takes two to tango** has become a modern-day proverb meaning 'both parties involved in a situation are equally responsible for it'. It started life as the title of a song written in 1952 by Al Hoffman and Dick Manning.

tank

You cannot get much more ordinary than a **tank** of water, but the word has exotic origins. In 17th-century English **tank** was the name given to a pool in India, going back to Sanskrit *tadāga* 'pond' and probably also influenced by the Portuguese word for 'pond', *tangue*.

In 1915 **tank** was used as a secret code word for the armoured military vehicles that were first being made. A *Times* column of September 1916 remarked: 'The name has the evident official advantage of being quite undescriptive.' A sleeveless **tank top** is not so called because it was worn by the driver of a tank, but because it resembles the top part of a one-piece swimsuit known as a **tank suit**, worn in 'swimming tanks' or swimming pools.

A drunk person has been **tanked up** since the 1890s. The comparison is with a vehicle filled with water or fuel from a tank.

tantalise

In Greek mythology Tantalus was a king of Lydia (modern-day Turkey) who killed his son Pelops. His punishment was to be forced to stand for eternity up to his chin in water which receded whenever he tried to drink it and under branches of fruit that drew back when he tried to reach them. **Tantalise**, which has been part of English since the 16th century, is based on his name. The same story is reflected in **tantalus**, a stand in which decanters of whisky, brandy and other spirits are locked out of reach but remain visible.

tap

A **tap** was originally a stopper for a cask. It controlled the flow of liquid, so the same word came to be used for the fitting which controlled the flow of water into a bath. Drink from a cask that was ready for immediate consumption was **on tap**. From the 1860s **tap** began to be used in reference to listening in secretly to a telegraph and then a telephone, from the idea of 'siphoning off' information. **Tap** in the sense of 'strike lightly' is a completely different word, which probably represents an imitation of the action in its sound.

taper

In Anglo-Saxon times a **taper** was a wax candle. The name comes, with a change of *p* to *t*, from the Latin word *papyrus*, because the pith of the papyrus plant was used for candle wicks. The verb was first used in the 16th century to describe the action of rising like a flame, and this picture led to the further idea of something 'tapering away' from a broad base to a narrow point.

tar

Tar is a thick flammable liquid distilled from wood or coal, and the Old English word **tar** may ultimately be related to **tree**. **Tar** or **Jack tar** has been a name for a sailor since the 17th century. It is perhaps an abbreviation of **tarpaulin**, which was also a nickname for a sailor – as well as being a waterproof cloth of tarred canvas, a tarpaulin was a kind of hat worn by sailors.

In medieval times an application of tar was one way of preventing infection. The expression **tar with the**

same brush comes originally from the practice of shepherds using tar to cover any wounds suffered by their sheep, to prevent infection.

To **tar and feather** someone was to smear them with tar and them cover them with feathers as a punishment. The practice was introduced into Britain in 1198, when Richard I decreed that it should be the punishment for members of the navy found guilty of theft. Since then it has sometimes been inflicted by a mob on an unpopular individual, notably against customs officials in the War of American Independence (1775-83), and by the IRA against people suspected of collaborating with the British.

tarantula

The Italian seaport of Taranto gave its name to the **tarantula**, a large black spider found in southern Europe. Its bite was formerly thought to cause **tarantism**, a psychological illness marked by an extreme impulse to dance, which affected many people in Italy from the 15th to the 17th century. The rapid whirling **tarantella** dance gets its name from the same source, as it was believed to be a cure for tarantism, with people dancing the tarantella until exhausted.

tarnish

Silver that is not polished will **tarnish**, losing its lustre. The word goes back to French *terne* 'dark, dull'. It has been part of the language since medieval times and the metaphorical use, 'to make less valuable or respected', has been established since the 17th century. In 1805, on the eve of the Battle of Trafalgar, Lord Nelson prayed that God might grant them 'a great and glorious victory; and may no misconduct in anyone tarnish it'.

tart

Today a **tart** is likely to be filled with jam or fruit, but in medieval times it was a savoury pie. In mid 19th-century slang it was an affectionate word for a woman (perhaps as an abbreviation of **sweetheart**), but by the end of the century it was being applied disparagingly to a prostitute or promiscuous woman. **Tart up**, 'to dress up ostentatiously', came from this use in the 1930s.

Tart meaning 'sharp to the taste', also found in medieval English, is a different word. It goes back to Old English and originally meant 'harsh, severe', especially in reference to punishment.

tattoo

The military **tattoo** sounded by a drum or bugle to recall soldiers to their quarters in the evening was originally written **tap-too** and dates from the 17th

Two warriors from the Polynesian Marquesas Islands show off their tattoos.

century. It comes from Dutch *doe den tap toe*, which meant literally 'close the tap'. The tap was the TAP of a cask, whose closure signalled that the time for drinking was over and soldiers should go home. **Tattoo** as a word for an indelible design made on the skin is a quite different word, which came into English in the 18th century from the Polynesian languages of the Pacific Islands – sailors and explorers such as Captain James Cook, whose journals are the first to record the word, observed the way that the Polynesians decorated their skin. See also TABOO.

tawdry

When we describe something as **tawdry** we are using a word with a colourful history. It was originally short for **tawdry lace**, a fine silk lace or ribbon worn as a necklace in the 16th and 17th centuries, a contraction of the original term **St Audrey's lace**. Audrey was a form of Etheldreda, name of the 7th-century patron saint of Ely, who was said to have worn many showy necklaces in her youth. When she became terminally ill with a throat tumour she saw her illness as retribution for her vanity. Tawdry laces, along with other finery, were traditionally sold at St Etheldreda's Fair in Ely, and their cheapness and poor quality led to the modern associations of **tawdry**.

tea

No drink could be more British than **tea**, but it did not enter the language or the country until the 17th century. The word goes back to Mandarin Chinese *chá*. A 'nice cup of tea' might be offered to someone feeling shocked and distressed, and **tea and sympathy**, used as the title of a play in 1953 and a film in 1956, has become a general phrase for comforting behaviour towards someone who is upset or in trouble. **Tea** became a meal in the mid 18th century, at first afternoon tea but then sometimes, especially in the north of England and Australia and New Zealand, an evening meal.

teach

In Anglo-Saxon times to **teach** was at first 'to present' or 'to point out', although the idea of instructing someone soon developed. The word shares an ancient root with TOKEN. The proverb **don't teach your grandmother to suck eggs** has been in use since the 18th century as a caution against offering advice to someone wiser and more experienced than yourself. Sucking eggs was something thieves did on a farm, as to suck the centre from an egg on the spot is the quickest and safest way to eat it surreptitiously. Many similar expressions have been invented down the years, such as **don't teach your grandmother how to steal sheep**, with the shared idea that an older person knows a lot more about cunning dodges than you do. The assumption here is that the longer experience of the older person brings wisdom, but the saying **you can't teach an old dog new tricks** associates the knowledge of years with rigidity, and an inability to take new things on board.

team

Some people are so fond of children that they say their ambition is to have enough to field a football team. This concept links to the original Anglo-Saxon meaning of **team**, which was 'the bearing of children'. From there it became 'a brood of young animals' and then 'a set of draught animals working together', which gave us the modern idea of a group of people or set of sports players in the 16th century. In the sense 'to be full of' **teem** is linked to **team**, but **teem** as in 'teeming with rain' is a different word altogether, which comes from Old Norse *tómr* 'empty' – the original sense was 'to drain liquid from'.

tear

The word **tear** meaning 'to pull apart' is found in Old English. To **tear someone off a strip**, or rebuke them angrily as if by pulling off a strip of their skin, was originally RAF slang, and is recorded from the 1940s.

The **tear** that you shed in distress is a completely different word, but still Old English, linked to Latin *lacrima* 'tear'. If you learn something **without tears**, the subject is likely to have been presented so that it can be learned easily. The expression appears in the title of a book for children published in the mid 19th century *Reading without Tears or, A pleasant method of learning to read*. Terence Rattigan borrowed the phrase for the title of his 1937 play *French Without Tears*. The person whose works were first called **tearjerkers**, in 1921, was James Whitcomb Riley, a US writer known for sentimental poems such as 'Little Orphan Annie'. See also CROCODILE.

storm in a teacup

The first **storm in a teacup**, 'a great deal of anxiety or excitement over a trivial matter', brewed up in the 19th century. But the idea goes back at least to the 1670s, with different wording such as **a storm in a cream bowl**. The equivalent in the US is **a tempest in a teapot**

tease

When you **tease** someone you may 'rub them up the wrong way'. This looks back to the original meaning of the word, since in Old English **tease** meant 'to comb wool in preparation for spinning'. We still use the same idea when we talk of **teasing out** tangles in hair or extracting useful information from a mass of material. The process was sometimes carried out using a particular kind of dried, prickly flower head, which is where the plant **teasel** gets its name.

teddy

In 1907 the **teddy** bear was the latest fashionable toy. Theodore 'Teddy' Roosevelt, US President from 1901 to 1909, was a keen bear-hunter, a fact celebrated in a comic poem published in the *New York Times* of January 7, 1906, concerning the adventures of two bears called 'Teddy B' and 'Teddy G'. These names were then given to two bears presented to the Bronx Zoo later in the year, and toy manufacturers saw an opening. Toy 'teddy bears' or 'Roosevelt bears' were imported from Germany, and became an instant success in America.

Teddy boys or **Teds** owe their name not to a Theodore but to an Edward. In the mid 1950s some youths began to favour a style featuring drainpipe trousers, long velvet-collared jacket, bootlace tie and hair slicked up in a quiff. The style was based on the fashions current in the early years of the 20th century in Britain, during the reign of Edward VII.

teetotal

The first part of **teetotal** has nothing to do with TEA, but is actually a way of emphasising **total**, by reproducing its first letter. It was apparently first used by Richard Turner, a member of the temperance movement from Preston, in a speech made in 1833. Early temperance reformers had limited themselves to suggesting abstinence from spirits, but this was an appeal to them to avoid all alcohol.

telegraph

The name **telegraph** was first used for a semaphore signalling device, consisting of an upright post with movable arms, invented in 1792 by the French engineer and cleric Claude Chappe. The word was based on Greek *tēle* 'far off' (source of words like TELEVISION and **telephone**, from Greek *phōnē* 'sound, voice') and *graphein* 'to write'. The first practical electric telegraphs were those of Sir Charles Wheatstone in Britain in 1839 and of Samuel Morse in the USA.

A **bush telegraph** is a rapid informal network by which information or gossip is spread. The expression originated in the Australian outback in the late 19th century. Bushrangers, outlaws who lived in the bush to avoid the authorities, used to rely on a network of informers, nicknamed the bush telegraph, to warn them about the movements of the police in their vicinity. See also GRAPEVINE.

television

The box that so dominates our lives was first demonstrated in 1926 by the Scottish inventor John Logie Baird, but the word was thought up before the design was perfected, in 1907. The first part of **television** means 'at a distance', and comes ultimately from Greek *tēle* 'far off'. The second part goes back to Latin *videre* 'to see'. C.P. Scott, a journalist and editor of the *Manchester Guardian* from 1872 to 1929, was unhappy about the formation, and perhaps about the invention: '*Television*? The word is half Greek, half Latin. No good can come of it.' It was first shortened to **TV** just after the Second World War.

tell

In Old English **tell** meant 'to count', a sense still seen in the term **teller** for a bank official. The meaning 'to disclose, reveal' does not appear until medieval times. To **tell tales out of school** is to gossip or reveal secrets about the wrongdoing or faults of someone else. As 'telling tales' to school authorities is a terrible offence in the eyes of schoolchildren, the expression is often used in the context of someone refusing to supply information or gossip. See also MARINE, TALK.

temper

The first sense of **temper** was 'a person's state of mind', either angry or calm. The word goes back ultimately to Latin *temperare* 'to mingle', and in medieval times the noun referred to the right balance in a mixture of elements or qualities. It was particularly associated with the thought of the combination of the four bodily humours (see HUMOUR) believed to control whether you were naturally calm, optimistic, melancholy or irritable – what kind of **temperament** you had.

temple

A **temple** has been a building for worship since Anglo-Saxon times, and comes from Latin *templum* 'open or consecrated space'. The **temple** which is part of your forehead is a different word, going back to Latin *tempus*, whose main meaning was 'time'. *Tempus* is the source of several words in English, such as **contemporary** and **temporary**. **Tempo**, which came to English from Italian, is now a musical term, but in the 17th century was used in fencing for the timing of an attack. **Tempest** also goes back to *tempus*, via Latin *tempestas* 'season, weather, storm'.

tempt

People were first **tempted** in medieval English – the word goes back to Latin *temptare* 'to test, try', which is the sense in the expression **tempt Providence**. To be unwise enough to test Providence, or your luck, is to invite misfortune.

In the Middle Ages **temptation** was particularly used in relation to the biblical story, in the Gospel of Matthew, of Jesus being tempted to sin by the Devil when he spent 40 days in the wilderness. Modern temptations are generally more trivial urges to indulge yourself. In 1892 Oscar Wilde wrote: 'I can resist everything except temptation' (*Lady Windermere's Fan*).

ten

The number **ten** goes back to an ancient root shared by Latin *decem*, the root of **decimal** and similar words. The rules of conduct given by God to Moses on Mount Sinai, according to the biblical book of Exodus, have been known in English as the **Ten Commandments** since the Middle Ages.

The common practice in schools of setting tests with ten questions has led to **ten out of ten** coming to mean 'completely right, perfect'. In the film *10* (1979) Dudley Moore played a Hollywood songwriter going though a midlife crisis who falls for a beautiful girl, Bo Derek, whom he rates as 'the perfect 10'.

tender

In the senses 'gentle and kind' and 'sensitive to pain or damage', **tender** is recorded from medieval times and goes back to Latin *tener* 'delicate'. It appears in a number of phrases relating to feeling for others. **Tender loving care** goes back to Shakespeare's *Henry VI, Part 3*: 'Go, Salisbury, and tell them all from me / I thank them for their tender loving care.' Its abbreviation **TLC** is comparatively modern, dating from the 1940s. The phrase **tender mercies** is used ironically to refer to attention or treatment which is not in the best interests of the recipients. It was probably originally a biblical allusion to a verse in the Book of Proverbs: 'The tender mercies of the wicked are cruel.'

The **tender** in 'an invitation to tender' is a different word that was originally a legal term meaning 'to formally offer a plea, evidence or the money to discharge a debt'. It comes ultimately from Latin *tendere* 'to stretch, hold out'.

tennis

Around 1400 **tennis** was the name for what is now known as **real tennis**, played on an enclosed court, but since the 1870s it has referred to the outdoor game also called **lawn tennis**. The name probably comes from Old French *tenez* meaning 'take!' – presumably the server's call to an opponent.

tenor

In medieval music the **tenor** part was given the melody, and therefore 'held' it, reflecting its root, Latin *tenere* 'to hold'. The **tenor** of something, as in 'the general tenor of the debate', also goes back to Latin *tenere*, via *tenor* 'course, substance, meaning of a law'.

tent

People have been using **tents** for shelter since the Middle Ages. The word goes back to Latin *tendere* 'stretch', since early tents were made of skins or cloth stretched on poles.

To be **on tenterhooks** is to be in a state of nervous suspense. A **tenter**, from the same Latin root as **tent**, is a frame on which fabric can be held taut so that it does not shrink while drying or being manufactured, and **tenterhooks** were the hooks or bent nails used to fasten woollen cloth in position. This tightening procedure had obvious appeal as an image for a person in difficulties or suspense, at first **on tenters** and later

on tenterhooks. The phrase has survived long after real tenterhooks disappeared.

terrace

In the early 16th century a **terrace** was an open gallery, and later it came to mean a platform or balcony in a theatre. A terrace of houses was originally a row built slightly above the level of the road – the first terrace of houses was mentioned in the 1760s, at first in street names like Adelphi Terrace. The source was a medieval French word meaning 'rubble, platform', based on Latin *terra* 'earth', the source of many other English words such as **terrain**, **terrestrial** and **territory**.

A **territory** was originally the district which surrounded a town or city and was subject to its laws. To say that something **goes with the territory** is to say that it is an unavoidable result of a situation. **Territory** here is probably used in the sense 'the area in which a sales representative or distributor has the right to operate', which developed in the US in the early 20th century. In Arthur Miller's play *Death of a Salesman* (1949), the central character Willy Loman tells his son that a salesman has to dream: 'It comes with the territory.' See also KOP.

anyone for tennis?

We think it the typical entrance of a sporty man in drawing-room comedy of the 1920s or 30s, but no one has actually said **anyone for tennis?** The closest is 'Anybody on for a game of tennis?', from George Bernard Shaw's *Misalliance* (1914).

terror

Like **terrible**, **terror** comes from Latin *terrere* 'to frighten' and goes back to medieval times. **The Terror** was the period of the French Revolution, from about March 1793 to July 1794, marked by extreme repression and bloodshed. The expression **reign of terror**, which may now be applied to any brutal exercise of power, was originally coined to describe this time. **Terrorist** also has links with this period, as the word was originally used to describe the Jacobins, the revolutionary group who were responsible for the repression and executions of the Terror.

Terrible once meant 'causing terror or awe', a meaning reflected in the name of the feared 16th-century Tsar of Russia Ivan the Terrible. The weakened sense 'very bad, appalling' gradually evolved from the start of the 17th century. Today parents talk of **the terrible twos**, a period in a child's development around the age of two that often involves defiant or challenging behaviour. The term is first found in the title of a film produced in 1950 for the Department

You've got mail

Once upon a time we relied on letters, telephones and face-to-face contact to communicate with other people. Now we are just as, if not more, likely to email via the internet or text – txt – on a mobile phone, introducing new forms of English.

Even the word email has generated a new 'e-vocabulary'. 'E' is short for 'electronic' and identifies anything done or used online, from e-banking and e-lancing (doing freelance work on a computer) to e-books, e-tickets and e-zines.

But it is not just words that have come over from the virtual world into general use. Thanks to its use in email addresses, the symbol @ has become the obligatory replacement for 'at' in text messages and slogans. Commonly known as the 'at sign', @ dates back to monks' writing rooms, where it was used as an abbreviation of the Latin word *ad*, meaning 'to', 'towards' or 'at'. The arrival of the internet brought it dramatically back into view. In 1971 the US computer engineer Ray Tomlinson was the first to create an email address in order to send a message from one computer to another in the same room. 'I got there first so I got to choose any punctuation I wanted', he has said.

Texting is necessarily the most abbreviated form of communication, as the small screen size of a mobile phone means that each message is restricted to an average of 160 characters. Speed is also important – the idea is to imitate real-life conversation as much as possible. As a result, the medium of the text message is one in which abbreviations and acronyms fulfil an important role (see opposite for some examples).

---

of National Health and Welfare in Canada, called *The Terrible Twos and the Trusting Threes*.

terse

In the early 17th century **terse** meant 'polished, trim, spruce', and when applied to language 'polished, polite', as in the description 'a terse and polite Latin poet of this period'. It goes back to Latin *tersus* 'wiped, polished'. The sense we have today developed from the idea of language from which everything unnecessary has been trimmed away, and which is concise and to the point – as in the historian Lord Macaulay's praise of a passage as giving 'an eminently clear, terse, and spirited summary'.

test

During medieval times a **test** was another name for what is now called a **cupel**, a shallow, porous container in which gold or silver can be refined or tested. The word goes back to Latin *testu* or *testum* 'earthen pot'. The original function of the container lies behind phrases like **put to the test** and **stand the test**. See also ACID.

The first cricket matches to be called **Test matches** seem to be have been those played between Australia and the touring English team in 1861-2. The term probably arose from the idea that the matches were a test of strength between the sides.

If someone reproaches an irritable friend for being **testy** they are using an unconnected word, which first meant 'headstrong, impetuous' and goes back to Old French *teste* 'head'. **Tetchy** has the same meaning but is again unrelated – it is probably a variant of the old Scots word *tache* 'blotch, fault', from French *teche*.

testicle

The ancient Romans felt that a man's testicles testified that he was male. They formed the word *testiculus*, from which we took **testicle** in the late Middle Ages, from Latin *testis* 'witness', the source also of **attest**, **protest** and **testify**. The testicles were the 'witnesses' of the man's virility.

text

A **text** is created when words are woven together, and the term goes back ultimately to Latin *texere* 'to weave', also the source of **texture** – which originally meant 'a woven fabric' – and **textile**.

Text, part of the language since medieval times, is a good example of how words develop new meanings in response to changes in the world. It is associated with the most traditional forms of the written word, but technological changes have also made the concept of **text messaging** familiar. You might think that the verb **text** (as in 'I'll text you when I get back') has only been in the language a short time, but here is

One drawback of both texting and emailing, which operate without the help of a tone of voice or facial expressions, is that the sender's intention may be misunderstood. As a solution, emoticons or smileys were born – combinations of keyboard characters designed to signal a facial expression or an emotion. Beyond the basic smileys of :-) and :-(for happy and sad are many fun and creative symbols (see box, right).

Children love communicating with their friends by mobile phone, so much so that in 2006 an eight-year-old girl was diagnosed with repetitive strain injury after too much texting. Some cannot help using text abbreviations and even emoticons in their school work, to the horror of lovers of good English. Many people H8 it, but plenty of others think SMS language is GR8, and slip the odd text abbreviation into emails or written notes.

TEXTING ABBREVIATIONS

AFAIK	as far as I know
BCNU	be seeing you
B4	before
BRB	be right back
CUL8ER	see you later
FYI	for your information
GR8	great
IMHO	in my humble opinion
LOL	laughing out loud or lots of love
RUOK?	are you OK?
TTYTT	to tell you the truth

TEXTING EMOTICONS

:'-(	very sad
;-)	winking
:-V	shouting
:-X	my lips are sealed
:-/	frustrated or sceptical
:-P	sticking my tongue out
:-D	laughing
O:-)	angelic
:-~	I have a cold
-:-{}	I have a moustache
8:)	I am wearing sunglasses

Shakespeare using the word 400 years ago in the context of inscribing something on a gravestone in large or capital letters: 'Yea and text underneath, here dwells Benedick the married man' (*Much Ado about Nothing*).

thank

People have wanted to **thank** each other since Anglo-Saxon times, and the word ultimately comes from the same ancient source as THINK. If you **thank your lucky stars** you not only feel grateful for your good fortune, but probably also feel that without help you would not have been successful. Since the early 19th century the phrase has become a light-hearted expression of an idea which people have sometimes taken seriously, the influence of celestial bodies on human affairs.

theatre

The earliest **theatres** were the open-air theatres of the classical world, first mentioned in English in the writings of Geoffrey Chaucer. People go to the theatre to watch a play, and the word itself goes back to the Greek *theasthai* 'to look at'. A theatre for surgical operations, or **operating theatre**, gets its name, recorded from the 1660s, because early rooms of this type were arranged like theatres, with banks of seats for observers. See also ABSURD.

theology see GOD.

thesaurus

It may sound like a dinosaur, but a **thesaurus** is a book containing lists of words with the same or similar meaning. The *-saurus* in the name of prehistoric reptiles is from Greek *sauros* 'lizard', whereas the source of **thesaurus** is Greek *thēsauros* 'storehouse, treasure'. In the late 16th century a thesaurus was a dictionary or encyclopedia – the current English meaning of the word comes from the title of one of the best-known works of reference, Roget's *Thesaurus of English Words and Phrases*, first published in 1852. See also TREASURE.

thespian

A **thespian** is an actor or actress. The dramatic poet Thespis, who lived in the 6th century BC and is traditionally regarded as the founder of Greek tragedy, gave us the word.

thick

The 'slow-witted' sense of the Old English word **thick** dates from the late 16th century. In Shakespeare's *Henry IV, Part 2* Falstaff says disparagingly of his companion Poins: 'His wit's as thick as Tewkesbury mustard'. A very stupid person might be as **thick as two short planks**, **thick as a plank** or **thick as a brick** – there is a play on **thick** in the usual sense 'deep from side to side' and the sense 'stupid'. **Thick** with the meaning 'very friendly', as in **thick as thieves**, comes from the sense 'very close together, tightly packed'.

To go **through thick and thin** is to go through everything that is in the way, ignoring obstacles or difficulties. The expression goes back to medieval times and originally probably referred to someone pushing their way both through a 'thicket', where trees grew closely, and 'thin wood', where the going would be easier.

thief

We have had thieves in the language since Anglo-Saxon times. The advice **set a thief to catch a thief**, meaning that a person who is dishonest themselves is most likely to recognise dishonest practices in someone else, dates from the 17th century. **Thieves fall out** expresses the view that an association based on shared dishonesty is likely to break down. It is a shortened form of the longer **when thieves fall out, honest men come by their own**, a 16th-century proverb implying that it is when thieves quarrel over their stolen goods that they are likely to be caught, and the goods recovered. See also HONOUR.

thimble see THUMB.

thin

The Old English word **thin** shares an ancient root with Latin *tenuis*, the source of **extenuate** and **tenuous**. An action which is unimportant in itself, but likely to lead to more serious developments is sometimes described as **the thin end of the wedge**. The idea here is of something being levered open by the insertion of the edge of a wedge into a narrow crack to widen the opening so that the thicker part can also pass through.

The thin red line used to be a name for the British army, in reference to the traditional scarlet uniform. The phrase first occurs in *The Times* of January 24, 1855, reporting a debate about the distribution of medals for the Crimean War in the House of Lords at which the Earl of Ellenborough had said: 'Nor were the services performed by the gallant 93d Regiment . . . to be forgotten – the services of that "thin red line" which had met and routed the Russian cavalry.' It has now become so much part of our language that the colour may be altered to change the meaning – **the thin blue line** can mean the police force.

thing

Just about anything can be called a **thing**, but in Old English it first meant 'a meeting, an assembly' or 'a court, a council'. The word developed though 'a matter brought before a court' and 'a concern, an affair' to its more general modern senses.

To **be all things to all men** can mean either 'to attempt to please everyone' or 'to be able to be used differently by different people'. The expression probably goes back to a biblical verse in the First Epistle to the Corinthians: 'I am made all things to all men.'

Odd sounds at night can be alarming, but if you are frightened you could recite 'The Cornish or West Country Litany', a traditional prayer which runs:

> From ghoulies and ghosties and long-leggety beasties
> And things that go bump in the night,
> Good Lord, deliver us!

This has given us **things that go bump in the night** to mean ghosts and supernatural beings.

think

The Old English word **think** is related to **thank** and **thought**. Hasty words can land you in trouble, and there is a traditional saying that warns you how to avoid this. **Think first and speak afterwards** goes back to the 16th century. Another proverb, **great minds think alike**, dates from the 17th century.

They think it's all over, now the title of a British TV sports quiz, is an extract from one of the most famous sports commentaries ever. Towards the end of extra time in the 1966 World Cup final between England and West Germany, with England leading 3-2, some spectators spilled on to the pitch as England attacked, thinking that the final whistle had blown. The TV commentator Kenneth Wolstenholme said, 'They think it's all over', whereupon Geoff Hurst scored and he continued 'It is now!'

A **think tank** is now a body of experts providing ideas, but it was originally a US slang term for the brain, recorded from 1905. A newspaper report in 1964 said that 'Truman . . . hoped to live to be 90 but only "if the old think-tank is working".' The modern sense appeared in the 1950s.

thong

For something that sacrifices comfort to fashion, it is perhaps fitting that **thong** should be related to **twinge**. In Anglo-Saxon times a thong was a shoelace.

After a certain age everyone can be struck by the gloomy thought that things ain't what they used to be. The phrase began as the title of a song by Ted Persons in 1941.

It then came to be used for any narrow strip of leather, and finally to any thin strip of material, from which came the modern use for minuscule underwear in the 1970s.

thorn

One of the earliest recorded Old English words, first found before AD 700. A **thorn in the side** or **thorn in the flesh** is a source of continual annoyance or trouble. Both expressions are of biblical origin. The Old Testament book of Numbers has a verse which reads: 'Those which ye let remain of them shall be pricks in your eyes, and thorns in your sides, and shall vex you in the land wherein ye dwell.' In the New Testament the Second Epistle to the Corinthians has: 'And lest I should be exalted above measure through the abundance of the revelations, there was given to me a thorn in the flesh, the messenger of Satan to buffet me.' See also ROSE.

thread

A word recorded from Anglo-Saxon times, and distantly related to THROW. The expression **hang by a thread** goes back to the 16th century, and comes from the legend of Damocles. He was a flattering courtier of Dionysius I, ruler of Syracuse in Sicily in the 4th century BC, who constantly told his master that he must be the happiest of men. Eventually the king decided to give Damocles a graphic demonstration of how fragile his happiness was. Dionysius invited him to a sumptuous banquet, but it was only after some time that Damocles realised he had been seated under a sword suspended by a single hair right above his head. The legend has also given us the expression a **sword of Damocles** for an imminent danger or ever-present threat.

three

An Old English word which shares an ancient root with Latin *tres* and Greek *treis*. Three close or inseparable friends may be known as **the three musketeers**. The original three musketeers were Athos, Porthos and Aramis, whose motto was 'One for all, and all for one'. They appear in the novel *Les Trois Mousquetaires* by the 19th-century writer Alexandre Dumas *père*.

The expression **the third degree** for long and harsh questioning by the police is American in origin, recorded from the beginning of the 20th century. The earliest reference, in *Everybody's Magazine* of 1900, runs: 'From time to time a prisoner . . . claims to have had the Third Degree administered to him.'

Perhaps in reference to the Holy Trinity, three is traditionally a lucky number, and this is reflected in **third time lucky**, used to suggest that someone should make another effort after initial failure. **Third time is the charm** is an American version of this saying. The same idea is probably present in the saying **the third time pays for all**, meaning that success after initial failure makes up for earlier disappointment.

Threescore is an old-fashioned way of saying '60'. In the Bible **threescore and ten** is given as the allotted span of a person's life. According to Psalm 90, 'The days of our age are threescore years and ten.' See also SHEET.

thrill

In medieval times **thrill** meant 'to pierce, penetrate', and the word is related to **through**. The sense 'to affect with a sudden feeling of excitement and pleasure' dates back to the 17th century, but it was not until the early 20th century that someone delighted could say 'I'm thrilled!'

The excitement of dangerous sports or entertainments, especially as experienced by spectators, is sometimes summed up in the phrase **thrills and spills** – which conjures up both hairbreadth escapes from danger, and accidents when escape is not achieved.

TYPICAL, YOU WAIT AGES FOR A MUSKETEER THEN 3 COME ALONG AT ONCE!

The first **thrillers** were exciting plays, performed in the 1880s. *Thriller* is the title of a record released by Michael Jackson in 1982 that has become the world's all-time best-selling album, having sold more than 100 million copies.

throw

An Old English word which first meant 'to twist' or 'to turn', and is related to THREAD. The sense 'to give a party', dating from the 1920s, probably came from the meaning 'to perform a leap or somersault', whereas the idea of 'throwing' a game or match is likely to be short for **throw away**.

When you withdraw from a contest you **throw your hand in**. The idea here is of a player in a card game throwing their hand down on the table as a signal that they are withdrawing from the game. The origins of **throw in the towel** or **throw in the sponge** lie in the boxing ring. Boxers or their trainers traditionally signal that they are conceding defeat by throwing the towel or sponge used to wipe the contestant's face into the middle of the ring. The earliest version of the phrase is **throw up the sponge**, dating from the 1860s.

To **throw stones** is to criticise someone. The phrase comes from the proverbial saying **those who live in glass houses should not throw stones**, meaning that those who are vulnerable to criticism about something should not criticise others. The earliest form of the saying is found in the 17th century. See also BABY.

thumb

Like **finger**, **thumb** is Old English. It shares an ancient root with Latin *tumere* 'to swell', probably because the thumb is a 'fat' or 'swollen' finger, and is also the origin of **thimble**.

The expression **thumbs up**, showing satisfaction or approval, and its opposite **thumbs down**, indicating rejection or failure, hark back to the days of Roman gladiatorial combat. The thumbs were used to signal approval or disapproval by the spectators – despite what many people believe, though, they turned their thumbs down to indicate that a beaten gladiator had performed well and should be spared, and up to call for his death. The reversal of the phrases' meaning first appeared in the early 20th century. In one of the stories

from Rudyard Kipling's *Puck of Pook's Hill* (1906), a Roman centurion facing a bleak future says to his friend, 'We're finished men – thumbs down against both of us.'

In Shakespeare's *Macbeth* the Second Witch says as she sees Macbeth, 'By the pricking of my thumbs, / Something wicked this way comes.' A sensation of pricking in the thumbs was believed to be a foreboding of evil or trouble. See also RULE.

tick

The **tick** in 'to tick all the boxes' and shown as a first meant 'to pat, touch' and goes back to medieval English, where it was related to **tickle**. This is the **tick** used to imitate the sound of a clock and in **ticker**, or the heart, a sense first used in the USA at the end of the 19th century.

The 'bloodsucking parasite' sort of **tick** is a different, older word which gives us the expressions **tight as a tick** or **as full as a tick** for 'very drunk', both of which refer to the way ticks swell as they gorge themselves on blood. Both forms of the phrase have the additional meaning 'be full after eating', but the more recent **tight as a tick** plays on two senses of TIGHT, which can mean both 'drunk' and 'stretched taut', as a tick is after it has had its fill of blood.

When you buy on credit or **on tick**, you are using yet another word, which is an abbreviation of TICKET. The ticket in question is an IOU promising to pay the money due, but there is also the suggestion of a pun on the reputation of moneylenders as 'bloodsucking parasites'. Both **on tick** and **on the ticket** date back to the 17th century, when credit was obviously as popular as it is today.

ticket

A shortening of an Old French word *estiquette*, which is also the origin of ETIQUETTE. A **ticket** was originally a 'short written note' and 'a licence or permit' – the use for a piece of paper or card giving admission or permission to travel dates from the late 17th century.

tide

In Old English a **tide** was a period or season, a sense surviving in **Eastertide** and **Shrovetide**, and it was not used in connection with the sea until the later medieval period. The saying **time and tide wait**

thug

The first thugs lurked not in city backstreets but in the forests of India. A **thug** was a member of an early 19th-century organisation of professional robbers and assassins who strangled their victims after pretending to be fellow travellers. The word comes from Hindi *thag* 'swindler, thief'. British thugs first appeared in 1830s Glasgow.

for no man originally referred just to time, with **tide** used as a repetition of the sense to add emphasis. Despite the great difference in their contemporary meanings, **tidy** is from **tide**. From the Middle Ages right up to the early 18th century it meant 'timely, seasonable, opportune', and acquired its current sense via the uses 'attractive, good-looking' and 'good, pleasing' around 1700.

tiger

The first reference to the **tiger** in English is found in around AD 1000, and the word goes back via French and Latin to Greek *tigris* – the beast was formerly found in Turkey and the Middle East, and would have been known to Europeans in classical times. The tiger is a fierce and dangerous creature, and to **have a tiger by the tail** is to have embarked on a course of action which turns out to be unexpectedly difficult, but which you cannot easily abandon. Having a **tiger in your tank** means that you have energy and spirit. The expression originated as a 1960s advertising slogan for Esso petrol, 'Put a tiger in your tank.' See also RIDE, WOLF.

Since the start of the 1980s the successful smaller economies of East Asia, especially those of Hong Kong, Singapore, Taiwan and South Korea, have been called **tiger economies**. The strength of Ireland during the 1990s led to its being dubbed the **Celtic tiger**.

tight

In early medieval times to call someone **tight** meant that they were healthy or vigorous. The senses we know today came along later, and it was not until the early to mid 19th century that the informal meanings 'stingy' and 'drunk' appeared. See also TICK.

A 'tight ship' was originally one in which ropes were tightly fastened. From this came the sense of a ship under firm discipline and control – which gives us the expression **run a tight ship**.

Tights are predominantly a women's garment, but they started life as tight-fitting breeches worn by men in the 18th and early 19th centuries. Dancers and acrobats then favoured them, before the first references to women's tights in the 1890s.

tile

A word which came into Old English from Latin *tegula*, and goes back to an ancient root meaning 'to cover'. The expression **on the tiles** was first recorded in a dictionary of slang published in 1887. The image conjured up is of a cat out on the rooftops at night, caterwauling and generally having a good but noisy time – just like the average Friday night reveller.

tilt

In its earliest sense, around 1300, **tilt** meant 'to fall, topple', and a jousting knight who **tilted at** a mounted opponent by riding with a lance levelled at his body was trying to knock him off his horse. This image of two armoured figures galloping towards each other is the source of **at full tilt**, 'with maximum energy or force'.

In the mock-heroic novel *Don Quixote* (1605-15) by Miguel de Cervantes, the hero Don Quixote sees a line of windmills on the horizons and takes them for giants, which he attacks. This gave us the expression **tilt at windmills**, meaning 'to attack imaginary enemies or evils'. See also QUIXOTIC.

time

To the Anglo-Saxons **time** and TIDE meant the same thing. Both **time immemorial** and its equivalent **time out of mind** were originally legal formulas. Their exact meaning was 'a time beyond legal memory', which was fixed by statute in 1276 as July 1, 1189, the beginning of the reign of Richard I. The idea was that if you could prove possession of a land or a title or right from that date there was no need to establish when or how it was first acquired. Not surprisingly, everyone but the lawyers soon forgot the specific meaning and both phrases developed the more general sense of 'a very long time ago', as in 'People have been yearning for happy marriages since time immemorial.'

We hear a lot today about the 'money-rich but time-poor' lives of many in the West, and the expression **time is money** has a very modern ring to it. But it seems to have been coined as long ago as 1748 by the American statesman and scientist Benjamin Franklin, in a speech entitled 'Advice to Young Tradesmen'. 'Remember,' he said, 'that time is money.' Before that the thought had clearly occurred to many over the centuries, as 'the most costly outlay is time' is attributed to the ancient Athenian orator and politician Antiphon. See also MOVE.

tin

The metal **tin** appears in the writings of the Anglo-Saxon king Alfred the Great. Use of **tin** to mean a sealed metal container for food or drink dates from the late 18th century. Tin is not a precious metal, and a number of phrases refer to its relative lack of value. To **have a tin ear** is to be tone-deaf. The term **a little tin god** for someone regarded with unjustified respect conjures up the idea of an idol made of cheap tin instead of gold or silver. In the early 20th century a **tin Lizzie** was an affectionate nickname for a car, especially one of the early Ford models. See also feature on ADVERTISING SLOGANS.

tinker

The reputation that **tinkers**, who travelled around mending pots, pans and other metal utensils, had for using bad language gave us the expression **not give a tinker's curse**, sometimes shortened to **not give a tinker's**. The verb meaning 'to attempt to repair or improve something in a casual way' was suggested by the improvised way that tinkers worked.

tinsel

Christmas would not be Christmas without **tinsel** decorations. Get the lighting right, and it almost seems to give off sparks, which illustrates its origin, Latin *scintilla* 'a spark', also the source of **scintillate**. In medieval times tinsel was fabric woven with metallic thread or spangles – it became something like our familiar shiny strips in the late 16th century. The idea of glitter was picked up during the 1970s in **Tinseltown**, a nickname for Hollywood and its cinema.

tipple

To **tipple** was originally to sell alcoholic liquor, not to drink it. It came in the late 15th century from earlier **tippler** 'a seller of alcohol', the source of which is unknown, though it may be related to Norwegian dialect *tipla* 'to drip slowly'. Emphasis moved to the drinker towards the end of the 16th century.

tissue

An Old French word that goes back to Latin *texere* 'to weave', the source of TEXT, **textile** and **texture**. **Tissue** was originally a rich material often interwoven with gold or silver threads – a long way away from the modern disposable paper hankie. From the idea of woven material came the notion of an intricate, connected series in the phrase **a tissue of lies**. The 20th-century product developed from **tissue paper**, thin soft paper used for wrapping fragile objects.

tit

Few words in English have such snigger-inducing contrasts in meaning. In the name for small songbirds **tit** is probably of Scandinavian origin and related to Icelandic *titlingur* 'sparrow'. It first appeared in English in the Middle Ages in the longer equivalent **titmouse**, though mice had nothing to do with it – the second element was originally *mose*, which also meant 'tit'. It changed to **mouse** in the

16th century, probably because of the bird's small size and quick movements.

In Old English a **tit** was a teat or nipple – it is from the same root as **teat**. In modern English it is a term for a woman's breast, a use that arose in the USA in the early 20th century. Since the 1970s British **tits and bums** and American **tits and ass** have suggested crudely sexual images of women. As a name for a foolish person, used since the 19th century, **tit** may be the same word, or it may have evolved from TWIT.

titanic

In Greek mythology the Titans were gods who were the children of Uranus (Heaven) and Gaia (Earth). Zeus, son of their leader Cronus, rose up against his father and defeated them to became chief god. Inspired by the Titans, **titanic** arose in the early 18th century with the meaning 'of exceptional strength, size or power'. The most immediate association of the word nowadays is with the *Titanic*, the British passenger liner that was the largest ship in the world at her launch and supposedly unsinkable. She struck an iceberg in the North Atlantic on her maiden voyage in April 1912 and sank with the loss of 1,490 lives. The expression **rearranging the deckchairs on the Titanic** refers to futile actions that do nothing to avert inevitable disaster.

titch

Harry Relph, who lived from 1868 to 1928, was a diminutive English music-hall artist whose stage name was 'Little Tich'. He acquired the nickname as a child because of a resemblance to Arthur Orton, notorious as 'the Tichborne claimant'. Orton had returned to England from Australia in 1866 claiming to be Roger Charles Tichborne, the heir to a title and estate who had been lost at sea, but was eventually tried and imprisoned for perjury. In the First World War British soldiers began to use **tich** or **titch** as a name for a small person.

toady

In the 17th century unscrupulous charlatans and quacks would try to sell their supposed remedies by demonstrating their powers. One technique was to have an assistant take the quack medicine and then eat, or pretend to eat, a toad – people thought that toads were poisonous and so were likely to attribute the assistant's survival to the charlatan's wares. Such an assistant was

Harry Relph – 'Little Tich'

a **toad-eater**. In the 18th century the word also came to mean 'a fawning flatterer', and in the early 19th this was shortened to **toady**.

toast

There is a connection between the toast you eat and the toast you make with a raised glass. **Toast** is based on Latin *torrere* 'to parch, scorch, dry up', the source also of **torrid** and **torrent** (a rushing or 'boiling' flow of water). 'To parch' was the earliest meaning of the English word, and before long it was used to describe browning bread in front of a fire. Drinking toasts goes back to the late 17th century, and originated in the practice whereby a drinker would name a lady and request that all present drink her health. The idea was that the lady's name flavoured the drink like the pieces of spiced toast that people added to wine in those days.

tod

The expression **on your tod** comes from **on your Tod Sloan**, rhyming slang for 'on your own'. Tod Sloan was an American jockey who made his name in the 1890s and was immortalised in this expression some 40 years later. An earlier parallel, used in Australia and New Zealand and first recorded in 1907, is **on your pat**, which is short for **on your Pat Malone**. Where it comes from is not altogether clear, but a popular ballad, 'Paddy Malone in Australia', was noted in the 1870s and appeared in a collection published in 1906.

toddy

Some palm trees have a sugary sap that is drunk in parts of Africa, South India and the Philippines, especially when fermented into an alcoholic spirit. This was the original **toddy**. The word comes from the Indian languages Hindi and Marathi and goes back to a Sanskrit name for an Asian palm, the palmyra. Travellers brought it back to the colder climate of Britain, and the **hot toddy** of whisky or some other spirit with hot water and sugar and spices has soothed many a cold since the late 18th century.

toe

An Old English word recorded as early as AD 700. To **toe the line**, 'to accept the authority or principles of a particular group', derives from competitors placing their toes just touching the starting line of a race.

Vagrants without proper clothing have long used rags wrapped round their feet as socks. Since the mid 19th century such a piece of improvised footwear has been a **toerag**. The term transferred to the unfortunate wearer later in the century, and nowadays **toerag** is an insult for anyone considered worthless or contemptible.

toff

Upper-class people have been called **toffs** since the mid 19th century. This is perhaps an alteration of **tuft**, once a term for titled undergraduates at Oxford and Cambridge, who wore a gold tassel on their caps. The associations of the word may have influenced **toffee-nosed** or 'snobbish', which was originally military slang. Toffee seems to have been a desirable commodity to soldiers during the First World War – **not be able to do something for toffee**, or be totally incompetent at it, is first recorded in 1914 in the mouth of a British 'Tommy'. **Toffee** is an alteration of **taffy**, now mainly used in North America for a sweet resembling toffee. The **Taffy** that is a name for a Welshman is quite different, representing a supposed Welsh pronunciation of the name David or Dafydd.

tog

To English-speakers nearly everywhere **togs** are clothes, but Australians, New Zealanders and the Irish specifically wear togs to go swimming. The word **tog** was originally 18th-century slang for a coat or outer garment, and appears to be a shortening of obsolete **togeman**, used by criminals to mean 'a light cloak' and coming from Latin **toga**, the loose flowing outer garment worn in ancient Rome. The **tog** that measures the insulation capability of duvets and clothing is the same word, which was adopted in the 1940s to match an earlier US unit the **clo**, which was an abbreviation of **clothes**.

toilet

You would not dream of putting what you wear in the **toilet**, but a toilet was originally a cloth used as a wrapper for clothes or a covering for a dressing table, from French *toilette* 'cloth, wrapper'. From the first meaning developed a group of senses relating to dressing and washing, including 'the process of washing, dressing and attending to your appearance', now rather dated, which is also expressed in the French form **toilette**. In the 18th century it was fashionable for a lady to receive visitors during the later stages of her 'toilet', which led to uses that would cause misunderstandings today, such as this by the dramatist Sir Richard Steele in 1703: 'You shall introduce him to Mrs Clerimont's Toilet.' People started using the word for a dressing room, and, in the USA, one with washing facilities, but it was not until the early 20th century that it became a particular item of plumbing, namely a lavatory. See also LOO.

token

'He gave him . . . a cordial slap on the back, and some other equally gentle tokens of satisfaction', wrote the novelist Fanny Burney in 1778. She was using **token** in the meaning it had had since Anglo-Saxon times, 'a sign or symbol'. In the 17th and 18th centuries there was often a scarcity of small coins, and tradesmen issued their own coin-shaped pieces of metal to exchange for goods or cash. Such a disc was a **token** as it 'symbolised' or substituted for real money. Use of the word for a voucher, as in a **book token**, dates from the early 20th century.

Tom

Like JACK, **Tom** has long been used to represent an ordinary man. The expression **Tom, Dick and Harry**, meaning 'a large number of undistinguished people', first appeared in an 18th-century song: 'Farewell, Tom, Dick and Harry. Farewell, Moll, Nell and Sue.'

During the 19th century the British army offered specimens of completed official forms using the name Thomas Atkins for the fictitious enlisted man. From the 1880s Rudyard Kipling helped popularise **Tommy** as a name for the ordinary – and much-exploited – British soldier. His poem 'Tommy' (1892) contained such lines as 'O it's Tommy this, an' Tommy that, an' "Tommy go away" / But it's "Thank you, Mr Atkins," when the band begins to play'.

The 'tommy' in **tommy gun** is not an anonymous private soldier, but the US army officer John T. Thompson, who conceived the idea of this type of sub-machine gun and financed its development. The designer, O.V. Payne, insisted in 1919 that it be called the **Thompson gun**, but by the late 1920s it had been domesticated as the **tommy gun**.

The cylindrical drum called the **tom-tom** is a different word, from Hindi *ṭam ṭam*. It came over to Britain in the 1690s.

*In the mid 16th century a **tomboy** was actually a boy – a rough or boisterous one. By the end of that century girls who enjoyed the rough games boys like could be tomboys.*

tomorrow

A word formed by the combination of **to** and **morrow** (see MORNING) in the 13th century, in the same way as **today** and **tonight**. Reflections on the future include **tomorrow is another day**, a 20th-century variant of **tomorrow is a new day**, recorded from the early 16th century. 'Tomorrow is another day' is remembered by many as the last line of the film *Gone With The Wind* (1939). The proverb **tomorrow never comes** was foreshadowed in 1523 when Lord Berners wrote: 'It was said every day among them, we shall fight tomorrow, the which day came never.'

tongue

Despite the difference in spelling, the Old English word **tongue** is ultimately related to Latin *lingua*, the source of LINGO and LANGUAGE. In the 18th century to **put your tongue in your cheek** meant 'to speak insincerely'. This came from a contemptuous gesture which involved poking your tongue in your cheek, and led to the expression **tongue in cheek**, 'in an ironic or insincere way'. Rude gestures move on over time, and nowadays people tend to press their tongue under their lower lip as a mild display of derision or dislike.

When the disciples were filled with the Holy Spirit after the ascent of Jesus into heaven, they were given **the gift of tongues**, the power of speaking in unknown languages. Members of Pentecostal churches believe that they, like the Apostles, can **speak in tongues**.

tooth

An Old English word from an ancient root shared by Latin *dens*, the source of **dental**, **dentist** and related words and also INDENT. To **fight tooth and nail** was in the 16th century to **fight with tooth and nail**. Although in a real fight this would mean 'by biting and scratching', the phrase is almost always used of non-physical struggles. See also HEN.

To **set someone's teeth on edge** is to cause them intense irritation. The expression comes from the Bible, and expresses the unpleasant sensation felt when you have bitten into something that is bitter or sour: 'Every man that hath eaten the sour grape, his teeth shall be set on edge' (Jeremiah).

top

Anglo-Saxon, and related to **tip**. The expression to **go over the top** originated in the First World War, when it described troops in the trenches charging over the parapets to attack the enemy. It gradually developed the meaning 'to do something to an excessive or exaggerated degree', possibly in reference to the huge numbers of soldiers who died in the conflict. Soon people were shortening it to simply **over the top**, and since the early 1980s it has been reduced even further to the abbreviation **OTT**, as in 'The film that gave Halle Berry the chance to make one of the longest and most OTT Oscar acceptance speeches ever.'

topsy-turvy

Things have been **topsy-turvy** since at least 1528. The term is probably based on TOP and **turve**, an old word meaning 'to topple over, overturn' – the extra *ys* are similar to those in **hurly-burly** and **arsy-versy**.

W.S. Gilbert, of Gilbert and Sullivan operetta fame, regarded the world as topsy-turvy, and in 1870, while on the staff of *Fun* magazine, introduced the word **topsy-turvydom**. In 1999 Mike Leigh wrote and directed the film *Topsy-Turvy*, based on parts of Gilbert's life and his relationship with Sir Arthur Sullivan.

torch

A **torch** in the original sense of 'an object soaked in an inflammable substance and carried as a means of illumination' was often made of twisted hemp or other fibres. This is still the American meaning, and reflects the word's Latin origin, *torquere* 'to twist', the source also of **extort**, **thwart** and **torque**. Only in British English can **torch** describe a battery-powered electric lamp, which Americans call a **flashlight**.

A **torch song** is a sad or sentimental song of unrequited love, whose name, used since the 1920s, comes from the phrase **carry a torch for**, 'to love someone who does not love you in return'. The image in **pass on the torch**, 'to pass on a tradition, especially one of learning or enlightenment', is that of the runners in a relay race passing on the torch to each other, as was the custom in the ancient Greek Olympic Games. The tradition of the torch relay is preserved as a prelude to the modern Olympics, with a team of runners carrying the Olympic torch vast distances across many countries until the site of the Games is reached.

tornado

A **tornado** was originally a violent thunderstorm over the tropical Atlantic Ocean. The word may be an alteration of Spanish *tronada* 'thunderstorm', influenced by *tornar* 'to turn', a reference to the shape of a 'twister'. See also TSUNAMI, TYPHOON.

torpedo

Although we think of a **torpedo** as speeding through the water towards its target, at the heart of the word's origin is the notion of slowness and paralysis. The electric ray, a sluggish sea fish that lives at the bottom of shallow water, produces an electric shock to capture prey and for defence. Its Latin name was *torpedo*, from *torpere* 'to be numb or sluggish', and when first used in English in the early 16th century **torpedo** referred to this ray. In the late 18th century the inventor of a timed explosive for detonation underwater gave it the name

torpedo, and this is the ancestor of the modern self-propelled underwater missile.

torso

Like BUST, **torso** at first described sculpture, referring to the TRUNK of a statue without the head and limbs. Charles Dickens, in *Our Mutual Friend* (1865), was one of the first to apply it to the living human body, writing of a man with 'too much torso in his waistcoat'. The word itself came from Italian, where it originally meant 'a stalk or stump'.

Tory

Most modern Conservative politicians and supporters in Britain would prefer not to dwell on the disreputable beginnings of their Party, but the term **Tory** probably comes from Irish *toraidhe* 'outlaw, highwayman'. In the 17th century English settlers in Ireland dispossessed many Irish peasants, forcing them to live as outlaws, and these were the first Tories. In 1679-80 Protestant opponents of the Roman Catholic James, Duke of York (later James II), who wanted to exclude him from succession to the Crown, gave **Tory** as an abusive nickname to his supporters. From 1689 people started applying the name **Tories** to one of the two great parliamentary parties, whose members were at first more or less identical with those 'Tories' who opposed the exclusion of James from the succession. For some time the Tories leaned towards the dethroned James II and the House of Stuart; but on the accession of George III in 1760 they abandoned this attitude, though they retained the principle of strenuously upholding tradition and authority. See also WHIG.

touch

A medieval word from Old French *tochier* 'to touch'. In modern French this is *toucher*, which is the source of **touché**, literally 'touched!', said in fencing to acknowledge a hit made by your opponent, and more generally in recognition of a good or clever point in a discussion.

In the mid 19th century **touch** developed a number of slang meanings among criminals. It described various ways of getting money from people, either by stealing, especially pickpocketing, or by some con trick. A **soft touch** was someone who was particularly easy to con or steal from, and even today the phrase is often used to describe someone who is always willing to lend money to a friend.

Someone **touched** is slightly mad or crazy. The sense has been used since about 1700, and was probably suggested by a line of Shakespeare's, from *Measure for Measure*: 'I am touch'd with madness.'

From the 16th century a **touchstone** was a piece of jasper or other stone used for testing alloys of gold by observing the colour of the mark which they made on it. Nowadays a **touchstone** is usually a standard or criterion by which people judge or recognise something. **Touchy**, 'easily upset or offended', may not be directly from **touch**, though it has been influenced by the word. It was probably originally an alteration of **tetchy** (see TEST).

tough

An Old English word related to **taut**. As a noun, meaning 'a rough and violent man or youth', it dates from the 1860s, in the USA. If you are **as tough as old boots** you are very sturdy or resilient. The earliest version of the phrase was **as tough as leather**, but any old leather does not seem to have been tough enough.

Before he became the British Prime Minister or even Party leader, Tony Blair made a speech at the Labour Party Conference in September 1993, when he was Shadow Home Secretary. The speech brought him to public attention and included the words: 'Labour is the party of law and order in Britain today. Tough on crime and tough on the causes of crime.'

towel

'I shall rub you down with an oaken towel', wrote Tobias Smollett in his novel *Roderick Random* (1748). Among **towel**'s former meanings are, in 18th-century slang, 'cudgel', as in the Smollett quotation. This led to a verb sense 'to beat, cudgel', which is now mainly used in Australia and New Zealand. The word came into English from Old French *toaille*. See also THROW.

town

An Old English word that in AD 600 or 700 meant 'an enclosed piece of ground' then 'a farm or estate' and 'a collection of houses'. **Town** gradually grew until by around 1150 it referred to a place of the size we might recognise today as a town.

In Oxford and Cambridge there has been long-standing hostility between the local inhabitants and incoming students, which in the early 19th century was formulated as the opposition between **town and gown**. The gown is the academic dress worn by university members, now required only on ceremonial or formal occasions. See also PAINT.

toy

A **toy** was originally a funny story or remark, and later a prank, trick or frivolous entertainment. The usual modern sense, of an object for a child to play with, dates from the late 16th century. Older women had taken up with younger men before the 1980s, but it took until then for the rhyming **toy boy** to appear. The origin of **toy**, like that of **boy**, is medieval but otherwise unknown.

track

A 15th-century word that perhaps came from the same Dutch source as TREK. The first meaning was 'a mark or trail left by a person, animal or vehicle' – the sort of tracks used by trains or (originally) horse-drawn coal wagons were described in 1805. The expression **the wrong side of the tracks**, 'a poor or less prestigious part of a town', originated in America from the idea of a town divided by a railroad track. In 1929 the humorist Thorne Smith wrote: 'In most commuting towns . . . there are always two sides of which the tracks serve as a line of demarcation. There is the right side and the wrong side. Translated into terms of modern American idealism, this means, the rich side and the side that hopes to be rich.' See also TRAIN.

talk of the town

Scandalous gossip has been **the talk of the town** since the 1620s. *The Talk of the Town* was also the title of a 1942 comedy film starring Cary Grant and of a 1905 stage musical.

trade

The medieval word **trade** came from German and is related to **tread**. It originally meant 'a track or way' and then 'a way of life' and 'a skilled handicraft' – the 'buying and selling' sense dates from the 16th century.

A **trade wind** has nothing to do with commerce. The term arose in the mid 17th century from **blow trade** 'to blow steadily in the same direction', or along the same course or track. Sailors thought that many winds blew in this way, but as navigation technology improved they realised that there are only two belts of trade winds proper, blowing steadily towards the Equator from the northeast in the Northern Hemisphere and from the southeast in the Southern Hemisphere.

traffic

A 16th-century word from French *traffique*, Spanish *tráfico* or Italian *traffico* that originally referred to commercial transportation of merchandise or passengers. The sense 'vehicles moving on a public highway' dates from the early 19th century. That bane of drivers, the **traffic warden**, first appeared in London in 1960. **Traffic calming**, a system of speed bumps and constricting chicanes also regarded as a bane by some, is a translation of German *Verkehrsberuhigung* and arrived on British roads in the late 1980s. See also JAM.

Nowadays **trafficking** implies dealing in something illegal, especially drugs, but in the mid 16th century to **traffic** was a neutral term meaning 'to buy and sell, trade'. By the end of that century, though, it had started to take on negative connotations.

train

Before railways were invented in the early 19th century **train** followed a different track. Early senses, from the mid 14th century, included 'a trailing part of a robe' and 'a retinue', which gave rise to 'a line of travelling people or vehicles' and later 'a connected series of things', as in **train of thought**. To **train** could mean 'to cause a plant to grow in a desired shape', which was the basis of the sense 'to instruct'. The word is from Latin *trahere* 'to pull, draw', and so is related to word such as **trace**, **trail**, **contract** and **extract**.

Boys in particular have practised the hobby of **trainspotting** under that name since the late 1950s. Others ridicule this solitary and apparently trivial pursuit of collecting train or locomotive numbers, and in Britain in the 1980s **trainspotter**, like ANORAK, became a derogatory term for an obsessive follower of any minority interest or specialised hobby. Irvine Welsh's 1993 novel *Trainspotting*, made into a film released in 1996, gave a high profile to the term. The title refers to an episode in which the main characters, both heroin addicts, go to a disused railway station in Edinburgh and meet an old drunk who asks them, in an attempt at a joke, if they are trainspotting. There are also other overtones from the language of drugs – TRACK is an addicts' term for a vein, **mainlining** for injecting a drug intravenously and **train** for a drug dealer.

Trainers were originally **training shoes**, soft shoes without spikes or studs worn by athletes or sports players for training rather than the sport. The short form began to replace the longer one in the late 1970s.

trappings

Animal traps have nothing to do with **trappings**, which go back to Latin *drappus* 'cloth', the source of **draper** and **drapery**. In the 14th century trappings were ornamental harness for a horse, but now people more often use the word in contexts such as 'the trappings of success' for the outwards signs or objects associated with a particular role or job.

trash

Popular culture is often called **trashy**, and this goes right back to the beginnings of **trash**'s history – one of the first things that the word referred to was bad literature. From the 16th century it was a word for various kinds of refuse, including cuttings from a hedge and sugar canes stripped of their juice, and domestic refuse became **trash** at the beginning of the 20th century. People have called others **trash** since the early 17th century – Shakespeare wrote in *Othello* 'I do suspect this trash / To be a party in this injury' – and in the USA **white trash** is a derogatory term for poor white people living in the southern states. See also GARBAGE, JUNK, RUBBISH.

travel

Keen globetrotters might reflect on how privileged they are to have aircraft, credit cards, internet access and all the other conveniences of modern travel, but others still regard it as torture. Well, 'torture' is at the root of the word **travel**, which came from **travail**, a literary word for 'painful or laborious effort'. The two forms were once interchangeable, and originated in an instrument of torture, called *trepalium* in Latin, that consisted of three stakes.

Robert Louis Stevenson, himself a keen traveller, was the first to express the view that **it is better to travel hopefully than to arrive**, in 1881. The idea that **travel broadens the mind** is also relatively recent, appearing first in 1900.

travesty

Both **travesty** and **transvestite** go back to Latin *trans* 'across' and *vestire* 'to clothe', and in the theatre a **travesty role** is still one designed to be played by a cross-dressing performer. The earliest use of **travesty**, which came through French *travesti*, 'disguised', and Italian in the mid 17th century, was 'dressed to appear ridiculous'. The usual modern sense, 'a false or absurd representation of something', developed from the word's application to literary parodies and burlesques. Academic interest in sexuality developed in Germany and Austria in the late 19th and early 20th centuries, and the immediate source of **transvestite**, recorded from the 1920s, was German *Transvestit*.

treacle

It is now a soothing kind of syrup, but **treacle** has the most unlikely original meaning – 'antidote against poison'. When the word entered medieval English from Old French *triacle*, which went back to Greek *thērion* 'wild beast', it was a term for an ointment made with many ingredients that counteracted venom. The idea of an antidote extended into that of a remedy or medicine, and later, by way of the sugar syrup used to make a medicine more palatable, into the current sense at the end of the 17th century.

treasure

A medieval word that came through Old French from Greek *thēsauros* 'treasure, store, storehouse'. This is also the source of THESAURUS, a type of book containing lists of words with the same or similar meaning.

A **treasure trove** is now a collection of valuable or pleasing things that is found unexpectedly, but it was originally a legal concept, which was abolished only in 1996. **Treasure trove** referred to valuables of unknown ownership that were found hidden, which were the property of the Crown. The term came from French, where the equivalent phrase meant 'found treasure'.

trek

Between 1835 and 1837 large numbers of Boers, discontented with British rule in the Cape area of South Africa, migrated north and eventually founded the Transvaal Republic and the Orange Free State. This was **the Great Trek**, which largely introduced the Dutch word **trek** to the English-speaking world. It came from *trekken* 'to pull, travel', from which TRACK may also derive. During the 19th century the word was restricted to South African contexts, but during the 20th migrated into international English for any long, arduous journey. The US science-fiction television programme *Star Trek* was not a success when it was first shown between 1966 and 1969, but has been popular since the 1970s and has given us **Trekkie** as a word for a Star Trek fan.

tribe

In the early days of ancient Rome the people fell into three political divisions. This division into 'three' (*tri-* in Latin) may be the origin of *tribus*, from which **tribe** descended, along with **tribunal**, **tribune**, TRIBUTARY and **tribute**. The first uses of **tribe** in English referred to the 12 ancient tribes of Israel claiming descent from the 12 sons of Jacob.

Boer families make the Great Trek across South Africa in the 1830s.

tributary

The idea behind **tributary** as a name for a river or stream flowing into a larger river or lake is the fanciful one that the smaller body of water 'pays tribute' to the larger one, a **tribute** being a regular payment made by one state or ruler to a stronger one. In reality it is the recipient of the tributaries' waters that depends on them for its flow and power. The word **tribute** goes back to Latin *tribuere* 'to assign', originally 'to divide between tribes', from *tribus* (see TRIBE).

trice

Unlike most *tri-* words, **trice** has nothing to do with 'three'. It comes from early Dutch *trisen* 'to pull sharply, hoist', and in the Middle Ages **at a trice** meant 'at one pull or tug' rather than 'in a moment, immediately'. By the late 17th century the original form of the expression had given way to the more familiar **in a trice**.

trick

A medieval word from Old French *trichier* 'to deceive or cheat', and related to **treachery**. A 16th-century sense of the word was 'habit', which is where the expression **up to your old tricks** comes from.

Children say **trick or treat** at Halloween when they call at houses threatening to play a trick on the householder unless a treat is produced in the form of sweets or money. The phrase first appeared in the 1930s in the USA, and in Britain has started to edge out the more traditional Halloween games, such as bobbing for apples. The Halloween festival is of pre-Christian origin, and is associated with the Celtic festival Samhain, when ghosts and spirits were believed to walk. The word **Halloween** is a contraction of **All Hallow Even** 'All Saints' Day' – **hallow** means 'a saint' and is related to HOLY. See also HAT-TRICK.

trilby

Trilby was the heroine of George du Maurier's novel *Trilby*, published in 1894. In the stage version the Trilby character wore a soft felt hat with a narrow brim and indented crown, which was immediately dubbed a **trilby**. Trilby falls under the influence of a musician called Svengali, who trains her voice by hypnotising her and makes her into a famous singer, although she had been tone-deaf before meeting him. A person who exercises a controlling or mesmeric influence on another is sometimes called a **Svengali**.

trim

The history and development of this little word are obscure. **Trim** appeared in Old English in the sense 'to make firm, arrange', but there is little record of it in the medieval period. From the 16th century, though, it burst on the scene to serve many purposes, relating to fitting out ships for sea, preparing a candle wick for use, repairing something, decorating clothing and cutting away the unwanted parts of something. A trim ship was well equipped and in good condition, which gave us the the sense of a slim and fit person having a trim figure. To a sailor to **trim a sail** means 'to adjust the sail of a boat'. On land to **trim your sails** came to mean 'to make changes to suit your new circumstances', from which we get a **trimmer** for an unscrupulous person who adapts their views to the prevailing political trends.

trip

The early Dutch word *trippen* 'to skip, hop' is the source of **trip**. The English word was initially used to describe not only stumbling by catching your foot on something but also dancing and nimble movement. The noun meant 'a light lively movement' before it became 'a short journey', originally a sailor's term for a short sea journey. The sense 'hallucinatory experience caused by taking a drug' was first recorded in the late 1950s. See also FANTASTIC.

trite

The idea behind **trite** is one of wearing something away by use and perhaps also of causing irritation through repetition. The word first appeared in English in the mid 16th century, from a form of Latin *terere* 'to rub'. An old meaning, now obsolete, was 'physically worn away or frayed'.

trivial

Latin *trivium* meant 'a place where three roads meet', and it is from this that we get our word **trivial**. Medieval universities offered a basic introductory course involving the study of three subjects – grammar, rhetoric and logic – known as the **trivium**. The earliest uses of **trivial** relate to this basic, low-level course, with the main modern meanings, 'commonplace, ordinary' and 'unimportant, slight', developing in the late 16th century. The plural of Latin *trivium* has also entered English as **trivia**. A crossroads, a place where not three but four roads meet, has a similar metaphorical relationship with CRUCIAL, a word which means almost the exact opposite of **trivial**.

The board game **Trivial Pursuit**, in which players answer general knowledge questions in various subject areas, was introduced in 1981. It had been invented two years previously by two Canadian friends, Chris Haney and Scott Abbot.

troll

Children have long been gripped by the Norwegian fairy tale 'The Three Billy Goats Gruff', where a troll lives under a bridge and tries to prevent the goats from crossing it, threatening to eat them. In Scandinavian folklore trolls are ugly giants or dwarfs that usually live in caves. The word entered English in the mid 19th century, and has no connection with the much earlier **troll** 'to fish by trailing a baited line along behind a boat' or 'to search'. Today internet users also 'troll', or send a provocative email or newsgroup posting to provoke an angry response. The origin of this **troll** is uncertain – its original sense was 'to stroll, roll', which might be connected to old French *troller* 'to wander here and there' or early German *trollen* 'to stroll'.

trolley

The first **trolley** was a low cart used for transporting goods such as fruit, vegetables or fish – not so different from the wonky-wheeled vehicle we push round the local supermarket when doing the weekly shop. **Trolley** started life in the early 19th century as an English dialect word, perhaps from **troll** in the sense 'to stroll or roll'.

The **trolley** in **off your trolley**, 'mad', has nothing to do with shops or with transporting patients along hospital corridors. This trolley is a pulley that runs along an overhead track and transmits power to drive a tram. If a tram becomes disconnected from the pulley, it is no longer under control. A similar idea is found in to **go off the rails**, meaning 'to start behaving in an uncontrolled or unacceptable way', from the image of a train leaving the tracks or being derailed.

trophy

Both **tropic** and **trophy** are ultimately from Greek *trepein* 'to turn'. In ancient Greece and Rome a **trophy** was a pile of the weapons of a defeated army set up as a memorial of a victory. Fortunately trophies now usually sit on mantelpieces or in cabinets to celebrate sporting success. An exception to this is the attractive young **trophy wife** of a successful older man, a term first used in the late 1980s.

By origin a **tropic** is a 'turning point', a point on the path through the sky that the sun can be seen to take through the year where, at the solstice, it appears to turn back again towards the Equator. The two parallel lines of latitude north and south of the Equator at this point are known as the tropics of Cancer and Capricorn, and the area between them has been called **the tropics** since the mid 19th century.

trouble

Our word **trouble** comes, by way of Old French *truble*, from Latin *turbidus* 'disturbed, turbid', source of **turbid** and related to **disturb**, **perturb** and **turbulent**. From the start, in the 13th century, it meant 'difficulty or problems'. 'Man is born unto trouble, as the sparks fly upward' is from the biblical book of Job, who was a virtuous man that God tested by sending him many troubles.

Most people now think of **the Troubles** in Northern Ireland as beginning in the early 1970s, but the same term applied to the unrest around the partition of Ireland in 1921, and in an 1880 glossary of words used in Antrim and Down **the Troubles** are defined as 'the Irish rebellion of 1641'.

The first **troubleshooters** had a very specific occupation. In the early years of the 20th century they mended faults on telegraph or telephone lines.

wear the trousers

The dominant member of a married couple wears the trousers, and has done since the 1930s. But long before that the phrase was **wear the breeches**, first recorded in the 16th century.

trousers

Scottish Highlanders and Irishmen once wore a **trouse** or **trouses**, a kind of knee-length shorts whose name came from Irish *triús* or Scottish Gaelic *triubhas*. The same words gave us **trews**, once similar to the trouse but now close-fitting tartan trousers as worn by some Scottish regiments. In the early 17th century people started calling the trouse **trousers**, on the analogy of **drawers**. Until the end of the 18th century men in Europe wore tight breeches – looser trousers were adopted by the working classes during the French Revolution, and the style imported to Britain by dandies like Beau Brummell. See also PANTS, TWEEZERS.

trousseau

The romantic **trousseau** conjures up an image of a blushing bride in flowing white or smart honeymoon outfit, but the original meaning might bring you down to earth. In the 13th century a trousseau was simply a bundle or package, and it did not acquire its modern meaning until the 1830s. The word derives from French *trousse*, an earlier form of which gave us **truss** 'a supporting framework' and 'a surgical support for a hernia'. See also HONEYMOON.

truant

In the 13th century a **truant** was someone who begged out of choice rather than necessity, what people used to call 'a sturdy beggar'. The idea of voluntary idleness led to its application in the later medieval period to children staying away from school without permission. The word came from Old French, but is probably ultimately of Celtic origin and related to Welsh *truan* and Scottish Gaelic *truaghan* 'wretched'.

truce

The old word **trow** meant 'belief, faith, trust' and had the same root as TRUE. In the early Middle Ages the plural form with *-s* applied to an agreement between enemies to stop fighting for a certain time, and this plural developed into singular **truce**.

truck

The **truck** that is a large road vehicle originally meant 'a wheel or pulley', and may be a shortening of **truckle**, which once had the same sense but now only refers to a small barrel-shaped cheese. It came from Latin *trochlea* 'wheel of a pulley'. To **have** (or **want**) **no truck with**, meaning 'to avoid dealings with', has no connection with the transportation of goods – here **truck** is from French *troquer* 'to barter'.

Since the 1920s US English has had the slang sense 'to move or proceed'. **Keep on truckin'** was the caption, first used in 1967, of a series of cartoons by the US artist Robert Crumb, who drew the cover of the Janis Joplin LP *Cheap Thrills* (1968). See also JUGGERNAUT.

true

An Old English word from the same root as TRUCE and TRUTH. It originally meant 'loyal or steadfast'. Over time this gradually led to the idea of being reliable or honest, and then to that of truthfulness. The idea behind **many a true word is spoken in jest** is found in Geoffrey Chaucer's *Canterbury Tales* in the late 14th century, but the modern form of the proverb first appeared in print in the 17th century. See also TWELVE.

trump

The word **trump**, 'a playing card of the suit chosen to rank above the others', is an alteration of **triumph**, which was once used in the same sense. The Latin source of **triumph**, *triumphus*, probably came from Greek *thriambos* 'hymn to the god Bacchus'. In ancient Rome a **triumph** was the grand entry of a victorious general into the city.

In some card games the trump suit is chosen before each game, while in others it is the suit of the last card dealt, which is turned over to show its face. This gives rise to the phrases **come** or **turn up trumps**, 'to produce a better outcome than expected', reinforced by the fact that a hand with many trump cards is likely to be a winning hand.

In the expression **the last trump**, **trump** is a different word, from the same origin, Old French *trompe*, as **trumpet**. The last trump is the trumpet blast that some believe will wake the dead on Judgement Day.

Officers making public announcements would sometimes blow a blast on a trumpet to get people's attention. To **blow your own trumpet**, or talk boastfully about your achievements, comes from the idea of going out into a public space and making an announcement about yourself.

trunk

Ever since English adopted **trunk** in the late Middle Ages, via Old French from Latin *truncus* 'the main stem of a tree', the word has branched out in several directions. The meaning 'a tree's main stem' is behind the sense 'the human body' and others with the notion of a central connection, such as **trunk road**. The 'chest, box' meaning arose because early trunks were made out of tree trunks. The circular shape of a tree trunk prompted another branch referring to cylindrical hollow objects, including, in the 16th century, the elephant's trunk.

In the 16th and early 17th centuries men wore **trunk-hose**, full breeches extending to the upper thighs and sometimes padded, worn over tights. The style went out of fashion, but in the theatre actors wore short light breeches over tights, which they called **trunks**. In late 19th-century America men's shorts for swimming or boxing took over the name. See also TOG.

truth

Our word **truth** goes back to Anglo-Saxon times and comes from the same root as TRUCE and TRUE. As with the latter word, it originally suggested qualities of faithfulness and loyalty. **Troth**, as in 'to plight your troth' or make a solemn pledge, especially in marriage, is simply a form of **truth**.

Many proverbs reflect on the nature of truth. Lord Byron was the first to popularise **truth is stranger than fiction**, in his poem *Don Juan* in 1823. The first verifiable instance of **truth is the first casualty of war** is an epigraph by the British politician Arthur Ponsonby in 1918: 'When war is declared, Truth is the first casualty.' One of the adages of the Dutch humanist and scholar Erasmus, writing in Latin, was *in vino veritas*, translated as **there is truth in wine**, and this

English version has continued in use, though the Latin form is probably more familiar. The idea itself goes back to Greek, and is attributed to the poet Alcaeus of the 6th century BC.

try

From Old French *trier* 'to sift', source also of **trial**. In rugby an act of touching the ball down behind the opposing goal line has been called a **try** since the 1840s. It got its name because a try gives the scoring side the right to try to kick a goal.

The cliché **try anything once**, indicating that you are willing to experience something new, dates from the 1920s. The British conductor Sir Thomas Beecham (1879-1961) is generally credited with 'You should try everything once except incest and morris dancing', but the composer Sir Arnold Bax reported a similar comment in a 1943 autobiography: 'You should make a point of trying every experience once, excepting incest and folk-dancing.'

You should try everything once except incest and morris dancing.

Sir Thomas Beecham

tsunami

The **tsunami** of Boxing Day 2004 made this Japanese word for a huge sea wave caused by an underwater earthquake known to everyone. It appeared in English in 1897, but for a long time remained largely restricted to specialist geological and oceanographical publications. It is formed from *tsu* 'harbour' and *nami* 'wave'. See also TORNADO, TYPHOON.

tucker

The idea of tucking into or tucking away food is behind **tucker**, the familiar Australian and New Zealand term for 'food'. It first appeared in print in 1858, for the daily supply of food of a gold-digger or station hand. See also BIB.

Tuesday

It is the ancient Germanic god Tiw who is the source of **Tuesday**. When Germanic peoples came into contact with the Romans they realised that their god Tiw was similar to Mars, the Roman god of war whose day was the third of the week, and started to call that day 'Tiw's day' or Tuesday. Other days of the week were formed in a similar way, with **Wednesday** being Woden's day, **Thursday** Thor's day and **Friday** Freya's day – Woden or Odin was the supreme god of the German and Scandinavian peoples, Thor the god of thunder, and Freya or Frigga the goddess of love and the night.

tumbler

The straight-sided drinking glass really does come from **tumble** 'to fall'. In the 17th century tumblers had rounded bottoms and would not stand upright, presumably so that the drinker would have to keep holding the glass and would drink more.

turban

The words **turban** and **tulip** are from the same source. Turkish people compared the flower of the tulip to the shape of the turban and gave the plant the same name, *tūlbend*, which they took from Persian *dulband*. The tulip made a spectacular impression, and cost a spectacular amount of money, when it came from Turkey into western Europe in the 16th century. At first forms such as **tulipan** and **tulban** existed alongside **turban** as the name of the headdress, whereas the name of the flower always appeared in the *-l-* form, and eventually monopolised that spelling.

tureen

The original form of **tureen** was **terrine**, from a French word for a large earthenware pot that goes back to Latin *terra* 'earth', source of TERRACE, **territory** and many other words. From its arrival in the early 18th century **terrine** referred both to a pot and its contents, but not long after its arrival the 'cooking pot' sense began to be spelled **tureen**, perhaps after the city of Turin in northwestern Italy. Nowadays tureens are usually oval with a lid and used for serving dishes such as soup. A **terrine** can still also be a container, but usually one that is oblong and steep-sided, used for cooking what we call a terrine, a mixture of meat, fish or vegetables allowed to cool and served in slices.

turf

The Old English word **turf** goes back to a root shared by *darbha* 'tuft of grass' in Sanskrit, the ancient language of northern India. The grass surface of a racecourse has led horseracing to be **the turf** since the mid 18th century. The **turf** in **surf and turf**, a dish containing both shellfish and steak, represents the lush prairies or meadows on which beef cattle graze. Since the 1950s criminals or street gangs have their own turf, an area of personal territory. This is a later expression than **turf off** or **out**, which is British slang from the late Victorian era and probably comes from the idea that the person 'turfed out' is kicked on to some grass.

turkey

The Christmas or Thanksgiving **turkey** did not originate in Turkey, but people in England who first encountered the tasty new bird in about 1530 could be forgiven for thinking so. The turkey had been brought to England by merchants from the eastern Mediterranean, whom the English called Turkey merchants because the whole area was then part of the Turkish Ottoman Empire. The new bird was called a Turkey bird or Turkey cock. Turkeys actually came from Mexico and were first brought back from there in about 1520.

The American phrase to **talk turkey**, 'to talk frankly and straightforwardly, to get down to business', was first recorded in the mid 19th century, when it had the rather different sense 'to say pleasant things or talk politely'. Although people have speculated about the origin of the expression, no one is sure where it comes from. Perhaps it is something to do with turkey hunters making gobbling noises, prompting the birds to respond in kind and give away their whereabouts.

turn

The origin of Old English **turn** is Latin *tornare* 'to turn', from *tornos*, the Greek word for a lathe. The sense 'a song or other short performance' developed in the early 18th century from the meaning 'an opportunity or obligation to do something', as in 'It's your turn', which is medieval.

Card games and betting combine to give us **a turn-up for the book** 'a completely unexpected event or occurrence'. **Turn-up** here refers to the turning up or over of a particular card in a game, while the book is one kept by a bookie to record bets made in a race. The **leaf** in to **turn over a new leaf**, 'to improve your behaviour or performance', is a sheet of paper in a book, not a part of a plant or tree. See also NARK.

turncoat

The original **turncoat** – a person who deserts one party to join an opposing one – is said to be a 16th-century duke of Saxony. His land was caught between French and Saxons at war with each other, so he donned a reversible coat, one side blue (the Saxon colour) and the other side white (the French colour), allowing him to quickly change his display of allegiance.

turtle

English sailors gave the **turtle** its name in the 1650s. They probably based it on **tortue**, an early form of **tortoise**, from French *tortue* and Spanish *tortuga* 'tortoise'. A boat is said to **turn turtle** when it turns upside down – because it then looks like the shell of a turtle, or because it is as helpless as a turtle flipped over on its back. **Mock turtle soup**, inspiration for the Mock Turtle in Lewis Carroll's *Alice in Wonderland*, is soup made with a calf's head, in imitation of turtle soup. The **turtle** in **turtle dove** is a completely different word whose source is Latin *turtur*, an imitation of the bird's cooing. 'The time of the singing of birds is come, and the voice of the turtle is heard in our land' is from the biblical Song of Solomon – a reference to the fact that the turtle dove is a migratory bird.

tutu

The female ballerina's costume gets its name from the French nursery. In French *tutu* is a child's alteration of *cucu*, an informal term for the bottom, from *cul* 'buttocks'. The outfit originally referred to was the short **classical tutu**, with a skirt projecting horizontally from the waist.

twain

Old English, a form of TWO. The comment **never the twain shall meet**, suggesting that two things are too different to exist alongside each other, quotes from 'The

Ballad of East and West' (1892) by Rudyard Kipling: 'Oh, East is East, and West is West, and never the twain shall meet.'

twee

A child's pronunciation of SWEET, recorded from the first decade of the 20th century. Originally **twee** was as complimentary as **sweet**, but people must have become more cynical and now it is intended as an insult, meaning 'excessively or affectedly quaint, pretty or sentimental'.

tweed

Tweed was originally produced in Scotland, where it was called **tweel**, a Scots form of **twill**. Around 1830 a cloth merchant misread this as **tweed**, a mistake perpetuated by association with the River Tweed, part of which forms the border between England and Scotland.

Tweed is traditionally worn by the English country gentry, and **tweedy** has been used since the early 20th century to suggest a robust, traditional kind of Englishness very popular in the USA. The actor and comedian Stephen Fry, often regarded as the quintessential English gentleman, wrote in his 1997 autobiography *Moab Is My Washpot*: 'My vocal cords are made of tweed. I give off an air of Oxford donnishness and old BBC wirelesses.'

Tweedledee and Tweedledum

The English poet John Byrom coined **Tweedledee and Tweedledum** in a satire of 1725 about the composers George Frederick Handel and Giovanni Battista Bononcini, musical rivals both enjoying success in London at the time. To **tweedle** is to play a succession of shrill notes or to play an instrument carelessly. Lewis Carroll picked up the names and used them for two identical characters in *Through the Looking-Glass*, and now they apply generally to any pair of people or things that are virtually indistinguishable. See also feature on LEWIS CARROLL.

tweezers

In the 17th century a **tweeze** was a case of surgical instruments. It appears to be a shortened form of **etweese**, a plural of **etui**, which was a term for a small ornamental case for holding needles, cosmetics and other articles that came from French *étui*. In the mid 17th century **tweeze** was extended to **tweezer**, while the plural **tweezes** became **tweezers**. **Trouse** became TROUSERS in much the same way. In the 1930s **tweeze** was re-formed from **tweezers** to mean 'to pluck with tweezers'.

twelve

You can express the number twelve as ten with two left over. This might seem a long-winded way to say it, but this is what twelve actually means. It is an Old English word from the root of TWO with a second element, also found in eleven, that probably expressed the idea 'left over'.

A jury in a court of law is traditionally composed of **twelve good men and true**. The 1957 film *12 Angry Men*, starring Henry Fonda, dramatised the story of a jury considering the case of a young man accused of killing his father, whom all but one juror initially assume to be guilty.

twilight

A medieval combination of *twi-*, a form of TWO, and **light**. What significance 'two' has here is not entirely clear, though perhaps there is the idea of half-light, between day and night. In Scandinavian and German mythology **the twilight of the gods** is the destruction of the gods and the world in a final conflict with the powers of evil. English also uses the German and Old Norse equivalents *Götterdämmerung* and *Ragnarök*, the first of which is the title of the last opera in Richard Wagner's Ring cycle.

Today a **twilight zone** is primarily an urban area in a state of dilapidation or economic decline, but the term will forever be associated with the US television series *The Twilight Zone*, first shown in 1959. Each episode of the series, created and presented by Rod Serling, offered a self-contained story with a science fiction or horror theme.

twinkle

As well as its original Old English sense 'to sparkle, glimmer', **twinkle** also meant 'to wink, blink the eyes' from the 14th to the early 19th century. The meaning 'the time taken to wink or blink' – a very short time, in other words – is just as old, but it survives only in **in the twinkling of an eye**, 'very quickly'. This is probably because the phrase appears in various passages in the Bible, including Corinthians: 'In a moment, in the twinkling of an eye, at the last trump.' A similar expression containing the same idea is **in the blink of an eye**.

twit

The kind of **twit** that is a silly or foolish person dates only from the 1930s and comes from an English dialect use that meant 'a tale-bearer'. It may come from **twit** in the sense 'to tease or taunt someone, especially in a good-humoured way', which is a shortening of Old English *ætwītan* 'reproach with'. See also TIT.

two

An Old English word from the same source as TWAIN, TWELVE, **twenty**, TWILIGHT and **twin**, an ancient root shared by Latin and Greek *duo*, source of **double**, **duo**, **duplicate** and other words.

The formula **it takes two to** — appeared in the 1850s in **it takes two to make a quarrel** and in the 1940s in **it takes two to make a bargain**. In 1952 Al Hoffman and Dick Manning wrote the song 'Takes Two to Tango', which, sung by Pearl Bailey, was a worldwide hit, giving **it takes two to tango** instant international currency.

Before the British currency was decimalised in 1971 twopence or tuppence was a standard sum. To **add** or **put in your twopenn'orth** is to contribute your opinion – **twopenn'orth** is a contraction of **twopennyworth** meaning 'an amount costing two pence', used also for 'a small or insignificant amount'.

> The saying **two's company, three's a crowd** was **two's company, three's none** in the 1730s.

tycoon

A tycoon is now a powerful businessman, but it was originally a Japanese ruler, and the word comes from Japanese *taikun* 'great lord'. Foreigners applied the title **tycoon** to the shogun, or military commander, of Japan in power between 1857 and 1868, and in the same period Americans nicknamed President Abraham Lincoln 'the Tycoon'. The word then extended to any important or dominant person, from the 1920s especially to a business magnate.

tyke

Since the later Middle Ages **tyke** (from Old Norse *tík* 'bitch') has been a term for a dog, especially a mongrel. A tyke became a rough or coarse man and then a **Yorkshire tyke**, 'a person from Yorkshire', before being used as an affection term for a cheeky or mischievous child. In Australia and New Zealand **tyke** is an offensive term for a Roman Catholic. Here it is an alteration of **Taig**, a Northern Ireland Protestant's insulting name for a Catholic, from the Irish name *Tadhg*, which has been used since the 17th century as a nickname for an Irishman.

typhoon

The fierce tropical storm brings together two sources, Arabic *tūfān*, which may be from Greek *tuphōn* 'whirlwind', and Chinese dialect *tai fung* 'big wind'. The Portuguese picked up the first in the Indian oceans, while merchants and sailors in the China seas would have encountered the Chinese expression. A wide variety of spellings appeared before the word finally settled down into **typhoon** in the 19th century. See also TORNADO, TSUNAMI.

tyrannosaur

The **tyrannosaur** or **tyrannosaurus** is the 'tyrant lizard'. The fossilised remains of this large carnivorous DINOSAUR were found in North America at the beginning of the 20th century, and the palaeontologist H.F. Osborn gave it the modern Latin name *Tyrannosaurus* in 1905, from Greek *turannos* 'tyrant' and *sauros* 'lizard'. The only known species of this type of dinosaur is the *Tyrannosaurus rex*, from Latin *rex* 'king'. The English rock band Tyrannosaurus Rex was founded in 1967 by Marc Bolan, but enjoyed its greatest success in the early 1970s when the name was shortened to T. Rex.

tyrant

In English a **tyrant** has always been a cruel and oppressive ruler, but in ancient Greece, where the word comes from, this was not originally the case. In the 6th and 7th centuries BC a tyrant, or *turannos*, was simply a man who seized power unlawfully. Since such tyrants were often taking over from despised aristocrats or kings they were not necessarily unpopular, and the word did not acquire negative associations until the beginnings of democracy at the end of the 6th century BC.

tyre

In the past wheelwrights strengthened the outside of the wheels of carts and carriages with curved pieces of iron plate, or strakes – a similar strengthening band is still fitted round the wheels of trains. The word for these strakes was the **tire**, probably a shortened form of **attire**, because the tyre was the 'clothing' of the wheel. Originally the spellings **tire** and **tyre** were interchangeable, but in the 17th century **tire** became the settled spelling, which it has remained in the USA. In Britain the development of the pneumatic tyre seemed to require some differentiation from the metal rim, and **tyre** was revived.

It comes from the title of the 1958 book *The Ugly American* by William Lederer and Eugene Burdick, which was released as a film starring Marlon Brando in 1963.

ukulele

The **ukulele** will forever be associated with the English comedian George Formby (1904-61). He accompanied himself on a banjo-like version (the banjolele) of the tiny four-stringed guitar while singing risqué songs like 'When I'm Cleaning Windows':

> The blushing bride she looks divine
> The bridegroom he is doing fine
> I'd rather have his job than mine
> When I'm cleaning windows.

The ukulele is a development of a Portuguese instrument called the machete that appeared in Hawaii in the late 1870s. Around that time a British army officer, Edward Purvis, acted as vice-chamberlain of the court of King Kalakaua. According to the story, local Hawaiians gave Purvis, a small, energetic and agile man, the nickname *ukulele* 'jumping flea'. When he took up the instrument he played with typical liveliness and with such success that they started to use his nickname as the name of the guitar.

ugly

The guttural ugliness of **ugly** is perfectly suited to such a negative word. It came into English in the 13th century from Old Norse *uggligr* 'to be dreaded', and had a stronger meaning than it does now, 'frightful or horrible'.

In one of Hans Christian Andersen's fairy tales the 'ugly duckling' is a cygnet hatched with a brood of ducklings that is jeered at and rejected for its clumsiness until it turns into a graceful swan. The tale appeared in English in a translation of 1846, and **ugly duckling** soon became a term for a person who turns out to be beautiful or talented against all expectations. The American entertainer Danny Kaye brought the idea to an even wider audience when he wrote and sang 'The Ugly Duckling' in a 1952 biographical film of Andersen's life.

In another fairy tale, *Cinderella*, the heroine has three ugly and unpleasant stepsisters who make her work in the kitchen. Since the late 19th century an **ugly sister** has been an unattractive person or thing or an undesirable counterpart. See also FAIRY.

More recent is the **ugly American**, the American who behaves offensively abroad. The original context of the phrase is more serious, that of Americans who adversely affect the lives of the people they live among in Southeast Asia.

ultramarine

The brilliant bright blue pigment **ultramarine** originally came from lapis lazuli, a rock brought from Afghanistan that was more precious than gold. The name **ultramarine** refers to these exotic and distant origins – Latin *ultramarinus* meant 'beyond the sea', and forms descended from it became the name for the pigment in most European languages.

umbrella

An umbrella is strictly a sunshade, not something to protect you against rain. The word came from the sunnier climes of Italy in the early 17th century, and goes back to Latin *umbra* 'shade'. Britain's wet weather meant that not much more than 20 years after the word's first appearance an **umbrella** became something to keep the rain off.

Another word from Latin *umbra* 'shadow' is **umbrage**, as in **take umbrage** or take offence. An early sense was 'a shadowy outline', which then gave rise to 'a ground for suspicion' and led to the current sense.

umpire

An **umpire** was originally a **noumpere** or arbitrator. People began to misinterpret *a noumpere* as *an oumpere*, just as they had taken *a naddre* as *an adder* and *a napron* as *an apron*. The word entered English in the Middle Ages from Old French *nonper* 'person who surpasses all others', which was related to PAR and **peer**. **Umpire** became a term in sports such as cricket and tennis in the early 18th century. See also UNCLE.

umpteen

Signals regiments in the army once used **umpty** to indicate the dash in Morse code (the dot was **iddy**). One slang dictionary states that this began in India, as a way of teaching the Morse system to Indian troops. The military term may be behind the use of **umpty** for an indefinite large number, recorded from the late 19th century and developing into **umpteen**, on the model of **thirteen** or **fourteen**, in the early 1900s.

uncanny

The Scots originally used **uncanny**, just as they did its positive equivalent **canny**, which comes from **can** and means 'shrewd, cautious', 'clever' or 'nice, pleasant'. **Uncanny** has always had overtones of the occult, and originally implied 'malignant or malicious'. The association with supernatural arts or powers led in the late 18th century to its application to people who were not considered safe to have dealings with – perhaps secretly they were witches or warlocks – but during the 19th century such superstitions diminished, and the word left Scotland to develop its usual modern meaning 'mysterious, weird, strange'.

uncle

Both **uncle** and **avuncular** came through Old French from Latin *avunculus* 'uncle on the mother's side'. In the late 16th century people started misinterpreting *an uncle* as *a nuncle*, and **uncle** developed a parallel form **nuncle** – the opposite of the process seen in ADDER, APRON and UMPIRE. In Shakespeare's *King Lear* the Fool addresses his employer Lear as 'nuncle'.

The expression **Uncle Tom Cobley and all** is used as the last item in a long list of people to emphasise that everyone possible has been included or considered. It comes from an old song called 'Widdicombe Fair', dating from around 1800, which tells the tale of seven men all on one horse on their way to the fair at Widecombe-in-the-Moor in Devon. The song lists the men's names, ending with 'Uncle Tom Cobley and all'. The independent use of the phrase itself did not develop until around a century later, in the 1930s.

Uncle Sam has personified the government or people of the USA since the early 19th century. He is often shown as an elderly man with white hair and a goatee beard, dressed in red, white and blue clothing, as in the 1917 recruitment poster captioned 'I Want You for U.S. Army', which was based on a British poster showing Lord Kitchener. The name is probably based on the initials US rather than a particular person called Samuel.

Since the 1920s **Uncle Tom** has been an insulting and offensive name for a black man considered to be excessively obedient or servile to whites. The original 'Uncle Tom' was an elderly slave who was the central figure of Harriet Beecher Stowe's 1852 anti-slavery novel *Uncle Tom's Cabin*. See also DUTCH.

uncouth

An Old English word that originally meant 'unknown'. For much of the history of **uncouth**, most people would not have used or understood its opposite, **couth**. This was only used in Scottish English, and meant 'kind, agreeable' or 'comfortable, snug, cosy'. Its negative equivalent **uncouth**, though, developed a fully independent life. It came to refer to unsophisticated language or style in the late 17th century and then to uncultured or ill-mannered people or behaviour. In 1896 the English essayist and critic Max Beerbohm was the first to use **couth** as a deliberate opposite of **uncouth** meaning 'cultured, well-mannered'.

Ungainly developed in a similar way. There is a word **gainly**, but it has never been common and its original meaning, 'suitable, fitting', now occurs only in Scottish dialect. **Gainly** came from the old word **gain**, which was used especially in the senses 'kindly' and 'convenient' and is of Scandinavian origin. Since its introduction in the early 17th century **ungainly** has thrived – criticisms are often more freely given than compliments.

underwrite

Originally, in the early 17th century, the emphasis of **underwrite** was on an insurer actually writing their name at the bottom or end of an insurance document. Nowadays the important thing is that they are guaranteeing to pay a certain sum if something is damaged or lost. In business contexts like these **underwrite** was probably a direct translation of Latin *subscribere* 'to write underneath', the source of **subscribe**, which people originally used in exactly the same way.

Union Jack

Some people will still tell you that the correct name for the **Union Jack** is the **Union flag**, since a JACK is strictly the small flag flown at the bow of a ship. Before the beginning of the 19th century **Union Jack** was indeed only a nautical term, with **Union flag** being the one in general use, but over the past 200 years objectors have effectively lost the battle. The flag itself was introduced to symbolise the union of the crowns of England and Scotland and was formed by surmounting the diagonal cross of St Andrew by the cross of St George. The diagonal cross of St Patrick was added in 1801 following the union of the parliaments of Great Britain and Ireland.

university

In Latin a *universitas* was a society or guild, and during the Middle Ages **university** first applied to an association of teachers and advanced students formed to give and receive instruction at a level beyond that of a school. In the 19th century **varsity** was a common colloquial form of the word, but now is used mainly to refer to university sports. The term survives in the annual **varsity match** played between Oxford and Cambridge at rugby and soccer, while in the USA a **varsity team** is a sports team representing a university or college.

unkempt

People have only **combed** their hair since around 1400 – before that they would have **kembed** it and their hair would have been **kempt**. These are forms of the old word **kemb**, which was eventually replaced by the related word **comb**. The term has survived, though, sometimes in the form **kempt** but especially in **unkempt**, which has come to mean 'untidy or dishevelled' rather than 'uncombed'.

unravel

The Dutch were the first to **ravel**, which originally meant both 'to entangle' and 'to disentangle'. In the early 17th century **unravel** added to the existing complexity. You might think that **ravel** would then have settled down as its opposite, 'to entangle', but that is not what happened. To **ravel something out** is still to untangle it, though on its own **ravel** means 'to confuse or complicate a situation'. Unravel the history of the two words if you can.

upper

The **upper** in **on your uppers**, 'very short of money', is the part of a shoe above the sole, covering the top part of your foot. Worn-out shoes tend to be a sign of poverty, and if all someone has left of their shoes is the uppers, they are likely to be in a very impoverished state indeed. The origins of **the upper crust** for 'the upper classes' are an object of debate. One of the most popular theories traces its roots back to medieval kitchens. When a loaf was baked the base, which was on the floor of the oven, tended to burn before the crust or top part was properly browned. The 'upper crust' would be cut off and reserved for the lords and ladies of the household, leaving the hard blackened remainder for the servants. There are no examples of the phrase being used of the upper strata of society until the 1830s, though. It seems to have been a popular US term around that time, and also features in a glossary of Northamptonshire words and phrases published in 1854, where 'Mrs Upper Crust' is explained as the nickname for 'any female who assumes unauthorised superiority'. It seems likely that **crust** is simply being used in the sense of 'top layer', not nearly as good a story as the first suggestion.

upside down

Until the 16th century things were not **upside down** but **up so down**, a phrase first recorded in the 14th century. Another alternative from the 16th century was **up set down**.

A special relationship

New words and phrases have been slipping into English from the USA for more than 200 years. Purists may bemoan Americanisms, but US culture continues to liven up the language.

In 1935 the BBC correspondent Alistair Cooke remarked in his weekly *Letter from America* broadcast that the average English-speaker uses dozens of Americanisms every day. Some American expressions have been in English for much longer than that. In the early 19th century a blizzard was 'a sharp blow or knock' or 'a shot' in the USA, and probably arose as an imitation of the sound of a blow. The sense 'a severe snowstorm' followed in the 1850s. At the start of the same century a rowdy was a rough, lawless man living in the backwoods, the remote forests beyond settled areas. The modern meaning 'noisy and disorderly' came about in the 1840s as a description of these people's typical manner.

You say sidewalk, we say pavement, you say DIAPER, we say nappy – and as for BUM and fanny, 'don't even go there'. Britain and the US often have different words for the same thing, and in many cases the US words originated in Britain. One example is fall for AUTUMN, and another is faucet, a medieval word from French *fausset* which has disappeared in Britain but is the usual US term for a TAP.

From JAZZ and blues to rock, PUNK and RAP, practically all the terms for popular music are US, as is the language of films. Americans rejected the French word CINEMA in favour of the more straightforward movies, recorded from 1903, and picture house or movie theatre.

Students are fond of a stunt, a word that originated as US college slang towards the end of the 19th century. The students first used it to mean 'a daring or athletic feat', but it is not clear where they got it from. In British English the word was first used by soldiers to mean 'an attack or advance', and by airmen in references to aerobatics.

Word-watchers in the USA noted burger in the late 1930s and 1940s. It must have been used mainly in speech and on menus, as examples of it in print do not appear until the 1960s. It is a shortening of hamburger, recorded since the 1880s, which was originally a Hamburger steak, named after the German city of Hamburg. The association with Hamburg began to be lost, and as early as 1940 ham had given way to beef, with the beefburger leaving no doubt as to its main ingredient. The development of burger as a separate word was probably influenced by the need to combat the restrictions on meat-eating imposed by rationing in 1943. This led to recipes for liver burgers, lamb burgers, veal burgers and even potato burgers being published in articles and advertisements of that year. The accompanying chips are another source of confusion, as chips in the USA are what the British would call crisps, and chips are French fries.

Yankee appeared first as an individual's nickname in the late 17th century, and may be from Dutch *Janke*, a pet form of *Jan* 'John'. In the mid 18th century it became a general name for a person from New England or any of the northern states, and during the Civil War Confederate soldiers applied it to their Federal opponents. Outside the USA people use Yankee or Yank indiscriminately for any American.

A dollar was originally a German silver coin, one that historians now call a thaler. The name comes from German *Thaler* or *Taler*, short for *Joachimsthaler*, which was a coin from the silver mine of Joachimsthal ('Joachim's valley'), now called Jáchymov, in the Czech Republic. People later applied the term to a coin used in the Spanish American colonies and also traded widely in British North America at the time of the American War of Independence. The new nation adopted dollar as the name of its monetary unit after achieving independence.

Inflation is to blame for the sixty-four thousand dollar question, originally the sixty-four dollar question. The top prize in the 1940s quiz show *Take It or Leave It* was at first $64, but by the 1950s had increased to $64,000. Nowadays something which is not known and on which a great deal depends is the sixty-four thousand dollar question.

the sixty-four dollar question

See also BLUE, GERRYMANDER, MACARONI, OK, ROCK, SILVER and features on BUSINESS JARGON, NATIVE AMERICAN WORDS and STREET SLANG.

uproar

The origins of **uproar** have no connection with roaring, either by lions or by the elements. The word came from Dutch, from *up* 'up' and *roer* 'confusion'. It sounded as though it could be a native English form, and people associated the second element with **roar**, shifting the meaning from its original sense of 'rebellion, uprising' to 'loud confused noise'. See also PANDEMONIUM.

uranium

Uranium is a rare radioactive metal found in the mineral pitchblende. The German chemist Martin Klaproth isolated the metal and called it **uranium** after the planet Uranus, which the astronomer Sir William Herschel had discovered less than a decade before, in 1781. Herschel himself had originally called the planet **Georgium sidus**, 'the Georgian planet', in honour of King George III, but the German Johann E. Bode proposed **Uranus**, the name of the most ancient of the Greek gods, to fit in with the well-established practice of using names from classical mythology. In the course of the early 19th century Bode's suggestion won the naming contest.

urchin

An **urchin** was originally a hedgehog, and the name, based on Latin *hericius* 'hedgehog', is still used in some English dialects. People started applying **urchin** to poor raggedly dressed children in the mid 16th century, though this did not become common until more than 200 years later. As a name for a marine invertebrate **sea urchin** harks back to the original meaning, referring to the spines on its shell.

usher

The primary function of an **usher** was originally to be a doorkeeper, and the word is based on Latin *ostium* 'door'. The duties of an usher extended to showing people to their seats, as ushers in a cinema or court of law still do, and from the mid 16th century into the 19th an usher could also be an assistant schoolmaster. The use of **usher** for someone assisting people at a wedding was originally American.

usual

The English words **use** and **usual** are both medieval and derived from Latin *usus* 'a use'. People have **used** drugs or been drug **users** since the late 1920s, a different idea from **user-friendly**, recorded since 1977.

The Usual Suspects is the title of a thriller released in 1995 and starring Gabriel Byrne and Kevin Spacey. It comes from a line in the Humphrey Bogart film *Casablanca* (1942): 'Major Strasser has been shot. Round up the usual suspects.' See also PLAY.

utopia

The English scholar and statesman Sir Thomas More wrote *Utopia* in Latin in 1516, depicting an imaginary island enjoying a perfect social, legal and political system. The name implies that such an ideal place exists 'nowhere', as More created it from Greek *ou* 'not' and *topos* 'place', the source also of **topic** and of terms such as **topography**, the arrangement of the physical features of an area. In the 17th century other writers started using **utopia** for other imaginary places where everything is perfect. The opposite of a utopia is a **dystopia** where everything is as bad as possible, a word formed in the late 18th century from Greek *dus-* 'bad'. George Orwell's *Nineteen Eighty-four* and Aldous Huxley's *Brave New World* are examples of dystopias.

A 1578 edition of Sir Thomas More's *Utopia* conjures up the fabled island.

someone who cannot think or communicate clearly. A **vagabond** was originally just a **vagrant**, someone who roams from place to place without a settled home, until it acquired the additional suggestion of 'an unprincipled or dishonest man'. Before it came to refer to impulsive changes or whims, as in 'the vagaries of fashion', vagary was used from the late 16th century to mean 'to wander' and, as a noun, 'roaming, a ramble'.

vacation
People did not really have holidays in the Middle Ages, and **vacation** was rest from work or occupation. The root of the word is Latin *vacare* 'to be unoccupied', source also of **vacancy**, **vacant** and **vacate**. The vacation then became the fixed time between terms when lawyers and university teachers vacate their premises and are free from formal duties. In North America it is the usual word for a holiday, a sense first used in the 1870s – there a **holiday** is normally a specific national holiday such as Thanksgiving.

vaccine
The English physician Edward Jenner (1749-1823) knew the folk tradition that milkmaids did not catch smallpox, and speculated that this might be because they had come into contact with the virus causing cowpox, a disease of cows' udders whose effect on humans resembles mild smallpox. In 1796 he took the risky step of deliberately infecting an eight-year-old boy, James Phipps, with small amounts of cowpox, and when the medical world rejected the successful result he repeated the experiment on several other children, including his own baby son.

The practice was eventually accepted throughout the world, and has led to the effective eradication of the smallpox virus. In 1798, writing in Latin, Jenner referred to cowpox as *variolae vaccinae*, from *vaccus* 'cow', and the beginning of the 19th century saw the words **vaccine**, **vaccinate**, **vaccination** and the beginning of the end of a deadly and disfiguring disease.

vague
A number of English words descend from Latin *vagari* 'to wander' and *vagus* 'wandering'. In the 16th century **vague** applied the idea of a 'wandering' mind to

valet
Rich men who could afford to employ a **valet** to look after their clothes had to be careful that he was also not a **varlet**, 'an unprincipled man', as the words are essentially the same. French *valet* 'attendant' and its early variant *varlet* are related to **vassal**, from medieval Latin *vassallus* 'retainer', which derived from a Celtic word. The first valets were 15th-century footmen who acted as attendants on a horseman.

vamp
Any self-respecting **vamp** is likely to wear stockings, and the two words have more in common than you might expect. From around 1200 the **vamp** was the part of a stocking that covered the foot and ankle, and from the 17th century the upper front part of a boot or shoe. The word comes from an early form of French *avantpied*, from *avant* 'before' and *pied* 'foot'. One of the cobbler's regular tasks was to replace vamps, and from the late 16th century the job could be described as **vamping** boots and shoes. This cobbling work gave rise to a general sense 'to improvise' and to the modern

use **vamp up**, 'to repair or improve'. The 'improvise' sense survives in jazz and popular music, where to **vamp** is to repeat a short, simple passage of music. The **vamp** who uses her sexual attraction to exploit men has more connection with necks than feet – this word is an early 20th-century shortening of VAMPIRE.

vampire

The best-known vampire is Count Dracula in *Dracula* by Bram Stoker, but these blood-sucking corpses of folklore had caught the public imagination long before the book was published in 1897. Writers had described their gruesome activities in English since the mid 18th century, and in 1819 *The Vampyre* by John William Polidori was a huge success. Polidori had been living with the poets Shelley and Byron in Switzerland when Mary Shelley conceived the idea behind her story of *Frankenstein*, and his novella appears to be the first about a vampire in English fiction. The word is from Hungarian *vampir*, perhaps from Turkish *uber* 'witch'. The 20th-century film industry gave vampires and vampirism a great publicity boost, as well as introducing the VAMP or **vampish** heroine.

The Vandals sack Rome in an engraving by Heinrich Leutemann (1824-1904).

van

The familiar words spelled **van** both refer to being on the move but are not related. The **van** that is a covered vehicle for transporting goods or people is a 19th-century shortening of **caravan**, from Persian *kārwān*, and can still mean 'a covered lorry' in North America. The earlier **van**, 'the foremost part of a group of people', is also an abbreviated form, from **vanguard**, whose first part was from Old French *avant* 'before'.

The workman's white van, often with 'Clean me!' written on the dirty rear door, is such a familiar sight that **white van man** has entered the language to mean an aggressive male van driver, or more widely an ordinary working man with forthright views. 'White Van Man . . . is the most feared driver on the road' wrote the *Sunday Times* in 1997 in one of the phrase's first appearances.

vandal

Today the worst thing a vandal might do is smash a few windows, but in the 4th and 5th centuries AD the Vandals were a Teutonic people that ravaged Gaul, Spain and North Africa and sacked Rome in 455. In Latin the name for a Vandal was *Vandalus*, which is also behind **Andalusia**, the southernmost region of Spain. The Romans overthrew the Vandals in 533 at the battle of Tricamarum, and like most victors set about discrediting their defeated opponents, so that the Vandals were branded as wilful or ignorant destroyers of anything beautiful or worthy of preservation. Our modern sense evolved in the 17th century, and **vandalism** in the 18th. See also HOOLIGAN, THUG.

vanity

In early use **vanity**, from about 1230, meant 'futility, worthlessness', with the idea of being conceited recorded a century later. This is the quality condemned in 'Vanity of vanities; all is vanity' from the biblical book of Ecclesiastes. The source of the word is Latin *vanus* 'empty, without substance', also the source of **vain** and **vanish**.

In Part I of *The Pilgrim's Progress* by John Bunyan, published in 1678, **Vanity Fair** is a fair set up in the town of Vanity, through which pilgrims pass on their way to the Eternal City. All kinds of 'vanity' – things of no real value – were on sale at the fair, including houses, honours and kingdoms. The 19th century took the name **Vanity Fair** to represent the world as a place of frivolity and idle amusement, most notably in William Makepeace Thackeray's novel *Vanity Fair* of 1847-8, which traces the progress of conflicting female characters, the clever and unscrupulous Becky Sharp and the gentle and unperceptive Amelia Sedley.

Vanity Fair has been the title of four magazines since the 1850s, in particular the current US magazine of culture, fashion and politics, founded in 1914.

From its earliest appearance in around 1300 **vain** has meant 'lacking real worth, worthless'. To **take someone's name in vain**, 'to use someone's name in a way that shows disrespect', echoes the third of the biblical Ten Commandments: 'Thou shalt not take the name of the Lord thy God in vain.' Since the late 17th century **vain** has also described someone who has a high opinion of their own appearance.

variety

The Latin word *varius* 'diverse' is the source not only of **variety**, in the late 15th century, but also of **variable**, **variegated**, **various** and **vary**. The **variety show** that consists of a series of different types of act is particularly associated with the British music halls, but the first examples of the term are American – the *Oregon State Journal* mentioned a 'variety troupe' in 1868. In the USA variety was first performed in saloons in front of a heavy-drinking male clientele, but when cleaned up and staged in more legitimate theatres it was transformed into VAUDEVILLE.

We have the 18th-century English poet William Cowper to thank for the familiar proverb **variety is the spice of life**. His poem 'The Task' contains the line: 'Variety's the very spice of life, / That gives it all its flavour.' The dramatist Aphra Behn, who had a similar idea around a century earlier, might possibly have inspired him. Her version, from the play *The Rover*, reads: 'Variety is the very soul of pleasure.'

vaudeville

Olivier Basselin was a 15th-century Frenchman from Vau de Vire, Normandy, who composed songs reputedly given the name *chansons du Vau de Vire*, or 'songs of the valley of Vire'. This was adapted to French *ville* 'town' and became *vau de ville* and later *vaudeville*, which was applied to a light popular song sung on the stage, the first meaning of **vaudeville** in English in the mid 18th century. Nowadays **vaudeville** refers to an entertainment featuring a mixture of acts such as comedy and song and dance that was popular in the USA in the late 19th and early 20th centuries.

veil

Our word **veil** is from Latin *vela*, plural of *velum* 'sail, covering, veil'. The first 13th-century uses refer to the headdress of a nun, and **take the veil**, or become a nun, appears about a hundred years later. Christian brides have worn veils since around the 3rd century, taking the custom from ancient Rome.

The expression **beyond the veil**, 'in a mysterious or hidden state or place', may call to mind the veil some Muslim women wear to conceal their face from view, but it comes from a different meaning of **veil** altogether. In ancient times **the veil** was the piece of precious cloth separating the innermost sanctuary from the rest of the Jewish Temple in Jerusalem. The idea soon developed of this cloth representing a barrier between this life and the unknown state of existence after death, giving rise to the current phrase.

velvet

The luxurious fabric **velvet** is noted for its smoothness and softness. Latin *villus*, 'tuft, down', is the source. **An iron fist in a velvet glove**, meaning 'firmness or ruthlessness cloaked in outward gentleness', has been current in English since the 1830s when it appeared as a saying of Napoleon's.

People gave the name **velvet revolution** to the relatively smooth change from Communism to a Western-style democracy in Czechoslovakia at the end of 1989. The similarly trouble-free division of that country into Slovakia and the Czech Republic in 1992 was the **velvet divorce**.

vendetta

Corsicans and Sicilians were the first to pursue **vendettas**. The word is Italian, and goes back to Latin *vindicare* 'to claim, avenge', the source also of **avenge**, **revenge**, **vindicate** and **vindictive**. It entered English in the mid 19th century.

veneer

'The yew especially is of late become very fashionable, and the goods fineered with it are certainly excessively pretty'. As this 1780 example shows, the earliest form of **veneer** was **fineer**. This word came into English through German *furnieren* from Old French *furnir* 'to furnish', and so is related to **furnish** and **furniture**. The idea behind it is that of 'furnishing' a piece of furniture with a thin surface.

ventriloquist

A **ventriloquist** speaks not with the mouth but with the belly. The word is based on Latin *venter* 'belly' and *loqui* 'to speak', from which **elocution** and **loquacious** also derive. Originally a ventriloquist was a person who appeared to speak from their abdomen because of spiritual possession. Its use to refer to someone who practises the skill for public entertainment dates from just before 1800, and ventriloquism later became a popular part of VAUDEVILLE shows.

verdict

After the Norman Conquest French became the language of the law in England, and many French legal terms entered English. One of these, **verdict**, first appeared in the 13th century. It came immediately from French, but goes back to Latin *verus* 'true', source also of **verify**, **veritable** and **very**, and *dicere* 'to say', from which **addict**, **dictate**, **dictionary**, **predict** and numerous other words derive

verge

Be careful when asking about the origin of **verge**. The answer could be embarrassing, not to say **verging on** the indecent. It came via Old French from Latin *virga* 'rod', and its first meaning in medieval English was 'penis'. This sense disappeared, to be replaced by 'a rod or sceptre as a symbol of office' and 'a boundary or margin', probably from the use of a rod as a boundary marker. The modern 'an edge or border' and 'a limit beyond which something will happen', as in 'on the verge of tears', are from the 17th century, as is the verb.

The church **verger** first took his name from the role of carrying a rod or similar symbol of office in front of a bishop or other official. Since the early 18th century a verger has also been a church caretaker and attendant.

vermilion

The name for this brilliant red colour and pigment goes back to Latin *vermis* 'a worm', source also of **vermin** and the pasta shape **vermicelli**. The reason for the unlikely connection probably lies in the red colours CRIMSON and **carmine**, which were originally extracted from the body of the kermes insect. People mistakenly thought that vermilion was also derived from an insect or worm, although its main early source was in fact cinnabar, a bright red mineral.

vermouth

One of the common ingredients of the aromatic wine vermouth is wormwood, a bitter-tasting shrub. Their names go back to the same source – **vermouth** came via French from German *Wermut* 'wormwood', which corresponds exactly to Old English

Wormwood

wermōd. People in the late Middle Ages modified this to **wormwood**, as if the word had been made by putting together two more familiar words **worm** and **wood**.

verse

In his poem 'Digging' (1966), Seamus Heaney resolves to carry on the family tradition of digging the soil by 'digging' himself, not with a spade like his father and grandfather, but with a pen. The link between agriculture and writing poetry goes way back to the origin of the word **verse**, as Latin *versus* meant both 'a turn of the plough, furrow' and 'a line of writing'. The idea is that of a plough turning and marking another straight line or furrow. *Versus* is also the source of **versatile** and **version**, and it is based on Latin *vertere* 'to turn', from which **vertebra**, **vertical**, **vertigo** and many other words such as **adverse**, **convert** and **pervert** derive. **Versed**, as in **well versed in**, is different, coming from Latin *versari* 'be engaged in'.

veto

The common people in ancient Rome chose 'tribunes of the people' to protect their interests. When these officials opposed measures of the Senate or actions of magistrates they said *veto*, Latin for 'I forbid'. The word **veto** entered English in the early 17th century for a rejection of a proposed act, especially one made by a law-making body.

via

The Latin word *via* meant 'way, road'. It survives in the names of major Roman roads, such as **Via Appia**, the chief road south from Rome also known as the **Appian Way**. The Christian Church also uses it in **Via Crucis**, another name for **the way of the Cross**, the journey of Jesus to the place of his execution at Calvary, and **the Via Dolorosa**, the route he is believed to have taken there and meaning 'the painful path'. **Viaduct** was formed from **via** in the early 19th century on the model of **aqueduct**. The modern sense 'by way of, through', as in 'London to Edinburgh via Oxford', arrived in the late 18th century.

vibes

In the Swinging Sixties people would **pick up** or **give out vibes**, using the word to mean 'an emotional state or atmosphere communicated to others'. **Vibes** is an alteration of **vibrations**, which had been used in a similar way since the end of the 19th century. Oscar Wilde wrote in 1899 in *The Importance of Being Earnest*: 'There is very little music in the name Jack, if any at all, indeed. It does not thrill. It produces absolutely no vibrations.' **Vibes** has also been used since the 1940s as another name for a **vibraphone**, an instrument resembling a xylophone.

vicar

The original **vicar** was a person who stood in for another – at first, around 1300, as an earthly representative of God or Christ, and then for an absent parson or rector. From there the vicar became the minister in charge of a parish where tithes or taxes passed to a monastery or other religious house, who paid the vicar as their 'representative' – a **rector** kept the tithes for himself. These meanings reflected the root, Latin *vicarius* 'a substitute', from which **vicarious**, 'experienced in the imagination through the actions of another person', also derives.

victory

A medieval word that came from Latin *victoria* 'victory', via Old French. The ultimate root was Latin *vincere* 'to conquer', also the source of **convince**, **convict**, **evict** and **vanquish**.

Dig for Victory was a British slogan of the Second World War which urged people to grow their own food. A radio broadcast of October 1939 urged: 'Let "Dig for Victory" be the motto of every one with a garden and of every able-bodied man and woman capable of digging an allotment in their spare time.'

A **Pyrrhic victory** is a victory won at too great a cost. **Pyrrhic** comes from the name of Pyrrhus, a king who from around 307 to 272 BC ruled Epirus, part of present-day Greece. Pyrrhus invaded Italy in 280 and defeated the Romans at the battle of Asculum in 279, though only after sustaining heavy losses to his army. After the battle he is said to have exclaimed: 'One more such victory and we are lost.'

Queen Victoria, who reigned 1837 to 1901, gave her name to the **Victorian** era. A support for **Victorian values**, often summed up as hard work, strict morality and social responsibility, is associated with former British Prime Minister Margaret Thatcher, who said in 1983: 'I was asked whether I was trying to restore Victorian values. I said straight out I was. And I am.'

vignette

In French a **vignette** is a 'little vine', and the word was once an architectural term for a carved representation of a vine, while in design and book production it refers to decorative depictions of foliage. From the mid 18th century a **vignette** became a design that shaded off into the background without a definite border. Restriction to visual features ended in the late 19th century, when the word assumed the modern sense, 'a brief evocative description, account or episode'.

Viking

The Vikings were seafaring pirates and traders from Scandinavia who raided and settled in many parts of northwestern Europe in the 8th-11th centuries. Scholars formerly assumed that the name came from Scandinavian *vík* 'creek, inlet' and referred to their setting out from the inlets of the sea, but it may well derive from Old English *wīc* 'camp', since formation of temporary encampments was a prominent feature of Viking raids. In 1975 the Americans gave the name **Viking** to two space probes sent to Mars, in recognition of the Vikings' fearless journeying and exploration. See also BERSERK, NORMAN.

villain

In medieval England a **villain** was a feudal tenant who was entirely subject to a lord or manor – this use is now usually spelled **villein**. People began to use **villain** as an insult implying that the person in question was a low-born rustic, and the meaning deteriorated even further to 'a person guilty of a crime, a criminal'. A bad character in a book was a villain from the 1820s. The word came from French and goes back to Latin *villa* 'country house with an estate or farm', from which **villa** itself and **village** also derive.

vindaloo

The **vindaloo** is one of the hottest curries, but the word is not Indian and does not imply spiciness. It probably derives from Portuguese *vin d'alho* 'wine and garlic sauce'. A vindaloo recipe is recorded in English in 1888, but it did not become familiar until Indian restaurants proliferated in the 1960s.

viper

Some vipers give birth to live young hatched from eggs within the parent's body, whereas the eggs of most snakes are expelled before they hatch out.

The name **viper** derives from this distinctive means of reproduction, coming from Latin *vivus* 'alive', as in **vivacious**, **vivid** or **vivisection**, and *parere* 'to bring forth', the source of **parent**. The phrase **a viper in your bosom**, 'a person you have helped but who has behaved treacherously towards you', comes from one of Aesop's fables in which a viper reared close to a person's chest eventually bites its nurturer. See also ADDER.

virago

The second chapter of the Book of Genesis describes the creation of Eve: 'And Adam said, This is now bone of my bones, and flesh of my flesh: she shall be called Woman, because she was taken out of Man.' In the Latin version of the Bible known as the Vulgate, the word Adam uses for Eve is *Virago*. This is not the insult it is now. *Virago* meant 'heroic woman, female warrior' in Latin and derived from *vir* 'man', the source of **virile** and **virtue**. **Virago** first appeared in English referring to Eve, but medieval man started using it in the scornful sense 'a domineering, violent or bad-tempered woman' that survives today. The Virago Press, founded by Carmen Callil in 1972 to publish female authors, harked back to the original meaning. See also AMAZON.

virus

A **virus** was originally the venom of a snake, and was an English borrowing of a Latin word meaning 'slimy liquid' or 'poison' that is also the source of **virulent**. Early medical practitioners did not understand the structure and properties of the virus, and used the word for a substance produced in the body as the result of disease. The modern meaning, 'a submicroscopic organism which can cause disease', dates from the late 19th century. The **computer virus**, the piece of code which can do such destructive things as corrupting the system or destroying data, dates from the early 1970s.

vital

Latin *vita* 'life' is the source of **vital** and also of VITAMIN. Medieval senses relate to the force or energy that is in all living things. A later meaning 'essential to life' evolved in time to describe anything regarded as essential or crucial, such as the vital organs, also known as **the vitals** from the early 17th century.

The British Prime Minister Benjamin Disraeli said 'There are three kinds of lies: lies, damned lies and statistics.' The only kind of statistics some men are interested in are **vital statistics**, usually understood now as the measurements of a woman's bust, waist and hips. This meaning has only been around since the 1950s, though, and for more than 100 years before that vital statistics were just the numbers of births, marriages and deaths in a population.

vitamin

In 1906 the British biochemist Frederick Hopkins proved conclusively that foods contain more than just carbohydrates, minerals, proteins, fats and water. He called these unknown constituents 'accessory factors'. The Polish chemist Casimir Funk took this further by identifying the 'accessory factor' in unpolished rice that prevented the disease beriberi as an amine, an organic compound derived from ammonia, and gave it the name **vitamine**. Funk formed the word from Latin *vita* 'life',

source also of VITAL, and **amine**. Other 'vitamines' were found , but by 1920 it was clear that not all were amines. The British chemist J.C. Drummond proposed, successfully, that the -*e* be dropped, and **vitamin** it is.

vodka

The name of the clear, strong alcoholic spirit claims that it is just 'water' – it is a diminutive form of Russian *voda* 'water'. Travellers to Russia brought the word, and perhaps also the drink, back to Britain in the early 19th century. See also WATER, WHISKY.

vogue

Fashion and rowing may not appear to have much in common, but Italian *voga*, from which **vogue** came in the late 16th century, derives from *vogare* 'to row, go well'. During the 17th century **vogue** was definitely in vogue, developing most of its current meanings. In the 1980s dancers in clubs began to **vogue**, imitating the poses struck by catwalk models – the word here refers to the glossy fashion magazine *Vogue*, which began as a weekly New York society paper before the US publisher Condé Nast bought and transformed it from 1909.

voice

A word derived from Latin *vox* 'voice' and related to **vocabulary**, **vocal**, **vocation** and **vociferous**. The Latin root survives in **vox pop**, 'an informal survey of people's opinion', which is short for **vox populi** or 'voice of the people'. When people refer to an ignored advocate of reform as a **voice in the wilderness** they are echoing the words of John the Baptist proclaiming the coming of the Messiah: 'I am the voice of one crying in the wilderness.'

volcano

In Roman mythology Vulcan was the god of fire, and a metalworker. A conical mountain with erupting lava, rock fragments, hot vapour or gas must have suggested his forge or smithy, and Italians named such a feature *volcano* or *vulcano* after him. A volcano in the Lipari Islands in Italy, noted for its periodic eruptions, still bears the name Vulcano. The word **volcano** entered English in the early 17th century.

vulgar

Latin *vulgus* 'the common people', the root also of **divulge**, is the source of **vulgar**. The original senses, from the late Middle Ages, were 'used in ordinary calculations', which survives in **vulgar fraction**, and 'in ordinary use, used by the people', which survives in **vulgar tongue**. The sense 'coarse, uncultured' dates from the mid 17th century.

waffle

Someone who waffles now talks on and on in a vague or trivial way, but in the 17th century to **waffle** was 'to yap or yelp', and then 'to dither'. It came from the English dialect term **waff** 'to yelp' (the same word as **woof**), and seems to have been used mainly in northern England until the modern meaning arose at the start of the 20th century. **Waffle** meaning 'a small crisp batter cake' is quite different: it comes from Dutch *wafel*, and before that Old French *gaufre*, the root of wafer. Gaufre also meant 'honeycomb', and this is probably the basic idea – the criss-cross indentations on a waffle or wafer look like a honeycomb.

waft

In the early 16th century **waft** meant 'to escort a ship in a convoy'. The current meaning, 'to move gently through the air', developed from the second sense, 'to convey by water', which was used several times by Shakespeare: 'I charge thee, waft me safely across the Channel' (*Henry VI Part 2*). **Waft** is from **wafter** 'armed convoy vessel', from German and Dutch *wachten* 'to guard'.

wag

The sort of wagging done by dogs is from the Old English word *wagian* 'to sway'. **Wag** meaning 'a joker' is a different word, dating from the 16th century, which first meant 'a mischievous boy or lively young man', and was often used as a fond name for a child. Showing the grim 'gallows humour' of the times, it probably comes from **waghalter**, 'a person likely to be hanged'.

In the 2006 World Cup a new meaning of **wag** suddenly became popular. The **WAGs** were the Wives and Girlfriends of the England players. The term had been used in the 2004 European Championship – on June 13 the Daily Mail wrote: 'Victoria Beckham was criticised for seeming to distance herself from the other players' partners, who have been nicknamed "Wags" (Wives and Girlfriends).'

wagon

The Dutch word *wagen* is the source of our **wagon**. It is related to **wain**, an old word for 'wagon' that is now mainly encountered in the name of the star formation **Charles's Wain**, now more commonly called the Plough.

If you are **on the wagon** you are avoiding alcohol. The original version of this expression was **on the water wagon**, which first appeared in America in the early 20th century. A water wagon was a sort of barrel on wheels which was used to water dusty streets. These vehicles had been around since the early 18th century at least, but it may have been the increasing popularity of the temperance movement in the latter part of the 19th century that gave rise to the phrase. Those abstaining from alcohol were encouraged to pledge that they were 'on the water wagon'. See also HITCH.

waif

In the 1990s a new look became popular for fashion models, epitomised by Kate Moss: the painfully thin, child-like girls were called **waifs** or **superwaifs**. The word **waif** can be traced right back to medieval law, where it was a term for a piece of property found without an owner, which belonged to the lord of the manor if it was not claimed – **waifs and strays** was an overall term for lost property and stray animals. It was not until the 1600s that **waif** first referred to a homeless or neglected person. The word is from Old French *gaif*, and before that was probably Scandinavian.

walk

An Old English word that originally meant 'to roll, toss' and 'to wander', and did not start to mean 'walk' until about 1300. The odd expression **walk of life**, meaning 'a person's occupation or position within society', probably derives from the use of **walk** to refer to the round or circuit of a travelling tradesman or official.

In Australian English a **walkabout** is a journey into the bush that an Aboriginal makes to re-establish contact with traditions and spiritual sources – to **go walkabout** is to go on such a journey. Since around 1970 the term has also been used of the informal strolls among welcoming crowds favoured by members of the royal family and visiting dignitaries. It can also mean 'to go missing, disappear', especially in the context of small objects such as pens, car keys and television remote controls which have frustratingly vanished from your desk, bag or sofa.

The Sony **Walkman**, a type of personal stereo using cassette tapes, was trademarked in 1981. **Walkman** was the generic term for 'personal stereo' until the release of the iPod MP3 player in 2001, and in 2003 Sony launched an MP3 Walkman. See also BLOOD.

wall

For as long as we have had somewhere to live we have had walls, so it is not surprising that **wall** dates back to at least AD 900 in English. It comes from Latin *vallum* 'rampart', from *vallus* 'stake', which implies that the earliest walls were defensive ones around a town or camp.

To **go to the wall** is now to fail commercially or go broke, but it originally meant 'give way' or 'be beaten in a battle or fight'. The idea may be that of a hard-pressed fighter retreating until he had a wall behind him and he could retreat no more – until he had his **back against the wall**. There may also be a link to the proverb **the weakest go to the wall**, which dates back to the end of the 15th century and is usually said to derive from the installation of seating round the walls in churches of the late Middle Ages.

Someone who is **off the wall** is unconventional or crazy. This is a quite recent phrase, first recorded in the mid 1960s, in the USA. One suggestion is that it refers to the way that a ball sometimes bounces off a wall at an unexpected angle.

The proverb **walls have ears** dates back to the early 17th century. A more rural version is **fields have eyes, and woods have ears**, which is first recorded some 400 years earlier.

Saying that **the writing is on the wall** means there are clear signs that something bad is going to happen. This is a biblical allusion to the description of Belshazzar's feast in the Book of Daniel. In this account Belshazzar was the king of Babylon whose death was foretold by a mysterious hand which wrote on the palace wall at a banquet. The words were *mene, mene, tekel, upharsin*, which no one could translate until Daniel was brought in. He told the king that the words meant 'God hath numbered thy kingdom, and finished it. Thou art weighed in the balance, and art found wanting. Thy kingdom is divided, and given to the Medes and Persians.' True enough, that very night the city was attacked by the Medes and Persians, and Belshazzar was killed.

wallet

Before the days of banknotes and credit cards a **wallet** was a bag, pouch or knapsack for carrying food, clothing or other provisions. Medieval pilgrims would carry them, and the earliest recorded use of the word is by Geoffrey Chaucer, in the prologue to the *Canterbury Tales*. The modern meaning did not turn up until the 1840s, in the USA. The word is from Old French, and is related to WELL.

wallop

Although the spelling is similar, **wallop** and **gallop** have very different meanings. Nevertheless the original meaning of **wallop** was 'to gallop', and the Old French sources of the two words, *galoper* and *waloper*, are related. It seems that there is something gratifying about the way **wallop** sounds that makes people use it in lively ways. The next sense to develop was 'to boil violently', and then 'to move in a heavy or clumsy way' and 'to flop about, dangle, flap'. The modern sense, 'to hit very hard', appeared in the early 19th century.

wally

You can say that **wally**, meaning 'a silly or inept person', is short for the name Walter, and that it was first used in the 1960s – beyond that nothing is certain. The most popular theory about its origin connects it with an incident at a pop festival where a chap called Wally became separated from his companions: his name was announced many times over the loudspeaker and was taken up as a chant by the crowd. In the 1970s hippies at gigs and festivals would certainly shout out

HOW WOULD I DESCRIBE MYSELF? ER... OFF THE WALL I GUESS

DATING AGENCY

'Wally!' in an exuberant and random fashion, and there was even a rock band at the time called Wally.

walnut

It is familiar to us now, but to the Anglo-Saxons and other ancient peoples of northern Europe the **walnut** was the 'foreign nut'. The nut they knew was the hazelnut, and walnuts would have been exotic imports from the Roman world of the south. The *wal-* part comes from *Volcae*, the Latin name for a particular Celtic tribe that the Germanic peoples came to use for all Celts (it is where **Welsh** and **Wales** come from) and eventually for anyone not of Germanic stock.

wan

An example of a colour word that has reversed in meaning, like AUBURN. As far as AD 700 **wan** meant 'dark, black', and it did not start to mean 'pale' until around 1300. As well as 'dark' it originally meant 'of an unhealthy greyish colour', particularly of the face of a person who was dead or affected by disease, and this notion of unhealthiness could have provided the connection with 'pale'.

wand

A word from Old Norse, and related to **wend** and **wind**, 'to move in a twisting way' – the basic idea seems to be of a supple, flexible stick. **Wand** did not have any connection with wizards and spells until about 1400, 200 years after it was first used. **Wander**, 'to move in a leisurely or aimless way', comes from a similar root.

war

Before the mid 12th century there was no English word exactly meaning **war**, which came over from Old French *guerre* and is related to **worse**. The Anglo-Saxons used *gewin*, 'struggle, strife'.

The war to end all wars was the hopeful but sadly inaccurate name given to the First World War. It is a misquotation of *The War That Will End War,* the title of a book by H.G. Wells published in 1914. It became famous when Prime Minister Lloyd George made this reference in the House of Commons on November 11, 1918, the day that the war ended: 'At eleven o'clock this morning came to an end the cruellest and most terrible war that has ever scourged mankind. I hope we may say that thus, this fateful morning, came to an

end all wars.' In 1904 Thomas Hardy wrote in *The Dynasts*: 'War makes rattling good history; but Peace is poor reading.' **Make love not war** was a student slogan of the mid and late 1960s, used by people opposing the Vietnam War.

Both **warpaint** and **warpath** are from the customs of North American Indians, who made up their faces before going into battle. **Warpaint** meaning 'make-up' is first recorded as early as 1869, while **on the warpath** in the sense 'very angry with someone' is from 1880. The first major trials for **war crimes** were those of 1945-6 in Nuremberg, where Nazi war criminals were tried by international military tribunal, but the term dates from 1906.

walrus

To the Anglo-Saxons the **walrus** must have looked a bit like a horse – they called it the *horschwæl*, 'horse-whale'. We owe our name for the creature to the Dutch, who took the same Saxon idea but reversed it: the *wal-* part is 'whale' and *-rus* is probably 'horse'.

ward

The words ward and **guard** share an ancient root, and used to share many of their meanings. **Ward** first meant 'the action of guarding or keeping watch', then 'custody, imprisonment' (**warder**, as in **prison warder**, is from the same root), 'the guardianship of a child' and 'a young person under the supervision of a guardian'. These meanings seem fairly logical, but the sense 'a room in a hospital' is different. The connection is the sense 'place that is guarded, section of a castle's defences', which became 'a prison' and then in around 1750 'a room in a hospital'.

wardrobe

It would cause plenty of confusion today, but a **wardrobe** used to be a toilet. The word comes from Old French *garderobe*, which was also used in medieval English. **Wardrobe** and **garderobe** both meant 'storeroom' and also 'private room, bedroom' and 'privy, lavatory'. The ultimate roots of both were **guard** and **robe**, so the modern sense of **wardrobe** is close to the basic meaning. It arose at the end of the18th century from an early sense, 'small room used to store clothing' – most of us no longer live in castles with whole rooms to store our clothes.

warlock

A **warlock** is not connected with war or locks, and was not originally anything to do with magic. To the Anglo-Saxons a **warlock** was 'an evil person, traitor', 'monster, savage' and 'the Devil'. The sense 'sorcerer, wizard' was originally Scottish, and only became more widely known when it was used by the novelist

Sir Walter Scott in the early 19th century. It comes from Old English words meaning 'agreement, promise' and 'deny'. See also WITCH.

warm

Such a basic concept goes back a very long way. **Warm** is an Old English word but can be traced right back to a lost root that was also the source of Greek *thermos* 'hot', which gave us **thermometer**, **thermostat**, and **Thermos** (flask). **Cold hands, warm heart** is a proverb first found in the early 20th century.

warren

Today it is a network of burrows used by wild rabbits, but in medieval times a **warren**, from Old French *garenne* 'game park', was a piece of land enclosed for the breeding of game, specifically rabbits and hares. Rabbits were brought to Britain by the Normans, and at first the animals were reared in an enclosed 'warren'. Presumably the rabbits (and hares) soon escaped and started to breed, and people realised that there was no need to make a special effort to keep them.

wart

The Anglo-Saxons suffered from warts – the word is first recorded around AD 700. The expression **warts and all**, meaning 'including features or qualities that are not appealing or attractive', dates back to the mid 19th century. The source of the phrase can be traced back to Horace Walpole's *Anecdotes of Painting in England* (1763), in which he recounts a request supposedly made by Oliver Cromwell to the portrait painter Peter Lely: 'Remark all these roughnesses, pimples, warts, and everything as you see me; otherwise I will never pay a farthing for it.'

wash

An Old English word that is related to WATER. Someone who is **washed up** is no longer effective or successful – they are likened to a dead fish or piece of wreckage thrown up on to a beach. The first example of the expression, from the 1920s in the USA, states that it is 'stage slang'. Similarly ineffective or disappointing is a **wash-out**, recorded from around 1900, which in RAF slang was specifically a person who failed a training course.

To **wash your hands** is a euphemism for going to the loo – a male equivalent of **powdering your nose**, used since the 1930s. To **wash your hands of**, or disclaim responsibility for, is a biblical allusion to the Gospel of Matthew. Pontius Pilate, the Roman governor of Judaea who presided at the trial of Jesus, was unwilling to authorise his crucifixion, but saw that the crowd were intent on his death. 'He [Pilate] took water, and washed his hands before the multitude, saying, I am innocent of the blood of this just person.'

wasp

Our distant linguistic ancestors had a word for the pesky insect the **wasp**, which can be traced back to an ancient root that also produced the Latin word for 'wasp', *vespa*. The ultimate origin may be a word that meant 'to weave', the connection being the way that wasps chew up wood into a papery substance that they use to constuct their nests. The Latin word *vespa* was carried forward into Italian and used as the name for the **Vespa**, the little motor scooter beloved by Italians, named for its hyperactive buzzing and to some ears almost as annoying as the insect.

A 1960s couple enjoy the buzz of riding on a Vespa scooter.

wassail

In the Middle Ages **wassail** was a drinking toast that literally meant 'Be in good health'. The polite reply was **drinkhail**, 'Drink good health'. Both words come from Old Norse, and were probably introduced by Danish-speaking inhabitants of England. By the 12th century they were considered by the Normans to be characteristic of Englishmen: in a work of 1190 the English students at the university of Paris are praised for generosity and other virtues, but are said to be too much addicted to 'wassail' and 'drinkhail'. Some things never change.

watch

In Old English **watch** meant 'to be or remain awake', and it is from the same root as **wake**. The connection with timepieces arose because in the 15th century the first watches were alarm clocks of some kind, whose function was to wake you up.

The watches of the night are the hours of night, especially as a time when you cannot sleep. A **watch** was originally one of the periods of time into which the night was divided for the purposes of guard duty. Ancient Hebrew guards had the toughest job, as their night was only divided into three, whereas the Greeks and Romans had four or five watches. The link with insomnia first appears in the writings of Sir Walter Scott, who wrote in his journal for January 1826: 'The watches of the night pass wearily when disturbed by fruitless regrets.'

water

The people living around the Black Sea more than 6,000 years ago had a word for **water**. We do not know exactly what it was, but it may be the source for the words used for 'water' in many European languages, past and present. In Old English it was *wæter*. The Greek was *hudōr*, the source of words like **hydraulic** and **hydrotherapy**. The same root led to the formation of Latin *unda* 'wave', as in **inundate** and **undulate**, Russian *voda* (the source of VODKA), German *Wasser*, and the English words **wet** and **otter**.

Of the first water means 'unsurpassed'. The three highest grades into which diamonds or pearls could be classified used to be called waters, but only **first water**, the top one, is found today, describing a completely flawless gem. An equivalent term is found in many European languages, and all are thought to come from the Arabic word for water, *mā'*, which also meant 'shine or splendour', presumably from the appearance of very pure water. People and things other than gems began to be described as **of the first water** in the 1820s. Nowadays the phrase is rarely used as a compliment: in a letter written in 1950, P.G. Wodehouse commented disparagingly on J.M. Barrie's play *The Admirable Crichton*: 'I remember being entranced with it in 1904 or whenever it was, but now it seems like a turkey of the first water.'

If you study a duck shaking its wings after diving for food you will see the point of **water off a duck's back**, used since the 1820s of a potentially hurtful remark that has no apparent effect. The water forms into beads and simply slides off the bird's waterproof feathers, leaving the duck dry.

Water under the bridge refers to events that are in the past and should no longer be regarded as important. Similar phrases are recorded since the beginning of the 20th century: 'Much water has flowed under London Bridge since those days' is from Wireless World in 1913. A North American variant is **water over the dam**.

The first uses of **waterlogged**, in the late 18th century, referred to ships that were so flooded with water that they became heavy and unmanageable, and no better than a log floating in the sea. A **watershed**, a ridge of land that separates waters flowing to different rivers or seas, has nothing to do with garden sheds: the second half means 'ridge of high ground' and is connected with **shed** meaning 'discard'.

weave

English has two words spelled **weave**. The one meaning 'twist from side to side' probably comes from Old Norse *veifa* 'to wave, brandish'. The other one is Old English and comes from a root derived from a source shared by Greek *huphē* 'web' and Sanskrit *ūrnavābhi* 'spider', or literally 'wool-weaver'. **Web** is a related word, first recorded in about AD 725. Nobody then could have visualised the **World Wide Web**, which was first mentioned in writing in 1990, in a paper by Tim Berners-Lee and Robert Cailliau, who are credited with its invention. See also YAHOO.

wedding

Both **wedding** and **wed** are Old English words that go back to an ancient root meaning 'to promise', and they are also linked to ENGAGE, appropriately enough. To **wed** was originally to engage or promise to do something, then to make a woman your wife by giving a pledge.

week

An Old English word that is probably from a base meaning 'sequence, series'. The seven-day week used in the Hebrew and then the Christian calendar corresponds to the biblical creation story, in which God created the Universe in six days then rested on the seventh. The Romans, who adopted it in AD 321, would have brought this week over to Britain.

'A week is a long time in politics' was first said by Harold Wilson, British Labour Prime Minister 1964-70 and 1974-6, at the time of the 1964 sterling crisis. He meant that a Party of government could be doing well at the start of a week but in disgrace at the end, or vice versa. Wilson came up with a number of memorable phrases, including 'the gnomes of Zurich', to describe Swiss financiers (1956), 'the university of the air' (1963) as a name for the Open University, which his government founded, and 'the pound here in Britain, in your pocket or purse or bank' (1967), which is often quoted as 'the pound in your pocket'. See also TUESDAY, WHITE.

weigh

The word **weigh** can be traced back to an ancient root that also gave us Latin *vehere* 'to carry', the source of **vehicle**. Early senses of **weigh** that are no longer used included 'to transport from one place to another' and 'to raise up', as in **weigh the anchor** of a boat or ship. The modern meaning probably comes from the idea of lifting something up on a pair of scales or similar device to weigh it.

weird

To Anglo-Saxons **weird** was a noun, spelled *wyrd* and meaning 'fate, destiny'. A weird was a witch or wizard, and the Weirds were the Fates, the three Greek goddesses who presided over the birth and life of humans. The adjective first meant 'having the power to control destiny', and was used especially from the Middle Ages in **the Weird Sisters**, who were the Fates, and later the witches in Shakespeare's *Macbeth*. The modern use, 'very strange, bizarre', as in **weird and wonderful**, dates from the early 19th century.

well

The **well** that means 'in a good way' and **well** in the sense 'shaft giving access to water' are two different Old English words. The first of these provides the first half of **welfare**. The start of **welcome**, on the other hand, is from a different Old English base, *wil-* meaning 'pleasure' – **welcome** originally meant 'a person whose arrival is pleasing'.

The title of Shakespeare's comedy *All's Well that Ends Well* was already an old saying when he wrote the play at the beginning of the 17th century. The first record of the proverb is as early as 1250.

People have been **well-endowed** only since the 1950s, but men could be **well-hung** in the early 17th century. At this time it meant 'having large ears' as well as 'having a large penis'.

Wendy house

The name for a toy house large enough for children to play in comes from J.M. Barrie's play *Peter Pan* (1904). In the play, which Barrie turned into the novel *Peter Pan and Wendy* in 1911, Peter and the Lost Boys build a small structure for Wendy to live in following their flight to Neverland.

west

All of the words for compass points are Old English. **West** can be traced back to an ancient root that also produced Latin *vesper* 'evening', also the source of the church service **vespers**, the connection being that the sun sets in the west.

Go west, meaning 'be killed', comes from the idea of the sun setting in the west at the end of the day, and became common during the First World War. The expression is also used more generally in the sense 'be lost or broken', and this is the meaning found in the American equivalent **go south**. The choice of a different compass point is possibly connected with the idea of something being on a downward trend, or perhaps **go west** sounded too positive, given the hopeful promise of the American West represented in the exhortation 'Go west, young man! Go west!', recorded from 1851.

The lawless western frontier of the USA during the period when settlers were migrating from the inhabited east was known as **the Wild West** from the 1840s, and was the setting for **westerns** featuring cowboys, Indians and cattle rustlers from about 1910. See also TWAIN.

whammy

A **whammy** is literally an evil influence or hex, formed from **wham**, which itself is an imitation of the sound of a forcible impact. The word has been around since the 1940s but is particularly associated with the 1950s cartoon strip 'Li'l Abner', in which the hillbilly Evil-Eye Fleegle could shoot a **single whammy** to put a curse on somebody by pointing a finger with one eye open, and a **double whammy** with both eyes open. **Double whammy** was popularised more recently by 'Labour's double whammy', a Conservative Party slogan in the 1992 general election campaign – if Labour were elected, the country would allegedly suffer the 'double whammy' of higher prices and higher taxes.

wheat

An Anglo-Saxon word related to WHITE, presumably on account of its pale colour. To **separate the wheat from the chaff**, meaning 'to distinguish valuable people or things from worthless ones' is a biblical concept. In the Gospels of Matthew and Luke John the Baptist tells the people that a being mightier than him will soon come and gather in the wheat, or good people, but ruthlessly burn the chaff. In several other passages God's anger is spoken of as driving away the wicked just as the wind blows away chaff.

The first part of **wheatear**, a small songbird with a white rump, is from WHITE rather than **wheat**. The second part seems odd, as birds have no ears – it is actually from ARSE, referring to the bird's rump.

wheel

The **wheel** was probably invented some time around 4000 BC in Mesopotamia (present-day Iraq). Its name, probably based on a word meaning 'to turn', moved east to India, where it produced Sanskrit *cakra* 'wheel, circle', and west, where it gave rise to Greek *kuklos* 'circle', the source of **cycle**. It is recorded in Anglo-Saxon English from about AD 900.

To **reinvent the wheel** is a 20th-century expression for wasting a great deal of time and effort in creating something that already exists. The **wheel** here represents an example of technology which is essential to any level of civilisation.

The phrase **wheels within wheels** indicates that a situation is complicated and affected by hidden influences. It is an allusion to a biblical quotation from the Old Testament book of Ezekiel. The prophet Ezekiel sees a vision in which four cherubs (winged angelic beings) appear, each with a weird-looking wheel: 'And as for their appearances, they four had one likeness, as if a wheel had been in the midst of a wheel'. The strangeness of the vision has led to some to speculate that what Ezekiel saw was a UFO.

Whig

The Whigs dominated the English political scene in the late 17th and first half of the 18th century. Originally opponents of the succession of James II and supporters of Parliament, they came to champion electoral and social reform. The first Whigs were 17th-century Scottish Presbyterians (religious dissenters) who were given their name by their opponents, the Tories. It was probably a shortening of Scots **whiggamore**, which came from **whig** 'to drive' and MARE – the idea was possibly that they were nothing better than horse thieves. In the mid 19th century the term **Whig** started to be replaced by **liberal**. See also TORY.

whimper

Like bonk, drum and hoot, **whimper** is another of those words suggested by the sound it represents. 'This is the way the world ends / Not with a bang but a whimper' is from 'The Hollow Men' (1925) by T.S. Eliot. See also WIMP.

whimsy

It sounds like it was invented by Lewis Carroll, but **whimsy** goes back much further. The first sense was 'a sudden fancy, a whim', in the early 17th century. The word comes from **whim-wham**, first recorded in the 1520s and meaning 'a decorative object, a trinket' and 'an odd notion or fancy'. **Whim**, which first meant 'a pun or play on words', also came from **whim-wham** in the 17th century.

whip

A word that came into English from old German and Dutch *wippen* 'to swing, leap, dance'.

The parliamentary **whip**, responsible for ensuring that Party members turn up and vote in debates, was originally a **whipper-in**. This is a term in hunting, where the whipper-in uses his whip to keep the hounds from straying. The short form **whip** is first found in 1850. A **whip-round**, or collection of contributions of money, is related, coming in the 1860s from **whip** in the sense 'a notice from a whip requiring MPs to attend a vote'.

Since the late 17th century a **whippersnapper** has been a young person who is presumptuous or overconfident. A **whippersnapper** is literally 'a person who cracks a whip' – the connection was probably that the presumptuous youngster was making a lot of noise but achieving little.

A **whipping boy** is a person who is blamed for the faults of others. Originally it was a boy who was educated with a young prince and, because it would not be right for a commoner to beat a royal person, punished instead of him.

whisky

The root of **whisky** is a Gaelic word, one to challenge the spelling skills of the most sober person – *uisgebeatha*, literally 'water of life'. The spelling **whisky** is first recorded in 1715, but more 'Gaelic' forms like **usquebaugh** and **usquebae** were used from the 16th century. Today **whisky** is the usual spelling for Scotch, and **whiskey** for Irish whiskey. Incidentally, two terms for **brandy** also mean 'water of life', Latin *aqua vitae* and French *eau de vie*, whereas vodka is a diminutive form of 'water' in Russian.

whistle

The first meaning of **whistle** was 'a small pipe or flute'. In **wet your whistle**, or have a drink, the whistle is your mouth or throat, as used in speaking or singing. The first example of its use is by Geoffrey Chaucer in *The Reeve's Tale*.

To **blow the whistle on** someone responsible for doing something wrong is to inform on them. The expression comes from the idea of a referee blowing a whistle to indicate that a player has broken the rules and that play must be stopped. When the expression was first used in the 1930s it simply meant 'bring an activity to an abrupt halt', but by the 1970s it had come to refer specifically to people exposing wrongdoing in government or industry.

In the 1930s a **whistle-stop** was a small, unimportant American town on a railway, where trains only stopped if they were requested to. If a passenger wanted to get off the conductor would sound a whistle to tell the driver he had to stop. A **whistle-stop tour** was one made by a politician before an election that took in even these small, obscure places.

white

The Old English word **white**, related to WHEAT, is used in many English phrases. A **white elephant** is a useless or unwanted possession, especially one that's expensive to maintain. The original white elephants were real albino animals regarded as holy in some Asian countries, especially Siam (present-day Thailand). The story goes that it was the custom for a king of Siam to give one of these elephants to a courtier he particularly disliked: the unfortunate recipient could neither refuse the gift nor give it away later for fear of causing offence, and would end up financially ruined by the costs of looking after the animal.

A **whited sepulchre** is a hypocrite. The phrase comes from Jesus's condemnation of the Pharisees in the Gospel of Matthew: he likens them to whited sepulchres, or whitewashed tombs, 'which indeed appear beautiful outward, but are within full of dead men's bones, and of all uncleanness'.

The white heat of technology is a phrase usually credited to Harold Wilson. What he actually said in a 1963 speech was, 'The Britain that is going to be forged in the white heat of this revolution will be no place for restrictive practices or for outdated methods on either side of industry.' See also WEEK.

The white man's burden, meaning the task of imposing Western civilisation on the inhabitants of colonies, comes from the title of a poem by Rudyard Kipling, published in 1899. The work, 'The White Man's Burden: The United States and The Philippine Islands', urged the USA to take up the burden of empire following its acquisition of the Philippines as a result of the Spanish-American War.

The festival **Whit Sunday** or **Whitsuntide** also comes from **white**. It is a reference to the white robes worn by early Christians who were baptised at this time.

wicked

A medieval word from Old English *wicca* 'witch'. **Wicked** is one of those words, like BAD, which has completely reversed its meaning, in the slang sense 'excellent, very good', first used in the 1920s.

No peace for the wicked is a biblical allusion, to the Book of Isaiah: 'There is no peace, saith the Lord, unto the wicked.' See also TENDER, THUMB.

wicket

The original kind of **wicket**, from Old French *wiket*, was a small gate or door beside, or in, a larger one. The cricketing wicket dates back to the 1730s, and was suggested by the shape of the gate. A **sticky wicket** is a cricket pitch that has been drying out in the sun after heavy rain. Because bowlers can make the ball turn a long way on pitches like this, they can be very difficult to bat on. Since the 1950s the term has been used more generally to refer to any tricky or awkward situation.

widget

The **widget** is first recorded in the 1920s in the USA, in the general sense 'a small gadget', and is probably an alteration of GADGET. In the early 1990s a **widget** became a specific sort of device used in some beer cans to introduce nitrogen into the beer, giving it a creamy head.

widow

The Old English word **widow** is descended from an ancient root meaning 'to be empty', which may also be the source of DIVIDE. A **grass widow** is now a woman whose husband is away often or for a prolonged period, but originally it was an unmarried woman who had been the mistress of more than one man: the term may have come from the idea of a couple having lain on the grass instead of in bed.

wife

The original meaning of **wife**, as early as AD 700, was simply 'woman', a sense which is still used in Scotland and in terms such as **fishwife** and MIDWIFE. **All the world and his wife**, meaning 'everyone' or 'a great many people', is first recorded in Jonathan Swift's *Polite Conversation* (1738). See also CAESAR, WOMAN.

wild

Both **wild** and **wilderness** are Old English words. The first sense of **wild** was 'not tame or domesticated', and **wilderness** means literally 'land inhabited only by wild animals' – it comes from Old English *wild dēor* 'wild deer'. This is the sense in *The Call of the Wild* (1903), a novella by the American writer Jack London about a pet sold as a sled dog that returns to the wild to lead a pack of wolves.

To the Anglo-Saxons **wildfire** was originally a raging, destructive fire caused by a lightning strike. It was also a mixture of highly flammable substances used in warfare, and a term for various skin diseases that spread quickly over the body. We use it only in the phrase **spread like wildfire**, 'to spread with great speed', which was suggested by Shakespeare's line in his poem *The Rape of Lucrece*: 'Whose words like wild fire burnt the shining glorie / Of rich-built Illion [Troy]'.

The obvious explanation for the phrase **a wild goose chase** is that it alludes to the difficulty of shooting wild geese flying fast and high in the sky. But early examples, from the late 16th century, refer to a sport of the time in which each of a line of riders had to follow accurately the course of the leader, like a flight of wild geese. See also DEER, VOICE, WEST, WOOL.

wimp

The origins of **wimp**, 'a weak and cowardly person', are a bit wimpish. The word seems to have originated in the USA in the 1920s, although it was not really used much until the 1960s. There was an earlier slang term **wimp** which meant 'woman', used at Oxford University in the early years of the 20th century: this could be the origin, or **wimp** could simply be an alteration of WHIMPER.

wind

A word that blew into English from a root that also gave us Latin *ventus*, the source of **vent** and **ventilate**. Like us, the Anglo-Saxons called gas in the stomach and intestines **wind**.

The proverb **it's an ill wind that blows nobody any good**, recorded from the 16th century, is often misinterpreted. It means 'few things are so bad that no one profits from them', and relates to sailing ships – if the wind was not blowing in the direction you wanted, it would be just right for someone somewhere else. To **get wind of** something, or begin to suspect that something is happening, comes from the idea of a hunted animal picking up the scent of a hunter.

The phrase **wind of change** was used by Harold Macmillan, British Prime Minister 1957-63, during a speech he made in Cape Town in 1960: 'The wind of change is blowing through this continent, and, whether we like it or not, this growth of [African] national consciousness is a political fact.' Macmillan is also famous for **you've never had it so good**. The full quote was 'Let us be frank about it: most of our people have never had it so good', said in 1957. 'You Never Had It So Good' was the Democratic Party slogan during the 1952 US election campaign.

window

The English first used the word **window** at the beginning of the 13th century, taking it from Old Norse *vindauga*, which literally meant 'wind eye'. Before that the Anglo-Saxons words were *éagthyrl* and *éagduru*, 'eye hole' and 'eye door'. Early windows would generally have been just openings in a wall, sometimes with shutters or curtains. The computing sense 'a framed area on a screen for viewing information' was first recorded in 1974, and in 1985 Microsoft released the first version of its Windows operating system. See also EYE.

wine

At heart **wine** is the same word as **vine**. Both can be traced back to Latin *vinum*, 'wine', which also gave us **vinegar** and **vinyl** – in technical use vinyl is a plastic created from a derivative of ethylene, which is a naturally occurring gas given off by ripening fruit.

Wine, women and song represent the pleasure-filled life of drinking, sex and carefree entertainment proverbially enjoyed by men. The expression was suggested by 'Wine and women will make men of understanding to fall away' from the biblical book of Ecclesiasticus, and 'Who loves not wine, woman, and song, / He is a fool his whole life long', a translation of an anonymous German fragment of poetry. See also TRUTH.

willy-nilly

Things have been happening **willy-nilly** since the early 17th century. Originally it was **will I, nill I**, meaning 'I am willing, I am unwilling'. **Shilly-shally** is similar, formed from 'shill I, shall I?', where 'shill' is just a variation on 'shall'.

wing

Before **wing** came into English during the 12th century, from Old Norse *vængr*, the term used was **feathers**. In a theatre the **wings** are the sides of the stage screened from the audience, where actors wait for their cue to come on stage: someone **waiting in the wings** is ready to do something at the appropriate time. To **wing it**, or do something without preparation, is originally theatrical slang, which meant 'to play a role without properly knowing the text', either by relying on a prompter in the wings or by studying the part in the wings between scenes. **Wing it** was used in this sense from the late 19th century, but did not acquire its more general meaning of 'improvise' until the 1950s.

On a wing and a prayer, 'with only the slightest chance of success', is from the title of a 1943 song by the American songwriter Harold Adamson, 'Comin' in on a Wing and a Pray'r'. He took it from a comment made by a wartime pilot speaking to ground control just before he made an emergency landing in his damaged plane.

wink

Today someone who winks closes and opens an eye quickly and almost imperceptibly, as the Portuguese footballer Christiano Ronaldo infamously did when his England opponent Wayne Rooney was sent off in the 2006 World Cup. In Anglo-Saxon times, though, to **wink** was simply to close the eyes. **Hoodwink**, meaning 'to trick or deceive', harks back to this original meaning. To hoodwink someone in the 16th century was to blindfold with a hood, before an execution or while attacking them. The modern metaphorical sense followed at the start of the next century.

To **tip someone the wink** or give them private information is an example of old underworld slang or 'rogues' cant' (see feature on STREET SLANG), recorded from the 17th century. It is probably the source of **tip** as in 'a useful piece of advice'. **Tip** here means simply 'to give, allow to have' – its use in sentences like 'tip me a shilling' led to the sense of **tip**, 'a sum of money given as a reward for good service'. See also NOD.

winter

The word **winter** is probably related to **wet**, with the basic idea being 'the wet season'. 'Now is the winter of our discontent' is one of Shakespeare's best-known phrases, from *Richard III*: 'Now is the winter of our discontent / Made glorious summer by this sun of York.' **The winter of discontent** was that of 1978-9 in Britain, when widespread strikes forced the Labour government out of power. In a *Daily Telegraph* interview on February 8, 1979, Prime Minister James Callaghan said 'I had known it was going to be a "winter of discontent".' The London *Evening Standard* had used the phrase in late 1978. See also CRISIS.

wire

The base of the Old English word **wire** probably meant 'to plait or weave'. In the 1850s people started taking of sending a message **by wire**, or by telegraph, or of wiring someone.

If a situation goes **down to the wire** its outcome is not decided until the very last minute. The expression originated in the USA in the late 19th century and comes from horse racing. Racecourses there have a wire stretched across and above the finishing line: a race that goes **down to the wire** is one in which the horses are neck and neck right to the finish.

wise

Both **wise** and **wisdom** are related to **wit**, and the three words share an ancient root meaning 'to know'. The -*wise* in **clockwise** and **lengthwise** means 'way, manner', but is ultimately related to the other **wise**.

Of the many proverbs and sayings relating to wisdom, **it is easy to be wise after the event** originated in the early 17th century, whereas **the price of wisdom is above rubies** comes from the biblical book of Job. In the USA a **wise guy** is a person who makes sarcastic or cheeky remarks to show how clever they are – a 'smart alec'. Since the 1970s it has also been a term for a member of the Mafia. See also EARLY, IGNORANCE, MAGIC, MONKEY, WORD.

witch

In Anglo-Saxon times a **witch** was originally a male sorcerer. The word then was *wicca*, which is the source of WICKED and has also been revived in recent times by modern pagans as the name of their religion, **Wicca**. A female witch was a *wicce*. A male witch would now be called a **wizard**, a word that comes from WISE – in the Middle Ages wizards were wise men or sages, only becoming magicians in the mid 16th century. See also WARLOCK.

The witching hour is midnight, the time when witches are active and magic takes place. The phrase is from Shakespeare's *Hamlet*. Hamlet himself declares:

Tis now the very witching time of night,
When churchyards yawn, and hell itself breathes out
Contagion to this world.

George Orwell was the first to use **witch-hunt** to mean 'a campaign directed against a person or group holding views considered unorthodox or a threat to society', in reference to Communists being persecuted in the Spanish Civil War (1936-9). Before that a witch-hunt was a real hunt for witches, though the term is recorded first in novels from the 19th century, long after witches were burned at the stake.

wobble

A German word first used in English in the mid 17th century. **Wobble** is related to **wave** and **waver**, and until the mid 19th century was generally spelled **wabble**.

To **throw a wobbly** is to have a fit of temper or panic. This is a recent expression recorded only from the 1960s, first of all in New Zealand, although **throw a wobbler** appears in the 1930s, in a US dictionary of underworld and prison slang. The image is of a person's body shaking with anger or fear.

woe

Many ancient languages, including Old English, Latin and Greek, had **woe** or a similar word – a natural exclamation made by someone unhappy or in distress.

The medieval word **betide**, meaning 'to happen', comes from the same source as TIDE, and these days is mainly found in the phrase **woe betide**, a light-hearted warning that a person will be in trouble if they do a particular thing: 'Woe betide you, girl, if you think this standard of rubbish is going to get you your eleven-plus!' (Meera Syal, *Anita and Me*, 1996).

wolf

The root of **wolf** also gave rise to Greek *lukos* and Latin *lupus*, the source of **lupine**, 'like a wolf'. The Greek word gave us **lycanthropy**, the mythical transformation of a person into a wolf or werewolf: the **were-** part of **werewolf** is probably from *wer*, the Old English word for 'man' or 'person'.

Wolves would have been much more numerous in ancient times, and would have been a constant menace to animals, especially sheep. Many phrases reflect the age-old battle between shepherds and wolves. The story of the shepherd boy who thought it would be funny to cause a panic by falsely **crying 'wolf!'** is one of the fables of Aesop, the Greek storyteller of the 6th century BC. The boy did it so many times that people stopped responding, and so when a real wolf did appear no one came to help.

To **keep the wolf from the door** is to have enough money to avoid starvation: the phrase has been used since the 15th century. To **throw someone to the wolves**, or leave them to be roughly treated, is surprisingly recent, though, being recorded only from the 1920s. The image here is of travellers on a sledge who are set upon by a pack of wolves, and decide to throw out one of their number to lighten the load and allow them to make their escape.

A **wolf in sheep's clothing** is a person or thing that appears friendly or harmless but is really hostile. This comes from the Sermon on the Mount, as recounted in the Gospel of Matthew, when Jesus says: 'Beware of false prophets, which come to you in sheep's cloth, but inwardly they are ravening wolves.' The Conservative leader Winston Churchill once dismissed his Labour opposite number Clement Attlee as 'a sheep in sheep's clothing'.

woman

In Old English the spelling of **woman** was *wīfmon* or *wīfman*, a combination of WIFE (which then meant simply 'woman') and MAN (which meant 'person'), so a woman was a 'female person'. **A woman's work is never done** and **a woman's place is in the home** reflect the traditional view of the sexes. The former was first recorded in 1570, as 'Some respite to husbands the weather doth send, but housewives' affairs have never

no end'. In response to such ideas, during the 1970s and 1980s some feminists decided that the usual plural of **woman**, **women**, had to be changed, because it contained **men**. They used **womyn** or **wimmin**, neither of which really caught on. The saying 'A woman without a man is like a fish without a bicycle' is sometimes credited to the American feminist Gloria Steinem but was probably just an anonymous piece of graffiti.

womble

'Remember You're a Womble' was a hit song in 1974 for the 'pop group' formed by the Wombles, long-nosed furry creatures that appeared in children's books from the 1960s and in a BBC television series from 1973. They had a 'green' message that was ahead of its time, as they went around Wimbledon Common collecting and recycling rubbish left by humans. Their creator, Elisabeth Beresford, claimed that their name came from one of her children mispronouncing the name of Wimbledon Common, but **womble** or **wamble** is actually a real English word that came from Danish and Norwegian in around 1300 and is still used in some English dialects. It first meant 'to feel queasy or nauseous' and 'to roll about', then in the 16th century 'to walk unsteadily'.

wood

The first meaning of **wood**, spelled *wudu* in Old English, seems to have been 'a tree', and is recorded in the epic poem *Beowulf* of the 8th century, although the sense 'small forest' was found soon after.

People **touch wood** (or in North America **knock on wood**) to ward off bad luck. The expression is recorded only since 1849. **Be unable to see the wood from the trees** is older, dating from the mid 16th century. Another phrase relating to the 'small forest' sense is **out of the wood**, meaning 'out of danger or difficulty'. This probably comes from the 18th-century proverb **don't halloo** [shout for joy] **till you are out of the wood**. See also NASTY, SPOON.

wool

The length of time that people have been shearing sheep and wearing the fleeces can be seen by the fact that **wool** is first recorded in Old English around AD 700 and can be traced back to a root shared by Latin *lana* 'wool' and Greek *vellus* 'fleece'.

The first person mentioned as trying to **pull the wool over someone's eyes** is an attorney, or American lawyer, in the mid 19th century, which implies that the 'wool' referred to is a lawyer's curly wig. The phrase may also be connected with the expression to **wool someone**, meaning to pull their hair or 'wool' as a joke or insult.

Someone **wild and woolly**, or rough and uncouth, is so called in reference to cowboys in the Wild West who wore shaggy sheepskin garments with the wool on the outside. The sense 'vague or confused' dates from the early years of the 19th century and draws on the idea of something woolly having a fuzzy, indistinct outline.

word

The word **word** is ultimately related to Latin *verbum*, the source of **verb** and **verbal**. 'In the beginning was the Word, and the Word was with God, and the Word was God' are the first words of the Gospel of John, which continues: 'And the Word was made flesh, and dwelt among us . . . full of grace and truth.'

To **eat your words** is to take back what you have said, especially in a humiliated way. The phrase is first found in a 1571 translation of a work by the French Protestant theologian John Calvin: 'God eateth not his word when he hath once spoken.' **A word in your ear** is of similar vintage, coming from Shakespeare's *Much Ado About Nothing*: 'Come you hither sirra, a word in your ear, sir'.

People sometimes say **a word to the wise** or **a word to the wise is enough** to imply that only a hint or brief explanation is required. The wording of the first English use, at the start of the 16th century, was 'Few words may serve the wise', although the concept was expressed much earlier than that in the Latin saying *verbum sapienti sat est*.

work

Work is connected with the Greek word *ergon*, which is the source of **energy** and also **surgery** (see SURGEON). **Wrought**, meaning 'made in a particular way', is the old past form of **work**, which people used where we now use **worked**. Wright, a common surname that means 'maker' and is found in words such as **shipwright** and **wheelwright**, is also closely related to **work**.

The first **workaholic** was mentioned in 1968. Since then we have had chocaholics and shopaholics, but the first word to be formed in this way from **alcoholic** was **foodaholic**, in 1965.

The wise statement 'Work expands so as to fill the time available' is known as Parkinson's law. It was first expressed by Professor C. Northcote Parkinson in 1955. Much older is the proverb **All work and no play makes Jack a dull boy**, which is first found in 1659. See also DEVIL.

world

The ancient root of **world** meant 'age or life of man'. The first part is the same as *were-* in **werewolf** – it means 'man' – and the second part is related to OLD. The Anglo-Saxons first used the word to mean 'human existence, life on Earth' as opposed to future life in heaven or hell.

America was first called **the New World** in 1555, and Europe, Asia and Africa **the Old World** at the end of that century. **Olde worlde** is a 'fake' antiquated spelling for old-fashioned things intended to be quaint and attractive, and dates only from the 1920s. The developing countries of Asia, Africa and Latin America were initially known as **the Third World** in the 1950s by French writers who used *tiers monde*, 'third world', to distinguish the developing countries from the capitalist and Communist blocs. The first use in English came in 1963.

The best of all worlds or **of all possible worlds** is from *Candide* (1759) by the French writer Voltaire. It is a translation of a statement by the ever-optimistic Pangloss, 'Everything is for the best in the best of all possible worlds'. The character of Pangloss, who remained constantly cheerful despite all the disasters that happened to him and his travelling companions, is a satire on the views of the German philosopher Leibniz, who believed that this world is the best of all possible worlds. See also OPTIMISM, OYSTER, WHIMPER, WIFE, YE.

worm

When it wriggled its way into Old English **worm** was spelled *wyrm* or *wurm*. The first meaning was 'serpent' or 'dragon', a sense still occasionally found in dialect and preserved in folk tales such as 'The Lambton Worm', which was adapted by Bram Stoker as *The Lair of the White Worm* (1911). **Worm** came to mean 'crawling animal, reptile or insect' and then, in about 1100, an earthworm or similar creature.

A **can of worms** is a complicated matter that is likely to prove awkward. The worms here are probably maggots – think of a fisherman on a riverbank with his wriggling bait tin. **The worm has turned** means 'a meek person has retaliated after being pushed too far'. The original form, in 1546, was 'Tread a worm on the tail and it must turn again'.

worry

At first to **worry** someone was to strangle them. The main current meanings arose quite recently, and the sense 'to tear at with the teeth', as in a dog worrying sheep, is much earlier. In Old English **worry** (or *wyrgan*, as it was then spelled) was 'to strangle'.

The Middle Ages saw the meanings 'to choke with a mouthful of food', 'to seize by the throat and tear' and 'to swallow greedily', and the 16th century 'to harass'. This gave rise 'to annoy or disturb' in the late 17th century and then 'to cause anxiety to'. The sense 'to feel anxious or troubled', as in 'he worried about his son', is not recorded until the 1860s, and was initially regarded as a rather informal use.

worship

The writings of Alfred the Great, King of Wessex from 871 to 899, are the first source of **worship**, which is literally 'worthship'. It initially meant 'good name, credit' and 'dignity, importance', ideas that survive in the title **your worship**, used for a high-ranking person such as a magistrate or mayor. The word was not found in the context of religious rites or feelings until around 1300.

Today we may **hero-worship** footballers or singers, but the term originally referred to the ancient worship of heroes such as Hercules, superhuman beings who were regarded as semi-divine and were often the subject of myths. The historian Thomas Carlyle was partly responsible for the modern sense – his lectures On Heroes, Hero-Worship and the Heroic in History, published in 1841, expounded his view that history is fundamentally the history of great men, who are worshipped as heroes.

wreck

When it first appeared in the 12th century **wreck** meant 'cargo or wreckage washed ashore from a wrecked or stranded vessel'. The word came into English from Old French *wrec*. The source was an Old Norse word meaning 'to drive' that was related to **wreak**, 'to cause a lot of damage or harm', and to RACK. A person in a state of stress or emotional exhaustion has been a **wreck** since the 1790s and a **nervous wreck** since about 1870.

write

The idea behind **write** in the ancient Germanic languages was 'to score or carve' – people in northern Europe would have written first by inscribing letters on wood. The original meaning in Old English was 'to draw or outline the shape of something'.

The first person to use the phrase **be nothing to write home about**, meaning 'be mediocre or unexceptional', appears to have been the comic writer Ian Hay in 1914. Hay was also a soldier who served in the First World War and was awarded the Military Cross, and it is likely that the expression was a military one. He also coined the expressions **funny ha-ha** and **funny peculiar** (see FUN).

If you say that a particular quality or feeling is **written all over someone's face**, you are echoing Shakespeare, as is so often the case. In *Measure for Measure* Duke Vincentio says: 'There is written in your brow, Provost, honesty and constancy.' See also WALL and feature on SHAKESPEARE.

wrong

An Old English word from Old Norse *rangr* 'awry, unjust', which first meant 'crooked, curved or twisted' and is related to **wring**. Until the 17th century the *wr-* would have been pronounced, and there was obviously something about the sound that suggested the idea of twisting – many English words beginning with *wr-*, such as **wrist**, **writhe** and **wreathe**, contain the notion.

Although to **get the wrong end of the stick** now means 'to misunderstand something', the original sense seems to have been 'to come off worse'. The example in *The Swell's Night Guide*, a guide to London low life published in 1846, gives an idea of what was wrong with the 'wrong end': 'Which of us had hold of the crappy . . . end of the stick?'

The proverb **two wrongs don't make a right** dates from the late 18th century. The Hungarian-born psychiatrist Thomas Szasz summed up the feelings of many when he said in 1973: 'Two wrongs don't make a right, but they make a good excuse.'

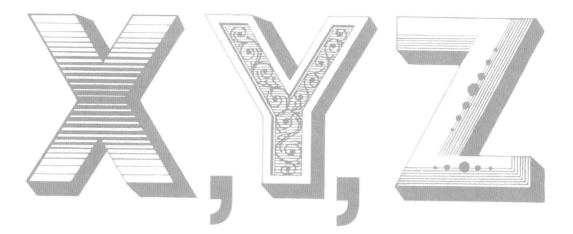

Xanadu

The exotic-sounding **Xanadu** has passed into the language as a name for any place of idyllic magnificence or luxury. It comes from the poem 'Kubla Khan' by Samuel Taylor Coleridge, which opens: 'In Xanadu did Kubla Khan / A stately pleasure-dome decree.' The Xanadu referred to is Shang-tu, an ancient city in southeast Mongolia which was the residence of the 13th-century emperor Kublai Khan. Coleridge claimed that he wrote the poem in 1797 at a farmhouse near Exmoor after an opium-induced dream. It is incomplete, as his train of thought was interrupted by the arrival of a 'person from Porlock', and was not published until 1816. His account may or may not be accurate, but it helped to create a literary legend.

Xmas

A term for Christmas that dates from the mid 16th century. It was originally only a written form, with X representing the initial letter of Greek *Khristos*, 'Christ', in the Greek alphabet. It is not possible to tell when people started pronouncing it differently with the sound of *x*.

X-ray

When the German physicist Wilhelm Conrad Röntgen discovered X-rays in 1895 he did not understand what they were, so he gave them the name *X-Strahlen*, with X conveying their unknown nature. German *X-Strahlen* translates as **X-rays**, and this was used immediately in English. Another name at the time was **roentgen rays**, in honour of their discoverer. The singular form **X-ray**, for an examination or a radiograph made using X-rays, dates from around 1900.

yahoo

The fourth part of Jonathan Swift's satire *Gulliver's Travels*, published in 1726, describes the country of the Houyhnhnms, who were intelligent horses. Their simplicity and virtue contrasts with the disgusting brutality of the Yahoos, beasts in the shape of men. Soon **yahoo** was being used for a coarse person or lout. In Australia the **Yahoo** is a large, hairy man-like monster supposedly inhabiting the east of the country. The name is recorded from the mid 19th century, and may have originated in an Aboriginal word, though Swift's Yahoos influenced the form in English.

The internet site and search engine **Yahoo!** was born as a student hobby in 1994 for two US electrical engineering students, David Filo and Jerry Yang. The site started out as 'Jerry and David's Guide to the World Wide Web', but the two friends felt it needed a less unwieldy name. **Yahoo!** stands for Yet Another Hierarchical Officious Oracle, but was chosen partly because the associations of **yahoo** with 'rough, uncouth' appealed to them. See also WEAVE.

yard

The **yard** that is a unit of length descended from Old English *gerd* 'twig, stick, rod', and has been the standard English unit of measure equal to 3ft since the later medieval period. The earlier standard was the **ell**, equal to 45in, succeeded by the **verge** during the reign of Edward III (1327-77), which was the equivalent of the yard. Since the Old English period this **yard** has also been a nautical term for a long spar for a square sail to hang from. See also SUN.

The other **yard** derives from Old English *geard* 'building, home, enclosure' and is related to GARDEN and **orchard**, and also to Russian *gorod* 'town', used in place names such as Novgorod. In Britain a yard is usually an enclosed piece of ground adjacent to a building, whereas in the USA it is the word for the garden of a house. In Jamaican English **yard** means 'a house or home', and among expatriate Jamaicans **Yard** is Jamaica. This is the origin of **Yardie**, used by Jamaicans for a fellow Jamaican, but since the mid 1980s in Britain to refer to a member of a Jamaican or West Indian gang of criminals.

yarn   see SPIN.

ye

In deliberately quaint names such as Ye Olde Tea Shoppe **ye** represents an imaginary old pronunciation of **the**. In the Middle Ages English used a letter called a thorn that indicated the sound of *th*. It looked rather like *y*, and came to be written in an identical way, so that **the** could be **ye**. This spelling was kept as a convenient abbreviation in handwriting down to the 19th century, and in printers' types during the 15th and 16th centuries, but it was never pronounced as 'ye'. See also WORLD.

year

This Old English word shares an ancient root with Greek *hōra* 'season, time', source of **horology**, **horoscope** and HOUR. A **leap year** is a year, occurring every four years, with 366 days instead of 365 and an extra day, February 29, added to keep the calendar in synch with the astronomical or solar year. The name, used from the 14th century, probably comes from the fact that in a leap year feast days after February fall two days later than in the previous year, rather than one day later as in other years, and could be said to have 'leaped' a day. The modern calendar is called the **Gregorian calendar**, named after Pope Gregory XIII and introduced in 1582. It replaced the **Julian calendar** first used by the Romans and brought in by Julius Caesar in 46 BC, because the calendar had slipped out of alignment with the astronomical year. Ten days were suppressed, and years such as 1700 and 1800 were only made leap years if they could be divided by 400. At the same time **New Year's Day** was changed from March 25 to January 1. Scotland adopted the Gregorian calendar in 1600, but England and Wales did not follow suit until 1752. See also CALENDAR, DOT.

yob

This is an example of 'back slang', where people say words as though they were spelled backwards. So **yob** is a reverse form of **boy** and originally, in the mid 19th century, simply meant 'a boy or youth'. Now a yob is a rude, noisy or aggressive one.

yellow

As with other colour words such as AUBURN and BROWN, the root of **yellow** probably referred to a wider range of colours than the modern word does. It shares an ancestor with GOLD, but is also related to **gall**, **bile** and the final element of MELANCHOLY, all of which derive from the greenish colour of bile. The yellow egg **yolk** was also related to **yellow**.

In the 17th century yellow rather than GREEN was the colour of jealousy, possibly with the idea of a jealous person being 'jaundiced' or bitter. The word **jaundice** is from Old French *jaune* 'yellow', and sufferers from the medical condition jaundice have a yellowish complexion. The colour is now associated with cowardice rather than jealousy, a link that began in the 1850s in the USA, perhaps in allusion to a person's face going pale with fear. Since the 1920s a coward has been said to be **yellow-bellied** or a **yellow-belly**.

yen

The vocabulary of drug users entered mainstream English before modern times. The **yen** in to **have a yen for**, 'to long or yearn for', originally referred to the drug addict's craving for opium. The word came from Chinese *yăn* 'craving' in the 1870s. The **yen** that is the monetary unit of Japan comes from Japanese *en* 'round'.

yesterday

Although **yesterday** is related to Latin *heri* and Greek *khthes*, both meaning 'yesterday', its base probably meant both 'yesterday' and 'tomorrow'. 'Yesterday' (1965), written by Paul McCartney and recorded by the Beatles, has been covered more times than any other song. It is a beautiful ballad with wistful lyrics about a former girlfriend, but would probably not have been so successful if McCartney had stuck to the original title. He came up with the melody first, and called it 'Scrambled Eggs' until he had written the words. See also JAM.

yeti   see ABOMINABLE.

yoga

The **yoga** that we know in the West is a simplified version of an ancient Hindu system of meditation, exercise and religious observance intended to lead to union with the divine. The word's literal meaning in the

Indian language Sanskrit is 'union', and it is related to English **yoke**, a piece of wood fastened over the necks of two animals to enable them to pull a plough or cart.

yomp

In 1982 Argentinian forces invaded the Falkland Islands in support of their claim to sovereignty, and in response Britain sent a task force to retake the islands. News reports quoted Royal Marines describing their march with heavy equipment over difficult terrain as they advanced to Stanley, the capital, and suddenly everybody knew what **yomping** was. Unfortunately no one knew where the word came from. People familiar with the terminology of rally driving identified it with **yump**, an alteration of JUMP supposedly suggesting a Scandinavian speaker and meaning 'to leave the ground while taking a bump at speed', but with the war long over its origin may remain uncertain.

yonks   see DONKEY.

young

'Youth is wasted on the young', said the Irish writer George Bernard Shaw. **Young** and **youth** are not young words – they are from the same ancient root as Latin *juvenis* 'young', source of **juvenile** and

Enough words already!

Yiddish, based on German dialect combined with words from Hebrew and Slavic languages, was spoken by Jews in central and eastern Europe before the Second World War. It is still used in Israel and parts of Europe and the USA, especially New York, and has added an extra special tang to English speech.

The most familiar Yiddish word may be nosh, 'to eat greedily', used in English since the late 19th century and deriving from Yiddish *nashn*. Foods worth noshing include bagels (ring-shaped bread rolls), lox (smoked salmon), matzos (crisp biscuits of unleavened bread) and that staple of huge American-style sandwiches, pastrami (seasoned smoked beef).

The opening *sch-* is characteristic of Yiddish words, including schlep (to go or move with effort), schlock (inferior goods or material, rubbish), schmaltz (excessive sentimentality, literally 'dripping, lard'), schnozz (the nose) and schtick (an attention-getting routine or gimmick). Most of these date from the early or mid 20th century, although schmooze, 'to chat intimately and cosily', is from the 1890s.

Yiddish words often express a certain attitude – oy vey! (oh dear!), enough with the kvetching (moaning and complaining) already! This use of already to express impatience is influenced by Jewish speech, and is a translation of Yiddish *shoyn* 'already'. It is an example of the way Yiddish has exerted a subtle influence on English. If you say you need something like a hole in the head you are translating the Yiddish expression *tsu darfn vi a lokh in kop*, used in English since the early 1950s. Other familiar idioms that are translations from Yiddish are it's OK by me and get lost!, both of which are first found in the USA.

Chutzpah is almost untranslatable – 'extreme self-confidence or audacity' is probably the closest approximation. A klutz is clumsy, awkward or foolish and a nebbish is a feeble or timid man, while a schmuck is foolish or contemptible – the word literally means 'penis', as does putz, also used to mean 'a stupid or worthless person'. On a more positive note, a maven is an expert or connoisseur, and a mensch a man of integrity and honour.

Although Yiddish is today associated particularly with New York, it has also influenced the speech of Londoners. Cockneys tell each other to keep schtum or silent, and call bad things dreck or rubbish and good ones KOSHER – a Hebrew word that was spread by Yiddish-speakers.

The -*nik* in words like beatnik is another Yiddish contribution to English. It was originally used in Russian to form words for people of a particular kind, and was taken up by Yiddish-speakers in the USA. Today we have terms such as kibbutznik, a member of a kibbutz or communal farm in Israel, and refusenik, a Jew in the Soviet Union who was refused permission to emigrate to Israel, or more generally a person who refuses to follow orders or obey the law. The beatniks were part of the subculture associated with the beat generation of the 1950s and early 1960s (see BEAT).

See also GAZUMP, GLITCH, SLAP, SMACK.

rejuvenate. **The good die young** is a proverb from the late 17th century, but the idea goes back to the ancient Greek playwright Menander, who wrote: 'Whom the gods love dies young.'

A **young turk** is now a young person eager for radical change, a meaning that comes from the **Young Turks** who carried out the revolution of 1908 in the Ottoman Empire and deposed the sultan Abdul Hamid II. Before that, though, a **young**, **little** or **terrible Turk** was an unmanageable or violent child or youth, and from the 16th century a **Turk** was a cruel or tyrannical man, a use reflecting prejudice against Muslims.

yo-yo

Crazes for particular toys are nothing new. Children in the early 2000s demand computer games and consoles, but in the late 1920s the **yo-yo** was the latest thing. Although toys resembling yo-yos were known in ancient China and Greece, the name probably comes from the Philippines, where the yo-yo had been popular for hundreds of years. It entered English in 1915, and became a verb meaning 'to move up and down, fluctuate' in the 1960s.

Yule

It is now just another word for Christmas, but **Yule** comes from the Old Norse word *jól*, a pagan festival at the winter solstice that lasted for 12 days. Germanic and Scandinavian pagans celebrated it in late December or early January, and when they adopted Christianity they simply changed the nature of the festival, turning *jól* into Christmas. In Old English **Yule** meant 'December or January' and also 'Christmas and its festivities'. The original **yule log** was a large log traditionally burnt on the hearth on Christmas Eve, nowadays replaced by a log-shaped chocolate cake.

yum

Since the 1870s our natural response to eating tasty food has been represented in writing as **yum** or **yum-yum**, and the delicious food has been described as **yummy**. In about 1993 **yummy** found a new use – a young, stylish, attractive mother, particularly a celebrity photographed with her cute child, was called a **yummy mummy**.

yuppie

The 1980s saw the rise of the **yuppie**, the 'young urban professional' or, as people later interpreted the initials, 'young upwardly mobile professional' (or 'person'). *The Yuppie Handbook* inaugurated their era in 1984, the year when the word is first recorded. It was possibly suggested by the **yippies**, a term for members of the Youth International Party, a group of politically active hippies formed in the USA in 1966.

The pattern of word formation that gave us **yuppie** spawned parallel terms. **Yumpie**, from 'young upwardly mobile person', had a short life in the 1980s before **yuppie** assumed its functions and its origins. **Dinky** or **dinkie**, from the initial letters of 'double' (or 'dual') 'income no kids', appeared in 1986 for a partner in a well-off working couple with no children – some allowed the y to stand for 'yet'. Two years later the **woopie**, the 'well-off older person', entered the language.

zany

Zany was the name of one of the servants in the improvised popular Italian theatre, the commedia dell'arte, which was popular from the 16th to the 18th century. The word is a Venetian form of *Gianni*, which itself is short for *Giovanni*. In its earliest uses in English, from the late 16th century, a **zany** was a comic performer who imitated the actions of a clown or acrobat in an amusing way, and **zany** described his entertaining behaviour. In time these old traditions fell out of use, but the word lived on as a description for unconventional or surreal comedians. See also PANTALOONS.

zap

In comic strips of the 1920s **zap** often represented the sound of a ray gun, laser or similar weapon. The sense 'to kill' has existed since the 1940s and 'to move quickly' since the 1960s. Since the early 1980s **zapping** has also meant the use of a remote control to operate a television or other piece of electronic equipment. This developed from the idea of moving quickly between channels during the commercial break or by fast-forwarding on a video combined with the notion of using the remote control like a ray gun to destroy the effectiveness of advertisements by zapping through other channels while they are on.

zebra

The **zebra** is related to the horse not only genetically but linguistically. The name of the striped animal is not from an African language, as was once thought, but via Italian, Spanish or Portuguese from Latin *equiferus* 'wild horse' – the root is *equus*, as in EQUESTRIAN. The **zebra crossing**, named because it is marked with black and white stripes, was introduced in Britain in 1949.

zenith

Like its opposite, **nadir**, **zenith** was originally an astronomical term deriving from Arabic, in this case from *samt ar-ra's*, 'path over the head'. In astronomy the zenith is the point in the sky immediately above the observer, and also, following this, the highest point reached by a particular celestial object, at which it is **at its zenith**. The modern general sense, 'the time at which something is most powerful or successful', developed from the astronomical use in the early 17th century. The **nadir** is the point in the sky immediately below the observer, and comes from Arabic *nazīr*, meaning 'opposite (to the zenith)'. The general sense, 'the lowest or most unsuccessful point', also developed in the early 17th century. 'The season reached a nadir with a record 7-1 home defeat to Brighton' (*FourFourTwo* magazine, 2001) is a good example of its use.

zip

As a name for a fastener **zip** dates from the 1920s. The idea of speed was already present in a 19th-century use representing the sound of something moving through the air rapidly. In the USA **zip** also means 'nothing, nil, zero'. This appeared in print in 1900, much earlier than the similar **zilch**, the first clear example of which dates from the mid 1960s, though **Mr Zilch** had been used as in indefinite name 30 or more years before. The US **zip code**, a postal code consisting of five or nine digits, is unrelated, being short for *Zone Improvement Plan*.

zoo

The first **zoo** was the Zoological Gardens in Regent's Park, London. It was established in 1828 in the gardens of the London Zoological Society, and was at first just for scientific study, but was opened to the public in 1847. Practically all English words beginning **zoo-**, including **zoological** and **zoology**, go back to Greek *zōion* 'animal', source also of **zodiac**. Most of the signs of the zodiac are represented by animals, such as Aries the ram, Cancer the crab, Capricorn the goat and Taurus the bull, and the name **zodiac** originates from this ancient mode of thought.

A family enjoy an elephant ride at Regent's Park Zoological Gardens – London Zoo – in 1900.

Acknowledgments

The Publishers would like to thank the following people and organisations for supplying photographs or other illustration:

Cartoon illustrations by Robert Thompson, www.robertthompsoncartoons.com

Feature illustrations by Anthony Sidwell Illustration, www.anthonysidwell.com

3 Columbia/The Kobal Collection   4 John Minihan/Evening Standard/Getty Images
5 The Art Archive/British Library   7 (top) Mary Evans Picture Library   7 (bottom) Photolibrary Wales/Rex Moreton   8 (top) Collections/© Chris Blyth   8 (bottom) National Portrait Gallery, London   9 (top) Mary Evans Picture Library   9 (bottom) National Portrait Gallery, London
10 (top) Library of Congress, Washington DC, USA/The Bridgeman Art Library   10 (bottom) Private Collection/The Bridgeman Art Library   11 (top) The Art Archive/Private Collection MD
11 (bottom) Photo by Bob Gomel/Time Life Pictures/Getty Images   15 Photo: 'Acme Rocket: Take 30' by Chuck Jones courtesy of Chuck Jones Center for Creativity and Warner Brothers Entertainment Inc. Clip and Still Licensing   20 Mary Evans Picture Library   27 Tony Ashby/AFP/Getty Images
29 © Bettmann/Corbis   37 © H. Armstrong Roberts/Corbis   44 Danjaq/EON/UA/The Kobal Collection   53 Hulton Archive/Getty Images   56 © Andrew Woodley/Alamy   58 Reader's Digest Association   62 www.istockphoto.com/Tomasz Zajaczkowski   69 Mary Evans Picture Library
76 © Najlah Feanny/Corbis SABA   80 Columbia/The Kobal Collection   84 VinMag Archive
86 © BBC   90 Mary Evans Picture Library/Tom Morgan   95 Mary Evans Picture Library
102 20th Century Fox/ The Kobal Collection   104 Image courtesy of the Advertising Archives
109 © Schloss Sanssouci, Potsdam, Brandenburg, Germany/Alinari/The Bridgeman Art Library
117 Image courtesy of the Advertising Archives   124 © Christophe Boisvieux/Corbis
127 John Minihan/Evening Standard/Getty Images   149 © Tony Lilley/Alamy   152 New Line/The Kobal Collection   156 Tim Graham/Getty Images   160 RDA/Getty Images   170 The Art Archive/Royal Automobile Club London/NB Design   174 © Leeds Museums and Galleries (City Art Gallery) UK/The Bridgeman Art Library   182 © Tom Hanley/Alamy   179 Image courtesy of the Advertising Archives   186 © Lake County Museum/Corbis   187 www.istockphoto.com
192 © Michael Nicholson/Corbis   193 Mary Evans Picture Library   195 www.istockphoto.com/Adam Przezak   206 www.istockphoto.com/Armando Frazao   208 © Popperfoto/Alamy
215 The Bridgeman Art Library   220 Public Record Office/HIP/TopFoto.co.uk   229 Evening Standard/Getty Images   235 www.istockphoto.com/Andrei Tchernov   238 Image supplied by Wikipedia   239 © Gianni Dagli Orti/Corbis   243 John Kobal Foundation/Getty Images
250 www.istockphoto.com/Richard Thornton   252 Reader's Digest Association   255 Warner Bros/The Kobal Collection   261 © Lynda Richardson/Corbis   267 Imagno/Getty Images
269 © BBC/Python Pictures   272 Fox Photos/Getty Images   278 © Robert Maass/Corbis
287 Mary Evans Picture Library   291 Hulton Archive/Getty Images   296 www.istockphoto.com/Amanda Rohde   301 www.istockphoto.com/Jo Ann Snover   303 Mary Evans/Rue des Archives
307 Evening Standard/Getty Images   323 Time & Life Pictures/Getty Images   330 © INTERFOTO Pressebildagentur/Alamy   340 Mary Evans Picture Library   346 Mary Evans Picture Library
350 Gordon Anthony/Getty Images   354 www.istockphoto.com   358 Frontispiece from the 1518 edition of Thomas More's Utopia   360 Heinrich Leufemann/supplied by Wikipedia
362 www.istockphoto.com/Alisher Duasbaew   368 Mary Evans Picture Library   382 Paul Martin/General Photographic Agency/Getty Images

The Origins of Words & Phrases was published by
The Reader's Digest Association Limited, London, using
material supplied by Oxford University Press, © OUP 2007

First edition copyright © 2007
The Reader's Digest Association Limited
11 Westferry Circus, Canary Wharf, London E14 4HE
www.readersdigest.co.uk

We are committed to both the quality of our products and
the service we provide to our customers. We value your
comments, so please feel free to contact us on 08705
113366 or via our website at:
www.readersdigest.co.uk

If you have any comments or suggestions about the
content of our books, email us at:
gbeditorial@readersdigest.co.uk

All rights reserved.

No part of this book may be reproduced, stored in a
retrieval system, or transmitted in any form or by any
means, electronic, electrostatic, magnetic tape, mechanical,
photocopying, recording or otherwise, without permission
in writing from the publishers.

® Reader's Digest, The Digest and the Pegasus logo are
registered trademarks of The Reader's Digest Association,
Inc., of Pleasantville, New York, USA.

The Origins of Words & Phrases was edited and produced
for Reader's Digest by Oxford University Press.

Concept Code: UK1220/IC/A
Book Code: 400-218 UP0000-1
ISBN: 978 0 276 44244 5
Oracle Code: 250011005H.00.24

FOR OXFORD UNIVERSITY PRESS

Project manager
Angus Stevenson

Editorial staff
Lesley Brown
Andrew Delahunty
Elizabeth Knowles

Picture research
Carrie Hickman

Art editor
Tim Branch

Production manager
Carol Alexander

Publishing manager, English Dictionaries
Judy Pearsall

FOR READER'S DIGEST

Project editor
John Andrews

Art editor
Louise Turpin

Editorial director
Julian Browne

Art director
Anne-Marie Bulat

Managing editor
Nina Hathway

Head of book development
Sarah Bloxham

Picture resource manager
Sarah Stewart-Richardson

Pre-press account manager
Penelope Grose

Product production manager
Claudette Bramble

Senior production controller
Deborah Trott

Printing and binding
CT Printing, China